Dedication

This book is dedicated to:

My life partner, Gary Roger Hicks, Jr.
My daughter, Susan Eliza Murray Keuchenberg and her family

My teachers in the Waverly City School District
who imparted to me a love of creative writing and American History:
Johanna Samson, Doris Young, Oscar Radigger, Nelvia Hunt, and
Janet Roberts

All the descendants of Peter Francisco, living and departed,

All Americans who wish to better understand
how we won our independence,
and how important it is we keep it.

With Special Thanks to:
Dale Neighbors and Tom Camden of the Library of Virginia
Heather Beattie and Jamie Davis of the Virginia Historical Society
Allene Phillips Hicks
Bill and Alice McDowell

Table of Contents

Forward

Part One...The Roots of Rebellion

Part Two ... The War for Independence

Illustrations and Credits
"The Battle of Cowpens" Cover

Forward

Meeting Peter Francisco

"Francisco's Fight"
An 1814 wood engraving – Public Domain

I first met Peter Francisco when I was a sixteen year-old student, the summer before my junior year at Waverly High School, in Waverly, Ohio. I was dragged to a family reunion held at the upper shelterhouse, overlooking where Pee Pee Creek forms Lake White. It was the Cisco Family Reunion.

I, a Murray, not a Cisco, did not understand why I couldn't spend that warm autumn Sunday afternoon water skiing with my friends, instead of sitting in the shelterhouse with a bunch of Ciscos I really didn't even know. I guess it was to please my grandma, Eliza Francis Cisco Murray. I just sat there and stared down at the lake below me, watching all my friends ski.

After the huge carried-in dinner was prayed over and eaten, some sort of distant relative, the Cisco lady who had arranged the reunion, stood up to give an amateur history of the Cisco Family. Even though

I was one of the few students at school who enjoyed history, and hoped someday to teach it, I could have cared less about the history of the Cisco family.

I sat and listened as the Cisco lady talked about what seemed to me to be a cross between a fairy tale and an old Norse saga of heroism. She spoke of a young boy, found on a river wharf in Virginia in 1765. He spoke no English, but wore an exquisite suit of clothes, and had golden shoe buckles with the letter "P" on one shoe, and "F" on the other. His history was unknown. Where did he come from? Why did he appear mysteriously on the wharf? What language did he speak?

She spoke on, with limited research, that he had been taken in and raised by an uncle of the colonial patriot, Patrick Henry. She said he witnessed Henry deliver his famous speech, *"Give me liberty or give me death!"* I was starting to become intrigued.

She spoke of how he fought in the American Revolution, and due to his large stature and strength, was known as *"the Virginia Giant."* She said General Washington actually had a special, larger-than-normal sword made just for him. He became good friends with Washington, LaFayette, Jefferson, Madison and Monroe. By then, I knew I wanted to know more about this man who I was apparently related to.

My Grandma Murray told me later that her father was born Robbin Francisco, but, due to a family feud, when they lived in Eastern Kentucky, he officially changed his family name to Cisco, dropping the "Fran."

Over the years, I took several trips to Richmond, Hopewell, and Buckingham County, Virginia. I visited Hopewell, where there was a bust of Peter at the wharf where he was found. I trespassed on his Locust Grove farm in Buckingham County, then very much dilapidated. I visited the Virginia Statehouse in Richmond, where he served as sergeant-at-arms for the Virginia Legislature, and visited his grave in Richmond's Shockoe Hill Cemetery.

Being a stamp collector, I was happy when the U.S. Post Office issued a stamp honoring Peter in its American Revolution Bicentennial series. The 18-cent Peter Francisco stamp was part of the "Contributors to the Cause" series. It showed Peter carrying a cannon on his shoulders during the Battle of Camden, South Carolina.

I knew one day I wanted to tell his story. When I decided my first novel would center on our nation's struggle for independence, I decided, who better to be the main character of my historical fiction **Cornerstone,** than this man I heard about at the Cisco Family Reunion in 1966?

Research proves Peter Francisco was indeed a real person, not a myth or legend, and played a large role in theAmerican Revolution, though overlooked by most historians. He is also a prime subject for the literary genre of historical fiction. Much of his life is obscured by lack of true evidence. Therefore, much of his story is simply the result of lore. One piece of the lore may say 'this,' while another says 'that,' depending upon what the later generations of descendants, or *wannabe* descendants wanted Peter to be.

Historical fiction is my preferred genre of literature. As my favorite American writer, Gore Vidal, led his readers artfully through the life and times of Aaron Burr, Abraham Lincoln, and others, using historical figures, mingling with fictional characters, to tell an easy to read story, I hope I have achieved the same enjoyable adventure for the readers of **Cornerstone**, and the future volumes I have planned.

Peter was indeed found on the wharf at City Point (now Hopewell, Virginia) in 1765. He was wearing elegant clothing (though well-worn), and had golden (or bronze) monogrammed shoe buckles. Most lore states he was around five years old when found on the wharf, though there is no proof of his actual age. I have made him eight to align his age more realistically with his involvement and interest in the pre-war politics of the day.

Historically, Peter was taken in by Judge Anthony Winston, and raised on his plantation. Some lore says that was in Hanover County, Virginia, while other lore says it was in Buckingham County. Some lore says Winston was a harsh taskmaster, and viewed Peter only as his property, his slave; while other lore says Winston was benevolent and took him in as a member of his own family, paying for Peter's schooling. I created a fictional plantation, Winston Woods, on the Pamunkey River in Hanover County, and molded Winston as benevolent, not as the harsh taskmaster.

Most research has Peter joining Washington's army in 1776, sometime after the Battle of Long Island. Lore says Peter served in the 10th Virginia Regiment, but even using military records, it is difficult to be certain, as records then were haphazardly kept, and regiments changed designation as events dictated.

I chose to have Peter enlist with his friend, James Monroe, into the 3rd Virginia. That would have meant he was with Washington's army evacuating New York for Pennsylvania, and Peter would have been with Washington at the crossing of the Delaware, and the Battles of Trenton and Princeton. Captain James Monroe, our future fifth president and lifelong friend of Peter's, was seriously wounded at Trenton.

Historically, it is known, Peter was wounded at Brandywine, and convalesced with the Marquis de LaFayette. He wintered with Washington's army at Valley Forge. He was also wounded at the Battle of Monmouth, at the storming of Stony Point, and left for dead at Guilford Courthouse. Washington had a special sword made for Peter, on LaFayette's suggestion. Washington referred to Peter as his "one-man army." That is well documented, and there is no historical debate to those facts.

A monument at the Guilford Courthouse battlefield attests to the fact of his heroism there. A Virginia historic highway marker marks the site of Ward's Tavern and site of "Francisco's Fight" in Nottoway County. There he singlehandedly fought the ruthless dragoons of the feared British officer, Banastre Tarleton.

Peter was called *"the Virginia Giant"* because of his great height and girth. The average colonial man stood only five feet six inches tall. Lore puts Peter's height between six-and-a-half and seven feet. I tend to favor the later, as even General Washington, who was a tall man himself for the times standing six feet two inches, saw him as a giant.

It is an historic fact that Peter had a farm named Locust Grove in Buckingham County, and married his first wife in December 1784. Their first meeting, courtship and marriage is in the opening chapter of the follow-up volume to **Cornerstone**. The second volume is set between 1781 and Peter's death in 1831.

During my career in building supplies, politics, travel, journalism, and the general work-a-day world, I would occasionally begin to get creative. Sometime in 1990, I wrote the first pages that would become chapter one of **Cornerstone**, titled *"The Wharf at City Point."* It sat in my files for two decades.

I seriously started writing **Cornerstone** when the last business I worked for closed down without notice on March 15, 2010. Shortly after that, I had a health issue, and lost my right leg. I started getting involved in genealogy, and had a personal vision shattered. *Nowhere in my lineage is Peter Francisco to be found!*

I was devastated. The Ciscos of my family are descended from one Ludwick Christoffel Franciscus, who was born at Grafschaft, Friesland, Niedersachsen, Germany, in 1680. He immigrated to Philadelphia, and died at Lampter Township in Lancaster County, Pennsylvania in 1757. I have no ancestral ties to Peter at all, however, I still feel a closeness and bond to the Virginia Giant.

My family research did prove I have an unexpected Murray family link to an important secondary historic player in **Cornerstone**. Through my tenth generation grandfather, Morgan James Murray (1665-1704), I am an ancestral cousin of John Murray, 4th Earl of Atholl, Lord Dunmore! My ancestral cousin turns out to be a real antagonist in **Cornerstone**. (Doesn't that figure!?!)

I hope this forward prepares you to begin your journey back to 1765, and the time when the most important cornerstone to our independence was laid. It will take you all the way to Yorktown in 1781, the day when the Scottish bagpipes played the song "The World Turned Upside Down"... and a lot that happened in between. Happy reading!

Jim Murray

Portrait of Peter Francisco
By the artist Joseph Westhall Ford, ca. 1828
Displayed on First Floor, East Wing of the
Virginia Statehouse, Richmond, Virginia
Courtesy of The Virginia Library

"Destruction of Tea at Boston Harbor"

by Nathaniel Currier (Currier & Ives New York) 1846

Part One
The Roots of Rebellion

❖ ❖ ❖

Chapter One

The Wharf at City Point

The darkness of the night was waning. The waves persisted with their melodious lullaby as they lapped against the stone rip-rap of the shoreline and the oaken pier posts holding the wharf's floor five or six feet above the river James. Gulls and terns were beginning to sing their cawing song, trumpeting the dawning of the new day...the last day of June, in the year of Our Lord seventeen-hundred and sixty-five.

The boy narrowly opened his eyes. He could tell the horizon's back-drop was now starting to show lighter hues of gunmetal gray instead of the tar-pitch black at his last stirrings. The aroma of yeast bread, rum buns baking, coffee, sausages frying in a cast iron skillet over cedar, no hickory wood chips, spurred his appetite.

He raised his head and craned to look east from the pile of huge, hard coiled nautical rope he had claimed as his bed for the past three nights. The golden ball of the sun was just barely peeking through on the horizon. It must have been about six o'clock in the morning, he thought. A handful of seamen from the three merchant ships tied at the far end of the wharf where the warehouse stood, were heading toward the tavern. After breakfast, they would load the bales of tobacco and other goods for market, and sail away to Europe.

The tavern was about halfway between the boy's nest atop the huge rope coil and the warehouse. He could see the tavern's kitchen was aglow with lanterns and the hearth was aflame. A steady white-gray stream of smoke rose from the red brick chimney, carrying its smorgas-bord of tantalizing aromas. That meant the large Negro woman was in the kitchen mixing up her Johnnycake batter. Her delicious rum buns would soon be ready for the seamen's breakfast. He laid his head back down on his interlocked fingers, gazing toward the heavens.

The boy was a stranger in this land, where he could understand no one's speech and no one could decipher his strange-sounding gibberish. He missed his young sister, Anamarie, and prayed to God constantly, she was safe. He smiled as he thought back to the very last time he had seen her.

She had been running along the seashore at the edge of their estate on the island of Terceira near the small seaport town of Sao Sebastiao. Anamarie was so beautiful, he thought, mentally picturing her run-ning, laughing and taunting him, to catch her if he could. Her long, shiny black curls trailed behind her as she ran along the white sand and turquoise water. She wore her new bright blue and gold dress as she ran several feet ahead of him.

His smile suddenly turned to terror as his vision continued. That had been the exact moment the strong, hairy arms of the burley pirate had grabbed him from behind. He saw the huge, hairy hand cover his mouth, muffling any cry for help. The pirate began carrying him off to the dinghy, hidden tied up at the estate's wharf.

"Run, Anamarie, run!" he cried in muzzled tones. Had she heard him? Had little Anamarie seen his capture as she had run ahead of him? Was she safe? He prayed so. Had she been able to run safely back to the villa? Papa would protect her, he thought.

That had been a whole month before, on the last day of May, Anamarie's sixth birthday. Did his father, Dom Carlos Antonio Fran-cisco, the wealthiest man in the Portuguese Azores, know of his son's taking? Why had it been so long? Why had no ships sailed to his res-cue? Would he ever again see his beautiful home on Terceira?

He wiped a small, salty tear from the corner of his eye and sat upright, dangling his legs over the coil of nautical rope. He saw the golden buckles on his black leather shoes, even in the waning moon-light...one large "P" on the left shoe for Pedro and an "F" on the right one for Francisco. They were of shiny gold and a gift from his father on his last birthday.

"What day is this?" the boy abruptly asked himself aloud. "It is the last day of June! ... My birthday!"

"Will this day bring my rescue?" the boy asked himself and God. "If not, what am I to do? What will become of me?" He sat and thought and smelled those wonderful aromas. Soon, his young playmate, the son of the mistress of the tavern, would come and play with him. The boy's mother would feed them breakfast. At least he would start this new day, his eighth birthday, with a full stomach.

The sound of clop-clop-clopping hooves of two horses and the rickety-racket of carriage wheels broke into the peaceful sounds of nature on the wharf. The carriage passed by the boy as he sat on the top of the coiled rope with his playmate, who had just arrived. The boys watched as the carriage pulled to the west side of the tavern.

Two men, dressed elegantly, alit from the closed carriage. The boys watched as the two men stood beside the carriage for several moments before entering the tavern, talking in words the boy of course, could not understand. They appeared to be businessmen, probably merchants, he thought. They both looked to be in their late twenties, both slender and tall. One had a bright orange-red head of hair, the other one, a sandy blonde. They were both dressed in waistcoats and knee breeches with white silk stocking and brass-buckled shoes.

The boy looked down again with pride at his own golden shoe buckles. He thought again back to that day of terror one month before.

He had dressed in his new suit of clothes for the very first time that day, as it was Anamarie's birthday breakfast and blessings at the cathedral. The suit of clothes consisted of olive-colored velveteen knee breeches and waistcoat, a white, puff-sleeved shirt and new black leather shoes with the year-old golden buckles now attached. After breakfast, the family would be going into town to the cathedral for Anamarie's birthday blessings from the bishop.

Just after breakfast, and with some time left before their departure for town, he and Anamarie raced to the shoreline for a few blissful minutes of play. That was, of course, the day he was kidnapped. The new suit of clothes and his golden shoe buckles were the only possessions he had from Terciera. He had now worn that same suit of clothes every day for a full month since the day of his capture.

The boys watched as the redheaded man patted the other man on the back and they entered the tavern.

The two men sat at a table near the entry from the kitchen and soon, the large Negro cook waddled through the kitchen doorway. She had an almost perfectly round, dark chocolate face, with large brown eyes, a small dot of a nose, and broad, thick lips. Her coarse, ebony hair was stuffed beneath a calico bonnet and her calico dress and apron flowed over her enormous frame of a body.

"Mista Patrick Henry! Why I do swear!" she said, greeting the elegantly dressed redhead.

"Auntie Savannah!" the attorney and member of the House of Burgesses returned her greeting. He turned to introduce his breakfast companion.

"May I present a colleague of mine in the legislature, the honorable Calvert McGowan." The blonde-headed gentleman rose and nodded.

"Now," Henry spoke, "How about stacks of your delicious Johnny-cakes, sausages, eggs and those delectable rum buns for the both of us?"

"I'll have 'em in a jiffy, Mista Patrick," Auntie Savannah giggled as she answered and waddled back into the kitchen.

Henry and McGowan, the only ones in the dining room except for a table of four hungry seamen seated by the window, resumed the conversation they had been having.

"Parliament sees the colonies as no more than slaves!" Henry started. "We are not 'real' Englishmen! The only 'real' Englishmen are residents of the isles…they who are represented in Parliament with votes. They forget we, nearly all of us here in Virginia, have roots, if not living relatives, in the shires of England and the moors of Scotland to this day. We founded this land as much for the English monarch and Parliament as we did for ourselves. Now they tether us with taxes and revenue stamps on most everything we need in order to simply exist."

"Patrick, we all agree the Stamp Act is a most vile piece of legislation, and one that should be repealed," answered McGowan. McGowan represented King George County in the so-called Northern Neck of Virginia, east of Fredericksburg. "But, you must admit the point is well-made by the crown."

"So, McGowan," Henry said, letting his red-headed temper rise, "you would vote to see Virginia march in lockstep with Parliament.

You would see Virginians buy their illegally imposed revenue stamps? I shall never do such!"

"We have no option save abiding by the laws rightfully enacted in London," McGowan defended his stance.

"The king wanting it does not make it right!" Henry's ire was now on fire. "The king wanted to send his armies to the American colonies! He wanted to fight a war against the French in Europe and here on our frontier as well! To pay for the war, the king now insists upon taxing our hard work and toil in the colonies beyond all extreme measures!"

The two men were best friends in the legislature. They sat in silence pondering their differences.

"We simply cannot stand against Parliament and king," McGowan tried to add reason to the debate between friends. "How can backwater Virginians convince the lords in London to repeal their damned revenue stamps? We must realize it simply cannot be done."

"Virginia is not alone, McGowan, do you not see that?" Henry calmly asked. "Dr. Franklin has led protests in Philadelphia. There is a man named Adams in Boston, many good men in New York and Maryland and Connecticut. If we all stand together as a united opposition to Parliament, we can convince the prime minister, the exchequer and King George himself, that this royal policy is no way to keep the royal empire together."

"All the colonies uniting?..." McGowan questioned thoughtfully, "...against the power of Parliament and King George?"

"There are voices growing louder and louder with each day in each of the colonies," Henry added. "With every new revenue stamp affixed to more goods, and now even to legal services rendered, there is talk of a special congress to meet in the late summer or fall, somewhere central to all the colonies, perhaps Philadelphia ... perhaps New York. Virginia must be represented and your support is vital to see to it."

"There just might be merit in considering such a congress," McGowan thought out loud. "I shall speak with Colonel Washington."
"Washington?" Henry questioned. "He is nothing but a benchwarmer in the legislature. His concerns are only for his fields and for his subsequent fortunes." Henry shook his head showing a great dislike for the fellow burgess from Frederick County.

"There is a limit to Col. Washington's vision," Henry continued. "Outside the realm of his Mount Vernon, he has no real knowledge, no expertise at all on any subject, no opinions and definitely no interest in muddying the waters between the Chesapeake Bay and the River Thames!"

"How can you say that, Patrick?" McGowan was astonished at his friend's disdain for the most important Virginia hero of the late war. "He fought heroically against the French and the Indians."

"Oh yes," Henry added snidely. "The great military genius of Colonel George Washington took a message from Governor Dinwiddie to the French commandant at some French outpost in the wilderness, demanding they vacate the land. The French laughed at him and run him off," Henry chuckled.

"He built that fort, what was it called? Fort Necessity?" Henry continued his argument against the hero. "It fell to a small advance party of Frenchmen and a handful of savages a few days after being built. As soon as he saw the French Fleur de Lis fluttering in the breeze, Colonel Washington waved his little white flag of surrender."

"But he led the successful retreat from Great Meadows after General Braddock was killed," McGowan argued. "He took command and saved the army."

"He certainly does know how to run from a fight," Henry said. "I will give you that."

"But Virginia listens to him, Patrick," McGowan came again to Washington's defense.

"Pity Virginia as she buys those damned stamps!" Henry said, ending the conversation as the pretty young mistress of the tavern, Christina Donnelley, entered from the kitchen with a tray of hot tea and biscuits.

"Gentlemen," Christina greeted her diners with a sweet smile, "shall you have tea?" The two men rose and nodded politely, having concluded their somewhat heated discussion of colonial politics.

"May I sit?" Christina asked.

"Certainly, Christina," Henry said rising, "Please grace us with your company this fine morning," He introduced McGowan to the pretty young widow who had caught his attention, being a bachelor himself. After pouring three cups of tea, she sat and faced Henry.

"Patrick, I want you to meet a child," she said and told the story of the young boy showing up mysteriously on the wharf three days before. She talked of how he spoke a language foreign to her but seemed similar in some ways to Spanish or Italian. She had fed him meals at the tavern and he played with her six-year-old boy, Joshua, though the two could only communicate through actions and smiles, not words.

"We need to find a place for him," Christina said pleadingly. "He sleeps on that coiled up old rope on the edge of the wharf. He is elegantly dressed, though it is clear the lad has worn the same clothing for weeks. I fear he has been kidnapped or abandoned here."

"Or perhaps a runaway, a stowaway aboard a European ship," Henry interjected matter-of-factly.

"I do not know," was all Christina could say sadly as she sipped from her teacup.

About that time the tavern door flew open and the two boys ran inside laughing.

"May we please have a rum bun to share?" her six-year-old son, Joshua, asked his mother.

"Absolutely not!" Christina said, rising sternly. "Not until after the both of you wash and finish the plate of johnnycakes and eggs Auntie Savannah has for you on the hearth. Now go on. Wash up!" She lightly tapped her son on his butt as he ran past her into the kitchen, followed by the new boy.

As the new boy was rushing past the table, Henry grabbed his arm strongly. The boy, startled, turned his head and looked square into Patrick Henry's eyes as if that same terror from his surprise abduction had returned to his world once more.

"Where do you come from lad?" Henry asked. "What is your name? Who is your father, your Papa?"

The boy understood the word "Papa" then smiled and spoke some words in his native tongue. Henry smiled and loosed the boy's arm. The boy rushed off, following his friend into the kitchen, turning his head back once toward Patrick, smiling as he disappeared through the kitchen doorway.

"Portuguese, I dare say," said Henry. "I believe that it was Portuguese he spoke. I have a client here at City Point, one Nicholas Souza. He is a Portugee himself."

"I know Nico," Christina said with a pensive smile, "the black-smith. I will send for him this very day. Thank you, Patrick. Thank you ever so much!"

A Link to Home

Nicholas Souza, a dark-haired, large-framed, swarthy man in his fifties, called "Nico" by everyone in City Point, had arrived ten years earlier. He had opened a blacksmith shop to continue his life's work. Nico had been apprenticed as a young boy in a village in Portugal. He lived alone above his shop, which sat about a half mile east of the wharf, one dirt road over from the waterfront.

He and his young wife Marianna had sailed from Lisbon in 1735, when they were both in their twenties, settling in Philadelphia. They were never able to have any children, and Marianna died suddenly of the fever in 1750. Nico, devastated by Marianna's death, could not remain in Philadelphia with all those memories of her. He hired onto a merchant ship and spent a year or more sailing between America, Europe and the Caribbean. When the ship made its final port call at City Point, before a planned docking in Philadelphia in the spring of 1755, Nico left the ship and made City Point his new home.

The swarthy older man was working the bellows at his hearth when a young boy entered the shop with a note from Christina. In the note she asked him to come to the tavern that afternoon.

Near the end of the day, the blacksmith walked onto the wharf. Christina saw him through the windows as he approached and wel-comed him at the door. They sat at the table by the window.

"Nico, you are Portuguese are you not?" Christina asked.

"Yes ma'am, from Portugal," Nico affirmed. "All of my fifty-three years, I have been a Portugee," he smiled.

"There is someone I want you to meet," she said. "He is just a little boy and speaks an exotic language. The lawyer, Patrick Henry, says he thinks it to be Portuguese. Could you confirm that and talk with him? He is such a mystery. If he has been lost, we want to help him."

She led Nico out onto the wharf where they spotted the boys play-ing near the warehouse. Christina pointed out the mysterious boy and Nico approached him. They began to talk and laugh and hug one another. Christina smiled with tears of joy. At last there might now be some way to communicate with the child, and truly help him. Christina sat and smiled, tears in her eyes.

After several minutes more, Nico sent the boy back to play with his friend and headed back to the tavern. Christina sat a tankard of rum in front of Nico. He began to relay the story of the boy's kidnapping from the Portuguese Azores by Dutch pirate slavers. He had been put to work on the pirate ship, with a cargo below deck from Senegal. When the ship off-loaded the slaves at Norfolk, the slave market master would not allow the boy to be auctioned off as a slave along with the Africans. Having no further use for the Portuguese boy, they spared his life and sailed up the James River that evening. The ship dropped anchor just below City Point. When it was well past dark, four of the pirates rowed him in a dinghy to the wharf, under cover of darkness, and abandoned him there.

Nico told Christina the boy's mother had died just a year before. "Like my Marianna, she died of the fever." Nico went on to say the boy's father was a wealthy landowner on the island of Terceira in the Azores. He had a younger sister and a papa he dearly loved and missed. That was all Nico could tell Christina about the boy, other than that the fine suit of clothes he wore had just been bought, and the golden shoe buckles with the "P" and "F" monograms had been a present on his seventh birthday. His name was Pedro Francisco. Nico had suggested to the boy he use the more English-sounding "Peter" and the lad agreed, liking the sound. "His name is now Peter Francisco and this day, June 30th is his birthday. He is now eight years old."

Christina bolted up and looked out the windows where the boys were playing. "We must have a birthday party tonight for young Peter Francisco! Indeed we must!" She turned and headed toward the kitchen, then turned back toward Nico. "You must come too, Nico. Savannah will bake a cake and we shall have a fine dinner for Peter on his birthday. Chicken? Lamb?"

"Caldierada!" Nico suggested as he stood. "I shall make it the Portugee way. That will be a real treat for the boy. It's a cod fish stew with clams, potatoes, onions and pin pin…little red peppers."

As Nico began to rush out the door, Christina yelled to him. "Can you be here by six?"

"Six o'clock," Nico nodded, "I shall be here with my Caldierada!"

Young Peter Francisco

Peter was surprised when he followed Joshua to the tavern for supper that night. There was a table set with a white linen cloth. The two young men, the one who had grabbed him by the arm and his friend were there, as was Nico, Christinia and a handful of others he did not know. He smelled the fish stew Nico had brought to the tavern to simmer on the hearth.

"Caldierada!" Peter shouted as he smiled. Nico had been right, Christina thought. The tastes of his homeland were a real treat for the boy.

Nico served as an interpreter for Peter, and explained to him his new friends in Virginia wanted to celebrate his birthday. That made Peter smile broadly. The cake Auntie Savannah had baked was delicious, but not as good as the rum buns she baked in the morning. They played games and talked about finding a suitable couple to take him in to raise as their own.

"He need not be a ward of the county," Christina said firmly. "He comes from refinement. We must not allow him less here."

"I shall speak to my uncle," Patrick Henry offered. "As the circuit judge, he can stall the county until a suitable adoptive family is found."

When the party broke up, Peter went back to the rope coil for bed. He had had a good day on his eighth birthday. He laid atop the coil, arms folded beneath his head. He gazed up at the heavens in the ebon firmament lit only by a pale moon and twinkling stars. He smiled. He now had friends in this new land and Nico to help him not forget Terciera. He went to sleep with a smile on his face.

It was not long before young Peter Francisco was spending more and more of his time with Nico, his countryman. Nico also would steal away from his blacksmith shop and spend hours sitting on the rope coils or on the edge of the pier, talking, teaching Peter, little by little, words and phrases in English the Virginians could understand. Nico had had to learn English himself when he and Marianna first arrived.

"There is not one thing worse than being in a strange land and not being able to speak the language of that strange land," Nico advised Peter.

Peter would walk with the older man back to the blacksmith shop after their conversations and lessons. Peter would stay and watch as his newfound friend worked at his forge. Nico was quickly becoming Peter's surrogate father. Peter was fascinated watching Nico pump the billows and pound the red-hot irons from the forge into their intended shapes.

Peter was a good student and a fast learner. The blacksmith had become a good teacher and a wonderful mentor to the lad. The older Portugee taught the younger Portugee some basics of conversational English. He had given Peter a slate and pieces of chalk to write phrases in his native tongue for Nico to translate and teach him how to speak the same phrases in English. Once he learned the words and phrases from Nico, Christina began to teach him the elementaries of reading and writing in English. He still played with his first friend in America, Joshua, but Peter's real fascination and goal now was to learn to speak, read and write his new language as a Virginian.

All that summer, Peter faced the reality of his circumstances. He missed Anamarie and his papa tremendously. He missed the estate he had known as home since his birth. While he dreamed of some day seeing a ship, sent by his father, docking at the wharf at City Point that would carry him back across the Atlantic Ocean to his real home, he knew that the dream was unlikely to come true. How would his father ever know Peter was well and living amongst new and wonderful friends at City Point? Peter knew his father probably accepted the reality that he could not have survived such a capture and kidnapping by the pirates, and was dead and thrown overboard at sea. He still greeted every ship that arrived at the dock, just in case.

Christina put a cot and quilts for Peter to sleep on in the storehouse just off the kitchen at the back of the tavern. Some nights, Peter slept above the blacksmith shop, on a bed made for him on the floor in Nico's room. He was well taken care of and never wanted for food or companionship.

Christina bought him several pairs of under garments, trousers and shirts, so he would have suitable clothing to wear playing. She had his fine suit of clothing laundered. With the constant wearing, the suit could not be returned to its original condition, but at least the laundress was able to put new life into it. Christina kept it in a cedar chest for when Peter might need it.

The real mission Christina embarked upon was to find a family who would give Peter a new and permanent home. She spent afternoons at the courthouse signing papers and keeping Peter from being taken as a ward of the county. She talked to the parson at the Anglican Church and interviewed certain parishioners, but none seemed just right for Peter. Oh, there were a handful of prospects, all fine Christians who could love Peter as their own, but none seemed financially equipped to take on the needs of the boy.

Christina loved Peter, but Peter needed a father as her own son Joshua did. Nico loved Peter dearly, but at his age, his health was not what it had been. He often said to Christina, "If Peter had come into my life when my Marianna was alive, we would have had a boy of our own!"

Judge Anthony Winston

Anthony Winston was a tall, slender, dashing figure with reddish-brown hair, more brown than reddish. He was a thirty-year-old land-owner in Hanover County, the biggest part of a day's journey north of City Point, south of Fredericksburg. He was a successful planter with hundreds of acres in tobacco for commercial sales in the colonies and for shipments to England. He owned about seventy slaves to tend to the work on his plantation.

Winston had been appointed a judge in 1760, by Francis Faquier, the Lieutenaant Governor, acting as Governor for the Crown Governor Jeffrey Amherst, who remained in England. He rode the circuit that included court duties in Hanover County and five others, including Prince George County with its courthouse at City Point. His judicial circuit brought him at least once each month to City Point.

Judge Winston had grown up with his one-year younger nephew, Patrick Henry. Like his nephew, the judge frequented Christina Don-nelley's Tavern on the wharf at City Point when his duties brought him to the banks of the James River. He favored Auntie Savannah's cook-ing and the comfortable featherbeds in the upper loft where he found lodgings.

"I hear from my nephew the young Portugee boy is doing quite well, learning to actually converse in English," the judge said to Christina one day in late August as he arrived at the tavern for two days of court duties in City Point.

"Oh yes, judge," Christina reported with pride. "He is such a good student and one can tell he comes from a home and a family of grand refinement."

"Now that he seems to be well on his way to becoming a Virginian," the judge inquired, "what is to become of him?"

"Well," Christina went on, "Nico says he is quickly learning to become a blacksmith."

"A blacksmith?" the judge seemed amused. "A noble trade no doubt, but is that not limiting the lad, assuming he is of noble parentage? I should think, the law, commerce, medicine, a profession more appropriate for such a boy. He should be schooled and trained up so as to make his own choices, don't you think?"

"That would certainly be wonderful for Peter," Christina said, "but that would take a generous and loving family with just as generous a bank account. Who might you know who could be a such ward for Peter?"

"Adella and I," the judge replied matter-of-factly.

Anthony Winston had married Adella Pope in 1756, when she was eighteen. Adella was a cousin of some sort of George Washington through their shared great-grandmother Anne Pope Washington. Try as the newlyweds did, they had never been blessed with children of their own. They had, however, taken on the parenting of the nine-year-old son of Anthony's older brother. Anthony and Adella had found great joy in young Zachary and were intrigued by Patrick Henry's stories of Peter Francisco. They felt Zachary needed a brother and from all they had heard about Peter, he might just be that brother for Zachary they had hoped for. The judge wanted to meet the youngster and broach the topic of Peter coming to live with him and Adella and young Zachary at Winston Woods.

"He shall certainly be raised properly, you can be assured," the judge noted. "He will be educated well and loved as a son of our own making." The judge seemed to be asking permission from Christina.

"I could think of no finer life in Virginia for Peter," Christina said with genuine happiness. "Let us go and you shall meet him now. If you favor him in the flesh as you seem to have been intrigued with him from Patrick's reports, then I agree wholeheartedly."

"Are you not forgetting the boy's favoring of me?" the judge wisely added. "I shall not agree based upon my own satisfaction with him, but he too must seem to be well-satisfied with the prospect of me being his father."

Peter and Joshua were playing near the warehouse as Christina and the judge approached. Christina pulled Peter aside and told him she had an important man for him to meet.

Peter and the judge sat and talked for a long time. They immediately bonded and Peter seemed pleased that someone so kind and so influential as Judge Anthony Winston would show such interest in him, and invite him to come live with his family on their plantation.

"What about Nico?" Peter asked. Peter felt somewhat confident in his abilities to communicate with the Englishmen in Virginia, but in Nico, he saw a connection with Terciera and his former life. He also felt safe knowing Nico was just a few steps away if he needed him.

"What if Papa hears news of me and sends for me?" Peter asked.

"What if I send word on a merchant ship bound for the Azores," the judge offered, "to let your papa know you are safe here in Virginia and available for him to send for you at any time?"

"You would do that for me?" Peter's dark eyes lit up. "You would really do that?"

"It shall be our goal," the judge said, putting an arm around Peter's shoulder, "reuniting you with your family. In the meantime, we shall see to your studies. As for Mr. Souza, well, I suppose there is always the need for a skilled smithy on a plantation."

Peter spent the next the next two days preparing to leave City Point for his new home.

He spent many hours with Nico.

"My new home is called Winston Woods," Peter said, "It is a big plantation on a river with a strange name...Pamunkey," Peter laughed. "Isn't that a funny name for a river?"

"Yes," Nico said laughing, "that is a funny name."

"I wonder if there are monkeys living in the trees," Peter said with a giggle.

"You shall see soon enough," Nico smiled.

"The judge said you could come too, and work as a blacksmith on the plantation," Peter added. "Could you? Would you please, so I do not miss you so."

"My health is not so good, Peter," the old man admitted. "And besides, here I work when I want to work and when I can work. I would not like to work for another. You can visit any time you wish when the judge comes here."

Peter hugged him, wanting him to come with him to Winston Woods, but realizing he could not.

"I will miss you," Peter planted a kiss on the old man's cheek.

"I shall miss you too," Nico said with a tear in the corner of his eye. "But I am so happy for you." He hugged him strongly.

Soon the judge's work at the courthouse in City Point was concluded for another month. His carriage pulled up to Christina Donnelley's Tavern. They would leave early the next morning.

After a hearty breakfast served by Auntie Savannah and a teary-eyed round of hugs and kisses, Peter and the judge were ready to leave. Peter, wearing the restored suit of clothes he had arrived in, and naturally wearing his golden shoe buckles with the "P" and "F" monograms, boarded the closed carriage. A small cedar trunk was loaded atop the carriage. It contained clothing and other possessions he had accumulated as gifts from Christinia, Patrick Henry, Nico and others during his two and a half months on the wharf since his arrival in late June. He was anxious to see this new home of his.

Winston Woods on the Pamunkey

Peter liked what he saw as the carriage left the main road just outside a small settlement named Hewlett. The carriage turned down a mile-long lane leading up to the manor house. The lane from the main road was bordered on both sides with majestic-looking trees, forming a leafy canopy over the lane as the horses clop-clop-clopped and the carriage jiggled back and forth down the lane.

Beyond the lane to the west was a huge tobacco field. Dozens of ebony-skinned Negro slaves, their faces and exposed arms glistening with sweat from the warm sun, were harvesting the tobacco leaves. Some were loading them into a wagon to be taken to the tobacco barn and hung to cure through the coming months. To the east were other fields of corn and grains with more slaves hard at work. The lane stopped at a circular drive in front of the huge manor house.

The manor house was red brick and two stories high with a third dormer-styled level above. Six Corinthian style columns held the two-story roof over the porch that swept across the entire south front of the mansion, wrapping around both sides. Six broad steps led up from the drive to the porch, and a white-painted wooden double-door stood in the symmetrical center of the main level of the house. Beneath the entry eave were six windows on either side on the first floor and eight across the second. Giant and ancient-looking trees surrounded the stately home.

A male Negro house servant opened the huge double-doors as the judge's carriage arrived. A pretty lady, with golden blonde hair framing her pretty, cream-like face with deep-set blue eyes and a beautiful smile, came out onto the porch, followed by a boy about Peter's age. As the judge and Peter alit from the carriage, Adella and young Zachary rushed down the steps and greeted them.

"This is your new mother," the judge said after giving Adella a kiss. Peter extended his hand to take and kiss hers politely. He nodded in respect and smiled at her as she smiled back at him.

"And this handsome young man," the judge said, "is your new brother, Zachary."

Peter shook hands with his new brother and they too exchanged assuring smiles. Peter was several inches taller than Zachary and a bit beefier, even though Zachary was a full year older. As they soon learned, their birthdays were just two days apart, Zachary having been born on June 28th 1756.

They all walked up the six steps, across the porch and into the mansion.

The house was of traditional Virginia plantation design, with an entry hall running south to north in the exact center of the ground level, with a dissecting hall running east from west. An elegant shellacked wooden staircase with an emerald green Persian carpet runner, with burgundy and golden designs, led to the upper floors and the bedchambers.

The foyer had the same carpet laid wall-to-wall and extended down both hallways in the same fashion. The first floor held sitting rooms, formal dining room and a smaller family dining room. Beyond the intersecting hallway was the inside kitchen and the office for the judge-planter who was master of the plantation. At the far north end of the entry hall was a wood and glass set of double-doors leading out to an expansive verandah overlooking the sleepy-looking, narrow and winding river with the strange name.

With what he had already seen, Peter knew this would be a wonderful place to live and to be schooled, until word reached his papa, and his papa would send for him.

He and Zachary would share a large bedroom on the second level. The room for the boys looked out over the river below and all the trees bordering it on both sides. The room's northern windows opened onto a verandah, which was actually the roof of the verandah below. They could play there, read and study, or just sit and talk. Zachary seemed to be a friendly sort and Peter felt they would soon become as close as natural brothers.

The judge knew it was time for some formal schooling for his two boys. Peter seemed to have a real thirst for knowledge and would be a good influence on Zachary. He had arranged for the pastor of the local Episcopal parish, the Rev. Abraham Gadsden, to be boarded on the plantation in exchange for his services as a tutor to the two boys.

Saint David's Parish was a relatively small parish with a church but no parsonage. The pastor was boarded around in the homes of the congregants, each taking turns one week at a time. Rev. Gadsden would now become a permanent resident at Winston Woods, having his own quarters on the dormer floor with a spacious bedchamber and across the hall, an office and library for his school and church preparations.

Classes would be held in the old smokehouse and begin the first week of September.

Rev. Gadsden moved in with all his meager worldly possessions, which did include several volumes on mathematics, science and nature, the classics, history, literature, and of course, religion. The boys had a full two weeks to play and explore and be boys before their first day of formal studies.

The thousand-acre plantation was a veritable wonderland for young boys in colonial Virginia. There were fields and forests to explore, a river to wade and swim in, and row boats to get to the other shore. There were barns and corncribs to hideout in. There was one adventure after another to be had.

The blue-colored and misty high mountains to the west, the Blue Ridge range of the Appalachian Mountains, were always there to beckon them. They dreamed of exploring the mountains some day, maybe next summer when classes would cease for the season.

Peter and Zachary spent the first days after Peter's arrival becoming great friends and playmates. Their days were full after the huge breakfast in the family dining room, served by the Negro servant Malcolm, his wife Mammy Jane, their twelve-year-old daughter Cassia and ten-year-old son Pearlie. The centerpiece of breakfast was generally baked ham from the smokehouse served with eggs, biscuits from the hearth's oven chamber, and a side dish of something called grits. Grits were a cooked concoction of coarse corn meal, very tasty to Peter when dollops of churned butter melted on top.

As breakfast was being cleared from the table, Peter and Zachary would go back upstairs to their bedchamber. They would go out onto the verandah and plan for their day's adventures while they waited for Pearlie to finish his morning chores of washing the breakfast dishes or sweeping out the inside kitchen.

The inside kitchen in colonial homes in the South was not where the food was cooked. It was only where the cooked food was taken from the detached cookhouse and plated to be served to the diners, and where the dishes were washed and put away. Too many colonial homes had burned to the ground due to errant embers or logs falling from the roaring hearth and engulfing the entire home in flames. Heat was another practical reason for having a detached cookhouse. In Virginia and the other colonies in the warmer climes of the South, spring, summer and autumn could bring unbearable temperatures. Heat from an inside kitchen with its hearth burning from before sun up till after the evening meal had been cooked, would add more heat to the natural sweltering heat of the day. At Winston Woods, the cookhouse was about twenty feet from the back door on the west side of the inside kitchen, with a roofed-over stone walkway connecting the two. The old smokehouse was about another twenty feet or so from the kitchen house. A new smokehouse had been built beside the butchering barn quite a distance from the house.

Soon Pearlie came out from underneath the verandah roof and yelled up to the awaiting boys. Some days, Cassia would join them if she had no chores in the sewing room that day.

Peter and Zachary rushed down the stairs as soon as they heard Pearlie's yells from below. Then they'd be off on the adventure they had planned for the day.

"We're going to the ravine today, Pearlie," Zachary announced. "Peter's never seen it."

They headed west along the riverbank through the dense stand of trees. They each claimed a limb, fallen from the branches above, to use as walking sticks and as weapons against the gangly briars they knew they'd be encountering along the way. The walking sticks were also needed should they come across a slithering snake or other critter they hoped not to encounter. Pearlie led the way as the guide, with Peter close behind, and Zachary guarding their rear flank.

After about a half-mile or so, they came to the famous ravine. The ravine dropped suddenly about twenty-five or thirty feet to a small stream emptying into the larger Pamunkey. There was a trail to the bottom, narrow and hazardous looking, but great for eight, nine and ten year-old boys set out for a day of adventure. Safely down from the wooded heights above, they crossed the shallow, narrow stream stepping on large rocks and pieces of flat slate each step of the way. On the far bank of the creek was a grassy flat mesa above the riffling waters. There they sat, proud of their successful trek through the woods and down the cliff.

Now they faced the climb up the other steeper side of the ravine.

"When we get about to the top," Zachary said, "Pearlie and I have a real surprise for you, Peter." Peter smiled, wondering what kind of surprise lay in store for him.

21

"Is that where I might see the monkeys of the Pamunkey River?" Peter joked. They all laughed.

About three-quarters the way up the west side of the ravine was a short narrow ledge path heading south around the hill. About fifteen feet off the main path stood a huge, ancient oak tree. Pearlie led the adventurers down the ledge path to the huge oak and pointed to a grapevine attached to a sturdy branch on the old tree. The end of the vine hung down to about three feet from the ground and was crooked and curved, a great grip for a boy to hold onto and swing out over the ravine and stream fifteen or twenty feet below.

Pearlie grabbed the end of the vine, backed up about eight paces and ran to the edge of the ledge. He swung out a good fifteen feet, sailing over the creek bed twenty feet below.

"That looks like real fun!" giggled Peter. "Can I try it?"

Peter took the vine from Pearlie, grasped it and did what he had seen Pearlie do. When his swing was over he said, giggling, "that was a little scary,... but that was so much fun!"

They took turns swinging on the grapevine for at least half an hour.

As Zack finished his last swing, Peter said, "I can now say I have indeed seen the monkeys of the Pamunkey, swinging through the trees. And I am one myself!" he laughed as the three adventurers headed back down the ledge path to the main path and continued their climb up.

Soon they were at the top of the ravine where trees gave way to a broad and flat field of barley. They rested beside a small spring beneath a large, spreading walnut tree standing alone at the edge of the field. They pulled out the packed pieces of fried chicken and slices of apple pie Pearlie had packed for them for the midday meal. They sat and ate and talked and laughed and drank the cold clear water from the spring. Faraway in the distance, running down the entire western horizon were those magnificent and mysterious-looking misty blue mountains.

"That's where our Virginians and the British soldiers fought those nasty Frenchmen and those savage Indians in the war," Zack told Peter as he pointed to the mountains. "The war was fought just on the other side of those mountains. The French and Indian War they called it."

They talked about the war and the stories of Indians burning the cabins and farms of white settlers, scalping the men, women and even babies. The savages boiled them, dead or alive, and ate their boiled flesh and guts and drank the bloody stew broth. The French and Indian War had just ended two years earlier, with the British taking control of all the land and the French being eradicated from North America. The tribes of Indians still lived and hunted there and butchered white settlers who dared to venture across the mountains, breaking the edict of the King of England, which forbade his subjects to settle west of the range.

The summit of the mountains marked the western boundary of the English colonies in America, of which Virginia was the oldest. As the mysterious blue mountains beckoned Zack and Peter, they also called out to many adults. Names like Michael Cresap, George Washington, Simon Kenton and Daniel Boone were on the lips and in the minds of those felt locked-in by the mountains. Those folks were yearning to see and settle the lands of the Kanawha River, the Ohio country, and the endless lands to the west.

It was said, a giant country lay west of the Blue Ridge and someday soon, now that the evil and greedy Frenchmen had been kicked out, would be free for the Virginians and other English colonists to settle.

There was said to be a huge river called the Mississippi, that ran all the way from the Gulf of Mexico at the French city of New Orleans, all the way north to the Great Lakes. There were tales of gold and other riches, and flat arable lands for farming, and plains for grazing. There were high western mountains, much taller and steeper than the Blue Ridge. Finally, there was the shoreline of the great ocean called the Pacific. The only white men who had been west of the Mississippi were French fur trappers and a handful of mountain men from the colonies.

Peter, Zack and Pearlie looked west and dreamed of what really might lie over the western slope. Was all they had heard true? They began dreaming the same dreams dreamed by men filled with wanderlust and the independence to create their own Winston Woods. They dreamed of making their own fame, fortune and comfort that came with owning their own land.

On their way back, after their fried chicken and cherry pie, the boys visited and played around at the stables, in the barns, and in the old smokehouse that had been turned into their schoolhouse.

It had been made ready for classes for the two boys. There was a desk for the teacher facing the boys. There was a bookshelf on the wall behind the teacher's desk and a large piece of black slate nailed to the wall next to the shelf. The boys would sit on a long bench with a wooden table in front of it. The classroom was sparse and harsh-looking, but the ideal setting for a colonial education. They sat on the benches at their makeshift desk and wondered what the Episcopal pastor would be like and how much they would learn from him.

The Trident of Neptune

Judge Winston had an office on the main floor of the mansion where he pored through his law books and kept current on the legal precedents coming down from the judicial benches in London and throughout the British realm. The responsibility he had been given was to adjudicate all forms of complaints, civil and criminal, in the counties where he was called to sit on the bench. He took his responsibility seriously, and knew, while the British system of justice was not perfect, it was, nonetheless, as fair as could be expected.

He scheduled two weeks each month to conduct court at the courthouse in Hanover. Those weeks he would ride to and from Hanover and dine and sleep at home each night. For ten days each month he would ride the circuit and be away from the plantation every night.

As the boys were about to start their schooling in the old smokehouse, the judge left on the circuit. He was to be in City Point for a special trial the next morning.

As soon as he arrived, he went straight to the wharf where he met a sea captain at Christina Donnelley's Tavern. The sea captain had loaded his ship with tobacco and was sailing at first light for London.

"There is a mystery I need your help in solving," Judge Winston approached the sea captain.

He told how Peter had been found on the wharf one morning in June. It had been determined the boy was Portuguese, from the island of Terceira in the Azores, and through an interpreter, had learned he had been kidnapped by Dutch pirates on a slaver which left him abandoned on the wharf at City Point.

"The boy is now with me," the judge said. "I need, for his sake, to get word to his family in the Azores, of his whereabouts and that he is doing well and is safe. Should they want to make arrangements to come for him, or for us to send him home, we shall make every such arrangement necessary."

The sea captain, Jacob Darwin, hesitated.

"How can I find the family? We port at San Sebastiao on our return trip in December, just for loading a few casks of Madeira Port. I really have no time to go gallivanting around, looking for a lost boy's family."

"From what we know, the task should not be time-consuming at all. His family is wealthy and well-known. Their estate lies very near San Sebastiao. It is reported the father is the wealthiest man in the Azores, a certain Dom Carlos Antonio Francisco. I will pay handsomely for anything you might be able to find."

Captain Darwin finally agreed and the two shook hands. Darwin said he would make the three-week crossing to London, be in London most of a week unloading the tobacco and loading the orders from Winston and the other Virginia planters. He would stop at Oporto on the Portuguese coast for casks of wine, and then at Sao Sebastiao, load on crates of bottled Madeira Port. The ship, 'Trident of Neptune,' would arrive back at City Point the second week of December, barring any unexpected delay.

Judge Winston would make the trip to City Point that same week in December, to tend to the business of the court and also to take possession of the items he had ordered from London for Winston Woods that the Trident of Neptune would be off-loading.

The Judge returned to Hanover County, pleased with the arrangements he had made. Regardless of the outcome of this investigation, the judge knew life would be better for Peter. If it worked out the way the judge assumed it would, Peter's family would send for their boy and Peter's life would resume again in the Azores. He was saddened to think that soon Peter would probably be leaving Winston Woods, and no longer be the joy he was becoming daily to Adella and himself, and especially to Zachary.

But the judge knew, it was all for the best. He assembled the family in the parlor after the evening meal upon his return. He told Adella, Zachary and Peter of the agreement between him and Captain Darwin.

"I want you all to know and to be prepared for the news, whatever it may be," the judge warned. "If it is God's will, this Christmas will be a time of great joy for Peter, and for us all, knowing he will soon return to the Francisco Villa, and be reunited with the family he so misses," the judge said, trying to lessen the sadness he knew Adella and Zachary must be feeling, and preparing them for the inevitable.

He turned to Peter. "I have fulfilled the promise I made to you, Peter, the first day I met you at City Point," the judge continued, "to do all in my power to get word to your family in the Azores, that you are with us and doing fine." Everyone in the room sat quietly as the judge spoke.

"When the Trident of Neptune arrives back at City Point in December, we shall then and there put an end to all the uncertainty Peter has had to ponder every day since his kidnapping. We will make any arrangements Peter's papa wants and see those wishes be carried out."

Adella spoke up. "Certainly we shall be happy, knowing our Peter is happy." She took Peter's hand in hers and patted it, tears beginning to well up in her blue eyes.

"We will share in Peter's joy, that's for certain. What a wonderful Christmas this will be for us all," he said rising to go into his office, hoping Adella, Zachary and Peter did not see the tears of sadness welling up in his eyes.

First Day of School

Rev. Abraham Gadsden was a tall, thin, lanky man, very pale in complexion, with sandy-brown hair, sort of unruly, unless plastered down with some sort of clear, greasy ointment. He was in his late twenties and had a pleasant sounding voice and large round blue eyes, pleasing to look at. The reverend had spent several days moving onto the dormer floor of the mansion, and brought with him several chests of books. The books were now filling the bookshelf behind his desk in the old smokehouse.

Each boy was given his own smaller slate, like the large black one hanging on the wall. The boys had watched the half-dozen slave men drag it out of the creek a week earlier. Rev. Gadsden also gave them each several pieces of white chalk to carry in a cloth pouch for his lessons. There were also bottles of India ink and quill pens for use on the plain yellow parchment paper stored in Rev. Gadsden's desk for special assignments.

Peter was anxious to learn more about the French and Indian War, fought just beyond the mountains, and what the land beyond those mountains was really like. He knew one day he would like to follow the life of an explorer, a real adventurer, a soldier, and claim thousands of acres for himself.

Zack was more interested in nature. Trees and plants and all the animals of the forests, fields and streams, had always been his passion. As the three boys took their hikes, Zack was always the one stopping mid-march to stoop down, spotting an unusual looking mushroom or a fern. The birds that flew by or a fish or crawdad beneath the clear rippling waters of the streams and river fascinated him. He was mesmerized by nature, all of nature.

The appointed day came and after a full breakfast with the family and teacher in the family dining room, Peter and Zack followed the tall, lanky Gadsden to the Winston Woods schoolhouse. The boys took their seats as Rev. Gadsden took his seat facing them.

"Boys," Gadsden started, "I have been secured by Judge Winston, as you well know, to guide your elementary educations. During this endeavor, I shall open your young minds to worlds unknown to you at present.

"You will learn first the fundamentals of basic mathematics and the proper skills of reading and writing. We shall be learning the proper and gentlemanly way to comport one's self in society, manners and competent conversation with others. These studies must be well implanted in you in order for us to continue onto more non-rudimentary subjects such as the sciences, the classics, history, and geography.

"We will, of course, study the Holy Scriptures for proper religious training for the salvation of your souls and the betterment of your being while placed here upon this earth by our Creator.

"We shall begin our daily studies," Gadsden continued as he stood, outstretching both arms as if signaling the two from his pulpit, to rise as well, "by reciting the Lord's Prayer."

Peter and Zack stood at their seats.

"Bow your heads in reverence to God Almighty and join me in the prayer:"

"Our Father, who art in Heaven, Hallowed be thy name
Thy kingdom come, thy will be done, on Earth as it is in Heaven.
Give us this day our daily bread
Forgive us our trespasses as we forgive those who trespass against us.
Lead us not into temptation, Deliver us from evil
For thine is the kingdom…and the power…
and the glory forever and ever
Amen."

The Stamp Act Congress

On the last Saturday evening in October, a formal dinner and ball was held at Winston Woods. The occasion was the return of the judge's nephew, Patrick Henry, from the Stamp Act Congress in New York. The congress, with delegates attending from several of the English colonies, had met to formally protest, and call for the immediate repeal of the Stamp Act. Patrick Henry would be the guest of honor and report on his experiences at the congress. Several other plantation owners in and around Hanover County had been invited for the evening to hear the report first hand.

George Washington of Mount Vernon, the famous fighter of the French and the Indians, and a distant cousin of Adella, would be an overnight houseguest along with his wife, Martha. The Washingtons had been invited to stop at Winton Woods en route to the capital at Williamsburg, where the official report would be delivered in more detail to the entire House of Burgesses on the following Tuesday. Washington had represented Fredericksburg in the colonial legislature since 1759.

Another houseguest and friend of the judge, James Madison, Sr. of Orange County to the west, would also be staying at least two nights. His wife, Nellie, and their eldest son, fourteen-year-old Jimmy, would accompany him. The Madisons would leave on Monday morning to return their son to the Innes Plantation in King and Queen County. Jimmy had been a student at the plantation school there for four years, under the instruction of Donald Robertson, a noted educator of colonial Virginia's boys.

The formal dining room at Winston Woods was cavernous and had not been used since Peter arrived at the plantation. The walls were painted a rich royal blue with white and gold molding and cornices. A huge golden carpet covered two-thirds of the hardwood floor where the huge table sat. Three tall windows, with velvety gold draperies tied-back, looked out toward the Pamunkey beyond the north wall.

On rainy days, the boys would sneak into the huge room and play with jacks, toy soldiers or playing cards on the hardwood dance floor. The dance floor took up the west third of the room, except for a small raised platform running alongside the dance floor in the northwest corner. There sat permanently a pianoforte, a harpsichord and a harp, with chairs and music stands now set up for a dozen musicians who would provide minuets for the guests' enjoyment on Saturday evening.

French double doors separated the southeast quarter of the ballroom from the pleasantly appointed ladies sitting room. A second set of French doors led to the gentlemen's brandy and smoking room, fashionably set in a more manly motif. Both sets of doors would remain open on Saturday evening to accommodate the arriving guests before dinner, and after dinner to accommodate those guests not taking to the dance floor for a minuet.

For the dinner party, the huge table had been set for nearly forty diners. There was beautiful china, crystal and flatware imported from London, in exchange for a good harvest of tobacco leaves. A massive island of autumn flowers and foliage arrangements with tall candles and china figurines, interspersed amongst the plants, would separate the diners to be seated on the north side of the table from those seated on the south side. Three crystal and brass chandeliers hung from the ceiling with ivory white candles to provide illumination for the diners and later, the dancers.

The Washngtons and the Madisons both arrived early in the afternoon on Saturday, and were shown to the rooms they would occupy. Fourteen year-old Jimmy Madison, would share Zachary and Peter's room. There was ample room in the large four-poster bed for the three boys to share.

Patrick Henry also arrived early with his fellow burgess and friend, Calvert McGowan. With the overnight guests and guest of honor's early arrival, there was plenty of time for visiting before the neighboring planters and their wives would start arriving. The judge and Adella invited their guests to join them on the verandah for conversation and cider.

"The Pamunkey is so beautiful here, judge," Martha Washington said as she stepped out onto the verandah. "I just love the Pamunkey. You know, I spent ten years sitting on my verandah at White House Plantation, looking out over the Pamunkey. Oh, it is much more broad there, but like here, it meanders and runs slow and peaceful, so idyllic."

Martha Washington had been born not far from Williamsburg in New Kent County in 1731. At eighteen she married Daniel Parke Custis, a much older man and wealthy landowner. The newlyweds moved into Custis' estate mansion called White House on the banks of the Pamunkey River in New Kent County. Her husband died in 1757. At age twenty-six, she found herself to be the wealthiest, marriageable widow in all of Virginia. She had inherited well-over ten thousand prime acres. She married George Washington in 1759, and became mistress of Mount Vernon, in northern Virginia, along the larger and even broader Potomac River.

"Now I sit on our piazza and gaze out over the Potomac and to the green hills and lands of the Maryland colony," she said and smiled.

The boys became excited as soon as they were told the hero of the French and Indian War, George Washington, was dining with them. They sat respectfully in awe of Col. Washington. They were disappointed a bit perhaps, that he didn't spend any time at all talking about his exploits in the wilderness during the late war. But they were still enamored just at the presence of such a great and famous man. They knew he had traveled to the land they had only heard about and fought the French and the Indians.

Washington was content talking with the judge and Mr. Madison about some of the new agricultural techniques he had recently read about in agricultural journals sent to him from England.

"Do you rotate your crops from year-to-year, judge?" Washington asked his host.

"I have started doing just that for the past two seasons now," the judge replied, "and the results are favorable indeed."

"And the soils shall thank you for it. They will be replenished year-to-year and be richly arable for generations to come," Washington inserted. "You must come and visit Mount Vernon soon. I can show you some new innovations I have added." Washington took great pride in his agricultural endeavors.

"It has been some time since I did last visit," said the judge. "We must make plans."

Nellie Madison joined Adella and Martha in a walk through the kitchen gardens while the men smoked their pipes and the boys headed off to show Jimmy Madison their grapevine over the ravine. Jimmy, though six years older than Peter, was a frail-looking and short young man. He barely came up to Peter's chin. Even Zachary was taller and stouter than the Madison boy. But Jimmy was very intelligent and spoke very much like an adult. He would soon be off to the College of William and Mary, Peter supposed, and embarking on a career in the law.

When the musicians arrived shortly before the guests would be pulling into the circular drive in their carriages, it was time for the boys to dress for the evening. Of course, Peter donned his olive green waistcoat and knee breeches, and a clean pair of white silk stockings. He attached the golden shoe buckles from the shoes he wore every day to his best shoes. The three boys dined in the small family dining room, out of sight and earshot of the grown-ups. After dinner was served and eaten, they joined the adults for the report Patrick Henry gave from the Stamp Act Congress.

Patrick Henry rose and spoke eloquently. He was becoming quite well known throughout Virginia as a marvelous speaker.

"Delegates from nine of the thirteen colonies met these past two weeks in New York to express the undeniable and universal opposition to the grievous actions of the British Parliament, embodied in the wrongly enacted Stamp Act.

"We are Englishmen all. Just as Englishmen in London or Coventry or Nottingham or Edinburgh support the government, so too do the Englishmen of Massachusetts and Pennsylvania and Virginia.

"Our complaint with the king and with Parliament is a just complaint. We will gladly share the burden with our cousins and grandparents still residing in the isles of Britain, but that sharing of the burden must be an equitable sharing. The colonies, with no voice and with no vote in Parliament, as our cousins and grandparents living in the isles do have, shall never uphold a tax levied upon us in the colonies, but not levied upon those cousins and grandparents in England, Scotland, Wales and Ireland."

There were nods of agreement, polite applause, and a few audible huzzahs.

"Why must we, Virginians, Marylanders, and Carolinians," Henry continued his report, "be burdened alone to replenish the king's treasury, depleted by a war of his own making ... a war fought upon the fields of Europe as well as in the forests of the American frontier?"

There was more agreement expressed from the diners.

"Without a voice and without a vote in Parliament, we are to accept, with no opposition, a tax on goods, home grown and manufactured, and a tax on services rendered, necessary to sustain our very existence. Stamps! Revenue Stamps! Tax Stamps! Unjustly considered and unjustly levied, must be repealed and repealed immediately!"

Henry accepted the energetic applause with a nod of his head and continued.

"That is the very message of the Stamp Act Congress. We are individual colonies and are unanimous in agreement and united in our purpose.

"The colonies, each and every one of them, shall stand together and raise a united opposition to the most burdensome acts of Parliament. We shall stand together to demand repeal immediately of the unnecessary taxations we are now tethered with, and we shall stand united to demand our rights as full Englishmen!"

The report from Patrick Henry ended as the diners raised crystal glasses of Portuguese Madeira Port wine to toast their guest of honor and his remarks. All seemed pleased with what they had heard of the work done by the delegates to the Stamp Act Congress.

Death at Winston Woods

One afternoon in mid-November, Rev. Gadsden ended classes early to allow the boys to enjoy some of the sunshine and unseasonable warmth of the day. Zack and Peter grabbed Pearlie and Cassia and headed down to the pier on the Pamunkey. The four climbed aboard the wooden rowboat and Peter took the oars. They were off on an afternoon adventure.

They rowed the boat downstream a ways, wondering when Rev. Gadsden would finally teach them something other than addition and subtraction, spelling and penmanship, and reading stories from the "Virginia Elementary Primer."

"When are we going to learn about all these fishes swimming in the Pamunkey?" Zack whined.

"What about the savage tribes of the Ohio country?" Peter joined in with his own complaint.

"At least you can learn somethin' and get an education," moaned Pearlie. "I wish't I could sit in the old smokehouse and learn somethin' like you."

"Why can't you go to school with us, Pearlie?" Peter asked, having never thought about it.

"He's a black boy, a slave!" Zack answered promptly. "Slaves can't be taught anything, except how to hoe and harvest and cook and clean!"

"Why?" Peter continued his questioning. "In my school at Sao Sebastiao, there was no difference between students, black ones or white."

"It just isn't done," Zack said, "leastwise not here in Virginia."

"Seems to me the slaves would be even better at their jobs if they had some education too," Peter said. "Pearlie, I'll tell you what. You and Cassia meet Zack and me everyday after we get out of school, and we'll teach you some of what we learn each day. What do you say Zack?"

"Sounds okay to me, but we have to ask papa first," Zack went along reluctantly.

"I ain't gonna be schooled," Cassia said. "Even the white girls don't have ta go ta no school. All we girls need to know is how to keep house, cook and make our menfolk happy. I know enough to get by."

"I will be there every day," Pearlie said and smiled.

As Peter rowed, they saw a toe headed boy of about their age, fishing off a dock on the north bank of the river. Zack yelled and waved at him.

"Gettin' any bites, Peter?" Zack shouted to the boy.

"Not a dang one! Not a gosh darned nibble!" the blonde boy with the cane fishing pole in his hand and his bare feet dangling in the water, yelled back. "I'm ready to call it quits for the day. What you doin'?"

Peter rowed over to the dock where the other Peter was fishing. The boy tied the rowboat to the dock, and Zack and Peter climbed out.

"Hello," the blonde boy said, staring at Peter and extending his hand. "I'm Peter Patrick. I live on the plantation here."

"Hello," Peter replied shaking the new boy's hand. "I'm Peter Francisco. I live with Zack and Judge Winston."

"I've not seen you before. So you're named Peter too?" Peter nodded and smiled.

The youngsters sat, dangling their feet over the dock and spent some time talking.

Peter Patrick was not the son of the plantation owners, the Maddens, but was the eight year-old son of the plantation's overseer, Buford Patrick. The Patrick boy had gotten no formal schooling, just hands-on education following his father into the fields and barns each day. He had a lot of time to sit on the dock and fish and go hunt mushrooms and berries or rabbits and squirrels. There were really no other boys his age to play with, but once in awhile he and Zack would get together and play. Peter and Zack promised the other Peter they'd come back as often as they could so he'd have more regular playmates to go off with on adventures. The new Peter showed them where he lived, pointing to the small clapboard house just a few yards from the dock.

The first day of December came quickly. The air was now getting colder. The skies were now more gray than blue. The sun still came through the clouds nearly every day but did not stay bright nearly so long. The trees had lost most of their leaves and the fields lay dormant for winter. The judge sat in his office in the mansion, knowing that soon he would be making his trip south to City Point. He knew the news coming aboard the Trident of Neptune would change his family life dramatically.

Zachary would view the return of Peter to the Azores with as much remorse as if Peter was his real brother and had died of some horrible disease. Adella would not take the loss of their newest son well, either. Both he and Adella had grown to love Peter as they loved Zachary. He was such an inquisitive young mind, a real joy to have living with them. As the judge closed a book that laid open before him, as if closing a chapter of his own life, he knew that coming news would take time for all to adjust to and accept.

"Why did I ever make that damned vow to Peter in the first place?" the judge spoke to himself. "Why did I contract with Captain Darwin to find his family?" The judge was regretting what actions he had put in motion. Still, he knew deep down inside his heart, that those actions were nothing short of what needed to be done in Peter's best interest.

Soon the silence and deepness of his thoughts was broken.

"Master Anthony," a Negro slave, the overseer's right hand man, Gulliver, rushed in, by-passing all normal manners and decorum. "It's master Richard, come quick!"

The judge shot up from his chair and followed Gulliver, at a fast pace, out the south entry doors and down the steps. They ran to the overseer's cottage, about a quarter-mile away, nestled amongst a grove of chestnut trees. They threw open the door to the small cottage and stopped in their tracks at the threshold. There he was, Richard Pohlman, appearing to be dead, lying face down on the floor. He had always been a hearty man, full of seemingly good health and energy befitting a man twenty years his junior. Without complaint or any indication of pain or illness, he now lay dead on the wood-plank floor.

The judge stooped over Pohlman's lifeless body. He gently rolled him over and then put an ear to his chest. He heard no heartbeat at all. The judge stood up solemnly. Quietly he motioned to Gulliver to help him lift the body from the undignified floor. They carried the body carefully to the freshly made bed and reclined the body, placing the head on the feather pillow. Pohlman had come with the plantation when the judge purchased it, shortly after his marriage to Adella.

The Negroes on the plantation seemed to love their overseer. He was not like many white men saddled with too much authority over slaves. The judge and Pohlman were of same mind in regards to treatment of the slaves. They were to be treated as the human beings they were. Yes, there was work on the plantation to be done, but both men felt more work would be done, and be done in a much more accomplished manner, if those doing the work were spared the whip and the shackles, and treated like field hands and servants, not as the "property" they were by law.

The judge had seen a harsher treatment of the slaves while growing up on the Henry plantation at Studley. As a boy, he knew some day he would own a plantation himself, and along with the plantation, he would own slaves. That was the economy of the southern colonies. He had seen far too many lashings with the taskmaster's whip on the naked backs of black men and even at times, black women. He had heard of many a white planter or task master having illicit relations with slave women, some even fathering children they would naturally cast off as slaves, never accepting them as their own sons and daughters.

Ruthless slave masters were not the judge's idea of how to oversee the work of any man, slave or free. He knew the human spirit required a great portion of respect and consideration, not simple-minded harshness at the vicious hand of an intolerant overseer. That was why the judge not only agreed to have Zachary and Peter share their daily lessons with Pearlie, but also to actually allow Pearlie to take lessons with them in the old smokehouse.

Richard Pohlman shared the judge's personal philosophy, and the slaves at Winston Woods were among the best cared for and most productive workers on any plantation in the colony. The judge's slaves had comfortable living quarters, and families were never to be split up. They were each given new clothing and shoes for Christmas and at Easter time, and were well fed. They were given what medical treatments they might need. As the members of his family were inoculated from diseases, especially smallpox, so were the slaves at Winston Woods.

Now Pohlman lay dead on the floor of his cottage. Where would the judge find another overseer with Pohlman's temperment?

The judge sent Gulliver in the carriage to the doctor in the Cedar Forks settlement, across the Pamunkey, so he would come and issue the death certificate. He told him to have the carpenter, Alexander, prepare a suitable coffin immediately.

There would be a funeral after three days, to make certain it was not a "false death" which had become all too common in colonial Virginia. Many, it seemed, assumed and declared dead, would begin to stir awake from a deep, sleeping sickness of some kind, moments before the lid of the coffin was nailed shut for burial. One wondered just how many sleeping men had been buried alive, to awaken only to find themselves in a coffins buried six feet into the ground? Richard Pohlman would not have a premature burial.

Pohlman had no family, but the Winston family and the slaves would be given an apt opportunity to bid farewell to him at a fitting Episcopal funeral, officiated over by Rev. Gadsden. He would be laid to rest in the plantation cemetery, which held the graves of deceased members of the Charles family, the former owners who had started the plantation eighty years before. Many former slaves were also buried there in the same small cemetery alongside the white folks.

A few days after the funeral, the judge was off to City Point. The news from Captain Jacob Darwin of the Trident of Neptune was not at all what the judge had expected.

Investigation in the Azores

On the thirty-first day of May 1765, a ship of Dutch slavers dropped anchor in the harbor at Sao Sebastiao on the island of Terceira in the Portugeece Azores. The Dutch pirates stopped under the guise of taking on final provisions for the rest of their sailing to Virginia, but were in fact on a mission of thievery. The target of their scheme was the rich estate of the wealthiest man in the Azores, Dom Carlos Antonio Francisco.

While the main crew loaded provisions, a small crew of thieves boarded a dinghy and headed for the villa to ransack and rob it of what worldly treasures they could pilfer. The pirates apparently abducted one of the children, the boy. The girl raced back to the villa out of fright, seeing her brother being carried off.

The thieving party made off with silver, jewelry and other treasures, and in the process, slit the throat of the wealthy Dom Carlos Antonio Francisco and two servants in the villa. When the girl ran inside the villa, she found her father dead, lying on the terrazzo floor of the courtyard.

Hours later, the bishop came to the villa because the family had not come to the cathedral for the young girl's birthday blessings. He found the horrific scene. The little girl was found hiding and trembling in terror under her bed. She was taken into Sao Sebastiao where she stayed in the convent, until her aunt, Louiza Bastion, arrived to take her to live with her in Lisbon.

Those were the grim details Captain Darwin passed on to Judge Winston in Christina Donnelley's Tavern that day. How would he tell such news to young Peter? More prevalent on the judge's mind was how eight year-old Peter would react to such news. Dreams of a young boy, sadly missing his family, hoping to return to his homeland someday, now shattered.

The judge paid the seaman handsomely for the completed investigation. The captain had secured handwritten affidavits from government officials and townsfolk stating to the validity of the report. There was no question Captain Darwin had earned the bounty.

There were also some items the captain had secured from the constable at Sao Sebastiao. Most were just items gathered at the estate, clothing and the like, nothing of any real value. Anything of value had been taken back to Lisbon by the aunt.

One item of special attraction was a golden pocket watch and chain, taken from the corpse of the slain father. Peter's aunt had no desire for any of the father's personal possessions. The constable had kept the watch safe in his office. This beautiful, elaborately etched gold watch would be a wonderful heirloom for young Peter. Would he give it to him now or would he give it to him on Christmas morning?

After his meeting with Captain Darwin, he inspected his inventory purchased in London from the proceeds of the fifty bales of tobacco his London agent, Douglas Canning, had sold for him at a handsome price. Everything seemed to have traveled well without damage. Among his purchases were new suits of clothing from London for everyone in the family, including Peter. There were provisions for the kitchen, spices, teas, sugars, and a sugar safe, a new mantel clock of gold filigree Parisian craftsmanship, and a few pieces of Chippendale furniture. There were also several crates of bottled Madeira Port wine for the dinner table.

There was a fine necklace and cameo brooch for Adella's Christmas gift and copies of new editions of books from the Gravesend Bookseller, Joshua Bodine. The judge loaded only some of the most expensive and smaller items into his carriage, and arranged with a teamster to have the bulk of the order delivered to Winston Woods within the week. The teamster would return to City Point with a load of some of the fruits of the plantation's fall harvest to sell in Richmond and at City Point.

The carriage ride back to Hanover County was one of grave thought and deep reflection on the news he had paid for so dearly ... news he did not expect ... news he was not prepared for himself, let alone news young Peter certainly did not expect. Scenes of that terrible day at the end of May on Terciera played and replayed over and over again in his mind as the carriage swayed and rickety-ricked on the dirt roads home. How would he relay that news, that not-thought-of news to young Peter Francisco?

If eight year-old Peter Francisco was anything, he was a strong lad, physically as well as mentally. He was a realist. He had feared Anamarie and maybe even their father and all their servants had all been murdered. He had never spoken aloud of those fears lest they come true. He tried to keep that possibility out of his mind. Everyday, he grew to realize the evil in the hearts of those men who had kidnapped him. If anything, upon hearing the news the judge had brought, he was relieved. Now he knew the truth, what had really happened that horrible day. He was so happy to learn that little Anamarie was safe and being well cared for in Lisbon by their aunt, their mama's sister. He only remembered seeing her once, when she attended his mama's funeral at the cathedral and burial in the cemetery. Peter was not alone in the world now, knowing little Anamarie was safe.

Of coarse, he grieved over the death of his father, who he had always loved and looked up to as a hero. But Peter was determined not to dwell on the grizzly facts. The entire family, along with Rev. Gadsden, helped him adjust to being the orphan of a murder. He had a few nightmares, with the remembered scenes of that horrible day playing out in his mind and waking him from otherwise pleasant sleeps. Peter knew he had to concentrate on his education and his new found life in Virginia.

"Peter," the judge spoke kindly, "you have a family here. This family loves you like you have been a part of it your entire life. We will always be here for you."

"Can we bury Papa here?" he asked.

"Well Peter..." the judge did not really know how to respond. "I am quite certain the family and his friends have made appropriate arrangements on Terciera for his burial beside your mama."

"I know that," Peter said. "I do not mean for you to bring his body here. Could we just have a stone in the cemetery, like the one for the overseer. A place I can go and talk to Papa and talk to God."

39

Adella ran to him, tears flowing as she had seen how Peter had been such a grown-up in hearing such tragic news. She threw her arms around him and said, amid salty tears, "we certainly shall bury your papa right here at Winston Woods. We'll do it first thing tomorrow."

"Could we not do it on Christmas Day?" Peter asked.

"That is a fine idea young man," the judge spoke up. "I will have Alexander prepare in the carpenter shop a fine coffin, and Gulliver will see to the digging of the grave. You, Peter, will select the exact spot of course, ... any spot to your liking."

Peter smiled, approving the details.

The judge thought that as soon as the father's possessions arrived along with the order from London later in the week, perhaps Peter would want to bury some of the clothing and other articles in the coffin, possessions that had been his father's. Perhaps that would make it more real for Peter. He decided then and there he would wait until Christmas day and wrap the gold pocket watch as a gift for his new son.

Christmas at Winston Woods

December was Adella's favorite month of the year. She loved the cool crispness in the air and the crackle of the logs in the fireplaces throughout the mansion. She enjoyed the aroma of freshly harvested chestnuts, roasting on the fireplace hearth in the sitting room each night after supper. But most of all, it was a time of celebration. The year was ending and a new one, with much hope, renewal, and promise, was about to start.

She was one colonial lady who spared nothing to decorate the mansion when the calendar turned to December. There were evergreen wreaths to make and decorate with bright red holly berries and bright-colored ribbons for the doors and every window. The island on the formal dining room table and the fireplace mantels would be transformed from the browns, yellows, golds and reds of autumn to the majestic greens of nature's pines, firs, and spruce boughs, arranged with holly leaves and berries. Candles would be made and dipped in wax, then dipped again in bright dyes ... reds, oranges, yellows, and blues to add a festive accent to the holiday greenery. In no time at all, the mansion would be ready to welcome Christmas.

A spruce, cut down by the house servant, Malcolm, was standing in its place in the parlor, ready for the decorations Mammy Jane, Cassie and Pearlie helped make. Bows were tied to the ends of the branches. Pine cones and clusters of nuts and berries were hung on the branches. An angel with golden corn silk hair and halo found its perch on the very top of the majestic spruce.

Peter and Zack joined in and made ornaments to hang on the tree ... birds of all species and color joined balls, stars, flowers and all sorts of shapes. Mammy Jane had shown them how to create the forms from pieces of torn-up paper dipped in a paste made of flour and water, and when dried, painted. All the guests stopping in over the holiday season would enjoy Adella's beautifully decorated home.

Soon it was Christmas Day. The judge and Peter had inspected the possessions of Peter's father, except of course for the pocket watch, which had remained hidden in the judge's desk drawer. Peter had decided to keep a vest and a pair of crafted leather boots that he remembered his father wearing. He was growing himself and soon would be able to wear the boots. He looked forward to that. But the rest of the clothing and other things gave weight to the coffin Alexander had built.

Peter had selected a spot beneath a willow tree on a knoll inside the cemetery for the gravesite. One of the stonemasons on the plantation carved an epitaph on a gray piece of stone in memory of Peter's papa and mama.

On Christmas Day, after the family's breakfast, the judge led Adella and the boys into the sitting room. There were gifts under the tree, wrapped for everyone.

The judge presented two wrapped gifts to Peter. The first was the new suit of clothes, a waistcoat and matching trousers of dark blue velveteen with gold trimmings. The second, smaller gift was the beautiful gold pocket watch Peter's father had worn.

"Papa's watch!" Peter shouted with excitement. "Look, it is Papa's watch," he showed it proudly. "Look, here are his initials 'C.A.F' Carlos Antonio Francisco, and here, behind the lid is a portrait of Mama, Dona Elainia Vasqueza Francisco!"

"The constable at Sao Sebasiao sent it for you Peter," the judge said.

"Thank you," Peter said. "It is like Mama and Papa are both here with me today. They are so happy I have been taken in by such a wonderful family." He smiled with real joy.

41

Christmas dinner was set in the formal dining room with Patrick Henry, his wife, Sarah, and their five children. Adella Winston's parents were also at the table, Carlton and Eliza Mannington Pope, and Adella's two spinster sisters, Edith and Eleanor. Rev. Gadsden arrived in time for dinner, after spending a week at the Campbelltown Academy in Washington Parish, to visit with his friend and noted educator Dr. Archibald Campbell.

The table was set for sixteen and they were served yams, corn, and green beans stored up for winter from the garden, biscuits, molasses, mashed potatoes, ham, roast beef, and a roasted turkey. Peter had never seen nor eaten that native American fowl. Peter liked it very much, especially the white meat of the breast and the dark meat of the huge drumsticks.

After dinner, all the guests attended the Episcopal service in memory of Peter's parents. The coffin was closed and resting on the verandah just outside the dining room. Four slaves in livery carried the shellacked coffin leading the funeral party.

Rev. Gadsden led the procession in his Episcopal robe and collar. Then came Peter in his new suit of clothes and his cherished golden shoe buckles, with Zack, the judge and Adella just behind. The rest of the dinner guests trailed behind.

When they arrived at the dug grave beneath the weeping willow on the knoll, Rev Gadsden stood on the opposite side of the coffin, facing the funeral party. He read a scripture and offered a short prayer. The judge read a eulogy he had written from what he knew of Peter's parents.

Peter went to the coffin, stood, bowed his head and prayed silently. He bent over and kissed the top of the coffin and laid a spray of magnolia leaves and holly berries on top. He made the sign of the cross as he had remembered from the Roman Catholic cathedral in Sao Sebastiao.

Four slaves lowered the coffin with ropes to the bottom of the grave. Each mourner passed by the coffin resting in its place for all eternity. Each took a handful of dirt and tossed it on the coffin, then made their way back to the mansion as light snow began to fall in the first flurries of the winter. They each passed by the beautiful headstone:

The Wharf at City Point

In Memory of
Dom Carlos Antonio Francisco
1740-1765
Dona Elainia Vasqueza Francisco
1742-1764
Both born in Portugal
Both died at Terciera the islands of the Azores.
Dearly Loved Parents of Peter and Anamarie Francisco

Chapter Two

Torrents of Protest

As London was preparing for winter and the Christmas season was fast approaching, the city was seeing, day after day, fresh new snow falling, adding to the heavy early snows already shoveled and piled up, forming huge white icy mountains along the city streets. The air was full of fresh coldness and abuzz with politics and debate.

"That damnable Rockingham is the cause of all these troubles," said Avery Nobles, owner of Nobles and Sons Imported Goods on Dover Street. He stopped his district's member in Parliament, Edward Braden, as they were passing by each other at Piccadilly.

"How did he ever think the American colonists would not rise up as they have against his tax stamps? Taxing them on the produce they grow and the few manufactures they toil over? Unheard of! Unheard of!" shouted Nobles. "And we merchants now suffer for it!"

"You are quite right, Nobles, quite right," replied the stunned Member of Parliament, not expecting a political debate in the streets, especially in the bitter cold of December.

"Well what is to be done, Braden?" Nobles tugged at his elbow as Braden attempted to go on his way. "I know this, if something is not done, my shillings and those of the other merchants will stay in our pockets when you campaign once more!" he shouted.

Braden turned back toward his constituent. "It shall be repealed and the colonies will have no further grounds for dissent. Tis bitter cold and I must go," he smiled and turned back walking down Piccadilly.

By the earliest days of November, word had reached London of the deliberations in America at the so-called Stamp Act Congress. This had been the first-ever concerted effort by the American colonies to unite together in defiance to a measure of Parliament, to which the king had given his royal assent. That colonial assemblage had called for the repeal of the hated Stamp Act.

Every merchant in London was of the same opinion as Nobles in their hatred for the Prime Minister, the Marques of Rockingham, and his Stamp Act on the colonies.

"Repeal the damned act so we can resume a healthy trade in the colonies," Avery Nobles said a few moments after his tirade aimed at Braden. This time it was Sir Jeffrey Amherst getting the brunt of Nobles' wrath.

"I am certain of that," said the handsome Amherst with a winning smile on his face. "There will be a vote to repeal very soon."

"And Rockingham must go as prime minister! Rockingham must go," Nobles added. "It was his damned bad idea to tax the colonies in such a hateful way!"

"That too, Nobles, I am certain of it," Amherst flashed another smile and walked away.

Every Member of Parliament was getting the same ambush from the merchants as they met on the streets, in the pubs and shops ... everywhere. Parliament had seen the anger in the colonies, now they were all being threatened by their constituents with the drying up of campaign funds and votes.

The Marques of Rockingham was to resign at the end of the year. William Pitt, the man who had led the opposition to the Stamp Act when Rockingham first introduced it, would replace him.

"How does the honorable Prime Minister expect the colonials to respond?" Pitt had asked on the floor of Parliament, as Rockingham presented the bill for a vote. "It shall raise little revenue but torrents of protest. How does the right honorable Rockingham even come to think we are just in taxing them on the products they raise and manufacture by the sweat of their own brows? It has never been done before, and should never be done in the future!"

Every parliamentarian remembered the banter between Pitt and the Prime Minister. Now William Pitt would save them from the debacle that had stirred incendiary emotions throughout North America, and to even start thoughts and talk of independence. Pitt would keep the Americans happy and Britain would not face losing her empire.

Beside the Hearth at the Hawk and Dove

As the snows continued to blow in London, Parliament assembled for the final time for the year 1765, two weeks before Christmas day. The House of Lords sat with the House of Commons to hear Rockingham's benedictory remarks, and to certify the election of the new Prime Minister, William Pitt. When the ceremonial work had been concluded and Parliament adjourned for the year, Pitt left the warmth of the Parliament building to trudge through the snows and seek refuge at the table closest to the fireplace at the Hawk and Dove Tavern in Drake Street nearby. Pitt had invited four others to join him before they each left for their home districts for the Christmas holiday.

Three members of parliament were invited to join the newly certified prime minister, along with the one man Pitt knew would become the most prominent member of his new cabinet. Lord Charles Townshend had perhaps the sharpest mind on economic matters in all of Britain. He was now in his early forties and had accepted the important cabinet post of Chancellor of the Exchequer with genuine relish. Townshend would direct all things regarding the treasury in the Pitt government.

Sir Edward Braden, the Member of Parliament who represented the London district of many merchants like Avery Nobles, was a heavyset gentleman in his mid-fifties, the same age as the in-coming prime minister. Sir Edward had boarded with Pitt at Eton, then at Trinity College in Oxford thirty-some years before, and was indeed Pitt's closest friend in London.

Lord John Murray, the fourth Earl of Dunmore, was a distinguished Scotsman who favored wearing the kilts of the Murray Clan to the more traditional powdered wigs and knee breeches of the English gentry. Lord Dunmore represented the environs around the important Scottish port city of Perth. Dunmore was quickly becoming a parliamentary leader, well respected for his ability to add reason and foresight, sought after or not, during the heated debates of Parliament. Dunmore favored Rockingham's ouster, and was an important early promoter of Pitt's ascension to lead the British government.

Sir Jeffrey Amherst was a genuine hero of the French and Indian War and well loved throughout the British Isles. Amherst played important roles in capturing the strategic Canadian cities of Louisburg, Quebec and Montreal. At forty-nine, he still cut a dashing figure. He was then serving the king as the current Royal Governor of Virginia. Amherst governed the Virginia colony in absentia, remaining in London to tend to his seat in Parliament. He left the actual governance of the colony to his Lieutenant Governor, the Virginian Francis Faquier.

The powdered-wigged heads of other parliamentarians and men of commerce, crammed into the crowded pub, craned to stare as Pitt and his friends took their seats at the table by the fireplace reserved for them. In the warmth of the fire, they lit clay pipes of Virginia tobacco and welcomed tankards of ale brought by the hospitable and busty serving wench, Castalia. Their plates of mutton chops and figgy pudding would soon be brought from the kitchen for them.

"Lord Rockingham's address this day was well-spoken and well-received." spoke Amherst between puffs on his clay pipe.

"Well-received, indeed," added Braden, "...if, for no reason other than it is to be the last we right honorable gentlemen shall ever hear from him."

"Sir Edward," Pitt spoke, reproaching Braden a bit jovially, "Rockingham is a great man and history will treat him well, even if he is not being treated so well by this age. He simply misread the pulse of the colonials with that damnable Stamp Act he so ardently promoted." The new Prime Minister took a healthy sip of ale.

"But the question we must all pose now," Pitt said after his swallow, "is, will the majority there seems to be in parliament currently for repeal of the tax stand when the vote is actually taken in the new year?"

"There is no doubt, Sir William," Braden led the discussion. "The colonials have well-made their case, and collectively so. The members I have spoken with on the matter, to a man I dare say, feel convinced repeal of the ill-conceived tax is far superior to the prospects of another war in North America ... and one that could cost Britain her colonies."

Amherst exhaled another puff of smoke and supported Braden's suppositions. "The right honorable gentlemen of Parliament will indeed rush to vote for the repeal, if only to prove they listen to and are there to serve the men of commerce who elect them. The very survival of the shops and counting houses depend upon keeping the safe, profitable and secure trade with the American colonies, safe, profitable and secure." He drew another taste of tobacco into his closed lips.

The Scotsman John Murray fidgeted in his seat, swirling the ale around in his tankard. Pitt noticed.

"Do you concur, Lord Dunmore?" Pitt asked the Scotsman.

"I can not help but wonder, Sir William," Dunmore spoke pensively and deliberately, "if the precedent we shall be setting with repeal will bring about a most undesired result. I for one feel we will all find ourselves in the awkward position of being seen as acting in obedience to the dictates of those who should be obedient to us. It is saying to the colonists, we were wrong and they were right. What fodder for those who would seek total rebellion from the crown? Are we not opening the door for every further act of Parliament to be called into question by other such colonial congresses? Would not a simple and more palatable amending of the original act provide the same desired outcome, and allow us to avoid appearing to be cowering to the dictates of the colonial rabble?"

Braden, red-faced by Dunmore's dose of reason, sprang with his voice.

"Tis no admission of anything fowl on our part, Dunmore. Tis simply seeing a temporary error we may have made and being the men enough to admit it and right it. Your amendment would not salve the feelings in North America. There must be a repeal and not a repeal shrouded by any other name."

"I agree," answered Ameherst. "There is no shame at all in following the clear will of those who elect us … our constituency. In fact there is much honor in doing so."

Pitt turned to his soon-to-be Chancellor of the Exchequer.

"Lord Townshend, you have not yet spoken one word. Will the current majority for repeal stand, or abdicate to amending it?"

All the gentlemen at the table turned to Townshend and awaited his response. Townshend, though nearly twenty years younger than

Pitt, was aging, probably due to his fondness for heavy eating as his girth seemed to attest. He brought a closed-lip smile to his face before he spoke.

"Tis my observation the tide is in for repeal and strongly so. It seems not to ebb nor flow. It is steady. Those in the precincts, not necessarily the right honorable gentlemen, make it so. And not as my friend Dunmore fears.

"Repeal is on the public mind. It is their call as much as it is the call of the colonial rabble," Townshend turned and looked directly into Dunmore's deep blue eyes. "...and a vile rabble they indeed are, Dunmore." He turned his head back to Pitt.

"The repeal will be viewed in the precincts as the one thing this government must do to strengthen not just our ties to our important commercial markets in America, but also to strengthen our hold over them and keep them loyal to king and country."

"Hear, hear!" agreed Amherst. "Lord Townshend is correct in his reading of the pulse of the man in the precincts. That man wants repeal because he wants our trade with the colonies to continue to be strong and profitable. That trade builds our treasury and that trade brings us our jobs and gives us the standard of life we hold so dear."

"But pardon me, Sir Jeffery," Dunmore dared challenge the strong case for repeal. "Few if any of those men in the precincts will relish in seeing the colonies dictate to Parliament. They have elected us to legislate. They will see no joy in having the tail wag the dog."

"Hear, hear! My dear Dunmore," chimed Townshend. "You do see what may well lie ahead. We must never be derelict in our duties to govern and we shan't!

"I plead for repeal, yes," Townshend carried on, "but not hastily, not until new legislation, more palatable to the colonials, to be sure, as well as beneficial to the treasury, has been prepared for passage. A new bill, an excise on the colonies, a right high one. We will have our cake and we shall eat it as well."

Pitt felt it time to add his opinion.

"I do support repeal and plan to have it. I support it, not because of the protests or the petitions from their Stamp Act Congress. As you all must recall, I voted with raised voice against the initial passage of the vile act. We have never before saddled the colonies we so want and need to keep, with a tax on products of their own toil and sweat. It was the wrong tax then, just as it is the wrong tax now."

In All Cases Whatsoever

As February turned into March 1766, Parliament was ready to vote on the repeal. Prime Minister William Pitt received a message from St. James Palace for a private audience with King George III. His Majesty requested Pitt to bring along his exchequer, Lord Townshend. The topic would be the planned actions of Parliament. Parliament was to vote on the repeal that Saturday, following the audience with the king on Wednesday.

After the morning session of Parliament on Wednesday, Pitt and Townshend boarded the coach sent for them from the palace.

"I feel the king shall be well-pleased with your plan." Pitt reassured Townshend. Pitt smiled in anticipation of the coming vote to repeal on Saturday.

"King George is young, but is a thinking man," Townshend stated with confidence. "I feel His Majesty will see the thought behind what we have planned. I surely feel he will understand just how the plan will produce the desired effect. As to our timetable for action," the exchequer continued, "I pray he can see beyond the impatience of his young age."

"The king is an impatient sort, "replied Pitt, "as I do suppose most kings, young or old, tend to be." He took a deep breath, and exhaled. "But, as you say, he is indeed a man of sound thought. Surely he will see the wisdom of patience and of not acting in haste as was Rockingham's dilemma."

The liveried coach drove through the gatehouse leading to the grounds of the ancient brick palace as the palace guards saluted.

St. James Palace was a dismal looking palace compared to the other fine palaces of other European monarchs. It was certainly not luxurious in the way most Londoners expected their king, the king of the greatest nation in Europe if not the world, to be living. The palace was steeped in history, dating back to Henry VIII and Elizabeth. In March 1766, it was showing its age.

George had been on the throne since the death of his grandfather, King George II, in October 1760. He was a young king at just twenty-three years when he married the rather plain-looking Charlotte of Mecklenburg in the Chapel Royal at St. James Palace in September 1761. His and his queen's official coronation was a few days later at Westminster Abbey.

The king did not reside at St. James, but used it to conduct business. It was closer to Parliament than his residence at Windsor Castle. In 1763, George had purchased the glorious Buckingham House as a city retreat for his family. That palatial home was then known as the Queen's House, because the queen spent much of her time there. George stayed there when Parliament was seated and he had business in the city. Most Londoners hoped the young royals would make Buckingham the permanent residence and palace of the House of Hanover.

But this day, William Pitt and Lord Townshend had been summoned to the faded and dismal Palace of St. James.

A liveried usher met the two distinguished guests at the door and led them up the dimly-lit staircase to the second floor, stopping at a closed door. The usher rapped once on the door, opened it, and stepped in to announce, "Your majesty, the right honorable William Pitt, Prime Minister of the King's realm and Lord Charles Townshend, Chancellor of the Exchequer."

The two men bowed at the doorway. The young king's eyes rose from the book he had been reading while seated in an armchair by the window. Without expression, the king raised one hand and motioned for his guests to enter. As Pitt and Townshend neared where the king was seated, the king motioned for them to take seats in the two armchairs facing the chair where he sat. As they took their seats, the king looked directly at the usher.

"Neville, brandy for my guests." Neville, the usher, bowed and left the room.

"So what is to be done in Parliament?" the king queried the two, looking directly at Pitt.

"If it please your majesty," Pitt spoke, "I should like to defer to Lord Townshend, the architect of our plan to deal with the colonies."

The king turned his head toward Townshend, nodding his head in assent, but still not smiling.

"Your majesty," Townshend spoke, "the Stamp Act which has caused such commotion and unrest in the colonies shall be repealed in the Saturday session."

"And the rabble rousing colonials win, sending the king's parliament running with tail between legs!" the kings said, pounding his fist on the closed book resting in his lap with a show of disgust at the thought. "'Tis a sad day when my parliament cowers to the demands of those it is elected to govern!"

"Your majesty," Pitt spoke repentantly, "repel is of the utmost importance, and your assent must follow."

"This king's assent is not to be given lightly!" the young king's temper was erupting.

"We must repeal," Pitt insisted, "so we can proceed with the plan of legislation Lord Townshend has devised."

"Yes," Townshend concurred, "the colonials will cheer the repeal and give us the time we need to set in place the plan that will once and for all time end all colonial dissent."

"Go on," the king said reluctantly, but intrigued.

"When news of the repeal reaches America," Townshend continued, "the colonies will raise cheers and set aside feelings of dissent for an important victory won. As the repeal is voted, so too shall be a second bill, the Declaratory Act. Its passage will go unnoticed in the colonies."

"How much of the revenue lost by the repeal will be replaced by this Declaratory Act?" the king questioned.

"Your majesty," Townshend answered, sensing the king's growing impatience, "...none."

"None!" the king roared as he shot up from his chair, the volume of Daniel Defoe's <u>Moll Flanders</u> thumping to the carpeted floor. "Has my government gone completely mad?"

The king walked to the window, peered out onto St. James Park for a few silent moments. Pitt and Townshend both shot up from their seats, as it was against protocol to remain seated if the king stood.

Pitt broke the short silence that hung on the room.

"Your majesty, I pray you hear us out."

The king turned abruptly to face the two most important leaders of his government.

"I will indeed hear you out!" the king took steps back to his chair, reached down and picked up <u>Moll Flanders</u>, "or I shall indeed have you both shown out, just as Rockingham was shown out!" The king sat down in his armchair and the two guests sat again.

Pitt began. "The Declaratory Act is not a revenue act at all, sire, but an important piece of political legislation, which will be the cornerstone for subsequent bills to insure the loyalty of the colonies, and the collection of the needed revenues from the colonies."

"Go on," instructed the impatient young king, turning to Townshend.

"The eventual new Revenue Act will bring more taxes into the royal treasury," Townshend stated, "and in such a way as to not create the wrath created by the Stamp Act."

"And when, Lord exchequer, shall this new revenue bill come to me for my assent?"

"By year's end, I should surmise," answered Townshend.

"By year's end?" the young king's patience was indeed wearing thin.

"Patience is of the essence," Pitt calmly inserted.

"I grow impatient with patience!" the king said, shaking his head.

The door from the dim corridor opened as Neville entered carrying a silver tray with a decanter of plum brandy and three crystal glasses. He sat it on a table near the armchairs and began to pour three glasses.

"The plan is for the colonials to have their time to cheer the repeal," Pitt went on to explain, "The repeal shall state current collections shall not expire for a few months, giving us the time to pass the new revenue bill. There is to be no wait for the new revenues to be collected."

"Lord Townshend's plan approaches the issue as a combination of revenue measures, as well as important political resolutions." Pitt nodded to Townshend to carry on.

"London merchants pay an excise on all goods imported into London," Townshend began to lay before the king more details of his plan. "Naturally the London merchants will pass the cost of the excise on to the colonials in the selling price of their goods. The colonials will pay an even higher excise when they receive the goods.

"Legislation will be passed banning all trade in the American colonies, except for trade with the merchants of Britain, ending the lower priced competition from the French and the Dutch."

"Go on," the king said as he thought about what he was hearing.

"We shall pass legislation to strengthen all duty collections in the colonies," Townshend continued, "and strictly prosecute all activities of smuggling and piracy."

"And how should the colonials then feel when subject to new and higher taxation than that imposed by the Stamp Act?" the king asked.

Townshend made his case that the colonials had always complained, but relented in paying the duties on imported goods, called external taxes; but their complaints turned to real protest over taxes on homegrown goods, called internal taxes, as was the case with the Stamp Act. The king sat in silence, taking in all he had heard and seemed to like what he was hearing.

"I wish to receive written reports from you, Townshend," the king said, "as this plan you are apparently the architect of takes its shape." He sipped from his glass of brandy. "In my estimation," the king added, "it shall be seen as masterful, or as a complete disaster, if your reading of the pulse of the colonials is off its mark.

"This Declaratory Act you propose," the king further inquired, "what is this wording the colonials will overlook in their celebrations of the repeal?"

"It simply states what has been our policy all along ... but with an added four words," Townshend stated. "It simply reaffirms the constitutional control Parliament holds over the colonies and legislation."

Pitt drew a copy of the one-sentence legislation from his case and read, "The Parliament of Great Britain, and only Parliament, shall legislate for the colonies in all cases whatsoever."

The king remained in silence, digesting each word, especially the importantly added four words ... in all cases whatsoever.

"Those four words added do solve the ambiguity. Masterful," the king said with a smile, "masterful indeed."

Cheers Raised in the Colonies

In early April 1766, newspapers from London arrived in the colonies aboard English merchant ships, carrying the long-awaited news of the repeal of the hated Stamp Act. Cheers did indeed go up in nearly every town as the news arrived. There were parades, celebratory gun blasts and fireworks, as well as political rallies with speeches ranging from a new feeling of really belonging to the king's realm to subtle cries for independence.

Judge Winston took the boys into Hanover for the planned celebration there.

"Do you know what all the excitement is about?" the judge asked Peter and Zachary as he led them down the crowded street in front of the courthouse.

"Cousin Patrick's work at the Stamp Act Congress," said Zachary.

"What about his work in the Stamp Act Congress?" the judge pushed for more.

"The Parliament repealed it," added Peter.

"Yes they did," the judge concurred. "And why is that cause to celebrate?"

"Because we've won our independence from Great Britain," Peter said.

The judge laughed. "No we have not won our independence," the judge clarified.

"Because we are about to be independent?" said Zachary.

"Perhaps," the judge said, "but now we are like every other citizen and subject of King George III. We are not taxed in a way others are not taxed. We are not taxed on the things we buy that are made or grown here in Virginia, just on the things imported from elsewhere."

The judge and his boys enjoyed the parade, the political speeches from Patrick Henry and others, the music and games. Peter and Zack tied Peter's right leg to Zack's left leg and won the three-legged race winning a whole cherry pie. They stayed to witness the fireworks, the first either of the boys had seen.

Williamsburg, Virginia's colonial capital, and the seat of the College of William and Mary, was the natural hub of political thought and debate in the colony. The taverns of the capital were popular centers for much of that thought and debate. With the repeal of the Stamp Act, there was much to celebrate as well as still more to think about and debate.

Three who regularly met together at popular Raleigh Tavern on Duke of Gloucester Street for meals, ale and political discussions were the famed Williamsburg lawyer and law professor, George Wythe, his friend, Francis Faquier, the acting Governor of Virginia who governed in the absence of Sir Jeffrey Amherst, and the young twenty-two year-old, tall and red-haired law student, staying and studying with Wythe, Thomas Jefferson of Albemarle County in the Blue Ridge Mountains.

Jefferson had been born in April 1743, at Shadwell Plantation near Charlottesville, on the eastern slope of the Blue Ridge Mountains. Being the eldest son of the family, he inherited five thousand acres and several dozen slaves at age fourteen, when his father died in 1757. He boarded for two years, starting in 1758, at the home of the scholarly minister James Maury in Fredericksville, about a dozen miles from Shadwell.

In 1760, Jefferson enrolled at the College of William and Mary. He was an ardent student, studying fifteen hours most days to soak up all the knowledge he could possibly soak up. After graduation in 1762, he moved from a room in the Wren Building to a room at the Wythe House where he began a five-year study of law.

Two members of the House of Burgesses, Col. Washington and his friend, Benjamin Harrison V of Charles City County on the north shore of the James River, joined them for dinner.

"What now, sirs?" Wythe questioned his fellow diners, "What now?"

"Oh, there is little doubt there will be new taxes to rear their vile heads at us," spoke Harrison.

The Harrisons were one of Virginia's earliest and most powerful families. A Benjamin led all five generations of Harrisons in America. The first Benjamin Harrison arrived at the Jamestown settlement in 1630. In 1726, Benjamin Harrison IV built the family mansion at Berkeley Plantation, where Benjamin V was born in 1730. Many of the Harrisons of each generation had served in the House of Burgesses and at other important colonial posts.

"Ben, I fear you to be accurate with your prophesy," spoke Washington. "Pitt is a decent man, but I feel he is advised by scoundrels."

"Scoundwels indeed," piped in the young Jefferson with his pronounced lisp, "and I feaw they will not shake theiw scoundwelly ways until they see a way to padlock all the colonial capitols and thwow the keys away!"

"It appears to me," said Faquier, "this is a glorious day of jubilee, to be followed quickly by a few weeks of calm before the ominous storm that is certain to strike."

"Bwing on the storm!" Jefferson added. "With it will assuwedly come ouw independence."

"Independence?" Washington questioned the young law student with the annoying lisp. "We have gotten the repeal we asked for. Let us give our cousins across the waves at least the opportunity to see more of the errors of their ways. I pray they now allow us the representation in Parliament we are afforded by the constitution. Let us be the full partners in sharing the great bounty of the world's greatest land."

A hush fell over the assembled diners at Washington's remarks. It was not long before Jefferson became the first to break the silence.

"Just how long, Colonel Washington, do you expect us to wait?" Jefferson chose his words cautiously to avoid any "R"s that plagued his speech. "Still yet, how much longew can a gove'ment seated in the old wowld, clinging to views that are old wowld in nature, gove'n the people of the colonies in the new wowld, people who came hewe to escape those vewy views?"

"Young Jefferson here," responded Wythe, "certainly has much to say worth lending an ear to hear."

"We came to these shores to worship as we see fit," added Harrison, "to escape the debtors' prisons, to seek the fortune and future that will bring to us the individual happiness we each seek. We need have no parliament along the River Thames to keep us on a short tether, and tax us on the labor we perform."

"We do live in exciting times indeed, gentlemen," Washington spoke in a tone signaling a retreat from his prior loyalty to the crown. "While I would hope we could reside here as loyal subjects of the king, and pursue the dreams and freedoms we all would cherish, I feel young Mr. Jefferson perhaps sees it all the more clearly than I."

"Let us toast what we do know," Wythe lifted his tankard of ale as he spoke. "We cheer the repeal of the vile Stamp Act. We hail what is now to come ... full and equal participation with the lords of London ... or independence from them!"

"Hear, hear!" the table toasted in unison.

"No Taxation Without Representation!"

From the repeal of the Stamp Act in March 1766, there was a much longer wait for new taxation to be levied upon the colonies than the king would have liked. No new revenue bill came until passage of the Revenue Act in June 1767. British merchants now held a total monopoly on trade with the colonies. The colonials could not, without facing arrest and severe prosecution, purchase any goods from any other foreign nation. If they were caught smuggling, God save them!

The next of Townshend's acts followed quickly. The Indemnity Act was passed to prop-up the East India Company, Britain's monopolistic importer of Asian tea. To make British tea more competitive against the cheaper Dutch tea, the excise tax on tea in London was totally lifted, while the duties the Americans paid for the imported tea doubled.

Provisions of the bill also strengthened the authority of customs agents to collect the duties. Writs of Assistance were authorized as warrants to search private homes and businesses. Not issued by a court, these writs were drafted by the customs officials themselves as they needed them. Armed with the writs, customs agents sought out any commodities where the proper duties might not have been collected. Private citizens not paying the duties would join those being arrested and prosecuted.

"The superiority of the mother country can at no time be better exerted than now," Lord Townshend spoke in the Parliament. His bills passed and he died suddenly in September.

Two other bills Townshend had created were passed shortly after the exchequer's untimely death. Both of the remaining bills dealt with tightening up trade regulations, stopping smuggling, collecting duties and prosecuting colonial offenders.

The Earl of Grafton succeeded Pitt as Prime Minister with the new year in 1768.

Lord Grafton's new government was aimed at harnessing the colonials and making them subservient to Parliament and king. Parliament created a new cabinet post, that of Colonial Secretary. Lord Hillsborough was appointed to the new post with the duty of reining in the wayward colonies.

Tempers were rising in the colonies over the Intolerable Acts, what the acts Towshend had authored were now being called.

A Pennsylvania legislator, John Dickinson, wrote a pamphlet, called "A Letter from a Farmer in Pennsylvania." In his pamphlet he wrote of the unconstitutionality of the Revenue Act, the Indemnity Act and all the other Intolerable Acts. He urged colonials to simply not pay the duties, and rise up in protest to any "taxation without representation."

"Is the Bwitish Constitution not in effect is Vi'ginia?" asked Thomas Jefferson at another evening at Raleigh Tavern. "We, as Bwitish citizens awe guawanteed we shall not be taxed at all, unless we have wepwesentation in Pa'liament."

"I have hoped and I have prayed," said George Washington, "that Parliament and King George would recognize that we, as British citizens, are constitutionally extended the right of representation. Without representation in Parliament it is illegal to tax us. But, I fear it shall never be."

The House in Craven Street

Benjamin Franklin was as well known and respected in Britain as he was in Pennsylvania and throughout the colonies. He had been to Britain for two extended stays as the agent to the crown representing the Pennsylvania colony.

He was first sent to London in 1757, and returned in early 1765. On his first trip, he had brought his illegitimate son, William, along with him. William had been the unplanned product of a tryst with what was called a low woman. When the child was born, the mother gave him to Franklin to raise. Franklin's common law wife, Deborah Read, was pleased to take the child into the home she shared with Franklin.

"This is the boy who helped me fly my kite in the lightning storm ten years ago," Franklin said to the king at an afternoon reception on the lawn at Windsor Palace in 1762.

"This cannot be the lad," the young king objected. "Ten years ago I was a young man of fourteen, and I do believe your son to be even older than I."

Franklin chuckled. "That was a tale conjured up by the fabulists," Franklin said. "T'was no boy in the lightning storm with me, but a man of twenty-one! See how they write and publish what they please, the facts be damned."

The king laughed with him.

"I am pleased to be once told the truth," the king said as he nodded to William. "If only my advisors could be men enough to tell me the truth!"

"Your majesty," the elder Franklin spoke again. "We shall be leaving the court for Philadelphia by year's end. I have heard through correspondence, you are soon to be in need of a royal governor for the New Jersey colony."

"Yes, Dr. Franklin," the king responded, "Governor Hardy shall resign on New Year's Day. Would you serve me in that post?"

"Oh no," Franklin chuckled again, "but I shall remain honored that you have suggested it. I was thinking of William here."

By the time Franklin and his son sailed off to Philadelphia, Franklin had a letter in his vest pocket signed by the king appointing William Franklin the Royal Governor of New Jersey.

After two years back in Philadelphia, he was again sent to the court of St. James in 1765. When he arrived, Franklin rented a house at 36 Craven Street in the center of London, a short walk from Covent Gardens. There he became like family to the landlady, Margaret Stevenson, and her family, and again renewed old friendships with many of the political leaders as well as men of commerce, the arts, science and medicine.

In April 1768, Franklin welcomed an old friend, Dr. Robert T. Leever. Leever was professor of medicine at the University of Edinburgh. He frequently visited London, and when so, stayed at Franklin's house in Craven Street. Leever was in his fifties and was an investor in a school of anatomy that had been opened just a few doors down in Craven Street, by one of his former students, Dr. James Beveridge. Beveridge was the son-in-law of Franklin's landlady. Franklin had stayed with Dr. Leever when he had visited Edinburgh with his son William, now the newly appointed Royal Governor of New Jersey.

On this visit, Dr. Leever was accompanied by two of his brightest students, Jeremiah Peebles of Nottingham, and Benjamin Rush of Franklin's hometown, Philadelphia.

When the three guests arrived, the butler led them to two rooms where they would be staying the next two evenings. Dr. Franklin was away for the afternoon at a meeting with the former Prime Minister William Pitt, but would be returning in time for the evening meal.

After tending to their baggage, the three guests walked to the anatomy school to pass the afternoon. They returned to the house with Dr. Beveridge for dinner. When they came into the house, Franklin met them and introduced them to the equally famous William Pitt, who Franklin had given a last minute invitation to dinner.

It was indeed quite a thrill for the young Pennsylvanian, Benjamin Rush, to be sitting at the dinner table with two of the most famous men in the world. The discussion around the table ran the gamut of science, medicine, the arts and, of course, politics.

"I fear what Grafton and Hillsborough plan will lead Great Britain to ruin," said Pitt.

"Will you lead the opposition?" Franklin asked.

"I have just introduced a bill to seat a representative in Parliament for each of the colonies," Pitt answered. "What more can I do?"

After dinner, Pitt left to return to his own house in Whitehall, and Leever, with his two students in tow, left on a nighttime stroll in Covent Gardens. As they left, Franklin invited them to join him in his third floor study when they returned from their walk.

Arriving back at the house in Craven Street, the butler led them to the third floor study where Franklin was waiting for them. As they walked into the study, a room lined on three sides by shelves and shelves, holding bound volumes on every imaginable subject, a large world globe on a wooden pedestal, three upholstered armchairs in one corner and a fourth, where Franklin sat, facing an open window. Franklin's long gray locks of hair were draped over the back of the chair. A stiff April breeze blew through the open window.

"Come in, gentlemen," Franklin said without turning away from the open window. "Join me in a most glorious and healthful air bath this evening."

The three approached where Franklin was seated and as they neared, saw the famous man to be as naked as on the day he was born.

At first the three guests were shocked by the nakedness of a plump and wrinkled sixty-two year-old male torso, but soon Franklin put them at ease.

"Here in this city," Franklin said, "I have discovered the most wonderful and curative powers of the air bath. If you never have experienced such pleasure, you must join me. Shed your clothing, gentlemen and pull up those chairs. We can share this wonderful breeze this night."

Soon all were naked, if a little red-faced, and seated in chairs facing the open window, seeing just how pleasant the breeze, rippling over their naked flesh, really was.

"My thoughts these days," Franklin stated as he and his guests enjoyed the breeze, "are trained on the present situation in the colonies. As much as I desire reconciliation with the mother country, what price are we to pay for it?"

"We do pray for reconciliation," Dr. Leever stated, "but I fear Parliament, with Grafton and Hillsborough now at the helm of the government, are, as Sir William said at dinner, leading us down the path of destruction."

"The meetings I have here," Franklin admitted, shaking his head, "give me little hope. Hillsborough is to be feared. He is a scoundrel."

Franklin turned to the young twenty-two year-old medical student from Philadelphia.

"What do you hear from Pennsylvania, Mr. Rush?" Franklin asked.

"The feelings are growing for independence," the young student answered. "Revolution, if necessary, is on many minds there, according to what I hear from home."

"Many here," spoke Rush's classmate, Jeremiah Peebles, "understand not why the colonials have no elected representatives in Parliament. They are not treated as all other British subjects are treated. Perhaps Pitts' bill shall pass. Would that not stem the tide of rebellion?"

"No taxation without representation," Franklin inserted to answer young Mr. Peebles, "that is now the cry rising up from the thirteen colonies. If Pitts' bill goes down, those four words may indeed lead to revolution, if King George, Grafton and Hillsborough do not take heed.

"That 'Letter from a Farmer in Pennsylvania' my friend John Dickinson has penned has truly gotten to Hillsborough." Franklin giggled.

The butler came into the room with a tray of tea. He poured and gave each of the naked men a cup and saucer.

"Ah," said Franklin, accepting the teacup, "a wonderful cup of hot tea, cooled with cream and sweetened with sugar, to end our discussions and lead us to our beds."

Benjamin Rush accepted his teacup and sipped, then replied, "and those new taxes on this very much-favored drink may well start our revolution."

Grafton and Hillsborough

"That infernal letter from that so-called farmer in Pennsylvania has lit the damned spark," Hillsborough stormed one evening in his parlor, as he sat with the Earl of Grafton after dinner. "Dickinson, is a politician, a legislator, not a farmer! He has promoted all forms of dissent throughout the colonies! Those damned Massachusetts ingrates in their legislature have reacted with that treasonous petition to the king. Now the other legislatures in America join the cause and ignite thoughts of rebellion, I mean a full-scale revolution throughout the colonies."

"They must be dealt with and dealt with immediately," Grafton responded.

"I think it is time to invoke the Treason Act," Hillsborough stated, as he rose to freshen their drinks. "It is, after all, still on record, having never been eradicated. It has stood since 1543, and in my estimation, needs to be given a good dusting off and put to good use in the colonies at once."

"Treason is not the actions of a legislature," spoke Grafton professorially, "but the actions of an individual acting outside the law."

"The Massachusetts colony is a hotbed of treason," Hillsborough erupted. "No doubt our Governor Bernard there can build a case against several individual radicals engaged in treason. They shall be arrested and detained, and by provisions of the old act, transported forthwith to London, and only to London, to stand trial for their actions against king and country." He handed Grafton a freshened drink, sat and sipped his own. "And we know full well what verdicts will be rendered. Heads will roll!"

"That should put the veritable nail in the coffin of rebellion, once and for all time," agreed Grafton.

"I have penned dispatches to each of our governors to do so as well," Hillsborough continued. "Each governor also is instructed to immediately dissolve any colonial legislature which acts in a positive manner regarding that damnable resolution passed in Boston. Governor Bernard has my instruction to dissolve the Massachusetts House of Representatives if it does not immediately repeal the resolution and send a second circular letter to the other legislatures rescinding it."

The spring of 1768 brought growing turbulence and defiance in Massachuetts. In April, Governor Francis Bernard did as instructed by Lord Hillsborough, and demanded the Massachusetts House of Representatives take back its call for repeal of the Intolerable Acts and rescind its letters to other colonial legislatures urging defiance. The Massachusetts legislature voted 92 to 17 to not repeal their petition to King George, and to not rescind its original letter to the other colonies. Bernard dissolved the legislature immediately.

To keep the colonies under control, Lord Hillsborough publicly announced his intentions to resurrect the two hundred year-old Treason Act that had never been used before. This was indeed seen in the colonies as another gross infringement of their constitutional liberties. Under provisions of the Treason Act, any colonial simply accused of treason could be arrested, taken to London and locked in the Tower of London waiting to stand trial. A guilty verdict would be inevitable.

Chapter Three

The Sons of Liberty

Colonials knew they could not just sit back and take all the abuses they were now seeing coming from the mother country. Three leaders of the Massachusetts Legislature met one evening soon after "The Independent Advertiser" announced in banner headlines the resurrection of the Treason Act of 1543. John Hancock, Samuel Adams and James Otis met at Sam Adam's malt house on Purchase Street in Boston.

"Hillsborough has proved himself to be the truest villain and the most vile opponent to liberty," Otis started the conversation. "Your writings in the Advertiser this day, Adams, speak volumes."

"He threatens us with the Treason Act, never used in its two-hundred year existence!" Hancock shouted, "stripping away any justice we now have for fairness at trial, because we speak opposed to the king and his Parliament."

"Hillsborough thinks the protests shall end out of fear of being accused, arrested and transported to the Tower and the courtrooms where the only verdict shall be guilty," added Adams, fetching his guests tankards of beer from the keg.

The Adamses had been well known for generations as among the finest brewers in the colony, though the truth be known, they simply prepared the malt for the brewers. Adams inherited the malt house when he was twenty-three, after his father died. The malt house was always supplied with kegs of beer from the brewers who made use of Adams' malt.

"There is no way we can simply sit idly by, seeing our liberties, freedoms and rights guaranteed in the constitution not be given to us in full, as if we were a conquered people," added Otis after a sip from the heady brew.

"We were each members of the Loyal Nine during the days of the Stamp Act," stated Hancock. "The nine secretly orchestrated some of the most effective protests."

"I was not a member of the nine," protested Adams. "Friendly to them, yes," Adams went on, "and supportive of their opposition, but I found some of their actions simply too violent."

"You simply let your Puritan morality step in the way, Sam," Hancock went on.

"The burning of Governor Hutchinson's home was simply beyond the reach of acceptable protest," objected Adams.

"I joyed in hanging in effigy the scoundrel Andrew Oliver the stamp seller on the Liberty Tree," chuckled Otis as Hancock and Adams joined in.

"That is what we need now," Hancock suggested.

"What good could nine secret patriots do to stem the tide?" asked Adams.

"Not nine, Sam, nine hundred!" Hancock made clear his vision, "from every neighborhood of the city, every county and village of the colony ... Hell, every colony from here to Georgia! Secret societies of patriots, swearing oaths to secrecy, distributing all forms of protest and encouraging freedom throughout, will protect us from any sustainable charges of treason. Let this latest threat to our liberty be answered swiftly by the very sons of liberty Hillsborough would aim to drag off to the Tower of London."

"The actions of these sons of liberty must be conducted with a mob of followers," Otis suggested. "There can be no visible leader, no one man nor three nor four men...no small number which could be arrested and charged. They cannot arrest an entire mob for treason, they are simply rioters."

"The entire town of Weymouth came out just days ago to taunt the tax collector there," stated Adams. "They captured him, sat him on a rail straddle-legged, covered him with tar and feathers and ran him to the limits of the town, where they ceremoniously dumped him on his ass alongside the road!"

"That's just how it must be, the whole town cannot be arrested for treason," affirmed Otis. "Had a leader been known, treason could have been applied to the action and the leader hauled off to England never to be seen nor heard from again."

"These sons of liberty are living in every town in these colonies," added Hancock. "They will quickly join, and they will be the ones to send the red coats running. Secrecy must be the watch word."

"I agree," said Adams, "secrecy, and a strict refrain against violence or bodily harm."

"Agreed," said Hancock. "If there be violence, let it come from the British, but let it be answered loudly and swiftly by the sons of liberty."

"And what better name for our secret society," Sam Adams thought aloud, "the Sons of Liberty."

Consequences Not Easily Foreseen

The American Customs Board headquartered in Boston, had asked Hillsborough for military protection so they could carry out their tax collection duties, following the reactions in Weymouth.

Hillsborough was determined to do all in his power to insure the Customs Board was able to collect all the duties of the Townshend Acts, and put down any riots, protests and other treasonous activities in Boston. Since Governor Bernard could not unveil one single man to charge with treason, Hillsborough felt strongly the army of the king could. He met with General Thomas Gage, the Commander-in-Chief of North America, and Sir Edward Hawke, First Lord of the Admiralty of the Royal Navy.

"It has come to this?" General Gage questioned Lord Hillsborough.

"It has sir," Hillsborough replied firmly. "These colonists are impeding, with all forms of obstruction, the very ability of our customs officials to perform their duties under the law. The collector in Weymouth was just the first to be accosted."

"What a sight that must have been?" Hawke chuckled. "A grown man, covered in feathers, run out of town on a rail, and dumped on his plump backside."

"It is no matter to laugh at," said the seriously affronted Hillsborough. "It has indeed come to this, sir, and it bodes to get no better. I suggest one regiment of the king's men should do quite well at re-establishing order in Boston."

"I fear the arrival of a regiment in response to the running out of town of a humiliated customs agent will only stoke the fires of dissension all the more," said the general.

"General are we to wait until the colonies ignite in flames of rebellion with us doing nothing to douse those flames?" Hillsborough nearly shouted at the hero of the French and Indian War who had served alongside the Virginian George Washington.

"Are you willing to accept the consequences of war?" Gage showed his own anger back to the Colonial Secretary.

"I know full well," spoke Hillsborough in calmer tones to the general, "the result may well lead to consequences not easily foreseen, but I see no less an alternative."

"We will see war then. You can count upon that," assured Gage. "But I do suppose, if it be war, then the better for us if we are already there with the army in place when it erupts."

"What about perhaps a more tempered and less threatening response," suggested the Admiral of the Fleet. "I should think the sending of a single battleship to be stationed in the harbor at Boston would represent the same authority, yet perhaps not in such a drastic form as the army of the king," suggested Hawke.

"When could a ship be dispatched?" Hillsborough asked anxiously.

"The Romney now sits at Portsmouth as we speak," stated Hawke, "and awaiting my orders, sir."

"I agree, Hillsborough," said Gage. "The sending of an entire regiment might just throw more fat into the fire. The Romney will serve nicely as a symbol of His Majesty's might, without seeming to be an over reaction to the times."

"Very well then," conceded Hillsborough, "we shall send the Romney, for the time being, that is. If the peace is restored, then there shall be no need for an army. If not, I will instruct you, General Gage, to be prepared to send such force as you shall deem necessary."

The Liberty Affair

On the 17th of May 1768, the HMS Romney, a fifty-gun battleship, sailed into Boston Harbor. Sir Edward Hawke, First Lord of the Admiralty, did as he suggested to Hillsborough and sent the Romney to keep the peace and protect the custom officials.

Late in the afternoon on June 9th, John Hancock's merchant sloop, Liberty, carrying a cargo of Madeira wine, moored at the wharf. Two customs agents were stationed aboard the sloop for the night to witness the unloading of the cargo. The following day, a third agent arrived to itemize the cargo of wine. The agent found the hold of the sloop was only about one-fifth filled with what the agent counted as just twenty-five pipes of wine.

"Were you men fast asleep last night when the bulk of the cargo was off-loaded?" Husted Bennett, the chief agent there shouted at the two men who had spent the night.

"No sir," stated the one.

"Not a wink sir," said the other.

"Did you inspect the hold when you first came aboard?" Bennett again barked his question.

"Saw no need to, sir," stated the one.

"No need at all, sir," said the other. "We stayed up all night playing whist right here on this barrel."

"You cannot convince me this ship sailed into port with but twenty-five pipes of wine, when the hold below can easily stow one-hundred-fifty!" Bennett shouted and left the sloop.

About an hour later, agent Bennett came back aboard with a contingent of sailors from the Romney.

"Is the owner of this sloop aboard?" Bennett shouted at a crewman

"John Hancock owns the Liberty," said the crewman. "He is at his chandlery, the House of Hancock, at the end of the wharf there," he said pointing in the direction of the three-storied building that stood where the wharf ended at the cobblestone street.

The officer of the sailors accompanying Bennett, Lieutenant Vernon Grove, approached the same crewman.

"Your name sir," the officer ordered.

"Douglas, sir," the crewman saluted, "Ebenezer Douglas."

"How many crewmen are aboard, Douglas?" the officer demanded.

"Eight, sir, including me," Douglas replied.

"Call them to assemble here," the officer ordered.

When the seven remaining crewmen had arrived and formed in a line, the officer asked each his name, age and birthplace. When he had gotten all the information he needed, he then gave a startling order to his men.

"Arrest these men!"

The men were placed in manacles and taken to the now-empty hold of the sloop. The officer ordered the sloop freed of its ropes and he himself piloted the Liberty away and tied it up alongside the Romney.

The men were taken aboard the Romney and presented to Captain Avery Mellencamp. The captain announced to the manacled eight, they were being impressed into service in the Royal Navy. Impressment was a policy that had not been in common use for years. It was the policy where a British officer could board any ship, military or otherwise, and impress any English-born males they wished into service in the king's navy. It had, until then, never been used in colonial ports.

Customs agent Bennett went to the House of Hancock and served John Hancock with a summons to appear at the Vice Admiralty Court on charges of smuggling.

Riots broke out in the streets of Boston as a result of the charges levied against Hancock and the impressments of Massachusetts men into the British Navy by Captain Mellencamp. The seamen taken off the Liberty were all born in Massachusetts, but born subjects to the king, and therefore forced into service under a rarely used policy.

The customs officials, fearing their lives as the riots broke out, evacuated Boston for Castle William in Boston Harbor. The Romney sailed the threatened customs agents to safety.

News of Hancock's arrest for smuggling spread throughout the colonies. Hancock hired a longtime friend, the thirty-three year-old Boston attorney, John Adams, to defend him against the smuggling charges.

While colonials in other colonies read newspaper accounts of the trial, the citizens of Boston continued to riot. The Sons of Liberty led the riots. That secret society had grown more rapidly than even the organizers had ever dreamed. The patriot colonials throughout North

America waited for the outcome of the trial. Cheers went up when John Adams was successful in seeing the smuggling charges against Hancock thrown out in September. That same day, news from England reached Boston that Hillsborough had ordered General Gage to send a force of the king's regulars, apparently to do what the men of the Romney could not do.

Samuel Adams, attorney John Adams' cousin, organized a convention of the towns in Massachusetts to meet and pass resolutions stating their opposition to the coming military occupation of Boston. Lord Hillsborough had suggested the placement of one regiment of British soldiers for Boston. He left the final decision as to just how many would be deemed necessary up to General Gage.

On October 1st 1768, the first of four full military regiments from England arrived in Boston. With the first regiment's arrival, the customs officials returned from their self-imposed exile at Castle William.

Tarred and Feathered

John Adams saw his fame as a patriot rising, especially after successfully defending his longtime acquaintance and onetime youthful playmate, John Hancock. Rarely were defendants appearing before the Vice Admiralty Court found innocent or saw the charges against them dropped.

Hancock had been born in Braintree two years after Adams. Hancock's father was the minister for the Adams family and the one who baptized Adams as an infant. As the boys grew, they played together on the Adams farms, which stood across the road from the parish church. When Adams was nine, Hancock's father died in the parsonage and the seven year-old Hancock was taken in and raised by an uncle on Boston's Beacon Hill.

As October neared its end, Adams invited Hancock to accompany him to his farm in Braintree. Adams wanted Hancock to have an enjoyable few days away from the activities in Boston. Adams would be celebrating his thirty-fourth birthday on Saturday, but the day the two left Boston, Adams would be celebrating his wedding anniversary. The two old friends left Boston around midday on the 25th.

"With the arrival of Gage and his regiment," Hancock said, "Boston shall be in flames."

"Not the city literally in flames, I hope," said Adams, "but I am certain the troops of the king will see our emotions inflamed."

"Oh they shall, John, they shall indeed."

"Revolution cannot be far off," Adams predicted.

"The correspondence I get, especially from Virginia," Hancock added, "tends to be running in that direction. I correspond with a young member of the House of Burgesses, one Thomas Jefferson. He reports the feelings for revolution and independence are running high there."

"Virginia is an important colony if revolution comes," Adams agreed. "With the two largest colonies, Virginia and Massachusetts for it, surely the other eleven shall enlist."

"We can be a nation of our own within the decade," Hancock predicted.

"Now we simply sit, fan the flames a might, and await the remaining three regiments to arrive."

When Adams and Hancock arrived, the pretty and petite Abigail Adams was seated in a chair under a spreading oak tree in the front yard, a bowl of red apples in her lap and a paring knife in her hand. Two children sat and played at her feet.

"John," Adams said to his friend, "this is Abigail, the beautiful wife I took as my own four years past this very day."

"Mrs. Adams," Hancock said, reaching out for her hand and bowing at the waist as she sat extending her hand to his. "You are indeed much too beautiful for this homely friend of my childhood." He bent down and kissed the top of her hand.

"It was not his appearance that made me love him, Mr. Hancock" Abigail offered, "but his spirit and his mind."

The two men chuckled at her remarks.

"And these are the two apples of my eye," Adams said, stooping down to hug his three-year-old daughter and pick up his one-year-old son. "This is little Abigail, but we call her Nabby," Adams said tousling her little blonde curls. "And this handsome young fellow is John Quincy, and naturally we call him Little Johnny."

After the introductions were made, Adams showed Hancock to the downstairs guest room in the red-painted New England saltbox style farmhouse Adams had built on the farm of his birth when he married

Abigail. With several hours of daylight remaining, the men decided on a trip to the pond to angle for fish and talk politics.

That day the customs agent, Husted Bennett, who had leveled the smuggling charges against Hancock, also made a visit to Braintree with three others, all armed with Writs of Assistance to rid the town of smuggled contraband. Bennett rapped on the door of the parsonage, across the road from the Adams farm. The United Parish Church was the town church, standing next to the parsonage. A servant opened the door and showed the four agents into the front parlor.

The parson and his wife came from the study to meet their unexpected guests.

"Rev. Lenox Andrew, Madam Andrew?" Bennett inquired.

"Yes," the aged minister responded, extending his wrinkled hand, but Bennett did not shake it nor extend his.

"This is no social call. I am Husted Bennett, agent for the collection of customs for the crown," he pompously said, reaching into his coat pocket and retrieving a writ. He handed it to the man of God.

"I am here to search for and confiscate whatever smuggled contraband I might find."

"How can you do such a thing?" the old Unitarian reverend protested.

"Please Lenox," his wife grabbed his hand with both of hers. "He shan't find a thing of that nature. Turn the other cheek, Lenox."

"This, my dear Mr. Bennett," the parson pulled his hand from within his wife's two, "this is the house of the parish of Braintree. We live simply and frugally with what our parishioner's provide to us. You can surely better spend your time in other homes."

"Step aside sir," Bennett held firm and the four agents brushed by them, two heading up the stairs, two heading for the kitchen.

Rev. Andrew's face flushed red. Veins in his head seemed to pulse. His wife led him to the settee and he laid down.

"Tilda, go." The pastor faintly spoke. "Go for help."

She kissed him on his throbbing forehead and scurried out the door and across the road to the Adams farmhouse.

Matilda Hopson Andrew was a few years younger than her husband of thirty-five years. They had had one son, Jonathan, who was married and pastoring a flock in Gloucester, north of Boston. They had been tending to the parish in Braintree for fifteen years and John and Abigail Adams were their closest neighbors and among their best friends.

Abigail was still sitting under the oak tree finishing her chore of peeling and coring apples for applesauce the children dearly loved.

"Abigail, come quickly," Matilda screamed as the frantic woman reached the other side of the road. "It's Lenox! He has collapsed!"

Abigail jumped up, the bowl of peeled apples flying to the ground. She sent Nabby to take Little Johnny and fetch their father at the pond. She ran toward Matilda and the two raced back across to road to the parsonage.

The minister was lying, seemingly lifeless on the settee. The women rushed over to him.

His wife grabbed his one hand in both hers and softly spoke his name, "Lenox ... I've brought Abigail ... Lenox ..."

The minister did not move nor speak. His eyes did not open.

Abigail stooped over his frame and took his wrist to feel for a pulse. There did not seem to be one, unless perhaps the faintest of one. She bent her head down to the old man's chest and placed her ear over his heart to listen. She held her palm near his nose to feel breath coming from his nostrils, but felt none. After just a few moments, Abigail raised her head. Matilda's face stared at Abigail, eyes big, wide, round, and inquisitive, showing the redness of tears, silently asked for Abigail's findings.

Abigail shook her head. "I am afraid I have heard nothing." Matilda began to sob with her fears of her husband's death seemingly confirmed.

"He's ... dead! He's dead!" she moaned.

The agents walked down the corridor outside the parlor and heard the new widow's pronouncement and sobbing. Bennett paused at the entry to the parlor as Matilda looked at him with tear-filled eyes.

"Pity," Bennett spoke callously, then led his men out the door and down the stairs.

Just then, Adams and Hancock came rushing into the parlor.

"Who were those men who nearly knocked us over as we were coming up the steps?" Adams asked.

"Murders!" Matilda shrieked, "... the customs agents who killed my husband!"

Hancock repeated the search for pulse and heartbeat Abigail had conducted and also found none.

"We must go to the physician to confirm the death," Hancock stated to Adams.

"You stay here with Matilda," Adams said to Abigail, then turned to Hancock. "I will lead you to Doctor Harding." The men rushed out.

Doctor Hezekiah Harding had a medical office in his home in the center of town, about a five-minute walk from the parsonage. Hancock had an eerie feeling and talked about it as he and Adams walked to the center of town.

"I remember that room too clearly," Hancock said, recalling when he was a boy of seven living in the parsonage. "My father collapsed on the floor in that very room twenty-four years ago. It was a hot day in the summer. I was running down the corridor and saw him lying there."

"I remember that day," Adams was reminded. "We had been fishing together at the pond and you caught a basket full of fish and ran to show your father. What a wonderful supper you were to have that day."

"That's correct," Hancock agreed. "I was so proud and anxious to show father my catch... but he was dead on the floor."

Doctor Harding was shocked at the news. "I just saw Reverend Andrew this morning," Harding noted, "and he looked well enough. It must have been the insolence of those damnable customs agents. Can you imagine harassing a parson and searching for smuggled contraband in his house?"

"Damnable actions," agreed Hancock. "Just damnable!"

The doctor pulled Adams aside and whispered in his ear.

"Go to Deacon Ledbetter, John," whispered Harding. "He's the leader of the Sons of Liberty. He needs to know about this."

"Send your friend to the parsonage with me, and you go fetch Ledbetter."

"Why do you whisper to me?" Adams whispered back to the doctor.

"In these times we must be careful who we speak to on such matters," the doctor whispered back.

"Do you not know my friend is John Hancock?" Adams asked Harding.

Startled, the doctor looked at Hancock then back to Adams and spoke aloud, "the smuggler?"

"He was cleared of those salacious charges, " Adams reminded Harding then again whispered in his ear.

"He organized the Sons of Liberty with Sam Adams and James Otis."

All three of the men got a good chuckle out of the whispered conversation.

When Adams and Hancock arrived at Deacon Josiah Ledbetter's home, Ledbetter had already heard about the customs agents being in town, but the news of Reverend Andrew's death was a shock. Not only was he the local leader of the Sons of Liberty, but was also the senior deacon of the parish church. Now he would have to take over Lenox Andrew's duties at the church until a new parson could be hired.

Adams and Hancock arrived back at the parsonage. Dr. Harding certified the death of the old minister and he and Malcolm Engel, the cabinetmaker who also crafted coffins for the dead, had moved the parson's body into the study until the coffin would be delivered in the morning. The minister's body would be prepared for burial and dressed in his Unitarian robe. The coffin would leave the parsonage the next evening to rest at the altar of the church until the funeral and burial in three days. The scare of a premature burial would be eliminated. He would then be laid to rest in the parish cemetery, directly across the road from the church, and just down from the rail fence of the Adams farm.

As the doctor and cabinetmaker left, Adams suggested they too leave and have their fourth anniversary supper.

"Tilda," Abigail spoke to her older friend, "I think you should sleep tonight at our home. There is no need for you to be alone all night on such a tragic day."

"I want not to be a burden," Mrs. Andrew replied. "I do not wish to leave Lenox alone."

Abigail put her arms around Matilda's shoulder. "Tilda, he is not alone this night, he is joyfully resting in the arms of our Lord."

Matilda did agree and the four walked across the road as autumn darkness was setting in upon Braintree. As they crossed the graveled road, they saw the center of town was lit with the torches of a mob, and the torches seemed to be approaching them. When they had crossed to the parish cemetery, they paused to await the coming mob and see what it was all about.

"Have the Sons of Liberty captured the customs agents?" Hancock wondered aloud.

"If so," Adams said, "I bet they tar and feather them, and run them out of town on a rail, like was done at Weymouth."

Abigail was excited at the thoughts of such a fitting demise for the damnable agents of King George. She rushed into the farmhouse and grabbed up Nabby and Little Johnny so they could witness this part of history in the making.

When the mob arrived in front of the parsonage, it stopped. Torches lit the night and all could see the mob had apprehended Bennett and the other three agents of the king. There were indeed pales of warmed up black tar and bags and bags of goose and chicken feathers.

Deacon Ledbetter, spotting John Adams standing at the gate to the cemetery, yelled out.

"Mr. Adams, might we borrow four rails from your fine fences as a suitable mode of transportation for these damnable fools to be run out of town upon?"

"You certainly may," Adams yelled back to Ledbetter. "You most certainly may."

Each agent was bound at the wrists and ankles and seated uncomfortably on a rail taken from John Adams' fence. Then came the tar, warm but not hot enough to cause great harm. The tar was brushed and broomed over the agents' clothing. Then nearly everyone in the mob, especially the women and children, took hands full of feathers and threw them on the warm tar-covered agents. Even Abigail, Nabby, Little Johnny and Tilda took part. Tilda, the newly made widow, grabbed a handful of goose feathers, walked up to agent Bennett, stared into his frightened eyes and threw the feathers at him. Tilda stared intently into Husted Bennett's narrow eyes. She stared for several silent moments, then, remembering Bennett's words to her as Lenox lay dead, she spoke the same angry word to him ... "Pity!"

With the four customs agents now appropriately attired for their evening's travels, men from the mob raised each rail holding a passenger. The mob turned around and marched the tarred and feathered agents back through the center of town and on out to the town's edge. There they were each ceremoniously dumped into the cranberry bog.

When the mob dispersed, the Adamses led Hancock and the widow Andrew into the farmhouse. It was an anniversary John and Abigail would not soon forget.

The Association

The British soldiers were not welcome in Boston in the autumn of 1768. The citizens were not happy seeing the red-coated soldiers always on the streets, every street of town, every hour of every day. They were always in small groups with bayonets fixed to their muskets.

Many were actually quartered in the private homes and businesses of the Bostonians. Others stayed on the wharf and on the ships in the harbor. Boston was certainly being punished for their defiance at seeing their rights taken away unconstitutionally.

The Sons of Liberty were ever vigilant and close-lipped, so no citizen patriot could legally be charged with treason. Hillsborough, in London, fumed at every dispatch from the colonies, all carrying the same news that his governors were unable to find any real evidence of specific individuals to arrest and charge with treason.

The new year of 1769 opened with the first all-out non-importation agreement between Boston merchants going into effect on January 1st. The merchants allied themselves to protest and would simply purchase no British goods whatsoever. Soon merchants in New York and Pennsylvania had their own non-importation agreements in place.

In Virginia, George Washington and George Mason opted not for an all-out non-importation agreement, but rather for a looser organized boycott of certain taxed goods from England. They led a growing movement in the House of Burgesses to pass a resolution stating simply the parliament had no constitutional power to levy any taxes on Virginians without consent from Parliament with a duly elected representative of their own voting.

The new royal governor who had replaced Sir Jeffery Amherst, Norbonne Berkeley Lord Botetourt, was well liked and seen as a diplomatic buffer between the colony and the crown. Boutetort was a heavyset man of fifty-one and, like Francis Faquier, made many friends in the

Virginia capital. However, Lord Boutetort did as he had been ordered by Hillsborough, and dissolved the House of Burgesses immediately upon passage of the boycott resolution. His friends in Williamsburg remained his friends because they knew he had no option but to do as he was ordered.

The Burgesses left the colonial capitol building and met in the Apollo Ballroom at Raleigh Tavern to decide the most appropriate action to take. The legislators adopted the organized boycott of British goods as proposed by Washington and Mason, and created an assembly to meet in rump session while the legislature officially remained closed. The rump legislature would simply be called the Association and Washington was elected to serve as its president

A Decision at Winston Woods

From the autumn of 1765 through the summer of 1769, life on the Winston Woods Plantation seemed a world away from the bitterness and political strife brewing between the colonies and the king and Parliament in faraway England.

The schooling of the boys and seeing to his plantation, when not riding the circuit in Virginia, were the main concerns of the judge. Taking lessons in the old smokehouse under the sharp eye of Rev. Gadsden for four years now, and going off on adventures of their own design when not at their schoolroom desks, motivated young Peter and Zack. Adella Winston's world was simply engulfed in the pastoral pleasures of life in rural in Virginia.

The boy from across the Pamunkey, Peter Patrick, now called "Pat" so as not to be confused with the other Peter, was a constant playmate, and had become a classmate of the boys at the Winston Woods School. His mama died a month or so after the overseer at Winston Woods died. The judge hired Buford Patrick from the Madden Plantation, and he and Pat lived in the dead overseer's cottage. The judge took over responsibility for Pat's education as part of Mr. Patrick's pay for coming to work. The slave boy, Pearlie, was also taking lessons in the old smokehouse

Rev. Gadsden had proven to be a good instructor of the basics, and gave the boys a good smattering of some of the studies the boy were anxious for ... especially history and nature sciences. They spent days in the spring and fall out of the confines of the classroom, studying plants and animals in their natural habitat. They had a favorite huge old chestnut tree to sit beneath when the professor lectured about history or they read the classics of ancient Greece and Rome. They had in-depth Bible studies and read and discussed popular literature from the writers of England and France. Gadsden read to them from various newspapers, articles about the goings on in the colonies and in England. The boys enjoyed debating the issues of the day in order to get some understanding about what the grown-ups were talking about in the parlors after dinner each evening. The formal dining room also became a part time classroom for honing their skills in the social graces and civility. They even had lessons in dancing a proper minuet.

The boys spent their summers tagging along with Pat's father in the fields and barns at Winston Woods. They even started helping out with some of the chores, even though there were enough slaves to do all the real work. Buford Patrick taught the boys to ride horses and shoot muskets, so they could help rid the fields of the occasional groundhog. They loved going off hunting squirrels, rabbits and wild turkeys. They fished in the river and streams, and still found time to swing on the grapevine over the ravine. One weekend in the early fall of 1768, the boys set out on their first overnight camping and hunting trip. They chose a glade in the forest beside a stream a few yards from the far edge of the hundred-acre barley field. They bagged a nice sized deer for the slaughtering.

By his tenth birthday in 1767, Peter began a rapid and startling growth-spurt. Everyone noticed he was growing out of the trousers and the shirts he wore. He was as tall as the judge himself at five feet eight inches, huge for a boy of ten. Peter had grown a good head taller than his three playmates, and seemed to be at least a-third again larger in weight and strength. For nearly a year, he had been wearing the boots the Trident of Neptune had brought to him from his papa's estate on Terciera. They fit him fine. Peter was being called "the Giant of the Pamunkey." By the time of the hunting trip, in fact, Peter was actually able to carry the slain deer, slung around his shoulders, all the way from their hunting camp back to the butchering barn at the hog pens.

One evening after dinner in the March 1769, Rev. Gadsden asked to have a discussion with the judge and Adella after the boys had gone to their room for the night.

"It is time we commence thinking about formally preparing the lads for William and Mary," Gadsden said.

"What course of study do you suggest, reverend?" asked Adella.

"Campbelltown Academy," Gadsden spoke without hesitation. "I am just not equipped to properly prepare the lads much further than I have already prepared them. Oh, I could stretch out another year in the plantation school, but to the detriment of the boys, I am quite certain. They should be learning more than I am equipped to impart to them. It will be more difficult for them to gain admission to college if that is your desire for them."

"What do you suggest then, reverend?" the judge asked. "I do wish they attend William and Mary some day."

"Most boys on Virginia plantations, from age eleven, begin their preparatory trainings, and by age sixteen are ready to enter college," Gadsden said. "Zachary will be thirteen and Peter twelve this summer. They are both on par with plantation boys of their age. Their training to date has been advanced. I just am not equipped to teach them more."

"And what about Pat?" the judge asked.

"He is catching up to where Peter and Zachary now are," Gadsen said. "He is a good student as well. Is he to be enrolled at Campbelltown as well?"

"We took it upon ourselves, the education of all the boys of Winston Woods," the judge took Adella's hand to his thigh and patted it, "I wish Pearlie could be enrolled as well, but do not expect Campbelltown would accept him."

"I am afraid not, sir," the schoolmaster replied.

"Well, I have certainly heard about the Campbelltown Academy," the judge said. "Is it truly the best choice for our boys?"

"There is no better instructors, in my estimation, than Dr. Archibald Campbell and his brother Matthew," affirmed the reverend. "The tuitions are fair and not inflated, even though the academy is by far the finest in Virginia, I feel."

"What are the specifics as to the timing and the arrangements?" Adella asked. "Will the boys need to be boarded away?"

"Campbelltown Academy is a full half day's journey through Bowling Green and Port Royal, across the Rappahannock into Washington Parish in the Northern Neck at Westmoreland County," spoke the judge to his wife. "Yes, the boys would board there during their school sessions, returning home only during the Christmas and Easter holidays, and of course in the summertime."

"As to their current studies," Gadsden added, "I propose a full class schedule through mid-May as normal. By then they should have all the benefit of the education I am prepared to give them. They should be well prepared for the more advanced studies and college preparation they will receive at Campbelltown. I will insure the Patrick boy will be at the same level as Zachary and Peter by that time.

"As to admission and other necessary arrangements," Gadsden continued, "I propose a trip to visit the academy at your earliest convenience, when the weather permits, of course."

"We shall see to it," the judge replied, and Gadsden left for his quarters on the dormer floor of the mansion.

Adella who was sitting on the settee with the judge put her hand on his and smiled a somewhat melancholy smile as he looked at her.

"Well, Anthony, it will be quiet around here shortly," she said. "Our boys are growing up and shall soon fly from the nest."

He put his arm around her shoulders. "It is for the best, my dear." He kissed her.

"I think so, too." She smiled again and said, "I believe God is blessings us. I believe I am with child." Adella's revelation caught the judge totally off guard.

"You are ... ... with child?" he managed to utter.

She just nodded in the affirmative. He kissed her and they went to bed.

Campbelltown Academy

In mid-April, the judge, Adella, Rev. Gadsden and the boys loaded into the carriage after an early breakfast, and headed out from Winston Woods. The sun was just rising. Peter looked at the gold pocket watch the judge had given him from his slain father. Peter was never without that watch from the day he had first been given it.

"Six thirty-five," Peter announced, as he closed the lid of the fob.

The carriage turned east and passed through Hewlett, then turned north to cross the Pamunkey River at a shallow ford for Cedar Forks. Peter checked his watch again as they were leaving Cedar Forks.

"Two minutes past seven," he announced.

The journey then headed east and then northeast to Bowling Green, where the judge, on occasion, sat for trials riding the circuit. The roads were relatively smooth for colonial Virginia, with hard-packed dirt from the horses and carriages that traveled from town to town. The day was dry and had been so for a week, so the roads were solid and dusty, not a boggy mire of mud. The countryside was rolling pastures with cattle and sheep grazing. Trees sprinkled the countryside and, in places, virtual forests of oak, spruce and pine.

They stopped for a mid-day meal of lamb chops and apple cobbler at the Prince George Tavern along the small wharf on the south shore of the Rappahannock River at Port Royal. After their meal, the traveling party walked to the ferry across the wharf from the tavern. The livery servants drove the carriage aboard the ferryboat and the passengers walked on and stood at the rail.

The final leg of their journey to the academy began. The countryside on the north side of the Rappahannock River was basically forested with dense pine trees until they finally arrived at the town of Oak Grove. They were in Washington Parrish. It was here that the grandfather of George Washington and his bride Anne Pope settled after their marriage. It was also here where George Washington had been born thirty-seven years before.

Peter checked his watch. It was five minutes past three in the afternoon. Their journey had taken eight hours and thirty minutes including two stops. Campbelltown Academy was about three miles east of Oak Grove.

There was not much of a town at Campbelltown. It was a very rural, pastoral setting. The academy was one large and long three-story, freshly painted, white clapboard building, with a separate two-story house, of the same architecture, sitting beside it. Both sat on the summit of a gentle rise well above the elevation of the road. Pine trees surrounded the school building and house. An inn sat across from the academy's gravel lane, which ran between two ten-foot high brick columns painted white, with a semi-circular sign attached to both columns forming an arch. The sign was painted with white lettering on a blue background: *"Campbelltown Academy"* in large letters with smaller letters beneath: *"Educating Young Christian Gentlemen since 1756."*

When the carriage pulled up the lane and stopped in front of the main entry, Gadsden exited the carriage to retrieve the headmaster, as the others climbed out of the carriage and took in the view from the summit.

"Well boys," the judge said, "this may well become your home for studies during the coming years. What do you think of it?"

"It looks like a nice enough place," Zack said. "but, I shall miss the Pamunkey."

"I hear the Potomac River is just a short walk from behind the campus," the judge said.

"I'm happy to think about new adventures in a new place," said Peter. "I will miss Winston Woods though."

Gadsden soon arrived back to the carriage with two men and two students.

"Judge Winston, Mrs. Winston," Gadsden said as he approached, "may I present Doctor Archibald Campbell." He introduced them to the famous instructor of young Christian gentlemen. Campbell was a white-haired man of about sixty years, with a medium height and a heavyset torso.

"We are so pleased to meet you Dr. Campbell, and have heard much good about you," said the judge, as he shook the headmaster's hand.

"And I am quite pleased as well to meet you, Judge Winston," Campbell said. "My dear friend Reverend Gadsden has spoken very highly of you and of the lads I see you have brought with you today.

"Permit me to introduce my much younger nephew, but just as capable an instructor as I, Matthew Campbell." The younger Mr. Campbell shook hands with the judge and bowed his head in recognition of Mrs. Winston.

"And our two eldest and best students," the headmaster said, "and both soon to be off to William and Mary, John Marshall of Germantown, and Stockard Samuels of Tappahannock. Both will commence their final year of college preparations as your lads commence their first term here in September."

"We are pleased with what we have seen thus far," the judge replied, after shaking hands with the two students.

"We are indeed," spoke Adella. "It is such a lovely setting. We are quite anxious to see the facilities here."

"Then why do we not start this very minute," the headmaster suggested. "If it pleases you, I thought perhaps Mr. Marshall and Mr. Samuels might show the lads the grounds, and then afterwards the interior rooms of the academy, while Matthew shows the two of you the classrooms, dining hall, dormitories and library in the main building. Reverend Gadsden and I shall meet with you in the parlor after your touring, and we shall retreat to my office to see to what arrangements can be made."

The adults headed into the academy as Stockard Samuels asked the younger boys, "Do you ride?" All three nodded enthusiastically indicating they did.

"Good, we will show you the stables and riding grounds." They headed around the east side of the main building and down the slope to the paddock.

"We have ample opportunities to ride and engage in fox hunts and other equestrian events," John Marshall spoke up. "The students here are assigned a steed of their own for their tenure here."

"We groom them and tend to their care," Samuels added as they walked inside the stable.

"Each of the students has his own horse to care for?" Peter asked energetically. He had never had a horse of his own, though he rode and helped curry some of the horses on the plantation. All three of the boys were good riders.

"Which of the three of you is the best horseman?" John Marshall asked.

"Pat is the best," piped up Peter.

"We are all quite good," Pat said magnanimously.

"Pat and Peter are better than I am," admitted Zack, "but, I enjoy it as much as they do."

"Good," Stockard chimed in. "Then you all shall really enjoy our Saturday rides."

The stable was a long building with stalls inside for about two dozen fine looking horses. The stable opened up into a large corral, fenced with neatly painted white boards. Beyond was a large open meadow with the same white board fence, which enclosed what appeared to be at least five acres for the horses to graze and the students to ride.

Samuels climbed and sat on the top rail of the fence. Pointing to the woods just beyond the fence at the far north side, "We have riding trails that run all the way to the Potomac."

"We have even ridden along the river all the way to the old Washington family cemetery at the Pope's Creek," added Marshall. All the talk of trail rides, fox hunts and such peeked the interest of each of the three boys.

From the riding grounds, the two upperclassmen led the boys back up the rise to the academy and showed them inside where, if they became enrolled there, would be their homes for the next three or four years.

As they entered the main door, the entry hall ran the width of the building with a two amply sized classrooms with rows of desks and slate boards behind the instructor's desk. Next was a small alcove of a parlor, where Gadsden and the headmaster were seated. Matthew Campbell was leading the judge and Adella down the staircase from the upper floors. The west side of the main floor held the cavernous dining hall, kitchen, and the office of the headmaster.

The wide staircase led to the second floor and held dorimtory rooms for the students. Each room had desks and single beds for two to four students.

"Usually," Marshall said, as they were in one of the rooms, "the new arrivals, the younger students, are assigned to the four-man rooms."

"The older students are two-to-a-room," added Stockard.

The staircase led on to the third floor where the bachelor Matthew Campbell lived in his quarters that took up the rear half of the west side of the floor. Just opposite Matthew's room was a huge library with shelves of books and study tables. The front half of the third floor was a long parlor-like room with study tables there as well.

The boys sat around tables in the library and their two guides told them about the classes they would be taking and what their days at Campbelltown would be like.

"The Campbells are quite superb instructors," noted Marshall. "They have tremendous knowledge to impart."

"The elder Mr. Campbell," Stockard added, "is a veritable fount of knowledge on every conceivable subject, while the younger is perhaps better at imparting that knowledge. He simply has a less formal manner about him and finds it easier to keep the interest of the students."

"How do the students call the Campbells?" Zack asked, "After all they are both Mr. Campbell."

"You simply call them respectively 'headmaster' and 'sir'," answered Marshall.

"And in the presence of others, students address other students as Mr." said Stockard. "I am Mr. Samuels and John here is Mr. Marshall."

"So I am Mr. Winston," said Zack. "These are Mr. Francisco and Mr. Patrick."

"That is the proper way to address a fellow student," said Mr. Marshall.

The three visiting boys were given one of the vacant rooms for the night. The judge, Adella and Gadsden were overnight guests of Dr. Campbell and his wife, Victoria, who lived in the fine house next to the academy building.

The boys took the evening meal in the dining hall with Stockard and Marshall, and met several of the students who would be back in September. After breakfast the next morning, the visitors got in their carriage and headed back to Hanover County.

"Well boys," the judge asked as they left the campus, "would you like to be students here in the September?"

"It is a nice academy," said Zack. "I am certain there are going to be some wonderful science and nature studies. Mr. Marshall said in the biology studies they actually cut up frogs and look on the insides."

"Yuck!" said Pat, "That's not for me. I don't much like cleaning the fish I catch in the Pamunkey, let alone cut open a gosh-darned frog!" Everybody laughed and chuckled.

"I look forward to the lectures in the classrooms," said Peter. "With all those pictures on the walls of Hannibal, and Julius Caesar, and the Battle of Marathon staring down. I don't want to miss a thing."

"Oh Peter, I'll have to keep nudging you in the ribs to keep you awake," said Pat, nudging him in the ribs. They all laughed again.

"Well boys, all three of you will be off to Campbelltown in September," the judge said and Adella and Rev. Gadsden smiled. "It is all arranged and paid for."

The Fox Hunt and the Barbeque

Social life on the plantations of colonial Virginia in the summer of 1769, was filled with cotillions, barbeques, fox hunts and such, hosted by one plantation, inviting friends and family and other plantation owners in the region. In early June, such an invitation arrived at Winston Woods. The judge announced to the family they were all taking a few days trip to Orange County, and staying with his good friend, James Madison, at Madison's plantation, Montpelier, at Madison Mills. Adella was indeed with child, and by the best estimation, about three months pregnant, due shortly before Christmas. It would be the last travel Adella would make prior to the birth of her baby.

Peter and Zack were anxious to visit their old friend, Jimmy Madison, who had spent overnights at Winston Woods every year, as the Madisons took their eldest son to and from his boarding school on the Innes Plantation. They were anxious to discuss his boarding school experiences, as they would be boarding at Campbelltown in September. Naturally, Pat was also invited to come along with the family to Montpelier.

The trip to Montpelier Station seemed nearly as long as the trip to Campbelltown and the roads, while not bad, were not nearly as accommodating to a carriage filled with five passengers. The trip went basically west. Following the Pamunkey from Winston Woods to the community of Bumpass. As they headed west, the Blue Ridge Mountains loomed ahead of them, sparking the imaginations of the boys. At their first stop, the boys got permission to sit atop the carriage to take in the mountain scenery and imagine just what really did lie beyond those high peaks.

"I bet we could walk there and back in a day," suggested Peter. "We could camp on top the mountains and return the next day."

"We'd be eaten up by the bears or scalped by those heathen Indians," said Zack.

"I hear there are caves and all kinds of places to explore," said Pat.

"We'd no doubt get lost, and they'd have to send out a search party for us," answered Zack.

"I really want to go there," said Peter. "Just beyond that mountaintop is the real frontier that goes all the way to the Pacific Ocean! I wonder if you can see all the way to the ocean from up there."

"I don't think so, Peter," Pat said. "I heard it's thousands of miles of plains and forests and mountains and even deserts."

When they arrived at the beautiful manor house, Mr. and Mrs. Madison, James and Nelly, greeted them, along with their seven children: eighteen year-old Jimmy and his three brothers and three sisters, right down to two-year-old Fanny. They were standing atop the entry porch in a real "stair-step" of siblings, standing in descending order from height, not age. The oldest boy, Jimmy, was third in line after his two younger brothers, Frank and Ambrose, due to Jimmy's short stature. At age eighteen, he was just barely five feet tall, if that. The other boys seemed hale and hearty looking. Jimmy was just barely an inch or so taller than his oldest sister, eight-year-old Nelly.

When everyone was outside the carriage and the boys had climbed down from their perch on top, Jimmy Madison, hurried down the steps to greet them.

"Hello Peter," he said to his friend. "Hello, Zachary."

"Do you remember Pat?" Peter asked, as Jimmy welcomed them for the first time to his home.

"Oh yes," Jimmy said, smiling at Pat, "I remember Mr. Peter Patrick. I am so happy you could come along too, Pat."

"I did not know you lived so close to the mountains," Peter said. "Perhaps we can hike up to the top."

"They are farther away than they appear," Jimmy informed them. "On foot it's a good day's journey just to the foothills, without even starting the two full days to hike up to the summit."

Peter and Jimmy walked toward the west with the mountains of the Blue Ridge in their view. Zack and Pat followed.

"It has to be so wonderful," Peter said, "living right on the edge of the frontier like this," Peter said. "What kind of world lies beyond those mountains, I wonder."

"When the French and Indian War was fought on that frontier, it was rather frightening for an eight-year-old boy living here," Jimmy said, as they paused at a large tree and sat down. "I had nightmares, vicious nightmares of savage Indians racing down the sides of those mountains and massacring all of us. It was a fright I shall never forget."

"Have you climbed to the mountaintop?" Peter inquired.

"No," Jimmy replied. "I have been to the foothills, but never climbed to the top."

Then the two older looking boys came and sat down with Jimmy and the Winston Woods boys.

"These are two of my younger brothers," Jimmy introduced them. "Francis, who we call Frank, and Ambrose."

"Jimmy has talked of you fellows," Frank said. "Do you really have a grapevine to swing on out across a ravine?"

"Yes," spoke up Zack, "The slave boy Pearlie and I discovered it one day. It's great fun."

"Do you ride?" Ambrose asked.

"Oh yes," Zack spoke, "but we'll have our own horses come September, when we enroll at Campbelltown."

"Oh yes," Jimmy interrupted, "I did hear you are all three enrolling at Campbelltown. You must be anxious."

"We are indeed," said Peter. "We visited there in April and liked it very much. The professors seem to be very adequate, so we are told, and seem like good men."

"Dr. Archibald Campbell is by far the most known educator in the colony," spoke Jimmy. "I have not been so blessed as to have had him as one of my tutors, but I have an older cousin who was a student of his. You shall meet him during your stay with us, Richard Taylor, he is coming for the fox hunt and barbeque on Saturday."

"Are you boys joining in the hunt?" asked Frank.

"We'd very much like to," spoke up Pat, "but we have only heard about them and know nothing about how they are run."

"There's nothing to it, if you can ride and stay in the saddle as the horses chase the hounds who chase the fox," offered Frank.

"I think we can all stay in the saddle," said Peter.

"Well we have a few days before the hunt," Ambrose said, "Frank and I will ride with you and get you familiar with the terrain."

"Are you not riding, Jimmy?" Peter asked.

"No," Jimmy answered. "I ride. I enjoy riding. But the rigors of a fox hunt are not suited to my frailties of body."

The boys spent the two days prior to the Saturday fox hunt exploring the areas of Montpelier Estate. They rode horses with Frank and Ambrose, taking the horses over downed logs and across streams, in preparation for the hunt, not knowing where the fox and hounds would lead them on the frantic chase.

Peter and Jimmy spent several hours just sitting beneath the spreading oak tree, talking about the new educational experiences that would open for each of them in September.

"It will be so exciting for you," Peter said one day as the two of them sat beneath the tree, "being in Williamsburg for your college studies at William and Mary, with all the excitement going on there."

"No," Jimmy added, shaking his head, "I am not enrolling at William and Mary. I will be enrolling at the College of New Jersey in the small town of Princeton, but near both Trenton and Philadelphia."

"All the way to New Jersey?" Peter questioned with excitement. "Why so far away from your home?"

"Peter, look at me," Jimmy said, a bit sadly, "look at me closely. I am eighteen years old. I am five feet tall. No taller than a ten year year-old. My body is a frail one. I weigh just eighty pounds. I am susceptible to every imaginable disease and malady known to man. The dank and damp climate of the lowlands of the Tidewater area where Williamsburg is situated, is very bad for me. I have visited there with my father three times, and each time, have come down with a fever and illness that sent me to bed for weeks. I cannot survive living in Williamsburg.

"The climate of the north should be much better suited for what it is that disables me in Williamsburg. I will be away from Virginia throughout my entire college years," Jimmy said. "I will not return home until my college degree is earned. Perhaps my health will improve in that more moderate clime and I, who knows, I could grow to be as hardy and as healthy as you."

"And as tall as well," Peter said encouragingly, slapping him on his back.

When Friday came, so did overnight guests for Saturday's planned fox hunt and barbeque at Montpelier. Patrick Henry and his family showed up from their Hanover County plantation of Scotchtown. Calvert McGowan arrived with Henrys. Five others came, all cousins of the Madisons from there nearby plantations in Orange County, the Taylors and the Bigelows.

The foxhunt was assembled for mid-morning on Saturday, and about twenty men in all saddled up, included the Winston Woods boys. They were ready for the caged fox to be released and given a small lead before the hounds, a pack of a dozen or more beagles with beautiful brown and black markings on their white bodies, were fast on the trail and yapping all along the way. The horsemen rode in pursuit. Peter, Zack and Pat joined the two Madison boys.

When the hunt ended with Richard Taylor taking the fox, the horses were given to grooms and the hunters joined the ladies and the children on the barbeque grounds for a succulent hog roast. The conversation naturally turned to the events in Boston.

"Four full regiments of British redcoats now occupy the port and town of Boston," said Patrick Henry. "We inch ever closer to revolution."

"I fear you are correct in your estimations, Henry," said Richard Taylor. "The British seem not to be ones to learn from their previous mistakes. They repealed the Stamp Act and saddled the colonies with more acts we have all found to be more intolerable than before."

"The colonies will never be given representation in Parliament," said Henry. "And the colonies, not one of them, shall ever concede full authority to Parliament! War is simply a matter of time."

Peter and Jimmy headed with plates of barbeque to the oak tree and sat. Soon Zack, Pat, Frank and Ambrose joined them.

"Have you heard of the Sons of Liberty in Boston?" Jimmy asked the boys of Winston Woods. "Have you heard how they burned an effigy of the tax collector on the Liberty tree and have run customs agents out of their towns after tarring and feathering them?"

"Yes," answered Peter. "Rev. Gadsden read articles in the 'Williamsburg Gazette' about the Sons of Liberty."

"What's an effi ... an effi ...," Ambrose asked.

"An effigy is like a stuffed scarecrow, made to symbolize a despicable person," Jimmy answered, "hung in the town square and set afire in protest."

"We need to do that, Jimmy," Ambrose said excitedly. "We could burn old King George!"

Jimmy continued his conversation. "We have organized a chapter of the Sons of Liberty on the plantation, in case the need arises and the redcoats get sent to Virginia. We want to be ready."

"You boys are members of the Sons of Liberty?" Peter asked. "How did you organize it?"

"We just did it, in much secrecy" piped up Frank. "We have eight members."

"We must do the same when we return to Winston Woods," Peter said to Zack and Pat.

"And we must do it at Campbelltown too," agreed Zack.

The Liberty Tree at the Corncrib

"So, we are all in agreement," Peter said to Zack, Pat and Pearlie, as they sat atop the pyramid of ears of corn in the corncrib at the edge of the cornfield. "The Sons of Liberty of Winston Woods is formed."

All the boys nodded.

"We must keep it our secret," Zack added seriously, "as no one must know, for fear we be apprehended, taken to London and hanged for treason."

"Agreed!" said the boys with a nod.

"I suggest this be our headquarters," said Pat. "It is the best place to keep our secrecy."

"Agreed," all said.

"What shall be our first action?" asked Pat.

"Well there are no redcoat soldiers here, nor customs officials to be run out of town on a rail," Peter said thinking, "but we do need something to do to let the plantation know we stand for liberty."

"Why not do as the Sons of Liberty at Montpelier have done," suggested Zachary, "and have a Liberty tree?"

"Splendid!" chimed in Pat. Peter agreed.

"There's a nice hickory nut tree right here beside the corncrib," said Pearlie.

"That's perfect," said Zack. "It is huge. It's top rises well above the roof."

Cornerstone

"Agreed," said Peter. Pat nodded and smiled.

"We need a sign to be painted and nailed to it," Pat added.

That afternoon, the boys went to the plantation's carpenter shop and found a nice piece of cut wood and two small cans of paint and brushes. The boys first painted the wood all a shiny white. When the white paint was dry, they lettered in Zack's best hand, 'Liberty Tree' in dark green. Grabbing a handful of large nails and borrowing a hammer, the boys went to the old hickory nut tree and nailed their sign to the trunk of the tree for all to see.

The boys met each day in the corncrib or at their favorite camping site just beyond the barley field. They discussed the happenings in Boston from newspapers the judge had brought home, and really felt left out of all the excitement then going on in Boston, far away in the north.

"We will be leaving for the academy next week," Zack said one day when the boys were at the campsite. "The Sons of Liberty must plan a protest of some sort before we leave."

"I was thinking the same," added Pat. "We need to burn an effigy."

"King George?" Zack offered, with a devilish grin.

"That might be viewed as just too treasonous," offered Peter. "What about that devil Hillsborough?"

"No, we need some one Virginians despise," said Zack.

"Governor Botetourt!" suggested Pat. "He claims to be such a friend of Virginia, yet he dissolved the House of Burgess over George Washington's boycott. Let's burn Botetourt."

"Perfect," said Zack. Peter agreed. They would spend the next two days making the effigy in the corncrib and hiding it out there until Friday. They had already planned to camp at the site on Friday, their last camping trip before heading off to Campbelltown on Sunday.

Pat commandeered an old pair of his father's work pants and a baggy shirt. Pearlie found an old straw hat. Zack snuck some old pillows from attic. They had the makings for the effigy of the dastardly governor. Pearlie suggested they recruit Cassia to sew it all together for them. She was, after all, a seamstress and a patriot.

With the scary-looking effigy sewn together and in need of stuffing, they took the "governor" to the hay barn and took great joy in giving some girth to the fat governor.

96

"Im glad the governor is a fat one," said Pat. "He needs a lot of stuffing and that will just help kindkle the flames when we burn the ole bastard!" The boys and Cassia laughed.

With the fat effigy stuffed, they painted red eyes, nose and mouth on the doomed dummy and hung a sign, "Governor Botetourt," around the neck. They hid the effigy in the corner of the corncrib, burying it with ears of hard golden field corn.

Friday came and the boys trekked across the barley field to their campsite they had now named "Fort Liberty." Cassia, since she had played an integral part in the creation of the effigy, was now initiated as the fifth member of the Winston Woods chapter of the Sons of Liberty. She would camp with the boys so she could take part in the glory of burning the effigy.

As darkness fell, it was time for the protest to begin.

They marched back across the barley field to the corncrib. Peter and Pat unearthed the effigy from its corncob grave and carried it out to the Liberty tree alongside the crib. When they emerged from the crib carrying the scary-looking fat stuffed effigy, Zack and Pearlie had lit two torches to give light to the dark sky, and eventually to send Governor Botetourt into the flames of Hell.

Peter and Pat strung the effigy to the trunk of the Liberty Tree and stood back. Zack and Pearlie, with their torches, approached the effigy for Zack to deliver the eulogy.

"Norbonne Berkeley, Lord Botetourt, Royal Governor of the colony of Virginia," spoke Zack, "may you burn in the flames of Hell!"

The boys lit the hay-filled effigy and the flames rose high as all cheered. They danced around the Liberty tree as the governor burned. What happened next, the Sons of Liberty did not expect.

The fat-stuffed torso of the governor proved to be more kindling than they had imagined. The flames were gorgeous as the shot upward, but soon a portion of the old hickory nut tree, alit in flames, dropped onto the roof of the corncrib. The roof of the corncrib was on fire!

Men from the slave cabins nearby saw the flames and a bucket brigade soon was on hand. So were Buford Patrick and the judge.

The vigilance of the slaves, with their ladders and buckets of water, could not save the corncrib's roof, but the fire was controlled before the structure was totally engulf and the corn stored for the winter feeding of the hogs was spared.

The secrecy of the Sons of Liberty had been exposed, and all the members unceremoniously received the spankings of their young lives. Had the Tower of London been nearby, they would have, no doubt, been locked away and tried for treason.

Pope's Creek

By the late fall of 1769, the boys from Winston Woods were settled in to their new life as students at Campbelltown Academy. Thirteen-year-old Zachary Winston, twelve-year-olds Peter Francisco and Peter Patrick, had been assigned to the four-man room at the west end of the second floor dormitory corridor. The fourth student sharing the room was a new student as well, eleven-year-old Jimmie Monroe, a local boy from Westmoreland County.

The Monroe lad was a slender, tall, attractive and athletic boy who lived with his parents, Spence and Elizabeth Jones Monroe in Fredericksburg. He had been born very near the academy in Washington Parish. He was a good student, even though he had had virtually none but the very basic of elementary training. His father was a successful planter and landowner who was also noted as an accomplished carpenter.

In the room next to theirs were the other three new students for the year, the youngest boys at the academy. Two were ten years-olds, Garrett Hicks and Malcolm Shepherd, from neighboring farms at Manassas in northern Virginia. The youngest was the seven-year-old nephew of George Washington, Bushrod Washington. Bush was extremely advanced educationally for his age. Bush's family lived in Fredericksburg, just a two-hour carriage ride from Campbelltown. Many weekends, Bush and Jimmie Monroe would return home after Friday classes, and return on Sunday evening before classes resumed on Monday.

Of the returning older students, John Marshall and Stockard Samuels were the upperclassmen shepherds over the new boys, and were lodged just across the hallway.

Peter enjoyed his studies, especially Latin, the classics and history, but his first love was his horse. He was assigned a beautiful white horse with a coal-black mane named Coronado in honor of the Spanish conquistador who explored the western wilderness of North America in search of the fabled Cibola, the city of gold.

One crisp fall morning, Peter woke early, and before breakfast, went to the stables to groom and "talk to" Coronado. The morning was chilly, but the air was fresh, like a true gift from God. Peter knew he and his friends would go riding. The morning had all the promise of a coming day of bright late autumn sun with another sliver of warmth before the skies would turn permanently gray and cold with winter. It was the second Saturday in November, the 11th. Perhaps one or two more such beautiful Saturdays would come in the next five weeks, before the academy would turn out for the month-long winter break. Peter, Pat and Zack would return to Winston Woods on December 16th, and classes would not resume again until Monday, January 15th, in the new year of 1770.

"I think we are riding along the Potomac today, Coronado," Peter said to the steed he knew understood every word he spoke. He grabbed the curry brush and began stroking Coronado's beautiful black mane. "You are such a beautiful horse, boy. I know you want a nice long ride today too." Coronado, as if answering his young master, nodded his head in agreement.

The door to the paddock opened and the young boys from Manassas walked in and approached Peter as he was gently using the brush on his friend.

"Peter," Garrett Hicks spoke, "can Malcolm an' I ride with ya taday?"

Peter turned his head, looking at the younger boys, still working his brush on the silky but course mane.

"I don't know, Garrett, I think it will be a long ride, all the way to Pope's Creek, I hear. Are you boys up for it?" Peter asked.

"I am," quickly came Garrett's response. "And I hope we're out all day!"

"Me too," stated Malcolm.

"Well then you best be seeing to your steeds," Peter instructed. "Talk to them. Make certain they tell you they want to go off on a full-day's expedition."

The younger boys laughed as they turned to go to their horses' stalls.

"They cain't talk," said Malcolm.

"Oh, but yes they can, at least Coronado does," Peter turned toward them, laying his brush down on a bale of hay. Peter turned back to Coronado and placed his two large hands, one on each side of the beautiful horse's face.

"What do you think about that Coronado?" Peter guided Coronado's face down to his. "These youngsters don't believe you can talk to me." Coronado had a playful look, staring into Peter's eyes. The horse just wiggled his head side-to-side, as if shaking his head in disbelief.

"See," Peter said, releasing his hands from Coronado's face and looking directly at the boys, "Coronado just cannot believe how you have had all these weeks to care for your own horses and still haven't heard a word they've spoken."

The boys stood, mouths open in wonderment, staring at Peter and Coronado.

"I will ask Stockard at breakfast if he thinks it wise we allow such a pair of dandies to accompany us today," Peter smiled and headed out of the paddock leaving the two younger boys to figure out for themselves how to listen and talk to their horses.

All the boys of the academy decided to ride that Saturday, being as Peter had predicted, "a fine day and one of the last we shall have before the snows blow." The youngest of the academy boys, Bush Washington, was especially excited to ride. He had not visited the family's ancestral home, or his cousin Gus who lived there, for over a year.

They arrived at the Washington estate just before noontime. Augustine Washington, called Gus, was the son of George Washington's oldest half-brother. Bush's father was George Washington's younger brother John Augustine Washington, called Jack.

Other than his uncle George Washington, the seven-year-old Bush had an aunt, Betty, and uncles Samuel and Charles. All, except the most famous Washington, lived in Fredericksburg near their mother, Bush's erasable grandmother, Mary Ball Washington. Samuel ran the Rising Sun Tavern in Fredericksburg, while Jack and Charles oversaw the Ferry Farm holdings of the family. His uncle George had inherited the entire estate at his father's death, but when he inherited Mount Vernon in Northern Virginia at his half-brother Lawrence's death, gave the Ferry Farm at Fredericksburg to his mother and brothers.

"Welcome, lads," Gus said to the riders as they cantered up the gravel lane before his redbrick mansion, the same home where Col. Washington had been born in 1732. "I have not seen this young man for near a year," indicating the youngest amongst the riders. "You do look hale and hearty for a lad of ... what? Six ... Seven?"

"Seven, Cousin Gus, and nearly eight," young Bush answered.

"And soon to be a well-educated young man," Gus noted. "And who are these other strapping young men you have thought to bring to your cousin's home this glorious autumn day?

Bush did the honors, introducing his fellow Campbelltown classmates.

They all dismounted and, at Gus' insistence, led the horses to the paddock for hay, water and a rest of two hours, before the return ride back to Campbelltown.

"Now, I shall have Matilda and Festus set plates for each of you, and you shall all join our family for the midday meal," Gus invited.

"But cousin," Bush spoke up, "we have packed dinners of fried chicken and cornbread muffins. I thought perhaps, on such a nice autumn day, we might have a picnic by the tombstones."

"Very well," Gus agreed jovially, "If you don't mind your cousin joining in on your feast, I'll have Matilda pack mine up and see if I cannot find a pie, ... no two," noticing there were a dozen hungry-looking, growing young men to be fed, "better make that three, and a gallon or so of cider."

Gus led the young visitors on their walk along the southern shore of the Potomac River for more than half-a-mile from the mansion house. There they came upon a clearing in the woods where a dozen or more tombstones protruded from the ground under a canopy of trees. This was the ancient burying ground of the Washingtons in America. Each found pieces of ground to sit and began partaking of the packed fried chicken, cornbread muffins and glasses of fresh apple cider the servant Festus brought with the three dried apple pies. As they sat, Gus entertained the students with stories of his ancestors in the New World.

"There," Gus pointed, "that tombstone is John Washington. John is Bushrod and my great-great-grandfather. He was the first Washington to immigrate to Virginia. That was ... oh let's see ... one hundred ... and ..."

"One hundred and thirteen years ago, cousin," piped up Bushrod.

"That is right," Gus chuckled, "In 1656 it was. His story is an interesting one I think you lads would enjoy."

"The Washingtons were connected in England with lineage through the royals from the time of Edward III. When the Roundheads of Cromwell overthrew the Stuarts, John Washington's father, Lawrence Washington, was rector of All Saints Purleigh Parish in Essex. The Washingtons lived well at stately Sulgrave Manor, until the Puritans of Cromwell took over and kicked him out of the position he had held for years in the church. It was said Lawrence was what they called, a common frequenter of alehouses." The boys chuckled at the history they would never get in the classroom. Gus joined in the laughter at his ancestry.

Gus continued his story. "Lawrence Washington was said to not simply visit the alehouses, daily tippling there, but also encouraged others to join him in that vice. He died in Essex in 1653.

"Great Great Grandfather John was one of two sons who worked to support their widowed mother. John signed onto sailing ships, bound for the Caribbean and the colonies to take British goods to sell, and load aboard spices, rums, sugar and molasses from the islands and tobacco from Virginia for resale in London.

"On one such trip in 1656, aboard the merchant vessel the 'Seahorse,' John plied this very river," Gus pointed out toward the Potomac. "The Seahorse took port at what is now Alexandria. The British goods were offloaded and the bales of tobacco from the plantations of Virginia were taken aboard. The Seahorse left the dock, only to have a gale come up unexpectedly upon them. The ship ran aground on a sandbar in the middle of the river and capsized.

"John, thinking his own life deserved sparing, swam to shore with the others. John saw it as a sign from Heaven. He had been enamored with the beauty of the land of Virginia, and now he was determined never again to return across the Atlantic to England.

"He met a prosperous landowner, Nathaniel Pope, and immediately went to work on Pope's holdings.

"He soon married Pope's daughter, Anne," Gus pointed to the tombstone beside John Washington's grave. "There, she lies beside him to this day, our great-great-grandmother Anne Pope Washington."

"This land here we now call Pope's Creek was a wedding gift from great-great-grandmama's father," young Bushrod added.

"She must be my and Peter's great-great-great grandmother!" Zack blurted seeming surprised at what he had just heard.

"And how so, lad?" asked Gus seriously.

"Our Mama is Adella Pope Winston," Zack answered, "the daughter of Carlton Pope."

"Indeed," Gus smiled with surprise. "Carlton Pope is my great-uncle. I am pleased to meet you Mr. Winston."

Zack was excited. He had met an uncle he never knew he had and had just seen the grave of his great-great-great grandmother! He could barely wait to tell his mother.

The boys enjoyed the tales of Gus Washington and soon were back at the paddock at Campbelltown.

When Christmas time arrived, Peter and Zack were anxious to be home for a whole month.

On Christmas morning, Adella gave birth to a beautiful baby daughter, Angelina Christmas Winston. The judge called her "my little Christmas angel."

Chapter Four

The Bloody Redcoats

The policies put in place under the Intolerable Acts of Lord Townsh-end made life, especially in Massachusetts, difficult and tense. The most threatening reality of life in Boston in 1770, was the continual presence of the despised red-coated soldiers, carrying their musket with bayonets attached, or sabers in hand, as they marched on maneuvers down the streets of town. The soldiers of the king were quartered in any houses in town where a spare and unoccupied room was found.

Captain Thomas Preston was one of those soldiers quartered in a private home. From the time he arrived in Boston in October 1768, his quarters were in the attached two rooms and hearth in the back of a house on Lewis Street near the harbor. The elderly couple, Caleb and Rowena Birney, owned the house, and did not mind Preston's presence. There was a private side entrance to the attached rooms, so they rarely saw him.

As events of life in Boston grew more and more under the control of the king's surrogates, bands of dissidents grew in many quarters. There were bands roaming the streets daily, who hated and feared the heavy presence of the "bloody" Redcoats. These were mainly gangs of boys and young men from the neighborhoods of Boston.

The Plug-Uglies were the rowdiest, made up of delinquents and ruffians who earned some money helping off-load cargoes from the English merchant ships in the harbor. William Samuel Winkman, called

"Wills," a strapping, good-looking, tall and muscular boy of nineteen, with coal black hair was their leader.

A band of free Negroes and mulattoes made up an active street gang, called the Phillipians, led by the freedman in his late forties, Crispus Attucks.

The rival gang to the Plug-Uglies was the Irish League. The Irish League was a smaller gang than the Plug-Uglies, but seemingly more feared, because of the pranks they played. They lived mainly in the hovels along the waterfront, as Irish Catholics were not well welcomed in Puritan and Protestant Boston.

John O'Malley Patrick Macneal, called "Jacky," was leader of the Irish League. Jacky was a slight-built, five-foot six-inch tall, nineteen-year-old, who had the face of a cherub with a larcenous smile. His large blue eyes and dark reddish hair gave a real hint to his true Irish heritage.

Jacky Macneal lived in the house next door to Caleb and Rowena Birney, and often saw the symbol of his true hatred, Captain Thomas Preston, as Preston entered and left the private side entrance door of his two-room quarters at the Birney home.

One late afternoon in January 1770, Jacky was returning to his home with two of his band of Irish Leaguers, Andy and Christopher Seider. Preston was standing at the door to his quarters and called out.

"Hey boy, come here!" He was directing his call to Jacky.

"What does that scurvy little bastard of a whore want?" Jacky asked the Seider boys.

"He's a damned Redcoat," said Andy. "You best go Jacky, if you don't wanna be the guest of honor at the gallows." He began to laugh, as his younger brother did as well.

"Oh, look at me," Jacky said. "I be a shakin' in me boots!" He started wiggling his legs and they all broke out in laughter.

"Come boy, I have a proposition," shouted Preston. "I mean you no harm."

"Oooh, a bloody proposition he 'as for ya Jacky, me lad," Andrew teased.

"He wants ya to wiggle yer arse at 'im like he saw ya a shakin' in yer boots," the younger Christopher teased.

Jacky slugged them both, then walked across the yard that divided the two houses. The Seider boys, laughing at the events, headed for their house on Prince Street.

"Come boy," Preston waved Jacky on toward him. When Jacky was standing at the Redcoat's door, Preston spoke.

"Lad," Preston said, putting his arm across Jacky's shoulders, "if you can run and find me a fine pint of some good Irish whiskey, I will pay you quite handsomely."

Preston dug a hand into his pocket and pulled out several coins.

"Two shillings. They are all yours boy, for a pint of the best."

"Make it three shillings, ya will, and it'll be the best damned whiskey to be found in all of this colony!" Jacky bartered.

Preston laughed at Jacky's audacity and shrewd bargaining skill.

"Three it shall be then. And be quick with it! Bring it here and knock thrice, so I know 'tis you." Preston tossed him a shilling. "Two more for you when I have the pint in hand."

Jacky ran down the street and out of sight.

Soon, with the pint for the captain in hand, Jacky walked back toward the Birney home. As he walked, thoughts of how he hated those damned red-coated soldiers of the king filled his mind. Why did they have to be so damned arrogant and hateful? Who gave them the right to run roughshod over Boston? Why the Hell were they here in the first place? He devised a plan. His larcenous smile spread across his angelic face. He raced to the shed out back of his house.

Inside the small outbuilding, Jacky put the pint of Charlie O'Brien's best Irish whiskey on a small workbench. He pilfered through his mama's jars she used to put up vegetables. Finding just the right jar, he went back to the pint of whiskey. He poured about a third of the whiskey into the empty jar. He then pulled down his pants, took his penis in hand, and pissed into the whiskey pint, filling the jar back to the top with Irish urine. When he finished peeing in the jar, he pulled up his pants, and with a spoon, stirred the pee into the whiskey. He did not want the Redcoat's first sip to be pure pee. Jacky replaced the cloth cover and string around the jar's top, so it looked to be untampered with.

He walked to the Redcoat's door, knocked three times, and the bloody Redcoat opened the door with a broad smile on his face and two more shillings in hand.

The captain lifted the pint jar and peered in at the glorious-looking beverage.

"Want to have a sip, boy?" he offered, thrusting the jar toward Jacky's face.

"No yer lordship, but thank ya all the same," Jacky said.

"My name is Tom, Tom Preston, Captain Thomas Randolph Preston of the 23rd Regiment of the Chippenham Guard," Preston thrust his hand toward Jacky.

Jacky took his hand, shook it politely, and said, "me, I'm John O'Malley Patrick Macneal the third, but you can call me Jacky."

"Well, Jacky Macneal, it is certainly my pleasure. If this is as good as you say tis, I will be calling upon you regularly."

"Oh it's good, alright," said Jacky boasting. "Tis like no other Irish whiskey in all the town, I can easily assure ya o' that fact."

Two days later the same scene reoccurred, as Jacky and the Seider boys walked up Lewis Street. Jacky was again summoned by Preston with his call.

Jacky had shared his story with Andy and Christopher about pissing in the whiskey. They all had a good laugh.

"Me thinks he's a wantin' more of that fine pisskey, I mean whiskey," Christopher said through his laughter.

"He surely is one piss drinkin' sorry sonofabitch'in bastard of an English whore, that one is," said Andy, joining the laughter.

Jacky walked over to Preston as the brothers headed for home. Had Tom realized there was Irish pee blended in with his whiskey? Would he be in for a deserved flogging? He approached with every caution, ready to race away if need be.

"Evenin' yer lordship," Jacky bowed at the waist.

"Indeed you were right, Jacky, ... that pint of whiskey was among the best I have ever swilled down," said Tom. "Some I have purchased, you could not tell from horse piss. That first jar I bought from you was oh so smooth. I detected a wee bit of saltiness that made it uniquely good. I must have another."

"Happy to hear ya enjoyed it, sir" Jacky smiled, laughing on the inside. "Four shillings it was, was it not yer lordship?" Jacky queried, trying to sucker the Redcoat.

"Three it was, and not a farthing more," Tom reminded Jacky.

"Oh," Jacky replied with a disappointed look on his boyish face. "But t'was worth four shillings, I dare say."

Tom laughed. "It was indeed, Jacky. It was indeed. Four shillings it will be. You be quick about it now."

Jacky ran off and returned soon, after making the brief stop in the shed to add his special wee bit of saltiness to the blend.

Every other day from then on, Tom Preston would call across the yard to Jacky to fetch him another pint of that wonderful Irish whiskey. Jacky enjoyed the ruse he was playing on the despicable Redcoat. Soon all the others in the gang knew about how the scurvy little red-coated bastard of a whore enjoyed the whiskey Jacky kept peeing in.

"He'd surely shit out one end and puke out the t'other, if he knowed he was a drinkin' me Irish piss, he would!" chuckled Jacky hysterically.

Jacky really thought the tall, slender, and handsome, blue-eyed, blonde-headed Captain Tom Preston, seemed not to be a bad sort at all. He was always nice to him, and always offered him a sip of whiskey, though Jacky always refrained from accepting. He wasn't about to drink his own pee!

The Prime Minister Dines with Dunmore

"That was a fine meal, Dunmore. My compliments to Lady Charlotte," the grossly rotund man, Frederick, Lord North, spoke as the gentlemen guests were retiring from the dinner table to the library for tobacco and brandy.

"And how did you find the haggis?" his host, John Murray, Fourth Earl of Dunmore, asked the obese man, soon to be the new British Prime Minister.

"I do believe it to have been the best haggis in which I have ever partaken," North replied. "Compliments to ma'lady's cook as well. One cannot imagine what a wonderful flavor is had by simmering sheep's pluck in that very sheep's own stomach after the slaughter! A glorious concoction your noble Scots ancestors have left to us."

Lord North was speaking of the traditional Scottish dish where the innards of a lamb are minced with onion, oatmeal and spices, then simmered for hours inside the slaughtered animal's stomach.

"I am so happy you enjoyed it, Lord Frederick," Dunmore smiled. "Many, knowing how it is prepared, opt not to even try."

"That simply leaves all the more for us who do enjoy it," said North. "I do believe I helped myself to three platefuls." He laughed, as did Dunmore

The Earl of Grafton grew tired of dealing with the rebellious nature of the American colonies, especially in Boston. He announced he would step down as the leader of the king's government on last day of 1769. Lord North was to become the new Prime Minister the first day of 1770. North had been a leader in the political circle of London for years, with a jovial and very likeable personality. He was an obese forty year-old, weighing well-over three hundred pounds, with a puffy, plump, round face, and always wore a curly, white powdered wig that appeared to be too comically small for his large head.

North had decided to keep several men who had served in the cabinets of Pitt and Grafton, especially Lord Hillsborough, serving ably, to his thinking, as the important Colonial Secretary. The British Empire of North America was the ultimate issue facing North as he prepared for his leadership.

Lord Dunmore, after eight years as the elected peer serving in the House of Lords from the district around the Murray clan's ancestral manor in Scotland's Forest of Atholl, County of Perth, coveted appointment to a governorship of one of the American colonies.

Dunmore knew a colonial governorship could bring personal wealth to the wealth he already had amassed. Land grants were easily sold to speculators at a huge profit. There were also many avenues open for bribes and other fees that went directly into the governor's purse.

He and Lady Dunmore had planned a dinner party during the Christmas season at the palatial London townhouse where they resided when Parliament was in session. North had accepted the invitation to dinner that evening, as did Lord Hillsborough and his wife Cassandra.

Dunmore also had a family connection with the soon-to-be Prime Minister. The Dunmores had an eight year-old son, George, Lord Fincastle, and a two year-old daughter, Lady Augusta. They had also raised two nephews, the sons of Dunmore's younger brother, William, who had died in 1762. The boys were both in their studies at Oxford: sixteen year-old Alexander and fourteen year-old Stephen Roderic Murray.

Dunmore took them and their widowed mother, Susannah Rose North Murray, in when William died. She lived permanently at their London townhouse. Susannah Rose was Lord North's favorite cousin.

"And how are the lads coming along at Oxford?" North had inquired of his cousin, as they earlier sat beside one another dining on the haggis.

"Quite well, Freddie," she replied. "Alex is at the top of his class," she said proudly. "Rodie is not quite the student Alex is, but Oxford seems to have given him a new attitude toward his education."

"Young Roderic has always been an impertinent child," added Dunmore. He noticed immediately Lord North's expression. The lord was not pleased hearing anything harsh about his favorite cousin's boys. "But he is such a joy," Dunmore quickly added. Lord North's frown turned into a close-lipped smile of approval.

"He is at that," inserted North, "a pure joy of boyhood personified. Do extend my love to both the lads, Susannah, the next time you see them. I must write to them."

"They will be arriving for the holidays on Monday," Susannah stated with a smile.

After dinner, as the gentlemen retired to the dark-paneled library, the ladies followed their beautiful hostess, Charlotte, Lady Dunmore, into the front parlor for pleasantries.

When the gentlemen had all found seats in the library, Dunmore offered a toast.

"I raise my glass to the coming age," Dunmore spoke. "May it be a long and successful tenure for our Prime Minister and for King George III."

The assembled gentlemen spoke "here, here's" as they sipped. North raised his glass in response.

"May Providence guide us." More "here here's" followed.

The discussions soon led to colonial politics and Lord North's coming agenda.

"The empire ... all of it ... must be strengthened and must remain loyal to crown and Mother Country. If that means the government here must rethink its policies, be more gentle or more harsh, as the case may be, then so be it. The British dream of empire shall continue.

"The idea of empire must guide us all," North continued from the leather armchair that he barely was able to fit his huge buttocks into.

"That will be the theme of these times. Dealing effectively with the colonials in North America is paramount. We can ill afford to lose our North American colonies.

"Britain is at the very portal of becoming the greatest worldwide empire ever ... greater than that of ancient Rome. It begins in North America and will spread upon every continent around this globe."

The Colonial Secretary, Hillsborough followed up. "We now have strong footholds on the African continent, and are competing quite well with the Dutch in the black slave trade to America."

"We have indeed," continued North, "and as well, we are growing stronger in India with our posts now at Madras, Bombay and Calcutta. Tea and spices make our London merchants very rich and very content."

"Why is there so much intolerance for our laws in America?" asked Jonathan Leeds, a parliamentarian from Portsmouth.

"They see our motives simply as being driven by commercial greed," said North flatly.

"Now they riot in the streets of Boston in protest to Townshends' marvelous plan we have put forth," said Dunmore. "We must be determined to end the insurrections in America, if we are ever to see our noble vision of empire realized."

"How can they not see they too shall share in the wealth of empire?" asked Leeds. "Mr. Prime Minister, how shall we deal with the current insurgencies in Boston?"

"Sternly, as we have; more sternly, if we must" North said in a fatherly manner, "but we must do a better work at expressing to the colonials the greatness of our realm that they share.

"Their uncles and aunts, cousins and grandparents are the very constituents we meet in the streets of London and throughout the isles. We must convince those constituents here that what is best for their American cousins, is a strong loyalty to king and country. They must be emissaries for us. If the riots turn to rebellion, and they become no longer part of the empire, they then lose all claim to the belonging and the amity of the greatest nation on the earth. The constituents here shall send that message to them, and it will be taken to heart."

Dunmore, seated in a large leather armchair alongside North, with Hillsborough in another on his other side, spoke. "What you say is so true. We must bring them back into the fold, but strongly and sternly, upon our terms, not upon theirs."

Hillsborough added, "We have in place the very legislation necessary to effectively enforce our laws in the colonies. Our agenda must remain. The example of firmness, being shown now in Boston, is being viewed in the other colonies as proof certain of our nation's power and resolve. As we contain the protests to New England, the other colonies shall split further and further away from the treasonous ones."

"And those who govern for us there," Leeds asked, "are they implementing your plan well?"

"I am, I must admit, not pleased with the lot of them," stated Hillsborough. "I ask them to find and bring to me just one man with the charge of treason on his shoulders, and they cannot. With all the mob protests, the riots, the running out of town on rails of our tax collectors, they tell me there is no leader to charge. They say they cannot arrest an entire town."

Dunmore added, "We must make certain the men we send to the colonies as our king's representatives, especially those holding executive power as royal governors, be men not rewarded simply for past services in Parliament and in the military. It appears they simply seek riches, captured from the colonies to supplement them in their retiring years. We must send men driven by the vision expressed this evening in this room. Empire ... expansion of that empire, with the vision of spreading the greatness of Britain to all the corners of the world, must drive them."

"Lord Dunmore has so eloquently put into words the exact thoughts I have on the matter," added Hillsborough. "Too many we send to America have indeed proven themselves more interested in personal riches than in securing the authority of Parliament and the crown in the colonies. They are little-liked among the colonials, and rightly so! The colonials see firsthand their greed to swallow up colonial lands as opportunists simply to resell it to the highest bidder. In that regard, we have become our own worst enemy."

"Here! Here!" cried Lord North, followed by a chorus of similar huzzahs. With that, the gentlemen began to leave the room and gather their wives and coats to ward off the bitter cold outside on their rides home.

"John," Hillsborough pulled Dunmore back as the others left the library. He spoke softly, "would you entertain the notion of putting your words into action?"

"I spoke only what I truly believe," replied Dunmore, "just that."

"Then I propose a governorship for you," stated Hillsborough. "I have just received news from New York of our governor's wish to return to England. I will, within days be suggesting an appointment for the king to make. Are you prepared to sail for America and serve there as your king's Royal Governor of the New York Colony?"

"That certainly comes as quite a surprise your lordship," responded Dunmore, hearing the offer he had hoped to hear all along. "I would certainly be open to give it my serious thought and consideration. Thank you for the honor of considering me."

Hillsborough smiled. "You shall, I do think, be summoned to St. James Palace soon after the new year commences."

John Adams, Esquire

John Adams had kept a law office on Tremont Street, just across from the commons in Boston, since being admitted to the bar in 1758. By 1770, Adams was one of the leading attorneys in Boston, having devoted a near total concentration on building his practice.

Adams lived and farmed on his land in Braintree with his wife Abigail and their three young children. Susannah, their third child, had celebrated her first birthday just before Christmas 1769. Abigail was the perfect wife for the young attorney. She was the daughter of a minister in Weymouth, and well read for a female of that era. She could conduct herself in brilliant conversations with her Harvard educated husband and his friends on nearly any topic. Politics was a favored topic of hers and that certainly suited John.

One February afternoon in 1770, with court business taken care of, Adams had made arrangements with his law partner, Josiah Quincy, to meet at a popular alehouse across the commons, for a little conversation and a drink or two before the ten-mile carriage ride back to the farm in Braintree.

Adams took a seat at a table with Quincy and his old client John Hancock.

"Will the new prime minister be an improvement over the last?" Hancock asked, as their conversation turned to politics in London.

"From what I read," said Adams, "Lord North has been a seeming friend to the colonies, but we saw how that office took away our friendship with William Pitt."

"Pitt was a friend to the colonies," said Quincy. "Then he steered through passage of every wit and whim that damnable Townshend could lay in front of him."

"Yes, I fear we trusted and huzzahed Pitt's elevation," said Hancock, "only to be saddled with those damnable Intolerable Acts."

"I fear it shall most probably be the same with North," sighed Adams. "Men seeing the colonials at first as fellow Englishmen, but after a few moments in leadership, feel the arm-twisting from the merchants and fellow members more. Instead of alleviating the hardships on the colonies, they simply add to them."

"That vile vermin in the London offices of the East India Company have the real power," Hancock added. "Lord North can never assume more power than the money-grubbers! He will be no better, no better at all."

"Watch our new prime minister attempt to paint pictures for us of the blessed life awaiting us all, if we but stay true to the king," said Quincy. "They are guiding us down the path to independence, they just do not realize that fact."

Hancock smiled at the thought. "This shall be the decade of our independence, gentlemen," The three men drank a toast to John Hancock's prophesy.

Abigail did not greet John at the door, as she usually did, when he arrived at home that day as the sun was quickly fading on the horizon. He wondered what was the matter.

"Abby, where are you?" he shouted as he looked around the empty house. Soon she appeared on the staircase, coming down, eyes red with sadness.

"It's baby Susannah," Abigail said. "She is burning with the fever." She found shelter from her fears in John's arms. They stood there several minutes at the foot of the staircase embracing.

"She has been ill since early afternoon," Abigail said. "Doctor Harding is upstairs with her now." They went up to the doctor and their sick baby.

Susannah died a week later and was buried in the Parish Church Cemetery next to the farm.

Jacky Macneal and the Captain

Jacky Macneal was enjoying the shillings he had been hoarding from Captain Tom Preston, and the shillings were piling up. Every third run Jacky made for the captain was simply a run straight to the shed. Not being a drinker much himself, he'd collect one-third of the whiskey with each pint he purchased from Charlie O'Brien, with his pee replacing the whiskey taken. By the third run, there was two-thirds of a pint of the pilfered whiskey waiting in the shed. He simply had to provide the missing one-third in Irish piss, and still get paid. As long as he could piss out a third of a pint, Tom would be none the wiser. Those four shillings for payment on every third run would be all his for the saving. Charlie O'Brien was selling his pints for two shillings, so Jacky was becoming a rich Irish lad.

He started feeling badly though for his prank, after all, Tom had been kind to him and seemed like a right good chap. Those guilty feelings would soon fade as Tom was just what he was, a bloody Redcoat who had no right to be in Boston, marching on the streets with his musket and saber in the first place.

One cold day in February, with snows laying high, Preston insisted, before Jacky went off on his run, that when he returned, he expected Jacky to come inside to share his supper and sip with him.

"I am not the evil man you think me to be simply because I wear this uniform," Tom said. "I know you sneak a tipple now and again. I can tell the cloth cover has been removed from the jar and replaced. I insist you come in, dine with me, and sip by my fire. I have a hearty lamb stew on the hearth. It will warm your insides on this cold and brutal day."

Jacky agreed he would, then left for Charlie O'Brien's. As he walked, he knew he could not tamper with the evening's whiskey. After all, he was not about to drink his own piss, and he had promised Tom he would at least take a sip or two with him by his fire. Would Tom miss the salty taste? He had a brilliant idea, he thought. He'd run to the shed and put a spoonful of brine salt in the pint from the canister his mama stored there for pickle making.

Back at Tom's door, he knocked three times and heard Tom call from inside.

"Come in Jacky, come in."

Jacky opened the door and walked inside.

The room was very warm from the hearth, a welcomed feeling from the cold. Tom was tending to the cast iron pot of lamb stew at the hearth. The aroma was wonderful. Tom was in a blousy white cotton shirt, open at the neck and unbuttoned midway down his chest. He had a pair of tan knee breeches on and was walking around barefooted.

"The stew is right ready," Tom announced. "Put the pint on the table and we shall enjoy some stew. Make yourself comfortable, Jacky."

Jacky put the pint (filled only with the best Irish whiskey in town this time, and a pinch of salt added for good measure) on the table, and took his scarf and coat off, stepped out of his wet boots and socks, and sat by the crackling hearth to warm his cold, wet feet. When his feet were nice and warm, he unbuttoned his shirt as well. He got up and sat at the table.

"Can I help ya with anything?" Jacky asked.

"No, no," Tom said, as he carried the pot and a ladle to the table. He took a seat and began ladling the stew onto the two plates.

Jacky was starving and dug right in. It was good. Jacky hadn't had lamb in months. He knew Tom's stew would better than what his sisters would come up with at his house.

The conversation at Tom's table was really each talking about his own circumstances. Tom learned Jacky was the only son of three children. His father had died some years before, and his mother struggled to raise him and his two sisters, both younger by two and four years respectively. His mother took in sewing jobs and worked as a maid and cook in some of the better homes on Beacon Hill. Jacky started the Irish League five years ago when the Stamp Act was being protested, but mainly to have some male companionship.

"I share me room with those two deplorable girls," Jacky said, as he consumed another spoonful of stew. "This here's the best lamb stew I ever ate! The shillings ya give me for me whiskey runs goes straight away ta Mama," Jacky said, with a rivulet of gravy from the stew trickling down from his chin.

Tom had not too different a story to tell Jacky. He was raised near the harbor in Portsmouth, England in a hovel of a home, even in worse condition than Jacky's. He was the youngest of three, and the only boy as well. His father, John Thomas Preston, a seaman, spent months at a time on the waves, and finally deserted the family and the ship he was hired onto years ago when the ship called at Bombay, so the family was told.

When Tom was an older teen, he was known to be lucky with the girls.

"I have since sworn off any dalliance with the fairer sex," Tom said, "because I am what you might say, just too lucky with the lasses."

"How can ya be too lucky with the lassies, now?" Jacky asked. "I be so awkward around any o' the girls I'd like ta ravish ... and would not know the first thing ta do with 'em even if ever I tried."

"Three lasses I bedded, and each of three lasses were then with child," Tom giggled.

"You are a father?" Jacky asked.

"Thrice a father, by three different mothers, and spread out only amongst three month's time." Tom admitted. "And three different fathers of those three different mothers all want nothing more than to see me swing from atop the gallows. That's why I ran off to Chippenham and joined the royal guard."

Tom was twenty-four, five years older than Jacky, but appeared young for his age, perhaps twenty, Jacky had imagined. Jacky looked younger than his nineteen years as well. Tom thought him to be maybe fifteen, that's why he used to call to him as "boy."

Tom took the pint in his hand, untopped it and poured two glasses. He gave one to Jacky, and Jacky sipped. It was smooth as it went down. Tom sipped his.

"That is good, smooth whiskey," Tom said, savoring his first swallow. A puzzled look came to his face.

"How is it," Jacky asked, noticing Tom's puzzled look.

"It certainly is good," Tom said, "...but...there just seems to be... something missing."

"Tastes good to me," Jacky offered, as he took a second swallow, "mighty smooth goin' down me gullet. Mighty smooth indeed it tis."

Tom sipped again. He savored it in his mouth, eyes wide open and lips tight as he seemed to swirl the sip in his closed mouth, as if searching for what was missing. He finally swallowed.

"The saltiness..." Tom observed. "That lovely saltiness seems to be lacking in this evening's pint."

Jacky felt the redness building in his face.

"I think tis plenty salty," said Jacky, hoping Tom would be convinced. Tom took another sip.

"No, most definitely, the saltiness is missing," Tom confirmed, "at least the light, sweet saltiness as before. There is a saltiness of sorts... but I think ole Charlie O'Brien has changed the salt.

Should he come clean and confess his sin to his new friend? Jacky's Irish Catholic conscience was getting the best of him.

"Tom, I have somethin' ta tell ya," Jacky began, "but first I do beg yer indulgence of an ignor'nt Irish lad."

"What is it Jacky?" Tom asked.

"Well, Tom," Jacky tried to soften the anger Tom was certain to aim at him. "When ya first ask me to make a whiskey run for ya... when I knew ya only as the devil himself in that damnable red coat of the king's...before I knew, mind ya, that ya was an alright fellow, not the scurvy bastard of a whore I felt ya first to be ... well, let's just say, I tampered with the whiskey I got fer ya. This night's pint is good an' genuine an' not tampered with a' tall."

"What did you do to it? Shake salt into it?" Tom laughed at Jacky's confession of the prank. "What did you do to make it so tasteful, Jacky?" He was still laughing, quite amused at Jacky's ingenuity and awkward confession. "You must tell me at once."

Jacky thought for a moment then said, "If ya say I must," Jacky said, taking the pint, now missing about a third of the whiskey. He stood at his chair facing Tom across the table, pulled his pants down.

Tom stopped laughing. His mouth gaped open as he watched what Jacky was doing right before his eyes. When Jacky had filled the jar and pulled his pants back up, he stirred the fresh concoction to blend it well, then handed it to Tom.

"Here," Jacky said with his devilish smile. "Try this!"

"Damn you, Jackie Macneal!" roared Tom. "I do not know whether to run you through with my saber or ... or ... or applaud your ingenuity and eventual honesty!" He started laughing and took the jar of pee-blended whiskey. He cautiously took a swallow.

"Now that, my friend, is a fine drink of whiskey," Tom smiled.

They both laughed and continued their conversation and drinking. Jacky took Tom's original and nearly full glass and slid it over beside his still nearly full glass.

"I gotta have somethin' ta drink," Jacky said with a smile. "I ain't about to drink me own pee! Thought I'd finish yer untampered with glass." Tom laughed and nodded his approval.

"You know, Jacky," Tom said as they sipped, "I do admire the protests you Americans are engaged in. I never thought about it when I first arrived, just thought you Americans were an ungrateful lot, willing to dishonor the king. He's a right fine chap, you know?" Tom questioned Jacky.

"Now how can 'e be such a right fine ole chap if 'e taxes us ta death an' won't even allow us to speak fer ourselves in 'is parliament?"

"Well that is a bad policy," Tom conceded, as he sipped some more. "I do hope and pray you Americans, you sons of liberty as they call you, win this fight. And a fight it's going to be. If you win your independence from England, well I can tell you this very moment, I want to stay here and become an Ameriucan and taste that independence."

As the night grew darker, Jacky mentioned he should probably leave for home and allow Tom get to sleep.

"It is late," Tom agreed. "But you know Jacky, I have so enjoyed your company tonight. I do wish it would not end."

"I can stay longer, if ya'd like," Jacky said, "I just thought ya might need a good night o' sleep before ya dress up in that fine red coat the king give ya an' go out harrassin' all the poor folk o' Boston tomorrow." They both laughed.

"Well, I suppose I do, but you know Jacky," Tom said, "and please do not think badly of me, but I have not slept beside another human being in my bed for three full years. I so enjoy lying beside another sleeping, breathing soul." Tom paused, hoping he had not said any-

120

thing Jacky would take as inappropriate…as something vile or appearing as a threat. Then Tom added, "would you stay the night?"

Jacky just stared at the handsome blonde sitting across the table smiling at him. Moments passed in silence. Jacky's mind went to times when he had slept in bed with the Seider boys and that was okay. He even had thought about doing more than just sleeping with another boy. He even admitted to himself that he had wondered what it would be like to be in such a circumstance with his rival, the dark-haired Plug-Ugly Wills Winkman.

Jacky, still not speaking a word, rose from his chair.

Tom stared at what move the boy was next to make. Jacky unbuttoned his shirt, took it off and tossed it on the back of the chair. He then unbuttoned his trousers and slid them down stepping out of them.

Tom still remained in his chair, silently staring at Jacky's every move. Jacky then turned and walked slowly into Tom's bedroom, wearing just his muslin long-john bottoms. He crawled beneath the covers.

Tom took a final gulp of the blended whisky, emptying the pint jar. He stood and shed his clothes, shedding them in a pile beside Jacky's. He put out the lantern and walked naked into his bedchamber to join Jacky beneath the quilts.

Death of an Innocent Boy

On the cold Boston afternoon of Thursday, February 22nd, an event occurred on the streets of Boston that pulled the colonials more and more toward the ranks of the insurgency.

Customs official Samuel Fielding entered the home of the widow Lucy Seider with a Writ of Assistance he had prepared. He ask to see documents proving she had paid the duty on the new glass panes she had installed in the front windows of her hovel of a house on Prince Street. Like so many others in Boston, she had not paid the duty. She had not even purchased the panes of glass.

"I have no documents," she said. "A neighbor brought the glass for my cracked windows from his place, and put 'em in hisself afore winter set in. I need not surely pay a tax on somethin' I didn't buy!"

"Someone must," Fielding answered sharply. "Who is this benovelent neighbor?"

"I would cause him no harm for doin' his Christian duty," the widow Seider shot back. "I do not owe you, so be gone!"

"Very well. Those two new panes of glass are then contraband and shall be seized," stated Fielding harshly.

"They will not be seized!" cried out her youngest son, Christopher. "You Britishers are fiends! You are the devil hisself!"

"Well, young man, we shall just see about that shan't we?" Fielding spoke as he left the house.

Christopher and his older brother Andy followed the customs officer down Prince Street, passing Paul Revere's house. Revere had been the neighbor replacing the widow's windows. He had taken it upon himself to look after her and her two boys ever since Mr. Seider died.

The customs official turned down Hanover Street. The boys continued to yell catcalls at the hated agent of England, as they stalked several yards behind him. After a block or two, Fielding turned up a narrow alley to the right. When Christopher saw him turn, he ran on up ahead of Andy, and turned down the alley. The customs agent grabbed Christopher, put his hands around the boy's throat, shook him and threw him to the ground roughly. When Andy caught up and turned down the alley, he saw his younger brother lying lifeless. Fielding ran, yelling back to the boys, "That will quiet your demon voices!"

Andrew stooped down to pick Christopher up, but there was no life left in the thirteen year-old's body. Fielding's grasp around Christopher's throat had been strong enough to choke the life out of his young tormentor.

Paul Revere, who had heard the taunts the boys had been chanting, rushed to the alley. Revere helped Andy carry Christopher's lifeless body to the widow Seider's home on Prince Street.

"My baby boy!" the widow Seider cried. "It's because o' that devil tax collector with his writ. What did he do to my baby boy? What did that devil do?"

She hugged her dead son, still in the arms of Paul Revere and Andy. They laid the boy's corpse on the settee in the parlor. The widow knelt on the floor sobbing and hugging her youngest.

Three days later a large crowd gathered at the Old Granary Burial Ground near the Boston Commons, for the burial of the lad. Most of Boston turned out for the sad service for a poor boy coming to the defense of his poor widowed mother. Britain would surely pay for the actions of the over zealous customs official ... just how was yet to be determined.

Crispus Attucks

One of the most vocal of the insurgents in 1770 in Boston was an unlikely sort.

Crispus Attucks was a half-Negro, half-Wampanoag Indian, living as a free black man in Boston for the past twenty years. He was about forty-seven, having been born into bondage in Framingham, west of Boston. His father had been John Yonger, son of a slave, captured in West Africa in the 1680s and brought to America. His mother, Nancy Attucks, was full-blooded Wampanoag, born in 1706 to two bondservants of a Colonel Buckminster.

Crispus had a relatively easy childhood, growing up in the manor house of the colonel. At the age of twenty-seven, with both parents dead, he was sold to Deacon William Brown, and was taken to do hard labor on Brown's farm near Framingham. After a few weeks under the lash of Deacon Brown, Crispus fled. Brown placed advertisements in the newspapers throughout the colony, with the description of the six-foot two-inch tall, burly mulatto run-away slave.

Attucks hid himself well. He signed onto a whaling ship for several months, until the news of his running away lifted. Returning to Boston, he hired out as a common laborer and began making a name for himself as a rope maker. For twenty years he lived in a small, plain house he built for himself near the harbor, and plied his trade to the ship's captains coming into and sailing from the harbor of Boston.

With the change in philosophy of Parliament, following the French and Indian War, to tax the colonials in order to make up the drain in the British treasury from the war, Attucks violently opposed the ruthless policies of the British. He talked with other freed Negroes and Mulattoes and convinced them they too had a stake in what the British were doing. They banded together as "the Phillipians," a gang to oppose the policies of Britain, and honor the murdered King Phillip of the Wampanoags.

When the Redcoats arrived in Boston, Attucks turned the Phillipians into a band of young men like the Plug-Uglies and the Irish League. He, nearing the age of fifty, became a leader the leaders of the other gangs looked to for guidance. Wills Winkman and Jacky Macneal often took notes from Crispus Attucks.

The day after the sad burial of Christopher Seider, Attucks called for a meeting at his home.

"The governor ain't gonna arrest that murderin' tax collector," Attucks said to a dozen or so who came to the meeting. "And if he did, he'd fin' some way ta see the charges dropped. They won't even give us his name so's we can avenge the young Seider boy."

"My brother did nothin' worth bein' murdered over," spoke Andy Seider, holding back tears. "Christopher was a hero. He ran that devil out o' Mama's house. I was there with him, runnin' down the street callin' him the scurvy bastard he was. I only wish I was right at his side when he turned down that alley. He would've been the one lyin' on the ground dead, not Christopher!"

"They will pay," Attucks said, putting an arm around Andy's shoulders. "We will get our revenge for your brother, you can count on that."

Tom Preston knew Jacky's two best friends were the Seider boys. He had seen the brothers with Jacky as he came home on the day of Christopher's murder. That was the day Jacky moved out of the room he shared with his two sisters, and moved in permanently with Tom. As they were dining on a Shepherd's pie Jacky had made, they heard the shouts in the streets with the dreadful news.

Jacky ran to the Seider's house where Christopher was laid-out on the settee in the parlor, awaiting the pine box coffin, being made by Paul Revere. Jacky attended the burial at the Granary Burial Ground three days later on Monday. Tom wanted to accompany Jacky, but out of fear of being recognized as a captain of the Redcoats, they both decided it best he stay away.

"Why ain't the Governor arrestin' that murderin' bastard?" Jacky asked Tom on Sunday evening. "Is that not proof enough that the damned Britishers are nothing more than evil scoundrels? The lowest of the low?"

"I know how sad and hurt you are, Jacky," Tom said, as they lay in their bed beneath the quilt. "These customs agents, the ones we are sent here to protect, are just as you say. ... scurvy bastards. All Englishmen are not to be judged by the actions of one Samuel Fielding."

Jacky bolted upright in the bed.

"Who? Who is Samuel Fielding?"

"The customs official who choked Christopher to death," Tom answered.

Jacky looked puzzled. "That name ain't been reported. The British are keeping it all hushed up. How did ya find the name of that vermin piece of buzzard shit?"

"You forget, Jacky," Tom said, leaning on his pillow with his hands folded beneath his head, "I am privy to much information. It was not difficult to find the name of the man who called upon Mrs. Seider of Prince Street on the 22nd."

Jacky smiled. He was pleased with Tom's brilliance in getting the name of the culprit and giving it to him. Jacky would make certain the newspapers on Monday would have the murder's name printed in big black letters.

"Ya know, Tom, there'll be revenge on this Samuel Fielding," Jacky flashed his devilish, yet angelic smile.

"Oh, I am most certain there shall be," answered Tom. "And I for one, as well as most of the men I command, will not bat one eyelid if that revenge was to be extracted beneath our very noses."

Jacky smiled at Tom and sunk back into the bed.

"See, Jacky," Tom said, as he slid his hand beneath the quilt and planted it on Jacky's abdomen, "not all of us are the evil scoundrels you make us out to be. Perhaps we are the lowest of the low, as attested to by my actions with you in my bed ... but not evil scoundrels."

Jacky smiled that larcenous smile that Tom was so growing to enjoy. Jacky slid his hand beneath the quilt and wrapped it around what Jacky liked to call Tom's "bayonet."

"I need to be getting to sleep soon," Tom said with a smile, his body wriggling beneath Jacky's grip. "I am officer of the day tomorrow at the Main Guard, and must be present for the roll call at six."

"Then that gives us plenty time" Jacky smiled more and winked. Tom hugged his new friend and they kissed.

Massacre at Boston

That following day, the fifth day of March 1770, Boston was crowded. The market stalls were filled. The offices around the Boston Commons and Government House were humming with business, and the street gangs were going about their duties of stirring up the rabble.

Tom reported for roll call at six, and assigned the various groups of soldiers in the Main Guard their rounds for the day. The Main Guard was located between Government House and the Customs House on King Street. The day was like any other.

Jacky left by seven o'clock on a mission. He went straight to Charles Eads' print shop near the harbor and gave the publisher of "The Gazette" the name of the murdering tax collector.

"The murderin' scoundrel's name is Samuel Fielding," Jacky told the publisher.

"How did you get the name, Jacky?" Eads asked. "The British say they know not who it was who visited the widow Seider."

"Oh, it's the right name for sure," Jacky said, "found out by a Redcoat hisself who perused the records an' found the name of the scurvy tax collector who visited the Seider home on Prince Street on the 22nd. It's truly verified an' it's the real thing."

The publisher smiled. "Good enough for me. I shall set the print now in big black headlines: "ARREST FIELDING!" and the Gazette will spread the name all over the town!"

Jacky smiled, and left the print shop. He headed across the street where he knew Wills Winkman, leader of the Plug-Uglies lived in an upstairs room.

"Wills, I have the name of the murderer..."

By half-past eight, he had gotten the publisher of the Gazette to set type naming the name of the murderer, and had informed Wills who would let his gang know the name. He now headed to Crispus Attucks' home so he could tell the Phillipians, and then to three other printers of newspapers. The Irish League was set to meet at ten o'clock. By noon, every patriot in Boston would know the name of the murderin' scurvy bastard!

Jacky left the meeting with his gang and knew his important work for the day was done. He would walk back to Lewis Street and visit for an hour or so with his mama.

"Are you comfortable at the Birney house?" his mama asked, as she made ready to go to the James Otis House on Beacon Hill. There was to be a dinner party that night, and she would not be returning until after the last guest had left.

"Oh yes, Mama, very comfortable," her son replied. "I'm leastwise not sharin' a room with two o' the most pesterin' girls the good lord ever put upon this earth!"

"Your sisters are not as ya say," Annie Macneal scolded her son. "Why they're the prettiest and most well behavin' girls I could ever 'ave asked for."

"Pretty? Them two?" Jacky said laughing, "an' well behavin' ya say? Well I could tell ya stories, but I won't, cause I don't wanna shatter your ideas of 'em." He hugged his mama and kissed here on her cheek. Annie smiled, knowing the truth was not as bad as Jacky said, but not nearly as good as she had said either.

"You gonna escort your old mama to Beacon Hill where the rich folk live?" she asked.

"I will go with ya far as the commons," Jacky said. "I'm meetin' the boys there after two."

At noon, Captain Preston assigned Private Hugh White to relieve Private Adam Ansley in the sentry box outside the Customs House. He had dispersed various eight-man units on a variety of maneuvers through the streets, to make the presence of the hated Redcoats plain. Order to be restored and the peace to be kept, was the order of the day. The day was very routine.

At one o'clock Captain Preston's subordinate officer, James Bassett, brought him a copy of the Gazette with the banner headline crying out for the arrest of Samuel Fielding for the murder of the Seider boy.

"Where the Hell did the publisher get Fielding's name?" Bassett asked his captain.

"If it is indeed the correct name," Preston said, taking the broadside to read.

"It says here," Tom said as he read, "a much reliable source said an agent at the Customs House revealed the name of the tax collector who harassed the poor widow Seider on Prince Street on the 22nd."

Tom put the paper on his desk and looked up at Bassett. "I fear there is a rat at the Customs House, and I fear the peace of this day may well be shattered. We best be on a most vigilant alert for the crowds." He smiled to himself, realizing Jacky had done everything he would have done, if he were not wearing the uniform of the hated Redcoats.

He rose and went to the window with Bassett. They looked out onto the grounds, the sentry box and the Customs House. All seemed to be peaceful, but the sidewalks were crowded.

"If those people, now walking peacefully about their business get wind of this, as they certainly shall, all Hell will break loose," the captain said to his subordinate.

Tom sat back at his desk as officer of the day. At two o'clock he heard yelling outside. He and Bassett again ran to the window.

Edward Gerrish, a young apprentice for the Boston wigmaker Donnell Simonton, was yelling at Lieutenant John Goldfinch as Goldfinch passed by the sentry box.

"There goes the thief!" Gerrish shouted, "The no good thief who fails to pay for his wig! Give me that wig you not-to-be-trusted bastard Redcoat!"

Most of the Redcoat officers patronized the wigmaker. The wigs both Preston and Bassett wore that day had come from there.

"Boy I paid in full to your master ... in full!" Goldfinch kept walking.

"You thieve, now you lie!" Gerrish continued his harassment. "You lying good for nothing sack of pig dung! You will pay in full, you can be damned certain of that!"

"Enough lad! Move on about your business," warned Private White on duty at the sentry box. "Move on and not another slander out of your mouth!"

"Slander is it, when I tell the truth!" Gerrish shouted even louder. "My business is with that conniving devil in that red coat!" Gerrish pointed at Goldfinch, walking up the stairs outside the Customs House. Gerrish headed down the street. Preston and Bassett took their seats again and returned pouring over paperwork.

Jacky had just arrived at the Boston Commons, and met up with Andy Seider and a half dozen of the Irish League.

"Have you seen the Gazette?" Jacky asked.

"We all have," said Andy. "Now the people of Boston will demand the arrest of the scurvy bastard!"

As the shift was nearing its end, about four o'clock, a noise of yelling again arose, and Preston and Bassett again came to the windows. Gerrish had returned, this time with what appeared to be two-dozen or more boys about Gerrish's age. Preston recognized Wills Winkman, leader of the Plug-Uglies. More and more boys came, it appeared, from all directions. This merited Preston and Bassett's total concentration.

"Arrest the murderer Fielding!" cried one.

"We know who he is," shouted another, "Arrest him!"

A chant went up, "Arrest Fielding! Arrest Fielding!"

From the office in the Main Guard, they could hear clearly what was being yelled at Private White by the several voices making a considerable din. They saw many of the boys throwing snowballs at the sentry box, and specifically at White. White came from the box and again warned Gerrish, "Tell your compatriots to stop and go home before all of you are sent to the Romney," White threatened to round up the gang members and have them impressed as seaman in the Royal Navy.

"I shall tell them one thing, me lord," shouted Gerrish, "Fire at will!"

At that, White raised his musket and swung it at Gerrish, hitting the sixteen-year-old with its butt and sending the lad to the ground. Gerrish writhed on the ground and screamed in the pain of his agony. Two other boys who rushed up to White, continuing the shouts, were Batholomew Broaders and Samuel Maverick. Gerrish finally rose to join them in the harassment of the private.

Then bells from the church steeples in that area began ringing. The residents knew when they heard the bells, other than on Sunday morning, it was a fire or some other emergency to be warned of. The streets swelled as houses, offices and markets emptied to see what the commotion was about. Hundreds started appearing on the streets. Preston and Bassett were alarmed now, and knew this mere shouting down of Goldfinch and the call for the arrest of Fielding was rapidly escalating to a full-fledged riot. Tom hoped Jacky was not going to get embroiled in the coming melee.

Jacky, Andy and the gang of Irish Leaguers, which had now grown to about a dozen, ran from the Commons toward the Customs House. They did not want to miss the arrest of Samuel Fielding.

Private White beat a swift retreat to the steps of the Customs House, but seemed to be trapped with the door now locked. He had nowhere to hide, nowhere to get to safety from the riotous throng.

"Corporal Weems," Preston ordered, "get six men and go to Private White's aid. Relieve him at once!" Weems rushed out, assembled the six men and had them fix bayonets. As a unit they ran to the sentry box. Preston and Bassett followed them outside.

The crowd of rioters had grown to between three and four hundred by the time Preston and his men arrived at the sentry box. White was still at the Customs House door banging to get in. Preston ordered the men to load their muskets, then as a unit, they marched to the steps of the Customs House to White's aid. At the Customs House, some-one inside finally heard the frantic pounding on the door, and quickly opened, then shut and re-locked the door, after White was safely inside.

Preston had his men form a semi-circular perimeter at the base of the steps. As the soldiers marched between the sentry box and the steps, and even after they formed the perimeter, rioters threw snowballs and any debris they could find to lob at the Redcoats.

Crispus Atuucks was now leading the riot. The rioters followed Attucks' lead and yelled as Attucks was yelling.

"Cowardly Devils!"... "Why don't you fire?" ... "Red-bellied bastards!"

Attucks threw a large piece of wood at the soldiers. It flew above Tom's right shoulder as Tom and Bassett were standing in command, between the soldiers in their semi-circle and the riotous crowd. The piece of wood hit one of the soldiers, Private Hugh Montgomery, squarely in the abdomen. He fell to the ground. When he rose to his feet once more, he yelled to his comrades, "Damn you, Fire!" then he let loose with a round from his musket. Hearing the shots fired by Montgomery, the others all joined in, apparentlty assuming Preston had given the order.

From the volley fired by the Redcoats, eleven men were hit. Three died instantly. Crispus Attucks was hit early with two musket balls lodging in his chest. He was the first to die, followed by Samuel Gray and James Caldwell.

Samuel Maverick, the Plug-Ugly who had harassed Private White, had made his way to the back of the crowd. He was shouting "Arrest

Fielding! Arrest Fielding!" Jacky and Andy Seider had spotted him as they came from the Commons. He was standing about ten feet beyond the sentry box, facing the semicircular perimeter of the soldiers in front of the Customs House steps. Jacky and Andy, and a few other Irish League boys, joined Maverick.

When the Redcoats fired their volley, a musket ball flew over the heads of the riot, hit the sentry box and ricocheted, hitting Maverick in the back of the neck. He slumped to the ground at Jacky's feet. Jacky and Andy reached down to help him. He was unconscious and bleeding profusely. They carried him away and put him under a tree across the street from the sentry box. Jacky stayed with Maverick, trying to stop the bleeding, as Andy ran for a doctor. Jacky saw Wills Winkman and yelled for him.

"Oh God!" Wills said, seeing his gang friend lying on his stomach under the tree. "Is he dead?"

"Not yet," said Jacky. "Andy went for a doctor." Jacky had pulled off his coat and was using it to apply pressure to the bleeding wound.

Andy returned without a doctor. Maverick died about an hour later, with Jacky still trying to stop the bleeding.

The four fatalities were taken from the site of the massacre and laid in state at nearby Faneuil Hall for the next three days. So Maverick's body could lay with the rest, Jacky and Wills carried his body to the nearby hall. Samuel Maverick was the only teenaged boy killed at the Boston Massacre.

The town turned out by the thousands to pass by and pay tribute to Crispus Attucks and the others. On Friday, March 9th, all were buried in the Granary Burying Ground, close to the fresh grave of young Christopher Seider.

Patrick Carr, an Irish immigrant of thirty, was the last victim of the Boston Massacre. He had been wounded that day, but lingered with his wounds, finally dying at his home two weeks later.

Awaiting the Consequences

Tom arrived late at the rooms he shared with Jacky on Monday evening the fifth. He had been detained at Main Guard to write his report as officer of the day on the day all Hell broke loose in Boston.

Tom hadn't seen Jacky at the riot, because Jacky had gotten no closer than the rear of the crowd. When he opened the door he saw Jacky sitting silently at the table, his head buried in his folded arms.

"I take it you have heard what happened today?" Tom said.

Jacky lifted his head, looked at Tom through his red eyes. "I was there. I saw you. I'm relieved you weren't hurt or killed."

Tom came to the table and Jacky stood up. They hugged for several silent moments.

"Why did it happen?" Jacky asked Tom. "I saw you just before you gave your men the order to fire."

"I gave no order to fire. I would never give an order to fire into a crowd of people, innocent or not!" Tom said, shaking his head. "It was the last thing I wanted. Please believe me."

"I want to, Tom, ... but I heard it m'self," Jacky insisted.

"I think it must have been Private Montgomery," Tom answered. "He had just recovered from being hit by a thrown slab of wood. All I know is it was not me."

"I believe you. If you say it was not you, I believe you," Jacky said and hugged Tom again. "I just got back here m'self," Jacky said. "I'm sorry I've had no time to fix anything fer supper yet. I'll put a chicken on the spit, if ya'd like."

"I don't much feel like eating any way," Tom said. He went into the bedroom and took his powdered wig off and put it on its stand. He pulled off his boots and hung his jacket over the chair. He slipped out of his uniform pants and put a pair of civilian pants on. He went back into the main room to the hearth.

"Ya know," Jacky said as they both sat by the hearth, "a good friend o' mine, Sammy Maverick, was shot and killed today." Jacky went on to tell Tom what had happened.

"You could have been the one shot!" Tom said, pulling Jacky to his side and putting an arm around him. "I am so thankful it was not you. Of coarse, I hate to know it was your friend. No damn it! I hate to think any one was killed today. It never should have happened. Things ... tempers got out of control. And for this to happen on my watch!"

Jacky had never seen tears in Tom's eyes. But they were there, streaming down his face. He put his arm around Tom's shoulders, and Tom's head rested on Jacky's shoulders. Jacky liked to sleep with his head on Tom's shoulder, but Tom had never been in Jacky' arms that way before. He liked holding Tom as Tom sobbed.

"Why did it end that way?" Tom said, as he raised his head after several minutes of crying on Jacky's shoulder.

"The way I seen it," Jacky said, "t'was just a natural occurrence, with men's an' boy's tempers and emotions gettin' out o' control." Jacky let his head go to Tom's lips and they kissed.

"I am just so happy you were not taken from me this day," Tom said as they kissed again.

"As you said, I assume it was simply a natural occurrence, brought about by men's fears," Tom said. "But, being the officer of the day, and in charge of my men, I fear I am to be held accountable, as I expect to be. Why did I ever send them out with loaded muskets and bayonets drawn?"

"But why should you be held responsible?" Jacky questioned. "If 'n the men fired without yer orders ta fire, ain't they to blame, an' not you?"

"To a degree, I suppose," Tom continued, "but I fear the burden of the blame shall lie squarely across my shoulders."

"That just ain't fair," Jacky said.

"It's been a horrible day, Jacky" Tom said, as he pulled Jacky up from the hearth. "Since there's no supper, and since neither of us are hungry any way, it must be time for bed."

"I think I'm just too upset to sleep," Jacky said.

"I do hope so," Tom smiled the first smile either had smiled all evening. Jacky smiled his mischievous grin and they walked hand-in-hand to the bed.

Thomas Hutchinson, serving a second tenure as the royal governor, sat in his residence. The day's events of March the fifth were still keeping the citizens of Boston in riotous turmoil. Word had spread of the events throughout the colony, and in fact, throughout all of New England and New York. How could these events, events of no one's planning, where a British officer accused of not paying for the service of a wigmaker, escalate into five colonials killed and eleven more suffering some sort of injury?

First, it was the death of that Seider boy, now this. Hutchinson knew his every move, any action he took, would have severe consequences.

He could not sit back as if nothing had happened. If the citizens of Boston did not feel their governor was seriously trying to make amends and pursue justice, this could spell the end to the empire in all of North America. Everyday of his indecision drove more moderate citizens closer to the patriot cause.

"There shall be arrests of British soldiers," Hutchinson said aloud, "and they shall stand trial before a jury of colonials, and suffer whatever verdict may come!"

Three weeks and a day after what was then being called the Boston Massacre, Hutchinson made his move.

The governor ordered the arrest of Captain Thomas Preston, his subordinate James Bassett, Corp. William Weems and the six soldiers who stood in the semicircular perimeter. They were bound over for trial on charges of murder. The governor in his announcement of the arrests, promised a fair and unbiased trial in Boston, with a jury of colonials to insure justice would be served. There was never any mention of an arrest warrant for Samuel Fielding the customs agent.

Tempers cooled at the actions of the governor. Those bloody Redcoats who fired into the crowd of Bostonians would be tried before a fair jury in the Superior Court. They were surely all to be found guilty and hanged ... each and every one of them!

There were no attorneys in Boston willing to defend the arrested soldiers. If the defendants were to be refused counsel, it would not truly be a fair trial. Sam Adams, perhaps the leading patriot of the day, knew that not only did Preston and his men require attorneys to plead their case, he knew they had to have reputable counsel. Sam Adams knew that if the defendants were not represented well, it could do great damage to the patriot cause.

Sam Adams went to speak with his distant cousin, the attorney John Adams, who had remarkably defended John Hancock from smuggling charges. John was known as a strong patriot, and was quickly becoming Boston's leading legal mind. With John Adams defending Preston, the governor and all in Britain could only view the trial as a fair one.

John Adams was surprised when his cousin appeared at his farmhouse in Quincy. He was doubly surprised when he was introduced to the man Sam had brought with him, the chief defendant, Captain Thomas Preston.

The three sat in the parlor as Mrs. Adams brought in tea and biscuits and joined them.

Sam presented his case to John and Abigail Adams.

"The patriot cause centers around fairness and justice for all. If in these circumstances, no capable attorney comes forward and represents the defendants, as none have and as all say they shall not, then how can the patriot cause be trusted?"

"I cannot...no I shall not," said John. "I shall lose every patriot credential I now hold should I do such a thing!"

"When you were admitted to the bar," Sam argued, "did you not swear an oath to give your best defense to each man who asked for it."

"Yes, Yes," John answered, "but that still allows for selection of ones clients."

"Based upon what?" Sam argued some more, "the man's ability to pay? If he is Catholic you can turn him down since you are Episcopalian? If he is a British officer and you are a Son of Liberty?"

When Sam Adams had concluded his case to the Adamses, Captain Preston asked to be heard. John Adams silently nodded his assent.

"I was indeed the officer of the day at the Main Guard on the fifth of March," Preston spoke. "I have met many citizens of Boston since first arriving here in the late autumn of 1768, and consider some among my best friends. I do not agree with all the laws our Parliament has burdened you with. Nor do I personally agree with the way the laws of king and country are carried out here, as I have personally witnessed. I am just a captain in the king's army, pledged to follow the orders of my commander.

"I came out of the Main Guard with my men that dreadful day, to attempt a restoring of order in the streets. I saw need for a military presence to quell the riotous atmosphere. I had no intention of ordering my men to fire. I gave no such order. Fearing the taunts and the hurling debris thrown at them, I am certain, out of fear for their own lives, the men fired without orders.

"While I say this not to escape the responsibility for the actions of my men, nor those five tragic deaths, I say it in hopes of your understanding of the temperament of the crowds that day.

"Am I not entitled to your counsel? Does your counsel not extend to a fellow Englishman? Am I and my men to be so denied?"

"As you know all too well, Sam," John Adams spoke deliberately, "I love the law and base any counsel I might give, and to whom I might give it, solely upon the rules that govern us. I have never, and hope I shall never be so blinded by political expedience as to evade the very spirit of justice.

"But, sir," turning to Preston, "do you know what you are asking of me? We are living in a time when I feel, as my cousin here feels, we in the colony are on the brink of perpetual slavery to the king, or on the converse, on the verge of freedom and independence unto ourselves. I have much love for the cause of freedom, and will not be able to help with this cause if my own kinsman and neighbors do no longer trust me. I am just now seeking election to the General Court, where I feel I can help amplify the cause. Defending the defendants in the horrific events of the fifth day of March will place me out of the graces of those citizens. No, I must not become involved. I cannot be a part of your defense."

"But, John," came the high-pitched and nasally voice of Abigail Adams, "Think about what you say. On the one hand you speak rightly, when you say you cannot be so blinded by political expedience as to evade the very spirit of justice. While on the other hand, the only argument you give is of that very forbidden political expedience. Is it not?

"I know not what the verdict shall come to be, and whether you or Sam or Captain Preston will be pleased or displeased by it. The one thing I do know is you shall never be comfortable with your own self if you make the decision not to give the counsel he so desires and he so deserves.

"You rightly know, there could be no better defense for the soldiers than the counsel John Adams can offer."

Chapter Five

The Quiet Time

Ironically, the day of the massacre in Boston, on the other side of the Atlantic, Prime Minister Lord North offered a bill to repeal all of the duties of the Intolerable Acts, except for the duty on tea. North personally saw the overall scope of the acts as being nearly as intolerable as they had been received in the colonies. But he held fast that Parliament must indeed hold the power of taxation over the colonies.

In the immediate aftermath of the massacre, John Hancock and Sam Adams organized a committee and met with Governor Hutchinson and the commander of the British troops in Boston, Colonel William Dalrymple.

"You were well warned, your excellency, that if a standing army of the king was quartered here, there would be uncontrollable turmoil that even we could not control." said Hancock. "Free men have no need to be subjected to a standing and occupying force of alien soldiers."

"There is no alien force of standing soldiers," retorted the royal governor. "We are all Englishmen. Need I remind you? When some Englishmen refuse the authority under which they hold their freedom, the soldiers are simply sent to remind them of their responsibilities. When they refuse to pay legitimate duties, and place fear of bodily harm upon those men assigned to collect those duties, the call for a standing army to enforce the law and the collections is indeed warranted."

"Under the constitution of Great Britain, the constitution you are charged with upholding," Sam Adams added, "there can be no taxation without consent, without representation, which we free men of Massachusetts have none."

"You here in America are unique," spoke Hutchinson professorially. "You do not have one representative in the Parliament. All the members of Parliament are there to vote your best interests."

"That is no representation at all!" fumed Adams.

"If these soldiers, four full regiments, responsible for the general emotions of the mob that rose up against them, are not now and forevermore removed from the streets of Boston," warned Hancock, "the events of March fifth will pale at the events to come."

"Is that a threat, Mister Hancock?" asked Hutchinson abruptly.

"No, your lordship, tis my simple thought, a simple fact, foreboding the reality to come," answered Hancock. "You are sitting upon what one could say is a powder keg. If the troops are not removed, there are ten thousand armed colonials ready to march. I do not think that is what you want."

"Of course, I do not want that!" said Hutchinson, knowing Hancock had padded the numbers of a potential armed revolt, but at the same time, knew the possibility did exist.

"The next move, dear sir, is within your hands," said Adams

Col. Dalrymple spoke up.

"If it shall calm the emotions of your citizens, Mister Hancock, Mister Adams, I feel then, removing the troops now quartered in the city to Castle William might better serve the interests of all."

"But is the daily presence of authority, not served better with the troops remaining here within the city?" asked the governor to the colonel.

"No more than the knowledge by the colonials that the troops are but a few oar strokes off the shore," added Dalrymple.

"Very well," spoke Hutchinson, as he rose to signal an end to the meeting. "If that will calm the fears and restore the peace, it shall immediately be done. Let their emotions be calmed!"

He turned to Dalrymple. "When can the total move be completed?"

"The troops can fully be removed from the city within the week," assured the colonel.

"Mister Hancock, Mister Adams," the governor spoke to the patriots, "will that soothe the tempers in the streets? Will that keep your ten thousand at home tending to their gardens and their chickens?"

The gentlemen shook hands and left to tend to their normal work.

The king gave his assent to the Repeal Act in April, and word reached the colonies in the middle of May. That truly signaled the coming of the 'Quiet Time.'

Return to the Wharf

When the session at Campbelltown Academy adjourned in late May 1770, Peter, Zack and Pat were anxious to return to Winston Woods. They gave their farewells to their fellow students. Stockard Samuels and John Marshall would both be going off to William and Mary in September. Peter knew he would miss the two older students who had been both mentor and friend to him. Still Peter was happy for them as they were both headed off to Williamsburg to live and study in the colonial capital during such exciting times.

Pat would not be returning to Campbelltown either in the fall. His father had asked the judge if he could stay at the plantation and get the real education that would better serve him in his future of being an overseer or a farmer in his own right.

The judge agreed with Buford Patrick's request. "It is your decision to make, Buford. I take no affront to that. But I ask first that you ask Pat his feelings. If your boy so wants to follow in your footsteps, I have no complaints with that at all. It is a noble profession you hold."

Pat was actually ready for that too. While he liked reading about the ancient Greeks and Romans, and learned to even enjoy dissecting frogs, he wondered how that would really help him in the future. He dreamed of some day heading west across the Blue Ridge and staking claim to land in the frontier to build his own plantation. He was anxious to start learning from his father all there was to know about cultivating the land and raising hogs and cattle.

After arriving back home to Winston Woods the first day of summer break, at the evening meal, the judge made an announcement that would surely excite the boys.

"We leave in one week for Williamsburg, where we will spend the entire month of June," the judge announced with joy.

"Williamsburg?" Peter immediately asked excitedly. "Williamsburg?"

"Yes, Peter, Williamsburg," the judge replied. "I think you boys need to visit our capital and feel the excitement that always permeates the air there."

"And we have an invitation to the Governor's Palace," added Adella proudly. "Lord Botetourt, shall host a summer evening with an elegant banquet set up on the grounds, and a ball to follow."

"Don't worry, boys," the judge chimed in. "You will not be arrested and tried for the treasonous act of burning the good governor in effigy. But I still feel the need for recompense from the both of you for the loss of a perfectly fine corn crib." They all laughed.

The week of preparation and anticipation flew by quickly, and soon the carriage was loaded with baggage and the trip began. They stopped after a day of travel at City Point where the judge had arranged for rooms at Christina Donnelley's Tavern. Peter had not been back in five years.

Peter was excited to see the wharf again. He talked nearly incessantly from the time they left Richmond until the carriage rumbled over the wooden planks of the wharf at City Point.

Peter wanted to show Zack the old coil of ropes where he slept. He wondered if Christina would remember him, and her son he mutely played with before learning to speak English. What about Auntie Savannah and her sumptuous rum buns? What about Nico Souza, the old Portugee blacksmith who taught him his first words in English? Would the wharf be as Peter remembered it or would it be changed after five years?

When the carriage pulled up in front of the tavern, Peter stuck his head out the side and looked around. It was just as he remembered it. Christina and Auntie Savannah had seen the carriage arrive and came rushing out the door to welcome them.

"My word, Peter Francisco!" said Christina, as Peter alit from the carriage, "Judge Winston told me how much you had grown, but I really did not expect to see such a tall and husky young man." She hugged him and kissed his cheek.

"You are certainly not the helpless little eight year-old Portugee boy I remember from ropes."

"Lord 'o mercy!" cried Auntie Savannah, wiping tears of joy from her dark eyes. "You sure is one giant of a boy! Come here and give your old auntie a hug." He did, as she wrapped her huge, flabby arms around him.

"Is that Joshua?" Peter asked, seeing a boy come out of the tavern.

"It is," Christina confirmed. "He is eleven, just about to turn twelve. My how the years roll by us," she exclaimed, looking toward the judge and Adella, cradling baby Angelica in her arms. Christina rushed to her.

"Oh and this must be your darling little Christmas Angel the Judge has told me about! May I hold the little darling?" Adella consented and handed the five-month old over to their hostess.

Peter had gotten all of his questions answered that had flooded his mind on the carriage ride from Richmond, all but one.

"What about Nico?" Peter asked. "Is the old blacksmith still here?"

"Nico Souza is very, very ill," responded Christina solemnly. "The doctors do not give the old man many more days upon this earth. He knows you are here and, if possible, would enjoy your company for a few minutes before you leave for Williamsburg in the morning.

The travelers went inside the tavern where Auntie Savannah had spread a marvelous table of food for them. The Judge and Adella took the main room on the second floor where the judge usually lodged when riding the circuit. The boys would share Joshua's room across the hall.

The next morning, Auntie Savannah had those marvelous and aromatic rum buns, fresh from the hearth, and a huge breakfast feast set out for the visitors. After breakfast, Peter, Zack and Joshua walked the short distance to the blacksmith shop, now closed, and the small rooms above where Nico was dying.

When Nico saw Peter, he knew him instantly and a twinkle came to his eyes.

"Pedro!" the old man cried out. "Pedro how you have grown!"

Peter rushed to his bedside and planted a kiss on the old man's wrinkled forehead.

"I hear you are not doing so well, Nico my friend," Peter said in sadness.

"I am not long for this earth, Pedro," he panted, showing signs it was difficult to get breaths. "I have lived a good life and I am ready to go and join my Marianna in God's Heaven."

"Nico, you were the first true friend I had when I arrived here," Peter said, tears welling in his large eyes.

"And now look at you," said Nico proudly. "You speak this language as if you have spoken it from birth." The frail old man took the young man's hand. "That gives great joy to me, Peter Francisco. I know you are ready for a successful life here in America."

"I wanted you so much to come live with us at the judge's plantation," Peter said.

"I would have liked that also," said Nico, "but soon after you left, my health began to fail. I would be no charity to anyone, especially not to the good judge. Has life there been as good as it appears it has?"

"Oh yes, Nico," Peter answered. "The judge sends both Zack, my brother, and I to Campbelltown Academy for our education. He takes us now to Williamsburg. He found the truth about my family, and now a grave with Papa's possessions is in the plantation cemetery. I visit Papa there every morning when I am home from the academy." Peter reached into his pocket and pulled out the beautiful gold watch his father had carried, and showed it to Nico proudly. He opened the fob and showed Nico the miniature of his mama.

"What a beautiful lady," Nico smiled. "She reminds me so of my beautiful Marianna, who I will soon join in Heaven. This all makes me feel so good," the dying man hacked and gasped and finally drew another breath. "Thank you so much for sharing this moment with me. I have thought about you near every day since you left. Go forth, Pedro, take possession of your future and make us all proud of you. You have made a dying man so happy."

Berkeley Plantation

Before noon the next day, the carriage turned off the main road toward Williamsburg and followed a bucolic country lane, bounded on both sides by huge and ancient trees, similar to the ones on the lane leading up to the manor house at Winston Woods. The carriage pulled round a circular drive in front of a stately red brick mansion, framed by immaculately manicured boxwood hedges. The judge disembarked and knocked at the door. A liveried servant opened the door and in walked the judge.

Soon the Judge appeared again at the door and motioned for all to step out of the carriage and join him. The judge led them into the parlor and they sat, waiting for their hosts to arrive.

"We are paying a brief courtesy on the hosts of our stay in Williamsburg," announced the judge. "This is perhaps the foremost family of Virginia, the Harrisons."

Then in walked a distinguished looking country squire and his lady, followed by a teenaged boy and girl.

"Welcome to Berkeley Plantation," said the gentleman to the judge, extending his hand. "This is my lovely wife Elizabeth, our oldest son, Benjamin, and third daughter, Lucy. How has the journey been thus far, Judge?"

"Just wonderful," the judge replied, "and but for your extreme generosity in the offer of use of your townhouse in Williamsburg, this trip would have been not so anticipated."

"Gladly offered, Judge, gladly offered," the gentleman replied. "And this must be the lovely Lady Winston, I presume." He reached for her hand and gave it a kiss.

"Oh, excuse my oversight," the judge said. "May I present my wife Adella and our daughter Angelica in her arms. These are my wards, my nephew Zachary and my adopted son, Peter, both in studies now at the Campbelltown Academy."

"So nice to have you here," spoke Lady Harrison.

"Campbelltown," said the host, "such a fine institution, and a wonderful headmaster in Dr. Campbell. I know you are not here long, so shall I have Ben show the boys around. Lucy can relieve Lady Winston of the infant, and we shall visit over teacups," the senior Harrison suggested.

"Come this way," the younger Harrison spoke energetically to Peter and Zack. "I will show you around."

"Do not tarry, Ben," spoke the father. "I am certain they will be anxious to travel on within the hour."

Ben led the boys down the front steps and around the mansion to the back lawn slopping down to the James River. It was a beautiful setting. They sat under a stand of stately trees and introduced themselves more fully.

Ben was fifteen, the sixth Benjamin Harrison in succession, since the ancestor Benjamin Harrison I arrived from England to Virgina in 1630. The immigrating Harrison had sat as clerk of the Virginia Council, and became one of the largest landowners in Virginia. He had bought the property where they were sitting, and it was originally named Harrison's Landing. The mansion was not built until Ben's grandfather, Benjamin Harrison IV, started construction.

"He was the struck by lightening under these very trees and died just there," the youngest Ben Harrison said, pointing to the spot where he had been told his grandfather met his maker.

"My father was the first Benjamin Harrison to be born here."

"It's not easy to be born into a long line of men you are expected to follow to greatness," said Ben. "I know I shall be the first great disappointment to my ancestors." They all laughed as Ben spoke of his future.

"Well, I am simply being realistic," said Ben laughing. "There is no way I can be the image of Papa. He has led the patriot cause from the beginning, protesting the Sugar Act, then the Stamp Act, and now those Intolerable Acts. He has already served in the Burgesses for twenty-two years."

"Are you not coming to the ball at the Governor's Palace?" asked Peter.

"Oh yes, we shall be there," answered Ben. "Father is expected, and the governor is, as father says, a quite good chap. We will arrive the day before the event and stay the night in the palace as guests of the governor."

"Is Governor Boutetort really a good man?" asked Zack.

"Quite a good gentleman, and quite a good governor, as governor's go that is," answered the young Harrison.

"We burnt him in effigy," admitted Peter. "Our Sons of Liberty chapter strung him up on our Liberty Tree, and burnt him to blue blazes, after he dissolved the House of Burgesses."

"And in the flames," added Zack, "the corncrib caught fire. We got the hide tannings of our lives!" They all got a good laugh out of that.

Summer in Williamsburg

The Harrison townhouse was an opulent residence at the corner of Duke of Gloucester Street, the main avenue of busy Williamsburg, and what was called the Palace Green. Palace Green led to the palace, with one street heading toward it and another heading back. A grassy area divided the two one-way streets. The famous Bruton Parish Church and several residences, including the home of George Wythe, sat on Palace Green.

For the entire month of June, the Judge and Adella would occupy one of the second floor rooms, overlooking the busy street below, while Zack and Peter slept in the one next door. The room across corridor was set with a crib, where baby Angelica would sleep and play, and Cassia would tend to her and sleep in that room, as would Pearlie. The fourth room would be for the Winston's house servants they had brought along, Malcolm and Mammy Jane.

As was the custom of the day, the Winstons traveled in a proper carriage while the household slaves traveled behind them in an open wagon with the food items and other baggage the party would need for the month-long stay. Lodging for the servants while on the road was generally out of doors, as it had been at City Point, where they, like Peter had done five years earlier, slept on the wharf. In Williamsburg they were able to stay in indoor accommodations.

The boys were anxious to explore the colonial capital. They usually included their friend Pearlie.

One day, the judge lived up to his promise and took the three boys on an outing of discovery to the ruins that were once Jamestown. They walked through the dense weeds and brush that had over-grown the area after the capital had been deserted. They saw the piles of brick and one lone standing chimney that was once where the House of Burgesses met.

"You do know the Burgesses is the oldest colonial legislature in America?" the judge asked as they searched through the ruins.

"And this is where it was burnt to the ground!" Peter added.

"They say," the judge schooled them, "A prisoner being held in a cell there, awaiting execution, felt he had nothing to lose, so he set the fire. That was in 1698, and seems to be the reason they decided to move the capital to Williamsburg in 1699."

They imagined the triangular-shaped fortress Captain John Smith had built to protect the colonists from the local tribes. They made their way through the briars and the brambles to the James River where Smith and the colonists had arrived in 1607, planting the first permanent English settlement in America.

When back in town, Peter and Zack spent hours walking down busy Duke of Gloucester Street.

"What do you think the governor had for breakfast in there today?" Peter asked Zack, as he boosted Zack up so he could look in the window of the dining room at the palace. "By the looks of the drawings I have seen of him," Peter offered, "I'd say a whole side of bacon, two of ham, a dozen...no two dozen eggs, a gallon of grits topped with two pounds of butter, and two dozen biscuits, smothered with molasses."

"Almost as much as you, right Peter?" Pearlie said. They laughed and Peter lost his grip, Zack falling into the bushes beside the window.

Zack got up and dusted himself off, and they ran back to the street, hoping not to have been seen peeping into the governor's window.

They walked all the way to the end of Duke of Gloucester Street, with the sidewalks busy with people. They came to the capitol building and walked inside.

"I like this better," Peter said. "I don't have to lift you up while you get to look inside."

"There is no way I could do the same for you," said Zack.

"You'd have to have Pearlie help you," Peter said.

"I don't think so," Pearlie retorted, "Not 'lessen you ordered me to as your slave boy an' threatened me with the whip." They laughed.

They walked down to the round chamber where the burgesses debated and deliberated the acts passed by Parliament, and went inside.

Peter turned toward Pearlie as the three boys walked inside the quiet room. "Pearlie, you reckon they allow the likes of you, a slave boy, inside?"

"I don't see no signs sayin' they don't," Pearlie said, as Peter playfully slugged his shoulder and smiled.

They saw the desks and benches where the burgesses sat. They saw the speaker's platform and the mace, the four-foot tall, slender ornate column, made of dark wood with silver entwining it, and a silver globe on top. It was the official symbol of the legislature.

"I wonder where cousin Patrick sits," asked Zack, sitting at a bench behind a desk.

"I wonder where Colonel Washington sits," inserted Peter. "I know where I'd like to be," he said running to the speaker's podium. He picked up the gavel, held it in his hand as if about to pound it on the podium.

"As ordered by Governor Lord Botetourt," he spoke in a theatrical voice, "I declare this body closed." He pounded the gavel. They laughed and left the hallowed chamber before being thrown out.

They walked back down Duke of Gloucester Street and sat on benches under a shade tree outside Raleigh Tavern. They sat and watched as gentlemen dressed in knee-breeches and vests entered and exited the popular tavern.

"I hear this is where Patrick goes to really debate the issues with other members," said Zack.

"I heard from Stockard, it's where they all go to drink ale and eat prime ribs," said Peter.

"It figures Peter would say that," Pearlie said. "Eatin's always on Peter's mind!"

"I'm a growin' boy," Peter defended himself.

"You sure are," Pearlie answered. Zack laughed.

"Let's go to the magazine on our way back," Peter suggested. Zack nodded and they got up and continued their walk.

The eight-sided red brick magazine pierced the sky like and broad, fat arrow. It sat just three doors down from the Harrison townhouse, back from the street in a grassy area where the militia encamped and maneuvered.

"That's where all the muskets and all the balls and all the kegs of powder are stored for when the militia needs them," said Peter.

"That's an awfully big building just to store a few guns and some powder kegs," Zack said.

"It'll take a lot of muskets and powder to fend off the Redcoats, if they leave Boston and come here," Peter explained. "And if they do come, the Virginia militia will surely send them all the way back to London!"

Peter was fascinated with anything of a military nature. His favorite studies at Campbelltown were listening to the younger Dr. Campbell lecture on great battles throughout history. Peter found it exciting, the stories of how nations fought other nations, and territories changed hands. His idols were all military leaders: Alexander the Great, Hannibal, Julius Caesar, William the Conqueror, Charlemagne and the hero of Spain, El Cid.

They spent several days walking around the College of William and Mary, and its impressive Wren Building. That building would be the home for John Marshall and Stockard Samuels in September. Someday Peter hoped to be among the students there. Zack was not so certain.

They visited the shops of Williamsburg where the judge had allowed them a small budget to charge purchases and have the merchandise shipped to the Harrison townhouse for his inspection and signature.

Peter's favorite store was the shop of Jonas Phillips, Bookseller. Peter signed for a volume, printed in London, dealing with Hannibal crossing the Alps on elephants, and the novel <u>Don Quixote</u> by the Spanish author Cervantes. Zack, too, purchased a copy of Izaac Walton's <u>The Compleat Angler</u>, and another book filled with drawings of fish, birds, and trees of North America.

Zack turned fourteen on the 28th and Peter turned thirteen on the 30th. Adella said they would celebrate both boys' birthdays on the 29th.

"I've had Mammy Jane prepare a special treat for you, Peter," Adella said, as the boys came down for breakfast to celebrate their birthdays.

Mammy Jane came through the door with a large platter of freshly baked rum buns with white, gooey icing crisscrossing the top and drizzling down the sides. Some were sprinkled with ground cinnamon and others with powdery sugar.

"They look just like Auntie Savannah's!" Peter said excitedly. He tasted one, dripping with icing, his favorite. "And they are just as good!"

"I coaxed Auntie Savannah to give up her recipe back in City Point," Adella proudly said. "That's Auntie Savannah's birthday gift to you."

"It is such a wonderful present," Peter said. "I will remember turning thirteen every time I eat one of these! I do expect them each morning at the breakfast table!" Everyone laughed.

The judge presented a wrapped present to each of the boys. Peter tore open a book about Alexander the Great, which excited him.

Zack opened his present. It held three tablets of white sketch paper, a box of charcoal pencils, and a small easel. He smiled, but was puzzled at the gift.

"I thought you might like to try your hand at drawing all those things in nature that excite you, Zachary," said the judge. Zack smiled, thinking he could now serious concentrate on the drawings he liked to sketch.

Let Us Put Aside Past Differences

Saturday, June 30th came too quickly for the boys. Soon they would be heading back to Winston Woods. First they would attend the evening gala and ball on the lawn at the Governor's Palace.

A deliveryman from J. Matthew Braden, the tailor, was expected to arrive with three boxes of new suits of clothing for the judge and boys to wear that evening. On their first day in Williamsburg, Adella insisted they be fitted for new clothes.

Adella was the officer on duty that day, and her orders had to be obeyed. When the boys left to enjoy the hustle and bustle of Williamsburg one last time before leaving for home early the next morning, she gave them their orders.

"You can go, so long as you are back here for your baths by one," she began her orders to them. "If you are not back in this house by the time the church bells chime one," Adella warned, "I had better find you locked up in the stocks in front of the courthouse, or I shall tan your hides myself and make new shoes from the leather! You will find my punishments much harsher than that of the judge, when the two of you burned down the corncrib!"

The boys obeyed and were back at the Harrison townhouse ten minutes before one

"There's lunch on the table," Adella greeted them at the door. "Your baths will be prepared when you finish. I want you to bathe, nap until about half past three, then dress in your new suits of clothes. The carriage will be here for us at half past four." She shooed them off to the dining room.

All things went just as Adella had scripted, and the finely attired foursome walked out of the townhouse and down the steps as the Westminster chimes of the Bruton Parish Church sounded half-past four.

They rode the short distance to the Governor's Palace in an open carriage, hired by the judge from the livery. The carriage driver and two liverymen, standing tall on the running boards, were crisply dressed in scarlet silk waistcoats, gray knee breeches with black trimmings and matching hats. It was an impressive sight as they rode down Duke of Gloucester Street and up the Palace Green, queuing in behind other similar carriages carrying the elite of Virginia to dine and dance with the governor at the palace.

The carriage waited in the queue of carriages as the guests in the carriages in front of them disembarked and walked elegantly across the front lawn of the palace to the entry doors. When it was finally their turn, the uniformed liverymen opened the small door of the open carriage and the four alit.

The Winstons got in line and walked into the palace. There they followed the line as it was led into a parlor where the Governor, Norborne Berkeley, the Baron de Botetourt, was seated in a throne-like chair on a raised platform to greet, with a courteous nod of his head, each of his constituents. His wife, Lady Botetourt, was seated in the second throne-like chair beside him.

The handsomely dressed palace valet introduced each guest as they arrived. The guest was then presented to the governor and his lady. The males bowed as their ladies curtsied. No one but the valet spoke as the string quartet played appropriate etudes.

"Judge Anthony Winston of Hanover County, Lady Winston, Master Zachary Winston, Master Peter Francisco," the valet spoke, and all bowed and curtsied as Adella had practiced with them, over and over earlier in the day.

"That was like it must be being introduce to King George III and Queen Charlotte," Peter said when they were safely able to speak, after leaving the palace through the rear French doors to the verandah overlooking the back lawn.

"Yes," the judge said, "this is as close to royalty as we have here in Virginia."

Tables, with bright white linen cloths, had been set on the massive manicured back lawn. China plates, silver and crystal adorned each. Ushers showed each guest to the table assigned for them to occupy.

When the Winstons were led to their table, there were elegantly hand-lettered cards on the plate at the seat with their name.

The table was set for eight diners. The Winstons would be dining with the George Washingtons. Judge Winston would dine between Zachary and Col. Washington. Martha Washington would dine between her husband and Adella. The Washington's daughter Patsy would be between Adella and Peter, with Patsy' brother Jacky seated between Peter and Zack.

After finding their seats, there was about an hour remaining before the banquet would begin, so they sat and talked, commenting on the arriving guests, several of whom all recognized, most of the others the judge was able to point out.

"That young man there," the judge pointed out, "the one in the emerald green suit of clothes, the one, not in a wig, the red-haired young gentleman, that's Thomas Jefferson, a young burgess from Charlottesville. He's standing with my old law professor, George Wythe, and the former governor Francis Faqueier."

"I do wish you had worn the wig, Anthony," Adella said in a scolding tone. "Most others are, and you do look the part of a judge when wearing it."

"Tis too warm and humid to my likings to be parading around in a powdered wig," replied the judge matter-of-factly.

"Oh you are simply yet a boy at heart yourself." Adella turned to Peter and Zack, "Now boys, you have met Colonel Washington and his wife Martha, but I expect you both to be on your very best behavior. Please speak only when spoken to."

"I did not think the colonel had children," Peter questioned.

"He has none of his own, but Lady Washington brought from her previous marriage a small son and daughter," answered the judge, still looking over the crowd as it arrived. "He duly took them in as his own. Oh, there, the heavyset gentleman coming down the verandah steps is the speaker of the house, Peyton Randolph. And there is Patrick, and McGowan just beside him."

"There are the Harrisons, Anthony, over there," Adella said, properly nodding, never pointing, in the direction where their hosts for the month were finding their seats. "I did not know Mrs. Harrison was a Bassett from New Kent County, and related to Lady Washington," Adella added.

"By marriage," the judge clarified. "Lady Washington's sister married Mrs. Harrison's brother."

"As I said," Adella shot back, "they are related."

About that time, the orchestra hired for the evening, began to play. Several of the guests made their way to the temporary ballroom floor set up in front of the orchestra, playing on a raised stage at the east end of the steps from the verandah.

"Are we permitted to go see Ben Harrison?" asked Zack.

"I would prefer you stay put," Adella said, matronly.

"How better, dear, for the young men to practice their social graces?" the judge suggested.

"Very well," Adella conceded, "but mind your manners and remember just where you are. No clowning. No running around or carrying on. Be perfect gentlemen and let us see what good students you have been."

Peter and Zack headed off in the direction of the young Ben Harrison.

"I am so very proud of those two young gentlemen," the judge said to his wife.

"I too," admitted Adella. "I feel so proud of just how they have both progressed so well. I do think it was a wonderful idea of yours to bring them on this trip, and expose them to society."

They watched as the boys, so handsome in their new attire, walked elegantly to the east edge of the lawn. Soon after the boys left, James Madison the elder, and two of his Taylor cousins from Orange County, stopped where the judge and Adella were seated. The judge rose as they approached.

"Well, Winston," Madison said extending his hand in greeting, "now that the duties on those damnable intolerable acts have been repealed, perhaps things will return to normalcy here in Virginia once more."

"I have not seen the actual wording," the judge replied. "It is a total and complete repeal of all duties, except those ones on tea, as I hear it."

"All but a reasonable duty on the tea," inserted Madison.

"We shall see just how reasonable the tea tax is," spoke Richard Taylor. "I fear those intolerable men of greed in the teahouses of London, and the greed that dwells within the offices of the East India Company, control us now. I fear the price on the tea will be exorbitant."

"We in the colonies are left to subsidize that greed," suggested the other Taylor.

About that time, the Washingtons began to descend the verandah steps. They were led to where the judge and Adella were speaking with Madison and the Taylors. Their sixteen-year-old son, John Parke Custis, familiarly called Jacky, and their pretty and petite fourteen-year-old daughter, Martha Parke Custis, called Patsy, followed the colonel and his lady.

As the Washingtons arrived at the table, all exchanged welcomes, and Lady Washington and the children took their seats. Taylor continued the conversation the gentlemen had been having.

"Colonel Washington, will this Repeal Act the king has assented to be of any real affect?" one of the Taylors asked.

"We certainly can hope so, Mr. Taylor, we certainly do hope so," answered the tall gentleman from Mount Vernon. "What matters is the intent. Is the true intention of Parliament and Lord North to allow the colonies to govern themselves, or shall the keeping of the tax on tea be their true intention to make precedent stand for their taxing authority over us? That remains to be debated down the street."

Soon the palace valet announced from the verandah for the guests to take their seats in preparation for dinner to be served. Peter and Zack returned after their visit with Ben Harrison.

"Zachary, Peter," the judge said, "You do recall Colonel Washington and Lady Washington, do you not?"

"Certainly," Peter said, politely bowing his head in the famed couple's direction. Zachary followed suit.

"These are my wards, Peter Francisco and Zachary Winston," the judge reminded the Washingtons, "and this young man," indicating the boy, "is their son, Jacky." The boys nodded at the boy. "And this charming young lady is their daughter, Patsy."

Seeing the pretty Patsy in her seat next to his seat, Peter introduced himself.

"Good evening," he said to Patsy, "I am Peter Francisico."

The fourteen-year-old girl with blonde curls tied in light blue ribbons framing her pale face with bright blue eyes, smiled and extended her hand for Peter.

"I am pleased to meet you Mister Francisco," she said sweetly.

Peter took her hand gently and kissed the top of it, as was the proper etiquette.

"I am the most honored guest of the governor this evening, to be seated beside the most beautiful young lady in attendance here this night."

The girl blushed and smiled as Peter released her hand. Lady Washington and the colonel seemed pleased at Peter's introduction and smiled at one another. With the niceties done toward the charming girl, Peter took his seat. The valet then came to the podium on the verandah once more to make his announcement.

"The most honorable Norbonne Berkeley, Baron de Botetourt, Governor of the Royal Colony of Virginia, representative of His Majesty King George III of Great Britain ... and Lady Botetourt."

The orchestra played a light air as the governor and his lady came forth from the palace. The guests stood at their seats and politely applauded the royal arrival. The governor and Lady Botetourt paused at the podium and received their guests' adulation with royal nods and waves, then descended the steps to the table on the raised dais between the guest tables and the verandah. Dining at the governor's table were bachelor house speaker Randolph, along with two other chosen couples already seated.

The governor was a stout man of fifty-two. His weight and a severe case of gout made it not easy to climb down the steps, or for that matter, walk at all. With him on the arm of his lady, it appeared she was propping up her obese husband.

The orchestra began to play lightly as dinner was being served by an army of liveried servants, carrying trays of roast beef, baked hams and fried chicken, complimented by bowls of vegetables and baskets of breads fresh from the palace hearths. Wine stewards strolled through with the wines selected for the banquet. The events of the elegant evening began in earnest.

As the diners dined on the lawn and the sun began to set, lanterns strung on garland ropes above the diners' heads were lit by lamplighters. Trays of desserts were then brought to the tables and the diners were sated.

154

When the dinner was ended, the speaker of the House of Burgesses, a huge rondundity of a man himself, beneath a rather odd looking white wig, strode to the edge of the platform where he had dined with the equally rotund governor.

"Citizens of the colony of Virginia, I am pleased to introduce to you a friend. Our governor is a true friend of Virginia and all Virginians. His Majesty King George III has blessed us in this colony with the appointment of such a man. He possesses a genuine love for the land and for his constituency. It is our hope he serves a long and benevolent term.

"He sits in a precarious seat. His orders from London have not always been to his nor to our liking. He has carried out his duties honestly and fairly.

"Because we have had a governor the likes of our friend here and our gracious host this evening, we Virginians have been spared the indignities suffered upon our fellow colonists in Massachusetts. We have not suffered under the day-to-day presence of His Majesty's troops, quartered in our homes and maneuvering upon our streets. We have not seen that occupation result in a massacre of our own citizens, simply driven by a desire for self-government." Randolph lifted his glass of Madeira and turned toward the governor.

"Raise your glasses, if you will, and let us all toast our most gracious host and our most beloved governor." All rose with glasses, cheered and sipped, then returned to their seats.

Following the toast, the governor rose, shook hands with Randolph as they met in passing, and replaced Randolph at the edge of the platform looking out over the assembled guests.

"Peace and quiet can now return to the dominion of Virginia," said the governor. "Let us never duplicate the tragedies of Boston. Let us never go so far in Virginia as to be ready to disassociate ourselves, and sequester ourselves from the birthright of our great and varied ancestry of England, Ireland, Scotland and Wales.

"My message this evening is the same to all in Virginia as it is to our government in London, the Prime Minister Frederick Lord North and His Majesty King George III. Let us commence this day to discuss the differences when we differ, respect the differences we may individually hold, and relinquish the greed and personal ambition we find in our souls, here and across the sea."

He again raised his glass to his seated guests. "Let us toast. Let us put aside past differences. Let us welcome peace."

As the governor waddled back to his seat and the guests quieted their applause, fireworks began to fill the black starlit sky overhead. Gasps to the brilliance of each rocket glaring with cinders of bright reds, and yellows and whites and greens, lit up the night and the already high spirits of the diners.

As the fireworks were still being shot into the sky, the orchestra struck up a minuet and several of the couples took to the temporary ballroom floor in front of the orchestra.

"Would you so honor me as to allow me to escort you on the dance floor?" Peter asked Patsy.

Patsy smiled, looked to her mother for approval. Lady Washington smiled and nodded her assent.

"I would be honored, Mister Francisco," she sweetly replied.

The two walked toward the dancers, Peter, towering over the petite Patsy as they walked. They joined the others on the dance floor, and although Peter had never danced the minuet in public with a young lady, did quite well. After dancing two minuets, they began to walk back.

"It is such a lovely evening," Patsy noted to Peter, her arm entwined through his.

"It truly is that," Peter replied. "And the fireworks in the sky were just magnificent."

"They were indeed, as meeting you was truly wonderful for me as well," Patsy added.

Peter's trip to Williamsburg was ending on a sweet note.

The Un-Educatable Jacky Custis

On September 6th the Winstons were again on the roads of colonial Virginia. With the boys resuming their studies at Campbelltown on Monday, September 10th, the judge and Adella had accepted an invitation from the Washingtons to visit Mount Vernon. Their estate in northern Virginia, lay just south of Alexandria, the major port on the

Potomac. They decided to make the visit to Mount Vernon en route to taking Zack and Peter back to Campbelltown.

Peter was anxious to visit Jacky, and especially, the pretty Patsy. During the summer Zack had started drawing any species of birds, fish and plants he came across. He had put his birthday present from the judge to good use, and was becoming a quite good artist. He wanted to spend time drawing while on his stay at Mount Vernon.

They arrived in the late afternoon on Thursday for their three-night stay. Soon after they arrived, Jacky took the boys on walk down the Potomac shore to the plantation wharf, and then further to his favorite spot to angle for bass, catfish and bluegills. As Peter and Jacky sat and fished, Zack put his line in the water, but concentrated on drawing. He spotted a graceful gray crane, fishing for minnows at the water's edge just a few yards beyond where he sat. He began sketching the beautiful bird.

"So you will be back to your studies within the week," Jacky said to Peter, as Zack sketched.

"Yes, we start classes at Campbelltown on Monday," replied Peter.

"I hear tis a good institution," Jacky added. "Uncle Austin gave the Campbells the land for the academy before he died. I visited the academy one time with Mama and Colonel Washington, returning from a visit at Pope's Creek."

"Oh yes," Peter said, "I have met your cousin Gus, a very nice gentleman. Several of our classmates rode our horses for a Saturday outing along the Potomac, and ended at Pope's Creek. Your cousin shared a picnic with us in the old cemetery and told tales of the early Washingtons in Virginia."

"Oh yes," Jacky said somewhat unimpressed, "I have heard all about the Seahorse running aground, and John Washington swimming ashore to marry Anne Pope. So romantic, I suppose." He shook his head arrogantly. "Thank the heavens, I am not, by blood, a Washington! I am a Dandridge, but mostly a Custis."

"You and Patsy, as well, so I've been told," added Peter. "Is that why you call him 'Colonel Washington' instead of father?" Jacky nodded.

Zack, still busy at his sketching, noticed a tug at his line in the Potomac and rose pulling out a nice, fat bluegill. He put it on a stringer to let it stay alive in the shallow water's edge. He would draw the bluegill after the crane was captured on paper, then return the fish to the Potomac.

"Nice bluegill Zack," Jacky said as Zack nodded silently and returned again to sketching the majestic bird.

"Yes," Jacky returned to answered Peter, "My real papa was the largest landowner in New Kent County, and one of the largest in the entire colony…near twenty-thousand acres and many slaves. We lived on the most beautiful tobacco plantation in all of Virginia, called White House."

"Was it not on the Pamunkey River?" Peter asked. "Winston Woods, where we live is also on the Pamunkey in Hanover County."

"It was," affirmed Jacky. "The Pamunkey was not near as broad a river as the Potomac, but it is, as I recall, a beautiful estuary. When Mama married Colonel Washington, I was nearly four and Patsy nearly two. We have lived here ever since."

"Are you going to study at William and Mary?" Peter probed.

"No," answered Jacky with a giggle. "I have no need for education and education certainly has no need for me," he laughed.

"I have boarded out short times in my sixteen years," Jacky admitted, "but was always successful in seeing to it that the professors gave up on me," he laughed. "In six years I have had a dozen tutors dessert me," his laughter grew more intense. Through laughter he continued. "My favorite success was with the one who wrote the colonel 'the lad is the most indolent and prissy young chap I have ever encountered. He is un-educatable!'"

All three boys laughed heartily, even Zack.

"I need not the formal education most need," Jacky explained, as their laughter subsided. "I have a marvelously huge fortune I have inherited from my Dandridge and Custis aunts and uncles. Tis more than I can possibly spend in a lifetime.

"Oh father died without a will, so Mama was taken well care of, inheriting his entire estate. I shall take my entire inheritance from the conservator, in less than five years time, when I reach maturity. In the meantime, what I need I get from Mama. I do not for the life of me know what I would do with an education. I do like to fish in the Potomac and shop for fine attire from Europe in the shops of Alexandria." He laughed his arrogant laugh again.

After a lavish dinner in the manor house at Mount Vernon, pretty Patsy entertained on the pianoforte in the parlor. Peter escorted Patsy on several walks during their three days at Mount Vernon. Had he met the young lady he would some day take as a wife?

Governor Lord Dunmore

Henry Moore, the Royal Governor of New York, who had expressed interest in retirement and a return to England, died suddenly, before Lord Hillsborough could accept the resignation. As soon as the news of Moore's demise arrived at St. James Palace, Hillsborough immediately made the easy decision to appoint John Murray, Lord Dunmore, to succeed the now-dead governor. In the meantime, Lieutenant Governor Cadwallader Colden, a New Yorker, would serve the colony of New York until Lord Dunmore could make the trip across the Atlantic to the New World.

Lord and Lady Dunmore began making arrangements centering around the children. Their eight year-old son, George, Lord Fincastle, needed to commence his education. Their daughter, two year-old Lady Augusta, would certainly be traveling with her parents to New York. Lady Dunmore would also soon be delivering a third child. The infant, Lady Katherine, was born in April. They would have to delay their trip across the Atlantic until mother and infant were hearty enough for the three-week-long journey.

They spent the summer at their estate, the seat of the Murray clan in the forest of Atholl in Scotland. John Murray's sister, Lucinda, and her husband, Clark Montgomery, lived there permanently as caretakers at the estate near Perth, while Lord Dunmore lived in London to tend to the business of Parliament.

The Montgomerys had three boys at the University of Edinburgh. They had attended Melrose Abbey for preparatory studies, as had Dunmore himself, and now, young George was to be enrolled there. Lucinda and Clark would also care for the young George at the Atholl estate when not being boarded at Melrose Abbey.

Dunmore decided his sixteen year-old nephew Alexander would serve him quite well as his private secretary while in New York. His younger nephew Roderic, at age fourteen, would also sail with them to

America, and be enrolled at King's College in New York to continue his studies.

On August 30th Lord and Lady Dunmore boarded the carriage along with Alexander, Roderic and their two young daughters for the journey to the port at Perth. There they joined their baggage, sent ahead, and took their staterooms on the ship "Pearl of the Perth" for their five o'clock departure for New York. They arrived in New York harbor twenty-two days later.

A smaller boat with a ceremonial canopy over two throne-like chairs, manned by eight oarsmen, rowed out to the ship for the arriving dignitaries. When Lord and Lady Dunmore were seated aboard the barge, the oarsmen headed for the Murray's Wharf, the newly opened wharf, built by merchant Jeremiah Murray, at the foot of Manhattan Island.

Lord and Lady Dunmore reveled in the pomp and circumstance of their welcome to the New World. Canons fired in salute from a British merchant ship at anchor in the harbor. They could hear the music of a band assembled on the awaiting wharf. Lord Dunmore, wearing the Murray clan's plaid tartan kilt and regalia, smiled broadly and proudly, as the tender boat rowed toward the city. When the party arrived at Murray's Wharf, Dunmore turned and took the hand of his lady, in a stylish silk gown of periwinkle blue with white with silver trim, stepped from the barge onto the red carpeted steps, laid out for the new governor's arrival. Their young daughter, Augusta, was dressed in clothing matching her mother, walked alongside, while the mother carried the infant Lady Katherine.

Acting Governor, Colden, the speaker of the New York colonial legislature, Henry Livingston, and the governor's chief advisor, Freyling Grayson, led the assembled crowd in applause as the Dunmores disembarked. The band played as the New Yorkers greeted the party of Lord Dunmore. Carriages were waiting to carry the new royal governor to his townhouse, just off the street named Broadway, at a smaller street named Wall.

When Dunmore was presented to the owner of the wharf, Jeremiah Murray, they shook hands, and Dunmore said, "I am somewhat disappointed, Mr. Murray." The wharf's owner seemed embarrassed.

"I thought certain, the good citizens of New York had already honored me, placing my family name upon this beautiful wharf." Dunmore continued to explain to the owner of the wharf, his family name was also Murray. Both men laughed, and wondered if they were closely related on their family trees.

Once at the residence, a smaller, yet lavishly furnished version of Murray's London townhouse, the arriving governor and the acting governor met with speaker Livingston and Freyling Grayson. Alexander accompanied Lord Dunmore to the meeting to take minutes. The younger nephew, Roderic, was anxious to take a stroll of the neighborhood to get a good look at the town that would now be his home.

"You come at a wonderful time," said Acting Governor Colden, "'tis a quiet time in New York, and I dare say in all the colonies of the king."

"Will the quiet be long in lasting?" inquired Dunmore.

"We shall see," Colden replied, "we shall see."

"On behalf of the elected legislature of the colony of New York," speaker Livingston offered, "I certainly welcome you as our Royal Governor. I speak for the members of the legislature when I say we all anticipate working with your highness for the common good." He bowed at the waist in respect to Dunmore.

"Mr. Speaker," said Dunmore, "I shall rely upon you, as liaison between the my station as governor and your colleagues in the assembly. I wish only to carry out the wishes of our king, and the will of our Parliament, with the best interest of my colonial constituents foremost in my mind."

"We pray for a long and amicable relationship with you as our governor," Livingston ended his comments.

Dunmore smiled and nodded.

"Now I believe I shall retire to the luxurious appointments you have seen fit to prepare for us," Dunmore spoke. "The journey across the waves has been a tedious one, though pleasant at times. I am most happy, as my family here is most happy, to be with you in New York. We shall expect the two of you and your ladies to dine with us on Thursday."

Turning to Grayson, Dunmore said, "And Mister Grayson, if you would be so kind, I would meet with you in the morning at nine."

"Very good sir," replied Grayson.

The three men of the colony left the new royal governor and his secretary. Dunmore walked through the rooms of the main floor and smiled, well pleased with his elevation to Governor.

John Adams for the Defense

John Adams knew he was doing the right thing, the thing he knew he really needed to do. The murder trial of Captain Thomas Preston was in its seventh day, the last day before the jury panel would decide a verdict.

"Were you on the grounds of the Customs House on the fifth day of March past," Adams questioned his final witness for the defense.

"I was sure there, alright."

Adams had spent months with his partner, Josiah Quincy, who he convinced to assist in the defense of Captain Preston and his men. Abigail had been constantly by his side too, during the months of preparation. She traveled with him between Braintree and Boston everyday, and helped at whatever needed to be examined or researched, until she had to remain at Braintree for a few weeks before their new baby was delivered. Charles Adams was born May 29th and, according to Doctor Harding, seemed to be a healthy child.

"And when did you arrive at the Customs House?" Adams asked his witness.

"Me an' me friends all heard the church bells a ringin' an' all the commotion at the Customs House, and ran from where we was at the commons, to see what was happ'nin'."

Adams had gotten the original case severed with one trial for Captain Preston alone, held in October, then one for the eight others in November.

Adams hired an investigator, Sampson Blowers, to help with selection of a good jury.

"We can ill-afford a seated jury with residents of the city" Adams told Blowers. "There is, I dare say, only ten-percent of the populous who would be fair and not biased against the soldiers. Rural men of Suffolk County are whom we must have as jurors. They are not near so close to the events of March fifth, and were not near so swept up in the emotions of that day."

As Adams fashioned the next question in his mind for the witness on the stand, he looked at the jury seated on his right. They all, to a man, seemed to be fair-minded Suffolk County farmers.

"And where, sir, were you situated, when you arrived at the scene?"

"We was a standin' in the back o' the crowd 'tween the mob an' the sentry box. We easily saw the Redcoat soldiers standin' in a line in front o' the steps o' the Customs House."

"And what was occurring when you arrived?" Adams asked.

"We saw a Mulatto man, name o'Crispus Attucks, fling a big ole slab o' wood at 'em. It hit one o' the Redcoats, an' he fell ta the groun'. Soon as he got up, the mob a started shoutin' at the soldiers, 'Why don't ya fire? Ya cowards, why don't ya fire?'"

Adams and Quincy also spent time in preparation examining an engraving made by Paul Revere, purporting to be a true depiction of the massacre. It had become popularly accepted throughout the colony. Everyone had seen it and took it for what really happened.

Blowers, the investigator, had found out Revere had not even been present as an eyewitness, but propagandized the depiction in order to inflame moderates toward the patriot cause. His depiction showed, without a doubt, Captain Preston drawing his saber and ordering the firing into the crowd.

"From where you and your friends were standing, were you able to see Captain Thomas Preston?" Adams asked the witness.

"We seen the Captain an' another officer standin' between the Red-coats at the steps an' the mob. They had their sabers in hand, but neither of 'em gave the order to fire."

"Then who did give the order to fire?" Adams pressed on.

"I heard someone, I dunno if it were a Redcoat or not, yell 'Damn ya, fire!' It weren't the captain nor was it the other officer."

"And what happened next? Adams asked the witness.

"Then, there was one shot fired an' all the rest fired after that first shot, all at the same time. That was all the firin' there was."

None of the eyewitnesses called before, by the prosecutors or by the defense, claimed to have seen Preston raise his saber and order his men to fire. They, without a doubt, heard what they assumed were shouted commands. They heard shouts such as "Damn you, fire!" and "Why don't you fire?" Neither John Adams nor Quincy saw any evidence that Preston had approved of the men firing, let alone ordered them to fire. Only Paul Revere's popular engraving attested to any role of mischief played by the captain.

"What happened next, Mister Macneal?" asked Adams.

"Well, that's when Samuel Maverick, a standin' right aside me, fell ta the groun'. See, a musketball fired over the heads o' the mob, hit the sentry box and bounced back, an' hit Sammy in the back o' his neck. He fell ta the groun' a bleedin' somethin' awful. I knelt down and tried ta stop the bleedin' but he died an hour or two later. Me and a friend, Wills Winkman, carried him to Fanueil Hall to be laid out with the others."

"Samuel Maverick," Adams turned and addressed the jury in his summation with Jacky remaining in the witness stand for effect, "was the youngest victim to die at what has rightly been called the Boston Massacre. Our witness here today, could very well have taken the ricocheted bullet his friend died from. John O'Malley Patrick Macneal, Jacky to his friends, was indeed an eyewitness to the events of the Boston Massacre. The patriot, and very good friend of mine, Paul Revere, the engraver, was not. No eyewitness to the events of that day saw what Revere engraved. No eyewitness heard nor saw Captain Thomas Preston raise his saber and give the command. He must therefore be adjudged by this jury to be innocent of any charge of murder."

The defense rested. On October 30th, John Adams' thirty-fifth birthday, Captain Thomas Preston was indeed acquitted. Tom would no longer spend his days and nights in the cell that had been his bed for seven long months. He would also no longer be a captain in the 23rd Regiment of the Chippenham Guards. Due to the charges filed against him, he was discharged from the army. With his acquittal, he was free now.

The Calm Before the Storm

"I cannot stay here in Boston, Jacky," Tom said when they met in his cell in the cellar of the courthouse, after his acquittal was announced by the jury's foreman. "Mr. Adams is taking me tonight to his home at Braintree, and will have a place I can stay."

"I want to be with you, Tom," said Jacky. "Can I come with you?"

"I want to be with you as well," Tom said, as he clung to Jacky's hand "You go back to Lewis Street and I will send a message to you letting you know where I am and I will send for you to come meet me."

They hugged and kissed one another before Jacky left to walk back to Lewis Street and wait. He hoped he would get Tom's message the following day. He missed Tom more than any thing.

Tom rode in the carriage with John and Abigail Adams and their three year-old son, Little Johnny, to safety at the Adams farm at Braintree. That evening, after dropping Abigail and the boy at the farm, John had the carriage take him and Tom to the wharf at Hingham, six miles east of Braintree.

"I have a good friend and old client, Obadiah Briley, at Hingham," Adams said as they rode. "He owns the tavern there and a fishing ship. I spoke with him on Sunday last, and he will put you up safely there. If you wish, he will hire you on as a fisherman, until your plans are more set."

"I should not use my own name," Tom said. "It has become too well-known in all of Massachusetts."

"That it has, that it has," said Adams, "and that is why I have given you an alias. You are to be called Tom Macneal."

"Tom Macneal?" Tom tried to protest... "but..."

"Tom Macneal it is," said Adams, not as a suggestion, but as a fact. "It was the first name that came to my mind. You can be Jacky's brother, cousin, uncle, I care not. But it will be less complicated when Jacky joins you. Fewer eyebrows shall raise."

Tom smiled, "You do think of everything, do you not?"

Adams smiled. "I have paid Briley for your week's lodging," Adams continued with the plan he had put together. "We shall write a message to Jacky and let him know where your are and when to come. I will have it given to him on Lewis Street."

When Jacky returned home the next afternoon from helping build a fence for the mother of the slain Sammy Maverick, he saw an envelope pinned to the door. He knew it was news from Tom. He could barely wait to get inside and read it.

Jacky,
Meet me soon as you can at the tavern called 'Pearl of the Clam' at the end of Hingham Wharf. I will be staying there.

Your brother,
Tom Macneal

"Your brother, Tom Macneal?" Jacky read that line over and over again. "He's taken me name!" Jacky said, smiling ear to ear. He had to make his way to the Pearl of the Clam at Hingham. "How do I get to Hingham?" Jacky asked himself.

He had a goodly sum of money saved up, near ten pounds, so he packed his and Tom's remaining belongings. The next day he bought for eight shillings, a rickety but dependable wagon from the widow Seider who had no use for it. She would have given it to Jacky gladly, but Jacky insisted she take the money.

Just down Prince Street, he bought an old mare from Paul Revere. Revere wanted three pounds for the horse, but Jacky struck a bargain at one pound four shillings. By noon the wagon was loaded with Tom and Jacky's possessions, and he headed the eight miles to Braintree, then the six more to Hingham and the Pearl of the Clam Tavern at the end of the wharf.

He spoke with the innkeeper, Mr. Briley. "I was told m' brother Tom Macneal is a stayin' here."

"You his brother called Jacky?" Briley asked. "Mr. Adams said you'd be a comin."

"Jacky Macneal, it tis," Jacky responded and thrust his hand to shake. Briley smiled and shook his hand. Briley looked at his pocket watch, then looked at Jacky. "Well lad, you have about two hours 'afore your brother gets here."

"Where's he at?

"He a fishin' on me boat. The boat will be in by six, after the sun's been down a spell."

"Can I leave me wagon an' horse tied up safely where it is an' get me a room for the night?" Jacky asked.

"If you don't mind sleepin' in the same bed with your brother," Briley offered, "you can just go ahead up to room three."

"That's alright with me," Jacky said. "I don't think Tom'll mind neither."

"Got a pot o' chowder…finest chowder you've tasted," Briley said. "Two shillings for a big bowl."

"Sounds good ta me on this cold day, an' nighttime's a comin',," Jacky said. "I think I'll just sit down right here an' eat me some o' that chowder while I waits for Tom."

"Want an ale with that chowder?" Briley asked, "or I have rum and the best Irish whiskey you've ever tippled."

"I'm not much a drinker o' whiskey," Jacky said smiling, "but I will have a tankard o' ale."

As Briley was bringing the ale and big bowl of chowder to Jacky, he stood and looked out the window. The fishing boat was docking.

"There's the 'Pearl' just now," he said. "They're early. Hope they got a good catch."

Jacky smiled, and tasted the chowder. "This chowder's good as ya bragged it ta be!" Jacky said. "Bring another for Tom."

Tom was glad to see Jacky in the tavern when he got off the fishing boat. They ate the chowder and went upstairs to room three.

"I have a plan, Jacky," Tom said, after they had gotten into the room, and gave each other welcome hugs and kisses. "I hope you will agree with it."

They sat on the edge of the bed and Tom laid out his plan. "John Adams gave me your last name, Jacky. I hope you don't mind."

"I'm glad John Adams gave you my name. O' course, I don't mind."

"If you agree with my plan, I shall keep the name 'Tom Macneal' for the rest of my life, and we shall pass as two brothers any where we go. If you object to my plan, I will once more find a new surname to use. I am just not safe in Boston, not just now at least," Tom went on. "I really do not know just how safe I am even here in Hingham. It is just too close to Boston and too soon after the trial, which was read about all over Massachusetts. How could I live in constant fear?"

"You should not live in fear, Tom," Jacky agreed. "It's just not fair."

"I love this New World of America, and want never to return to England," Tom said. "I am taken in with the patriot cause. I have seen justice, having been tried for murder in a patriot court, before a patriot jury, which saw justice in giving my acquittal. I am no longer an Englishman. I am an American and wish to remain so."

Jacky smiled at Tom, pleased with what Tom had been saying.

"I feel I need to find a settlement far enough away, where there will be little chance of me ever being mistaken for that captain of the army who most feel deserved the gallows."

"But where shall we go?" Jacky asked.

"We? Are you certain? Are you prepared, Jacky, to not be in Boston, to not see your family? Are you certain?" Tom asked.

"I wish to be with you...wherever you go I wanna be there with ya."

"Are you trying to quote the scriptures, 'whether thou goest I shall go'?"

"Yes I shall," Jacky answered. "I hope there was never any doubt 'bout that in yer mind."

Tom took Jacky's hand and smiled broadly. "I had so hoped to hear you say this, but I had to hear it voluntarily, and sincerely coming from you."

"Where," Jacky smiled with excitement, "where shall we go?"

Good News for Dunmore

In Virginia, the fifty-two-year-old and obese royal governor, Norborne Berkeley, Lord de Botetourt, succumbed to the pains of indigestion, and died in his sleep October 15th in the Governor's Palace at Williamsburg.

The colony was shocked at news of his passing. Botetourt had been well liked compared to the royal governors Virginia had seen. He had a pleasing disposition and firm family ties to Virginia. The acting governor, until a royal replacement could be named, was William Nelson, Botetourt's lieutenant governor, from Yorktown.

Virginia was the largest and most profitable of all the English colonies in America. Appointment as royal governor of Virginia was the most sought after seat in the New World. With the appointment came real financial and land grant probabilities for the fortunate appointee. Lord Hillsborough knew this, as did the newest royal governor in America, Lord Dunmore, who had just arrived in New York a few months before news of Botetourt's untimely passing arrived.

Dunmore was a capable politician and a strong adherent to Parliament and the king. If anything, he was loyal and would not be intimidated, should the current 'Quiet Time' rekindle into flames of dissent and rebellion. Dunmore would be the best man possible for

Hillsborough and Lord North to approach King George with as their choice for the royal governance of the prime colony in North America. Hillsborough's correspondence with Dunmore had encouraged him to be prepared for the move from New York in the summer.

The Murray family wealth had increased in just the short months since Dunmore's arrival. Freyling Grayson, who had served both of his successors, Henry Moore and Cadwalder Colden, went to work immediately for Dunmore. During that time, Grayson had brought in nearly fifty thousand pounds in kickbacks from merchants and other fees and duties collected. He had also secured lucrative land grants of some twenty thousand acres up the Hudson River Valley and in the Catskill and Adirondack Mountains. He had obtained a massive grant of more than fifty thousand acres around Lake Champlain in New York, in the disputed lands of the Vermont Green Mountains, claimed by also by the colony of New Hampshire.

Dunmore did not receive the official appointment from London until August 1771. The Dunmores arrived at Williamsburg, their new capital, aboard the ship "Mercy" on September 25th.

Most leaders of the Virginia House of Burgesses were pleased with the appointment of Lord Dunmore. As a member of the House of Lords in Parliament, he had built a reputation as a skilled political mind. He was greeted as the new royal governor with great fanfare when he and Lady Dunmore, accompanied by his their daughters and nephews, arrived at Williamsburg. William Nelson, the acting governor presided along with speaker Peyton Randolph.

The 'Quiet Time' continued.

A Cabin on Assonet Bay

On their journey away from the Boston area in their horse-drawn wagon, the new 'Macneal brothers' passed into a beautiful forest near the upper reaches of the Fall River Valley, overlooking Assonet Bay in the Rhode Island colony. The waters of three tributaries of the larger Fall River formed three fingers of land jutting into the bay before the broad Fall River started its journey to the larger Narragansett Bay, then out into the Atlantic. It was there, in the forest overlooking the waters of the bay, that Tom and Jacky made camp.

They threw together a lean-to attached to the side of the wagon, with a large canvas roof. They gathered stones from the water's edge and wood from the forest to build a fire ring just outside the lean-to. They stored up firewood while there was still daylight, enough to last through the night, which had omens of coldness.

Quilts and blankets, gathered by Jacky from his mama, Mrs. Seider and Mrs. Maverick, would make a warm nest for the cold night.

Game seemed plentiful. Deer, squirrels, rabbits, raccoons, otters and muskrats seemed to be everywhere. Tom and Jacky bagged two plump rabbits and a squirrel for supper, and roasted them on spits over the fire ring they had built.

An idea came to Jacky, as he and Tom snuggled in together for warmth, and to requite each man's months of longing to be beside the other.

"We had no problem shootin' our supper tonight," Jacky said, "an' earlier, a few miles back, were some fields with grouse an' pheasants."

"And I saw several wild turkeys," added Tom. "I would have enjoyed a venison steak tonight, if we had come across a deer before we saw those rabbits."

"An' you know there's plenty fish in that bay," Jacky added.

"And your point, my young brother?" Tom smiled.

Jacky sat up, pulling some of the covers with him. "It's November. It'll be hard gettin' hired on day fishin' boats, an' we'll spend what money we have rentin' a room in the town," Jacky said.

"Why don't we build a cabin of our own ... right here ... it's flat enough land, an' we could save all the rent we would be charged in town. We could hunt game, dress it, salt it down, an' sell it in town. We could fish here too, an' sell the fishes."

Tom sat up in the makeshift bed, evidently in thought at what Jacky had suggested.

"We could sell the hides and fur as well," Tom said slowly and deliberately. "We have most of the tools we need to raise a cabin, and there are definitely ample trees to be felled for logs for it. We could make enough, I dare say, during these coming months of winter, to provide for us well. Perhaps in the late spring, when the hunting may be more scarce, we will move to town and hire on to fishing boats. But then again, maybe not."

He turned and smiled at Jacky. "I like your idea."

Jacky smiled broadly that Tom had liked his idea for their future. Tom kissed him on the forehead and Jacky laid his head on Tom's shoulder. They fell asleep, anxious to get started.

Chapter Six

The Word Not Spoken

It was the Quiet Time, but still there were voices of dissent in the colonies. The remaining tax, the one on tea, though relatively small, was still seen as a tax unlawfully passed without representation in Parliament by the colonies. Most merchants simply would not purchase tea and did not offer it for sale. The one word on every patriot mind was "independence," but it was never spoken in the halls of the legislature, only in the taverns and parlors of private homes.

Josiah Quincy published an essay in the "Boston Gazette" where he urged continued support of the boycott, stating *"break off all social intercourse with those whose commerce contaminates, whose luxuries poison, whose avarice is insatiable, and whose unnatural oppressions are not to be borne."*

Similar articles and essays appeared in Sam Adams' "Independent Advertiser" and other patriot newspapers throughout the colonies.

John Hancock, the leading Boston merchant and member of the House of Representatives, also wrote that accepting and paying the one remaining duty imposed by Parliament would only justify Parliament's right to enact new and higher taxes at will, without colonial approval. *"Anyone who supports the tax on tea is an enemy to America!"* Hancock wrote.

Those who did buy tea, bought it through the black market of Dutch tea smuggled in.

In November 1772, Sam Adams formed a Committee of Correspondence in the Massachusetts Legislature, to begin corresponding with the legislatures of the other colonies, as a way of uniting the dissent they each felt. Royal Governor Hutchinson of Massachusetts, immediately saw this as nothing short of a covert attempt by the patriot leaders to further the cause of American Independence throughout all thirteen of the colonies. When the House would not disband the covert committee at his order, he dissolved the legislature.

When the new year of 1773 came, Hutchinson called for the legislature to meet in Boston. He felt his dissolving of the legislature in November had served its purpose, and he himself would open the new session with an address of warning for all to hear.

At the opening session, Hutchinson took the podium. His address spoke of the past three years of calm, quiet and peace in the streets of Boston and across the colony of Massachusetts. He pointed to the magnanimous actions of Lord North and Parliament in the repealing of duties to alleviate the financial burden on colonials. He looked to a future of Englishmen living in America, continuing to be Englishmen, and sharing in the fullness of the government with undying loyalty to George III.

Then he made his carefully worded warning to the legislators. *"To deny the supremacy of Parliament is dangerously close to rebellion. I know of no line that can be drawn between the authority of Parliament and the total independence of the colonies."*

A deafening hush feel upon the legislators. John Adams whispered to John Hancock, sitting beside him.

"Did the Governor not just utter the word, until now never spoken aloud in this chamber…*independence?*"

"He did indeed," smiled Hannock. "He did indeed!"

Hancock immediately rose from his seat on the floor and began applause. John Adams joined, as did every member assembled.

The governor smiled at first, thinking the adulation was for him. But why? He wondered what had sparked this applause during the portion of his speech intended as a warning? He looked down at his notes. The phrase *"total independence of the colonies"* glared up at him. He knew he had made a grave mistake. He had just, then and there, opened the door to talk of independence. His faced began to glow red with embarrassment. Had he just opened the floodgates of revolution for all the British colonies in North America? He picked up his papers and without another word, turned and exited the chamber as the applause grew louder and louder.

"Total independence of the colonies" soon became the public cry of the patriots. The Quite Time was now coming to an abrupt end.

In May, Parliament passed the Tea Act of 1773. It was designed to alleviate the East India Company's growing tea surpluses, stacking up on the piers along the Thames, due to the success of the American boycott. The boycott in America had been devastating and Dutch tea smugglers were too covert for capture.

The Tea Act allowed the East India Company to ship tea directly to the American colonies without first porting at London. The new act rescinded the duty collected in London. It would be assessed in the colonies on top of the colonial duty. The tea now would be shipped to only a small, government-created monopoly of tea merchants in Boston, Philadelphia, New York and Charleston. The unsold surplus tea sitting on the Thames wharfs would be the first sent to the colonies.

In June 1773, Sam Adams received copies of letters, sent from Hutchinson to London, urging the leaders of Parliament to put in place *"an abridgement of what are called English liberties"* in order to assure the supremacy of Parliament in the colonies.

As Adams read the letters publicly on the floor of the legislature, boos and hoots demanding recall of the governor rose. A resolution to Parliament and the King, calling for Hutchinson to be recalled was passed.

The Trip Back to Lewis Street

For two and a half years, Tom and Jacky profited with their enterprise of hunting, fishing, trapping and selling game, fish and hides in the towns of Fall River, Providence and New Bedford, all within a few hours journey in their wagon from their cabin on Assonet Bay. The cabin was primitive, but grew to become very comfortable for the two friends and partners who all their acquaintances knew as 'brothers.' They soon erected a small smoke house to cure the game meat and a shed cellar built into the hill to store the salt barrels for the cured meat and fish for market.

They easily sold their goods to taverns, inns and markets in the towns they serviced. The large variety of game and fish gave them a good income and a good stash of cash saved on hand. The mammals provided two sources of income for the young men: meat and pelts. Beaver, otter, rabbit and bear pelts were easily sold to the merchants, to be shipped off to furriers in London, Amsterdam or Paris. Pheasant and turkey feathers were also in demand to hat makers, as well as porcupine quills for the makers of quill pens.

Tom and Jacky were frugal with their earnings, stashing the savings in a small wooden keg buried beneath the plank floor of the cabin. They also had a milk cow and kept a few chickens for eggs, and an occasion pot of chicken and dumplings. A small garden plot grew corn, beans, potatoes, carrots and squash. In season they gathered wild berries and nuts from hickory, walnut and hazelnut trees.

The only cash money they spent was for black powder for their muskets, (they made their own musket balls) salt, flour, a few spices, and a pint or two of Irish whiskey on occasion. By the summer of 1773, the little wooden keg held more than two hundred pounds sterling. The average yearly wage in the colonies was about forty pounds.

Twice a year, Jacky took about ten days and returned to Boston to visit his mother. He made these trips usually in March and August. He always took an agreed upon amount of cash with him to help out his mother and pick up what needed supplies he and Tom wanted from Boston. Jacky always brought back copies of the "Boston Gazette" and Sam Adams' "Independent Advertiser" to keep Tom up on the political tone of Boston.

In August 1773, Jacky had just turned twenty-one. His oldest sister, Hannah, at nineteen, was married and lived with her husband, Drake Enfield, on his farm just east of the town of Lexington. They had a one-year-old daughter, Myra. Jacky's youngest sister, Caroline, at seventeen, had married a local ne'er do well, Johnny Kilkenny, and lived near the wharf. They too had a child, six-month-old Calvin. Caroline did visit their mother at least once each week, but for the most part Jacky's mother, Annie Macneal, at forty-two, was alone in the house on Lewis Street. She still took in sewing, cleaned homes, and cooked for the wealthy on Beacon Hill. When Jacky visited in August 1773, he didn't realize how his life would soon change.

"Mama," Jacky called out from the kitchen door when he arrived at the small home on Lewis Street that Monday afternoon. "Mama, tis me, your son Jacky!" he continued his announcement. There was no sign of anyone in the house. The door was open and he walked in, "Mama? Are you at home, Mama?"

He walked through the kitchen and into the front parlor, still not seeing nor hearing anything.

He walked into the downstairs bedchamber where his mother slept. There she was, lying fast asleep on top of the quilt.

"Mama?" he said much more quietly. "Mama?"

An eye opened slightly. Her face appeared much older than her forty years would suggest. Jacky noticed how quickly she had aged, just since his last visit in the spring. A slight smile crossed her lips.

"Jacky, me boy." She uttered, seemingly taking every morsel of strength her tired body could muster. She raised both arms toward him as if begging for a hug. He bent down, hugged her and planted a familial kiss on her cheek.

"Are you ill, Mama?" he asked with great concern.

She slithered her frail body up and began to sit on the edge of the bed. "No more today than any other day, son," she answered. "Tis so good to have you home, boy. It must be March."

"August, Mama," Jacky corrected her. "I dare say I've never felt this warm o' weather in March."

She chuckled. "Silly old me," she said. "O' coarse tis August and time for me son to pay me a visit." She kissed him on his cheek.

The two went from her bedchamber into the parlor, then to the kitchen. "Go sit out yonder, in those chairs 'neath the shade tree," she said. "I'll get us glasses o' me blackberry punch. We'll sit an' visit 'afore ya gotta be leavin' again."

"I ain't goin' no where soon," Jacky said, "I'll be here a full week."

"Now go! Be off with ya, an' mind your mama now!" she said. "I'll fetch the punch an' join ya."

Jacky went and sat in a chair beneath the old elm tree and knew he had never seen his mother in such a state of weakness. "She's so slow an' shuffles her feet as she walks," he thought as he sat there. "She's quite ill or else she's just been workin' too damn hard."

He saw her coming slowly out of the kitchen with two glasses of punch she'd made. He ran to her and took the glasses out of her trembling hands. "Mama, let me help ya with these," Jacky said.

"I ain't helpless, ya know," she protested. "Very well, take 'em." She handed him the glasses. She sat in a chair beside him and began to speak. "So how is your life in the woods?" she asked.

"We're doing well," Jacky said. He reached in his pocket and pulled out a cloth pouch tied with string. He tossed it in her lap. "Sixty pounds sterling," Jacky said proudly, as the pouch landed in her lap.

"What a good son ye are!" she said and smiled. "That's a half year's wages from the Borden mansion alone, and then some!" She giggled.

"Mama, you are working too hard," Jacky said, concerned.

"I must work boy, or I shall surely be residin' in the Granary Burial Yard," she smiled and chuckled.

"Mama, I'm concerned for you, I truly am," he pleaded. "You're either workin' too hard or you're ill with some malady. Which is it?"

She patted his hand and wheezed. "I'm the same ole work horse I've always been an' ain't ready to be turned out to pasture."

The subject changed. "Ya know little Caroline's married and moved off?" she said.

"Yes, Mama," Jacky said.

"An' she has a beautiful little baby boy name o' Calvin," she looked up to the sky and smiled with pride.

"An' a worthless husband in that worthless scamper Johnny Kilkenny!" Jacky said.

"Oh yes, Johnny Kilkenny," his mother answered, "a fine boy if ever there was one."

Jacky realized his mother was in a world of her own as they spoke.

"What do ya hear from Hannah?" Jacky asked.

"Hannah! Why boy I see you more often than I ever lay me eyes on that one. Hannah!" She made a face.

"Well then, we'll just ride out to Lexington in me wagon and pay her a visit, we will," Jacky said. "We can take Caroline and the baby along as well."

"That'd be nice boy. That'd be real nice."

"I don't know why ya don't leave this ole house where you're all alone?" Jacky thought aloud. "You could move to the farm at Lexington and be well taken care of by Hannah and Drake."

"No, no, boy. I'll never leave this place!" she said tormented by the thought. "Why if 'n yer dear father returns an' finds me gone, he'd know not what to do."

"Me father?" Jacky was shocked and a bit scared "Me father's been dead fer years!! He's buried in the Granary yard."

"Oh no dear son," she spoke. "He's just been delayed. He will be home ... very soon."

Jacky knew then and there his mother was ill. She was losing her mind. Her body was failing and had failed a hundred fold, just since March. They would make a trip to Lexington and he would convince Hannah and Drake to take her in.

The College of William and Mary

When the summer of 1773 began to come to a close, Peter and Zack were busy preparing to move from the pastoral quaintness of a rural Hanover County plantation to the most thriving metropolis in the colony, Williamsburg. They had spent four years at Campbelltown Academy, and in the May, both had passed the dreaded entrance exam, and were admitted to the September term at the College of William and Mary.

Zack excelled in nature sciences and was getting quite good drawing specimens of nature. He was set on a course of study to become a botanist or horticulturalist. If he had his way, he'd spend the rest of life just making sketches, but the judge insisted he pursue a career with a more financially sound future.

Peter was less certain which direction he wanted to follow. He had mastered the languages, excelling in Latin, Greek, French and Spanish. He also immersed himself in the classics and history, especially military history. He was also an excellent debater. Most who knew him expected a career in the law. If he had his way he'd start on a career in the military, or leave for the western frontiers and become a mountain man, like the ones he'd read about.

The boys spent weeks packing trunks and making ready to join the students at the second oldest college in America, located at the end of Duke of Gloucester Street, in the colonial capital. The times were exciting on the political level, and now, with the Tea Act of 1773 in force, and thoughts of independence being spoken openly, things promised to get even more exciting. The so-called Quiet Time had been put to rest.

At age sixteen, Peter was a giant among the students, weighing 240 pounds and standing six feet ten inches tall. He stood heads above his fellow students as well as his professors at Campbelltown. Adella and the judge hoped his growth spurt was over.

Their first day at the Wren Building on the campus, Zack and Peter were shown to the room they would occupy for their years of study. It was a nice room with two beds, two desks and chairs, and ample room for their trunks. Classes would not start for three days, so they had some time to reacquaint themselves with the city they had so enjoyed three summers before. They were also scheduled for meetings with professors and upperclassmen during their early days of orientation to college life.

That first day they were to meet their upperclass mentor, the student who would serve as each boy's advisor for his first year on campus.

Peter was happy to learn the name of the upperclassman assigned to be his mentor. It was, Stockard Samuels, his first real friend and mentor at Campbelltown. The scheduled meeting between the two old classmates was a happy start to Peter's career in college. They met at Raleigh Tavern and enjoyed the prime rib and tankards of ale.

Zack, being the more shy and introverted of the two boys, dreaded his meeting with a strange older student who was to be his mentor.

"Can you not come with me, Peter?" Zack begged.

"It will be fine, Zack, you'll see," Peter responded. "Then we'll go into town for the afternoon. I'll stay right here and wait for you."

Zack finally got up the nerve and walked out of the room, down the corridor and one flight of stairs to the library where he was to meet his mentor. He had his ever-present sketchbook under his arm.

"You must be Zachary Winston," said an older student as Zack entered the room. "My name is Justin Sloan, and I am to be your upperclassman mentor." He extended his hand and the two shook hands, Zack, dropping his ever-present sketchbook on the floor.

"What is this?" Justin said, stooping to help Zack retrieve the book of sketches.

"I draw nature," Zack said, as they stood and began walking to a library table.

"May I see?" asked Justin politely.

Zack handed the book to his new mentor as they sat, and Justin began thumbing through the sketches Zack had drawn.

"These are quite good," Justin said, "excellent actually. You should have them published."

The meeting was longer than Zack had expected or hoped it would be, but the time sped by. Zack and Justin were hitting it off nicely. Justin was nineteen and in his final year. He lived on a plantation in Buckingham County, west and south of Richmond. He was studying to become an educator, and shared Zack's love of nature.

The two talked about Zack's classes and professors. "You will like professor Crowe," Justin said. "He is fond of taking the class out of doors to study botany. That will no doubt become one of your favorite studies."

"I hope for a good class and a good professor for zoology," Zack said.

"Oh yes, and you shall," Justin answered Zack's thoughts. "Professor Hugh Langston. He is one of the favorite professors here. He will be your instructor for natural sciences, and biology as well."

"And I know just the man who can help you get these sketches published," Justin said. "He is a bookseller on Duke of Gloucester Street, Jonas Phillips." Zack smiled broadly.

"I bought a book with nature prints from Jonas Phillips," Zack said. "We spent the month of June here three summers ago."

"Show them to him and ask if he thinks they are publishable, as I think they are," Justin said, as the two students stood and ended their first meeting. Zack was pleased with his new friend and mentor. He told Peter all about the meeting and they headed off to Duke of Gloucester Street.

Taking Care of Mama

"I don't think I'll ever go back there again," Jacky said, as he and Tom sat at the table they kept under the big willow tree overlooking the bay. It was Jacky's first day home from his visit to Boston and his mother's house on Lewis Street.

"Mama's not well an' you'd think her daughters would be there ta take care o' her," Jacky went on. "But, no, they are both too damned selfish and too damned busy with their own useless lives!

"Mark me words, Tom, Mama will not last out the winter," Jacky added sadly. "She has worked herself to the nub, she 'as. Hardly got outta the bed the entire time, an' when she did, all she'd do was worry 'bout when me dead father might be a comin' home. He died near fifteen years ago an' layin' in the Granary yard! I fear she's lost 'er mind, she 'as."

"I am so sorry to hear that," Tom comforted Jacky. "Both your sisters are now married and live close by..."

"An' they can't be bothered with the ole woman who raised 'em!" Jacky said in anger. "We rode out ta Hannah and Drake's fine farm at Lexington," Jacky told of the visit.

"I felt certain, Hannah, bein' the oldest an' all, an' with a fine house an' husband, would see the need to bring Mama ta stay with her. But no, Hannah is now again with child an' fears she needs lookin' after more'n Mama. She said 'Mama's comfortable on Lewis Street, an' she just wants to stay put.' Stay put an' just pass away in her sleep some night.

"I tell you Tom, Mama is ill ... feeble o' body an' feeble o' mind. Hannah doesn't want a demented ole woman 'round her child. That's the truth o' the matter...a selfish, inconsiderate, ungrateful woman, that she is!"

"And Caroline?" Tom added. "Is her husband not planning to go away to sea. Will she not be alone and willing to stay with your mother on Lewis Street while he's away?"

"Knowin' Caroline as I do, an' all too well, I might add," Jacky added, "She'll be spreading 'er spindly legs for any Jack Tar what crosses her path! I'm just as certain she welcomes months alone an' free from that rotten, no account bastard of a husband, that low life poor excuse of a man, Johnny Kilkenny, being away ta sea. She'll be havin' the time o' her life, she will! The last thing she wants is ta have ta tend ta a sickly ole woman. I'd be surprised if she didn't try ta saddle Mama with takin' care o' her baby, Calvin!"

"Then we shall go," Tom said with authority. "If your mama is in such a state, with no one else to tend to her, we must go and take care of her ourselves."

Jacky was stunned. His mouth dropped to his chin as Tom spoke. Why would Tom so easily give up the life they had shared for the past three years in the wilderness at Assonet Bay? "But what about all this?" Jacky asked, sweeping his arms around their homestead, "What about you bein' found out?"

"I think no one will remember me...remember who I was then," Tom said. He got up from his chair, held his hand out to take Jacky's, and they walked, hand-in-hand, toward the edge of the small bluff, looking through the sparse stand of birch, willow and pines, to the cobalt blue waters of Assonet Bay. The leaves were still vibrant and green, but soon, all but the leaves of the pines would change to the golds and reds and browns of autumn, and soon after, the gray-white bitterness of cold winter would set in.

"I know your heart is here with mine," Tom said, "but your heart too is sad ... sad for your mother, and sad for the state she has come into. It grows very sad, knowing she may well not pass through this coming winter.

"Your place is with her," Tom added, "and my place is with you. You know, 'whether thou goest'..."

By the first week of September, Tom and Jacky had packed the wagon with all their belongings, as well as hides from their storehouse and three barrels of cured meat. Tom had sold the homestead and buildings for twenty pounds sterling, to two brothers they had befriended, who, like Tom and Jacky, hunted and trapped in the forest, and lived in a cliffside cave about four miles to the northwest of the bay.

Tom and Jacky rode the day and a half journey to Boston, and in mid-afternoon on the second day, arrived at the Macneal home on Lewis Street. They found Jacky's mother in bed and not well at all. She was warm with a fever and coughed and wheezed as mother and son attempted conversation.

"Mama," Jacky said, sitting on the edge of her mattress, "Tom an' I have come ta take care o' you."

"I need no one ..." she said as he held her hand. "I can care for m'self as I 'ave always cared for m'self ... But tis so good o' you an' Tom ta come. I love you so, but what I need now is me rest, so I can clean the Borden Mansion t'morrow… They expect me." She coughed a few hacks and turned back over onto her pillow.

Jacky rose and went to Tom, waiting in the parlor. "She's much worse than even before," Jacky said, "an' by the look o' things it 'pears she's not eaten in days. I think she's slipping fast. Come, I'll show ya ta our room an' you can unpack."

"First, Jacky," Tom said, "what if I stir up a broth. Perhaps that will nourish her some."

Jacky smiled. "Perhaps," he agreed and led Tom to the kitchen.

Tom and Jacky put a chicken to stew over the hearth and when it was finished, Jacky took a bowl of broth into his mother. She woke and seemed to take the broth well, propped up in bed as Jacky spoon-fed his mother. She was still feverish and when finished, went back to sleep.

Jacky joined Tom in the chairs under the tree where Jacky had sat with his mother a few weeks earlier.

"I have been reading in the Gazette where the tensions here in Boston are near as volatile as they were before the massacre in front of the Customs House," Tom commented. "It seems the tax on tea is not being well taken here in Boston."

"I hear the dissention runs deeper now," Jacky said, "somethin' about the governor takin' away the rights o' the people, as if they was no more than slaves." Then a voice called out from the street.

"Jacky? Jacky Macneal is that you?"

It was a familiar voice from Jacky's past, Wills Winkman, leader of the one-time rival gang of Jacky's Irish League, the Plug-Uglies.

"What the Hell does it matter to a damned Plug-Ugly," Jacky shouted back as Wills crossed the yard toward them. Jacky rose from his chair, smiling and extending his hand.

"Well are you not just as horrible ugly as last I remember?" Wills said as the three laughed.

"Have a seat Wills," Jacky said. "This is me long-lost cousin, an' trappin' partner, Tommy Macneal. Tom, this is Wills Winkman."

"Pleased to meet you, Wills," Tom said, shaking Wills' hand, thinking in his own mind how Jacky's quick-thinking had relegated him from older brother to long-lost cousin. "I have certainly heard of you from Jacky here."

The three sat and sipped some Irish whisky Wills had in a flask in his hip pocket. They talked about the health of Jacky's mother.

"Has she seen a doctor?" Wills asked. "I will have my uncle, Paulus, stop in tomorrow. Perhaps he can look at her and give her some medicine."

They also talked about the politics since the Tea Act came to pass. "Those damnable British are now forcing us to buy their tea and only from the governor's sons' at a high price," Wills said. "The taxes we pay go right into their pockets, not the King's treasury. The king and Parliament now pay the salaries of the governor and judges. The legislature has no control at all now. There are soon to be no rights at all for any colonials."

"There are but few rights we colonials have now," Tom said, sounding very much the patriot he had become. "That is just why Jacky and I have been in the forest hunting and trapping for three years. I hope some day to go away from the settlements in the colonies altogether, and live free on the frontier …someday." Tom had not mentioned his dream yet to Jacky, and saw a rather surprised look on Jacky's face.

"Oh but to be free from the chains of bondage the British want to bind us with," said Wills. "The two of you ought to join our meeting tomorrow night. Remember Sam Adams and John Hancock? Well, they are the leaders of our group of about two hundred. I know you've heard of the secret society, the Sons of Liberty. Well, that's our group. You'll see a lot of old friends, Jacky, and hear about our plans for independence. Come if you can. It will begin at seven o'clock in the long room above Benjamin Edes' Print Shop down at the harbor. Oh, by the way, I am an apprentice printer for Mr. Edes." Wills was soon on his way.

"That was some good whiskey Wills had," Tom commented. "Do you think he pissed in it?" They both laughed.

"I don't think so, but if ya want, I could run off ta Charlie O'Brien's an' buy us a pint o' our own."

"Only if you let me watch you pee in it and blend it the way you do so marvelously," Tom said, pulling out a few coins from his pocket. Jacky smiled and started off.

"Wait!" Tom shouted. "When did I get demoted from brother to long-lost cousin?"

Jacky turned after a few steps toward the street, and said, "I thought it best at the moment. Everyone in Boston knows I 'ave no brother. While we're here, you best be me long-lost an' happily-found cousin."

Tom smiled and praised him for his quick thinking. He waved Jacky on his way. "Be off with you, cousin!"

Jacky again headed toward the street then turned back to Tom, "When I get back I want to hear these plans o' yours to take off for the real frontier."

Jacky returned in a few minutes with the pint. The two went inside and lit the whale oil lamp in the parlor. Jacky brought an empty glass from the kitchen, poured about a third of the fresh and unadulterated whiskey into it, and placed in on the table. He looked up at Tom, smiling his larcenous smile, and put the pint of whiskey down beside the glass, now just two-thirds full.

After Jacky had 'blended' the whiskey, they sat in the parlor sipping.

"Now what about the frontier?" Jacky asked.

"I also read in the Gazette you brought home from your last trip, that tens of thousands of colonials are ignoring King George's edict of 1763, prohibiting white settlement west of the summit of the Appalachians and the Alleghenies," Tom informed Jacky. "What an opportunity that would be for a couple of enterprising young men who knew hunting, trapping and fishing!

"It is virgin land, Jacky, and there for the taking. The first to arrive will become the men of wealth, power, and land when the hordes come, as they will come.

"And there's no real rush to go," Tom was quick to say. "We can take care of your mama, as long as she needs us to care for her. Then, when we are not needed here, we can head toward Fort Pitt and lay claim to some land on the Ohio River. We can do there what we've been doing at Assonet. We can open a trading post for settlers heading west, a day or two's journey west of the fort, when they will be ready to see white folks again, and replenish some of their spent supplies."

They talked into the wee hours, then climbed the stairs to go to bed, and enjoyed each other's company until the sun began to rise.

Wills Winkman had done as he had said he would, and in the morning, after Jacky had prepared a breakfast and spoon-fed his mama some oatmeal, there was a rap on the door. Tom welcomed Dr. Paulus Winkman, carrying a black leather valise. He was there to see Annie Macneal. After his examination, the physician met with Jacky and Tom in the chairs beneath the old oak tree.

"Consumption, I feel," said Dr. Winkman. "I fear it is but a matter of time. I doubt there would've been a thing I could've done for her if I had seen her a year ago. It appears to have been eating at her for years."

"Is there nothing that can be done for her?" asked Tom.

"I fear very little can be done," he spoke in uncertainty. "Her lungs appear congested and her pulse is weak. We can administer a regimen of bleedings, but I cannot legitimately say it will be of any great cure. To me, bleedings do nothing. They may relieve some maladies temporarily, but more often than not, simply speed death."

"I can do nothing for me mother?" Jacky asked pleadingly.

"I am so sorry to say that what you are now doing is but all you can do. Make her as comfortable as is possible. Feed her regularly soups and broths and things easily digestible. The oatmeal you served her today is good. She needs some sustenance aside from liquids. That will ease some of the pain she has to be suffering. If you feel she be in extreme pain, perhaps a sip of whiskey, mixed with a spoonful of honey will help."

Student Life in Williamsburg

Student life in Williamsburg in 1773 was based on lectures and a heavy dose of classroom lessons, shared with the unavoidable political goings on of the colony. Peter especially found the distractions invigorating. He read "The Virginia Gazette" thoroughly. He began to steer his education toward the events outside the classrooms of the Wren Building.

Stockard Samuels invited Peter to discussions at the Raleigh Tavern. Stockard would be leaving his formal studies in May, but would be remaining in Williamsburg, reading law and studying at the home of George Wythe, as his friend, the burgesses from Albemarle County, Thomas Jefferson had done. Stockard hoped some day soon to be elected as a delegate himself from his district in Essex County at Tappahannock.

"The goveno' has shown his opposition to ouw committee of co'espondence when he dissolved the house in Mawch," Jefferson said, in his stuttering fashion one evening, as Peter and Stockard joined him and a few other delegates for dinner at the tavern. "But ouw committee wemains, and shall wemain until we have ouw independence."

"Nothing is left save the issue of independence," spoke the delegate from Charles City County, Benjamin Harrison V. "The governor of Massachusetts, in opening the recalled house in Boston, spoke thus. There can only be complete authority of Parliament, or total independence for all the colonies."

"He spoke true," added Stockard. "It was dangerous of him to do so, but he spoke the truth."

"And Amewican independence shall come," agreed Jefferson, "by edict of King George himself, or by Lowd No'th and the Pa'liament ..."

"Or by revolution," came the voice of Patrick Henry, as he approached the table.

"Join us Patwick," invited Jefferson, "and add you' welcomed voice to ouw discussion."

Henry sat and said, "The Tea Act will be the final act of Parliament, before the colonies from New England to those on the rice plantations of Savannah, join forces and say 'tis enough!"

"We shall see what welcome the colonials give those seven ships of the East India Company, loaded with thei' su'pluses of tea, bound fo' ouw shores," Jefferson stuttered.

"They shall arrive soon," said Henry, whose oratorical voice was easier on the ear than the pediment Jefferson spoke with.

As Stockard and Peter rose to leave, Peter recognized a familiar face, sitting and dining alone. He went to him.

"Jimmy," Peter spoke, "Jimmy Madison?" Madison interrupted his concentration on a platter of steamed clams and smiled.

"Peter Francisco," Jimmy rose as he recognized the tallest person in the room. "It has been years." They shook hands.

"I am enrolled at the college and this," he motioned to Stockard, "is my mentor Stockard Samuels from Tappahannock." Stockard and Jimmy shook hands. "Will you not sit and we might catch up with each other," Jimmy asked. The two students sat.

"What brings you to Williamsburg? When did you return from New Jersey?" Peter asked.

"I graduated in two years," Jimmy said, "but remained an added year to have private studies in Hebrew and philosophy with the college president, John Witherspoon. I returned from New Jersey to Montpelier last spring, and for a year have been reading the law. That brings me here for a short month of studies under the professor, George Wythe. Father arranged it for me."

"Impressive," spoke Stockard. "When do you become a member of the bar? I will begin my studies with professor Wythe next year."

"I do not actually expect to practice the law," Madison added. "I have studied law simply to gain more knowledge of the law. I shall leave the courtroom and all its trappings to barristers such as you."

"Then what career have you chosen for yourself?" Stockard inquired more.

"I will see just what change these political times shall bring, and then decide," Madison said.

"And you Peter? What career have you in mind" Jimmy asked.

"Well, Jimmy, as you are waiting to determine that as the times may dictate," Peter said, "I am content absorbing what I might, and put it to good use as the times may lead me."

"Politics? … The law perhaps?" Jimmy quizzed.

"Perhaps, Jimmy, perhaps," Peter answered. "But if Parliament and king stand in the way of our independence and we face war," Peter spoke, "I should think a military rank of some sort might suit me well. I have read about the great battles of world history, I think now I might wish to smell the powder for myself. "

After a few minutes, and making plans for Peter and Zack to get together with Jimmy on Saturday, Stockard and Peter walked back toward the Wren Building.

"This Jimmy Madison is some sort of a genius, I should think," offered Stockard. "I cannot imagine such a young boy, already graduated from the College of New Jersey, and no doubt prepared already to pass the bar. He is what, no more than your age, sixteen, I dare say."

"Do not let his short height and less than one hundred pounds of weight trick you," Peter said. "My friend James Madison, Junior, is a full six years my senior. But you are correct in your observations about his being a genius."

Zack was having a much more pleasant experience as a student at William and Mary than he experienced at Campbelltown Academy. At Campbelltown, Zack really felt he did not fit in well with the other students. He felt a bit of jealousy in how well Peter had gotten on with the other students, the older ones as well as the younger boys. But now at college, none of that jealousy and self-pity raised its head in Zack's mind. Peter was again Zack's best friend, and near as much a brother as a real brother could ever have been. They shared a sleeping and study room, and shared fun times away from the Wren Building. As Peter listened to and talked politics with the likes of Thomas Jefferson, George Washington and Zack's cousin Patrick Henry, Zack had new friends he shared interests with.

Zack enjoyed being with Justin Sloan, who had indeed become a friend. One day after classes, Justin knocked at Zack and Peter's door.

"I have some wonderful news," Justin spoke. "The bookseller Jonas Phillips wants very much to see your sketches! All of them! Gather them up and let's be off!"

The two classmates walked hurriedly out of the Wren and down Duke of Gloucester Street to the wood-framed shop, painted a sky blue hue with white trim.

"These are, as you said they were, Mister Sloan, quite good, quite good indeed," said Phillips, examining the sketches Zack had made. "I do propose we have them published."

"Is there a possibility?" Zack asked surprised.

"There is I should think," Phillips said, looking up from a perfect sketch of a grouse in a harvested field of corn. "Mister Murray, do you have a moment? Could you please come and look at these drawings?"

A tall boy, slender of frame, came from uncrating a new arrival of books he had been stocking on the shelves. "Take a look, please," Phillips asked the young man who appeared to be about Zack's age. "What do you think? Should these be published?"

The boy took his time flipping through the pages, closely examining each sketch.

"This one is especially lovely," said the boy, with a decided Scots accent, "this crane at water's edge. Oh, and this skunk! What a wonderful rendering! By all means they should indeed be published. They would easily sell at Bodine's at Gravesend in London."

"Is there also prose to go with the wonderful sketches?" Phillips asked Zack.

"No sir," Zack said, "I sketch. I am not an artist with words."

"Well," Phillips said, scratching his chin in thought, "we must remedy that. We must have a libretto for this opera of nature sketches you have drawn."

"Could I offer my abilities," the young man spoke. "I have had essays published, and a little poetry as well. I have a good education in the species, and could turn out a readable and accurate prose to go along with each." He looked directly at Zack. "With your assistance, naturally."

"Is that agreeable with you Mister Winston?" asked Phillips.

"It is, indeed," Zack smiled at the prospect of seeing his sketches published.

"My name in Roderic Murray," the boy said, extending his hand to Zack. "I studied at Oxford, with one year at King's College in New York, before enrolling here. I have lodgings in the Wren."

"I have seen you in the dining hall, and in the library. I am Zachary Winston," Zack said shaking his hand, "but please simply call me Zack, as my friends all do."

"I look forward to working with you on this project, Zack Winston," Roderic said.

As Justin and Zack walked back to the Wren, Justin asked Zack if he really knew who this boy, Roderic Murray, was. Zack indicated he did not. "He is the nephew and ward of Lord Dunmore, our governor. His older brother, Alexander, is the governor's personal secretary," Justin said. "You, my friend, are destined to be traveling in a fine society."

Ships Filled with Chests of Tea

By the autumn of 1773, seven English tea ships, loaded with surplus tea from the wharfs along the Thames, were authorized, under the Tea Act, to sail for the colonies. The Tea Act set deadlines for the ships of the East India Company, to unload their cargoes to the assigned government-approved monopoly of agents, have all the duties for the tea collected, and sail away. The deadline was twenty days from the arrival in the colonial port. If the deadline was unmet, the cargo would be confiscated by customs, and the shipping company would lose everything.

On Monday November 26th the English ship Dartmouth arrived in the Port of Boston with a full cargo of one hundred twenty-two chests of tea. Upon word of the Dartmouth's arrival, Sam Adams had a circular printed and sent throughout Boston, calling for a mass meeting in opposition of the tea cargo, to be held at Faneuil Hall three days later on Wednesday.

While Jacky and Tom lived in the house on Lewis Street taking care of Jacky's dying mother, they took turns working as day fishermen on the boat the Octopus, with one staying and tending to Annie, while the other went off to sea for the day. Jacky spent more days at the house on Lewis Street, fishing only one or two days each week, just to be able to breathe in some of that salt-sea air. Sunday was their one day together, both staying close to the house.

Annie had her days, but they were rare. Most of the time she spent in her bed, being spoon-fed chicken broth, chowder and consommés, after a breakfast of oatmeal, steamed rice or cornmeal mush. On occasion, there seemed to be a need for a small glass of whiskey, unadulterated of coarse, except for a spoonful of honey.

On her best days, she would rise up, wrap a housecoat around her, and sit in the parlor looking aimlessly out at the street. Her illness robbed her of anything more than brief periods of energy. She was slipping away fast. There were few visits from Jacky's sisters.

On Monday afternoon, Tom walked in from a day of fishing. He hung his coat on the hook by the kitchen door and pulled off his boots. He sat at the table and laid one of Sam Adams' circulars on the table.

"What's this?" Jacky asked, picking it up and reading it out loud.

Attention all citizens of Boston and the environs!
Attention all Patriots!
A mass meeting is called for seven o'clock,
Wednesday, November 29th - Faneuil Hall
to discuss the arrival of the English tea ship Dartmouth.
There are more on the way!

*The citizens of Boston shall determine what actions must be taken
to ensure the free exercise of our individual rights as
citizens of Great Britain and subjects to King George III.
All are welcome! All shall be heard!
Samuel Adams, John Hancock.*

Jacky looked at Tom and smiled, tossing the circular back on the table. "We must go!" Jacky said. "Have you seen the ship?"

"We saw it in the morning as we sailed out," Tom said. "It was weighing anchor about four miles from the harbor. I got a good look at her when we moored. She's a beautiful ship and appears to be loaded with many chests of tea."

"We can go Wednesday to the meeting," Jacky said. "I'll have Mrs. Maverick sit with Mama, as she sits with her when we go to the Sons of Liberty meetings."

"Good," Tom said. "If you want to attend, we shall. Now what is that aroma I smell coming from the hearth?"

Jacky smiled, headed to the hearth, and opened an oven door. "A fine Irish Shepherd's Pie, it tis," he said proudly, inhaling the aroma, then shutting the door once more before opening a second oven door. "An' a dried apple pie fer dessert!"

On Wednesday, Tom got home to share dinner with Jacky. When they were finished, Maddie Maverick came to sit with Annie, and Jacky told her to help herself to the pot roast and apple dumplings left over from their supper, but still warm on the hearth. They left for Faneuil Hall. The streets were filled as they walked toward the hall. Thousands of people had turned out from their invitation by circular. So many came in fact that Jacky and Tom barely made it just inside the hall's door.

"We've too many people!" Wills Winkman shouted, as he started coming out the door as Jacky and Tom were trying to enter. "Help us move the crowd to the Old South!" He asked as he saw the Macneals and smiled. Wills turned toward the crowd, which was trying to get in.

"We've too many! Move to the Old South!" Wills shouted. They followed Wills' lead, yelling to the people still arriving, "Move on to the Old South! Move on to the Old South!"

When they made it the few blocks to the Old South Meetinghouse, Jacky and Tom clung near Wills and took seats at the edge of the raised stage. Sam Adams and John Hancock were seated just behind the rostrum. Soon they saw Andy Seider and Jacob Maverick, the younger brother of Sammy who had been killed at the massacre. They spotted Paul Revere and two of his sons.

Soon the crowd came to order and Sam Adams took the rostrum. Adams delivered remarks, stating "the end of Britain's colonial hold over the American continent is nearing its end..." Applause broke out throughout the hall.

"And the reason for Britain's loss of America is Britain herself!" There was more applause. "The question here this evening is what is to be done with the chests of tea aboard the Dartmouth?"

Hancock approached the rostrum. "Those wishing the tea to be unloaded, with taxes paid on it to the governor's two sons, who are the only official merchants appointed by King George and their father the royal governor, signify your pleasure with a shout of 'yea'!" Not an utterance was heard in the packed hall of three thousand.

"Those wanting ... No, those demanding the governor instruct the captain of the Dartmouth to hoist anchor and sail away from this free port, signify your pleasure with a shout of 'Yea'!" The Old South Meetinghouse rocked to the rafters with the shouts of "YEA!"

With that polling of the feelings of the mass meeting, Sam Adams asked his cousin, the attorney, and now a member of the House of Representatives, John Adams, to read a resolution for adoption by the meeting. Adams read the resolution, which called for a petition to the governor to order the Dartmouth to sail away immediately, without unloading one chest of tea. It also called for the creation of a committee of thirty vigilant and hearty men to be stationed on the wharf to watch the activities aboard the Dartmouth.

The resolution passed with a resounding and deafening shout of 'YEA!' from the crowd."

"Well, boys, you ready to join the cause?" Wills spoke to Jacky and Tom.

"Of course we are," Jacky said.

"What can we do?" asked Tom.

"Well, Paul Revere's son, Apollos and I are going to be in charge of the committee watching the Dartmouth," Wills said. "Can the two of you take a shift each day?"

"We'll do what we can," said Jacky.

"We will gladly do it," Tom added.

"Good," Wills said as he got up. "Head straight away to Benjamin Edes' Print Shop. The side door is ajar. Go up to the long room above the shop and wait for us. I have to round up more. We'll be there soon. There's a bowl of grog on the table. Help yourself."

With that, Wills headed into the crowd. Tom and Jacky rose from their seats and headed toward the harbor.

"Well," Tom whispered to Jacky as they walked, "apparently the face of the dastardly Captain Preston has been erased from all memory. Not even his defender, the quite capable John Adams, recognized his face, sitting just in front of him, as he took the rostrum."

A quiet voice came from behind them. "I did so indeed, sir," came the soft voice. The two Macneals stopped dead in their tracks and turned. The short attorney was standing in front of them with a smile.

"I spotted you in the throng as I was reading the resolution," stated Adams. "It is so good to see you Tom. You look well," Adams smiled. "You look well." The two shook hands and continued their walk with Adams alongside.

"I am a patriot and America is now my adopted home," Tom relayed to Adams.

"And America is the better for it," stated Adams.

Adams left them after about one block's walk, assuring his former client his true identity was safe with him. Jacky and Tom continued on to the side door at the print shop. If there had ever been any doubt, they were now truly, Sons of Liberty!

A Tea in Boston

"This tea will be safely offloaded and the duties shall be collected!" Governor Hutchinson beat his fist on top his desk, when news of Sam Adams' mass meeting was reported to him the next morning by a loyalist member of the legislature, Ezra Poindexter.

"Send for Dalrymple," Hutchinson barked at his secretary. "I knew moving the entire army of occupation to Castle William would bring disaster. We shall have every single soldier marching maneuvers throughout this god-forsaken city!"

"Captain Ralston McKay of the Dartmouth is here to see you sir," an aide said.

"Send him in," Hutchinson gave his permission.

"Captain," spoke Hutchinson, as the handsome and athletically built captain of the Dartmouth entered his inner office, "how soon can the cargo be offloaded?"

"By the news I have received from your citizens here in Boston, I doubt it shall be offloaded at all," the captain spoke bluntly.

"Balderdash!" The governor stormed, and again slammed his fist on his desk. "That tea is to be offloaded and the duties collected on it immediately. Is that clear?"

"Oh, it's clear alright," the captain spoke, "but you saying it does not make it happen."

"I shall have your hide!" Hutchinson barked at the seaman. "I am the governor here, the agent of the king, and I command you to go about your duty."

"As you wish, your highness," McKay bowed and began to leave. "I will be going about my duty, and I shall be hoisting anchor and sailing to some more favorable port."

"I forbid you to sail. You may not see my orders as applicable to you, but I can and I do forbid you to sail the Dartmouth from our port!"

The Dartmouth did not sail away, nor was one chest of surplus tea offloaded from her cargo holds.

Wills Winkman and Apollos Revere's committee, called the Mohawks, split up into three eight-hour shifts to vigilantly watch all the actions on and around the Dartmouth. Each man met in the long room above the print shop with Wills and Apollos before starting their shift, and again reported back at the shift's end. The punch bowl was always there and always filled with a good grog.

Jacky and Tom worked each night through the night, reporting in the long room at eleven o'clock, sitting on the wharf near the Dartmouth until seven in the morning. Four others joined Jacky and Tom on their watch. Tom would leave and board the Octopus at half past six for a day of fishing, and Jacky would report to Wills or Apollos, before heading to Lewis Street and fixing breakfast for Annie and Maddie Maverick, who had agreed to sleep in the parlor just outside Annie's room.

As the deadline set by the Tea Act for the Dartmouth to be unloaded and sail away neared, two other ships arrived from England with their cargoes of tea, the Eleanor and the Beaver. It appeared nothing would change. The governor, using the force of the army, still holding fast on the island in the harbor, would confiscate the tea from the Dartmouth.

The Mohawks needed to devise a series of plans for whatever circumstance might transpire. Most evenings of the last week before the deadline, there was a planning session held in the long room above the print shop. Sam Adams and John Hancock hoped the governor would relent and avoid a riot in the streets, or worse.

"It is not now the time for war," Sam Adams warned. "We have not the arms, nor, at present, the organization. If this be the result, Massachusetts would stand alone from the other colonies, and lose our fight."

"I disagree," said Hancock. "I feel it is time to piss or pass the pot!"

"Let us piss, then Hancock," Adams said laughingly, "but let it be Hutchinson, Lord North, the Earl of Hillsborough, and King George himself who lead us to war ... war when our friends in Connecticut and New Jersey and Virginia and Georgia will be willing to join the fight."

If Hutchinson continued to refuse to allow Captain McKay and the captains of the Eleanor and the Beaver to sail away, the Mohawks would carry out their plans, and be the ones confiscating the surplus tea, not the Redcoat soldiers of the king. There would be a meeting at the Old South Meetinghouse the evening of December 16th. If at the meeting, Adams and Hancock thought the plan should be carried out, Adams, from the rostrum, would say, "this meeting can do nothing further to save the country." That would be the signal for Wills, Apollos and the Mohawks to go ahead.

As was expected, nothing changed the royal governor's mind. The Dartmouth faced its deadline. The captain and crew of the Eleanor and the Beaver watched and waited.

On Sunday December 16th early in the evening, Jacky, Tom, Wills, Paul Revere and his son Apollos, and about three thousand more flooded into the Old South Meetinghouse. Sam Adams rose to the rostrum and informed the assembled multitude that the royal governor had once more, just moments before the gavel called the mass meeting to order, refused to allow the Dartmouth to sail away from the Port of Boston.

Adams paused, then said: *"This meeting can do nothing further to save the country."*

That was the signal to Wills Winkman and the Mohawks. They rose and left the building. Soon nearly everyone who had attended the meeting swarmed to the wharf. They knew something was about to happen.

The Mohawks were now numbering nearly ninety, and all headed to the long room above the print shop. There each had stored a bag of costumes for the night they knew would come. They stripped off their clothing and climbed into the costumes each had brought ... loincloths, leggings of buckskin and vests, feather bonnets and armbands. They painted their faces with war paint and picked up bows and arrows or tomahawks and headed out the side door of the shop.

There they formed in groups. Wills and one-third of the men would board the Dartmouth. Apollos and his third would board the Eleanor, while Tom and Jacky led the final one-third to board the Beaver. Each group had torches lit to light the way to what they each knew would eventually be liberty.

Yelling and war-whooping their way to the harbor, the crowds from the Old South were there to join in the yelling and whooping, as the Mohawk braves each boarded the ship they were responsible for commandeering.

Wills, aboard the Dartmouth, Apollos on the Eleanor, and Tom and Jacky aboard the Beaver, each raised a chest of tea for all on the wharf to see, and heaved it over the side and into the brine water of Boston Harbor. All the Mohawk braves followed suit, lifting chests of tea and heaving them over the side until, after three hours of mischief, three-hundred and forty-two chests of surplus tea bobbed like buoys through the harbor and out to sea.

The battle for American liberty and independence had been set off.

Chapter Seven

The Lure of the Frontier

On Lewis Street, Annie Macneal died four days after the tea party. She died peacefully in her sleep on Thursday, December 20th, and was buried on the morning of Christmas Eve in the Granary Burying Ground beside her long-dead husband.

Jacky was the only one of her three children to say goodbye to her, as he had done without saying it everyday since he and Tom had returned. In fact, Jacky's sisters did not show up at the house on Lewis Street, where they all were born and had grown up, until the day before the burial.

Hannah came on the 23rd with her husband, Drake, and toddler, Myra, from their farm at Lexington. They spent the night before the burial in the house with Jacky and Tom, as Annie's corpse, prepared for burial by Mrs. Maverick and the neighbor ladies, was laid out in a wooden coffin Paul Revere had crafted and set in the parlor. Caroline, who lived just a few blocks away near the wharf, only showed up at the burial ground with baby Calvin. As a surprise to everyone, her husband, Johnny Kilkenny, had just returned that week from being away at sea, and went to the graveyard with Caroline.

Friends of Annie from Lewis Street came to the burial, as did the family of James Otis and Henry Borden, whose palatial homes on Beacon Hill Annie had cleaned and cooked for. Wills Winkman and Andy

Seider were there with several of Jacky's old Irish League buddies, as was Paul and Apollos Revere.

On Christmas Day, Jacky and Tom were home alone, and the subject of their future was the discussion.

"King George and Parliament are not going to sit idly by and not punish all of Massachusetts for the tea party," Tom spoke. "It will be something terrible, not the simple occupation by a few soldiers like I was part of back in '68."

"When do we leave?" Jacky said, without emotion of any kind. "I've no reason to stay in this horrible excuse of a town. I have no family here, just two poor excuses of sisters I wish to erase totally from me memory!"

"Are you certain, Jacky?" Tom quizzed his partner.

"I've never been more certain o' anything in me life," Jacky said. "I miss the peace an' solitude of Assonet Bay an', as I said once before, whether thou goest ... "

Tom smiled, hugged him, and gave him a kiss. He left the parlor, but soon returned. He laid out a map he had purchased from a Boston bookseller. He pointed to a spot just west of Fort Pitt in far western Pennsylvania, the very edge of civilization.

"Here is where I would like to eventually build a permanent home for us," Tom said.

The plan Tom put forth was to sell any thing they did not absolutely need for the trip into the frontier, along with any of Annie's remaining possessions. Hannah had taken some of Annie's china as mementos. Caroline wanted nothing. Jacky and Tom would take any quilts and blankets, a bed and mattress, and some pots and pans from the hearth, as well as a few other small pieces of furniture and items they might have use for on the frontier ... whatever fit in the wagon.

"Yesterday at the cemetery," Jacky said, "Mr. Borden made a generous offer of sixty pounds sterling to buy the house. I'll go see him for it tomorrow."

They decided to fit the wagon with a canvas top, nailed to wooden trusses forming a roof to keep their load dry, and give them a warmer and drier place to sleep on their journey. They would load the wagon with salt barrels around the sides, with chests of clothing in front, and set up the bed and mattresses in the center of the wagon. Tom felt the preparations would take three weeks, maybe a full month, and that they could be easily ready to leave Boston as early as the middle of January.

"The sooner the better," Jacky said.

"The sooner the better, indeed," Tom added. "If the British see I am here, I fear they will impress me back into the army, like those rats impress colonials into the navy. I am an American now, and owe no allegiance to any king or any parliament."

"But should we plan our trip during the snows?" Jacky asked, "or winter here, then go?"

"The ground's now frozen," Tom answered, "and travel will be better and not as slow as when the March rains mire up the primitive roads ahead of us." We can hunt and trap along the way, and sell our catch in New York and Philadelphia. The hunting should be good."

Jacky agreed and was anxious to set out.

They left January 20th heading toward the wilderness. They arrived at the small frontier settlement surrounding old Fort Pitt on March first. Jacky smiled, for the first time in months, not being plagued with sadness and thoughts of a dying mother.

Independence ... or the Frontier?

In Williamsburg, Lord Dunmore was pleased that the Boston Tea Party, as it was being called, was Hutchinson's mess to deal with and not his own. He had seen an amicable relationship with the Virginians, for the most part, and save for a handful of radical patriots, the general tenor of attitudes in the colony seemed unlikely to support an all-out rebellion. Soon after the news of the tea party arrived in Williamsburg, Dunmore met with his two most-trusted civilian advisors, John Connolly and Andrdew Lewis.

"It will please me to no end to have this incident of unrest isolated to New England," Dunmore spoke. "Regardless of Thomas Jefferson and his damned committee of correspondence, I feel we shall not see rebellion here."

"I do feel you read the events correctly," spoke Lewis. "The landed gentry of Virginia, with few exceptions, stays loyal to the king. They want no such breaking away from the greatest nation on the globe. It is simply the upstarts, the Jeffersons and the Henrys, who fan the flames of rebellion.

"Hutchinson may have opened the floodgates of rebellion when he uttered the word 'independence' opening his legislature. Is he mad?" Lewis asked.

"Hutchinson is such a fool," raved Dunmore. "Until he drew that line in the sand between the authority of the king and independence ... total independence, he said ... that word had not been used at all in the public discourse of these times ... spoken or written. Now it is everywhere!"

"Well we can hope, as the king and Lord North arrive at the appropriate punishments for Boston," spoke Dunmore, "those Virginians who do wish to remain Englishmen will begin speaking up, lest the same penalties to be assessed in Massachusetts be assessed here as well."

"There is one way we in Virginia might change the subject away from the tea party and independence," John Connolly interjected into the conversation.

"If there is such a way to do that," Dunmore seemed intrigued, "please do not keep it from me."

"I have brought a friend with me today, Simon Kenton, a frontiersman from the Kentuck," said Connolly. "He's waiting in the anteroom. He arrived last evening. I saw him at Raleigh Tavern, and I think you'd be interested in what he has to say."

"Show him in at once," ordered Dunmore.

Connolly went to the door and Kenton walked in, dressed in a suit of buckskin clothing, a coonskin cap on his head, and a rifle in his arms.

"Connolly made the introduction. "Governor Lord Dunmore, may I present Simon Kenton of the buffalo trace in Kentucky, on the Ohio River."

"Mister Kenton," Dunmore spoke, "Mister Connolly thinks I might be interested in what you have to say."

Kenton searched for the best words, then started. "As you know, Lord Dunmore, the king issued an edict after the French war, prohibiting settlement on the western side of the mountains," spoke the frontiersman. "Many in Virginia and Pennsylvania have in the past few years ignored the edict in search of prime homesteads in the west."

"Yes, yes," Dunmore spoke, somewhat put off by Kenton's words. "Thousands have snubbed their collective noses at our good and wise king, we know, we know."

"Well governor," Kenton went on, "these men and their families have heard the stories of land for the taking," Kenton continued. "With the French ceding claims, and the British government taking control, they have headed west to settle the frontier lands, claimed by charter in the colonies. Virginia holds the land of Kentucky where there are several settlements already, and the Ohio country is on many minds."

"They are law breakers, simply put," said Dunmore, dismissing whatever it was the frontiersman wanted to express. "They are as much the criminals as the so-called Mohawks of Boston are."

"Many act because they feel pinned-in along the seaboard," Kenton argued on. "They want to migrate west. They want to be removed from all this talk of rebellion in the east, and want to seek peaceful lives in freedom away from it all. But now, the tribes are feeling threatened. They burn the homesteads and massacre the settlers for their scalps. Just like before the war with the French, they spare no soul, not women, not babies."

"These are their lands, their hunting grounds," Dunmore argued. "Now they hunt the criminal colonials who reject the edict of the king. How, Mister Kenton, can this be any solution to our present concerns?" asked Dunmore condescendingly.

"Kenton speaks a truth," inserted Connolly. "The idea of safe and free settlement of the vast western frontier lands is, I dare say, a more popular idea to near every Virginian, than talk of independence. While the idea of independence is gaining some support, and somewhat rapidly I might add, the idea of western land settlement is by far more dreamed of among the populous.

"My lord," Connolly went on, "you could turn the discussion totally away from independence, by proving our British government would do all things necessary to end the threat of the savages on the frontier, and in doing so, open those western lands to safe and free white settlement."

"One day soon, those lands will need to be cleared and populated with British Americans," added Kenton. "While I do not know how I truly feel about the idea of American independence from England,

I do know what they feel, because I share those feelings. I feel free and independent, when I am on the frontier lands."

Dunmore thought and thought some more. Finally he said, with a pensive smile, "We shall speak of this more fully in the days to come."

Lord Dunmore started to see the plan Connolly and Simon Kenton had laid out to him. The governor saw a way to divert the attentions of Virginians away from treasonous thoughts of independence, and toward more personal thoughts of new homes on the beckoning frontier.

"If these affairs in Massachusetts turn to rebellion, as it is feared," Dunmore spoke to Connolly, Lewis and Kenton two days later, "and if the attentions of the Virginians are turned to the west, Virginia will not be so readily inclined to the patriotic cause. With Virginia, the largest and most important colony not taking part, the coming rebellion can be contained in Boston and it shall be short-lived."

"I have traveled amongst the tribes there, in Kentucky, and north of the Ohio River," said Kenton. "Many of the tribal leaders are reasonable men and can be dealt with. The Mingo and the Delaware are the most peaceful of the tribes. The Mingo chief, called Logan, has given me lodgings in his very own cabin many times. He is respected among the other leaders of the other tribes. Logan is convinced it will better for their people to welcome the white settlers, and live peacefully as neighbors.

"The Shawnee and the Miami tribes are the ones who will be the problem," Kenton continued. "Cornstalk, their main chief, has a hatred for the whites. He will be convinced only in battle."

"Then battle it shall be," said Dunmore. "In this war we can select who we will battle. If the battle takes us to the savages on the frontier, and brings an end to the Indian threat to white settlement, we just might turn the attention away from independence."

"Connolly, I want you and Lewis to prepare a plan for our actions against the savages, ready to execute by May," Dunmore spoke. Turning to Simon Kenton he asked, "and Mister Kenton, will you be returning to the Ohio country?"

"Yes, I hope to leave at daybreak," Kenton answered.

"Will you return to Williamsburg in the spring, and report the attitude of the tribal leaders to me before we commence our plan?"

"I can, if it will lead to the opening of the west," Kenton said.

"You can be assured that is our intention."

The Closing of Boston

Things were tense in Boston as the year 1774 opened.

In London, the East India Company wanted compensation for the tea thrown into Boston Harbor by, what Governor Hutchison had called "an act of a lawless mob." Opinions through the streets of London were heavily against the colonials in all of America.

Lord North, his secretary of state Lord Dartmouth, and his colonial secretary Lord Hillsborough, were summoned to St. James Palace for an audience with King George III.

"How shall these colonials be dealt with?" the king asked, showing his agitation and impatience. "This kingdom cannot abide by such open acts of treason against the crown. I want that Hancock man and that Samuel Adams arrested under the Treason Act! I will send our army to every rebel colony!"

"Your majesty," Lord North spoke, "the opinion of your government, sir, is to bring harsh punishment to the colony of Massachusetts, and to the colony of Massachusetts alone."

The king listened without expression.

"I beg Lord Hillsborough be heard on the matter," North spoke. The king nodded.

"There is not cause to penalize twelve other colonies, when the actions were the actions of Boston and of Boston alone," stated the colonial secretary. "Now is the time to replace your majesty's royal governor in Massachusetts. Your royal governor could have averted many of the tempers in Boston with a more reasoned approach. Lord Dartmouth has an opinion to add."

The king looked at Dartmouth and nodded.

"Your majesty, I have taken the liberty to approach General Gage, your commander-in-Chief of the army in North America. He has agreed to make himself available, by May, to take the reigns of your royal government in Massachusetts himself, in time to oversee the punishment deemed necessary by your majesty."

"And what is that punishment I shall deem necessary?" the king asked.

"If I may, your majesty," spoke the prime minister, "the colonials of Massachusetts are to be dealt with and dealt with severely. The port of Boston shall be closed, and shall remain closed until the private property of the East India Company, the tea thrown into the harbor, shall be paid for and paid for in full.

"Self-rule, as chartered in 1691, has been abused by the colonials, so it shall be revoked in that colony.

"No customs officer or government official, civil or military, charged with murder, shall be adjudicated anywhere, excepting for here in London.

"A military force, adequate to enforce the peace in the streets, shall be dispatched there, and quartered in the cities and towns of the colony at the sole expense of the colonials.

"These actions your government is ready and able to take, shall be a true warning to the other colonies," North added, "and to also show our benevolence, as it were, we shall extend, under law, a civil government of self-rule to the colonies in what was once French Canada. Doing such shall show to the southern colonies that the same self-rule can eventually be theirs ... if they accept the authority of Parliament and your majesty the king."

"Let it be done," assented the king.

"Welcome Strangers!"

"Welcome strangers," said the lanky man in his forties at the trading post at Fort Pitt. "Where you a comin' from?" Fort Pitt was the old French Fort Duquesne, built right between where the Allegheny and Monongahela Rivers formed the Ohio River.

"Boston," spoke Tom, as Jacky started looking over the provisions in the post they might need building their cabin. "My name's Tom Macneal and this is my brother Jacky."

"Nate Nevers, that's my name, an' I'm the owner o' this here tradin' post," the older man said, shaking Tom's hand.

"Boston, ya say. Well there's been a lot goin' on, from what I read in the papers from Philadelphia. Where ya headin'?" Nevers asked.

"Into the Beaver Valley, north of here," said Tom.

"Beautiful land up there," Nevers said. "You fellers hunters and trappers?"

"If there's plenty to hunt and trap," Tom added.

"Oh that there is," Nevers chuckled. "I pay 'tween four shillin's an' a pound fer pelts, dependin' on what it is o' course. Or I'll barter o' course."

"Sounds fair to me," Tom shook his hand. "I have a load of beaver, rabbit, deer, and fox pelts in the wagon now."

"Ya don't say. Let me see 'em," Nevers said. They went out and Nevers bought all the pelts Tom showed him.

"That gives you twenty-two pounds. I can pay ya cash or run ya a credit," Nevers said.

"That is certainly a fair price, and credit will be fine," Tom said. "Just write it down. Could we camp here for a day or two, as we go off and explore the Beaver Valley?"

"Any wheres ya like," said their new friend.

On March 5th, they left the fort and journeyed four or five hours to the northwest, following banks of the Ohio River.

"Tis the most beautiful land I ever seen," said Jacky, as they drove their wagon along the western and southern shoreline of the great river. "Tis all ya imagined and said it'd be, Tom."

"It is indeed, and more so," Tom replied, with a large smile spreading across his face. "It is beautiful, and the forests are full with game, and the river is full with fish."

They stopped at a clearing near the river, as the Ohio turned west. There they saw a forested bluff, rolling down steeply from the summit, then more gently to water's edge. They selected the site for their camp, and began gathering up wood and rocks for a fire ring. They had arrived and were very happy with what they had found.

The First Day of June, 1774

By late May, Hutchinson was on a ship sailing for England and General Gage was the new royal governor of Massachusetts. Gage immediately announced the closing of the port of Boston to begin on Friday the first day of June.

In Virginia, Lord Dunmore announced his plan to retaliate against the savage tribes of the frontier for their massacres and scalpings of Virginia settlers who had crossed the mountains to plant peaceful homesteads in the west. In May, Dunmore ordered Connolly to lead an expedition from Williamsburg, and capture Fort Pitt from the Pennsylvanians. Connolly was ordered to rename it Fort Dunmore.

Paul Revere, whose many functions for the patriot cause included being a rider used by the Massachusetts Committee of Correspondence, immediately rode to New York with Gage's edict closing the port of Boston. From New York another rider rode with the news to Williamsburg, and one from Williamsburg rode south to New Bern in North Carolina, Charles Town in South Carolina, and on to Savannah in Georgia. Within four days, all thirteen colonies were aware that the important port of Boston would be closed on the first day of June, and martial law would be in effect in the city of Boston.

On Thursday, May 25th, a rider sped into town, up Duke of Gloucester Street to the Capitol, dismounted and ran into the building. He asked for Thomas Jefferson, and was directed to a small room off the main chamber where Jefferson and Calvert McGowan were discussing a resolution.

The rider gave the pouch to Jefferson. Jefferson read it and tossed it to McGowan.

"General Gage has closed the po't of Boston!" said Jefferson.

"Now," McGowan said, "they have acted."

"And all that needs to be done," Jefferson added, "is to pwepa'e fo' wa' and independence."

Several of Jefferson's compatriots from the house met that night at Raleigh Tavern. Peter and Stockard were there, as the men they so admired discussed the news from the post rider.

"This calls fo' swift and decisive action, gentlemen," Jefferson spoke.

"I say, yes, a swift response," answered Washington, "but carefully thought, with words carefully chosen."

"I suggest we pass a resolution tomorrow," Washington offered. "Let us be quick to express our disgust. I suggest we set aside the day the port is to be closed as a day of prayer and fasting. But let us not create a severing of our ties with Dunmore."

"Dunmore be damned!" shouted Patrick Henry. "Let us act! Let us act now! A petition to Dunmore is called for demanding the port remain open to commerce! If the port in Boston is closed, how long before our ports be closed as well? How long before we in Virginia starve at the hands of Parliament?"

"We can ill afford to sever ties with Dunmore," stated Benjamin Harrison, on a rational note. "More is at risk than the closing of the port of Boston. It is indeed a dastardly act and must be addressed, but addressed by men of reason, not by men with emotions raging."

"The colonel and Hawison have just weasoning," inserted the lispy voice of Jefferson. "We awe near weady to call fo' a congwess to meet as a confedewated unit of thi'teen colonies. But thewe needs be yet some time."

"I agree with the colonel's rationale," spoke McGowan. "We must not shoo away the moderates.

Speaker Randolph then spoke, after having sat silently listening.

"A resolution, as Washington has suggested, a day of fasting, humiliation and prayer, on June first, is in my mind the proper course of action, with no other message or action proposed, at the time. Let ours be a civil and reasonable response."

Peter was angry as he and Stockard walked back to the Wren.

"Why not fight? Why not commence this war now?" Peter asked.

"Washington's thoughts are well placed," Stockard said. "Dunmore is well-liked, but if the actions of the radicals rule, those now being moderate to the cause for independence shall isolate themselves more so. There will be riots and Dunmore will be forced to put down their revolt. As even Jefferson said, we are not ready at this very moment to rebel, but that time is coming, and quickly so. Biding our time is prudent. If Dunmore is fool enough to react negatively to a simple resolution of peace, the fight may well be on."

Williamsburg had planned a celebration, a ball, hosted by the House of Burgesses in honor of the beloved Lady Charlotte Dunmore, now three months pregnant with a fourth child. The children living in the Governor's Palace had become a sheer delight to the colonials of Williamsburg. The young governor's lady was endeared to them for her pleasing and friendly personality. Lord and Lady Dunmore were loved and respected by the citizens of Williamsburg and throughout the Virginia colony.

The ball was two days away on the 27th, and it would go forward. The Judge and Adella had already arrived in the city with little Angelica. They rented rooms at the comfortable inn on Duke of Gloucester Street. They had another reason for traveling to Williamsburg. Classes at William and Mary were ending, and Zack and Peter would be coming home to Hanover County for the summer. Also, the book of Zachary's sketches was to be available for the first time on June first.

Zack and Rodie Murray were now best of friends. Zack spent many afternoons and evenings at the palace, as he helped Rodie with the prose for his sketches in his nature book. The published edition of The Nature of Virginia would be on the shelves at Jonas Phillips' bookshop on June 1st.

On the morning of May 26th, the House met and adopted the resolution honoring the colony of Massachusetts with a day of fasting, humiliation and prayer. The House sent the resolution immediately to Lord Dunmore at the palace. His secretary, Alexander Murray, read it aloud to his uncle the royal governor.

Dunmore said little. He sat at his desk for Alexander to write his response.

"Mr. President Randolph and gentlemen of the House,

"Having read your resolution, proposing to mark Friday the first day of June, as a day of fasting, humiliation and prayer as being an appropriate response from your body to news you have received of the closing of the port of Boston, I demand you rescind this resolution immediately, it being viewed as incendiary and treasonous.

"If you fail to obey my official order, the House of Burgesses of the colony of Virginia shall immediately and forthwith be dissolved and forbidden to conduct any further business."

Alexander wrote the response in his best hand, gave the document to his uncle for his signature, then melted wax for the official seal and handed it to the courier to deliver it to the Capitol.

The motion to rescind the original resolution failed, and the House was dissolved on the eve of the of Lady Charlotte's Ball.

While Lord Dunmore's reaction to the resolution seemed extreme, most members of the House welcomed it. Feelings were still positive for Dunmore, and especially for his lady and children. The ball went on as planned, even with the hosts being the members of the dissolved House of Burgesses.

When Friday, June first arrived, Zack woke up early. That was the day he would see, for the first time, his sketches in print. He and Peter, along with Stockard Samuels, Justin Sloan and Rodie Murray, walked down Duke of Gloucester Street to Jonas Phillips' bookshop. The books were to have arrived during the early morning hours. Their plans were to pick up copies of the book *The Nature of Virginia*, and head to the inn where the Judge, Adella and little Angelica were staying.

As they walked, they heard the muffled beating of drums in the distance. As they passed the Palace Green where Bruton Parish Church stood, they saw a parade marching toward them down Duke of Gloucester Street. The parade of the members of the dissolved House of Burgesses was led by the bearer of the symbolic mace, followed by Speaker Randolph and the entire body of the House, all dressed in their waistcoats and knee breeches with black armbands around each delegate's upper arm. The governor's banned day of fasting, humiliation and prayer in support of the citizens of Boston was being observed, regardless of the feelings at the Governor's Palace, or in London for that matter. The citizens of Williamsburg turned out to observe and show their support. The street was crowded.

The students paused and watched as the delegates passed by. There was George Washington in his freshly-powdered wig, marching between two bare-headed, red-haired members, Thomas Jefferson and Patrick Henry. Eight boys from the town, strapped with drums, beat the muffled cadence, marching behind.

Stockard remarked, "It appears the governor's words are not being abided."

Stockard had forgotten he was standing beside the nephew of the governor.

Rodie surprisingly shouted respectfully toward the marching burgesses, "Long live the House! Long live Virginia!" A cheer from the crowds rose up.

Stockard looked at Rodie, somewhat in dismay, without speaking more.

"Oh, I love my uncle dearly," Rodie turned toward Stockard and explained, "as much as a nephew might love an uncle, but I fear I love Virginia just a bit more."

Stockard gave him a smile, a pat on the back and a huge hug.

After the parade, the students continued their walk to the bookshop.

Surprisingly, the Judge and Adella were already on the sidewalk, glaring into the display window beside the bookshop door. They were just too anxious to see the new book to wait for the boys to come to the inn.

The display window already was filled with stacks of the new book, and a half-dozen books opened to various drawings of the crane in the Potomac, woodchucks, bluegill fish and others.

"Look, Zack," Rodie pointed to the window, "Jonas could not wait for me to decorate his window! He has done a right fine job of it."

There they were, beautifully bound copies of the book, bound in a deep forest green with gold leaf lettering, _The Nature of Virginia_.

Inside the shop, Jonas greeted them energetically.

"I told you, Mr. Winston," Jonas spoke to Zack as he exuberantly shook the student's hand grasped inside both of his. "Your work was well-worth publication!" Jonas led him to a box with a dozen of the books waiting for Zack. He picked one up and looked at the bound cover:

The Nature of Virginia
Sketches by Zachary Winston
Narrative by Roderic Murray

Zack immediately handed a volume to each of his friends, and one each to the judge and Adella. They all thumbed through the pages and commented on the sketches.

"They are so lifelike," came Adella's comment.

"I think my favorite is the crane in the Potomac River," said Peter.

"Oh no," added Justin, "the best by far is the raccoon."

"I like the squirrel eating the hickory nut," said Stockard.

"I have no favorite," said the judge judiciously, "I rather enjoy them all."

"I feel everyone in Williamsburg will agree with the judge," spoke the bookseller. "They are already on the shelves and shall be featured prominently in my window for weeks."

Zack smiled with a great deal of self-satisfaction, and turned to Rodie.

"And the prose on each page is just right, thank you Rodie," he smiled at the governor's nephew and his new friend.

"Thank you, Zack, for such beautiful subjects to describe in words." He smiled at his new friend.

On their way back to the Wren, the boys walked to where the crowd had gathered at the church. They found space near a window to look in and hear the goings on of the dissolved House.

The fat Speaker Randolph had called the rump session to order, after prayers for the poor colonials of Boston had been lifted heavenward.

Randolph recognized the member, Calvert McGowan, who offered a resolution calling for the assembling of the Continental Congress, made up of delegates from each of the thirteen colonies, to meet in Philadelphia, a location central to all the colonies. The resolution set the date to convene as Wednesday, September fifth, just three months away.

George Washington rose to second the McGowan Resolution.

With little debate, the members voted their assent to the passage, and ordered Jefferson's committee of correspondence to send riders with the printed resolution to the other twelve colonies.

Patrick Henry rose to offer a second resolution condemning the closing of the port of Boston.

"These latest acts of Parliament are coercive to the constitutional rights of the British citizens of these colonies.

"All shipping in or out of the port is now suspended and must be resumed immediately," Henry spoke to polite nods and calls of "here, here" throughout the pews of the parish church.

"General Thomas Gage, now as the king's royal governor there, has brought harsh and severe martial law to the colony, and that coercion of colonial rights must end.

"The Massachusetts Government Act, if allowed to survive, that shall end eighty-three years of colonial self-rule, as expressly laid out in the colony's charter of 1691, and no elected representation whatsoever shall be recognized for that colony. It must be repealed at once!

"Soldiers of the king, the King's Regulars, are quartered in whatever private hearth, home and residence of the citizens of Boston they so deem necessary, and at the expense of those private citizens. This untenable occupation must end forthwith!

"In Massachusetts, customs and government officials have been given the right to commit murder, and not fear justice upon our shores nor in our courts. Adjudicating such a crime must be dealt with in the colony, not as Parliament now insists it be, in London!"

George Mason of Alexandria seconded Patrick Henry's resolution to petition the king to repeal each of Parliament's Coercive Acts.

Calvert McGowan rose to offer a third resolution calling for a Virginia Convention to be held in Williamsburg, during the first week of August, for the purpose of electing delegates to the Continental Congress in Philadelphia.

Jefferson rose to submit to the burgesses for consideration his writings entitled *"A Summary View of the Rights of British America."*

Before adjourning the rump session, Speaker Randolph offered to have the delegates continue to meet, as need be, in the Apollo Ballroom of Raleigh Tavern, until the governor would eventually lift the dissolution.

On the Banks of the Ohio

"We couldn't 'ave found a more beautiful spot on earth for our homestead," Jacky said to Tom, as he took another bite from the roasted duck, which had a few hours earlier been fishing near water's edge. "We 'ave a great new home here."

"Yes," Tom answered, "and our neighbors at Pittsborough around the trading post seem to be friendly enough."

"They are friendly folks, 'specially that Nate Nevers," replied Jacky.

By the first of May the two had built a large cabin, raised off the ground eight feet, with the back wall laid up with stone from the river, and built back into the steep slope of the hill. Across the front of the forty-foot long and twenty-foot wide cabin was a ten-foot wide roofed over verandah, where Tom and Jacky ate their meals when the weather was warm enough.

Beneath the verandah, a cellar for storing cured meats, pelts, salt barrels and other provisions to store, ran under the entire cabin. Outside the cellar door, all the area under the verandah was open for other storage, with the ceiling being the verandah floor. The verandah faced the Ohio River bank, about fifty yards down the gentle slope.

The inside of the cabin had two bedrooms, on either side of the front door. The one on the northeast corner was a room for any overnight guests. It was smaller than the one on the northwest corner where Tom and Jacky built their bedroom. That was where Annie Macneal's bed and chest of drawers now sat.

The main room was a big open area, facing the stone back wall and huge hearth. It was very comfortable for the two men.

By the first day of June they had built a shed barn and a smokehouse. A fenced in an area by the barn was for the horse and two milk cows they had bartered for from Nate Nevers. They built a small chicken coop for the two-dozen hens and one rooster they got bartering with some of the settlers at Pittsborough. They planted a vegetable garden and had corn, potatoes, beans, carrots, onions and other vegetables already sprouting.

Before they had left Boston, they loaded as much of Annie's furniture as they could. There was a table and four chairs, a smaller table, two upholstered armchairs, a small settee, a four-drawer chest of drawers, a mirror, and a large woolen hooped rug.

"I've an idea," Tom spoke, as they sat on the verandah, enjoying the sun setting over the Ohio Country to the west. "I've been thinking about it since we left Philadelphia," Tom explained. "Since your mama is so much responsible for us making this journey to the very edge of civilization, and for the comfort and warmth we share atop her mattress and beneath her warm blankets and quilts, not to mention all the furnishings in our home, why should we not honor her memory and name this place after her?"

"Mama'd like that," Jacky smiled at his partner. "I'd like that too."

"Then it is settled," said Tom. "Welcome to…" he thought for a moment or two, "welcome to Annie's Port."

"Annie's Port," Jacky thought for a moment and smiled broadly. "I like it. Annie's Port it shall be!"

The Ohio River mystified Tom. It seemed to sing a mystic siren's song to him. Tom had dreams of exploring the forbidden Ohio Country. King George III recognized the land on the western and northern shore of that great river as tribal lands of the North American Indians, and any Englishman was forbidden to go there, let alone settle there. There were tales of some heroic frontiersmen who had gone there, men like Daniel Boone and Simon Kenton, and they told of endless supplies of game and rich, fertile farmlands.

"I really want to explore that river," said Tom, as he and Jacky sipped their whiskey on the verandah under the dark night sky, filled with shimmering white stars. "I want to see the lands forbidden to us."

"There are some settlements there a'ready," Jacky said. "I read about 'em in them newspapers from Philadelphia."

"Yes, in the western Virginia lands south of the Ohio," Tom said, "the land they call Kentucky. But it is still far too dangerous to settle north of the river in the Ohio Country. I still think we could journey a day or two down the river, and take a look for ourselves. I know it cannot be long before the whole of the Ohio Country is open to us. I want to be ready."

"Remember that flatboat we seen on the Susquehanna, as we were crossin' Pennsylvania?" Jacky asked. Tom nodded. "Why not build our own flatboat?"

"I was thinking more of a smaller vessel we could paddle," Tom interjected.

"But a flatboat, like the ones we seen, have plenty o' room for storin' all the hides an' furs an' other bounty we might need ta carry back here with us. 'Tween you an' me, we know how ta build near anything. We can have a flatboat an' a smaller one too, if we want, in the case we come across a smaller stream to continue our explorations inland."

Within three weeks they were tying down a small canoe they had built, onto the deck of their new flatboat, named the Annie Macneal, packing some needed supplies for cooking and hunting, and pushing off the shore, beginning their voyage downstream on the mighty Ohio River.

Ho-Tawa

Tom and Jacky left Annie's Port on June 21st and two days later, went ashore where a rather large river emptied into the Ohio from the north. They slept aboard the flatboat in the small cabin built in the center of the fifteen-foot long and twelve-foot wide boat. The next morning, they found a cove on the south shore where they could hide the flatboat from possible discovery by the Indians they had heard tell of. They loaded some supplies in the canoe, covered them with canvas, and paddled across the river to the mouth of the smaller tributary on the north shore.

They paddled up the smaller river for about six or eight miles, where they came across a sandy beaching area with a broad and flat grassy clearing. They went ashore, pulling the canoe safe enough onto the shore so it would not drift away and leave them stranded.

They pitched the small tent Tom had made out of canvas and made a fire ring. Then they headed into the woods to explore. They saw the area was filled with game, more even than roamed in the woods around Annie's Port. They refrained from using their muskets for fear of savages hearing the gunfire. They decided to return to the camp and fish for their dinner that evening.

"This land is even more plentiful than I had ever imagined," said Tom, happy so far with their journey. "Why don't we continue upstream for a day or two, and when he head back, stop here again and do some hunting for Nate Nevers?"

"Maybe we can fin' some buffalo upstream," Jacky added ... "maybe some Indians too."

They went to sleep.

The June morning wasn't cool and crisp, it was cold and damp from a mild overnight sprinkle of rain that had fallen. There was no warmth from the fire ring when Jacky rose first, Tom still lying sound asleep. The sun was just starting to shed a little light on the dark morning. Jacky slipped into a pair of pants and, still shirtless, snuck out the tent flap, sealing it tight behind him so as not to allow too much of what little warmth remained inside to escape as Tom slept.

Jacky picked up a stick near the fire ring and squatted at the once raging fire. Now, only a few bright orange-colored embers were still aglow, with more embers glowing hidden beneath a covering of dark gray ash. At least, Jacky thought, there were still remnants of heat and fire.

Jacky was surprised that the rain, even as light as it seemed to have been, had not doused it totally. He stirred the remaining embers and laid two logs on top to try to catch the damp bark and kindle the logs. He stacked two more on top the first two, running the opposite direction to create a draft, then threw on some dried leaves and weeds from the tender bag. They first smoldered and smoked, but soon the flames started again as the logs caught fire in a blaze. Jacky sat with the stick in his hand, poking the logs, and added a couple more once the fire had convinced him it would continue and be warm for when Tom woke.

He thought about the beautiful land Tom had led them to. They had, as far as Jacky was concerned, found the most beautiful spot on earth possible to build their homestead at Annie's Port, alongside the winding Ohio River, as it wound through the floor of the Beaver Valley.

This campsite here was also a beautiful spot, like so many other lands they had seen on their journey down the Ohio. He sat on a log, stirring the fire and smiling, thinking how fortunate he was to have befriended that red-coated bastard of a whore, Tom Preston, er, he meant to think 'Tom Macneal," since he had never spoken the name 'Tom Preston' aloud since the creation of his brother 'Tom Macneal."

He felt so happy with Tom, and knew he and Tom would be together forever. Even with society in the colonies expecting a man to take a wife and have children, Jacky knew his world would always center around Tom, another man. They could do just that here on the frontier, away from the norms of proper society in Boston, New York or Philadelphia, even in the smaller settlements like Fall River and Lexington back east.

He stirred the fire once more, then decided to return to his bed inside the tent and beside the man he had grown so accustomed to. He stood and walked toward the water to take a good pee before returning to his bed. There was some time before the sun would be well up, and the darkness of the night would be totally gone. After finishing the task at hand by the riverside, he turned to walk back toward the small tent.

As he turned, he was suddenly stopped in his tracks and speechless.

Standing about six feet, directly in his path, was a young Indian boy. The boy seemed to be in his teens, he thought. The stranger was dressed in buckskin pants and was wrapped in a warm-looking blanket. Moccasins were on his feet and his dark hair fell across his shoulders. He did not have a fierce or threatening look about him, in fact his blue eyes seemed almost vulnerable. But, since Jacky had never seen an Indian before, he still felt fear.

The two stood there, face-to-face, through long moments in silence. Jacky knew he could not understand any words the boy might utter, and thought it worthless to try to speak himself, though he wanted desperately to let the Indian know he and Tom meant him no harm. Even though he knew all this, he surprisingly heard his own voice come forth.

"How long you been standin' there?"

That was stupid, thought Jacky.

"Since after you and the other man went into your lodge," the Indian boy spoke perfect English.

"You speak English?" Jacky asked, surprised at what he had just heard.

"I was born English," the Indian boy spoke. "I have been Mingo for four years now."

Jacky extended his hand, "My name's Jacky Macneal."

The Indian boy shook his hand and spoke, "Jacky Macneal, a good name. My Christian name is Davy Danielson. My Mingo name is Ho-Tawa, White Feet."

"Come," Jacky said, "sit with me by my fire."

The two walked and sat on two logs near the fire, now emitting a nice warmth and a good crackle.

"How did you come to be a Mingo?" Jacky asked.

"I was born sixteen years ago in Cumberland in the colony of Maryland," Ho-Tawa explained. "When I was ten, my father moved us west to a tract of farmland along the Monongahela River, a few days journey south of Fort Pitt, in the land the king had forbidden whites to settle.

"When I was twelve, my father let me go with him and two other men who lived beside us in our settlement at what was called Smithtown. We went off on a hunting trip.

"On our second day away from our settlement, the Shawnees came. Papa and the other men were killed and their scalps taken. I was taken captive."

"You seen your father an' the others killed before yer eyes? ... an' scalped? ... You had to 've been scare't ta death!" Jacky said.

"I was certain I would be killed when the five braves took me to their camp on the Scioto," Ho-Tawa answered.

"Why were you spared?" Jacky asked.

"The chief, Cornstalk, feared the whites would come for me and there would be a useless war. He traded me to the Mingo Chief Logan for two horses.

"Logan is a great and gentle man, and the Mingos are not a tribe of warriors. They know the whites are going to come, and the Mingos will welcome them and live in peace with them," Ho-Tawa said.

"You will see," the Indian boy went on. "I will take you to Logan."

"Don't know 'bout that," Jacky said. "We just came into this land o' yours to explore. It's a beautiful place. We have a cabin on the Ohio River in the Beaver Valley, north of Fort Pitt."

"I saw you and your friend float down the Ohio on your big boat," said Ho-Tawa. "I saw you stay on the boat at night, and watched you hide your big boat in the cove. You hid it well. I saw you cross the Ohio in your canoe the next morning, and saw you paddle up the Muskingum."

"The Muskingum?" Jacky questioned.

"That is the Indian name for this river," Ho-Tawa said, "Mus-king-um."

"So you followed us up the Mus-king-um?" Jacky asked.

"Yes, and through the woods where you did not use your muskets to shoot the deer there. I watched you as you set your camp and fished and cooked your fish and ate. I watched from the shadows as you talked and then went inside your lodge to fall asleep.

"I spread my blanket near your fire, and kept it going through the night," the boy said. "The rains came, but I kept your fire going."

As the two talked, Ho-Tawa suggested he take them to Chief Logan of the Mingo tribe.

"Logan will welcome you as he has welcomed many whites before," said the Indian boy. "If you plan to visit the Ohio Country again,

Logan will be your friend. He will approve of you hunting and trapping, as long as you do not waste what you kill."

Soon Tom, awakened by Jacky talking to a stranger, pulled back the flap of the tent. He came up on them as they were talking about Logan and the Mingos.

"Who is your friend here, Jacky?" Tom asked, seeming somewhat startled at the presence of a young Indian sitting and talking with his young partner.

"Tom, this is Ho-Tawa, his Christian name bein' Davy Danielson," Jacky introduced Tom to Ho-Tawa.

"Ho-Tawa, this is my brother, Tom Macneal," Jacky said.

"I am pleased to meet you Tom Macneal," Ho-Tawa extended his hand and their introduction was sealed with the handshake of friendship.

As the three sat there around the fire, daylight broke with the beckoning of a warm early summer day, and the promise of bright sunshine and white fluffy clouds floating lazily on a powder blue sky. Tom could not take his eyes off the peaceful, glassy surface of the Muskingum River. The river was calm and still at their camp, like a mirror. It reflected the branches of the trees and even the dark pink, almost red blossoms of the small trees dotting the shoreline. This was indeed paradise.

"Yes," Tom said as the three talked over a breakfast of eggs and jowl bacon Jacky had made, "indeed I want to meet your Chief Logan," he answered Ho-Tawa. "I need his friendship and long to make many trips back to this place. How far away is his village?"

"In your canoe," Ho-Tawa pointed, "we can be there by midday. Logan is just upriver perhaps five, six miles."

Tom rose and looked at Jacky, "Well, if you would like, Jacky, we can break camp here and be off to meet the noted Chief Logan."

Soon they pushed off in the canoe. The river was pristine as it wound through the miles of their journey. They saw huge turtles on the shoreline or basking in the sun atop a fallen log.

"I shall teach you to make a wonderful soup from those turtles," said Ho-Tawa to Jacky. "There shells are used for many things. I will show you."

They came across a doe deer and her fawn drinking at water's edge as they passed by. They saw beavers working to build a dam on a smaller tributary as they paddled by. The river wound but generally ran in a basic northwestern route. After an hour or so, the river wound in a sharp turn nearly due south. There they came ashore for a rest.

"I know this place," said Ho-Tawa. "I will show you where the sassafras roots are."

"Sassafras?" Jacky questioned, "What is sassafras?"

"To make the best tea you ever have tasted," Ho-Tawa spoke, "And there may be some mushrooms, after that rain we came through, with the sun now warm and bright. We shall see."

Ho-Tawa led Jacky and Tom on a root and mushroom hunt. The sassafras was easy. Many small bushes with their distinctive leaves were growing in the woods just a few yards from where they had beached the canoe. Ho-Tawa dug down with his knife and, using his hatchet, chopped off several roots, enough to give Jacky and Tom several good pots of the flavorful tea, but not too many as to kill the growing bushes.

Jacky was excited to learn just how to take the roots and not totally destroy the small tree where it grew. He had also seen those distinctive leaves before, especially back at Annie's Port where he knew they were plentiful, just behind the cabin on the steep hillside. The roots would probably bring a decent price at Nate Nevers' trading post too.

"I hope we can see some mushrooms," Ho-Tawa stated. "They should be up after that rain." He began walking slowly and carefully, looking down at the ground as he spoke.

Tom and Jacky started imitating the moves Ho-Tawa was making, eyes toward the earth as they took small and cautious steps.

"Look for a gray or sometimes yellowish sponge in the shape of a cone popping up from the leaves," Ho-Tawa instructed.

"Is this one?" asked Jacky, pointing to a whitish umbrella-like fungus.

"No!" said Ho-Tawa in a warning tone. "That one is poison. Never eat those."

"What about this?" asked Tom.

"Yes!" Ho-Tawa rushed to what Tom had spotted. He pulled it up gently from the soil and leaves. He held it up.

"This is a mushroom you can eat and will enjoy much!" Ho-Tawa said pleased. "This is a big one!" It was about six inches tall. "Most are much smaller, perhaps only half this size," explained their guide.

He handed the first mushroom of the hunt to Jacky to put in the pouch with the sassafras roots.

"Now, look here, all around," said Ho-Tawa. "Where there is one there are many, but hard to see."

They all looked and found, as Ho-Tawa had suggested, many.

Soon they were back in the canoe and paddling south. Ho-Tawa said just after the river turned again back to a northwest, Logan's village was just a half mile more on the west side bank.

Chief Logan was all Ho-Tawa had said. Logan made Jacky and Tom feel extremely welcomed in his village. Tom was carrying one of Annie Macneal's quilts, wrapped up in a bundle. He and Jacky had put together a few items as a gift offering for the chief, before they left camp. With humility, Logan gratefully took the gifts Tom and Jacky presented him, and made the gift-givers smile at his genuine appreciation, especially for the tin of molasses, which was extremely rare north of the Ohio. After the successful mushroom hunt, they had included the three dozen or more fungi they had picked earlier that afternoon. Ho-Tawa had said Logan considered the wild sponge mushrooms a rare delicacy and was one of Logan's favorites.

Logan had his daughter prepare them by cleaning them, dipping them in an egg yolk and milk mixture, dredging them through cornmeal, and frying them with melted lard in Logan's new gift of a cast iron skillet from Boston.

Tom and Jacky agreed to Logan's hospitality of lodging in his cabin. Logan's daughter soon served them a supper of fried mushrooms, squash soup, venison stew and Ho-Tawa's sassafras tea, as they sat with the chief and three of his sons.

"This tea is wonderful," Jacky said to Ho-Tawa. "With sassafras roots so plentiful, why've we been importin' all that tea from the British?"

"And I do say," Tom added, "the mushrooms are delectable, and everything is simply wonderful."

After supper, they sat around the fire with Logan and his sons.

"The white man comes," Logan said, as Jacky, Tom and Ho-Tawa sat beneath a huge spreading oak tree in the center of Logan's village. "He will come, and soon this land will be a land civilized by the white man.

"Logan will welcome the white man," the chief went on. "Logan's people will welcome the white man as they have welcomed you. The Mingo want to live in peace with our white brothers.

"Manitou has given this land to no one person, to no one tribe. The white man does not understand that, nor do many of the tribes here," said the aging chief. "Logan knows the white man wants peace, as do the Mingo. Other tribes see it differently. They fear the white man will not live with Indians as neighbors and friends. The white man will want land to own, enough to provide for his family. Too many tribes feel this land can only be their lands, and will not welcome the white man as a neighbor, but as an enemy. They will rise up and cause war.

"Logan knows the Mingo and the Delaware and the Shawnee can never stop the white man. Logan only wants his people to continue to live in peace, after the coming of the white man.

"Hunt upon this land, my brothers, for there is plenty," Logan said. "Tell your white brothers, Logan and the Mingo want peace and do not wish for war."

Tom and Jacky spent more than a week in Logan's village, making friends of Logan's four sons and the husbands of Logan's three daughters. They made other friends among the men of the Mingo village, that numbered just under two hundred, as best they could determine.

When the time for them to return to Annie's Port came, the evening before, after supper, Tom, Jacky and Logan talked before retiring to the feather and cornhusk mattresses in the rafters.

"Logan loves Ho-Tawa as he loves all his sons," Logan said, as something was apparently weighing upon the chief's mind.

"Ho-Tawa is a happy boy, but his happiness is clouded in uncertainty. He witnessed the young Shawnee warriors kill and take the scalps of his father and uncle. His uncertainty comes in the night in dreams of his mother, his younger brother and his small sister.

"Logan has for four years become his family, but Logan knows of his uncertainty."

The chief took his hands and placed one in Tom's hand and the other in Jacky's.

"Can Logan ask you to take Ho-Tawa when you go in the morning, take him to your home on the Ohio, and then to his family left behind at the place called Smithtown?"

The night was forever ending, as Tom and Jacky laid awake on their mattress, thinking about Logan's wish. What were they to do? What if, when they found Smithtown, if they could find it at all, the mother had left with her younger children? What if they had been massacred as Ho-Tawa's father and uncle had been massacred? What then? But then, how could they say 'no' to Logan, the generous chief who had been so hospitable and only wanted for peace?

Morning came and Tom and Jacky pushed the canoe off the shore into the waters of the Muskingum. Ho-Tawa was sitting in the canoe in front of the bounty from their days of hunting along the Muskingum. He would now be returning to the white man's civilization, such as it was, at place called Annie's Port.

Who is the Commandant?

After a few days back at Annie's Port, they made the trip to the fort. They decided to make the trip on the river in the canoe. Instead of a four-hour overland ride pulling a wagon, the canoe trip upriver took a little less than two hours.

Nate was pleased to see them, and was excited with the fresh stores of game meat and hides he needed to trade. He was fascinated with the sassafras roots. He had heard of the tea made from sassafras, but had himself, never tasted it. Jacky boiled a pan of it on the trading post hearth for Nate to sample.

"Other than this good tea, how did ya enjoy that journey into the Ohio Country?" Nate asked.

"Tis by far the most beautiful land these Irish eyes 've ever peered upon," said Jacky.

"It is everything we had expected, and much, much more," said Tom. "The game is plentiful and the vegetation unspoiled."

"An' ya met Chief Logan, did ya?" asked Nate.

"We not only met him, we did, but we shared his cabin fer a full week," answered Jacky.

225

"A finer, gentler man I dare you to find anywhere," added Tom. "That leads me to ask you Nate, have you heard tell of a settlement, south of the fort a few days' journey, called Smithtown?"

"Smithtown?" the bearded and lanky merchant repeated, scratching his chin and thinking. "On the Monongahela? Yes ... yes, I have heard tell of it. I believe it lays just this side of where Pennsylvany becomes Virginy land. Never been there, min' ya, but I do believe so."

Tom and Jacky told Nate of Ho-Tawa, captured by the fierce Shawnee four years ago, and their promise to Logan to find his family, if any remained.

"Seems like I heard tell of that massacre of some hunters from the Smithtown settlement, and the disappearance of a boy," Nate recalled. "I can't be sure. There's been so many massacres and scalpin's by them savages. I just don't know for certain any how."

"We will be wanting to travel down there," said Tom.

"Where's the boy now?" Nate asked.

"This is him right here," Jacky said, introducing the merchant to the boy. "Nate Nevers, meet Davy Danielson, otherwise known as Ho-Tawa."

"Why you don't look like you been raised by the savages, boy," Nate said, looking at the sixteen-year-old, dressed in pants and a colonial frontier shirt, with his dark hair cut in the fashion of the frontier by Jacky.

"I am he," replied Davy. "I was captured by the Shawnee whose chief, Cornstalk, traded me to Chief Logan of the Mingo for two horses."

"Well don't that just beat it all," said Nate. He turned to Tom. "Anything you might need for the journey takin' him home to his mama will be provided for you Tom."

About then, a man dressed in frontiersman's garb walked in the door of the trading post. He saw Tom, Jacky and Davy talking with Nate and said, "Who is the commandant of this fort?"

Nate went toward the man, wiping his hands on his apron and extending a hand.

"I am Nathaniel Nevers, an' I'm the proprietor of this here trading post," Nate said. "Though there ain't no real fort now these days."

"I am pleased to make your acquaintance," the stranger said as he shook Nate's hand. "I am John Connolly, agent for the royal

226

governor of Virginia, Lord Dunmore. Are you the man in charge of this outpost?"

"As much as there is a man in charge of this here outpost," Nate said.

"There is no garrison of troops here?" Connolly asked.

"Oh, there's a handful of militiamen when the need arises, but, no there is no garrison of troops here."

Connolly withdrew a parchment paper from his jacket and presented it to Nate.

"Be you whereby informed, as of this, the first day of July, in the year of our lord seventeen-hundred-seventy-four," Connolly spoke, "this outpost, formerly named Fort Pitt, shall from this date forward be known as Fort Dunmore, and by virtue of the charter of Virginia, is hereby governed by Virginia."

"What's to become of me and of my tradin' post here?" Nate asked.

"Unless you challenge the authority of Lord Dunmore and the king, nothing," stated Connolly with great authority.

"I could give a damn whether this is Pennsylvany, Maryland or Virginy," said Nate. "As long as not one nail from that barrel or one pint o' whiskey is taken from me, I don't give a damn. Hell, I'm from New York any ways."

Everyone laughed as Nate continued.

"Now your lordship, might I show you to suitable quarters?" Nate bowed comically to Connolly who laughed.

Connolly had walked back to the door and motioned for another man to enter. Nate recognized this second frontiersman.

"Simon Kenton! You old son of a polecat!"

"Hello there Nate," Kenton said. "Where should the men make camp?"

"Oh have them pitch their tents just any where they please," said Nate, looking out the door and seeing about three hundred men that would now be the garrison of Fort Dunmore.

Nate introduced Tom, Jacky and Davy to John Connolly and to his old friend Simon Kenton.

"Simon, you know, these three just returned from spending a few weeks with your old friend, Chief Logan," Nate said. Simon immediately went to them and shook their hands.

"How is my friend, Logan?" asked Kenton.

"He seems to be in good health," said Tom, "and as you might suppose, treated us with the hospitality of his cabin on the Muskingum."

"Logan is an intelligent and peace-loving man," Kenton added. "How well do you know the Ohio Country?"

"This was our first journey there," said Tom, "but Davy here was a captive of the Shawnee, traded to Logan."

"For two horses," said Jacky with a snicker.

"No, Macneal," Kenton corrected Tom, "Ho-Tawa was traded for his life, and Logan knew that well," said Kenton hugging Davy. "It has been too long since I last saw you with Logan on the Muskingum."

"Yes, it has been," said Davy, with a huge smile. "Logan asked Tom and Jacky to attempt to take me home." Kenton smiled and turned to Tom and Jacky.

"If we have the time before Lord Dunmore arrives," Kenton said, "Perhaps I can join you."

"We must talk," Kenton said, turning to Tom and Jacky. "I think you will want to join us in the campaign Lord Dunmore has planned."

"We would be pleased to welcome you to our homestead in the Beaver Valley," offered Tom. "If you desire a comfortable lodging while here, we are just a couple hours by river to the northwest."

"I know the Beaver Valley well," said Kenton. "I had my eye on that place for a settlement of my own, but I was drawn to the bluffs above the Ohio near the Blue Licks of Kentucky. The game is plentiful. There is where the buffalo are to be had."

"Will you come and stay with us?" Jacky asked.

"It sounds inviting," said Kenton. "Let me talk with Connolly, and if he feels my constant presence is no longer needed until Lord Dunmore arrives in late August. I will at least join you for supper tonight, if that invitation includes supper, that is."

"We are leaving presently and will expect you," said Tom.

It was still two hours before darkness would fill the summer sky, when Simon Kenton walked up the stone laid steps from the river's edge to the verandah of the cabin on the hillside.

As a venison roast was on the spit over the open hearth and beans, carrots and potatoes, flavored with onions and jowl bacon, were cooking in a pot. A pan of biscuits was starting to rise and a second pan of cornpone was being placed in the oven. A pot of sassafras roots were brewing.

Jacky, Tom and Davy showed Kenton around Annie's Port. They showed their guest the cellar packed with barrels of salted down meat and brine barrels of fish from the river. There where sides of deer and wild boar hogs hung to cure in the new smokehouse they'd built. They showed him the flatboat, the canoe, and the old buckboard wagon that had got them all the way from Lewis Street in Boston.

After dinner, they sat on the porch with glasses of whiskey, and Kenton laid out the plans Lord Dunmore had for eradicating the problems with the tribes in the west.

"Dunmore seems to be a driven man who takes his position very seriously," said Kenton. "I do not care what motives, hidden or otherwise, the man may have," he said pensively, "so long as the result is a western frontier open to settlement ... safe settlement, not harassed by the more savage tribes. I have faith he will succeed.

"He has dispatched a man I have no real faith in, a Col. Andrew Lewis, with about eleven hundred men to cross the Blue Ridge range in Virginia, and cross the western Virginia wilderness, following the Kanawha River to its mouth on the Ohio, a day or so beyond where you paddled up the Muskingum to Logan's Village.

"The governor himself, will lead a second army of about equal size to what's now at Fort Pitt...er...Fort Dunmore, as I guess it is now called." Everyone laughed at the vanity of the royal governor.

"When will Dunmore arrive?" asked Tom.

"If he leaves near the start of August," Kenton calculated, "he should be here by the start of September. He will wait at the fort for scouts to inform him of Lewis' position, then march south to join the two armies together at the mouth of the Kanawha.

"They plan to cross the river and engage the Shawnee somewhere near the Scioto River," Kenton went on. "After a victory over the most feared of the tribes, the Shawnee, scouts will be sent into the interior to treat with the more peaceable tribes, the tribes who tend to share Logan's philosophy. With all the tribal leaders meeting and making their marks on the treaty, the Ohio and Kentucky lands will then be safe for white settlers."

"It sounds to be a reasonable plan," said Tom. "From what we saw of the Ohio Country, we plan to lay claim to a settlement there as soon as it is safe from the Shawnee. As wonderful as this land around Annie's Port is, the beauty and bounty we saw there seems unending."

Dunmore is going to need men like the three of you to join the campaign," Kenton added.

"I think we should, Tom," said Jacky.

"I feel we must," said Tom.

"I know I must," said Davy. "I owe it to Logan."

Keep Me Kindly in Your Daily Prayers

Classes ended at William and Mary the week after the burgesses marched down Duke of Gloucester Street for their day of fasting, humiliation and prayer for the citizens of Boston. Neither Zack nor Peter looked forward to spending the summer at Winston Woods, and miss all the excitement going on in the capital.

Zack, now a published artist, had applied to become an apprentice for Jonas Phillips at his bookshop, replacing Rodie Murray, who was hired to help edit and write articles for Alexander Purdie at the "Virginia Gazette."

Peter, uncertain still about his future, hoped to convince the judge to allow him to stay in the capital too, if only to look after Zack and keep him company. The judge, of course, was expecting both boys to return to the plantation with him, Adella and Angelica. There were two days left before the Winstons would leave Williamsburg, so Zack and Peter, delaying the announcement of their hopes for summer until the last moment, decided to make their plans clear at dinner that evening.

As they walked down the street to the inn to join the judge and Adella for dinner, they passed by the Lansing and Boyd Mercantile on Duke of Gloucester Street. Zack pointed to a sign in the window, which read "Apprentice Wanted Inquire Within."

"Peter," Zack said excitedly, "look!"

Peter read the sign, looked at Zack and smiled, then immediately walked inside the store he had been in many times before. That was just what Peter needed if he was to convince the judge to allow him and Zack to stay the summer in Williamsburg. Zack stood outside and peered in through the window, watching. He saw Peter speaking briefly with Linwood Boyd, who Peter knew not only from the store, but also from many evenings of political discussion with Stockard and other patriots at Raleigh Tavern. Zack saw them smile and shake hands. He knew Peter had secured the position, ... as long as the judge concurred.

"What do you mean you do not want to return with us to Hanover County?" the judge virtually fumed, as the boys sat at the dining table in the tavern. They had not seen him so angry since they caught the corncrib on fire burning Governor Botetourt in effigy.

"You are, both of you, returning to Winston Woods for the summer, and that is the end of this discussion!"

"But, father," Zack had always called the judge 'father' even though Peter always called him judge, "it is the opportunity I need to expand upon my future career as an artist and writer."

"Zachary, you have published some brilliant sketches, son," the judge admitted calmly, "I am indeed very proud of you, but I thought you would enjoy the summer at home, drawing more."

"I have drawn the nature of Hanover County, all of it," Zack said. "I need to expand to other subjects...people, events...and this is the place to do so."

"But as for Peter? Does Peter sacrifice your company for the entire summer?" the judge posed a question aiming to paint Zack into a corner of guilt.

"Tell him Peter, tell him," Zack smiled.

"I too have found a career to follow," Peter announced, "that of a merchant. I have also obtained the position of apprentice at the Lansing and Boyd Mercantile, here in the capital," Peter said boldly. "It is mine, with your approval that is, sir. I very much want to become a merchant."

The judge sat speechless. Adella sat speechless. The serving lady brought their dinner.

Zack and Peter dove into the plates set before them ... pot roast with cooked vegetables and egg noodles for Zack ... fried chicken with potatoes, cooked vegetables and gravy in Peter's first plate, broiled fish with more vegetables and egg noodles on his second one.

Adella picked at her turkey and dressing, while the judge pondered over his halibut steak.

After the plates were cleared and glasses of Madeira Port were served, the judge rendered his verdict.

"Young gentlemen, I feel the months of July and August are not too much for your mother and I to look forward to, and expect your company at home," the judge spoke as if speaking to two defendants seated before him. "However, I have always been of the opinion that the very best education for career preparation is an actual working within the realm of that chosen vocation. Is there no better college than that of the book shop of Mister Phillips or the mercantile of Misters Lansing and Boyd in the city of Williamsburg?"

Peter turned to Zack and Zack turned to Peter, both beamed ear-to-ear.

"But there is one provision to my verdict," the judge continued.

"This is but a portion of your education, and you shall attend to a full class schedule, each of you, when the summer ends."

Then Adella spoke.

"I shall surely be saddened with my two boys not with us during the summer," she said, "but I am pleased with the judge's verdict, and am happy, very happy for you both. But I have news of my own. I am again with child."

The judge was again shocked to hear her announcement, as much as he had been shocked to hear the news earlier from the boys.

"Darling, are you certain?" he asked. She smiled and nodded. "When shall our child be born?"

"Again in December," she beamed with joy of how she had revealed her secret to the three men in her life.

The next day Peter went to see Linwood Boyd at the mercantile. Boyd was pleased to have Peter as an apprentice to learn the trade of a merchant. Boyd showed Peter a room off the back of the store, and offered it for Peter and Zack to stay for the summer months. The room was small, but room enough to set up cots for them to sleep on and a table and some chairs. They were able to use Mr. Boyd's outdoor hearth to cook on. Boyd was a bachelor and lived in rooms above the mercantile. His partner and cousin, Robert Lansing, was married with three children, and lived in a house several blocks away.

The next morning at breakfast with the Winstons before they left for Hanover County, another issue was brought up.

"Peter, I pray your decision to become a merchant has laid aside any such ideas you might yet entertain about a future life as a soldier," the judge broached the subject he had so many times heard Peter fantasize about.

"There is nothing to be excited about carrying a musket and bayonet, a saber or a knife against another man," the judge went on. "There is no real glory on a field of battle, only horrific agony, fear and pain.

"In these times, speeding by rapidly toward who knows what, perhaps to revolution, to war, I want one promise from both of you, but especially from you, Peter. That promise is that you fend off any temptation to join the militia, or the army if one is formed, or any military company of any kind, until you have reached maturity at age twenty-one."

"Four years?" Peter questioned. "Is that not harsh? If we are invaded and I, a very able-bodied and strong man, am held by a pledge not to take up arms, is that not unfair? Unfair not just to me, father, but to my country as well?"

"You know my fears, Peter," the judge spoke solemnly. "Are you able to give to me that pledge?"

"I will wholeheartedly pledge to you, the man who took me off the rope pile on the wharf at City Point, and raised me as his own son," Peter spoke, "that I will never take up arms except for under two conditions."

"And what might be those two conditions you would set?" the judge was pleased with Peter's ability to debate, and wondered why the law did not appeal to him.

"Unless the cause is a just cause I believe in with all my whole heart," he said, then added, "and unless I first announce my intentions to you, seeking your blessings."

The judge said nothing for several long, silent minutes. Then he rose, and went to where Peter was sitting, pulling the tall and muscular Peter from his chair. The judge embraced his son with the proud hug of a true father.

The summer was better than either of the boys expected. Zack began a love of prose. His first love was still sketching the things he saw, especially plants and trees and fish and birds and mammals of all sorts. But now he wanted to sketch more. He knew his next publication would be an illustrated book of more than simply nature. His initial publication had sold-out and a second, larger printing was ordered. He also had a London bookseller Rodie had arranged.

Zack spent days when not expected at the bookshop, drawing buildings in the capital and scenes of some of the patriot leaders walking down Duke of Gloucester Street or debating at tables in Raleigh Tavern.

Peter was in his element at the mercantile. He stocked the shelves, displayed newly arrived items in the huge front windows of the store to tempt passersby, and handled the till when a customer made a purchase. He even started getting comfortable with the mathematics of helping keep the books for the company. He hated classes in mathematics at both Campbelltown and at William and Mary. He simply did not find numbers interesting at all, not like the written accounts of the French and Indian War. Now, seeing the application of numbers to the success or failure of the mercantile, he saw numbers being put to use in a practical and real fashion. Yes, Peter would some day be like Robert Lansing and Linwood Boyd, and own a mercantile store of his own.

Rodie was also an almost constant companion of Zack and Peter. Rodie was becoming more and more a patriot with every passing day he worked at the print shop, setting type for the "Virginia Gazette." A large majority of the words printed in the Gazette were not received well at the Governor's Palace, where his uncle held court and threw editions of the paper into the palace fire. Rodie soon grew to not much like his uncle. He also knew that if he had been a colonial all his eighteen years, he'd be pitching tea chests into the James or York Rivers, if that had been called for as it had been called for in Boston.

Peter was hesitant to invite him to political discussions at Raleigh Tavern, lest Peter's compatriots see Rodie to be no more than a filthy spy for his filthy uncle. But Rodie did accompany Peter on several occasions with Stockard and Mr. Boyd, and the patriots welcomed him and did not watch their tongues in his presence. Instead of going back to the palace each night where he shared a room with his older brother Alex, many nights Rodie would sleep on the floor in the room behind the mercantile with Peter and Zack.

At the palace on the last day of June, Lord Dunmore instructed Alex to send for a messenger. He sent for Col. Lewis, Col. George Rogers Clark, a young militia leader from Kentucky, and the frontiersman, Michael Cresap, for an important meeting at the palace at nine o'clock the next morning. Dunmore also had Alex arrange a small, private dinner that evening with Col. Washington and his lady.

The Washington's arrived at the Governor's Palace for their private dinner with Lord and Lady Dunmore. Though the Washington's had dined with the royal governor on several occasions at the palace, this was the first time they would be the only guests... just them and the Dunmores.

Washington admired Lord Dunmore, in fact he quite liked him as an individual. Washington knew just how politically astute Dunmore was, though he was not the diplomatic sort his predecessor, Lord Botetourt, had been. John Murray, Lord Dunmore had impressed Washington even before he arrived in Williamsburg.

"He wants me to disavow the call for the Continental Congress and attempt to have me dissuade others to do so as well," Washington said to his wife, as they awaited the Dunmores in the parlor. "I shall not, under any circumstance, concede to Dunmore on that issue!" Martha did not respond.

"He wants my advise on how to handle the savages on the frontier. There will certainly be a war with the Shawnee. He wants me to lead our forces. I cannot. I will not!" He waited, but there was still no response from Martha, who sat and listened intently to every possible reason her husband could give for the invitation to dine alone with Dunmores at the palace.

"Perhaps 'tis nothing more than one gentleman with holdings, discussing with another, the agricultural advances, and how best to profit on a plantation in Virginia," Martha, in her soft and sweet voice added her thoughts.

Then the gilded double doors were flung open by the palace valet, and in walked the governor on the arm of his lady. Dunmore, as always, cut a dashing figure in his Murray family tartan plaid kilt, calf-high white Cardigan hose, and a white blousy dress shirt with scarlet red vest. Lady Charlotte was with child, but appeared as glamorous and beautiful as ever. She wore a lavender gown with white lace, with her golden curls falling down beyond her creamy white shoulders.

Dunmore went directly to Martha.

"Lady Washington," the lord spoke and took her hand, "Williamsburg has indeed missed your beauty and company during your convalescence at Mount Vernon." He kissed the top of her gloved hand.

"We were delighted to hear of your arrival at our capital this week," Dunmore put her arm in his to lead the small dining party into the lavish dining room. Col. Washington followed Dunmore's lead and took Lady Charlotte's arm.

Soon a splendid dinner of roasted pheasant, vegetables, greens and consommé was served. Conversation was light during the course of the dinner meal, until after the desert dishes, which had held slices of coconut cake with vanilla cream between the layers, had been taken away.

"Shall we retire to my study for tobacco and brandy?" Dunmore suggested. Washington nodded and followed. Lady Charlotte led Martha to the music room, where they sipped tea and engaged in social conversation, while a musician serenaded them softly on the pianoforte.

The men took seats in leather armchairs alongside the empty hearth of summer.

"Col. Washington I shall get immediately to the reason I have asked you, and you alone, to dine with me this evening," said Dunmore. "I have an important meeting tomorrow and I want to hear from you this evening before hand.

"You, and you alone, among my acquaintances here, have a proven knowledge of the frontier and of the savage tribes which inhabit there. I ask your opinions, your thoughts, as you know the frontier. And, dear sir, how you would suggest this colony approach those issues and events of the present."

Washington thought for a brief moment.

"Your lordship," Washington spoke, "I fear a war on the frontier, with especially the Shawnee tribe, is inevitable and not to be avoided.

"During the immediate past ten years," Washington continued, "it is reported tens of thousands have left the eastern colonies for free farmlands and homesteads in the vast lands of the west. The presence of the white settlers is seen as a threat to the native tribes. Now we read weekly of massacres, the burning of farms, the savage practices of taking scalps and captive little children."

"That is my issue, Colonel Washington," spoke Dunmore. "I am about to commence a campaign I hope shall rid the threat of the savages from the frontier lands of Virginia. I ask for your feelings and your advice.

"I have sent John Connolly north and west with some three hundred men. As we sit here this evening, Connolly sits safely as commandant at Fort Pitt, now renamed Fort Dunmore. Virginia has now claimed that land from the Pennsylvania Colony."

"I salute you, Lord Dunmore," Washington raised his brandy glass. "That fort is on Virginia soil, according to our charter. It sits on the land Governor Dinwiddie sent me to drive the French out, which started our French and Indian War."

"I intend to send Colonel Lewis, with eleven hundred men, west across the Blue Ridge to the mouth of the Kanawha. I will send another thousand to join Connolly, and the armies shall meet at the Kanawha.

"You know the wilderness, Washington, and how the savages fight a certain type of warfare unfamiliar to the European ways of war," Dunmore went on. "You were a young man when, had Braddock but listened to you, as you tried to warn him of just how those vile savages fight in any but conventional manners, I dare say Braddock would have died at home in his bed instead of on the road to Fort Duquesne."

"Braddock was a fine man," Washington added, "but failed to imagine how a war could possibly be fought and won in such a fashion, with the enemy using the tactics of ambush and snipers behind trees."

"You make my point for me," Dunmore said. "I need you to command the forces of Virginia, to make peace with the tribes and bring peace to our Virginians settling now on the frontiers."

"I am indeed honored, your lordship, with the faith you place in me," answered Washington, "but I must, out of necessity and personal concerns, decline that extreme honor."

"You agree with the campaign, do you not?" asked Dunmore.

"Most assuredly I do," spoke Washington, "but my concerns must be first and foremost for my wife, and those concerns force my refusal."

"You have deserted her to Williamsburg these past weeks as she was ill," Dunmore argued. "The campaign shall be a short one, surely she can survive your absence that long."

"There is nothing I would relish more than leading Virginia forces against the Shawnee," Washington said. He then told the governor the sharp hurt in his heart.

"You see, my lord, Martha and I have not been blessed with children of our own, as you have been so blessed. She brought into our marriage two small children I have raised as my own. The apple of my eye has always been her daughter, the younger of the two. Little Patsy suffered her entire life with fits and seizures. A more beautiful young lady has never breathed.

"One year ago this month, after she rose from the dinner table, I can remember it as if it had been just last evening," Washington continued, a small tear appearing in the corner of his eye, "she seemed in better health and in much better spirits than I had seen her in weeks. There were none of the usual signs of a fit coming on. We went into the small parlor, and Patsy sat the pianoforte, planning to entertain us with her music. Just Martha and I were there. Her one-year older brother, Jacky, had married and was then living on his own farm in New Kent. Patsy smiled at us as we sat for her intimate little recital.

"She played but a few chords then began to shake, and fell from the bench to the floor. I rushed to her and began to tend to her as I have done so many times before. She spoke not a word…made not one moan nor growl."

Washington stopped, without a word, for a long silence. "She expired within just two minutes, with that precious little smile on her precious little face."

"I am so sorry," Dunmore responded. "I had not heard of your tragedy at Mount Vernon."

"Lady Washington took to her bed for weeks, no months, with servants bringing her meals and tending to her," Washington spoke, wiping tears. "She has grown somewhat stronger, yes, but ever so slightly. She stayed away from Williamsburg during the past season, and just arrived days ago to accompany me back to my plantation. I do hope your lordship can excuse me from this great honor you have extended to me. Lady Washington's health depends upon me spending this time with her."

"I shall, colonel, I shall," said the Scotsman.

"With you being unavailable, and with good cause, I shall lead the forces to Fort Pitt, I mean Fort Dunmore, and meet up with Lewis' force at the Kanawha myself. I will however, wish from you as much advice and stories of the Indians during the war with France as you can give."

"Col. Lewis, you are to prepare your army to begin your march on Sunday, the last day of July," the governor started. "You shall head across the Blue Ridge and into the frontiers of western Virginia. You shall then head directly to the Kanawha River, and follow it to its mouth into the Ohio. There you are to camp and await my re-enforcements.

"Col. Clark," the governor turned to the frontier militiaman, "you will have circulars printed calling for volunteers to build an army to join our forces at Williamsburg. Enlist men in every county, and return to this city with them before Lewis marches. I will personally lead that army and do say as much in the circular."

Rodie set the type for the circular Col. Clark handed him, calling for volunteers to join Lord Dunmore in his campaign against the Shawnee. Rodie took a copy to Peter and Zack that night at the room behind the mercantile.

"We must volunteer, Peter, we must!" said Zack.

"I can not go back on my word," Peter sadly answered his friend.

"Peter, this is just what you want," Zack said, "to march with the army. To go into a battle, not like boys at play, but a real battle!"

"You were there, Zack, when I promised the judge," Peter said, knowing deep down inside he wanted nothing more but to volunteer, and rid the Ohio Country of the savages who massacred and scalped defenseless settlers, even women and children. He really did want it more than anything he had ever thought about.

"I gave him my word," Peter said emphatically.

"I am going," spoke Rodie. "Even if it is being commanded by my uncle."

"I am going too," Zack announced. "Father will not say a thing. He will be amazed that I want to be in the army, which I do not really want to be. I want to see the Ohio Country, and draw it for all the folks here in the colonies to see."

"You know I have got to go," Peter admitted. "How can I do it? How can I hold to my pledge to the judge, yet not let this opportunity pass me by?"

The next day, Zack, Rodie and Peter stood in the line in front of the table set up in front of the courthouse, with Col. George Rogers Clark sitting facing the volunteers. They each signed the recruitment forms and became members of the army of Lord Dunmore.

As students, still enrolled at William and Mary, and the campaign not expecting to return to Williamsburg until well after the opening day of classes in September, they each had to get written approval from the college registrar. The registrar was the beady-eyed, and mostly bald, skinny man of at least fifty, Jeremiah Pohick. Pohick, feeling nothing but pride to see so many students at the college want a release from classes, temporarily, to assist Lord Dunmore clear the west of the savages, signed his permission without thinking twice.

Peter, in an attempt to uphold his promise, penned a letter to the judge.

"I think often of you and would never with aforethought deceive or do anything to lessen what I hope are your good thoughts of me. There is an opportunity arising for me to help in a cause most righteous. I know you will concur, when you receive the word I, your humble son, have volunteered and shall march with our good governor, Lord Dunmore, in his noble campaign to rid the threat of savagery on our western frontier.

"Being a victim myself of savagery nine years ago, being kidnapped from my loving family against my will, and being brought here, I can do nothing except volunteer for this service.

"I know you will support, if with reluctance, my decision to do thus, and I beg you to keep me kindly in your daily prayers."

Marching with Dunmore

On the last day of July, the city of Williamsburg turned out along Duke of Gloucester Street to cheer and applaud, as the eleven hundred men under the command of Col. Andrew Lewis marched toward the Blue Ridge Mountains. Peter, Zack and Rodie were on the sidewalks cheering with the throngs, knowing the next morning, they would be repeating the same scene, falling in behind Lord Dunmore, as they marched to the northwest. They were excited and knew they would get very little, if any sleep that night.

When the men of Col. Lewis' army had marched out of town, the three boys walked down the Palace Green to the tent they had pitched on the grounds of the Governor's Palace. As they walked, they ran into a familiar face.

"Peter Patrick! Is that you?" Peter yelled.

"It is!" said Zack. "What brings you to Williamsburg, Pat?"

"To march with Dunmore, I guess, an' to keep a promised eye on the two of you," said Pat. "The judge, he ain't too pleased with you two errant lads a runnin' off ta war, so he sent me to be your guardian!" Peter slugged him on one shoulder, Zack slugged him on the other.

"Where's your tent?" asked Peter.

"I don't have no tent," replied Pat.

"Well, I guess you can tent with us," invited Zack.

"I'll commandeer another tent," said Rodie. "Pat and I can share it."

Rodie extended his hand to shake with Pat, as Zack introduced him to the governor's nephew.

"You're the governor's nephew? Really?" asked Pat.

"I am," admitted Rodie, in a rather quiet voice, "but I do not wish my family lineage to be public knowledge. Let that just remain our secret." He glared at Zack for even telling Pat. Few of the men in the army knew Rodie to be the governor's nephew, and Rodie wanted to keep it that way.

The men of Dunmore's Army provided their own pants, shirts, jackets, socks and shoes, coats and hats. They were issued tents and bedding from the quartermaster, and wagons of provisions would follow the men as they marched. They were each issued muskets, powder and musketballs.

They assembled in their units on the grounds of the palace by half-passed seven on the morning of August first, waiting for the royal governor to appear at the verandah, and take command of his army. The drummers began a cadence and, as Lord Dunmore appeared at the palace door, the bagpipes and fifes began playing a Scottish march, in Dunmore's honor.

The Lord made a striking appearance, Zack kept the image fresh in his mind so he could sketch it when the unit rested. Dunmore wore a Scottish tam-o-shanter on his head with a fancy black plume-like feather. He was dressed with a white puffy-sleeved shirt under a vest made of the same Murray family tartan plaid as his kilt. His white Cardigan wool stockings covered his calves, leaving his knees exposed, and emerald green garters held the Cardigans in place. He did not wear boots, but more comfortable, low-rising walking shoes. He carried his own haversack on his back, like his men did. A sword was in a scabbard around his waist, and he held a walking stick in his right hand.

Dunmore was at the center of the verandah as the fifes and drums ceased.

"Gentlemen, I am proud, as your governor, to lead you in this campaign," Dunmore spoke. "We depart this hour on a valiant mission to end, once and for all time, the savage slaughter of innocent Virginians on the frontiers of this colony. A civilized people cannot live under constant fear of uncivilized neighbors. When we return to this city, we shall have secured every inch and acre of our Virginia lands for safe and secure settlement. Let us begin our campaign without further delay. God save the king!"

"God save the king!" echoed each of the twelve hundred souls assembled there to meet up with the three hundred more Connolly had waiting at Fort Dunmore.

The men marched in ranks down Duke of Gloucester Street to the cheers, yells and huzzahs of the throngs turned out, now two days in a row, to watch the brave army of Lord Dunmore march off to the dangerous frontiers.

The march along the roads of the colony was easy. In a week they camped at Cedar Forks in Hanover County. The judge and Adella brought Buford Patrick and were standing along the dirt street as the army marched by.

"There's Peter!" Adella cried out, as she spotted his head above the rest of the soldiers, "and there's Zachary right beside him, and Pat too!"

When the army passed by, the Judge took Adella's hand, and he and Buford Patrick rushed with her, following until the army halted to make camp.

"Well, there are the two young scoundrels who cannot keep their pledges to me," said the judge to Peter and Zack, after the command "At ease!" had been shouted.

"I did send a letter," Peter said, as the judge was hugging him.

"And you both are certainly in our daily prayers," added Adella, as she received her hugs.

"I am still not pleased with you two marching off to a war with the tribes," said the judge.

"It is a cause we do truly believe in," said Peter.

"Dunmore's aim is a worthy one," added the judge, "and...well..." the judge stumbled for the right words, still with a blank expression on his face. "I just wish I were marching with you." He hugged both boys and a smile of pride and approval came across his face.

A week later, the army arrived at Winchester, the last town before crossing into the western frontier. Dunmore had maps of the route Washington had traveled in 1753 from Winchester to the present site of Fort Dunmore. Travel became more difficult and slower, with few roads other than mere paths through the forests and up then down steep mountains. There were rivers and streams to ford and always the fear of an Indian ambush.

The army enjoyed a much-needed two-day rest at the site of Fort Necessity in Great Meadows, where General Braddock had been killed by ambush during the French and Indian War.

Leaving Great Meadows, the army marched into Fort Dunmore on the eleventh day of September. There had been no incidents along the campaign route, thus far, and the army looked forward to several days at the fort. It had taken the army of Virginians forty-one days to march from the colonial capital city to Fort Dunmore, where they joined the three hundred men under Connolly at the confluence of the three rivers.

Fort Dunmore

The day after the army left Williamsburg, the Virginia Convention met at the Capitol. Delegates were chosen to travel to Philadelphia for the convening session of the Continental Congress, set for September 5th. Just prior to the arrival of Dunmore's army at the fort, a post rider had delivered news from the Congress.

In his private quarters at the fort, Dunmore read the report. There was no news from the opening day's session, but Dunmore learned who the delegates from Virginia were. The convention in Williamsburg had elected, for the most part, moderate men of basically good judgment. George Washington was one of those chosen, as was the venerable speaker of the house, Peyton Randolph. Randolph, Dunmore learned and smiled at the news, had actually been elected to preside over the congress. The only radical amongst the Virginia delegation was that vile man, Patrick Henry.

"At least that damnable, lisping, red-headed Jefferson, was not elected!" Dunmore said aloud to himself. He had left his nephew and secretary, Alexander, behind at the palace.

Dunmore tossed the newspaper aside, leaned back in his wooden chair with his fingers interlocked behind his head. He smiled and thought out loud, "The real news will be from the frontier, and this dream of revolution and independence will soon fade."

Zack had found all sorts of subject for his sketches, starting with Lord Dunmore himself, decked out in his Scottish kilt. Zack had added buildings and portraits to his sketches as well. As the army passed near something Zack wanted to sketch, he made mental notes, then at the next rest, would make simple drawings. In camp for the night, Zack would pull out his sketch book and add touches to the drawings he had made that day ... soldiers, mountain tops, scenic outcroppings of rocks, trees, and of course, animals.

Peter was feeling the camaraderie of the unit. His personality lent to that, and he soon began collecting more and more friends. It seemed, everywhere Peter would go to sit around camp, a crowd would follow him.

Peter Patrick dreamed of finding a place to return to after the campaign, to settle and build a fortune for himself. He spotted a beautiful valley with a stream running through it on their second day out of Winchester. He saw an old sycamore tree, seeming to stand sentinel to the land, so he drew out his long-bladed knife from its sheath and carved his initials into the trunk, *Pee. Pee. 1774,* making what was called a tomahawk claim to the land.

"When this is over," Pat said to Rodie, Zack and Peter watching him, "Someday I'm comin' back here and claimin' this place as my own." He did the same thing, making tomahawk claims, at least twice more, before the army settled in at Fort Dunmore.

After the army had been at the fort for two days, a rider rode into the fort to see Lord Dunmore. He had news Dunmore was waiting for.

"I left the army as it was crossing the Ohio River at the mouth of the Muskingum," stated the rider as Dunmore spread his maps on the table.

"It is here, my lord," the rider said, pointing to the mouth of the Muskingum on the Ohio side of the river.

"What possessed him to cross the river? And it appears to be days the off-course of his ordered camp on the Kanawha!" Dunmore fumed, pointing to the mouth of the Kanawha. "He had explicit orders to wait … to wait for my further orders."

"He received a scout's report of a tribal village a day's journey up the Muskingum," said the rider. "Having reached the Ohio well-ahead of schedule, and just a three day's journey from the Kanawha, he decided to survey the area," he concluded his report.

"When does Lewis expect to return to the Kanawha from this unauthorized adventuring?" Dunmore was more than dissatisfied with what he had thus far heard.

"He should be camped at the mouth of the Kanawha River by the twentieth."

Dunmore looked at the map. "That's in just nine days!" Dunmore roared. He pointed to the mouth of the Kanawha and traced a trail to Fort Dunmore. "My men shan't have the rest they so deserve!"

"Can we march fifteen hundred men from the fort here to the Kanawha encampment of Lewis' army within eight days?" Dunmore asked John Connolly.

"I would think it possible," said Connolly, "but it would be a hard march."

"I do not want them sitting targets for an ambush!" Dunmore roared. "There is little doubt the Shawnee are not now well aware of his adventures to that Indian village, and all surprise has vanished!"

Dunmore gave the courier his orders. "Carry the news to Lewis, and order him to sit firm and expect us on the twentieth. I do not wish to arrive and find he is off on another unauthorized foray into the Ohio forests. Is that understood?"

"It is your lordship," the rider said, bowing his head in deference to Dunmore.

"You shall leave at first light," Dunmore said. "That is all." The rider left.

Dunmore turned to Connolly, "Send for Kenton. Do we know his whereabouts?"

"We do, your lordship," spoke Connolly. "He is three hours from the fort at a cabin in the Beaver Valley. I shall send for him immediately."

"Did no one think to have the most-able frontiersman I have to be here when I arrived?" Dunmore scoffed. "I need him here and must now wait six, perhaps eight hours to see him? Order all the men to be ready to march at first light. Tell Kenton I need him here immediately," Dunmore instructed him.

Kenton arrived at the fort with Jacky, Tom and Davy near three o'clock the next morning. Dunmore was awakened and Kenton was shown in. When Kenton returned to Tom, Jacky and Davy he said, "I learned some news that troubles me.

"Colonel Lewis has disobeyed Dunmore's orders, and crossed the Ohio. He marched on Logan's village up the Muskingum.

"Lewis seems to me an army officer wanting fame, and I fear for Logan and his people. Who knows what terrible fate might have befallen our friend with such a glory-seeker leading eleven-hundred armed men into his village!"

"Logan would have welcomed the soldiers as he welcomes all white men," Davy said assuredly.

"Ho-Tawa, do not be so certain, that Lewis would even accept that welcome."

Ambush on the Kanawha

Lord Dunmore led his army west from the fort toward the east shore of the Ohio, then followed the river south toward the Kanawha. On the morning of the last day of the march, and about fifteen miles from the Kanawha, they stopped for a thirty-minute rest.

Zack was anxious to go to the water's edge and look across the broad, greenish waters of the Ohio River to the rolling hills on the

246

north shore. Of course, he had his sketchbook out and began drawing an outline of the sketch he'd finish later. He noticed a boy, dressed in buckskins with a colorful headband around his black trimmed hair, and a necklace of buckeye nuts around his neck. The boy squatted at the river's edge, cupping his hand for a drink of water.

After a couple drinks, the boy suddenly stood upright, dumped the water from his hands, and stared down river. He squatted again with his ear just inches above the water's crest. He stood again and pointed down river.

"There is gunfire in the distance," Davy shouted. "Musket fire ... many muskets."

Rodie, with Peter and Pat, were just behind Davy, approaching the water.

"What did you say?" Peter asked the boy who he had seen in camp but did not know.

"There is gunfire," Davy repeated. "I can hear it on the water's surface."

"Are you certain?" asked Rodie.

"Yes," Davy said. "Logan said I had a keen sense of hearing. I used that sense often as a tracker when I lived with the Mingo."

"We need to inform my uncle," Rodie ran off immediately.

"You lived with the Indians?" Peter asked Davy.

"Yes," Davy said, and told the boys his story before Rodie came back with Lord Dunmore.

"Tell me what you hear on the water, boy," commanded Dunmore.

"Gunfire ... much gunfire. A battle rages ... ten, perhaps fifteen miles downstream."

What Davy had heard on the water's surface was the ambush Lewis' men were suffering at that very moment at the hands of Chief Cornstalk and the Shawnee.

Braves, with painted faces, had been waiting for the white men to march from their camp to the banks of the Ohio. They had spotted the camp from the smoke of their campfires the night before. A scouting party had crossed the Ohio and spied upon them as they camped. When the camp broke, around ten in the morning, they began their short march to the mouth of the Kanawha to await Dunmore. Braves were seemingly behind every tree and bush. They sprang out from the woods, surrounding the white men on three sides, with war whoops filling the air, and tomahawks flashing in the morning sun.

Lewis ordered his men to fire and the battle raged.

Dunmore called his men to order and renewed the march at a faster pace. They marched for nearly three hours. Dunmore had Davy at his side, and every mile or so, ordered Davy to again go to water's edge and listen to inform Dunmore if the battle was still raging. Davy returned each time with the same news ... "There is much gunfire still."

Cornstalk, with his nephew, Chickseeka, led the Shawnee at the Kanawha ambush.

The Shawnee held the upper hand in the battle for more than four hours, killing forty-six of Lewis' men, wounding more than one hundred, and another one hundred were taken as captives or deserted. The day was all but lost for the Virginians under Lewis when Lord Dunmore in his kilt and fifteen hundred re-enforcements arrived to attack on the rear of the Shawnees.

Knowing he was out-numbered and now out-flanked, Cornstalk flew the white flag of truce. The musket fire ended, and Dunmore, with Simon Kenton and Ho-Tawa by his side as interpreters, approached Cornstalk and Chickseeka.

"I have met with defeat this day," Cornstalk said humbly, as Ho-Tawa interpreted. "I beg for your mercies and for peace."

"The mercy I shall give you, Cornstalk, is that of your life and the lives of your braves still standing," Dunmore said through Ho-Tawa. "Our mission here is for peace, not war."

"In twenty day's time, you, and all the leaders of the Ohio tribes, shall come and a peace shall be commenced that day." Ho-Tawa again spoke in Cornstalk's tongue to the great chieftain who had, four years earlier, sold him to Logan for two horses.

"Meet us that day where the Scioto River flows into the Pickaway Plains."

"We shall meet that day," spoke Cornstalk, "and there will be peace."

Cornstalk and Chickseeka turned and rode their horses away from the battle, heading north as their horses swam straight across the wide river.

Not one shot was fired after Cornstalk saw Lord Dunmore and the re-enforcements at his rear. No one in Dunmore's army saw any battle action, except for the last acts of battle as they approached. None took part in the battle, not Peter Francisco, who had hoped to feel the sense of battle for the first time, not Jacky Macneal, not John Murray, the fourth Earl of Dunmore. No one.

As soon as the Shawnee were back across the Ohio River, Dunmore ordered camp be set up, as he wanted a day or two to tend to the wounded, send searchers out for any deserters, and see why Colonel Lewis had blatantly disobeyed his very clear orders.

Dunmore immediately convened a council of his military advisors, to discuss the battle and plans for the treaty with the tribal leaders. Of course, the council included the errant Col. Lewis, Col. George Rogers Clark, and the frontiersman Michael Cresap. Simon Kenton also sat in, as did Ho-Tawa.

"We fought, gentlemen, not on our terms," said Dunmore, with a tone of disappointment in his voice, "but were forced to fight on the terms of the enemy. We brought these armies many miles, through the difficult terrains of the wilderness. But for the timely arrival of the army of my re-enforcement, this day would have ended in extreme disaster and loss.

"Our arrival from the north saved the day and won the battle without one more shot being fired," Dunmore congratulated his timely arrival at the Kanawha to avoid certain defeat and the mass slaughter of Lewis' men. "We have won the battle, we must now fashion the peace that will justify our war.

"Nothing short of total acceptance by the tribes that this land is indeed Virginia land, and the white settlers will be unmolested in their activities of settlement," stated Dunmore. "I shall draft the documents of peace under those terms and under those terms only."

"Now to the matters of our remaining campaign," Dunmore laid it out. "We cross the river here with a flotilla now being built. We shall march up the Scioto four days to the Pickaway Plains. We shall build Fort Charlotte there to meet the tribal leaders. We will then march back triumphantly to Williamsburg with the peace." Dunmnore had laid out his plan to his officers. There was silence as Dunmore decided then how to deal with Lewis' rash insubordination.

"Now, Col. Lewis, what provoked you to disobey my orders?" Dunmore asked immediately.

"Having arrived on the Ohio River many days ahead of schedule," Lewis spoke, "and having previous reports from frontiersmen that the Indians had a large village north of the mouth of the Muskingum River, I, acting admittedly with no authorization from your lordship, decided to lead a company to the village to survey the activities there.

"When we arrived at the village, it had already been laid to ruin. Not a lodge, nor soul, had survived what appeared to have been a massacre, most probably at the hand of the Shawnee or some other tribe. We reversed our course, crossed back over to the south side of the river and came immediately here to await your coming."

"So your insubordination resulted in nothing except to lay open to the Shawnee the arrival of our armies," Dunmore scolded.

"Orders are given to be followed and followed for a purpose," Dunmore went on. "I have no doubt the cause of the ambush and near-loss of an entire army, is the direct result of your insubordination," Dunmore looked directly into the eyes of the colonel.

"You are hereby relieved of your command! Col. Clark, along with Col. Cresap as his subordinate, will take the command forthwith!"

"May I ask the colonel for some details of his findings?" asked Kenton. Dunmore nodded.

"This was the village of Chief Logan of the Mingo?" Kenton asked.

"That is what we were informed," replied Lewis.

"Were you able to find out what has become of Logan?" Kenton probed further.

"In meeting up with a hunting party of Virginians from a settlement on the New River," Lewis added, "the rumors were that Logan himself had been away from the village, but no one survived the burning of the village. It is also rumored that Logan has moved himself to the west on the Pickaway Plains."

"Kenton, can you ride and locate Chief Logan?" Dunmore asked, "and tell him of our need to have him present for the treaty signing?"

"I will take Ho-Tawa with me, if you approve," Kenton said.

"Yes, yes, by all means," Dunmore agreed, "and meet with us on the Pickaway Plains before our scheduled date of the fifteenth."

Kenton left and the council ended.

"Pee. Pee. 1774"

The journey to the mouth of the Scioto took eight days with the army camping for two days in a huge meadow beneath a tall outcropping overhanging the steep hills the men called Hanging Rock. Zack spent his time sketching the impressive stone ledge high above the river below. He also added touches to many of the other sketches he had drawn along the way. His favorite was of the Indian boy with his ear at the water's surface.

At the mouth of the Scioto, the army turned north, up the wide inland river valley. Dunmore was in the lead boat, followed by the flotilla carrying about four hundred of the men. The vast number of soldiers marched up the west bank of the river, led by Clark and Cresap.

After the second day of the march up the Scioto, the army stopped for a full day and two-night rest.

"Your uncle even carries his own haversack," said Peter to Rodie, as the boys sat around the campfire and ate supper fished from the waters.

"He is assuredly in his element," said Rodie. "He has, until now, only read of military exploits that seem to so thrill him. I am certain he wants to do as is expected of him."

"If he gets the treaty he wants," said Zack, "we will certainly be welcomed back to Williamsburg as triumphal heroes."

Peter and Pat went exploring on their own after supper while a couple hours of daylight remained. They were camped beside where a rather large creek emptied into the larger river. Peter and Pat headed west along the tree-shaded creek for a half-mile, then climbed a small embankment and walked through the narrow strip of forested creekside, until it broke into an open plain.

They sat and rested and enjoyed the beautiful, untouched scenery. To the east, across the Scioto, high hills seemed dark blue in color, like the Blue Ridge Mountains of Virginia, only not so high. To the west were more high hills, perhaps five miles distant. In the middle was a large, flat, treeless plain that stretched from the river to the high western hills. The plain seemed to run all the way to the horizon to the north.

"This is by far the most beautiful piece o' land I've ever seen," announced Pat. "This has to be the richest river bottomland soil 'neath these weeds." Pat walked into the field and bent down to dig with his knife a handful of soil. He raced back to Peter.

"Look Peter!" Pat dropped the handful of soil into Peter's hand. "Have ya ever seen such rich, dark, moist soil before? I've seen none so rich in all of Virginia!"

"It is like no soil I've ever seen," Peter agreed.

"It's just like God made it...untouched by furrow or plow!" Pat said excitedly, as he stood and gazed across the plain. "Imagine bein' the first man to harvest this land! Just imagine it!

"Framed in by these beautiful hills!" Pat went on. "This is the place I'll return to," Pat said. "Yes, this is the place that will someday be mine, the estate of Peter Patrick!"

He drew out his knife, walked back to the huge walnut tree standing near the creek as it rushed toward the Scioto, and again began to carve Pee Pee 1774 for the eighth time on his march.

As Pat finished making his final tomahawk claim in the walnut tree's trunk, Rodie and Zack followed up a deer path through the trees.

"Look!" Rodie pointed to the tree as they approached, "Peter Patrick has laid claim to yet another plantation." He started giggling. "Mr. Patrick is destined to be the largest damned land-holder in the Ohio Country, as soon as it is safe to settle."

"Laugh as you will," Pat said, "but look, look at this place! I will be back here someday. This place makes all the rest look like grown-over patches of briars and brambles." They all stood and gazed out over the endless plain.

"I do not laugh at you, Pat," Rodie apologized, as he gazed across the plain Pat and Peter had discovered. "This is land I myself would be proud to claim and cultivate."

Rodie turned toward the creek, flowing with clear cool water. "But now, I must take relief, and what better thought than to christen Peter Patrick's Creek with a little Scottish pee-pee of me own." He walked to the creekside and emptied his kidneys in an arc of golden pee, streaming into the clear water of the creek below. The three others joined Rodie creekside pee-ing themselves.

As they pee-ed, someone said, "We now christened thee, Peter Patrick's Pee Pee Creek!"

Chief Logan

Two days after leaving the camp at the newly christened Pee Pee Creek, the army reached the southern edge of the Pickaway Plains. Dunmore commanded a small stockade be built and named in honor of Lady Dunmore. By late afternoon the next day, Fort Charlotte stood, ready for the visiting chieftains who would arrive in two days.

Kenton and Davy had met them when the army first arrived.

"Logan is safe," said Kenton to Dunmore when they met aboard his flatboat. "But he is not today the man of peace he has always been known to be," Kenton added.

"Is he to hold out and must be vanquished, as Cornstalk has been?" Dunmore asked the frontiersman.

"Logan has been vanquished alright," Kenton added, "and not by the Shawnee."

"In early July, he was away with a hunting party," Kenton told the story Logan had told him. "An armed party of white men, not the Shawnee, came into his village and laid the torch to it, burning the village to the ground, raping many of the women before brutally scalping them and murdering them as they slept defenselessly."

"Not even one child was spared," added Ho-Tawa. "Logan has lost every member of his family. His sons and the husbands of his daughters, his grandchildren, all have been killed."

"He is with a handful of braves who were with him on his hunt for buffalo," continued Kenton. "Only a three of the women escaped the village in the night, and found Logan within one mile of this place. That is where he has remained."

"Did Logan receive word as to who the leader of the massacre was?" asked Dunmore.

"One you know all too well," Kenton informed the governor. "Michael Cresap."

"Cresap! Send for that scoundrel immediately!" Dunmore barked at Connolly.

Cresap was nowhere to be found. Apparently, fearing he was soon to be found out for his deeds, had deserted the army and fled. No one had seen him since they had broken camp halfway up the Scioto.

Dunmore, reviewing in his mind all that Kenton had told him, knew Logan would not be among the chiefs arriving to sign the treaty he had prepared. He called for Kenton to meet with him in his quarters at Fort Charlotte.

"Connolly is tracking Cresap, and is ordered to hang him on the spot! I want you to take me to Logan," Dunmore said. "All I know of this Chief Logan is, deep in his soul, he is a peace-loving and reasonable man. I want him to know Michael Cresap will be dealt with, and dealt with swiftly and justly. I want to show him how deeply we share his personal grief."

The next morning, Dunmore, dressed in a fresh suit of Murray tartan plaids, was ready to walk the long mile to where Chief Logan was living. Kenton met the governor and brought with him Davy, Tom and Jacky Macneal, all who had personal relations with the old chieftain. Dunmore's nephew was there to ask his uncle to allow him to go along with his three friends. Dunmore, who was pleased Rodie had marched with him on the campaign, agreed to the request.

"Your lordship," Rodie said, "may I present Zachary Winston, Peter Francisco and Peter Patrick."

"I have heard that name before," Dunmore said, nodding to Zack. "You are the artist of the book <u>The Nature of Virginia</u>, are you not?

"Yes, your lordship," answered Zack.

"I have thoroughly enjoyed your wonderful renderings, as well as the prose added by my talented nephew." Dunmore smiled at Rodie. The lord was not one to give out accolades readily. "Lady Charlotte, as well, has been well-pleased with the book. We have purchased a full crate of the books, and have sent them to all our friends in England and Scotland. Do you have your sketch book with you today?" Dunmore asked as Zack nodded.

"Then you must sketch this noble Chief Logan."

The nine set off on foot for where Kenton and Davy had met with their old friend.

When they arrived, Logan was seated on a blanket beneath a huge and ancient elm tree. He welcomed the fourth Earl of Dunmore as his friend. They spoke, but Logan held fast to his decision not to take part in the treaty signing at Fort Charlotte. He appreciated Lord Dunmore coming to him personally, and agreed to have his words written down as a speech to both the Virginians and the tribal leaders expected the following day.

Davy did not have to interpret, as Logan spoke English as well as his native tongue. Dunmore asked his nephew, Rodie, to take down every word Logan spoke:

"I appeal to any white man to say if ever he entered Logan's cabin hungry, and he gave him not meat; if ever he came cold and naked, and he clothed him not. During the course of the last long and bloody war, Logan remained idle in his cabin, an advocate for peace. Such was my love for the whites, that my countrymen pointed out as they passed, and said, 'Logan is a friend of the white men.' I had even thought to have lived with you, but for the injuries of one man, Colonel Cresap, in cold blood, and unprovoked, murdered all the relations of Logan, not sparing even my women and children. There runs not a drop of my blood in the veins of any living creature.

This called me for revenge. I have wrought it: I have killed many: I have fully glutted my vengeance.

For my country, I rejoice at the beams of peace. But no longer harbor a thought that mine is the joy of fear. Logan never felt fear. He will not turn on his heel to save his life. Who is there to mourn for Logan?---Not one."

Chapter Eight

If Our Grievances Are Not Met

As Dunmore was treating with the tribal leaders of the Ohio Country in October, the delegates to the First Continental Congress had returned to their respective colonies when the Congress adjourned that same week. The delegates viewed their deliberations as a success, and a giant step toward the re-establishment of colonial rights, or the alternative, total independence.

Petitions from Philadelphia sailed to the Parliament and to King George III in London, laying out the grievances needed to be addressed once and for all time. The delegates added a stern and serious warning to the petitions they sent:

"If our grievances are not met, we shall assemble once more in the city of Philadelphia on the tenth day of May, 1775, to further address the situation within which we have been placed, and act upon the remedies necessary to correct the conditions alien to our common rights as Englishmen."

In Boston, when the delegates arrived home, the royal governor, General Thomas Gage, cancelled a previously scheduled meeting of the General Court. Under the terms of the hated Massachusetts Government Act, Gates' actions permanently dissolved any elected legislature in the colony.

Sam Adams, John Adams, John Hancock, Josiah Quincy and other patriot leaders of the legislature met in rump session and created the Massachusetts Provincial Congress, despite the governor's actions. The Provisional Congress immediately elected John Hancock as president, and established "minuteman companies" throughout the colony, to be ready at a minute's notice, should the need to defend the colony arise.

Wills Winkman was an early volunteer in his local minuteman company in the Boston Harbor area. Wills recruited other volunteers for the minutemen, and was made assistant commander to Miles Reynolds, the company's captain. A meeting was called for the long room above Benjamin Edes' Printing Shop, to organize the minutemen of the harbor area. Prior to the meeting, Wills met with Captain Reynolds at his home.

"We have now about two dozen volunteers in the harbor precinct," said the captain. "We need perhaps an additional two dozen here, where there will undoubtedly be much activity by the British."

"We can easily fill that number, Captain, and more, as we did for the tea party," offered Wills, as the captain's charming daughter came into the parlor with a tray of tea and muffins.

"Tea and cakes, sir?" the petite teenaged girl with beautiful golden curls encircling her cream-colored face asked Wills. He looked into her deep blue eyes and smiled at her.

"I do not mind if I do," Wills said, taking a teacup in one hand and reaching for a muffin with the other, not taking his eyes off hers. She smiled with a blush, turning red in the face.

"As far as I can determine, the goal of the company is to train the minutemen for actions they may need eventually to perform," the captain continued. "We need to be vigilant in monitoring the every move of the British. If there is an all-out invasion, we shall warn the countryside."

The men finished their conversations and left the house for their meeting. As they walked together, Wills turned to the captain.

"Captain, your daughter is one of the most beautiful young women I have seen in Boston."

"Why thank you for the compliment," Miles said. "She is seventeen, a well-mannered and quite well-read young lady. I am most proud of my eldest daughter, Priscilla."

"Priscilla? That's such a lovely name," Wills thought aloud. "Perhaps the time might come when, with your permission of course, I might call upon her, Priscilla, from time to time," Wills boldly stated.

"Perhaps. We shall see," responded Miles happily, yet cautiously. "Do not stand on formalities with me Wills, please call me Miles."

The room had a good crowd when Wills and Miles entered. Miles called the meeting to order.

"We have done good work in getting the volunteers we now have," Miles spoke, "but we still need double our present number."

"We can double our members in a week's time," came a voice from among the volunteers.

"Kind sir," Miles spoke, "would you be so kind as to identify yourself?"

"Pardon me gall, sir, me name's Kilkenny, Johnny Kilkenny," spoke the young man. "I live across from the wharf, and fish from the boats that come an' go everyday. The men onboard those boats can be amongst us within a week."

Wills had heard Jacky talk of this Johnny Kilkenny, who had married Jacky's youngest sister. Jacky had referred to him as a "ne'er do well" and a "low life bastard". Kilkenny did not seem like a ne'er do well to him. At least, he was apparently a true patriot and ready for the fight.

"Well, Mr. Kilkenny," said Miles, "we do welcome any of those sailors and fishermen you can attract."

"While surveillance and espionage is our main duty," Wills addressed what would be expected of the minutemen, "we also need hearty men to train in musketry, hand-to-hand combat, and other activities of war, should war break out, as we expect it will."

"And good horsemen," Miles added, "to ride the countryside, if the need arises to warn the citizens there."

The meeting ended as the men gathered around the grog in the punch bowl, which added to the popularity of the long room being the favorite place to meet.

Wills approached Kilkenny at the punchbowl.

"I was impressed with your offer to help secure volunteers," Wills said, extending his hand. Johnny accepted his hand and shook it, smiling.

"My name in Wills Winkman," Wills spoke, "and I believe you said your name is Johnny Kilkenny."

"Johnny Kilkenny it is indeed," Johnny answered. "I've heard your name, Winkman, one o' the Mohawks aboard the tea ships, I believe. I was on a four-month sailin' in the Caribbean."

"You married Caroline Macneal, I believe," Wills added.

"I did indeed," Johnny said, a bit taken aback. "Are you one o' the many who've had a turn with me wife?"

"No, no, not at all," answered Wills, turning a bit red-in-the-face. Wills had been somewhat attracted to Caroline, before she married Johnny, but lost interest quickly, hearing she liked the private company of young men so much that she'd been with many.

"I know her only because I am a friend of your brother-in-law, Jacky Macneal."

"You know Jacky, now do you?" Johnny asked, relieved. "Jacky's an odd boy. Ya know he ran off with some man, an' they live on the frontier some place in the woods, doin' I suppose what two men alone together in the woods, with no females to be had, might do."

"Yes, Jacky and his cousin Tom joined us Mohawks for the tea party," said Wills.

"'Tis his cousin he's left with?" Johnny asked, as Wills nodded. "An' the two of 'em were Mohawks? Jacky dressed up like an Indian?" Johnny laughed. "Now if that don't just beat everything I ever thought about ole Jacky! He did? He really did that?"

"Oh yes, he and Tom led the Mohawks aboard the Beaver, while I was in charge on the Dartmouth," offered Wills. Johnny extended his hand again to shake hands with Wills.

"Wills Winkman, it has indeed been me pleasure a meetin' ya," Johnny said, and they left for a pub around the corner.

And the Crowds Came Out in Force

Lord Dunmore and his valiant army were due to arrive in Williamsburg near noontime on Wednesday, November 30th. All of the townsfolk were excited as they went about their morning chores, so as not have chores waiting for them if the celebrations continued into the night. Wagons and carriages brought many people from the outlying areas to join the citizens of the capital, to welcome the heroic governor back from his campaign amongst the savages of the Ohio frontier. The inns were crowded, and it was difficult to find a table at the taverns.

The talk throughout the colony was of the success of Lord Dunmore's campaign in the frontier, and the apparent peace he authored to end the fear of massacres and scalpings of white settlers on the frontier.

News from the campaign had arrived in Williamsburg sporadically while Dunmore was away. Riders had been sent back from the campaign, as Dunmore had to keep in touch with Alexander and his aides in Williamsburg, and officials in London, on a variety of matters. Dunmore had agreed to allow his nephew, Rodie, send his writings, documenting events along the way, to be published in the Virginia Gazette to keep the people informed.

George Washington, who felt a frontier war was imminent, but due to family circumstances had turned down the offer to lead the army, applauded the treaty when he read it as being "conclusive and certain, and I dare say it will be of lasting duration."

Another legislator, no friend of Dunmore, the fiery patriot Thomas Jefferson, had been so impressed with Logan's speech beneath the elm tree on the Pickaway Plains, that he stated, "I may challenge the whole orations of Demosthenes and Cicero to produce a single passage, superior to the speech of Logan, a Mingo chief, to Lord Dunmore."

The House of Burgesses met in the morning at the Capitol, and would assemble on the palace grounds to applaud their governor as he marched down Duke of Gloucester Street. Washington was named to lead the welcoming escorts to greet Dunmore at the edge of town.

The students at William and Mary were excited that the day of pomp and circumstance meant no classes for the day. The new students had not arrived before Lord Dunmore led the army down the streets on the way to the frontiers. Several students from Campbelltown were now among the new students, and were anxious to see their governor, but more so, to see their former classmates, Peter Francisco and Zack Winston.

Jimmie Monroe was now enrolled at the college, as was the young prodigy, Bushrod Washington.

"I can hardly wait to see Peter and Zack," Jimmie Monroe said excitedly, as the two found a good place to stand along the Palace Green. "I was so impressed when I walked past the bookseller's window, and saw copies of The Nature of Virginia, and saw the name Zachary Winston emblazoned upon it!"

"It is a quit good volume," noted Bush, "quite wonderful indeed. He is a fine artist."

"I also cannot wait to see if old Peter Francisco has grown even taller than his giant height of six foot and ten inches," added Jimmie.

"I bet he's now bigger in girth as well," responded Bush.

Finally, the sounds of the bagpipes, fifes and drums announced from down the street, the approach of the army. The crowds on the sidewalks were exploding with the pent up excitement. The combined armies of Dunmore and Col. George Rogers Clark marched up Duke of Gloucester Street to the thunderous cheers. Dunmore was naturally decked out in his finest Murray family tartan plaid kilt and full regalia. He was the first to come into sight. Dunmore walked ahead of his men, alongside Washington and the escort committee, down the cobblestone street with his walking stick in hand, carrying his own haversack on his back as he had done for weeks.

Then came Colonel Clark and the other leaders, Colonel Lewis and Simon Kenton. The troops followed with a number of Shawnee captives, encountered on the march back from Fort Charlotte to Williamsburg.

As Peter, Pat and Zack marched by, Jimmie Monroe yelled, "There they are! There's Peter and Zack! Hey, there's Peter Patrick, too. Remember him?"

"Hey Peter! Hey Zack! Hey Pat!" the two boys from Campbelltown shouted and waved, getting the attention of their former classmates.

When the soldiers entered the palace grounds and Dunmore mounted the platform, Speaker Randolph welcomed him.

At the Governor's Palace, a platform had been built and decorated as a suitable viewing stand from where the governor's children and his palace staff cheered him as he returned the conquering hero of the west.

Lady Dunmore was absent from the welcoming celebrations for her husband. She had just, the day before, given birth to a lovely and healthy baby daughter.

"You have taught them a lesson which the savage beast was a stranger to," said Speaker Randolph, as he welcomed Dunmore, "that clemency and mercy are not incompatible with power."

The governor spoke briefly as he was, without a doubt, anxious to see his lady and one-day-old daughter.

"We have successfully completed what we set out to do," spoke the governor. "Your husbands, brothers, sons, cousins and grandsons have been my joy to lead. They performed in the marvelous fashion of the gentlemen they are. Now, I beg you my leave so I might attend to husbandly and fatherly duties. It has been too long since I have had the pleasure of looking into the lovely eyes of Lady Charlotte," then he added, "and I have of course not seen my new daughter, who by the way shall aptly be named Lady Virginia." The crowd on the lawn and in the street screamed their approval at first hearing the chosen name for the governor's new baby girl.

At the podium, the governor received delegations from Norfolk, Chesapeake, Portsmouth, and other towns.

Before Lord Dunmore left the podium, the fifes and drums started playing, and the troops began their march by. The governor and the dignitaries stood, saluting the men as they passed in final review. Dunmore had not seen such love and admiration shown to him during his days in America. He was, that day, enjoying the height of his popularity. It would not last.

As the army disbanded for the last time on the drilling field at the magazine, Jimmie Monroe and Bush Washington caught up with their old friends. They all walked together back toward the Wren, where the underclassmen were lodged. Peter and Zack had no home to return to. Peter was certain someone else had taken his room behind the mercantile during the four months they had been in the west.

As they walked down the street Peter wanted to stop in the mercantile and see his mentor Linwood Boyd. The other boys waited outside and talked to Pat and Zack about their experiences.

"Did you see a lot of savages?" asked Jimmie. "They are damned demons, aren't they?"

"We saw our share," said Zack, "but most of them are not, as you say, 'damned demons.' The Shawnee are the fierce ones who have no respect for others. The others seem quite friendly."

"Did you make a lot of sketches, Zack?" asked the young Bush.

"I did indeed," Zack answered enthusiastically. "I especially enjoyed sketching Chief Logan as he delivered his speech to Lord Dunmore beneath the old elm tree on the Pickaway Plains."

"Dr. Campbell bought a copy of your <u>Nature of Virginia</u> for the library at the academy. We have all committed those sketches to our memories," Jimmie said.

"It would please me more," Zack said, "if you'd buy your own copy. I could use the royalties." They all laughed, as Peter came from the mercantile. He waved a key at Zack.

"Mister Boyd kept the room for us for when we returned," Peter was thrilled to announce. "And after a few days of rest from our adventures, my old position is waiting for me, between my studies, of course."

"I hope Mr. Phillips is as generous and protective of my job," said Zack.

"Well, I know I am secure with Mr. Purdie," said Rodie.

"If not," said Peter, "you can always become the spoiled nephew of royalty, and wile away your days at the palace," Peter added as they all laughed.

"And get lazy and fat...stout like Peter," Zack suggested amid the laughter.

"Let's go to our room and unload these haversacks," Peter said.

It was good to be back in Williamsburg.

Christmas Eve 1774

Christmas was quickly approaching, and the citizens of Williamsburg used the holiday time as a continuation of the celebrations that had begun with Lord Dunmore's triumphal return on the last day of November. Lord Dunmore was enjoying the adulation he was getting from the townsfolk, and even from many of the leaders of the House of Burgesses. But the latest dispatches from London, awaiting him when he returned to the palace, troubled him.

Lord Dartmouth, the British Secretary of State, was displeased with not just the news of rebellion growing in all of the colonies, but also with Dunmore's adventuring on the frontier, contrary to the king's edict. The letters from Whitehall weighed heavily upon Dunmore's mind the entire month of December. On Christmas Eve, he decided to put those letters to rest, and reply to Dartmouth, laying out the peoples' thoughts in the colony, and defend his own actions in the west.

After Christmas Eve dinner at the palace, Dunmore took his secretary, Alexander, into the library. Alexander sat at the writing table while Dunmore sat in an armchair beside the fire, crackling below the marble mantle. Dunmore, deep in thought, re-read in his mind the scolding Dartmouth had rendered to him. He re-thought the responses he would have Alexander put to ink and parchment.

He too, had seen the cause of the patriots gaining more and more support from the once silent men of fortune who had always remained loyal to king and country.

"Many families of influence in Virginia remain loyal, but fear they can be of little avail against the turbulence and prejudice which prevails throughout the country," Dunmore dictated to Alexander. He went on to explain that the associations enforcing the boycott on luxuries and tea from England "with the greatest rigor, haul in offenders, and expose them to outrageous and lawless mobs.

"Men of fortune and prominence join now equally with the lowest and the meanest."

Then he went on to discuss what he saw as the most threatening new occurrence: "Every county is now arming a company of men to be employed against the government, if occasion requires," stated Dunmore. He called Virginia "an armed camp."

Dunmore moved then to defend his actions on the frontier. He viewed the edict of King George II, the present king's grandfather, forbidding settlement beyond the rise of the mountains as just and wise. The thoughts being it would be much easier to control the colonies in the compact area east of the mountains than it would be if the western lands were heavily populated.

However, Dunmore thought, the people living east of the mountain crest knew of those open lands and would not be held back. The Americans were not ready to have any government keep them from settling the frontier lands.

"They do not conceive that government has any right to forbid their taking possession of a vast tract of frontier land."

He discussed his plan to march west was simply to turn the colonial mind away from thoughts of total independence, and toward a western frontier, open for safe settlement. He discussed the grand reception he had been given in the colonial capital. "Even the patriot leaders, Washington and Jefferson, have been won over." Dunmore honestly felt that the colonials, seeing the British government rid the frontier of the Indian threat, would prove the benevolence of the government of the king, and thoughts of independence would eventually fade.

Dunmore concluded the letter to Dartmouth, proposing a series of harsh measures be taken to secure the British hold on all their American colonies. Dunmore suggested cutting off all trade with the colonies, blockades of all the ports, as Boston had been successfully closed, and virtually to "starve the Americans into submission."

"I Know Not What Course Others May Take..."

January 19th 1775, was a day in Williamsburg for solemnity and gala. The day started with the townsfolk again lining Duke of Gloucester Street and the Palace Green to politely applaud the elaborately ornate, closed carriage of Lord Dunmore, pulling away from the Governor's Palace, with uniformed liverymen at their posts, and six beautiful white horses with plumed pink headdresses and shiny brass tack. The royal governor, his lady and their children, were going to Bruton Parish Church for the christening of the two-month-old Lady Virginia.

The rector and parish leaders stood at the door, dressed in black robes, as those guests invited to observe the holy service formed a cordon on both sides of the walkway, leading from the street. George Washington and his wife Martha were amongst those specially invited, as were Peyton Randolph, the Benjamin Harrisons and Hartwell Caulder, a Loyalist delegate from Richmond. They would also be accompanying Lord and Lady Dunmore back to the palace for a lavish christening brunch.

The ceremony lasted the biggest part of an hour, with scriptures read, prayers prayed, and the sprinkling of holy water on the infant's forehead, amid shrill whimpers from tiny little lungs. The rector announced, "I christen thee, Lady Virginia Charlotte Elizabeth Murray."

Soon the parish church was empty, and the governor's carriage, followed by dozens more, was headed to the palace. After the niceties around the dinner table, Lord Dunmore invited his male guests into the library where a roaring fire was blazing in the fireplace.

"I wish to thank you so much, governor, for graciously inviting Lady Washington and I to share in this day with you and Lady Dunmore," said Washington, as they entered the library.

"And we are so pleased Lady Washington was well enough to join you this day," replied Dunmore.

"From the time we received your invitation," Washington said with a smile, "that was all Martha could talk of. It will soon again be the anniversary of our losing darling Patsy, and I feel this, the christening of your beautiful baby daughter, has been what Martha sees as her time to lay her own sadness behind her."

"Lady Dunmore and I both greatly cherish the two of you and joy in your company," admitted Dunmore. "I hope the times we live in now will not create a chasm between us."

"I do feel any chasm that might arise between us," Washington said, "can be bridged."

As all the men found drinks and seats, Dunmore brought up one issue on his mind.

"Gentlemen, I fear there is one issue I must broach today," stated Dunmore. "Since I have been so honored as to have been sent to Williamsburg, there have been differences amongst us, but those differences have never grown so much as now. Allow me to speak openly and honestly to each of you, my friends.

"Since my return from the frontier, I have found, throughout the colony, a virtual armed camp," Dunmore said. "I know not why there seems to be such threatening animosity growing between us. Is there to be no trust? Are there to be armed men in our streets?

"This is not Boston. There are none of the king's regulars marching patrol on our streets. Our harbors are not closed, not on the James, not on the York, Rapahannock nor the Potomac. Why then are these so-called committees of safety forming in every county of Virginia? Why is there a call for these local militias? Am I not a man who can be approached?"

The men sat in silence, pondering the words of their friend Lord Dunmore.

"Your Lordship," Peyton Randolph finally spoke, "you have not a thing to fear from the activities of these committees. They simply are formed to insure the peace, if, and only if that need arises. That has always been the right of the British citizen to band together with other local citizens to protect the communities from any such emergency."

"And what sort of an emergency, Randolph, do you expect?" asked Dunmore, somewhat insulted.

"At present," Benjamin Harrison came to the speaker's aide, "none. But should such an emergency arise... a revolt of the slaves, pirates raiding, gangs of highwaymen. There has been such a local militia here in Williamsburg for many years. The other counties simply wish the same."

"And, yes," Randolph boldly added, "the possibility of a standing army of the king's regulars is much to be feared. Yes, your lordship, that is a clear and potential danger we must be vigilant against."

The room returned to silence...several minutes of silence, before Lord Dunmore stood.

"Gentlemen," Dunmore spoke and smiled, "I speak for myself and for Lady Dunmore ... and for my darling baby daughter, Lady Virginia, when I thank you heartily for accepting our invitation to share in this day with us."

The stage was set. The governor had laid his fears on the table... the fears of Virginia being the armed camp he had reported to Dartmouth that it was.

Every man in the room knew this would be the main issue of the coming second Virginia Convention, slated for March. By March, the delegates all knew the springtime would bring the robins and the crocuses, but also would bring Virginia closer than ever before to rebellion.

Peter and Zack were happy to be back in Williamsburg, living in the room behind the Lansing and Boyd Mercantile. Peter kept busy with his studies, and even busier stocking the shelves, tending to customers, and working in the office on the store's books. He was really enjoying the work at the mercantile, and knew one day he wanted a mercantile of his own.

Zack was working at the bookshop, and started learning the work of a bookbinder. There was soon to be another book published. The author of the book would be Roderic Murray with the title <u>Marching with Dunmore</u>, chronicling, as a firsthand account, what was now being called "Lord Dunmore's War." Zachary Winston would be credited with his sketches this time, and they would share the royalties. This time Zack's sketches were of white settlements burned-out by the Shawnees, scenes of the natural beauty of the wilderness, soldiers on the march, the battlefield at Point Pleasant after the fight, the army marching along the banks of the Scioto River, and Chief Logan, sitting beneath his elm tree on the Pickaway Plains.

Peter and Mr. Boyd continued meeting several times a week at Raleigh Tavern and debating revolutionary politics with patriot leaders. The second Virginia Convention was drawing near, and Boyd asked if Peter wanted to join him in Richmond for a few days of business. Boyd said they would stop by St. John's Church, where the convention was to be held, and listen to some of the fiery speakers. That was all Peter could talk about for the weeks leading up to the convention.

"You ought to grab that sketchbook of yours and a whole parcel of charcoals and come with us," Peter hounded Zack. "The sketches you draw are so life-like! You should be there to draw it for publication."

"But I cannot write any thing anyone would want to publish," protested Zack meekly.

"I can write," piped up Rodie, "and really I want to be there. I want to write some essays and articles from what goes on there. I feel it is all going to be so important!"

"Does your uncle know?" Peter queried the nephew of the royal governor.

"No," Rodie squirmed a bit. "I will no doubt lose my bedroom at the palace if he finds out. I will have to sleep on your floor permanently...but that will not be so bad!"

Wednesday, March 22nd came, and Linwood Boyd, with Peter Francisco seated beside him on a loaded buckboard wagon, pulled away from in front of the mercantile, and headed down Duke of Gloucester Street before the sun rose. Zack and Rodie were seated in the bed of the buckboard, with their backs resting against the seat for the drivers. The wagon was loaded with deliveries for a mercantile in the smaller town of Richmond. They arrived in Richmond by early afternoon.

On their way into town they passed the churchyard of St. John's Episcopal Church, the site of the convention.

They unloaded their cargo for a Richmond merchant, and found lodgings for the night in a corner of the hayloft at the livery stable. At dinner in a tavern Wednesday evening, they dined with Patrick Henry and Hartwell Caulder. Caulder had sat in on some of the famous debates at Raleigh Tavern, and seemed to be coming closer and closer to the patriot cause, even if reluctantly so. Caulder lived on a plantation near Richmond.

"Are we going to have our own patriot army in Virginia, Patrick?" asked Boyd, as the diners finished their desert of apple dumplings.

"The counties are all organized through the local committees. I have just organized the Hanover Militia myself," said the red-haired delegate. "Each county is well equipped, should the king send his regulars."

"That will not happen," inserted Caulder, ringing Loyalist tones. "There is no need for a standing army, ours or that of the king."

"But Mister Caulder, if the king's navy sends the king's men to Yorktown or to the James, shan't we have arms ready to defend ourselves from occupation?" asked Peter. "Should we not be prepared as those in Boston could not be?"

"Tis my very point, Peter," Henry spoke. "Those in Boston did not prepare. They were taken in by a false a sense, promoted by the loyalists that no such thing as the king's army coming could ever occur. Like our good friend Caulder here is promoting. They have learned the lessen, and now, according to what missives come to us, are ready for the next shoe to drop."

"Having a patriot militia present and visible in the streets, will only encourage Lord Dunmore to convince Dartmouth to send those troops we all fear," warned Caulder.

"Do we know as a certainty that my uncle has not already so requested?" Rodie added.

"That will be the debate tomorrow at St. John's," said Henry, "to encouraged and form an armed resistance or not."

"We've no cause, no just cause," said Caulder emphatically, "to smack the hands of the king, the governor, and parliament, before there is such an act."

270

"So we wait umtil it is too late, with no militia?" Boyd questioned.

"Caulder, you have come to our side on many issues," said Henry. "I see you not as the unthinking Loyalist you have been in the past, but see you now as a soon-to-be-patriot. How can you not now see there is to be war? And when it comes, should we not be ready for it?

"You flaunt your nose at the governor just by your presence here at the convention," Henry added. "Our stated and published purpose for the convention is to elect delegates to the Second Continental Congress. Dunmore issued, just two days ago, an official proclamation, warning each and every one of us not to elect delegates at all. You are here. Are your intentions to elect delegates or not."

"Of course, I shall vote on delegates, Patrick, I plan to vote even to send you," answered Caulder. "The Continental Congress is not proposing a standing army."

"It shall, Caulder, it shall," answered Henry. "And I believe it shall be one of the Congress' first acts."

Thursday, March 23rd saw crowds heading to the church and churchyard for the historic meeting.

Peter, Zack, Rodie and Mr. Boyd could not get into the packed church, but found standing space outside the two windows closest to the front of the sanctuary and speaker's podium. Zack laid his sketch book open on the sill of the second window, giving him a good vantage of the speakers and the assembled delegates. Rodie laid his note pad on the first window, Peter standing beside him. Mr. Boyd found a spot on the opposite side of the church, standing with his merchant friend from Richmond.

Delegates were elected to represent Virginia in Philadelphia on May 10th. Washington, Harrison, Randolph, and Henry were all re-elected. Thomas Jefferson was elected to fill a vacancy.

Then came the debate on arming the colony in more than the simple way now being done by the local committees.

Benjamin Harrison rose to present a resolution for the Continental Congress to create the Continental Army, if the grievance petitioned by the last Congress had not been agreed to in London.

Caulder took the podium in opposition, articulating the same arguments he had given at the tavern the evening before. Others spoke for, and a few spoke against. The convention seemed divided enough to make passage by two-thirds of the delegates seem uncertain. Patrick Henry had made several informal arguments in support of Harrison's resolution, but had not spoken from the podium. Before Randolph called for a vote on the resolution, he recognized Henry, who had indicated he now wished to speak.

His lengthy oration was heard with not another sound coming from the pews. Not a huzzah. Not a hiss. Nothing at all heard, except for the stirring words the animated orator was speaking, with impassioned tones and motions accentuating his major poinys.. He came to the end of his words and spoke fervently:

> *"Is life so dear, or peace so sweet, as to be purchased*
> *at a price of chains and slavery?*
> *Forbid it, Almighty God!*
> *I know not what course others may take; but as for me,*
> **Give me liberty ... or give me death!"**

The convention was quiet for a moment, then, the Loyalist, Hartwell Caulder, bolted to his feet and punched his fist into the air as he cried, *"To Arms!"*

"To Arms! To Arms!" one by one the men stood and yelled. *"To Arms! To Arms!"* until every delegate, every soul standing at the opened windows and doors of the church, every lady, with parasol standing beneath the trees, and every child playing tag in the churchyard was joining in.

"To Arms! To Arms!"

Shots Heard 'Round the World

"Give me liberty or give me death!" Lord Dunmore read the remarks Patrick Henry made at the Virginia Convention, and threw the Virginia Gazette article, written by his errant nephew Roderic, into the fire. "He asks for liberty or death?" Dunmore fumed to Alexander. "He shan't have the former, but I shall most happily give him the later!"

As a result of Lord Dunmore hearing of the overwhelming support of the resolution, asking the Continental Congress, as a whole, to make preparations for an armed resistance, not simply in Virginia, but throughout all thirteen of the colonies, with the creation of the Continental Army, the governor knew the handwriting was on the wall.

John Hancock and Sam Adams knew the same as they led the Massachusetts Provincial Congress in the winter and spring of 1775. There was much communication between Gage in Boston and Dartmouth in London. By February, the leaders of Lord North's government had recognized an inevitable state of rebellion existed in the American colonies. All that was left and waited for was an actual event that would lead to a full-scale revolution.

Among the dispatches from Gage to Dartmouth in London was the news that Massachusetts was amassing arms and munitions in preparation for war. The so-called "minutemen" were to be found in every city precinct and village across the colony. According to Gage's best estimate there were some sixteen thousand patriot militiamen in Massachusetts. The colony was a powder keg waiting for the fuse to be lit.

On April 12th Gage received his orders from Dartmouth. He was to arrest *"the principal actors and abettors in the provincial congress, whose proceedings appear, in every light, to be acts of treason and rebellion."* Gage was also to find the stores of munitions in the colony and confiscate them immediately in the name of Great Britain.

Hancock and Adams, fearing arrest before they could safely make their way to Philadelphia as delegates to the Second Continental Congress, moved the sessions of the Provincial Congress in April to the town of Concord, fifteen miles north and west of Boston. The two patriot leaders took up residence in the home where Hancock had spent part of his boyhood, five miles to the east in the village of Lexington.

Wills Winkman called a meeting of the harbor precinct minutemen, seeing more activity and overhearing the talk of soldiers on the wharf and in the taverns. Something was about to happen to get the soldiers this fired up.

In the long room above Benjamin Edes' print shop, the men gathered on the afternoon of April 13th.

"There is something coming from the Redcoats," announced Wills, "I do not yet know what is coming, but something sure as Hell is getting ready to happen."

Dr. Joseph Warren, one of the patriot leaders who helped organize the minutemen, was present and seated between Paul Revere and Captain Reynolds.

"There is a stir in the air," Warren spoke. "It appears that Gage is anxious about the arms and munitions stored at Concord. It seems apparent, the regulars will move on Concord, and I would hasten to say, within just the next day or so."

"Our riders are ready at a minute's notice to warn the countryside," said Revere. "As soon as we can discover the plans, we shall ride."

"How will we know when the plan has been discovered, and what that plan shall be?" Wills asked. "We need to be the first warned, and know the warning is real."

"We need to set a plan to alert the riders when they should mount up and ride," Revere suggested.

"The tower of my church, the Old North Church, is seen from all parts," offered the church's sexton, Robert Newman. "It could easily be the beacon for such a purpose, and not arouse the attentions of others."

"I agree and I support such an idea fully," spoke up John Larkin, the church's deacon.

"But what signal shall we wait to see?" asked Wills.

"The espionage I have received leads me to believe," spoke Warren, "a force of regulars will be bound for Concord. We know not whether that force of the regulars will travel to Concord by way of the Charles River to Watertown, then overland toward Concord, or strictly by land from Boston. In order to alert the minutemen along the way, we need to wait until it is known which route shall be taken, and when they should be preparing to march."

"We shall keep all light from the tower of the Old North until that evidence is made clear," stated Deacon Larkin. "The moment Mr. Warren confirms it to me, there shall be one lantern glowing from the tower, if the Redcoats move by land, and if by the river, two lanterns will be aglow. One if by land ... two if by sea."

"As soon as the lanterns glow," agreed Warren, "be prepared to immediately mount and ride your assigned routes."

"That will be easily seen in Charlestown and all along the harbor precinct," stated Wills. "That will be our sign, one if by land ... two if by sea!"

The men all agreed, and all had the routes for their ride to warn the countryside.

As the meeting broke up and the punchbowl was being emptied of its grog, Wills walked down the outside stairs. He walked toward the harbor and his rented rooms above Sarah Eskridge's house. As he passed by the mercantile near the wharf, he almost knocked over a young lady leaving the shop with a half-dozen boxes.

"Oh I beg your pardon, miss," Wills said, and recognized immediately, it was the beautiful Priscilla Reynolds, daughter of his captain in the minutemen.

"How silly of me, Mister Winkman, I should have been looking before stepping," she said, with a flirtatious giggle. Wills stooped to pick up the boxes she had dropped.

"The least I can do is treat you to tea and biscuits at the inn," Wills managed to speak an invitation to her. "I remember well when you served tea and biscuits to me. Then I shall carry these awkward boxes home for you."

"The least I can do is accept your gracious invitation."

The two strolled off in the direction of the inn, with Wills toting the boxes for the petite object of his affections.

There was no signal on Sunday, nor on Monday night. Having heard Warren's words, they had expected the signal from the Old North Church would have been lit by then.

An hour or so before dusk on Thursday, the 18th of April, Wills again ran into Priscilla, and this time invited her to his rented rooms above the Eskridge house. Wills' mind was anywhere but on the tower of the Old North Church. He had a guest in his private rooms … the prettiest seventeen year-old lady he had ever laid his twenty-five year old eyes upon.

Wills poured the tea from a pot on the hearth and set out a pan of muffins. The two sat and sipped, ate and talked about…well about just things.

"I have been smitten by you since you first served me tea and cakes, when I was your father's guest," said Wills boldly, not knowing what sort of response he would get from the beautiful Priscilla.

"I too have looked upon you fondly, even when you were not in my actual sight," admitted Priscilla.

"I have longed for this day," Wills said, "when I could be alone with you, and get to know you, and see if my imagined thoughts are true."

"Wills, you are so sweet," she blushed. "I too have had such hopes."

Wills got up from his chair and walked toward Priscilla, reaching out his hands for hers. He pulled her up from her chair at the table. They stood there, face-to-face, staring into each other's eyes and smiling, still holding hands, Wills brought his face to hers, and they kissed.

After a few moments, the two young lovers were shed of their clothing and in Will's feather bed truly getting to know one another.

"I imagined it would be like this," admitted Priscilla, as she smiled, lying in his arms after their lovemaking.

"It was your first time," Wills said, in his most pleasant tone.

"Did I perform as you had expected I might?" she asked.

"I knew no more of what to expect than you," Wills admitted, with his face turning a bit red. "It was my first time as well."

She kissed him and he gladly received her lips.

"I told my mama I would not do such as we have done, until I did that with the man I would marry," Priscilla admitted. "And I have kept my word."

"You would make me the happiest man in Boston ... in all of the colonies ... in all of the world!" Wills shouted as he rolled over on top of her to kiss her again, "if you would agree to marry me."

"Marry you, I shall," accepted Priscilla, smiling as she rolled him off her. "But you will just have to satisfy that little fellow," looking down at his erection, "on your own." She scooted off the mattress and into her dress. "I must go before I am too late in arriving at home, and am forbidden ever again to be out after darkness has fallen."

Wills smiled, as he layed naked on the bed, pulling the quilt up over his body, watching his true love dress to leave.

"Would you meet me tomorrow?" Wills asked.

"I will attempt to get away and meet you ... in the Commons ... near the pond ... near three o'clock," she smiled and winked at him. She left the bedchamber and was out of sight in the main room. He heard her open the door, then immediately began working his sexual desires out from his body.

"One lantern," Priscilla said quietly, standing in the doorway, gazing out to the dark night sky. "Did you hear me Wills?" She came back across the floor of the main room and stepped back into the bedchamber.

"I said," Priscilla began to restate her observations, but her observations were distracted to that of a naked Wills, head laid back on the pillow, eyes closed, sweat beads on his forehead, as he pumped his erection vigorously. He saw her and his face turned bright red.

"As... I ...was saying," Priscilla said slowly, as embarrassed as was Wills. "There is one lantern in the tower of the Old North Church." She smiled at him, turned and closed the bedroom door behind her.

About the time Priscilla was leaving Wills' rooms, Dr. Warren and Captain Reynolds were knocking at the door of Paul Revere's house.

"Revere," Warren spoke, "our intelligence states the regulars are moving in fact on Concord with the intent of not simply confiscating the arsenal, but of also arresting Hancock and Adams under the Treason Act. They must be warned and warned immediately, or our cause could be ended by daybreak."

"The lantern was just placed in the tower moments ago," Revere added. "One if by land, the regulars are marching to Concord. I was just getting ready to mount and be off. You caught me in time."

"Ride with all haste," said Warren. "Take the post road, the shortest path to Lexington, and warn them to seek safety. Do not delay!"

Johnny Kilkenny was already at the meeting place he had arranged with Wills for when the lantern would be hung in the tower. Wills arrived ready for the ride, but would much more enjoy having been able to stay in the warmth of his room with Priscilla, naked in bed beside him. He would have to wait until three o'clock the next afternoon, if Priscilla was able to slip away.

The two rode northwest on the Somerville Road, shouting at every house and farm along the way.

"The Redcoats are coming! The Redcoats are coming!"

They would see lanterns flicker in response, and see many men dressed and with musket in hand coming out the door to head to their appointed company assembly area.

"The Redcoats are coming! The Redcoats are coming!"

They shouted as they rode from Somerville to Medford, then turning west for Arlington.

"The Redcoats are coming! The Redcoats are coming!"

From the town of Arlington, Wills and Johnny turned south. Arlington was the closest point to Lexington and Concord they would ride. They were in Arlington turning back toward Boston by midnight.

At about that same time, Paul Revere dismounted his horse at the manse where John Hancock and Sam Adams were staying. Revere knocked on the door, and Hancock himself answered and showed him in.

"The British are making their way on foot to Concord, and the arsenal to confiscate our arms," stated Revere. "You need to flee to safety," Revere added. "They have warrants for your arrests. Under the Treason Act they will ship the two of you off to London!"

"I will not flee like a coward," stated Hancock, with patriot pride. "I mean to command the men waiting for those bastards in their red coats to appear."

"Dr. Warren tells me you must vacate this place," Revere delivered the message.

"Hancock, we must go," agreed Sam Adams. "You and I both are much more important to this cause in the politics of the war that starts here this night, than upon the battlefields. We must go and we must leave at once."

"I shall not flee from here, the home of my boyhood," Hancock asserted, "until I cause the death of at least one of those bloody red coated bastards! I shall not!"

The argument continued for more than an hour. At half-passed midnight, the rider Billy Dawes arrived, and shortly thereafter, Dr. Samuel Prescott.

"Excuse the lateness of my arrival, gentlemen," stated Prescott entering the manse. "I am just now returning from a lady friend's house, and fear it is a most awkward hour." Everyone laughed at the elderly doctor's admission.

Eventually, near two o'clock in the morning, Hancock allowed reason to take over, and threw off the desires to personally kill as many

British soldiers as he could. He and Adams packed up their belongings, along with their families, and headed to a new refuge. The wanted men escaped from certain arrest at Lexington to the rural farmhouse of a preacher, midway between Lexington and Concord, a mile or so from the main road, near the small town of Lincoln.

As the riders were returning from their rounds in Boston, at Lexington, Paul Revere, Billy Dawes and Dr. Prescott headed to Concord to join the minutemen assembled on the green.

"Halt!" came orders from a British officer as they approached Lincoln. "Who goes there?" The three patriots were immediately taken and detained. Prescott spurred his horse and jumped a stonewall alongside the road to escape. He was off in the distance, free in no time.

Dawes attempted the same, but as the horse's hoof hit the top of the wall, Dawes fell to the ground. Dawes lay on the ground as the British patrol took Revere at gunpoint for questioning, and then led him back toward Lexington. As the patrol and their captive approached Lexington, the sun was just beginning to peek through the darkness. Morning was breaking and the sounds in the distance of heavy musket fire startled the patrol. The three-man patrol confiscated Revere's horse and set him free.

Revere took off on foot, walking through a cemetery, then a mile's worth of pastures and woodlands, before he arrived at the safety of the farmhouse where Hancock and Adams were.

Captain Drake Enfield, one of the three leaders of the minuteman company of Lexington, the brother-in-law of Jacky Macneal, was the first of the few casualties of the brave and valiant stand taken by the heroic minutemen on the Lexington Green. Their actions against the king's regulars were successful in delaying the advance of the redcoats on their way to the arsenal at Concord.

At Concord, the minutemen stood their ground and the British retreated, without capturing the armaments, or without capturing and arresting John Hancock and Sam Adams. The retreating Redcoats faced the constant threat of guerilla sniper fire from the forest, all the way along their route back to Boston.

Farmers and common colonial citizens held their ground that Friday morning, April 19th at Lexington and Concord, against the mightiest army in the world. It was the shot heard 'round the world, and the defenders could now truly call themselves 'Americans.'

The Unsheathed Sword

Soon after the failure of the regulars to seize the arsenal and the armaments at Concord, General Gage issued a general amnesty to all the colonials involved in the events at Lexington and Concord.

"Lay down your arms, and return to the duties of peaceable subjects," was the amnesty offered by the royal governor. All colonials could accept the amnesty, and have life go on as it had under the British. All colonials were offered the amnesty, all except for John Hancock and Samuel Adams. Few accepted it. No one wanted to return to the way it had been.

That same week in April, Lord Dunmore made preparations of his own. The powder, muskets, swords and other armaments of the Williamsburg Militia were stored in the magazine by the field where the militia drilled. The munitions were kept under lock and key, with the only key being held by John Miller, a trusted city official. Dunmore sent for Miller and ordered him to turn over the keys to the magazine.

"I cannot, sir," said Miller. "The militia entrusted the key to me. I shall unlock the magazine only upon their orders, as I have always done."

"You shall obey my orders," said Dunmore. "I am the government in Williamsburg."

"I repeat, your lordship," Miller continued his protest. "So long as I am the keeper of the key, I shall obey only the militia."

"I have authorization to use the Treason Act," Dunmore threatened. "I shall immediately order your arrest, and you shall sail off to London, be locked in the tower, and judged guilty by a London jury of right honorable and loyal subjects to the king."

Miller argued no more. He handed the key to Dunmore and left the palace. He went straight to Mayor John Dixon. Dixon assembled the militia on the drill field and gave orders to post four men to stand guard at the powder magazine around the clock, to prevent Dunmore from successfully spiriting away the precious munitions.

Fifteen Royal Marines from the HMS Magdalen, at anchor in the James River, led by Lt. Henry Collins, camped for a few days and nights in the wooded park behind the palace. Collins sent spies to monitor the militiamen guarding the magazine. Collins waited for a time when the militia would tire of boredom and abandon their posts.

The guards assigned the night watch on April 20th played into Collins' hand, as the Westminster chimes from Bruton Parish signaled midnight.

"We could be safe and comfortable in our own beds this night," complained Carlton Baker, one of the guards.

"Not a mouse is stirring in Williamsburg this night," agreed Joshua Hampton, another guard.

"And it has been so for the past nights, ever since we were stationed here," Baker added.

"The governor is not gonna pilfer the munitions," Hampton stated. "He's the governor, not a thief."

"I am going back to my farm and my wife, now soundly sleeping in our bed." Baker said.

As Collins wished, the guards left their posts.

At two o'clock, Lt. Collins ordered his marines to the magazine. The marines loaded fifteen barrels of gunpowder onto the governor's wagon, then left town, heading down Quarterpath Road to the landing on the James River. A light-sleeping militiaman was awakened by the sounds of a wagon on the cobblestone street. He went to his window and saw the governor's wagon loaded with the barrels. He ran next door to alert the captain of the militia. Soon, militia drummers began beating an alarm, rallying the militia to assemble.

The wagon had been spotted about halfway down Quarterpath Road. The militia gave chase, but the wagon filled with arms was already unloaded onto the Magdalen, when the militia caught up.

As day broke, Mayor Dixon, went to the palace with the aldermen and council members, demanding the return of the town's property. Dunmore refused and said he felt the gunpowder would be safer in his control.

"If an emergency arises," Dunmore said, "such as the slave revolt, you tend so much to fear, the powder will be at your disposal within one hour."

Riders spread the news immediately throughout the colony of the actions the governor had taken, smuggling the gunpowder from the magazine.

The day's issue of the Virginia Gazette on Monday, April 24th was one of the most important issues Alexander Purdie and Rodie Murray ever published. The Gazette carried the first printed news of the failed attempt of Gen. Gage to confiscate the arsenal at Concord, and of the brave stand taken by the minutemen at Lexington and Concord. The article was read and re-read by everyone, and the morale for the impending rebellion was elevated to new heights.

But more damning to the British was the article releasing the actual letter Lord Dunmore had written to Lord Dartmouth on Christmas Eve. When the citizens read Dunmore's urgings to Dartmouth to cut off all trade and blockade all ports, with the intention being *"to starve the Americans into submission,"* the revolution began in fact, then and there in Williamsburg.

On Wednesday, May 3rd the Hanover Militia marched into Williamsburg to demand the gunpowder be returned to the magazine. Patrick Henry, as the militia's commander, authorized the campaign himself. The same day, Lord Dunmore, hearing of the approach of Patrick Henry's militia, sent his family to his private hunting lodge, Portobello, along the York River. Only Alexander and Dunmore remained at the palace.

Rodie had, just the week before, been banned from the palace, and banished from the Murray clan. Dunmore had assumed it was his nephew who had furnished the publisher a copy of the letter sent to Dartmouth. Actually, the letter was released to the London papers, and copies of those newspapers found their way to the colonies.

Dunmore subjected his nephew to a heated cross-examination, and found him guilty of treason.

"You may carry the name of Murray with you," John Murray, Fourth Earl of Dunmore, head of the Murray Clan in Scotland, and the royal governor of Virginia spoke his sentence, "but you shall never ever again be claimed as a member this noble family! You are damned fortunate I do not have you arrested for treason and carried off to the Tower!" Those were the last words spoken between uncle and nephew.

On May 6th, Dunmore issued a proclamation stating, *"a certain Patrick Henry and a number of deluded followers, organized as an independent company and put themselves in a posture of war."*

The proclamation went on to threaten the emancipation of the slaves in Virginia, and that if Henry or any other militia company caused any harm to him, his family, or other royal officials, Dunmore would burn the city of Williamsburg to ashes. The proclamation defaming Patrick Henry increased Henry's already high esteem and prominence in the colony. The threat to emancipate slaves and burn Williamsburg to the ground only served to further fanned the flames of rebellion, and bring more and more Loyalists to the Patriot cause.

Alexander Purdie printed a broadside stating:

> *"The Sword is now Drawn and God knows when it*
> *shall again be Sheathed!"*

Being a student at William and Mary was not conducive to studies in the spring of 1775. Students heard the debates and saw the revolution building with each day.

On May 4th, Jimmie Monroe joined with Peter Francisco and some older boys, and broke into the magazine, hauling off many of the remaining muskets, swords and other equipment. The governor was not amused, and instructed some of his palace guards to set a trap inside the magazine. The guards set four shotguns, ready to be triggered, if such a culprit tried to haul off the remaining arms. A few days later, some of the students again broke in. The buckshot wounded three, but the rest were able to confiscate the remaining muskets.

After protests to the governor from the mayor and a crowd of angry townsfolk gathered on the palace grounds, Dunmore was forced turn the keys over.

In the wee hours of June 8th, Dunmore himself fled Williamsburg under cover of darkness to rejoin his family. Lady Dunmore and the children had been sequestered away at Portobello for over a month. For safety's sake, Dunmore led his secretary and family aboard the HMS Fowey, a British warship at anchor at Yorktown.

Lord Dunmore sent word to the House of Burgesses to continue with business as usual, and bring to him, aboard the Fowey, whatever bills were passed requiring his signature.

The burgesses demanded Dunmore return to the palace. His suggestion they come to him was not reasonable and would not happen.

As June came to a close, the students of William and Mary, and many of the younger residents of the city made plans of their own. They met at Raleigh Tavern. Caullen Dixon, the son of Williamsburg's mayor, and one of the three boys injured in the trap at the magazine, called the meeting.

"Our esteemed governor has fled, and we cheer his departure," Dixon said, opening the meeting. All the boys assembled cheered and applauded. The Campbelltown boys were among them.

"The Governor's Palace has sat unoccupied for the past seventeen days," Dixon went on.

"He's a scurvy coward," shouted Jimmie Monroe to more cheers and applause.

"He ran away under the cover of night with his skirts flapping in the wind," added young Bush Washington.

Zack laughed, trying to picture Dunmore running out of the palace doors to an awaiting liveried carriage, with his Murray family tartan plaid nightgown flapping about his knees. That might be a sketch he should consider, he thought. He'd have Rodie print it in the Gazette.

"As our noble representative of the king fled for his life," Dixon went on.

"Without life nor limb ever being threatened in any way," came a shout from one of the students.

"Yes, indeed," affirmed Dixon, "without any such threat. He left a store of arms behind."

The room grew quiet with a hush.

"Dunmore took from the magazine a large quantity of our muskets and swords," stated Dixon. "At this moment, those very confiscated arms that belong to the city of Williamsburg, are locked away in the palace. He apparently was so much afraid the night of his exodus, he forgot to have them taken with him!"

"We must take them back!" shouted Monroe.

"We must!" agreed Peter, "before he sends the marines for them!"

"How do we know for certain they are still at the palace?" asked Monroe.

"I saw them there myself," came a hardly ever heard voice at these rallies, that of Zack Winston. "I was at the palace, just yesterday, doing a sketch. I peered through the windows and just inside the main door, in the foyer, were stacked a treasure of muskets and swords."

"I saw them there too, the last time I visited my uncle," spoke Rodie Murray, "the day that scurvy little coward of a man expelled me from my own family. There were at the least four or five hundred muskets, and a large number of sabers, swords, and bayonets, and bags and bags of balls, all there in the foyer."

"We cannot wait another day," said Monroe, "lest the marines come from the Fowey in the still of the night, and take them like they took the gunpowder before."

"We cannot wait another hour," shouted Peter. "Every moment we wait to act, we stand to lose, and the king's men stand to win. What is your plan, Dixon?"

"As you have all said, we cannot wait," Dixon began to lay out his plan. "We should leave from here and, with all in agreement, go directly to the palace. We shall break out the windows where Zack Winston saw the arms, and cart them away. We shall need one wagon and horses to carry them away back to the Magazine. It is safe now."

"There is a team and wagon at the livery owned by the mercantile," Peter offered. "I can go straight away and get it, and have it in front of the palace in twenty minutes time."

"I have an easier way for us to get inside the palace," offered Rodie. "There is a hidden window behind the boxwood bushes at the rear of the palace. I used it many times to sneak in and out unnoticed. There is no lock upon it. I can get in and unlock the back doors from the inside. Peter can pull the wagon up to the back verandah, and the arms can be easily and secretly loaded, with no detection from prying eyes."

"Then is it settled?" Dixon asked. "Are all in agreement?"

Shouts and applause went up, and the plan was put into action.

Well before the boys would return for their normal suppertimes at the Wren or with their families, all the muskets, swords, sabers and bayonets, with nearly one thousand pouches of musketballs, were safely stashed back inside the Magazine.

That was June 24th, and that day all the town's attentions were turned to the far other end of Duke of Gloucester Street. The House of Burgesses had announced its last session. The house would dissolve itself, breaking all influence King George III and his parliament had over them.

Dunmore had sent a messenger from the Fowey, stating only he, not the delegates themselves, could dissolve the legislature, and that if the delegates did as they intended, it would be considered in London an all-out act of rebellion.

On July 29th, Lady Dunmore sailed to Scotland with the children. Dunmore and Alexander remained on board the Fowey in Chesapeake Bay. Dunmore was still the appointed royal governor, and had no intentions of abdicating his title. He headquartered himself at Kemp's Landing on the river just south of Norfolk. Norfolk, with a majority of the citizens remaining loyal to the king, welcomed the royal governor to his new capital in exile.

The Second Continental Congress

The first order of business for the second Continental Congress was determining officially if Parliament and the king had made any attempt to address the grievances laid out by the last session of Congress.

The president of Congress, Peyton Randolph of Virginia, read the list of grievances: the right of assembly and petition, trial by a jury of one's peers, protection from the presence of a standing army, and the right to elective representation on any issue dealing with taxation.

"Neither the right honorable men sitting upon the River Thames," stated Massachusetts delegate John Adams, "nor George III sitting in St. James Palace, have addressed one of the enumerated grievances."

"Here, here!" came the cries from all the delegates.

"That being the general sense of the delegates," president Randolph announced, with gavel in hand, "I hereby declare the second session of the Continental Congress open for further business." He rapped the gavel to more cries of "here, here!"

Randolph, the rotund and aged man who commanded great respect from his colleagues, had not been of good health upon leaving Virginia for the Congress in Philadelphia, and had not traveled comfortably or well.

After the close of the first day's session, Randolph asked the one delegate he admired most from the first Congress to dine with him.

John Adams had been a favorite of many delegates the year before, and was honored to dine with the president.

"Adams," Randolph said, as the two men began their suppers, "I fear my age, my general health, and my rotundity are getting the better of me."

"I could not agree at all with you, Randolph," insisted the lawyer from Braintree, "especially after seeing how vigorously you articulated your remarks at our the opening session this day."

"I appreciate the words of one I do so admire," Randolph said, "but believe me, Adams, when I say I doubt I shall breathe the autumn air again. I intend to announce my desire for another to be elected as the president."

"I pray you reconsider," the shocked and stunned John Adams said. "Who shall replace you?"

"You ... your cousin Sam ... that John Hancock fellow," Randolph suggested. "Someone from the colony you represent. You of Massachusetts, who have been so subjected to the vile oppressions of Parliament and King George."

"But the colony of Virginia is so important in the leadership of this cause," Adams reflected. "If a Massachusetts delegate replaces you, a Virginian in the presidency, will this not seem to the other colonies as a play for power on the part of my delegation?"

"Virginia will stand beside our brethren in Massachusetts throughout this cause," Randolph spoke, "and I feel the others shall, as well."

Adams thought through the main course of his meal and into desert, then offered a possible solution.

"I am not one who would relish the seat of president," Adams began. "I am invigorated standing on the floor and expounding what views I possess, and debating with the South Carolinians and the Georgians.

"Cousin Sam, as devoted a patriot as he is, I feel he is not a prime choice to succeed you. Hancock, on the other hand, is one who could be an effective president, if he will have it, and I see no reason why he should decline such the honor."

"Then it is settled," Randolph spoke, "John Hancock will be the president."

"Oh no, it is not quite so simple, Randolph," stated Adams firmly. "First, he needs to be consulted and in agreement, and second, we must create an invaluable leadership role for the colony of Virginia; and I think I have just the answer."

"Then speak," Randolph seemed intrigued. "Speak."

"Congress is soon to create the Continental Army," Adams went on. "The army needs a commander-in-chief to direct the war and capture the victory. Since the Congress adjourned, I have concentrated on the one best man to serve in that role. There is none in any colony to fit that order other than your own Col. Washington."

Randolph thought on the possibility of his old friend, the forty-four-year-old George Washington. Washington really only had limited military service, but the service he had provided for Governor Dinwiddie, and then General Braddock during the French and Indian War had been legendary. He certainly had the aura of heroism and folklore around him. Others would volunteer to follow him.

"There are the names of others with more proven military acumen," stated Randolph. "There is talk among the delegates of Horatio Gates and Charles Lee, both of whom have tested experience in the British Army."

"We need an American military mind to lead an American army," stated Adams firmly, "and a Virginian for political reasons."

"Why is my decision on the matter needed?" Randolph asked. "Of course I could support Washington as our commander-in-chief, but I am but one."

"If we do not have Washington and Virginia leading us on the battlefields, then we must have you, we must have Virginia leading us in Congress. Massachusetts and Virginia will lead this new country through this coming revolution. No other two colonies can do so."

On May 24th, John Hancock of Massachusetts was unanimously elected to replace the retiring Peyton Randolph as president of the Continental Congress. Days later, Congress authorized the creation of the Continental Army to be established with twenty thousand men.

It was time to have Washington named to lead the army just created by Congress. Adams invited Washington to dine with him on the evening of June 14th.

"Colonel Washington," Adams began the discussion as the two leaders dined, "you must be the one man to lead our army."

"I would be honored," Washington responded, "but are there not others who have more certain military experience than I?"

"You have the experience needed," stated Adams firmly, "and the name and reputation to rally the men and bind thirteen states together. Had Braddock listened to your advise in the Great Meadows, he may well be this day leading the King's Regulars in Boston, instead of being a mere footnote in history.

"I wish to place your name before Congress tomorrow as commander-in-chief. I seek a unanimous confirmation, but I need your assistance."

"I will not campaign for the honor," Washington spoke dismissively. "While I would relish in accepting such an honor as you propose for me, I shall not campaign, nor speak one word in my own behalf."

Adams smiled. "Speak not one word colonel. Just wear the magnificent uniform you wore the first day of the quorum, and you shall leave our august body with the command, and with the rank of general."

On Thursday, June 15th John Hancock recognized his fellow Massachusetts delegate, John Adams, who offered a bill to create the office of Commander-in-Chief of the Continental Army, and to place George Washington's name in nomination to fill the position, with the rank of general.

Adams, being the effervescent orator he was, gave a flowery nominating speech on Washington's behalf that ran for more than an hour. Adams glorified Washington so that the humble Washington, dressed in his uniform, as requested by Adams, became so embarrassed as Adams spoke, he got up and left the floor, not to be further embarrassed as his fellow delegates considered his appointment.

The election of Washington was unanimous. Upon his election, Washington resigned his seat and begged leave of the Congress. Within days, Washington, in his uniform, left for Massachusetts, to join the army assembled at Cambridge, just north of Boston.

Pennsylvania delegate, John Dickinson, asked the captain of the local militia to assemble a company of Pennsylvanians to escort Washington to Cambridge. The citizens of Philadelphia lined the cobblestone streets of the largest city in America, and cheered General George Washington and his escort company on their ride out of town.

Wills and Priscilla

Ever since the lanterns lit the Boston darkness in April, Wills Winkman and Priscilla Reynolds met nearly every afternoon or night at Wills' rooms in Sarah Eskridge's house by the wharf. One June night, while they were again together, she lay naked beneath a sheet on Wills' bed. Wills, on his knees besides her, gently rubbed her stomach.

"Do you think it is a boy or is it a girl? He asked Priscilla, as his hand made circular motions on her bare stomach above where the baby grew.

"I could care not," she said sweetly and smiled, "only that tis healthy and tis your child." He bent over and kissed here.

"We need to be wedded," he said gallantly. "I will talk with your father this very night." She began to sob. "What is it?" Wills asked. "Do you not want to be my bride?"

"Father will want a proper engagement, and a wedding in the church," Priscilla said.

"Yes," Wills answered, "and I want that as well."

"By the time a proper engagement is ended, I shall not be with child, we shall already have a child," Priscilla sobbed. "I will be disgraced, and they will call our darling baby a bastard!"

Wills sat bolt upright on the bed.

"Then we shall run away and wed," Wills offered. "After the battle we shall have tomorrow at Bunker Hill, we can ride off to … to … to Gloucester. No one there knows us. We'll be wed and come home within two days. And just pity the fool who ever calls my child a bastard!"

"Run off and get married?" Priscilla queried.

"Why not? I am to join the troops at Cambridge," Wills said. "I will rent a home for us, and we shall live there. He bent over her and kissed her. They layed there for more than an hour, just holding each other nakedly on the bed that warm afternoon, and planned their escape for the next week. The next day, Wills would report to General Artemis Ward to help defend the redoubts on the heights of Breed's Hill.

On June 17th, the second day of Washington's journey from Philadelphia, as he was riding between Morristown, New Jersey and New

York, the Battle of Bunker Hill was taking place in Boston. Washington had been pleased with the dispatches from New England since the Battle of Lexington and Concord. The fervor for war was lit, and the soldiers who were now the beginnings of the Continental Army, were amassed around Harvard Yard at Cambridge. In May, Ethan Allen and a band he called the Green Mountain Boys from Vermont, along with a military man, Benedict Arnold, leading some militiamen from Connecticut and western Massachusetts, stormed the British Fort Ticonderoga, on the southern shore of Lake Champlain, and captured it and its valuable cannons. Washington wanted those cannons at Cambridge for his plan to rid Boston of the Redcoat Army.

To prevent the King's regulars from fortifying Charlestown from Boston Harbor, the patriots, led by General Rufus Putman and Colonel William Prescott, built redoubts on the summit of Breed's Hill. The object of the British was the adjacent Bunker Hill. In an effort to dispel the patriots, the British force began a march up the hills.

"Don't fire till you see the whites of their eyes," Col. Prescott ordered, as the Redcoats approached. The valiant efforts of the patriot soldiers proved they knew how to fight, even though the day belonged to the British.

Many citizens of Boston turned out to watch the battle from another neighboring hilltop, as the brave and grossly out-numbered patriots fought the gallant fight. Among those witnessing the battle was Abigail Adams. She brought the three oldest of her and John's four children, to watch history unfold. Their oldest, Nabby, was ten, John Quincy was eight, and Charles was five. The youngest and last of the children, Thomas Boylston Adams at age three, remained with his grandmother in Weymouth.

Priscilla Reynolds came too with her mother and sisters. They watched the Battle of Bunker Hill from the hilltop as Abigail Adams and her brood did. They watched the British Redcoats march up the hill, and saw the smoke of muskets as the two armies neared each other. Somewhere in that distance was Wills, soon to be Priscilla's husband, and Captain Reynolds, her father, soon to become a grandfather.

There were but a handful of American causalities, but among them, Captain Miles Reynolds. Wills and his friend and fellow patriot, Henry Knox, carried their dead captain to a wagon to be transported to the Reynolds home for preparation and burial at the Granary Burial Ground.

Wills' plan had to be rethought as they waited for the funeral and burial. Mrs. Reynolds was devastated with the death of her husband. There she was, alone, left to care for and support three daughters without the loving companionship and financial support of a husband.

The day after the funeral, Wills and Priscilla were again naked on his bed.

"We need to act fast," Wills said, "for us as well as for your mother and our child."

"What do you mean, dear?" Priscilla asked, "I cannot think of leaving her at this moment."

"She needs a man to be her protection and her support," Wills said. "I will be that man."

Priscilla shot up in the bed.

"You? Marry my mother?" Priscilla asked, with her face red in anger.

"No!" Wills said, sitting up and grabbing her bare shoulders. "Don't be silly! I will marry you." He kissed her. "It will be out of necessity now," Wills explained. "We will talk frankly with your mother tonight. We will be wedded, and I will move the entire Reynolds family to a house, not rented rooms, in Cambridge, safely away from the dangers of this city."

Priscilla smiled broadly, "You would do that? You would, as a newly-wedded husband, marry not just me, but my mother and two younger sisters as well?"

They kissed, sank back onto the mattress and made love.

Washington at Cambridge

On June 20th 1775, General Washington rode into Cambridge. He received a warm welcome from the citizens lining the cobblestone streets, as the general and his escort passed by. He wished to ride through Boston itself, but that was too dangerous, as Howe kept his headquarters there. The war was on and George Washington was anxious to begin making plans to win the independence of the American colonies.

The army was more than twenty thousand men when Washington arrived. It was mostly made up of the New England militias, now commanded by General Artemas Ward, General Rufus Putnam, and his brother General Israel Putnam. The army at Cambridge was largely an undisciplined and disorderly band of men. There was no sense of unity or brotherhood among the troops, as militiamen from Connecticut argued and fought with the men from Rhode Island, while New Hampshire men did the same with those from the Maine district of Massachusetts. Washington knew his army was not yet ready to march and perform upon the fields of battle.

A temporary headquarters on the Harvard College yard had been prepared for the general when he arrived. The army was quartered in tents and lean-tos, spreading across the yard and throughout the neighborhoods nearby. Officers occupied rooms in some of the buildings of the college, and had commandeered homes of loyalists who had already fled to England.

Soon, Washington selected one of those deserted homes as his permanent headquarters. The loyalist merchant, John Vassall, had sailed for England shortly after the Battle of Lexington and Concord. Vassall had built the luxurious house in 1759. It was three stories and painted a golden hue with crisp white trim. It was the most beautiful house on Brattle Street, just a block or so from the Commons.

The new commander of the American Army was organizing his general staff, and laying plans for a siege of Boston, to drive the British out, as well as making plans for a total war of revolution. The men he relied upon most heavily in those early days were General Ward, the Putnam brothers, and Lieutenant Henry Knox.

Wills Winkman found a small house near Brattle Street, standing vacant from the former loyalist owners, now safely back in London. Soon after General Washington arrived, Henry Knox suggested that Wills serve, at least temporarily, as his secretary at the headquarters. General Ward endorsed the idea, and Washington accepted the suggestion. Wills, with the rank of private, spent many hours taking minutes in strategy and planning sessions with Washington, Lt. Knox and the generals.

Henry Knox, like Wills, was a twenty-five year-old Boston native. His father had died when he was twelve, so he was forced to support his widowed mother. He had a self-taught academic bent toward the military, and especially the artillery. He witnessed the Boston Massacre, and joined the Boston Grenadiers. He had been active in the Sons of Liberty, where he had met and befriended Wills Winkman. He served at the Battle of Bunker Hill, just before General Washington arrived to take command of the army at Cambridge.

Wills enjoyed his new life with his new family in the rented house on Landsdowne Street. Priscilla knew the baby would probably come in February, as the date of inception, as best she could figure, had been in early May. For the sake of propriety, she claimed the birth should be in late March or early April, since her wedding to Wills had been held in the parlor of their new house on the last day of June. If the actual birth was a month, or even six weeks earlier, that could be easily explained as a bit premature, and no reason for the term 'bastard' to be used, or for the prevailing Puritan suspicions to surround the newlyweds, as having been the slightest bit improper during their brief courtship.

Eudora Reynolds was well over the sudden battlefield death of her husband, and was keeping busy helping Priscilla with the housekeeping chores of a bride, and preparations for childbirth. The two younger daughters, Amanda and Eleanor, were fourteen and twelve, and enjoyed all the excitement in the streets of Cambridge, with the twenty thousand-plus soldiers assembled and preparing for a revolutionary war.

The Cannons of Ticonderoga

Washington quickly developed a liking for his secretary, and offered Wills the permanent position with him, along with the rank of lieutenant. Wills had his office in what had been the front parlor of the Vassall House. Every visitor coming to see General Washington came to Lt. Winkman to be shown in to Washington's office, the former gentleman's study, that could only be accessed through Wills' outer office.

Every day, various officers of the army were either summoned to Washington's headquarters, or came on their own, with something on their minds they wished to share with the commander-in-chief. Wills became quite familiar with most, and friends with many.

One day, the first week of November, Ward and Knox walked up the steps of the Vassall House and into Wills' outer office.

"The general is ready for you," Wills greeted the two, rose from behind his desk, and walked to the door to Washington's private office. He knocked twice and opened the door.

"General Ward and Lieutenant Knox are here, sir."

"Send them in, and please, lieutenant, join us," came Washington's voice.

Washington was anxious to discuss an issue that had weighed heavily on his mind for weeks, and he wanted Wills there to take notes.

"We are in dire need of artillery if we are to send the British army into their ships, and out of our harbor," Washington opened the discussion. "There are, according to the reports I have received, some fifty cannons captured, and sitting idly in the New York wilderness at Forts Ticonderoga and Crown Point," Washington noted.

"Fifty-nine, sir, to be precise," Knox spoke up, "Forty at Ticonderoga and another nineteen at Crown Point."

"We need those pieces of artillery here," insisted Washington. "Three hundred miles away sit the very key to our victory here in Boston."

Turning directly to Knox, Washington continued. "Henry, I wish for you to plan immediately to take a company of men and retrieve those cannons. Bring them here so, as spring breaks, the British will awaken one day to see those cannon barrels looking down upon them from the heights of Dorchester."

"That cannot be done," spoke Ward, "not as winter is setting in upon us, and the snows will be deep in the mountains. This is not Virginia, General Washington. This should have been undertaken in July ... or August."

"It can, most assuredly, be done," Knox said, not wanting to disrespect his superior, General Ward. "Begging your pardon, General Ward, but I have thought of nothing else since receiving those same dispatches myself. How strategic a necessity it is for us to get those pieces of artillery here. I can do it, and have them here in ample time."

"How do you propose doing such a thing, Knox?" Ward asked smugly, not believing it possible at all. "The terrain opposes you, as does the winter calendar."

"Oxen and sleds," calmly commented the young Knox. "We will make the return with enough yoke of oxen pulling sleds, with a cannon and supplies on each."

Washington pondered Knox' plan for several moments. Could it really be done? What other way would be more feasible to get fifty-nine greatly needed cannons from forts in the frontier to Cambridge? Washington raised these questions silently in his mind, as Ward brought up various oppositions, with Knox answering each.

"What would be a realistic timetable?" asked Washington.

"We could leave here within six day's time," Knox spoke, showing he had a workable plan. "We would be at the forts before November ends, secure the oxen from the farmers in the area, build the sleds, then be on the way to Cambridge by the middle of December. We can be back here with the cannons by the middle of February. It will be a slow trudge, but I am certain we can do it.

"I will need a company of one hundred and thirty," Knox continued, "a supply wagon, and a purse of one hundred pounds sterling. I shall send scouts ahead to contract for the oxen, and congregate them at the forts for the trip back. Loaded and yoked, I surmise we could average six, maybe even seven miles per day, with the artillery."

He stood and looked at the map laying across Washington's desk. He started with his finger on Fort Ticonderoga.

"Driving down the west shore of the Hudson to Albany," Knox laid out the route, "we shall cross the river there, and head due east across the Berkshires back to Cambridge."

"Artemas?" Washington looked to the elder general for his thoughts.

General Ward, thought, digesting Knox' plan. He took a deep breath "If any one man can execute such a plan," he shook his head in disbelief, "it is Henry Knox."

Washington turned back to Knox. "Then it is agreed," Washington said, as he stood and offered his hand to Knox. "Go forward with the plan as soon as is practicable. Wills, draw up the appropriate orders for Lieutenant Knox to conscript the one hundred thirty men he needs, and papers for the quartermaster to allocate a wagon and supplies enough for the maneuver. I shall have a purse with the funds required to purchase the oxen."

Washington put an arm around Knox' shoulders.

"Henry," Washington spoke, "if you can succeed in this important endeavor, as I have every confidence you shall, I shall commission you a colonel in the Continental Army, and make you my commander of the artillery for the entire army."

The men rose and prepared to leave.

"Oh, Mrs. Ward would skin me alive if I forgot to invite you to Thanksgiving at our home," General Ward spoke to Washington.

"Thanksgiving?" Washington questioned.

"Oh yes," Ward answered. "We in Massachusetts have adopted the celebration the Pilgrims brought to America in 1621. Our congregation celebrates Thanksgiving this year on the twentieth."

"I shall be delighted," said Washington. "I will be interested in how you might celebrate Thanksgiving differently in New England… from the way we celebrate it in Virginia."

"Thanksgiving in Virginia?" Ward seemed to chuckle.

"Oh yes, General Ward," Washington said. "Virginians gathered at Harrison's Landing on the James River to celebrate Thanksgiving for twelve years of permanent settlement…in 1619…two full years before your ancestors, the Pilgrims."

At Kemp's Landing, the exiled royal governor of Virginia issued a proclamation offering freedom to any African slave willing to turn on his colonial master, and join the British Army. Dunmore reversed his previous stand on slave issues when, several months before, he refused to sign to a bill passed by the House of Burgesses outlawing the slave trade in the colony.

Dunmore created the Black Loyalists and the Ethiopian Regiment out of the hundreds of newly emancipated Virginia slaves. The emancipation, and the dependence on freed slaves as the military arm of the governor, did not sit well with many of the Loyalists in the environs of Norfolk and Portsmouth.

In the autumn of 1775, an epidemic of smallpox hit hard along the Virginia coastline. Several died, even with the new inoculations to prevent the disease. The hardest hit segment of the population was that of the slaves. No emancipated slave, now in red coat uniforms, had been inoculated, and more than five hundred of the eight hundred men of the Ethiopian Regiment died.

At Winston Woods, all of Judge Winston's slaves were inoculated, and none had to be taken to the old cemetery.

In December, Dunmore, using the Black Loyalists and the remaining Ethiopian Regiment, attacked the settlement at Great Bridge, south of Norfolk and Portsmouth. Dunmore suffered a defeat, and afterwards, lost what remaining Loyalists who had stood with him after the emancipation proclamation. As a show of revenge for his defeat at Great Bridge, on January first 1776, Dunmore laid the torch to Norfolk and Portsmouth as his last acts in Virginia. He sailed away to New York the next day.

The Smithtown Settlement

Around the first of May, 1775, Tom had a load of hides to take to Nate Nevers at the trading post. Jacky and Davy stayed at Annie's Port to plow the garden and make it ready for springtime plantings. They also wanted to collect some sassafras and ginseng roots, and harvest some hemp leaves to dry. Davy showed Tom and Jacky how the Mingo burned the dried leaves in their pipes.

"It is a relaxing smoke," Davy said the first time he introduced it to Jacky and Tom, "not harsh nor bitter like the tobacco grown in Virginia. You smoked it when you smoked Logan's peace pipe on the Muskigum." They soon were passing their own peace pipe most evenings on the verandah after dinner.

The sun was setting as Tom returned later than expected, but Jacky and Davy had supper ready. They sat around and talked for an hour or so, smoking the pipe with dried hemp leaves, then Davy, tired from the work he had shared with Jacky that day, went to his bed in the spare room. Tom and Jacky soon went to bed themselves.

"I didn't want to mention this earlier, while Davy was up," Tom said, as he was getting undressed and crawling into bed. "I wanted to talk first to you."

"What is it?" Jacky asked, as he undressed and got into bed with Tom. "You sound so serious."

"Well, it is serious," Tom said, "and will be a great surprise to Davy. I just wanted to tell you first. Isn't that what's right...us not surprising the other with something that is for us to both decide upon together?"

"Of Coarse," said Jacky, snuggling into Tom's shoulder.

"Nate Nevers talked to a man this week who knows Smithtown." Tom announced.

"Did he live there?" Jacky shot up in bed. "Did he know the Danielson family?"

"No, he just seems to roam the area," Tom said, "but the main point is Nate now knows exactly where to find Smithtown. It's about two and a half days straight down the Monongahela from the fort, and about two miles inland, after we come across a small trading post on the river."

Jacky slipped back down in bed. "When do ya wanna go?"

"I was thinking we'll both tell Davy at breakfast, and plan to take a week or two and head off soon, say Friday or Saturday?"

Davy was excited, though seemed a little hesitant when Tom and Jacky told him of their plans at breakfast.

"Yes, I do want to go to Smithtowm," Davy said, "but I know not what it may bring."

"We know there is all too much that remains uncertain in your thoughts," said Tom, "but I am just as certain, whatever it is we find there, will end some, if not all of the uncertainty that now plagues you."

They left Annie's Port early on Friday morning for Nate Nevers' trading post. The Monongahela was as broad as the Ohio, when it turned and snaked south. On Monday, they came across a small trading post on the river. The man at the trading post was new to the area and knew nothing of the Danielson family. He told them to walk the path along the winding creek to find the settlement.

"I remember this place," Davy said, having been gone from his family's farmstead for five years. "I used to fish and play in this creek with my friend Jasper. Our farm is right on the creek bank as we arrive at Smithtown." He picked up the pace, seeming anxious now to see his old home. Tom and Jacky followed Davy's pace.

They stood in front of the cabin beside the road with a split-rail fence and a large field, plowed and ready for planting.

"This is the farm," Davy said nervously as he stood on the lane staring at the cabin.

"Should we go up and see if anyone is here?" asked Jacky. Davy just nodded.

All sorts of possibilities flooded his mind. Was he to at last be reunited with his mother, brother and sister? The settlement was still there, so the Shawnees had not massacred and burnt it. There was nothing else to do but see if his family was still there.

"Howdy folks," a scruffy man of about forty came out the door of the cabin. "Ya plannin' on settlin' here?" the man asked.

Tom, seeing Davy had not recognized the man, went forward extending his hand.

"This is the Smithtown settlement, is it not?" Tom asked.

"What there is of it," the man chuckled. "Many have left, but others come. Come on," he waved at Jacky and Davy motioning for them. "Come on up, all o' ya, an' sit on the porch." Jacky and Davy walked to the porch and sat.

"We're actually looking for a Mrs. Danielson, who we think once lived in this cabin," said Tom.

"Oh, she used ta all right," said the man who introduced himself as Justus Brewer. "Me an' my wife Hester bought this here place from 'er two years ago."

"She was sure pitiful," the man said, shaking his head. "Her man an' young boy was kilt by Injuns. She had two youngin's, a boy an' a beautiful little girl. It was all she could do to work this farm herself with no man to help out. She married a stranger come ta town, an' I think they were headin' off ta som'ers back in Virginny."

"Is there any one here who might know for certain?" Tom asked.

"Well, her best friend was Sarahy Small. Her husband was kilt the same time," the man said. She lives the next farm over," the man pointed down the lane toward the settlement.

Davy stood, "I remember Sarah!" Davy said. "Her son, Jasper, was my best friend here. She will remember me, and know where Mama is if any one does know."

"Lordy mercy, boy" the man said, "you the boy they all said was kilt?"

Davy looked at the man. "Yes, I am Davy Danielson. I was taken captive by the Shawnee."

"Lordy sakes alive!" Brewer shook his head.

Tom and Jacky followed Davy as he led the way to Sarah Small's farm, just down the dirt road.

Sarah was in her plowed garden with three children, planting corn. When she saw the three walking toward her farm, she stood and wiped her dirty hands on her apron. She stood like a statue staring. "Jasper," she said quietly, "would that there be yer ole playmate Davy?"

The boy looked up from his planting. "No, Ma, Davy's dead." He went back to his work.

"Sarah!" Davy shouted out and waved. He started running toward her.

"Davy Danielson! It is you!!" she shrieked, spreading her arms wide to welcome him. He ran into her open arms. They both cried. Jasper came running too. His old playmate was not dead after all!

"Your mama surely did miss ya, Davy," Sarah said, as she sat with Davy, Tom and Jacky, and her boys Jasper and Evan, and daughter Josie. "She didn't wanna leave here, fer she knew ya were alright some hows, and would come home some day. But that man she married," Sarah shook her head, "Clinton Deerfield, he insisted they go all the way back ta his farm near Richmond."

"And what about Jacob and Susannah?" Davy asked of his siblings.

"Jacob was growin' like a weed, last I saw 'im," Sarah said, "an' little Susannah, why she was gettin'prettier by the day."

Davy smiled, and told Sarah about his life with Logan for four years, and now at Annie's Port.

"You men hunters?" she asked Tom and Jacky.

"Yes ma'am we surely are," answered Jacky.

"Well, there's game o'plenty 'round these parts," Sarah said. "You're sure welcome ta stay on a spell ... long as you'd like. There's a hayloft in the barn, makes a comfortable bed. I heard tell they saw a herd o' buffalo a grazin' 'long Hickory Creek 'bout a week ago."

"We'll stay the night," said Tom, "but we need to get back soon."

"Very well," Sarah said rising. "If Jasper here'll go out and wring a chicken's neck, I'll put a pot on the hearth an' we'll have us a mess o' dumplin's."

Davy went off with Jasper to wring a chicken's neck.

After breakfast the next day, Jasper Small walked back to the trading post with Davy, Tom, and Jacky. Sarah sent him to pick up a sack of corn meal. She cried as they left, tears of joy that Davy was alive and well, but tears of sadness that her friend Deborah Danielson had not been there to greet him.

Davy said his goodbyes to Jasper, and climbed in the canoe with Tom and Jacky.

"I now know Mama, Jacob and Susannah are alright," he said, with a big smile. "That mystery is gone. I have the both of you to thank."

"We simply did what we said we would do," Tom said. "Perhaps next summer we just might head toward Richmond."

After their return to Annie's Port, they headed out again for the Ohio Country. They loaded their flatboat and took the Ohio to the mouth of the Scioto, and followed the Scioto upstream, a good day's journey. They made their camp near where a creek emptied into the Scioto. There were high hills on both sides of the river, and a broad, flat, treeless plain, running parallel to the Scioto, which was a natural grazing place for deer and other game. One day, walking along the creek bank heading west toward the hills in the distance, they saw initials carved into a walnut tree: "Pee. Pee. 1774."

"Look Tom," Jacky said, pointing to the carved initials in the trunk of the tree. "A tomahawk claim, that's what it's called. I bet these were carved here by someone marchin' with us an' Dunmore."

"Well, you're probably right," Tom said. "He surely did pick a beautiful place for his homestead someday."

A day or two later after breakfast, they started walking across the plain. Davy grabbed Jackys upper arm to have him stop.

"Buffalo," Davy said in a whisper. The three stood and marveled at the giant bovine grazing on the tall grass of the plain.

"Where there is one," Davy said in his whisper, "there is a herd. Shoot one and the rest will stampede away."

All three tamped powder and musket balls in their muskets. All three took aim and fired. The huge behemoth dropped into the sea of grass.

Christmas Visitors

As the snows of December began to blanket the landscape of New England, General Washington was anxious for news from Henry Knox.

Washington had received several reports from Knox, and knew he had arrived at Ticonderoga November 25th. He also knew Knox had secured the oxen they needed for the return trip, and was building the sleds to carry the fifty-nine cannons the oxen would pull across the mountains. But was he still on schedule, and had he left for Cambridge on December twelfth, as his last dispatch indicated he would?

Washington was also looking forward to Lady Washington's arrival in Cambridge. It had been five long months since he had last seen her the day he left Mount Vernon for the Continental Congress. Only letters, which took two full weeks to be delivered, provided his only link to his wife.

He had arranged for her to spend the entire winter with him in Cambridge. His old friend from the French and Indian War, Dr. Hugh Mercer, and his brother-in-law, Fielding Lewis, both of Fredericksburg, would escort her and her son Jacky Custis, along with Jacky's young wife Nellie Calvert, on the week-long journey north. Washington's sister, Betty, Colonel Lewis' wife, would also be traveling with their eight year-old son Lawrence.

"Wills, I know not exactly when to expect Lady Washington and her traveling party to arrive," Washington noted to his secretary, who was quickly becoming like a son to him. "Might you inspect the guest rooms and make certain Frederick and the staff have made everything ready for them."

"I have already done so, sir" Wills spoke. "Lady Washington will of course, share your bed chamber, and the second floor study has been converted to a pleasant sitting room for her. The young Custis boy and his wife will be at the top of the staircase on the third floor."

"Good," said the general chuckling, "I do not much like my stepson's company, and placing his room as far away as possible is quite ingenious. Could you not exile him to the cellar?" They both laughed.

Wills went on. "The Lewises shall have the bed chamber next to yours, with their son the next, and Dr. Mercer will be just across the corridor. The linens are crisp and clean, and flower arrangements are in each of the rooms, along with pine boughs, holly berries, ribbons and candles on each mantel. There is a good stack of firewood beside each fireplace and the tender boxes all filled with kindling."

"It appears you have considered everything. I do so appreciate it." the general nodded and changed the subject. "If Knox started back on the twelfth, tis now the eighteenth, why have we not heard from him?" Washington asked.

Frederick, the Black freedman who oversaw the household staff, came into the general's office.

"The midday meal is set, general," Frederick said.

"Good," Washington looked up and smiled. He started to rise, "Come join me Wills, I do so detest dining alone." They sat down to a tureen of clam chowder and plates with thin-sliced steaming roast beef, carrots and green peas, and a platter of fresh-baked dark rye bread.

Frederick came in as the chowder was being ladled into bowls.

"There is a rider..." he said

"From Knox? I hope," the general interrupted excitedly and started to rise.

Frederick shook his head, "from Mrs. Adams of Braintree."

Washington sat back down, disappointed. "Hand it here." Washington took it and laid it aside. When the meal had been eaten, he picked it up and handed it to Wills.

"See what the lovely Mrs. John Adams wishes me to know, now. As you know she does have opinions."

Wills read aloud:

"I have just enjoyed an hour in the company of Lady Washington. Her carriage stopped here en route to you at Cambridge. We so enjoyed conversation and tea. The carriage should arrive on Brattle Street before the sun sets... Abigail Adams."

Marching to Valley Forge
By the artist William B.T. Trego, 1883 [PD-US]

Part Two

The War for Independence

Chapter 9

Johnny Kilkenny Goes to Sea

Johnny Kilkenny was a frequent supper guest at the Winkman house during those months in Cambridge. So regular were his visits that a spare room in the attic was always ready for his use, if the late night discussions and card games ran into the wee hours.

Johnny and Caroline had gone their separate ways. Caroline always had her eyes fixed on those of the opposite sex, and Johnny knew, all along, the days of his marital life were numbered.

"She's a real whore, she is!" Johnny confided in Wills. "She spots a man's frame in a sharp-fitting pair o' sailor pants, an' she won't let up till her legs're spread wide for his dingdong to slide in an' out o' her wretched an' smelly glory hole! I'm through with that lowly bitch an' hope never ta lay me eyes upon 'er again!"

"What about your son?" asked Wills.

"Oh, thank the Lord she had 'nough sense to give little Calvin to 'er sister," Johnny added. "I doubt ever so much the lad is of me own blood any way, the way she whored 'round even then. I'm well done with that scurvy daughter o' the devil, I am!"

Wills and Johnny looked forward to the coming conflict, though they hoped it would be brief. They knew the adventures that lay before them would bring about freedom and better times. Wills was close to the high command of the American strategies and, the day after Christmas, brought Johnny some news he knew Johnny would like.

"The general received a dispatch from Congress," Wills spoke excitedly. "Congress has created the Continental Navy, and has appointed a commander-in-chief of the new navy...one Esek Hopkins of Rhode Island."

"A navy?" Johnny asked just as excitedly. "Now that's the life fer me! Where do I sign up?"

"The commodore will be fitting out a fleet of vessels in Philadelphia to keep the Chesapeake Bay free of British raiders," Wills said. "No firm details are ready as yet, but Washington is certain they will be soon forthcoming."

Johnny smiled, knowing he was more suited to the life at sea than that of marching through the backwoods of America, fighting for independence.

"Should I leave this shiverin' cold place an' head straight 'way fer Philadelphia?" Johnny asked Wills for advice. "I'd never forgive ye if I missed me chance."

"Wait till I can get more news from the general," Wills offered. "There are too many worthy seamen in Massachusetts for Hopkins not to send out the general call for volunteers. I would speak to your captain now and advise him of your plans. He will have to release you from your terms with the army."

"Terms?" Johnny asked. "There's no terms to me service here. I just showed up an' was assigned to Captain Davis. I never signed nothin'. I just came ta fight fer the cause. If he gives me any shit, I'll be off, I will, on the post road south fer Philadelphia!"

"You can't desert, Johnny," warned Wills. "They'll come for you and you'll spend the war in the stockade, or in a grave, after they swing your scurvy Irish neck from the gallows."

"I can't desert from somethin' I never 'fficially joined in the first place!"

"Just give me a day, no, two days," Wills offered, "and I promise I will have more details. But you talk to Captain Davis, just the same."

Johnny spoke to the captain the next day, and the captain agreed that if official word came from the navy seeking enlistments, he would take it straight to General Washington to get him furloughed for enlistment in the navy.

New Year's Day 1776

The celebration of New Year's Day came, and naturally Johnny celebrated at Wills and Priscilla's house. George, Martha and their Virginia guests celebrated as it was not just the first day of the year 1776, but also the last day before everyone but Martha would be returning to Virginia. The general would be happy to see them leave so he and Martha could enjoy the winter and spring months without guests always underfoot.

Jacky Custis and his wife of three years had not yet had any children. Washington thought it to be a blessing. Nelly was a charming young lady, even if she seemed to have the same social arrogance as Jacky, she being a Calvert of Maryland and all. Jacky had been a huge disappointment to Washington, but allowed Martha to spoil her only son. After the death of darling Patsy just two years earlier, George accommodated Martha in every way.

Within months, on his approaching twenty-first birthday, Jacky would have total access to the considerable fortune he would inherit from the wealthy Custis family. In the meantime, Martha's money, and money gifts from Dandridge and Custis aunts and uncles, supported his lavish lifestyle. He wore only the best clothing the gift money could buy, and lived in a world of cotillions, balls and salons. He wasted away his time on every form of frivolity. Washington knew not what to do with Jacky. Jacky had no education, nor any profession, save that of a member of the landed gentry.

"General," Jacky addressed his stepfather, "how do you abide this dreadful weather here at Boston? I much prefer the milder climes of Virginia."

"Well, Jacky," Washington responded, as the two sat with Hugh Mercer and Fielding Lewis beside the fireplace after their New Year's day dinner, "I must endure it out of duty. Tis here my command sits, so tis here I shall endure the weather."

Washington began to tell of the extreme conditions Henry Knox and his company were facing at that very moment, suffering through the snowdrifts in the Berkshires to get the fifty-nine cannons safely from Ticonderoga to Cambridge.

"What a fool this Henry Knox must be," added Jacky. "That is the work for common men, not leaders." Washington was growing more and more impatient with the arrogance of the lad.

"Leaders lead their men," Washington said abruptly. "They do not sit idly around the warmth of a fireplace, while their men trudge through the snows and slush of winter. Oh I wish I were there, right alongside Henry Knox," turning directly to Jacky with a distinct glare of disgust in his eyes, "who, by the way my young man, is no fool! He is one of the most brilliant minds in the army. Why no one knows more about artillery and how to effectively use it. It might do you some good if I sent you to meet Knox, and accompany him on the remainder of his heroic journey. What do you say, Jacky?"

"Mama would not permit it," the arrogant stepson mustered a good dose of prissiness. "What good would come from such a thing, anyway?" He rose and excused himself with a flair.

"It is beyond me," Washington said somberly, shaking his head after the boy had left the room, "how one boy could grow to become such a wastrel! There is not one element of self-responsibility, let alone duty, honor or civility in that boy's being."

"It may not yet be too late, George," spoke Mercer informally to his friend of nearly two decades. "The army can provide the education for manhood the boy seems to lack. Make him your secretary, an aide of some sort. Get him away from his hearth and home for the campaigns of this war and make a man of him."

"That is an excellent idea," added Washington's brother-in-law, Fielding Lewis. "We in the family have always worried and fretted over our Martha's boy. He is a Custis, not a Washington after all."

"I shall think upon making him the offer," said Washington, "I shall indeed...some day. But I shan't just yet. Presently, I simply can think of nothing more pleasant than his departure in the morrow." The three men chuckled.

"Lewis and I would like to recruit a regiment in Fredericksburg," said Mercer. "The spirit is certainly there. Virginians want to fight alongside of you, George."

"'Tis all the talk in the colony," Lewis added. "With you the commander-in-chief, Virginians want to share in that glory."

"Use this spring and summer to recruit a regiment of Virginians," Washington said. "Train them well, for I simply now have the boys from the farms and the street gangs of Boston, who have no discipline and quarrel amongst themselves.

"When the cannons arrive from Ticonderoga and Crown Point," Washington began laying out his plan for the war, "they will be placed at Dorchester Heights, overlooking the British fleet in the harbor and the city below. I feel Howe will want to vacate the city without a fight, when he awakens to see cannon barrels looking down upon him. But if a fight is required, we shall win! It is our soil upon which we fight.

"Then, with the British gone, we shall move quickly on to New York, and fortify that city to keep the British at sea," he concluded. "The British will be forced to negotiate, and with sentiment in England turning away from prospects of another long and expensive war in North America, independence will be given... so do not tarry raising that Virginia regiment, or you shall surely miss the war altogether."

Wills had seen the general's stepson nearly every day of his visit. He had not been impressed with what he had seen.

"Never in my lifetime have I ever met a boy, I refuse to call him a man," Wills described to Johnny and Priscilla, as they sat around the table New Year's Day, "than that sissy of a boy Jacky Custis. He has the haughty arrogance of every Britisher I have ever come across. I am surprised he doesn't protest to Washington that they should be fighting for the King, not against him."

"Well, Wills," spoke Priscilla sweetly, "I hear he and his dainty little bride will be off to Virginia tomorrow."

"And not a moment too soon!" Wills added. "Lady Custis is like her husband's twin."

"I leave tomorrow as well," spoke Johnny.

"What?" Wills questioned.

"Yes, I've gotten the blessin's o' Capt'n Davis, an' a letter signed by General George Washington hisself, addressed to Commander Esek Hopkins."

Wills smiled a demon smile. "I wondered just when you might share your good news with us."

"You knew o' this?" Johnny asked.

"Yes, fool," Wills said laughing, "who do you think penned that letter and gave it to the general to sign?"

"You knew an' ya didn't tell me?" asked Johnny, put off by Wills' secrecy.

"I wanted you to break the news to Priscilla and me in your own time and in your own way," Wills said, still laughing. "Besides, I knew Captain Davis would see you sooner than I would to give you the news. You would have had to wait until today for me to give it to you."

Johnny smiled. He was proud he had been granted the furlough, and did not have to look over his shoulder and behind every bush for bounty hunters, seeking a deserter during his entire journey to Pennsylvania.

"You are to report to headquarters at eight in the morning to escort the Washington party to Philadelphia," Wills added details Johnny had not known.

"You know more'n I do," Johnny said.

"Eight letters, similar to the one Captain Davis gave you, were signed by the general, all furloughs to the navy, and all forming the escort for Dr. Mercer and Mr. Lewis, as they take the general's sister, nephew, and, of course, that arrogant and poor excuse of a man and his wife, John Parke Custis and Nellie Calvert Custis, to Philadelphia. There you are to be relieved to report to the navy, and replaced by a guard from Pennsylvania to continue the Washington party on to Mount Vernon."

"Escort duty for General Washington's fam'ly!" Johnny spoke proudly. "That'll be sure an honor an' an easy duty indeed."

"Yes," Wills smiled broadly. "I shall finally be rid of that louse Jacky Custis, and I bequeath him to you for the next week's journey."

"If he's the pain in me ass, as you say," Johnny laughed, "I'll have ta just give 'im what he needs," he said grabbing his groin. "He'll then see what a real pain in the ass I can be!" They all laughed.

"Don't be doing that, Johnny," Priscilla said, still chuckling. "He might enjoy it too much, and expect your services all the way to Mount Vernon!"

Martha looked beautiful to him in her pouffy, white muslin sleeping bonnet, as she laid propped up on pillows in the four-poster bed in the master chamber. The general changed into his nightshirt, and climbed onto the plush mattress, covering both with a quilt. He leaned over to her and kissed her. Her sleepy eyes opened slightly, and she smiled up at him.

"This is my New Year's Day present, dear one," George said, smiling at Martha, "having you with me in my bed, and with me for the next four months. Just the two of us, alone."

"I could not imagine spending Christmas and the entire winter away from you," Martha spoke, as the mid-forty year-olds kissed, beginning again to feel like newly weds.

"Did you bank the fire?" she asked, between kisses.

"Tis banked," he replied, and kissed and hugged her again.

Henry Knox and His Cannons

February 12th ended with news from a rider that Henry Knox and his expedition would arrive near midday the following day.

The Continental Army was now split at two encampments, with about half the men remaining at Cambridge on the north shore of the Charles River, and half stationed a journey of less than an hour to the south and east at Roxbury. It was decided the cannons and mortars could more easily remain hidden from prying British and Loyalist eyes at Roxbury than at Cambridge. Too many of General Howe's aides had shown up to parlay with the American general in Cambridge, and total surprise was the key to Washington's plan. Washington wanted the British to leave Boston without a skirmish of any kind, if at all possible. Surprise was of the essence. If the arrival of the cannons went undetected, Washington felt Howe would be shocked at the sight of cannons aimed down at him, the city, and the harbor, and would wisely decide to evacuate without the loss of ships or men.

Wills penned a letter to Knox for the general's signature, before leaving headquarters at the Vassall House for the evening. The letter instructed Knox to halt his return at Waltham, an hour's journey west of Roxbury. There, Washington would personally welcome Knox home. The cannons were to be off-loaded from their sleds at Waltham, and would then be rolled along on their own wheels to Roxbury. To silence the creaking wooden wheels as they rolled over the rough dirt roads, each wheel would be shod with straw to muffle their sound. It would take the biggest part of the day of the 13th to muffle the cannon wheels, so the cannons would arrive in Roxbury, undetected, the following day.

Wills accompanied Washington and about a dozen others as they made their way from Brattle Street to the farm of Alexander Coulter on the western edge of Waltham. An advance party had come to Waltham earlier that day to set up a headquarters for the day's activities. When Washington arrived, he was shown to the front parlor of the Coulter farmhouse. Just after the general was served a midday meal of pot roast, a rider came in with news Knox would arrive within the hour.

Washington smiled and nodded at the report, and finished his meal. Artemas Ward, who Washington had placed as commander of the troops quartered at Roxbury, arrived as the general finished and walked to seats on the porch of the farmhouse.

"Artemas," Washington said, "in a matter of minutes the cannons of Ticonderoga and Crown Point will be here." He smiled at the prospects, and gazed down the lane of the farmhouse for any sign of the expedition.

"As I said months ago," Ward said, "if there was any man who could complete such an impossible mission, it would be Henry Knox."

"And, Artemis, I will do as I said," Washington went on. "Today, Lt. Henry Knox becomes Colonel Henry Knox, Commander of Artillery for the Continental Army."

"A good choice, general," Ward agreed, "a good choice, indeed."

The first horses came into sight with the plump figure of Lt. Knox at the lead. Knox halted at the porch with the first of the oxen behind him. Knox saluted the general.

"General Washington," Knox spoke, "I am pleased to deliver to the Continental Army forty-three cannons, sixteen mortars and ample ammunitions from the forts at Ticonderoga and Crown Point for the defense of Boston."

The 3ʳᵈ Virginia Regiment

Hugh Mercer and Fielding Lewis spent January making plans for the recruitment of a regiment to join the Continental Army. Broadsides were printed and circulated throughout the counties, announcing the regiment's creation. Recruiting tables would be set up in the towns for able-bodied young men to enlist, and for the inductees to assemble on the commons in Williamsburg on the first day of June, for a two-month basic training exercise. They hoped to join Washington by September at the latest.

At Williamsburg, it was difficult for the students at William and Mary to concentrate on academics, as the whole continent was reeling for war. The broadsides Mercer and Lewis circulated in Williamsburg were all the talk at the college.

"I cannot learn anymore with a war going on," said Jimmie Monroe. "I can always resume my studies after the war ends. I am going to be the first to enlist with Mercer!"

Peter and Zack debated the idea during the early weeks of the recruitment campaign. They still shared the room together at the mercantile, where Peter was still working with Boyd and Lansing.

Zack was still working at the bookstore, and saw his sketches published in a second volume, The Fight for the Frontier. Rodie had written the volume, which was originally to be titled Marching with Dunmore. Since Dunmore was now viewed as a villain in Virginia, the title was changed to insure good sales in the colonies. The earliest volumes, printed with the original title, were quickly shipped off to Gravesend Booksellers in London. After all, Dunmore was viewed as a real hero across the Atlantic, and sales there were excellent.

"I think we should both enlist and fight side-by-side as we did in Dunmore's War," said Peter to his adopted brother.

"We saw only ten minutes of battle," Zack said, "and that was enough for me. Afterall, I am an artist, and want to sketch."

"With the army," Peter argued, "you can sketch history as it happens, and not be a prisoner to birds and fishes and all the other critters. You'll see Philadelphia, New York, and perhaps even Boston. Come on, let's go to the recruiting station tomorrow and march with Colonel Mercer."

Peter could imagine nothing more exciting than the battlefields of a war. Zack had wanderlust, and wanted the peace, quit and tranquility of nature.

The door to their room opened. It was Rodie.

"Friends, I come to invite the both of you to join me at Raleigh Tavern this night," he smiled. "There is a man, an extraordinary man, I wish you to meet," he looked directly at Zack.

Ansley Magruder was a tall, lean-framed Scotsman of about thirty years, dressed in buckskins, with long reddish-brown hair falling to his shoulders. He had a noble nose set between weather-chapped lips, and big dark blue eyes with heavy brows. He spoke with a decided Scottish accent.

"Rodie me lad," Magruder rose, as he saw his new friend approach the table where he was seated. "An' who are these two strappin' young men?" Looking at Peter and his size, Magruder continued, "Tis a giant of a man, I do declare!"

Rodie introduced Zack and Peter to Magruder, and they all sat.

"I met Mr. Magruder this afternoon at the Gazette," Rodie spoke. "He's returning to Philadelphia from escorting a party of what they call in America, Scotch-Irish settlers to Carolina."

"To the Waxhaw, me lads," spoke Magruder, "and I dare say there's no lovelier a place on the face o' God's earth. It straddles the border 'tween the two Carolinas, 'mid the rich dark green pine tree forests, and creeks babblin' like a symphony, as pudy as ya please, as they run to'ard the sea. Beautiful land it tis...beautiful indeed. ... an' far away from all the damned Britishers here 'long the seashore."

"Mister Magruder will be..." began Rodie.

"Please, lad, call me Ansley, as me dear ma did, 'till she passed on, bless her soul," Magruder interrupted.

"Ansley will be leading another group of settlers in the spring," Rodie went on. "This is our chance Zack, just what we've waited for."

Peter seemed puzzled at what Rodie had said. 'What plans?' Peter asked.

"A real expedition, Peter," Rodie was about to reveal close-held dreams Zack had only spoken of to him. He turned toward Zack.

"The real adventure you've dreamed of, Zack, into lands not yet seen by many, and sketched by none!" Rodie spoke excitedly. "We can join in on Ansley's party when it comes through Williamsburg in late May. We can travel with him through the North Carolina colony, through the Great Dismal Swamp, the barrier islands off the coast, up the inland rivers. The nature! The birds and creatures, strange to this land! Can you imagine it? I have spoken at length with Ansley, and he says we are welcome to go with him."

"I will be starting my basic training as a soldier at that time," Peter interupted. "I'm enlisting in Colonel Mercer's regiment first thing tomorrow. I thought you and Zack would be joining me."

"I thought you would, Peter," said Rodie. "And I know you've dreamed of that. You'll be living out your dream, while Zack lives out his."

"What happens when we get to that place, ... that Waxhaw place?" asked Zack.

"We can put together a party of our own, and go on into Spanish Florida, and all the way to New Orleans, if we chose," answered Rodie, "all the way to the Mississippi River!"

"How long will the journey take to get to the Waxhaw?" Zack asked, directing his query to Magruder.

"Well," pondered Magruder, "I reckon from Williamsburg, ... oh, say 'tween forty and fifty days, dependin' on nature an' the elements, o' course. There are few good roads."

Zack was taken by visions in his mind of all the nature he had never before seen, but would now be able to sketch.

"And are there those in the Waxhaw who have journeyed to New Orleans, if we decide to continue?" asked Zack.

"Indeed there are me lad," spoke Magruder. "One in particular, a tradin' post man who goes there each year. I'm certain he'd be a lovely guide to the Mississippi River's delta lands. An' then there's Spanish traders from New Orleans what come there too."

The next day came and Peter stood alone in the line at the recruiting station set up in front of the Wren.

Don't Tread on Me

"Gentlemen, how might I be of service?" spoke the sandy-haired handsome, athletic looking man behind the desk in the house on Chestnut Street, across from the Pennsylvania Statehouse where the Continental Congress was meeting.

"We're furloughs from the army, just arrived here from Cambridge, with letters from General Washington," said Johnny Kilkenny as the spokesman for the eight furloughs he traved with.

317

The officer rose and smiled, extending his hand to Johnny.

"I am pleased to meet you," the officer said. "I am Captain Dabney Fortune, Chief Recruiting Officer, Continental Navy."

"Johnny Kilkenny, sir," answered Johnny, and the others followed suit. When the greetings were ended, Johnny laid thei letters from George Washington on the desk. Captain Fortune examined each, then rose with the letters.

"Please take seats," the captain said, pointing to some bench seats against the wall. "I shall be back momentarily with your papers and your orders." He turned and opened the closed, white-painted door at his rear, entered the room, and closed the door behind him.

"Did ya hear 'im? Our orders!" Johnny near shouted to the others. "That letter from ole General Washington surely did the trick!"

"I bet we'll be a sleepin' in the barracks t'night," said Danny Laws, a fisherman from Salem.

"'Tween sheets and 'neath a nice wool blanket," added another furloughed man, Torbie Brinkman, the son of a ship builder from Rhode Island.

"I just hope the food's good," piped in Perry Langston, a merchant sailor from New London.

"I just want ta fin' me a big-breasted Philadelphy lass," added Joshua Lane, youngest of the furloughs at eighteen, but the most experienced sailor of the lot. He had been a Gloucester whaler since he was fourteen.

"What on earth would ya ever do with her, Josh, if ya did find one?" joked Matthew McKee, a twenty-one year-old graduate of Yale from New Haven, "play tiddlywinks with her?" All the boys laughed, as Josh turned red and the white door opened.

An older man, short in stature with a round face and huge pointed nose, dressed in a uniform of sorts, led the captain out of the back room. The boys all stood at attention and saluted. The older officer returned their energetic salutes and said, "At ease gentlemen, I am pleased to welcome you fellows. I am Commander Esek Hopkins, and we welcome you to our squadron."

Captain Fortune gave them their orders to report to their ship, the Enfield. "I am also the captain of the Enfield," Fortune said, "and am happy to have you each with me."

"Give your orders to the boatswain on duty." said Fortune, "The first mate, Jeremiah Trevost, will show you to your quarters."

The young men were soon walking the wharf along the Delaware River. The navy had three man-o-war vessels, and had confiscated five merchantman vessels and tobacco boats, all to be refitted for action as gunships. That was the extent of the new American fleet.

After passing by the three man-o-wars, the Hornet, the Wasp and the Alfred, the five ships being refitted came next. The Enfield was the second vessel they came upon, moored between the "Oglethorpe" and the "Calvert."

The Alfred appeared to be the largest, but not by much. It also appeared to be the flagship, flying a large flag with a yellow field. In the middle of the field was a coiled diamondback rattlesnake in black, with thirteen rattles, preparing to strike from a perch on a bed of green grass. Words emblazoned in black below the coiled snake warned *"DONT TREAD ON ME"*. The other ships each had a smaller flag with thirteen alternating red and white horizontal stripes, and a slithering black rattlesnake across the middle with the same warning inscription.

A uniformed sailor, the boatswain, wearing white trousers, a red and white horizontally striped shirt, dark blue jacket, and a dark blue brimmed hat with a white ribbon tail, guarded the gangplank at the Enfield. He saluted the boys as they stopped at the ship. The boys returned the salute, and Johnny handed the boatswain their orders from Hopkins. The sailor looked over the orders and said, "Follow me." He turned, and the boys, in single file, followed him.

The First Mate, similarly uniformed, less the hat, was on the main deck. The boatswain saluted his superior, handed him the orders, turned and left as he had come. As soon as the First Mate read the orders, he looked straight at Johnny and smiled. Johnny smiled back, recognizing the young man in the uniform.

"Johnny Kilkenny!" the officer said, extending a hand. "It has been what, two years, since we sailed together on the Aristocrat?"

"It has been that indeed, sir," said Johnny, shaking the hand of an old acquaintance.

"Well," the sailor announced to the entire gang of boys, "you are certainly a welcomed sight aboard the Enfield. Kilkenny and I sailed aboard a merchantman to the Indies a while back. We shall have to reminisce over some of those old times," he directed his eyes and smile to Johnny. "But now we have to complete the refitting of this old tobacco boat and four others, and make them worthy gunboats within the month."

"Come, I will show you men to your quarters." He started to lead the men toward the steps that went below deck. He turned midway to the steps.

"By the way I am your First Mate Jeremiah Trevost from Boston."

During the coming days, the new furloughs were put to work finishing the refitting of the five merchantmen. All the ships being refitted bore the names of men admired by the patriots throughout the colonies.

The Faquier was named in honor of the former governor of Virginia, who befriended the patriot cause. Faquier had died in 1768.

The "Quincy" was in honor of Josiah Quincy, the rabid patriot attorney from Boston who had died just the year before, while visiting England to confer with the few parliamentarians who seemed to support independence for the colonies.

The other two ships were the "Oglethorpe," named for the original proprietor of the Georgia colony; and the "Calvert," for the original proprietors of Maryland. The "Enfield" was named in honor of the first patriot to die in the first battle of the war at Lexington, Captain Drake Enfield. Johnny was proud to be stationed on a ship named for his brother-in-law, the only member of the Macneal family he ever really liked, except for what Wills Winkman had told him about Jacky and Tom.

The furloughs also took drill training as well as artillery training, to be able to effectively use the cannons and mortars along the gunwales of each of the eight vessels. They soon were in uniforms of their own, and packed their duffle bags with clothing, shaving razors and other necessities they would need for the cruise.

On Saturday February 17th all the ships had been refitted and were gleaming with fresh coats of shiny white paint. The three hundred newly unformed sailors of the first naval squadron assembled in ranks with their captain on the wharf in front of their ships. A regiment of two hundred thirty marines marched by with fifes and drums playing. They halted at the reviewing stand built in front of the Alfred.

Commander Hopkins followed a second fife and drum corps, wearing a new and more regal uniform, tailored to his specific design by a Philadelphia clothier. Hopkins, along with General Samuel Nicholas, commandant of the marines, and John Hancock, president of the Continental Congress, passed by the men standing at attention in front of their newly refitted ships. The delegates of the Continental Congress followed next.

After Hopkins had led the distinguished guests to the reviewing stand, the sailors marched up the wharf, passing by the stand, taking in the applause and cheers of the hundreds of townsfolk who had come out for the ceremonies of the day.

When the review of the ships and sailors concluded, the sailors boarded their ships and took their individual stations, ready to sail away. Then the twenty-to-thirty marines assigned to each ship came aboard. The moorings were loosed and anchors weighed. The Albert led the fleet from the harbor, as the assembled guests and townsfolks gave the first American naval squadron a fitting send-off.

As the ships passed by, heading downriver to the sea, the delegates and the crowd on the wharf smiled, threw hats in the air in celebration, and cheered. The sailors aboard ship watched and spotted some of the more famous delegates.

"There's John Adams!" Johnny cried out, standing along the portside gunwale beside his first mate Jeremiah Trevost.

"Sure enough," answered Trevost.

"There is my old governor," shouted Torbie Brinkman. "That old man there is Stephen Hopkins, the older brother of our commander. He was the governor of Rhode Island."

The morale of the men aboard ship was high. The morale of the citizens of Philadelphia was just as high, as was that of the delegates to Congress.

Cannon salutes came from shore on both sides of the river, as the ships passed by Camden, New Jersey, on the east, and Chester, Pennsylvania, on the west. The colonials standing on the riverbaks were as much excited at having a navy, as the sailors of the new Amewrican Navy were excited to be part of it. Similar salutes followed as they passed the Delaware cities of Wilmington and New Castle, and along the coast near Dover and Milford. When the Delaware River was at its broadest point, emptying into the Atlantic, small boats came out from Lewes on the Delaware shore and from Cape May in the New Jersey colony to escort the fleet. They fired muskets into the air in salute of the American ships. In late afternoon the squadron steered south along the coast of Delaware and Maryland until, at dusk, they were alongside Assateague Island in Chesapeake Bay off Virginia.

Johnny spent much of the day developing a friendship with his old sailing friend from the Aristocrat. Johnny and Jeremiah had not really been close friends. Trevost, four years older than Johnny, was more tightly linked to a couple older crewmen at that time. Johnny, being a younger and less experienced as a seaman, knew Jeremiah simply as the seaman in charge of the crew of twelve. He was happy to see the familiar face, and Jeremiah seemed to be someone who might serve him well in his hopes of eventually becoming captain of his own ship.

"Kilkenny," Trevost spoke to him, as Johnny was about his duties, "take a break. Come with me to the foredeck and let's get reacquainted."

Johnny left his post and followed Trevost up the steps and to a bench outside the pilothouse. They sat there for at least an hour as the Enfield plied the coastal waters.

"It is a blessing having someone with the real skills of a seaman aboard," began Trevost, "especially one I at least have some familiarity with."

"How long you been with the navy?" Johnny asked.

"After leaving the Aristocrat," Trevost said, "I headed to Newport and signed on with Captain Hopkins. We sailed together on his privateer, smuggling in Dutch tea. What a great time that was! I shall some day tell you what it was like running the blockades," Trevost laughed. "The captain's older brother was then the governor of Rhode Island, and later went off to Congress with the idea of creating a navy. He promoted his brother the captain as the commander-in-chief. I have a long relationship with the commander, and with his brother, and became close with our present Captain Fortune. Fortune had sailed with Hopkins for many years and was his first mate."

"Capt'n Fortune's the one what accepted me furlough from General Washington," Johnny said proudly.

"Yes he was. What have you done since leaving the Aristocrat?" Jeremiah asked Johnny.

322

"I got meself married to a whore what walked the wharf," Johnny said. "T'was the biggest mistake o' me young years." Jeremiah laughed.

"She kept a lookin' fer other men's comp'ny the entire time. I kept a lookin' fer another ship an' started hirin' onta fishin' boats. Finally I signed on a four month cruise, doin' the triangle, Boston to Jamaica to London. When I returned, the day after the tea party at Boston," Johnny said, "I then hooked up with the minutemen an' rode warnin' the patriots in the countryside 'bout the Redcoats movin' on Lexington an' Concord. Drake Enfield, the first one kilt an' namesake o' this old tobacco boat, was me brother-in-law. Right fine man Drake Enfield was."

"That is interesting," Jeremiah said, "you knowing Enfield and all. How long were you serving with Washington?"

"Since the first day he arrived at Cambridge," Johnny answered. "Me best friend, Wills Winkman, is his secretary, an' he told me Congress created a navy. I knew, right then an' there, I wanted to be a sailor, not a soldier. He spoke to Washington 'bout me an' the rest is history."

"Well, Kilkenny," Jeremiah said, as he was starting to rise and return to his duties, "I have arranged for you to dine with me in the Captain's Quarters tonight. I see ambition in you, and know you are going to be important to this navy."

Dinner call came when the squadron was anchored along Assateague Island, not far from Virginia and the mouth of Chesapeake Bay. Johnny dressed and headed to the Captain's Quarters.

The dinner was hot and good and served on real plates, as opposed to the tin mess kit plates and cups the seamen were used to. Captain Fortune sat at the head of the six-man table with his first mate, Jeremiah Trevost, at the other end. Johnny was seated on Trevost's left, beside the chief gunners mate. Across the table were the chief of artillery and the ship's pilot. Johnny seemed somewhat out of place, being the only diner not a major officer on the ship. But at the same time, he was pleased to be the only midshipman dining with the captain and his officers.

After dinner was eaten, brandy was served as conversation began.

"Kilkenny," spoke the captain, "what brings you to our navy?"

"Sir," Johnny spoke, hoping to really be able to have remained silent, not wanting to be awkward in his speech, "I love the sea, I do, an' life aboard a ship."

"Well said," replied Captain Fortune. "I feel you speak for us all. Trevost here speaks very highly of you and of your capabilities. Would you be open to a new assignment?"

"I will serve where ever ye think best, sir," Johnny waited with anticipation for the next words from Captain Fortune's lips, but added, "I'm a growin' tired of swabbin' them decks." The others around the table chuckled.

"Very well then," the captain smiled, "we'll give the mop and bucket to another. You are now my assistant ship's pilot. Meet your superior. Johnny Kilkenny meet Thomas Folger."

Folger, who was seated directly across the table from Johnny, stood and extended his hand across the table. Folger was a man a little older than Johnny, with blonde hair and bright blue eyes. He had a broad smile, and showed a perfect mouthful of gleaming white teeth.

"Report to the pilothouse on tomorrow's duty," Folger said, as Johnny smiled with pride and joy.

"Aye aye, sir," Johnny said, giving the obligatory salute.

Aboard the Squadron

Commander Hopkins was at the desk in his quarters aboard the Alfred studying maps with General Nicholas.

"My orders are to patrol the Chesapeake for British vessels," Hopkins stated in a tone that displayed his annoyance. "Mr. Hancock fears a landing of the fleet somewhere here," Hopkins pointed to Baltimore, "and an overland invasion with the prize being the Congress at Philadelphia. I feel the British fleet will stay in New England, and when Washington sends them running from Boston, they'll high-tail it off to Halifax to lick their wounds and regroup. We'd be wasting our time bottled up in the Cheasapeake!"

"A politician playing the role of military strategist cannot be taken seriously," stated Nicholas. "We bottle up our small squadron, such as it is, in the Chesapeake, and we become an easy prey for the British." Nicholas pointed at the mouth of the great bay.

324

A small force of British warships can easily blockade us in for the war's duration," Nicholas advised.

"I can only agree with you," replied Hopkins. "I intend to keep this squadron on the move. We shall take advantage of our speed. As Washington is in charge of the army at Cambridge, free to design his own war strategies, I intend to use my rank to set the strategies at sea!"

"So what do you propose?" Nicholas asked.

Bending over the maps, Hopkins began to point as he spoke.

"We shall make port at Norfolk tomorrow," Hopkins announced. "To build morale for the patriot citizens there, in that once hotbed of Loyalists, and to show them our crisply-uniformed men and the cannons on our decks. Remember, they suffered the torch of Dunmore.

"We will the next day sail to the James and do the same for the folks of Williamsburg. We will be a presence in the Chesapeake Bay, but a brief one, and one that is moving.

"We shall visit Baltimore, then turn back to the sea, and follow the coast line down to Ocracoke in the Carolina outer banks, to New Bern, then Charles Town and Savannah.

"We shall sail to the very edge of Britain's new province of East Florida. I do wish the Spaniards still controlled Florida and the city of Saint Augustine. Perhaps there is where that damnable Dunmore stowed away the munitions he thieved before leaving Virginia. They could very well be in the fort there. Castillo de San Marcos, they call it.

"Would it not be wonderful, Nicholas, if we could return to Philadelphia with those munitions for Washington's army?"

"It would indeed, Hopkins," stated Nicholas, "It would indeed."

Returning to his plan, the commodore ended by saying, "Then we shall turn from the very edges of our southern border on the St. Mary's River, and sweep north all the way to Portland in the Maine District, and on to the St. Croix River bordering New Brunswick, with Nova Scotia in our sights."

"We shall be at the ready for any British sloops to commandeer. We have cannon power and speed on our side. We can outrun any of those larger British vessels. Flexibility is the key and surprise is our strategy. We must be prepared to follow whatever intelligence we might obtain. The army needs munitions and the navy needs vessels. That shall be my goal."

Johnny's first day as the Enfield's assistant pilot was short, as the squadron arrived the wharf at Norfolk by nine o'clock in the morning. The town was just starting to build back from Lord Dunmore's New Years Day torching of the city. The wharf was not yet rebuilt, so the squadron sailed just west to the sister city of Portsmouth, and moored there for the day.

The townsfolk greeted the squadron, and told of the devastation they had suffered after Dunmore, defeated and humiliated at Great Bridge, turned on his once-loyal friends and laid the torch to the thriving port.

"That damnable Dunmore used the slaves he emancipated from our own plantations to carry the torches," said one former Loyalist of Norfolk. "I saw three of my best field hands set the torch to the chandlery."

The next day, the squadron sailed west up the James to the original spot where, in 1607, Captain John Smith had put to shore and built Jamestown. Johnny took several turns at the pilot's wheel. The wheel felt to be part of his hand, and there was a comfort knowing he was able to steer the ship. The wheel became part of his being, and when he held the wheel, a special oneness with the ship developed.

As word spread, the citizens of close-by Williamsburg headed down Quarterpath Road to the wharf to greet the ships. Peter Francisco led his friends, now signed-up for General Hugh Mercer and Colonel Fielding Lewis' 3rd Virginia Regiment.

"That would be the life," Peter said, looking at the men in their smart-looking uniforms.

"No Peter, the navy is not for your," piped up Jimmie Monroe. "As much the giant as you are, you'd sink the damn ship!"

Garrett Hicks, and Malcolm Shepherd, the old classmates from Campbelltown, had just enlisted when they came for a visit to Williamsburg. They laughed at Peter's expense.

"You'd have ta have your own ship, special built, Peter," added Garrett.

"You'd be a sufferin' continual headaches," said Malcolm, "after forgettin' ta stoop down an' bangin' that big ole forehead of yer'n, jest a tryin' ta go through those low doorways!"

"An' seasick too, oh m' God!" Garrett finished the taunting. "You'd be a heavin' yer vittals all over the main deck an' t'other sailors'd get danged tired o' swabbin' yer vomit, an' in no time a'tall would have yer big ass a walkin the gang plank!"

"You'd be a swimmin' with Neptune an' them mermaids!" added Malcolm.

Peter took their ribbing in jest, as he had gotten used to his pals poking fun at his larger-than-normal size. He was now a full seven feet tall and weighed two hundred eighty five pounds.

"No, Peter," Jimmie concluded, "tis the army for you for certain. If you'd been with Henry Knox bringing those cannons from Fort Ticonderoga, you could have done the work of three of those yoked-up beasts!"

Jeremiah invited Johnny to tour the colonial capital with him. They took a mid-day meal and some tankards of rum at Raleigh Tavern. Sitting in the tavern in their uniforms, they were the center of attention. A businessman stopped at their table.

"Welcome to Williamsburg, gentlemen," said the stranger. "I am Linwood Boyd, part-owner of the Lansing and Boyd Mercantile down the street."

The sailors introduced themselves and invited the friendly merchant to join them at their table beside a window. After several minutes of rum and conversation, Boyd turned the conversation to his real intentions.

"I heard from a very reliable seaman, a captain of a merchantman, that Lord Dunmore has hidden away great stores of munitions he stole from the magazines here and at Portsmouth and Norfolk, and I have knowledge as to their whereabouts," said Boyd.

"And where is this stolen cache hidden?" asked Trevost.

"According to the captain," Boyd answered in a whisper, "in the Bahamas, at the two forts on New Providence Island at Nassautown. He was there on a recent commercial voyage, and saw it with his very own eyes. Cannons, mortars, wagonloads of barrels of powder, and other munitions, all stolen from the colony of Virginia! That damnable bastard! May he rot and burn in Hell!"

Late that afternoon, after having been back aboard the Enfield for about an hour, Johnny was summoned to Trevost's cabin. Trevost was still hearing the words of the Williamsburg merchant, ringing in his ears. What espionage those words, from a seemingly reliable source,

contained! The whereabouts of Lord Dunmore's cache of stolen gunpowder and munitions, taken from Virginia powder magazines, along
with vital cannons and mortars, was the prime question on every military mind in the colonies. Trevost had heard the scuttlebutt from the
high command, that Commodore Hopkins was bound and determined
to find that loot, and take it back for use in George Washington's Continental Army.

"I have spoken with Captain Fortune," Trevost said excitedly, not
being one to go around the chain of command, "and we are dining
tonight at the captain's table aboard the Alfred ... we two, along with
Captain Fortune. Commander Hopkins and General Nicholas are anxious to hear, first hand, the news we learned today about Dunmore's
cache of arms."

"What?" Johnny asked, not believing what he had just heard.

"We might have just stumbled across the news that will win this
war before it really gets started," Trevost said.

Captain Fortune, Trevost and Johnny walked down the gangplank
of the Enfield, down the wharf at Jamestown, then up the gangplank
of the flagship Alfred. They were shown to the Captain's Quarters for
dinner. Commander Hopkins was anxious to hear the intelligence.

"So how is it," Hopkins started the conversation, as the door
was shut behind his dinner guests, "that a first mate and an assistant pilot from a refitted tobacco boat can learn of this treasure trove
of stolen munitions, when any source I have gives me nothing but
speculation?"

"Go ahead, Mr. Trevost," ordered Captain Fortune, "tell him what
you have told me."

Trevost repeated what he and Johnny had learned at Raleigh Tavern
from Linwood Boyd.

"What says the munitions of Lord Dunmore remain at Nassau?"
asked General Nicholas.

"That I do not know sir," replied Trevost. "I simply know what I
was told. Captain Edwards had arrived here just days after leaving the
Bahamas, and left here just two days ago.

"What safer place to hide them?" Hopkins said. "The British know
they are safe there, and easily available if needed.

"I have only put in at Nassautown a handful of times," Hopkins recalled. "It is a safe harbor, with a long and narrow outer island protecting it. Why the British never fortified the outer island is beyond me. The two forts lie behind the barrier island."

The six dined on seafood and pudding, and continued the discussion after desert and brandy was served.

"Lord Dunmore has now left the Chesapeake for New York and London," Hopkins noted. "Our army is in dire need of those stores, and now it is up to the Navy and the Marines to retrieve them!" He sipped his brandy. "This night we end our patrolling in the Chesapeake, for there is nothing to patrol," the commander spoke. "At first light we sail south to the Bahamas!"

The Battle of the Bahamas

From the Chesapeake Bay, Commander Hopkins plotted the cruise to the Bahamas. It would take more than a full week, possibly ten days. With good conditions, the squadron could be in the islands off the coast of British East Florida by the first day of March. The eight ships sailed with the Alfred out front, and the yellow snake flag flapping proudly in the breeze.

Johnny shared duties at the helm with his immediate superior, Pilot Thom Folger. Thom and Johnny were soon best friends, and sometime on their first day in the open Atlantic, sailing south toward the Bahamas, Johnny moved his dufflebag and personal effects into the pilothouse to share more comfortable sleeping quarters with Thom.

They sailed along the coast of the outer banks of North Carolina, making a brief stop at Ocracoke, where, nearly seventy years earlier, a raid sponsored by Virginia Governor Spotswood, captured Edward Teach, the feared pirate Blackbeard. Teach was killed and decapitated. His severed head hung on the mastarm of the Virginians' ship for all to see.

The squadron then made port at the North Carolina colonial capital of New Bern, west of the Outer Banks, up the Neuse River. With the royal governor having fled at the outbreak of revolution, the patriots and general assembly took over his lavish home, Tryon Palace. The new patriot governor hosted an impromptu reception for all the sailors of the new navy at the palace.

Next was a port call at Charles Town on the South Carolina coast, the largest port in the southern colonies, and after that, Savannah in the most southern of the colonies, Georgia. The squadron stayed moored along the Savannah River for two nights to gather more intelligence, if possible, about Lord Dunmore's stolen arms.

With the most northern islands of the Bahamas lying less than one hundred miles south of the former Spanish city of Saint Augustine, the squadron sailed as far as the St. Mary's River boundary between the colonies and British held East Florida.

On the 28th of February, ahead of Hopkins' schedule, the squadron sighted Grand Bahama Island, and split in two smaller flotillas. The Alfred led the Hornet, Faquier and Enfield around the north shore of the large island, while the Wasp led the Oglethorpe, Calvert and Quincy along the southern coastline.

The waters were calm and beautifully clear, to where Johnny and Thom seemed as if they were merely steering the Enfield on a sheet of clear blue glass. The sun on the last day of February was warm, and beat down on them as they piloted the ship. The sands of the beaches on shore looked like white powder, framed by tall palm trees, adorned on their tops with only a few dark green fronds.

"See them trees over there, Thom?" Johnny said, pointing to the shore, "the ones not standin' straight up like the rest."

"Like a big wind blew 'em over halfway to the ground?" Thom asked.

"Yea," Johnny answered. "Them all have coconuts up in their tops. When the Aristocrat was at Jamaica, me an'a friend o' mine shimmied right up one of 'em an' knocked some down. We chopped the green husk off 'em an' laid 'em out to dry on the ship for a week or two. When they was dried, we punched holes in 'em with our knives, and drunk out the milk. Then we busted 'em open, and scrapped out all the white coconut meat. We chewed on coconut fer days. It was sure good.

"I hope we get some time at Nassautown after we take back that powder," said Johnny. "I'll take ya over to the island 'cross the harbor an' we can climb fer coconuts an' swim in that water. You swim don't ya?"

"Like a fish," replied Thom. "I've never been in the islands before till now," said Thom, "just the cold waters of the rocky coast of New England and the Maritimes. I'd like to go pickin' coconuts!"

During the early daylight hours on Friday March first, the squadron was back together. Hopkins sighted Little Abaco, which was detached from the larger island of Great Abaco by a small inlet. Cruising the western coast of the bigger island, Commander Hopkins sighted through his spyglass, two large sloops tied at a mooring at what appeared to be a banana plantation. Hopkins ordered the pilot of the Alfred to pull closer, and as they approached, Hopkins conferred with Nicholas and sent a small raiding party ashore to capture the two moored ships.

The owners of the vessels came running from the planter's house when they saw strange sailors aboard their boats. When they saw the eight navy vessels in the channel, they stopped dead in their tracks. They were immediately held in custody by ten musket and bayonet-wielding marines.

The commander and the general were rowed ashore as Johnny and Thom watched from the helm of the Enfield.

"Well," Thom said, "there's two more ships for the Continental Navy."

The commander and general walked up the plantation's pier where the owners were being held beneath a coconut palm at the end of the wooden pier.

"Where do we stow prisoners 'round here?" asked Johnny.

"There is a brig cell below deck on the Alfred, Wasp and Hornet," Thom said. "But I hear tell General Nicholas has a personal code of takin' no prisoners."

"He sets 'em free?" Johnny asked.

"No," Thom answered, his eyes rolling skyward to the mast-arm where mutineers are hung.

"Oh," Johnny said, realizing Thom's intent, and apparently General Nicholas' preference.

Johnny and Thom watched as the two owners were led to the two moored sloops and escorted up the gangplank to join the sailors and marines already on board. Soon the commander and general were rowed back to the Alfred, and the two sloops sailed away with the American flotilla.

The morning was beautiful with a calm gentle breeze. Thom and Johnny shared the duties at the wheel in the pilothouse. The squadron sailed around the southern tip of Great Abaco Island. All the men had been informed they would be landing on New Providence Island by mid-afternoon, and storming the fort just east of Nassautown. The Battle of the Bahamas was soon to start.

"Land the Landing Force!"

Esek Hopkins had commandeered the two sloops and temporarily impressed the owners into service in the Continental Navy, ordering them onto their own sloops, under guard with eight marines on board each sloop. The sloops, the "Green Turtle Cay" owned by Gideon Lowe, who also owned the plantation that took up the entire small island of the same name, and the "Abaconian," owned by Lyman Seymour, the largest landowner on Great Abaco Island. Lowe and his family had stayed the night at the Seymour house the night before for a dinner among friends.

Hopkins had hoped to find something like the two large sloops. He knew if the full squadron was seen approaching Nassau, alarms would sound. Hopkins wanted surprise. The north side of New Providence Island, where Nassautown sat, had no view of the open sea to the north, due to the long and narrow barrier island. He planned to enter the remote inlet between the two islands from the east, not passing in front of Nassautown. Fort Montague, the larger of the two forts, set less than a mile east of the town. With the two sloops as the decoy, Hopkins felt the squadron could arrive without alarm.

The squadron left immediately after the capture of the sloops. Hopkins estimated they would be in sight of New Providence within the hour. Nicholas knew his marines would make easy work of taking the forts.

As soon as the flotilla entered the eastern inlet, the owners of the two captured sloops, as if on cue, jumped from where they were told to stand on the portside of the boats. They dove into the crystal-clear water. With the sailors aboard the sloops busy at their posts, and not wanting the sound of shots fired to alert the fort, the owners made it to the shore safely, and ran for the fort to warn of the impending raid.

The squadron continued down the inlet and dropped anchor in front of the fort. The marines boarded skiffs and were lowered to the water, Nicholas then called out in a loud booming voice, the command he had been waiting to issue for days.

"Land the landing force! Land the landing force!"

The skiffs rowed to the beach in front of the Fort Montague. Saber and musket-toting marines scrambled into the water and rushed onto the beach. They raced to the gates of the fort, and with not a single shot fired, the gates of Fort Montague opened.

The Battle of Nassau was won, and the first amphibious landing by an American military force had been a success.

Within the hour, Nicholas and Hopkins were inside the fort, surveying the bounty of their capture ... fifty or more cannons and mortars and a fair amount of captured powder and musket balls. Hopkins and Nicholas met in the commandant's office with the fort's captured commander and two of his aides. Hopkins named Captain Dabney Fortune the new commandant of the fort, with a company of two-dozen sailors and fifty marines to hold the fort for the Americans.

"Are these the munitions stored here by Lord Dunmore?" Hopkins asked the young British commandant, who was now relieved of his command.

"Some of them," replied the tight-lipped commandant.

"Where is the gunpowder? At Fort Nassau?" Hopkins continued his interrogations.

"I know not what may or may not be at Fort Nassau," answered the commandant, in an air of British superiority, which did not sit well with Nicholas. Nicholas drew his saber and held its sharp tip on the commandant's neck.

"That is no answer, lad," Nicholas scoffed at him. "You best answer the admiral of the fleet!"

"Yes, yes...," the now nervous young man spoke rapidly.

"The stores from Virginia are at the fort, ... except the gunpowder, some of the gunpowder, that is. Some has been taken away to Halifax. It was taken just yesterday. The rest remains. They are hidden in the buried magazine, ...beneath the floor of the commandant's office. There too are as many cannons and mortars there." The commandant now, with the saber tip near to puncturing the life out of him, could not have been more talkative, nor could he have spoken any quicker, divulging all.

Nicholas released the saber with a slight twist, causing a small rivulet of bright red blood to course down the young man's flesh, toward his bright red coat.

"Now, see," Nicholas smiled, "that was quite simple, and I dare say only a might painful."

"Be off!" Hopkins barked at the commandant and his officers. The three scurried out the door where they were grabbed by a handful of marines and taken to the fort's brig to join the rest of their thirty men who failed to defend Fort Montague.

"Let us strike while the iron is hot," said Hopkins.

"I would be in total agreement," concurred Nicholas, "but the men, while there was no resistance today, are exerted, if not physically, then mentally. I feel we quarter here for the night and give them rest on land. They will be renewed for the fight tomorrow, if a fight at all comes."

"Very well," agreed Hopkins. "I shall send emissaries to the governor in the town, to see if he is amenable to foregoing a fight."

Emissaries were not needed. A delegation from Nassautown arrived soon, carrying a white flag of truce. Led by the lord mayor and speaker of the assembly, they came bearing an invitation from Lieutenant Governor Montfort Browne. Browne requested the pleasure of the company of the commanders and their staff, for a dinner at his residence on the hills behind Duke Street. Hopkins immediately accepted the invitation and dismissed the delegation.

Then he thought about the two sloops. With the owners deserting their own ships at sea, he had now no intentions of returning the Green Turtle Cay, nor the Abaconian, to the owners. He sent for the two men from the Enfield who he felt indebted to for the intelligence that had brought the first victory to the new navy. The First Mate, Jeremiah Trevost and the assistant pilot, Johnny Kilkenny were given command of the two newest ships of the fleet, and both given the rank of captain.

The lord mayor of Nassautown greeted them at the town limits, and paraded his guests through the heart of Nassautown, and up the steep winding road behind Duke Street to the palatial residence of the lieutenant governor. A military band from Fort Nassau was assembled on the front lawn to welcome the Americans with pomp and circumstance.

Lt. Gov. Browne, donning a freshly powdered wig and sporting a lime green light-weight dinner jacket, trimmed in gold brocade, and darker green knee breeches with white stockings, met them at the portico and led them through the house to a side lawn. The lawn was neatly clipped and set with white-clothed tables and candelabras for the impromptu outdoor dinner. A string quartet was playing for the guests as they arrived and took seats. The view was magnificent.

"We cannot see Fort Montague, which you have now possessed, but," said the host, turning to the west and pointing, "there lies Fort Nassau, just beyond the edge of town."

"And the cache of powder and munitions stolen from Williamsburg by Lord Dunmore," Hopkins asked, "is there awaiting us?"

"Some do say so," stated the governor a bit hesitantly, "but I do not know. I am after all, simply the lieutenant governor. It is a pleasant view I have from my home, do you not agree?"

"It is beautiful indeed," said Hopkins.

Dinner was a meal grilled in the manner of the islands. Chickens were placed on grates over an open fire, a favored cooking practice from the Spanish islands called barbacoa. Heavy pots hanging on hooks above the grates contained vegetables. Bowls of rum mixed with citrus juices were on each table. Two-dozen black servants brought platters of food to the guests.

"Commodore Hopkins," Browne started, having finished his meal, "may we now discuss the return of the two sloops?"

"What two sloops might you be speaking of?" queried Hopkins.

"You do know quite well what sloops I speak of," Browne giggled as he spoke, "the Green Turtle Cay and the Abaconian, of coarse. They are the private property of two of the Bahamas' most respected landowners. They must be returned at once."

Hopkins looked puzzled.

"Why I have no such sloops bearing those odd names in my navy," Hopkins replied.

"But sir," insisted Browne, "you captured those very sloops, tied up at their private wharfs, and impressed their owners to serve as pilots."

"Oh," Hopkins replied, "those two sloops. I am afraid you are gravely misinformed. We came across the two sloops moored as you say at the pier," Hopkins recounted the story. "Misters Lowe and Seymour offered the sloops to us, and even came along with us as we sailed to Fort Montague.

"Lowe and Seymour both, apparently changed their minds, and jumped ship. They both deserted their own vessels, leaving them to surely crash upon the shoals. Thankfully I had stationed able sailors to rescue the reeling ships, or they would certainly have been lost. Those ships were deserted and now, by tradition and rule of the waves, are the property of the American Continental Navy, and shall remain so.

"May I introduce you to their new captains?" Hopkins asked. "This is Captain Jeremiah Trevost, captain of the newly commissioned ship "Providence," and this is Captain Johnny Kilkenny, captain of the newly commissioned ship "Cambridge."

"But sir," Browne was insulted, "I must protest."

"Shall you order your garrison at Fort Nassau to open its gates for us at daybreak tomorrow, so we can claim the munitions, rightly our property, robbed from Virginia by Dunmore?"

"As I said," Browne re-iterated, "I have no standing to do such a thing. I am simply the lieutenant governor."

"Then we shall arrive at daybreak tomorrow," Hopkins said, "and take it as we have taken Fort Montague this day, with sabers drawn and muskets at the ready."

Hopkins and Nicholas stood, signaling the end the evening's pleasantries, and the Americans marched back to their new quarters at Fort Montague.

The next morning, the marines and sailors marched through Nassautown to the gates of Fort Nassau. Nicholas called out, ordering the gates be opened. Again, without one shot fired, the Continental Navy and Marines had a second bloodless victory.

General Nicholas demanded the keys to the secret magazine beneath the commandant's office floor. Dunmore's stash was indeed there, less a few dozen barrels of gunpowder that had already been spirited away to Halifax two days earlier. There were also fifty or more cannons and mortars at the fort, some British to be sure, but all were taken.

Later in the morning, General Nicholas took a detachment of marines and entered the chamber where the assembly was meeting. He gave orders for two marines to enter the chamber and arrest the lieutenant governor who was speaking from the podium. They led him away in chains.

Then an escort of marines led General Nicholas and Commodore Hopkins into the chamber and up to the podium. Nicholas addressed the parliament, meeting in an emergency session.

"Gentlemen," Nicholas stated. "We, the American Continental Navy and Marines, mean you no harm. We have come for one thing and just one thing. That is the retrieval of the munitions of war stolen by John Murray, 4th Earl of Dunmore, while serving as His Majesty King George III's royal governor of the colony of Virginia. We shall be in your colony but a few days.

"The lieutenant governor has been removed, and I shall oversee the safety and commerce of the colony during our occupation here. That occupation shall be brief and peaceful. We invite the people of this colony to join us in our fight for American independence." None took the offer.

Dorchester Heights

On the night of March fourth, Col. Henry Knox led his men as they rolled the cannons on their wheels, muffled by straw, from the barns of Roxbury to positions he had selected on Dorchester Heights. Col. Knox ordered the barrels of the cannons and mortars to aim down from the heights to the city of Boston below and the ships of the king's royal navy at anchor in Boston Harbor. Knox himself selected each placement for the artillery, to make certain General Howe and his men would see the full effect of the arms captured at the forts in New York.

As the sun rose, alarm bells began to ring throughout the town, waking all Loyalists to the threat staring down upon them. Through their spyglasses they could see the cannons, and saw thousands of continental soldiers in formation, with musket and bayonet in hand. There too, very recognizable, was General George Washington, astride his white steed, Nelson, surveying the fortifications, and looking down threateningly on the Loyalists below.

"This is not Breed's Hill!" roared Howe to his staff. "Our troops barely won that day facing but a few colonial defenders. Now we stare up the noses of those cannons! Those damned cannons! Where the Hell did Washington get those damned cannons?"

Howe had arrived in Boston six months before to replace General Gage as the commander-in-chief of North America, and Governor of Massachusetts. His older brother, Richard, Admiral of the Royal Navy, joined him with a large portion of the fleet.

For the better part of two weeks, the scene remained the same. Each morning the citizens of Boston woke to the thousands of continentals in threatening formation, with their muskets and bayonets, and the artillerymen with their torches and tampers poised to rain down terror upon them.

"Not a single ship at anchor in the harbor is safe!" roared Admiral Howe. "One carefully placed cannonball could wreck havoc on any one of them at any time!"

"What is that damned fool Washington waiting for?" asked Gen. Howe of his brother. "Why has not one cannonball been hurled at us?"

Loyalists and soldiers alike slept with an open each night. Commerce stopped, and the job of packing up began. The ships would be ordered out of the harbor soon, hopefully before the threat from atop the heights would become real devastation. How long would the siege continue? Only one man knew that answer and that one man was George Washington. General Howe had never before been on that side of a siege. He did not much like it, and he would not allow mass devastation to conquer his army and navy. He made arrangements to evacuate Boston, so he could live to fight another day.

Loyalists, if left behind, would surely become prisoners of the Americans. They too would be evacuated.

On the thirteenth day of the silent siege from Dorchester Heights, Washington, on his steed as he had been each day, oversaw his men in formation with their muskets and bayonets, and the artillerymen, newly trained for the action. He gazed down to watch through his spyglass as the soon to be evacuated soldiers and Loyalists boarded the ships. Soon the anchors were up and the fleet began to sail from Boston Harbor. By dusk on Sunday, March 17th, neither a British warship nor a British soldier remained in Boston.

Washington's plan had been brilliant and had succeeded as hoped. The Royal Navy ships were bound for Halifax in Nova Scotia. The next morning, for the first time, Washington rode into the center of Boston itself and surveyed the city, now won back from the British with no cannons fired. The townsfolk cheered him as he and his officers rode by. He stationed half the men from Roxbury and Cambridge to be encamped on the wharf and in the city proper.

That evening, Washington hosted a dinner at the Vassall House for his staff, which now included generals Nathaniel Greene, Horatio Gates and Charles Lee. Greene was a loyal friend and supporter of Washington. Gates and Lee were both cool and arrogant toward their commander-in-chief. Both men felt they were far superior in battlefield strategy than Washington, and both felt greatly slighted by Congress for unanimously appointing Washington to the prized leadership position.

"Gentlemen," Washington spoke after dinner, "we have made an important stride for our country. We now direct our total effort toward the New York colony and the island of Manhattan. We shall build upon Long Island the needed fortifications to repel any attempts by the British to establish a foothold there."

"What makes one think Howe will not return here if the army leaves?" asked Gates.

"It seems foolhardy to me as well," added General Lee, "not to think it likely the Howes shall return to this undefended city."

"The British selected Boston to put down a rebellion. We came here and have won that war. We shall now select where the war shall be next fought, and not be found forced to race to where the British wish to fight." responded Washington, showing he was very much in command. "New York is central to the colonies, and their strategy shall be to try and divide the colonies in half by taking New York. They shall not take New York without a fight!"

"I agree," stated Greene. "If our army remains detached in New England, as the two of you so suggest, the British, by taking New York and fortifying the Hudson Valley from Canada, will split the colonies in two, with the army bottled up in New England, and the Congress in danger in Philadelphia."

"So you would open New England to renewed British occupation? Has this city not suffered enough?" Gates again argued.

"We must fortify Manhattan," Greene re-iterated, "and prevent the British from effectively dividing us and conquering us."

"Gentlemen, that is precisely why our aim must be Manhattan," added Washington. Then sounding a conciliatory note toward his political foes, Gates and Lee, he continued. "The experiences you gentlemen have had in the British Army are vital to me. We need a chain of fortifications on Manhattan, Long Island, and on both sides of the Hudson River. We must fortify the harbor, and make it difficult for their ships to pass into the interior. I shall soon send you to direct that effort.

"If we succeed in keeping the British from dividing the colonies in two, by keeping them off Manhattan and out of the Hudson Valley," Washington laid out his strategy, "the diplomats can then begin their work, and we can all return to our farms and other commercial endeavors, as free men in a free nation."

The Munitions of War

Johnny Kilkenny now commanded his own ship with the rank of captain. The Cambridge was a large sloop that had sailed the triangular trade route for Mr. Seymour. It transported kegs of rum, barrels of sugar and other spices, and harvested bananas and coconuts from the Caribbean islands to sell in the North American colonies. There the ship loaded tobacco, rice, indigo and other colonial commodities, bound for sale in England. The American commodities were sold in London, and the ship, loaded then with European goods not manufactured in the colonies or in the Caribbean. This triangular trade built fortunes for Seymour and others in the islands. Now, the Cambridge would carry the captured arms of war to the Continental Army in New England, and then be refitted as a war ship for Commodore Esek Hopkins' navy.

The Cambridge was large and could quarter over one hundred men, with a broad and long main deck that could easily house two-dozen pieces of artillery. On it's sailing from Nassautown, it had a compliment of just twenty-four men, and the main deck carried twenty of the captured cannons and smaller mortars. Below deck were stored some of the captured barrels of valuable gunpowder.

Jeremiah Trevost, the captain of the Providence, oversaw an equal number of artillery pieces and barrels of gunpowder. The rest of the artillery was aboard the other ships.

On March 22nd, the fleet made port at Charles Town, South Carolina, and dispatches were sent immediately north to Cambridge to advise Washington of the captured munitions, and to arrange for a rendezvous. On the 25th, the fleet sailed into the James River so the citizens of Williamsburg could see and celebrate the arms recaptured from Lord Dunmore. The fleet put out for Philadelphia on the 26th, bound north for New England, and a rendezvous with Washington's army.

Washington was enjoying all the news he was getting in March 1776. With the placement of the captured cannons on Dorchester Heights, having convinced General Howe and his brother the admiral, to evacuate Boston on the 17th, eleven days later, the rider arrived on Brattle Street with the dispatch from Commodore Hopkins.

Wills Winkman received and read the dispatch. He rushed into Washington who was meeting with Col. Knox, Generals Greene, and Rufus and Israel Putnam. The generals were planning the movement of nineteen thousand troops from Boston to New York. One thousand would remain behind in Boston under the command of General Artemis Ward.

"Begging your pardon, sir," Wills announced, "But this dispatch just arrived from Commodore Hopkins, and needs your immediate attention." He handed the dispatch to Washington, who put on his spectacles and silently read it and smiled with closed lips.

"Commodore Hopkins has just captured one hundred and three cannons and mortars in the Bahamas, of all places, and a tremendous store on munitions and gunpowder." Washington looked up from the dispatch. "That gunpowder was the powder stolen from Williamsburg by Dunmore." He looked back at the dispatch. "He is currently en route to us." Washington handed the dispatch to Knox who began reading it himself.

"What glorious news we have this day!" Washington said. He turned to Wills and smiled.

"Have a seat lieutenant," Washington spoke to his secretary. "We need to reply immediately.

"Henry, I think the Continental Army now has the sufficient arms to defend New York from a British invasion," Washington said triumphantly.

"This is extremely good news," crowed Knox. A huge toothy smile stretched nearly ear-to-ear across his fat round face. "I can hardly wait to actually hear cannon fire."

Martha Washington planned to leave for Mount Vernon on April 1st with the army slated to begin their march to New York one week later. With the arrival of the new artillery pieces and gunpowder, Washington wanted to speed up the move.

"I do not want those pieces sitting on the docks," Washington stated. "They are too valuable to leave them open to recapture."

"Why not have Hopkins deposit them with Lee and Alexander in New York?" General Greene suggested. "They will be building the fortifications there. They shall be safe there, and we shan't be bogged down with them as we march."

"No," said Washington emphatically. "I want those pieces with the army. The army can transport them easily." He looked up from the maps and smiled at Knox.

"We have the greatest mover of artillery right here with us, do we not, Henry?" Knox nodded and smiled.

Washington pointed to the map, "Hopkins will receive our dispatch in three days at Philadelphia. We can meet him here on the fourth," he said, pointing to the small port of Charlestown on the Rhode Island coast, off Block Island Sound."

"Wills," Washington instructed, "pen a dispatch immediately. "Commander ... The news you have given this army is extremely well received. Congratulate your men, as I do congratulate you. Let them know how indebted our nation is for their heroic actions in the Bahamas. ... The army, marching en masse, shall reconnoiter with you at the port of Charlestown on the Block Island Sound on the fourth day of April. ... Washington."

A rider from Washington's headquarters at Cambridge arrived at Hopkin's headquarters at Philadelphia on the 28th. On the second day of April, the squadron again sailed north, per Washington's instructions. The ships arrived at Charlestown on the Rhode Island shoreline on April 3rd, and began off-loading the arms for Washington to take possession on the fourth.

Washington's new plan called for him and the entire Continental Army to escort Lady Washington as far as New York. They would leave from Cambridge and march directly to Charlestown to meet the squadron.

The general escorted his lady from the coach to tour the pier alongside him. It was crowded with the cannons, mortars and the barrels of gunpowder that had been spirited off by Lord Dunmore, while Washington had sat in the legislature in Williamsburg. Now they had been recaptured and taken from the Bahamas.

The Washingtons toured some of the ships of the squadron, and met Hopkins and General Nicholas on board the captured sloop, now named the Cambridge.

"I want to congratulate the both of you, in your victory in an unplanned campaign," Washington said with a broad smile. "Acting as you did, hearing where the munitions Dunmore pilfered were hid, you acted and succeeded. You proved beyond any doubts your ability to strategize and act. Our superiors, the Congress," he placed a cordial arm around Hopkins' shoulder, "are not in the field, and should never direct our actions, except in the broadest sense."

"We simply learned where the munitions were," said Hopkins, "and had to act before it was all carried to Halifax, as several barrels of powder had been."

"And I hear we have a prisoner," Washington turned to Nicholas.

"Lt. Gov. Browne is a scoundrel of the first order," stated Nicholas. "He claimed to hold no real power. He was no assistance to us, even after the marines stormed and took Fort Montague. We decided, since he was so unimportant, we would rid the Bahamas of him. It was my great privilege to march into the legislature and have him placed in leg irons and chains before the delegates assembled there."

"Even with, as he claims, no real power," said Washington, "he shall be valuable to us in negotiations or a prisoner exchange." Washington smiled, knowing he had a bargaining chip in the lieutenant governor appointed by the king. He also had the artillery needed for his plans for New York.

"The lieutenant governor is now the lonely guest of the Williamsburg Magazine," Commodore Hopkins informed Washington. "The first prisoner of war taken from the British is now moulders where the gunpowder Dunmore stole once rested."

"How fitting," Washington smiled. "The good citizens of Williamsburg, I am certain, will be pleased to keep watch over him."

Wills accompanied the Washingtons on their tour at the Charlestown wharf. He was anxious to see his old friend Johnny Kilkenney, and saw him when they went aboard the Cambridge.

"You old devil of a lowly Irishman!" Wills said as he shook Johnny's hand.

"Tis good ta see ya, Wills," Johnny smiled, "but them are fightin' words, don't ya know?"

"I expected you might end up some day captain of your own ship," Wills admitted, "but never imagined that it would happen so soon."

"Just how long now were ya willin' ta wait?" Johnny asked with a devilish grin. "The way things're goin' now, with you advisin' Washington an' me advisin' the commodore, this here war ain't ta be a lastin' long, I dare say! So how's that beautiful Priscilla of yers?" Johnny asked.

"Still beautiful and a wonderful mother," Wills answered.

"So the baby's here, ya say!?" Johnny crowed. "Another ornery litt'l Winkman in this world? When?"

"Reynolds Miles Winkman, we call him Rennie, came into this world on the twentieth day of March," Wills proudly announced. "He is now all of fifteen days old."

The next day, Johnny, at the helm of the Cambridge, Trevost, at the helm of the Prtovidence, and Thom Folger at the helm of the Enfield sailed south to Philadelphia for refitting. The rest of the squadron was to enjoy a two-week rest at Providence, following the weeks at sea. The commodore was looking forward to a few days with his family at his farm nearby.

That day the army marched, pulling wagons and rolling cannons under the capable guidance of Henry Knox. The carriage carrying the general and Lady Washington down the post road into the colony of Connecticut, led the army.

The army arrived on Manhattan Island after six days on the New England roads. General William Alexander had prepared a headquarters for Washington on the street called Broadway, near Wall Street and the Trinity Church. The headquarters was the former townhouse of a Loyalist who had fled to London. It was an easy walk from the headquarters to the Arsenal Battery at the southern tip of the island.

General Alexander had been sent by Washington from Cambridge to assist Gates and Lee in planning and building the New York fortifications. Alexander was born in New York in 1726. As the eldest male offspring of the first Earl of Stirling in Scottish peerage, he claimed the vacant title, 3rd Earl of Stirling, when visiting Britain in 1763. The British House of Lords did not accept his claim without assent by George III, which did not come. For the rest of his life he preferred being called Lord Stirling.

On April 13th, the refitting of the Cambridge and the Providence was in its fifth day. Kilkenny, Trevost and Folger were enjoying the largest city in the colonies, and awaiting orders from Hopkins at Providence. Trevost bought a copy of the pamphlet, Common Sense, written by Thomas Paine. It had become the most purchased and read pamphlet throughout the colonies since its January 1776 publication. The English author had laid out the reasons colonials had debated for a decade or more, the issue of independence, and freedom and liberty for all mankind.

On that same day, four British warships arrived at the mouth of Narragansett Bay, setting up an effective blockade of Rhode Island, bottling-up seven of the ten ships of the fledgling Continental Navy.

The Howe's Bring the Fleet

As soon as the nineteen thousand men of the Continental Army had arrived and settled into new quarters on Manhattan Island, the prime question on the mind General George Washington, all of his officers, and every soldier in camp, was when would the ships of the British fleet appear upon the horizon.

Washington found his headquarters on Broadway as comfortable as he found on Brattle Street. On their first evening in New York, the Washingtons went to prayers at Trinity Church, just down the street from the headquarters. They entertained Knox, and generals, Greene, Israel Putnam, his brother Rufus Putnam, and Lord Stirling. Washington made plans for a visit to Long Island to inspect the fortifications Gates, Lee and Stirling had built. The visit would be in two days, when Lady Washington would leave on her journey the final distance back to Mount Vernon.

"Is the city well-defended?" ask Washington of Stirling, knowing Congress had meddled and changed Washington's orders. Congress dispatched Lee with his men on some petty matter to South Carolina, and had asked Gates to come to Philadelphia.

"The fortifications are coming along, sir," was Stirling's only response.

Washington was notably not at all pleased.

"Congress meddles and the British could arrive in days!" Washington fumed. "Charles Lee, with his friends in Congress, I am certain, planned his own absence, just to allow our plans to fail, as he predicts they shall. Horatio Gates, too, has many friends in Congress, and now there he sits! Fortunately, I know men like Gates and Lee. All they are seek is personal glory, damn the cause!"

Washington found the fortifications not halfway complete. The most complete of Lee's projects were the redoubts, barricades and bastion atop the summit at Brooklyn Heights. To Washington's satisfaction, the work there done by Lee was the prime real estate in the heights to be used in defense of Manhattan, across the East River. The name given to the fort was Fort Stirling.

Gates and Lee had started three additional forts east of the village of Brooklyn, Fort Putnam, Fort Greene and Fort Box. They were barely started. There was also a planned Ft. Defiance near the southwest coast of Long Island. Over all, the sites Gates and Lee had selected met with Washington's approval...the work done did not.

Three days after Stirling escorted Washington on the tour of Long Island, Washington held a conference with his general staff. General Greene had taken the Putnam brothers on a tour north along the westside of Manhattan, while Stirling and Washington had headed across the East River to Long Island. The purpose of the conference was to compare notes in preparation for the coming British.

"Lee and Lord Stirling have begun good works," Washington opened the meeting. "With the needed men now necessary to complete the job, the island defenses should be ready before the end of May."

"The Putnams and I see a great need for fortifications along the Hudson as well," spoke General Greene. "If the British, in their ships, are able to encircle and trap us on Manhattan, we need a defense to the west to prevent them from establishing a land base north of the island."

"That has always been my plan," Washington stated. "Have you located sites on both shores? How soon could they be in place?"

"The sites we have located to keep the British bottled-up in the harbor, could be realized within, I would say, one month's time," Greene answered.

"We have selected two sites," Israel Putnam added. "One, the main defense, would be on the bluffs of the Hudson, just a mile north of the main city. The other lies on the New Jersey shoreline, a little to the south. British ships will indeed have a difficult way of it, should they try to ply the river north."

"Start them both immediately," Washington ordered. "Take what men you need. I fear the Howe brothers will not wait long."

By the last week of June, Washington made an inspection tour of the main defense, called Fort Washington, sitting high on the bluffs, with cannons looking down on the river. Across the river stood Fort Lee. Washington insisted it bear the name of the general who found argument with every strategy Washington authored.

"It shall give him a bigger head than he now has," Washington smiled, as the generals around him laughed.

"Fine work, Greene," Washington said as he stood at the highest point of the fort, peering into his spyglasses at the river below. "Both forts shall serve us well."

"We can now rest assured," Greene replied, "the British shall not easily encircle us and end the war early."

When Washington returned his headquarters, Wills Winkman met him with a dispatch from Boston. Gloucester fishermen, who made regular trips to Halifax, had spotted the British fleet leaving the harbor and sailing south.

Washington read the dispatch.

"It is about to begin, Wills," Washington spoke calmly. "The intelligence here states the fleet has left Halifax, and has been heading south, for near two weeks. They could arrive at any time."

The very next day, forty-five British ships appeared on the horizon, dropping anchor in Lower New York Harbor. The British had now arrived.

General Howe stood on the main deck of his flagship, alongside his brother, the admiral. Both men, with spyglasses, scanned the terrain on shore as the fleet made its way into the harbor at New York.

"I would certainly enjoy being a fly upon the wall in Washington's headquarters, as he looks out to sea this day," noted the general, "and shakes in his boots, seeing the fleet of the Royal Navy arrive at his threshold."

"As much as we did shake in our boots at Boston?" his brother questioned, "seeing those damned cannon barrels trained upon us in the harbor, from high atop Dorchester Heights?"

"I did no such a thing!" the general scoffed at his brother, lowering his spyglass. He held the spyglass up to his eye once more. "The time to retreat was the simple reality of that time. Those cannons simply made it so. Today, we are in the position to dictate, with grand superiority. We have lived to fight another day. This is that other day."

"Washington has no navy," the admiral spoke, "such as it is, it is bottled up at Narragansett. How many troops has he?"

"Our intelligence says somewhat over ten thousand, at best," replied the general, "and no adequate fortifications, with little artillery. We shall make quick work of them."

Within a week, the size of the British fleet was increased to one hundred and thirty ships. On July 2nd, Washington received word from his spies, the British were off-loading thousands of troops on Staten Island, making a land base there. What was General Howe's plan, Washington wondered. Would Howe invade Manhattan as Washington felt he would? Would he once more flee and attempt to strike at Philadelphia to the south? What would Howe do?

The Call for Independence

The four British warships blockading Narragansett Bay were the product of a bill passed in Parliament in February. Known as the Prohibitory Act, it authorized the Royal Navy to blockade the entire North American coastline, and effectively end all colonial trade. It was Dunmore's urgings to Lord Dartmouth to starve the Americans into submission.

In Congress, John Adams welcomed the act, if not the blockade. He began calling it the "Act of Independency." He said the British Parliament had, with that bill, declared American independence by viewing the thirteen colonies in the light of an enemy nation, therefore an independent nation.

"This is a complete dismemberment of the British Empire," Adams spoke in Congress. "They have authorized our own independence which, as of this day, we have not the needed delegations, authorized by their respective legislative bodies, to support independence. That situation," Adams continued, "shall soon be reversed."

The rules of Congress gave each state one vote. After issues were debated, each delegation would poll its members, and the state vote would reflect the majority thought in that delegation. The colonial legislatures also gave instructions to their delegates on important issues, such as independence. The delegates were either given instructions to support a call for independence, or to oppose it. At the time, five states had instructions to oppose independence: Delaware, Maryland, Pennsylvania, New Jersey and New York. No delegation had instructions to actually introduce legislation calling for independence.

Adams went to work, lobbying each of those colonies to revise their instructions to the delegates. Adams threatened that if they did not, Congress would no longer recognize those legislatures, and establish new ones, friendly to the cause of independence.

It was soon also learned King George had hired mercenary soldiers from Prussia, the Hessians, to add numbers to the king's own army in North America. This cavalier decision of the king became incendiary in the minds of colonials.

"He claims to be our king, and appeals to us to accept him as such," spoke Adams in Congress, "yet he hires the most barbaric of mercenaries to annihilate our citizens, when he controls the most powerful army in the world...the British Army. Now we must fight not only the Redcoats, but also the bought-and-paid-for barbarian Germans!"

On April 23rd Chief Justice William Henry Drayton of South Carolina declared, "George III, King of Great Britain, has no authority over us, and we owe no obedience to him." South Carolina's delegation now had the authority needed to support independence.

On May 4th the Rhode Island Legislature passed a resolution of its own declaring Rhode Island independent of Great Britain.

On May 15th the Virginia State Convention was held, and independence was the main topic of discussion. After adopting a new state constitution, they took the boldest step, and instructed the Virginia delegation to Congress "to propose to that respectable body to declare the United Colonies free and independent states, absolved from all allegiance to, or dependency upon, the Crown and Parliament of Great Britain."

When the news from Virginia was spread through the colonies, things happened fast. Virginia delegate Richard Henry Lee proposed the resolution from Virginia in Congress on June 7th. Lee's resolution received a second from John Adams, and after four days of debate, was approved by a majority.

On June 11th Congress established a committee of five men to draft the declaration. Robert Livingston of New York and Roger Sherman of Connecticut joined Benjamin Franklin, Thomas Jefferson, and John Adams, with the duty of drafting a declaration.

The committee met that same day in a tavern across Chestnut Street from the Pennsylvania

Statehouse. Jefferson was given the task of writing the first draft.

Jefferson sequestered himself in his rented upper floor rooms at the Graf House, at Market and 7th Street, two blocks from the hall. He struggled for the right words, and with what he felt should and should not be included in such an important document. He decided before declaring independence, there had to be justification for a people to do such a thing. He decided upon "the Laws of Nature and of Nature's God" entitle "man" with that right to be independent.

Next he penned the preamble. He coined the phrase *"unalienable rights"* and defined those rights as being *"Life, Liberty and the Pursuit of Happiness."* In the preamble he went on to state: *"whenever any Form of Government becomes destructive of these ends, it is the Right of the People to alter or abolish it."*

Jefferson went to great lengths to list all the egregious practices the king and Parliament had yoked upon the colonials, against both colonial and British constitutions. From there, Jefferson addressed the many efforts of colonials to appeal to the king for consideration and reconciliation, and the disappointments that always followed such appeals.

In his conclusion for the declaration, Jefferson used some of the strong words in the Virginia resolution that *"these United Colonies are, and of Right ought to be Free and independent States; that they are Absolved from all Allegiance to the British Crown..."*

The last line of the declaration showed just how strongly united in the cause of independence those men were, adding their signatures to the bottom for King George to see. The king would see the American colonies were indeed united ... *"We mutually pledge to each other our Lives, our Fortunes and our sacred Honor."*

After a little over a week, Jefferson came out of his private quarters and met with his four other committee members for their suggestions and revisions.

On June 28th, the committee's revised draft was introduced in Congress. Congress ordered the document to "lie on the table."

While Jefferson was sequestered in his rented rooms at the Graf House, Adams had been speaking, one-on-one to his fellow delegates.

He knew the legislatures of Delaware, New Hampshire and Connecticut had each been authorized to vote for independence, and they would.

In Pennsylvania, the Loyalist legislature had been replaced by a new patriot legislature. The new legislature declared the colony's independence from Britain.

The Maryland delegation to Congress had walked out when Adams' resolution to replace all legislatures not in favor of independence. A convention in Maryland convened and ordered the delegates back to Congress, allowing each to vote his own mind on the issue.

In New Jersey, William Franklin, the illegitimate son of Benjamin Franklin, was the royal governor. Unlike his father, Governor Franklin was strongly loyal to the king who had personally given him the appointment in 1763. He was not about to see his colony forsake his king. On June 15th, Franklin, being unhappy with the New Jersey Provisional Legislature, called the pro-independence body "an enemy to the liberties of this country."

Hearing this, the legislature issued a warrant for the governor's arrest. After Franklin was taken into custody, the legislature named a new delegation to Congress with explicit instructions to vote for independence.

In New York, the provincial legislature evacuated the city as the British were in the harbor. The legislature would not reconvene until July 10th. The New York delegation would remain impotent on the issue of independence.

Adams knew, from his individual talks with the delegates, that a vote on the Declaration of Independence would be favorable.

On the first day of July, John Adams impatiently rose on the floor of Congress.

"Let us now take the declaration off the table, and have a vote upon our independence," Adams made the motion. "Why, my dear gentlemen, do we wait to claim the independence that is our right?"

"Let us wait to declare our independence," spoke the Pennsylvanian, John Dickinson. "When we do declare independence, it will be war full on. We must wait until we have secured the alliances and loans from the other European nations we need in order to conduct war."

"What nation in Europe shall give us the amity and the loans," Adams questioned, "if they view us simply as yet a territory of Britain, with simply grievances against the king? As Britain sees us as an enemy nation, let us be just that...an independent and enemy nation!"

A vote was taken. Pennsylvania and South Carolina voted to delay. New York abstained, having no instructions from their legislature, as did Delaware, whose two delegates in attendance were split.

The other nine colonies voted as Adams knew they would, to go ahead immediately. The next day, some delegations wished for another vote, as things had changed in their delegations.

Edward Rutledge convinced the South Carolina delegates to change their vote to delay, to a stand for immediate independence.

The third Delaware delegate, Caesar Rodney, arrived in Philadelphia. His vote was for independence, so the tie was broken and Delaware voted for immediate passage.

In the Pennsylvania delegation, John Dickinson and Robert Morris agreed to abstain from the delegation caucus, allowing the five remaining delegates to vote three in favor of immediate passage and two opposed.

Only the delegation of New York remained unheard on the matter. All other delegations wanted immediate passage of the Declaration of Independence.

"This day, the second day of July," John Adams spoke with all the exuberance he could muster, "shall be celebrated throughout the new nation each year hereafter, with great celebrations, parades, fireworks and oratories, as the day of our nation's birth!"

A distinctive southern voice spoke, "We have voted to declare independence, and all are in agreement. We now must determine if there need be changes to the draft as presented to us. I rise to express much disfavor in one particular line in the proposed declaration." The voice was that of South Carolina's Edward Rutledge. The issue he found disfavor in, was the ban on the slave trade Jefferson had authored.

"How can we declare independence, if a large portion of our society shall not benefit from the same freedoms as their white masters?" questioned Jefferson, a slaveholder himself.

The debate lasted all afternoon and through most of the following day.

"Mr. Jefferson of Virginia," stated Rutledge, in the final hours of the debate, "may feel we cannot have our independence without extending full freedom to the slaves. I can count votes, Mr. Jefferson, and while we all want independence from Parliament and king, we shall never have it if the southern states vote against it, simply because of this ban you insist upon."

Benjamin Franklin, a strong anti-slavery proponent, rose to speak.

"Mr. Rutledge, and all my dear friends from the South," Franklin spoke, standing and leaning on his walking stick, "independence without your colonies which depend upon the slave economy, as has been the reality for generations, would not be the independence we shall want, or be willing to fight a war to obtain. The thirteen united colonies must remain so...united. I personally find that peculiar institution of slavery wretched, but in the name of union, I propose a motion to strike all reference in the document espousing any banning of the slave trade."

After that revision was made, to Thomas Jefferson's dismay, the revised document was adopted on the fourth of July. The United Colonies were now indeed, the United States of America.

Franklin sent a written copy of the declaration to the Philadelphia printer, John Dunlap, with instructions to print broadsides for general circulation. The "Dunlap Broadsides" were circulated throughout the new states. Every city and small town held public readings, the first being on the steps of the Pennsylvania Statehouse, from that time called Independence Hall.

When in the Course of Human Events...

On July eighth, a rider tied his horse to the hitching post outside Washington's headquarters on Broadway. Wills took the packet from the courier straight into Washington.

"They have done it!" Washington rose excitedly from his desk, smiling after reading the dispatch from Congress. "They have done it, Wills! They have indeed done it! The Congress has declared independence from the king and Parliament!" Washington handed the broadside to Wills to read.

"That, my lad," Washington said, as Wills began to read the declaration, "is what all this fighting is for. I am instructed by President Hancock of the Congress to have a public reading of the declaration before my troops and the citizens of New York."

Wills drafted a release to the "New York Advertiser" to announce a public reading of the 'Declaration of Independence' at six o'clock the following evening, July ninth, to be held at the city commons near the Bowling Green, in the lower portion of Manhattan.

As the British continued deploying their troops from the ships to encampments on Staten Island, the citizens of New York gathered with the troops on the commons. A platform had been erected and stood about five feet above the ground. General Washington led his generals onto the platform as fifes and drums played a military tune. He rose to address the crowd of about ten thousand of his nineteen thousand men, and a thousand or more citizens of New York.

"We have, just yesterday, received important news from the Congress at Philadelphia," the general spoke. "This news," Washington continued, "will better state our just cause, and the reasons for our army, and our past and coming struggles with Great Britain. I have asked my aide, Lieutenant William S. Winkman, to read to you assembled here, the Declaration of Independence of these United States of America, just passed by the Congress."

Wills rose and stood at the podium as Washington stood beside him. Wills began to read.

"When in the Course of human events, it becomes necessary for one people to dissolve the political bands which have connected them with another, and to assume among the powers of the earth, the separate and equal station to which the laws of nature and of Nature's God entitle them, a decent respect to the opinions of mankind requires that they should declare the causes which impel them to the separation."

Wills paused in his nervousness, reading the historic document for the first time, before a sea of people. He looked out into that sea for a moment, then focused his eyes again on the document and continued his reading:

"We hold these truths to be self-evident, that all men are created equal, that they are endowed by their Creator with certain unalienable rights, that among these are Life, Liberty and the Pursuit of Happiness."

There were cheers and huzzahs rising from throughout the assembled masses in the commons.

Wills read the complete document to much adulation from the crowd. When completed with the reading of the new declaration, that defined the new United States of America, Washington shook his hand and attempted to end the public reading with a few inspirational words of his own, but the crowd of newly declared independent citizens and soldiers immediately became a riotous mob. The mob marched, en masse, to the nearby Bowling Green, where there stood a huge bronze statue of King George III, riding upon his horse. Ropes were brought and tied to the legs of the horse and the waist of the king. After a few hearty tugs, the statue came toppling to the ground amid taunts and cheers from the mob.

Members of the mob beat the statue with whatever they could find, to render the iconic work of heroic art unrecognizable. It soon lay in many pieces, strewn across the grounds of the Bowling Green. The head, decapitated from the sovereign's torso, was taken away. Those with the head of the king, walked the several blocks to the yard in front of the popular Fraunces Tavern. There they drove a five foot high stake into the ground, and hung the bronze head of King George III for all passersby and patrons of the tavern to see. The rest of the metal from the statue was scooped up into bags of burlap to be sent off to a foundry in Connecticut, and made into musket balls to be used against the army of King George.

We Hold These Truths to be Self-Evident...

Similar events were held in every town and city in the colonies to proclaim independence from Great Britain. On the same day Wills Winkman read the Declaration of Independence on the commons of the city of New York, similar public readings were held in Trenton, Newark, Hartford, Providence and Boston to the north, and in Baltimore, Annapolis, Alexandria and Williamsburg to the south.

In Boston, Abigail Adams, of course with her four children in tow, stood in the shade of a giant tree in the Boston Commons, to listen as the venerable president of Harvard College, the Rev. Samuel Langdon, read the document. Abigail was indeed happy at the work her husband and his colleagues in Congress had completed. But in her listening, she did not hear all she wished to hear. The independence spoken of said "all men are created equal." Had John not insisted upon that independence being extended to the African slaves in the South and, most importantly, to the females? In her many letters to her husband in far away Philadelphia, they corresponded regularly on many of the political issues. Abigail always included one sentence in each of those letters ... "Remember the ladies!" She would write him a new letter as soon as she returned with her brood to Braintree. She celebrated independence, but not her own.

In Williamsburg, the men of the newly formed 3rd Virginia Regiment had assembled on the capitol grounds in May to begin their two and a half months of basic training exercises. Col. Hugh Mercer announced they would be marching out on August 5th to join Washington's army at Manhattan by the first of September. The first week for the new recruits was an exciting time in Williamsburg. The town was filled with visitors wanting to witness the Virginia State Convention, where the new state constitution was drafted, and the issue of independence was furthered with fiery oratory.

Peter Francisco and Jimmie Monroe shared a tent at the soldiers' encampment where they trained for combat with several of their fellow Campbelltown students. John Marshall and Stockard Samuels were there, as were the farm boys from Manassas and Hanover Counties, Garrett Hicks, Malcolm Shepherd, and Peter Patrick.

Jimmy Madison was also in town, but not in the regiment. James Madison, Jr., as he now preferred to be called, had been elected a delegate to represent Orange County at the state convention. Madison spent many hours at the camp with the regiment during his stay in Williamsburg.

"Virginia is now the first and only delegation to Congress," Madison announced, "with instructions to not simply support independence, but to actually introduce a resolution in Congress to declare independence."

"Will the British accept such a declaration," asked Peter, "and just let us be?"

"I say they will," said Marshall. "I do not think London wants to fight another costly war in North America."

"You mean there won't be no war after all?" asked Garrett. "I really wanna kill me some Red coats!"

"They will not accept any declaration our Congress pens," said Stockard firmly, opposing the conciliatory assumption of Marshall.

"They were humiliated by General Washington and fled Boston. There will most definitely be a war, so keep training, Mr. Hicks."

"I feel you are most correct, Samuels," said Madison. "As the king and Parliament thumbed their noses at the Olive Branch offered by the Congress last year, they will absolutely thumb their noses at our declaration of independence."

"So we will march in August to join Washington in New York?" Peter asked excitedly.

"Yes," said Madison, "you will soon be marching off to war. Today, the convention elected all delegates to our convention to make up the lower chamber of the new state's assembly, until popular elections can be held. So I shall remain here to pass the laws."

"So you now are a burgess!" Peter congratulated his friend.

"Well," Madison explained, "we no longer use that title associated with our colonial experience. We are now simply called delegates. And tomorrow, we in the House of Delegates, will elect the first true governor of Virginia, not a Dunmore appointed by the king." Madison looked directly at Peter. "Your cousin, Peter, Patrick Henry, has the support and will soon be living in the palace down the street from which Dunmore fled."

Patrick Henry was elected by the new legislature as the first governor of the state of Virginia. He did in fact take his seat at the palace on July fifth, and three days later received the Declaration of Independence from Congress. He announced a public meeting for the citizens of Williamsburg to hear the document read on the front lawn of the palace at four o'clock the afternoon of July ninth. He, himself, using his great oratorical skills, would read the document his friend, Thomas Jefferson, had penned, before a huge throng of his new constituents.

Independence on the Frontier

News from the east was slow arriving at Fort Pitt, and it arrived on anything but a regular schedule. Nate Nevers ordered copies of Philadelphia papers when he sent wagons east for more provisions for his trading post. Once a week, a post rider from Mercersburg arrived with mail for the Pittsborough settlement and sometimes newspapers came.

Tom and Jacky always tried to get all the news from back east they could, when they visited Nate. They discussed what they read about the Congress in Philadelphia and the events around Boston. It was an after dinner entertainment for them most evenings, while they sat on the expansive verandah, sipping whiskey and passing a pipe filled with dried hemp or tobacco.

"Was your sister not married to an Enfield?" Tom asked Jacky one evening in late May.

"Yes, Drake Enfield," replied Jacky. "He's an alright sort, not like that good fer nothin' Johnny Kilkenny what married Caroline. O'coarse, I guess Johnny got as bad as he gave."

"The reason I asked is I read in the paper I brought today from Nate's, that one Drake Enfield was the first patriot killed on the Lexington Green," Tom said.

Jacky was stunned and just sat there for a moment shaking his head in disbelief. "It sure figgers, the good ones take the bullets an' the scoundrels live ta tell 'bout it. I sure hope this war that's sure a comin'stays far away from here."

"It should," said Tom, "unless the British in the forts Davy speaks of stir up the tribes and send them on raids of our settlements. If that happens, Jacky, we may have to get involved."

"The Redcoat soldiers are in the frontier," Davy re-iterated. "They have forts to the north at Detroit and Michilimackinac. They are also to the west at Vincennes on the Wabash, and Cahokia and Kaskaskia along the Mississippi. As the tribes fought with the French, many will fight alongside the British against the Americans. They fear when the Americans come to the Ohio Country, the tribes will be driven across the Mississippi."

"I still want to go into the Ohio Country some day and settle there, so we can operate a trading post for the settlers," Tom spoke again of his dreams. "We can build flatboats and sell them to the settlers heading west. Somewhere on the Ohio, near the Scioto, would be a great location. By the time the settlers get that far, about halfway to the settlements in Kentucky, they'll be anxious to see white folks and probably need to buy some supplies by then."

"I sure liked the looks o' that tomahawk claim to that plain we saw on the Scioto," said Jacky. "That'll sure make someone a rich bottomland farm."

The war in the east was just delaying their plans for the time being. In the meantime, they would hunt and amass furs and hides, cure meats and preserve other foodstuffs for sale to Nate Nevers, until the settlers started coming.

"Are there a couple o' varmints here, name o' Macneal!" a loud voice pierced the quiet of nature one afternoon in mid-July.

"Kenton!" Davy shouted and ran toward his old friend. Kenton and Col. Clark had tied their canoe at the dock and began walking toward the cabin.

Tom and Jacky came out of the smokehouse where they had been curing some game.

"Kenton, you ole cuss!" Jacky shouted back when he saw his old friend.

Tom and Jacky rushed to greet the two frontiersman, and invited them to rest on the verandah and stay for supper and overnight if they wanted.

"What brings you boys out here?" Tom asked, shaking hands with the guests.

"Congress and Patrick Henry," Kenton answered.

"There's gonna be a big celebration at the fort tomorrow," Kenton said, as the five men took seats on the porch.

"A celebration?" Jacky asked.

"Yep," said Kenton. "The Congress has declared the independence from the king for the whole United Colonies ..."

"We're not colonies no more, Kenton," Clark corrected him. "We're the United States of America!"

"'scuse me...Colonel Clark," Kenton corrected himself and continued. "Every settlement in these here United States of America, are celebratin' with a public readin' of the declaration they drafted, signed and sent off to King George. Nate Nevers is spreadin' the word in Pittsborough, and at two o'clock tomorrow, everyone's to turn out and bring eats. Nate's dug a pit and has four hogs an' a steer roastin' in it. It oughta be a day to remember."

"Well, Jacky," Tom spoke, "the war hasn't reached us here yet, but it does seem that independence has. Of course we will go to the fort and celebrate with our neighbors."

"That's sure good," said Kenton, digging into his side pouch and pulling out one of the broadsides. "Here, Tommy me boy," Simon handed it to Tom. "You might want to read over it a time or two. Nate Nevers wants you to read it tomorrow to your neighbors."

After a supper of Ohio River bass and catfish, rolled in corn meal and fried in lard in the big cast iron skillet over the hearth, fried mushrooms, and wild greens and green onions wilted with bacon grease, the five sat back on the verandah as the darkness of night came. They sipped whiskey and smoked, as Clark and Kenton painted a glorious picture of the new Kentucky settlements down the Ohio. Tom, Jacky and Davy agreed to join them in the fall at the Blue Licks to hunt the elusive buffalo.

When everyone had gone to their beds for the night, Tom and Jacky took to their bedroom and laid down on the mattress. Tom wrapped one arm around Jacky, as Jacky laid his head on Tom's shoulder.

"Can you imagine what our neighbors at Fort Pitt tomorrow would think if they knew the person selected to read 'the Declaration of Independence' to them for the very first time would be the former British Captain Tom Preston, infamous and hated leader of the Boston Massacre of 1770?"

Jacky rolled over and hugged him, planting a kiss on his forehead.

"How proud though, they'd be," Jacky said, "if they knew you then got dressed up like an Mohawk Indian and threw tea into Boston Harbor." They both chuckled and fell asleep.

Journey to the Waxhaw

Zack sat in the old rustic longboat as Rodie poled him and seven Scotch-Irish settlers through the brackish green waters of the Great Dismal Swamp. He had his sketchbook on his lap and a charcoal in hand. He wanted to put an image of the scene unfolding before him on a glade as the boat approached and slowly passed by. Zack rushed enough of the image onto the sketchpad to spur memories in his mind's eye and bring the scene to life later when they made camp, and he'd add those details to it. The fat and fury brown mama bear was frolicking with her two small cubs underneath a beautiful old live oak tree, dripping with Spanish moss.

The day through the swamp, which stretched across the Virginia-North Carolina border, kept Zack busy. He had never seen a seemingly endless swamp like this one. Huge trees with mystically shaped trunks, looking like knights of the Crusades, pirates, and demons of all kinds, stood tall as if sentinels looking down upon the travelers. Knobby knees of cypress protruded eerily out of the water. There were unusual reptiles, amphibians, fish and birds. Each had been captured in charcoal. Zack imagined it to be some prehistoric land of dinosaurs. Zack's mind was filled with these images and he would detail them each when he had the time.

The Magruder party of Scotch-Irish settlers had arrived in Williamsburg the last week of May. Zack and Rodie were packed and ready for their adventure.

The Scotch-Irish were a misunderstood race. There was no such thing as "Scotch-Irish" in Scotland. There they were simply Scots who had lived, generation after generation in Scotland. They were Presbyterians. When the Catolics, then the Anglicans, then the Puritans of Oliver Cromwell ruled England, these people fled across the Irish Channel and planted homes mainly in County Antrim in the North near the main port of Carrickfergus. The Irish Catholics welcomed them, but banned them from actually living in their Irish Catholic towns. The Scots fended for themselves and huddled together in Presbyterian settlements of their own making. After a hundred years or so living in Ireland as second-class citizens, they were prime for new lives in the new world of America.

When they arrived at Philadelphia, they were registered as Irish immigrants because the migrated from Ireland. They protested as they were Scots, not Irish, and the Irish were not readily accepted in most of the colonies, because of the Catholic faith of most Irish. The immigration officials in Philadelphia created the new "nationality" of Scotch-Irish, to differentiate them from the true Irish.

Not trusting the English at all, they journied to the far western or southern frontiers, as soon as they could. The Waxhaw was known to them as a hub for Scotch-Irish immigrants. Most of the settlers Ansley Magruder led to the Waxhaw already had cousins or other relatives and friends already living there. There they were far away from the established cities along the coast, and could have a safe place to plant roots. While the colonies were fighting a war for independence, the Scotch-Irish on the frontier already seemed to have it.

From the swamp they trudged through the coastal regions of North Carolina on foot, and took boats to Ocracoke, one of the barrier islands along Cape Hatteras. Zack saw the ocean for the first time. He sketched the great sand dunes, the powerful waves crashing into the sandy shore, the playful little white birds with long, skinny legs that darted across the sand at the edge of the surf, leaving the tracks of their footprints in the sand.

The only real city they visited was New Bern, the colonial capital of North Carolina. New Bern reminded Zack of a smaller Williamsburg. The opulent red brick Tryon Palace was on the scale of the Governor's Palace at Williamsburg, but newer. It had just been completed a couple years before the royal governor fled back to England. Zack sat on the lawn in front of the circular drive, set up his small easel, and put every detail of the splendid residence on paper.

Their travels up the Nuese River, inland through the piney forests, and then overland on foot to the Catawba River, gave Zack more of nature to sketch. There he saw an ancient and ugly-looking reptile Magruder said was called an alligator. He had never seen such a prehistoric looking animal before. The trip ended along the Catawba, which took them to the Waxhaw settlement.

"Six more fam'lies a needin' homes, I've brought ya Thad," Magruder said to the leader of the settlement, Thad Henderson, as the settlers stood outside the Waxhaw Trading Post, which the seventy year-old Henderson had opened twenty years earlier.

"I got families lined up to take 'em all in till they select a homestead, an' we raise their cabins for 'em," the old man said.

"I also brung two young men wantin' to stay here a spell, an' then head off to the Spanish lands," Magruder added.

"They speak English, don't they?" old Thad asked. "No one don't speak Spanish 'round here, least much that is."

"They do," Magruder said, "They're Virginians, headin' to'ards the Mississip on an adventure."

"I bet the widder Jackson'll take 'em in for a spell." Magruder followed Thad inside.

Soon, a leathery-skinned, lanky woman with dark reddish-brown hair, hanging down across her shoulders, came out of the trading post. A young boy, tall for his age, with unkempt dark red hair was with her, carrying a box filled with provisions.

"You be the fellers a headin' to the Spanish lands?" she asked in her montone voice.

"Yes ma'am, we are," said Rodie. "I'm Rodie Murray and this is Zack Winston."

"I be Betty Jackson," she said, "an' this here's me youngest boy, Andy. You're welcome ta take meals with me and me boys, an' sleep in me barn loft, as long as you needs. Come on along now." They walked with Betty and Andy to their cabin down the dusty lane.

Betty and her husband had sailed to Philadelphia from Carrickfergus with their two sons in 1765. They joined an expedition to the Waxhaw, where some of Betty's cousins had already settled. When Betty was pregnant with a third child in 1767, her husband, Andrew, was killed when a tree fell on him and crushed him to death. He and some of the other men were lumbering for the settlement. Their third child was born one month after the father's death. Betty named her new baby, Andrew, after his dead papa.

"Tomorry there's a big celebratin' we're a havin'," she added. "Andy here is ta read somethin' from that Congress up at Philadelphy. The whole settlement'll turn out for the pig roast ole Thad's a providin'. There's ta be fiddle-playin', an' dancin', and somethin' or another they be a callin' indy-pendence."

"Independence?" Rodie questioned excitedly. "Is the war over? Did the British run away and give us the independence we've been wanting?"

The widow just shrugged her shoulders, not knowing what the young man was talking about. "I don't pay no mind a'tall ta sech as that. I reckon you'll see tomorry."

"So Andy's reading the resolution tomorrow?" Zack asked, smiling at the lad.

"Yep," Andy said, "I do it all the time. Whenever newspapers come in, Thad has everyone show up and I read 'em aloud to them that cain't read."

The next day everyone showed up in front of the trading post. Thad's grandson, Micah, lifted Andy up onto a four-foot high stump of a felled tree so all in the settlement could get a good look at him, as they heard about the independence Congress had given them. Zack sat on barrel outside the general store and captured the historic event in charcoal.

Zack and Rodie enjoyed the days at Waxhaw. They joined in and helped raise six cabins for the newly-arrived settlers of the Magruder party. Zack had plenty of time to take those rough drawings from their travels and add the finishing touches. No one in the settlement was planning a trip to New Orleans any time soon, so the boys waited.

Chapter Ten

I Only Regret ...

"Damn it to Hell!" shouted General Washington at his headquarters on Broadway, the morning of July 13th. "We built those forts on the Hudson to prevent this very thing!"

"Under the cover of night, two of their ships, carrying soldiers ... the Lord alone knows just how many ... did slip by, unnoticed by anyone at Fort Lee or at Fort Washington! Where have they landed their army? Where have they set up their base on the Hudson? Do our guards there sleep on their watch? Do they not know the British Fleet is at our door!"

The situation was tense at Washington's headquarters all morning and into the afternoon. As officers arrived throughout the day, Wills Winkman showed them in to see Washington, if they seemed to have any sense of intelligence whatsoever. One had only the names of the two British ships that made the stealth nighttime passage ... the Rose and the Phoenix. Intelligence as to the numbers of soldier aboard ranged from "just a handful of Red Coats and a few Hessians" to "more than a thousand of their best from the Black Watch." The only reliable intelligence came from a patriot farmer from Tarrytown.

"Those damned Redcoats are swarming all over my farm, and all the farms in the area!" the farmer told Washington.

In the early afternoon, a uniformed British officer, flying the white flag of truce, was rowed to the Arsenal Battery at the southern tip of Manhattan. Major Joseph Reed met him.

"Who goes there?" Reed barked, as the British officer stepped onto the dock.

"Lieutenant Phillip Brown," the officer replied, "official emissary of General Lord William Howe." He saluted Reed, and Reed returned the salute.

"And what is your business, under this flag of truce?" asked Reed, harshly.

"I have official correspondence from the Commander-in-Chief of the British Army in North America," replied Brown, taking an envelope with waxed seal from his coat, handing it to Reed. Reed took it and instructed Brown to wait. Reed left and walked the several blocks to Washington's headquarters, as four bayonet-wielding soldiers kept an eye on Lt. Brown.

Wills greeted Reed at the door. Reed discussed with Wills the lack of protocol on the way the official correspondence from the British general had been addressed.

"Those arrogant British bastards cannot even address General Washington with the dignity and protocol he so rightly deserves," said Reed. Wills took the envelope and looked. In a nice and formal hand was simply written "Geo. Washington."

"General Howe has seen fit not to address our commander with his official title," Wills said, "and he simply abbreviates even his given name!"

At that moment, Washington came from his office, having heard Wills and Reed talking. "What do you have there?"

"An emissary of General Howe has arrived at the battery with a correspondence," said Wills, handing the envelope to the general.

Washington took the envelope, looked at the way it had been addressed, looked up at Wills and Reed, and smiled. "Should I accept this? Would you accept this?

"Addressed as it is so chauvinistically addressed," Washington answered his own query, "by the one we so scared into running away from Boston, I should think not." He handed it back to Wills, who handed it back to Reed. Reed saluted Washington and left.

Reed approached Brown, pacing impatiently on the edge of the wharf, fenced in, as it were, by the bayonets. He handed the unopened envelope back to the British officer and spoke: "There is no one here by that address."

"Tis for your commander, George Washington!" Brown shouted in a rage. "It is from his Lordship, General William Howe, Commander-in-Chief of the British Army of North America, and emissary of King George III!"

"As I said, sir," repeated Reed calmly, "there is no one here by that address. Perhaps you should return it, unopened as it is, to the sender, and find a more adequate and appropriate address."

Brown stormed off, back into his dingy, and it pushed off. Reed and the Continental soldiers stood by and laughed at the expense of the arrogant British.

The next day, the soldiers posted on the wharf saw the same dingy approach with the same Lt. Brown, standing with the same little white flag of truce. Brown saluted Reed, and Reed took the second wax-sealed envelope and walked back up Broadway to Washington's headquarters.

After a few minutes, Reed returned again with the unopened envelope. The second envelope was simply addressed: "George Washington, Esquire, Etc. Etc. Etc."

"Again, my dear sir," spoke Reed, "there is no one here by that address."

Brown protested once more, then sailed off again to the hoots and cat-calls of the American soldiers on the wharf.

The next day, three boats neared the battery and an officer, noticeably of higher rank than the humiliated Lt. Brown, stepped ashore.

Reed approached and shouted out, "Who goes there?"

The officer answered, "Colonel James Patterson, adjutant to the Commander-in-Chief of the British Army in North America, General Lord William Howe, requesting an audience with General George Washington, Commander-in-Chief of your American Army."

Patterson saluted, and Reed escorted the commander's adjutant up Broadway. At last, the second-in-command of the British army had addressed General Washington with the respect due his office.

Patterson and Washington met behind closed doors for just a few minutes, then Reed escorted the colonel back to the wharf.

"Well, General Howe did not demand our surrender, at the least," Washington chuckled, then turned to Wills. "Howe has magnanimously offered us all full pardons." Washington smiled and turned to walk back into his office. He turned again to Wills. "I told him as plainly as I could, those who have committed no fault desire no pardon." He smiled again and closed his door behind him. The war would indeed continue.

The Blue Licks of Kentucky

Jacky, Tom and Davy set off down river to join up with Simon Kenton and George Rogers Clark, to hunt buffalo at the Blue Licks in Kentucky. Before Kenton and Clark had left Annie's Port in mid-July, they set the date of August 15th to meet at the Blue Licks.

A week down the Ohio River, they made camp a mile or so west of the mouth of the Scioto River, the farthest point west Tom and Jacky had ever traveled. The site they chose for their camp was on the north side of the river with a gradual slope up from the water. Beyond that was an open field, then dense forests started upthe steep and rocky hills. The Kentucky side of the river had steeper forested hills, seeming to rise right out of the water.

The area's landscape was dominated by one huge rocky hill with a tall outcropping at its summit. The top of the huge rock was dome-shaped, with a ledge hanging out over the hill twenty or more feet, looking like the head and beak of a giant bird. The evening the Macneal party made camp there, several large black ravens were circling above. They named the spot Raven Rock.

"This would be a wonderful spot for a trading post after the war," Tom said, as they ate a supper of two plump rabbits, roasted on a spit over the campfire.

"Macneal's Raven Rock Tradin' Post," Jacky said, seeing the sign in his mind. "I think you're right, Tom. It's a natural landin' for flatboats, an' a good week away from Fort Pitt. Time for them settlers ta restock some an' stretch their legs a spell. I'm gonna make a tomahawk claim to it right now."

He got up and took his hunting knife out of its sheath. He walked over to the big buckeye tree beside where they had built their campfire.

"This is a signal mountain for the Shawnee," Davy told them. "They build their signal fires on the ledge up there," Davy said, pointing at the raven's beak. "They send signals to the Chickasaw and the Cherokee across the Ohio."

"Will we see any Shawnee or Cherokee on this trip?" Jacky asked Davy, as he started carving.

"I doubt we see any," Davy answered Jacky's question, "but if any are here, they will see us."

"I dunno if I like the sound o' that?" Jacky said, blowing the cut wood chips from the first initial he had carved.

"Don't worry," Davy assured Jacky, "They will only spy to see if you intend to bring harm. Remember, I saw you two full days before I let you see me." They all laughed.

"I doubt the Shawnee are now a threat here, after Dunmore's treaty." Davy continued.

"I have heard many Shawnee have broken the treaty," Tom said. "It seems Cornstalk has led many Shawnee west to the Wabash, but a new chief, Blue Jacket, remains in the Ohio Country with many who view Cornstalk as a traitor for giving up their Shawnee claims."

"Blue Jacket," Davy said seriously. "I know him. He was the one who captured me; he and his friend, Pucksinwah. He was then Cornstalk's chief warrior. His name is Se-pet-te-ka-nathe, Big Rabbit. They call him Blue Jacket because he wears a blue cloth coat. He and Pucksinwah are to be feared."

Davy blew the final wood chips from the tree trunk and admired his work: "Tee. & Jay. 1776."

"Well, Tommy me lad," Jacky came back and sat down at the campfire, pleased with his work, "This land is claimed!" The three friends chuckled. They shared whiskey and hemp, and talked until the night sky had been black for an hour, then turned in for a good night's sleep.

Two days later, they found the spot on the river where Kenton had told them to land. It was where the river made its third turn north, after the mouth of the Scioto. They came ashore on the Kentucky side of the river. Just as Kenton described, there was a small creek emptying into what seemed like a natural harbor, with a flatboat moored hidden in the canebreak. A wide and beaten path ran up the side of the low rise, then disappeared inland. That had to be the buffalo trace Kenton had told them about. Kenton said the buffalo would swim across the river from the Ohio Country, and travel inland to the salt licks.

"This has got to be Kenton's landing," said Tom. "From what he said, if we take that buffalo trace straight up the hill, across a narrow plain, then up a larger and steeper hill, we'll find his cabin. It should be about four miles from here."

"I cannot wait to see my friend Simon Kenton," said Davy.

"I can't wait ta kill me another buffalo!" said Jacky.

"Don't forget the elk too," Tom added. "Kenton said the Blue Licks are teeming with all sorts of game. The hides and the meats we dress will bring a good price from Nate Nevers. Let's get going."

They moored the flatboat under the spread out hanging branches of a large weeping willow, and carried their muskets and knives, putting their large haversacks with provisions on their backs. They began the trudge up the slope.

"Well ain't you a sight fer sore eyes!" came a cry from a cliff above the trace as the three neared the top of the steeper hill's summit.

"Kenton! Is that you?" shouted Jacky.

"No, it's General George Washington!" came the reply, as Kenton jumped from the twenty- foot cliff to the dusty trace just in front of them. He picked himself up, dusted himself off, and said, "O' course it's me. I'm the only white man in these here parts! The worst o' yer trip is over. My place's just 'round the bend. You made it just in time. We're meetin' Clark an' Boone at the Blue Licks day after tomorrow."

"Daniel Boone?" Tom asked, showing excitement, thinking he would be meeting the famed frontiersman.

"The one and only Dan'l Boone!" answered Kenton.

After two nights at Kenton's cabin, the party headed south. Kenton had horses for each of them, and a mule to bring back the game they planned on hunting. They rode off, following the buffalo trace for about twenty miles when they spotted a burned out cabin, just off the trail.

"What ya s'pose happened there?" asked Jacky.

"The damned Shawnee!" Kenton said.

372

"Moses Kemper was my closest neighbor. He an' his wife Molly settled here last fall. There's a big spring just down the rise. They sure picked a beautiful place for a homestead. I helped 'em raise the cabin.

"When I returned from Annie's Port," Kenton continued, "I learned a Shawnee raidin' party had snuck up on 'em an' burnt the cabin, an' scalped 'em both. Those filthy savages!"

"So what I heard is true," Tom said. "Many Shawnee did not leave with Cornstalk."

"You heard right," Kenton said. "The orn'riest of 'em stayed."

In late afternoon they made camp on the bluffs overlooking a broad flat glen in the forest at the Blue Licks. The Blue Licks were large, naturally exposed salt outcroppings, where the wildlife came to lick the exposed salt. The whole area provided them plenty of grazing and water from the Licking River. Deer and elk were plentiful, and their buckskins brought a good price. There were bears, raccoons, possums, squirrels, and other varmints to skin for pelts and sides of meat to eat, but the main draw was the buffalo.

"Yep," Kenton said, "the buffalo have been plentiful here since June. I know it won't be long 'til you fellers start seein' 'em."

"An' start shootin' 'em, I hope!" added Jacky. "That buffalo we shot on the Pee Pee Prairie on the Scioto fed us near all winter, an' the hide brung top dollar."

An hour or so before sunset, the remainder of the hunting party was spotted, riding across the glen below the bluffs. They watched as four men approached.

George Rogers Clark had come to Boonesborough from his cabin on Corn Island at the falls of the Ohio River. Daniel Boone and two others from Boonesborough joined Clark on their forty-mile trek to the Blue Licks. Hezekiah Borders, the preacher who had followed Boone on the initial expedition to build Boonesborough, and Borders' sixteen-year-old son, Levi, were along for the hunt.

The hunting party had a feast on their first night. Boone's party had bagged several pheasants on their way. Davy had spent an hour gathering some luscious looking blackberries, some wild greens, wild carrots and green onions. After their supper, the nine men sat around the fire. They passed around a flask of whiskey and a pipe filled with dried hemp Jacky pulled out of his haversack.

"Have there been any more raidin' parties," Kenton asked Boone, "since the one what took little Jemima?"

"Not 'round Boonesborough," said Boone.

"There's bound ta be some this winter," added Clark. "The British Governor Hamilton up at Fort Detroit will make damn sure o' that."

"Hamilton's sure stirrin' 'em up," said Boone. "He's doin' ever'thin' he can ta keep 'em all stirred up, an' makin' allies out o' 'em fer the Redcoats."

"How's little Jemima doin'?" asked Kenton.

"No worse fer the wear," answered Boone.

"Who is this little Jemima?" asked Jacky.

"Tell 'em about 'er Dan'l," Kenton urged the fabled frontiersman, who loved to tell a good tale.

Boone took a draw from the pipe, passed it on to Preacher Borders, and began the story.

"Well, Jemima's m'daughter, leastwise I claim 'er as m'own. Fourteen years ago, I was gone from our settlement in the Yadkin Valley on a huntin' trip inta the Ken-tuck' an' Ohio countries. Becky, m'wife, fearin' I must o' surely been kilt, as she hadn't heard hide ner hair o' me fer more'n a year, started up with m'brother, Ned. Becky was soon with child, and that's how I foun' her when I finally did return...ready to drop that youngin' in a day or two. That youngin' bein' Jemima.

"Now, I got no apologies a'tall from m'Becky fer her givin' me up fer dead, an' a layin' up with ole Ned. All I got from 'er was scorn fer not returnin' when she 'spected I would. All Becky'd say ta me was 'Dan'l, you'd had better o' stayed ta home an' got it fer yourself, 'stead o' bein' gone an' lettin' your own brother get it!!'" All the listeners roared with laughter at what Boone had said.

"I reckon Becky had cause," Boone continued with a smile. "I took little Jemima as m' own an' raised her up. She's m' favorite youngin' of all ten.

"Well, one Sunday in early summer," Boone continued, "after Preacher Borders here finished one o' his fire-an'-brimstone sermons, some o' the girls decided ta go ta the river behind the stockade an' pick 'em some wild flowers. Most o' the youngin's stayed put on shore, a pickin' flowers there. Jemima an' her two best friends, Fannie an' Betsy Calloway, the older girls o' the bunch, got inta a boat an' paddled 'cross the Ken-tuck River ta where they had seen a great stan' o' posies on the fer bank.

"When they got through the canebreak an' close ta shore, five savages, two Shawnees an three Cherokees, led by a fierce Cherokee name o' Hanging Maw, grabbed up the three gals an' carried 'em off inta the woods.

"When told by the scare't-ta-death little gals what came a runnin' back ta the fort, me an' Colonel Calloway put tagether a rescue party an' were fast on their trail. That was no easy chore, follerin' a trail laid down by the savages."

"Well, we tracked 'em two full days and finally saw signs that were fresh," Boone continued the true tale. "On that mornin' o' the third day, we saw the smoke from their fire. As we came upon'em an' hid in the woods, we seen 'em makin' a breakfast of fresh buffalo tongue. It sure smelt good, an' we was sure hungry. We figgered they must've been the ones who had kilt that buffalo we'd seen half cut-up a ways back. Them takin' time to get what they wanted out o' that ole buffalo prob'ly gave us a chance ta catch up to 'em.

"Surprisin' 'em was all that was on m'mind," said Boone, "an' the timin' was right. I had me a clear shot at one o' them Shawnee, tendin' to the buffalo tongue over the fire. I took that shot. He fell right inta that fire face-down dead.

"Then I heared little Jemima a cryin' out 'that's m'pa's gun!' I knew Jemima was all right. We fired two more shots, both hittin' their targets smack dab. The two live savages took off a runnin' fer the blue blazes through the woods.

"All the gals was fine," Boone said proudly. "And the buffalo tongue surely made us some good eatin'. Betsy Calloway, up an' married one o' the young bucks in the rescue party jus' last month. Her sister, Fannie, is a-courtin' another o' the rescuers," Boone ended his tale.

"An' little Jemimy is a-courtin' Flanders Calloway," inserted Preacher Borders, as a footnote. "Dan'l's gonna have a new son-in-law and most sure a new grandbaby soon."

"He may claim to be called o' the Lord," said Boone of the preacher, "but you best not be a beleivin' a damn word comin' outta that man's mouth, lessen the good book's right there an' opened in his hand! … Jemima is a lookin' fer a husband, that she is, but Flanders Calloway is not gonna be no son-in-law o' mine. I'm a thinkin' on invitin' Davy here, to come back to Boonesborough with me ta meet m' little Jemima. Now Davy Danielson would fer certain make her a right fine good husband."

The men all laughed and began teasing Davy about Boone's plans to marry Jemima off to him. They soon went to sleep to get rested for a full day of hunting.

After a successful week of hunting, Jacky and Davy helped Kenton build a travois for each horse and the mule to pull behind them on the trip home. The travois was a canvas platform attached to two long poles, harnessed to the horse. Kenton, Tom and Jacky took back with them the hides and caracsses of two elk, six deer, two bears, two buffalo, and several other smaller critters.

Davy decided to go to Boonesborough and get introduced to Jemima.

"I ain't looking to be married," said Davy, before leaving Jacky and Tom at the camp. "I'll be back at Annie's Port sometime in the winter. I want to spend some time with Dan'l and see his settlement."

On the trip home, Jacky and Tom were once more camped at Raven Rocky, the place they had discovered and laid claim to on the trip down river.

"Do ya think Davy'll get married to Dan'l's daughter?" Jacky asked Tom, as they lay together in their tent.

"Never can tell," answered Tom. "I'm sure gonna miss him."

"Me too, but maybe he'll stay at Boonesborough a spell, then head back home to Annie's Port, like he said.

"When do ya think this land might ever be safe ta settle?" Jacky asked Tom. "When do ya think this war will ever really get started so it can get over with?"

Tom rolled over on his side and wrapped an arm around Jacky's chest. He smiled at Jacky, who was smiling that mischievous smile Tom had grown so used to since they had first met six years earlier.

"I have no idea," said Tom, "but I do know, some day we will have the Macneal Trading Post right here at Raven Rock." He kissed Jacky.

"Until then, I guess we will just have to sit back and wait for Washington and Howe to start and finish the war," Tom said.

"An' hope Gov'nor Hamilton up at Fort Detroit don't bring the war here to us," added Jacky.

Arrival of the Spaniards

"Senora Jackson," proclaimed the visiting Spanish trader, Alejandro Tamayo, "I have not dined on such marvelous barbacoa since we left New Orleans."

"And such a wonderful flavor your molasses add," agreed his partner, Joaquin Avila, as they ate with the widow Jackson, her three sons, and their two visitors from Williamsburg.

"Tis the honey," the widow said, accepting the compliments with a blush in her leathery face.

"For this wonderful fiesta you have so graciously allowed us to share with you," added Tamayo, "I have some jars of habaneras and cayenne for your cocina…your kitchen."

"Thank ye, Senor Tamayo. They'll sure be put ta good use 'roun' here," she answered. "Me youngin's, alls they wanna do is sleep an' get inta trouble an' eat…then eat some more."

Tamayo and Avila were the sons of the owners of the largest mercantile and trading company in New Orleans. They tried to make two trips each year to the frontier settlements in the Carolinas and Georgia. They traded for tobacco and other produce grown in each of the settlements where they traded. They docked their flatboat on the landing of the Catawba River the first week of August. They had spices, rum, wines, rice, coffee, bolts of cloth, and other goods from not only New Orleans, but also from the islands of the Caribbean and from Spain.

The widow Jackson had ten bales of tobacco and traded her crops for some cloth to make her a dress or two, and some shirts and pants for her growing boys, as well as some refined sugar, coffee, and other kitchen needs. She invited the visitors to supper at her homestead, so she could introduce the two Spaniards to the two Virginians.

Betty Jackson prepared a recipe, called "barbacoa," she had gotten from the Spaniards a few years earlier. She put a large pork butt from the smokehouse into a cast iron pot, and simmered it as the pot hung on a tripod over an open fire set up in the yard. When it was nice and tender, she took it out of the pot, pulled it into strings of meat with a fork, and placed the stringy meat back into the pot to simmer in a sauce made of molasses, honey, some diced peppers, and onions.

"Where do you head from the Waxhaw?" Rodie anxiously asked, as Betty brought an applesauce cake to the outdoor table.

"This is the farthest point on our journey," said Tamayo. "We leave here the day after tomorrow. We will stop in Pensacola and Mobile on or journey back to New Orleans."

"Zack and I wish to travel to your city," added Rodie. "Might we join you on your return trip?"

"We travel light, I am afraid," commented Tamayo. "It is a tiresome journey, more than a month's duration."

"We traveled seventy-eight days to get here from Williamsburg," added Rodie. "Have you seen Zack's wonderful drawings? He's an artist, and wants to draw New Orleans and the Mississippi River country. Go get your sketches Zack. Let them see."

Zack went to the barn loft and returned with some of his finished works, and a copy of his published book.

The Spaniards enjoyed the drawings. They spent most of the evening looking at each one of them, realizing just how talented Zack was.

"I believe our fathers would enjoy these so much," commented Avila. "What do you think, Alejandro?"

"Do you draw portraits?" Tamayo asked noncommittally.

"He does indeed," said Rodie. "Show him Chief Logan."

"The famous tribal leader Logan?" asked Tamayo. "Logan sat for you?"

"I was there with Dunmore when Chief Logan made his speech beneath the giant elm tree on the Pickaway Plains," Zack said proudly.

Within a month, Alejandro and Joaquin tied up the flatboat at the wharf in New Orleans, loaded with bales of tobacco and other sought-after commodities from the frontier settlements. Zack and Rodie helped off-load the cargo on the dock. Zack's sketch books were full of drawings from along the way...the inland rivers and forests with moss hanging from the live oak trees, the Gulf of Mexico, the towns of Pensacola and Mobile, and finally, the delta of the great Mississippi River itself.

Zack and Rodie were invited to share a room in Casa Tamayo, which was adjoined to Casa Avila by a courtyard. The two owners of Mercado

Tamayo y Avila were business partners and best friends, who had come from San Juan, on the island of Puerto Rico, to New Orleans.

To Zack and Rodie, this city was a world away from Virginia.

The Opening Battle

Washington remained at his headquarters most days, well into the evening. He met with his most-trusted generals, as the Americans waited for General Howe to make his next move. For the next six weeks, after the offer of a general pardon was summarily dismissed, the British sat on Staten Island, in total control of New York Harbor, and amassed a great army of thirty-two thousand men.

"What we must have is intelligence." Washington added, "to match the intelligence the British apparently seem so capable of gathering against us."

Rufus Putnam offered an answer to Washington.

"There are several cadets from Yale College in my army," Putnam said. "I have been impressed with not simply their zeal for the cause of freedom, but also for their seeming ability to mix into the people on the streets, in the taverns, in the shops, not as soldiers, but as common townsfolk. These young men, I feel, could give us the covert army of spies we need."

"In your estimation, Putnam, would these young men be willing to go behind enemy lines, and pass as loyalist townsfolk?" Washington posed the question.

"In my estimation, they would relish in the opportunity, and succeed at it," replied Putnam.

"I would very much enjoy meeting with them as soon as is possible," Washington added.

Washington was impressed with young Captain Nathan Hale, when they met the following day. Hale was a handsome young man of twenty-one years, with square jaw, piercing blue eyes, and light flaxen hair, with dark brown eyebrows. He was a man taller by several inches than the average man, standing just under six feet, with a slight, but muscular and athletic frame.

Hale explained he had enlisted with his one-year-older brother Enoch, and best friends, Benjamin Tallmadge and Elisha Bostwick, all four of whom had graduated Yale College in 1773, and had been teachers in Connecticut schools before enlisting.

Like Rufus Putnam, Washington saw Hale possessing the common sense intellect to be able to easily pass as a loyalist behind enemy lines, without being discovered as a spy. He had the agreeable good looks and dispositions that could easily attract new friends, friends even among soldiers in the Redcoat army, and learn the plans of the British.

On August 22nd, things began to change. At five o'clock in the morning, an advance landing party of four thousand British landed on the southern tip of Long Island. By noon, a total of fifteen thousand Redcoats, led by General Charles, Lord Cornwallis and General Sir Henry Clinton, were headquartered at the Long Island village of Flatbush.

Washington had split his forces with half of his nineteen thousand men, under General John Sullivan, reinforcing Long Island, and half remaining to wait on Manhattan for the eventual invasion. Washington received faulty information from his officers that the total number of British on Long Island was only about eight thousand, half what was actually in place.

Washington met with his staff with the maps laid out before them. The general laid out his plan.

"Israel Putnam shall defend from here," pointing to the bastion of Fort Stirling, on the Brooklyn heights. "He will command the siege against the approaching British below. We have six thousand men there.

"Sullivan and Stirling shall command from here," Washington pointed, "Guana Heights, one hundred-fifty feet above the British, to lay siege and inflict as many causalities as possible as they approach Brooklyn. They will also defend the three main roads: Stirling, with five hundred men on the Gowanus Road here to the west, Sullivan, with one thousand on the Flatbush Road in the center, and on the Bedford Road to the east with eight hundred. The less significant road, and the one more difficult for troop movement, the Jamaica Pass, should easily be held with but a handful of militiamen on horseback.

At nine o'clock the night of August 26th, Sir Henry Clinton began his advance from Flatbush. With ten thousand men, they marched to the area surrounding Howard's Tavern, where the Jamaica Pass began.

To not arouse American suspicions, they left camp at Flatbush with their campfires still burning. Without firing a shot, they easily captured the two dozen American militiamen and their horses, who were Washington's sole defense of that route to Fort Stirling.

Israel Putnam was awakened at Fort Stirling at three in the morning with news of the British advancing up the Gowanus Road. Putnam lit signal fires to warn Washington, who was still at Manhattan. Washington arrived at Brooklyn Heights at nine o'clock, to find the men at Guana Heights were now in retreat, heading for the main American army at Brooklyn Heights. Washington watched through his spyglass as the retreating Continental troops were engaged in bloody hand-to-hand combat. The Americans were forced to swing their muskets and rifles at the Hessians running after them. The Hessians immediately killed the Americans they had captured, running them through with bayonets.

"Good God," Washington lamented, pulling back his spyglass, after witnessing the slaughter, "what brave men I must this day lose!" Three hundred Americans were killed, and one thousand taken as prisoners. The British lost only fifty-nine men and the Hessian lost five.

Howe ordered a constant bombardment of the hilltop bastion on the afternoon of the 27th. During the night of the 29th Washington ordered the clandestine evacuation of the entire army from Fort Stirling. As the British had done when they left Flabush, Washington ordered all the campfires to remain burning, so as not to tip off the British. The evacuation was carried out in waves, with the wounded and infirm the first to be taken to the Brooklyn Ferry on the East River at eleven o'clock in the evening. The regular troops would follow in waves beginning at four on the morning of the 30th. Washington and his staff, with Wills Winkman beside him, were in the last boat from the ferry, arriving safely back on Manhattan Island at seven o'clock.

Nathan Hale

The British remained alone on Long Island, and Washington knew it was simply a matter of time before the enemy would make a landing on Manhattan itself. Washington knew he would soon be moving the entire army somewhere to the north. What Washington still was lacking was reliable intelligence as to the specifics of the British plan.

"Captain Hale," Washington rose and approached the boy, extending his hand for a shake, "sit, please sit. I have an important mission, and I thought of you." Captain Hale took the seat beside the chair Washington took at his large rolltop desk.

"The British are soon to land on Manhattan," Washington stated the obvious. "We know not when. We know not where. I need a man to covertly go behind the lines of the enemy, infiltrate their confidence, learn what they know, under the guise of a loyalist enraged by the audacity of the patriot cause." Washington turned in his seat, looking squarely into Hale's eyes.

"I will not order you to embark upon such a mission," Washington warned the young captain. "By the common rules of war, the man who accepts this mission loses all protection of the army. He, if discovered and captured, is not considered an enemy combatant, but an illegal combatant. There is no trial. There is, in most cases, simply a hanging."

"I shall undertake it gladly," Hale spoke without hesitation. "I shall gladly pose as a loyalist ... a graduate of Yale College, as I am, seeking to educate the loyalist children of Long Island. I shall obtain the intelligence you need."

After it was agreed, they entered the outer area where Wills sat at his desk. Hale saluted his commander-in-chief and left for his quarters on the Bowling Green.

Wills gave the general some news he was indeed anxious to receive.

"A regiment from Virginia is marching to us from Elizabeth."

"The 3rd Virginia Regiment?" Washington queried.

"Yes sir, it is the 3rd Virginia Regiment," Wills replied.

"It will be so good to see my old friends," Washington smiled. "I hear they have recruited, fitted and trained these men in Williamsburg...young, strapping, patriotic lads, many students at William and Mary, much like the young Col. Hale. It will be good to welcome them!"

The 3rd Virginia Regiment marched to Washington's headquarters on Broadway. Peter Francisco, Peter Patrick, Garrett Hicks, and Malcolm Shepherd were all under the command of Lieutenant James Monroe.

General Washington himself met the regiment, and greeted them with kind words, conversation, and many handshakes. The men were assigned to quarters at Fort Washington, where they were to await further instructions.

"Damn it all!" Garrett Hicks said, as the newly arrived soldiers sat around the campfire their first night at the fort. "If we'd a started this here march just a week earlier, we'd've already seen us a hell-for-certain battle!"

"Yes, Garrett," said Monroe, "and instead of marching up the post road safely, as we have, we'd have been running with those damned Hessians fast upon our asses!"

"Or drown'ded in them swampy bogs," said Pat.

"Or be a sittin' in a prison camp, starvin' ta death," said Malcolm. "I fer one am sure glad we missed that damn battle on Long Islan'."

"I would have sure liked to swing my musket like a club over the head of one of King George's paid-for Prussians!" said Peter.

"Hell Peter," added Garrett, "as big a giant as ya are, you'd've thrown down that there musket an' picked up one Hessians by his legs, another by his shoulder, spun 'em 'roun' above your big ole ugly head a time or two, an' flung 'em clean inta the swamp!" The boys hooted and hollered, imagining such a sight.

"Well, the way things appear," Monroe said, as the laughter died down a bit, "we shall be on a field of battle soon enough I should think. We best rest up a bit before again we march."

"Come here, Hicks ... Shepherd," Peter said, standing up, exposing his full seven-foot height. "Let me practice with the two of you, in case I feel the need to hurl some Hessians." The campfire crowd erupted in more laughter.

Nathan Hale, dressed in the clothing of a New England schoolteacher, crossed the Brooklyn Ferry, and rode his horse, Valliant, to the Billings Tavern at Flatbush. He paid for a week in a room at the tavern. Hale spent several hours each of the next few days dining and drinking in the tavern, which was always crowded with British soldiers. He easily made acquaintances with a handful of men, and soon gained their trust, as being no one to fear, but there was no news yet for Washington.

"Nathan!" one of those men Hale had befriended, Captain David Grayson, shouted out to him as he entered the tavern one evening.

"Any luck securing that teaching position?' Grayson asked, as he stood, placing his hands on the table where Nathan sat with a glass of wine.

"No, David," Nathan replied, "I am sore afraid I have yet to be discovered by the gentry here on Long Island as a suitable educator for their young gentlemen."

Nathan decided to shed his normal manly persona, and presented himself in a somewhat refined and effeminate manner. He had heard talk that many British officers were inclined to seek out such young men for companionships. While Nathan had no such leanings, he felt it was a way to seem harmless, and make his new friends loosen their guard when around him.

"I fear, riding these dusty roads with the sweltering sun beating down upon me, just wilts me! I simply melt under this Hellish heat, and perspire in such profusion. How can I present myself pleasantly?" Hale poured out the persona of the character he had created.

"Well," replied the young officer, "I would hire you, if in fact, I had children of an educatable age."

"Thank you so for your encouragements," Nathan said, patting Garyson's hand.

"Have you dined yet this evening?" Grayson asked.

"I have been patiently waiting," Nathan said, "hoping for a suitable companion to sup with."

"Might I be so bold as to invite myself to sup with you?" Grayson asked with a smile.

"Indeed you might," answered Nathan, returning a sweet smile from his eyes and lips. "I do so enjoy the supper companionship of such a bold gentleman."

They dined on prime rib and vegetables, followed by several glasses of claret, and tankards of ale.

"This obscene war these so-called patriots are waging, simply scares me, and is the sole cause of my current distresses," Nathan stated, sipping his claret.

"How so?" asked David, taking a fresh tankard from the serving wench.

"No one feels the times are conducive to education," Nathan sipped again. "How can thinking men, educated men, and men of refinement, condone battlefields and the slaughter of their peers? No cause is worth the horrific conditions of war."

"I am educated ... from Eton," said David, beginning to slur his words from the ale. "I am a thinking man, ... I think so any way," he took another gulp of ale, "and as you say, young man, I am a man of refinement ... and proper breeding, ... back in London that is, and I find the battlefield most invigorating."

"Invigorating?" questioned Nathan. "How can anything be invigorating, if its very outcome could result in injury, in loss of limb ... in death? Oh Heaven forbid it, I find nothing romantic about it a'tall." He sipped his claret, nursing it so as to remain sober, watching his friend getting more inebriated with every gulp of ale.

"The thought of independence does not invigorate you, as it seems to invigorate the men of the Continental Army?" Grayson asked, still with a smile.

"I should say not!" Nathan was quick to reply. "Independence would isolate us from the very society that makes us British citizens ... the most civilized people on the earth! Imagine men, common men, rubes, and backwater illiterates, leading a nation! ... with not one speck of royal blood flowing in their veins, and the sophistication which that upbringing affords ... why the very thought alone is terrifying to me indeed!"

"Well, Nathan," Grayson blurted, "with the news I received this day, I feel that there shall be peace very soon here in New York, if not throughout the entire continent."

"You are privy to such news?" Nathan inquired with great intrigue, and a sly boyish grin. "Do tell." Nathan leaned across the table toward Grayson.

"Oh, I cannot, Nathan," Grayson turned a bit red-faced, realizing he may have said things best left unsaid. "Do not attempt to get me in trouble with General Howe."

"General Howe, the Commander-in-chief of the king's army?" Nathan excitedly pushed for more. "You simply must tell me more! You know me well enough to share the news with me, do you not?"

"Perhaps, " Grayson said as he took another gulp of ale, "perhaps." He then leaned with his elbows on the table, nodding for Nathan to come closer to hear the choice news.

The next morning, Nathan dressed, and went downstairs for an early breakfast.

"How easy was that?" Nathan thought to himself, proudly, of how he had gleaned some wonderful news for General Washington. Afterwards, he mounted Valliant and rode off. He boarded the Brooklyn Ferry for Murray's Wharf, and rode up Broadway to Washington's headquarters

Major Winkman showed Hale into Washington's office immediately.

"Hale," Washington greeted his spy, "What news have you brought me?"

Nathan sat at the same chair he had used before, crossed his leg to remove one shoe and stocking. Out fell his message for the general. He picked it up from the floor and read it.

"British forces from Long Island shall land on the island of Manhattan in the early morning hours of September 15, 1776," Nathan read.

"Three days from now," Washington thought aloud. "That gives us time. Go on."

"They plan to make landfall with an advance force at Kips Bay," continued Nathan.

"Kips Bay?" Washington said, as he thought aloud, "good, a landing near where we sit."

Nathan looked up to see Washington's approval of the news he had delivered.

"Did your source say how large the landing party shall be?" Washington asked his new and very efficient spy.

"I shall try to find that out," Nathan said, "but I did wish to get this to you immediately."

"May I have your notes?" Washington said, as he reached toward Nathan.

"Do you read Latin, sir?" Nathan inquired.

"Latin? Why no," Washington admitted laughingly. Nathan showed the notes he had scrawled on paper before leaving his room at the tavern. They both laughed.

"Well, I shall have Lt. Winkman transcribe as you translate. He can be trusted."

Nathan was back at the Billings Tavern in Flatbush before darkness set in. Col. Grayson smiled from a table, as Nathan entered and walked toward him.

"What a day this one has been!" Nathan spoke in a weary and exasperated tone. "I think my stay at Flatbush might be a short one, if this day's example is any indication."

"Well, from what I hear," Grayson said, "you might very soon be seeking a benefactor on Manhattan Island itself."

"What news have you heard that makes you think so?" asked Nathan.

"If we might find a place away from all these prying eyes and ears," Grayson said, taking a gulp of ale, "we could discuss the news I know will encourage you. You have a room here, do you not?"

Nathan thought he might be approached by one of his friends to come to his room, but had, so far, avoided that circumstance. But if Grayson had more detailed information that would help Washington, he saw no other alternative. He would just have to fend for himself, if things began to get on out hand.

"I do, and have an adorable bottle of blackberry brandy, waiting for us on my bedstand," Nathan said. "I am at the room on the left, at the far end of the corridor. I shall go up first. Follow after you finish your ale. I shall leave the door slightly ajar." Nathan smiled and left the crowded tavern.

"Our landing shall result in the total expelling of the patriot army from the entire colony of New York ... in just a matter of days," Grayson said, as the two sat on the edge of Nathan's bed.

"Are you certain the army will land with sufficient numbers to do that?" Nathan asked. "I hear near every day new armies march to Washington from the Southern colonies, and the Bowling Green there is crowded with tents."

Grayson laughed. "Just let those farmer-soldiers, untrained as they are, try to repel Sir Henry Clinton, and four thousand of the king's finest soldiers!" The two laughed.

They finished off the "adorable" bottle of brandy, then Grayson surprised Nathan.

"I wish I could stay the night here with you, Nathan," Grayson said, "but I must be back at camp soon."

Nathan was extremely relieved he would still not have to fend off awkward advances the captain might make.

"Perhaps another time," Nathan suggested with a smile. "I am so spent from this day's heat and dust, I want just to bathe and sleep."

The British did land four thousand at Kip's Bay on the 15th, following an advance shelling from the navy, forcing the two thousand defenders of the landing site Washington had sent, to immediately flee north. Washington had, the day before, evacuated most of the city, making a camp at Harlem Heights in the extreme north of the island. During the landing, Washington rode from Harlem Heights to Kips Bay, and attempted to stop the mass retreat of the Continental Army, which now also included Israel Putnam's entire army at the battery.

"Are these the men with which I am to defend my country?" Washington shouted in defiance of the cowardice actions of the men in retreat.

By the afternoon, an additional nine thousand British and Hessian soldiers had landed, and the remaining citizens of New York City welcomed Howe and his commanding general Sir Henry Clinton. The patriot flags were quickly lowered and burned, and the Union Jack raised over the important city.

General Clinton stopped his march just south of where Washington was now headquartered at the Harlem River. The next day the two armies met. Washington, with just under three thousand men, including the fresh recruits of the 3rd Virginia Regiment, and British Major General Alexander Leslie, with five thousand, faced off.

Washington, who had been given orders from Congress not to burn New York, but to not find it necessary to hold it, commanded his men into an orderly retreat north across Kings Bridge. Washington wanted no further losses on the battlefield until he could amass a more potent army.

Gen. Leslie, seeing the retreat, instead of commanding the bugler to sound "charge" ordered the sounding of the well-known call of a foxhunt "Gone Away." Leslie planned it as an insult and humiliation for Washington. It was widely known, Washington was avid foxhunter and would recognize the melody immediately. The buglers playing "Gone Away" signified the "fox" to be in full flight with the "hounds" hot on the trail.

Washington was outraged. Many of his men shared the insult as an outrage. Washington abruptly ordered his army to turn from its retreat and charge the Redcoats, pushing the British all the way back. The Americans reclaimed their original position, and won the day. At the end of the day the Americans suffered thirty killed and one hundred wounded, while the British saw more than ninety killed and nearly four hundred wounded. It was the first clear victory for Washington's army since the British sailed out of Boston Harbor.

In the early morning hours of September 21ˢᵗ, a fire broke out in the Fighting Cocks Tavern in Whitehall Street of lower Manhattan. Heavy winds quickly spread the fire from rooftop to rooftop. Residents grabbed what personal effects they could save, and huddled together in the grass of the city commons. The fire raged throughout the day with devastating results. One full quarter of the city was burned. Between four and five hundred homes, shops and other building burned to the ground, including the old Trinity Church, and the house General Washington had used as his headquarters.

Gen. Howe had, a day or so earlier, taken residence east of the area in a more rural setting at Beekman House on Turtle Bay. With no indication of who set the fire, Howe declared martial law over the city.

Nathan Hale, still attempting to gather more intelligence on British troop movements, had been waiting for his friend, Col. Grayson, to report back to him on a strategy meeting he was to sit in on that day, the day of the Great Fire of New York.

Nathan had retruned to the Billings Tavern at Flatbush two days earlier. He had been fortunate in having avoided any uncomfortable situations with Grayson. Grayson, while he hinted at wanting more from Nathan, seemed awkward and a bit too shy to force the issue. Grayson arrived late in the afternoon, and they shared an early dinner.

"I apologize for this early liaison," Grayson started the conversation, "but I did want to see you before my company marches. I have to be back at camp soon."

"Marching?" Nathan queried. "To where shall you be marching?"

With the tavern not crowded, Grayson decided to tell Nathan of his meeting, without fear of being overheard.

"General Howe plans to move his operations to New Rochelle, Mamaroneck, and Rye," Grayson said softly, "in preparations for taking the American arsenal at White Plains within the month.

"I tell you this, Nathan," Grayson said, "so you shall feel safe in joining me there very soon. I shall be posted in the town of Rye." He smiled at Nathan. "The rebels will be put down and the war ended. Manhattan is where we shall find a teaching position for you."

Grayson left after they finished their early supper. Nathan went to his room and wrote his Latin encrypted note, and secured it in his stocking. He wanted to ride that evening and relay the intelligence to Washington at Harlem Heights. He grabbed his haversack and walked down the stairs into the tavern.

When he reached the door to go and mount Valiant, a hand grabbed his shoulder.

"Do not turn around, Mr. Hale," came a gruff voice from behind him. "We shall talk once outside." Nathan continued out into the courtyard of the tavern.

The man in a redcoat uniform led Nathan to a bench underneath a huge shade tree. The night sky was dark with few twinkling stars.

"We have been watching you, Hale," the man said. "With the help of one of your old classmates at Yale," the man nodded toward a young man near Nathan's age, standing beside the water pump, "we are placing you under arrest as a spy."

"A spy?" Nathan began to laugh and stand, as the man put his hand on Nathan's shoulder and pushed him back down to the bench. "How dare you treat me so?" Nathan protested in his effeminate persona. "I have never been man-handled in such a barbaric fashion."

"Levering!" the soldier shouted and motioned for him. When the young man came to where Nathan was seated, the soldier asked, "Do you know this man?"

"I do, Captain Roberts," the young, paunchy girthed man answered, "at least I did know him at Yale. This is Nathan Hale."

"And what do you know of him, Levering?" the captain asked.

"Well, sir," Levering spoke, "he graduated top of the class the year before I graduated."

"Did you befriend him?"

"Yale is a small college, sir," Levering said, "so I did know him, but we were not as you say, friends. He was among the athletic boys, which I was not."

"Athletic, you say?" Roberts questioned, looking at the effeminate appearing Hale. "You expect me to believe this dainty boy to be athletic?"

"At school," Levering insisted, "he was most athletic."

"Go on, Levering, tell me all you know of mister Nathan Hale."

"Well, sir," Levering went on, "aside from being a most intelligent student, he was the leader of the patriots there, the Sons of Liberty."

"That's all, Levering," Roberts said. "Mount up. We shall ride tonight, and if our conclusions are right, we shall both be well-paid." Levering went to where his horse was tied.

Roberts turned to Nathan. "Levering, here, also says you've been quite the friend of our friend Captain Grayson. Is he freely giving you the news you take to Washington?" Roberts began his interrogation. "Or has he been simply an unwitting dupe?"

Nathan sat silently.

"Your old classmate, Alamander Levering, a Loyalist of Danbury, says also, your friendship with Col. Grayson has been a nighly one, before we landed at Kips Bay," Roberts said. "Then you disappeared for a week, only to reappear again two days ago. What news are you to carry to Washington now?"

Nathan still sat silently.

"What favors do you allow Grayson for the intelligence he gives you? I do give him credit. You are a most beautiful young man. Who knows what secret plans I might have divulged for a tryst with you in your bed," Roberts said with an evil grin. Nathan turned his head.

"It may not yet be too late," Roberts went on. "I could tell Levering to go back to camp. It would be such a pity to see a beautiful boy, such as yourself, swing from an apple tree with a rope around his neck. We could enjoy your bed for thirty minutes, maybe an hour, then you could be off with the news Grayson gave you this afternoon. No one would be the wiser. And I know I would be quite satisfied. What do you say?"

"I say," Nathan turned his head back toward Roberts and spoke in his normal voice, "it is true what they say about you Redcoats. You do so enjoy the company of young men lying with you in your beds!"

Roberts' evil grin turned to anger. He slapped Nathan with the hard blow of the palm of his hand across Nathan's cheek.

By ten o'clock, Major Roberts and Private Levering had Nathan, at Beekman House and at the door of General Lord William Howe. The general himself interrogated the lad, and was convinced of Nathan's guilt, even though there was no physical evidence.

"Take him to the greenhouse out back at the garden, and have him quartered there," Howe commanded Roberts. "Strip him down, and if no evidence of the high crime is found on his person, lock him there, and the two of you return to the tavern. Search his room for evidence. Report to me immediately with your findings."

Roberts took Nathan to the greenhouse and led him inside. Roberts released him from his manacles and shackles, and stripped him of his clothing. Nathan stood there, naked, except for his stockings. Roberts pushed the naked boy onto the cot made ready for him. Roberts removed the stockings one-by-one, and as the last stocking was rolled down Nathan's left leg and off his foot, a folded piece of paper fell to the ground.

Roberts reached down and picked up the evidence. He opened it and looked at the Latin letters.

"Cleaver," Roberts stated, looking directly into Nathan's eyes. He started shaking his head. "Poor boy, every graduate at Eton is required to read Latin." He re-folded the paper and put it inside his jacket.

"Tis a great shame, boy," spoke Roberts. "I regret you will be hanged by your lovely neck in the morning."

On the morning of September 22nd the sun rose bright with the promise of another sweltering autumn day. Nathan was left to sleep naked on his stomach, with only a sheet atop him, with both hands and feet manacled to the cot.

Around seven o'clock, the door was unlocked, and a uniformed officer he had not seen earlier, came in. He introduced himself as Major John Montresor, a Loyalist American soldier with the British army.

"I am here to help you with your preparations," Montresor said. "Let us get you dressed."

After Hale was once again fully clothed, Montresor asked if Hale had any requests.

"A Bible?" Nathan spoke, "and an Episcopalian clergyman?"

"I shall see," Montresor said, left and soon returned.

"I am sorry, Hale," Montresor announced disappointedly. "You are to have no visitors, and there is no Bible to be found. Is there anything else?"

"May I write two letters?" Nathan asked. "I wish to write my mother and my brother Enoch."

"That I can assist you with," the kind officer said and left again, returning with paper, two envelopes, a quill pen and a bottle of India ink. Nathan sat and penned the letters as Montresor stood and watched every word the prisoner penned.

It was then time. Montresor took both letters, and the guards came to escort Nathan Hale down the post road to the Artillery Park, alongside the Dove Tavern. At the park there was an old apple tree standing in a small orchard. A large wooden crate stood directly beneath the noose, tied to a sturdy limb. Quite a crowd of soldiers and loyalist townsfolk had assembled for the hanging of the patriot spy.

Nathan's feet had been freed of the chains that had bound him throughout the night. He breathed the fresh crisp air of the autumn morning, and felt the warmness of the early morning sun on his face. He loved the autumn time best of all the four seasons. If this would be his last day on God's earth, praise be, it was a glorious September morning, he thought, as he was led to the apple tree. What he would give for one juicy bite out of that ruby red apple that he spotted still hanging on its branch!

He was placed atop the wooden crate, and a young teenaged black boy, Billy Richmond, a fugitive slave and loyalist, looped the noose over Nathan's head, and cinched it around the young spy's neck.

When the former slave boy hopped off the crate, his acquaintance of the night before, Captain Roberts, approached Nathan at his gallows.

"Are you Captain Nathan Hale of the Continental Army?" asked Roberts aloud for all to hear.

"As I said last night before General Howe," Nathan spoke with the rope about his neck, "I am Captain Nathan Hale of the Continental Army."

"You have now the opportunity to make your dying speech and declaration," instructed Roberts.

Nathan stood there, straight of posture, head held high, not shivering in fright, not regretting anything except his capture. He had been loyal to the cause of liberty and independence. He did regret not being able to live to see that liberty and independence won, but knew his mama would, as would Enoch and his ten other brothers and sisters back in Connecticut.

He spoke but a few words:

"I am satisfied with the cause in which I am engaged.
I only regret that I have but one life to give for my country."

The Hurricane

October's days were filled with sweltering, suffocating heat and sticky humidity in New Orleans, unlike October in Virginia, where the heat of summer was ending with much more comfortable weather, making the air fresh and renewed.

Zack and Rodie enjoyed the busy port town with all its French and Spanish influences. They found it strange that the Spaniards had not replaced the French language when they took over control of Louisiana in 1763, but simply melded their own Spanish with French. The boys enjoyed some of the new tastes they the found. Instead of drinking tea, Rodie and Zack grew to favor coffee flavored with a local root called chicory. Rodie, who spoke excellent French and passable Spanish, took a part-time job at the busy market, Mercado Tamayo y Avila. The huge marketplace building, built of wood and coquina shell stucco, took up a full city block between the main town square and the Mississippi River bank wharfs.

The boys leased the large, unused and empty space on the second floor of the massive building. It had huge windows looking out over the busy riverfront and the main town square, dominated by the large Roman Catholic Church. Their leased space also had an outside covered stairway with a private entry.

After the boys cleaned the cobwebs and dust from their new home, they got free lumber from the warehouse and partitioned the one large room into three. They created a studio for Zack just inside the entry door, a large sitting room behind it, and a bedroom beside the studio.

Enrique Tamayo, Alejandro's father, encouraged Zack to concentrate on painting to sell portraits and nature pictures from some of his best sketches.

"There is a market for portraits and the wealthy families will pay dearly," said Senor Tamayo. "There is now no favored portrait artist here. Your sketch of Chief Logan proves to me you have the talent. I shall bring the business to you. Have you ever worked in oils?" he asked.

"No," Zack replied, "only in charcoals."

"I have all the oils and brushes you need at the mercado," the merchant said. "You can get what you need, and pay the bills as you sell your art. If you created this beautiful crane in oils," he said, looking at the sketch he liked most, "a larger rendition of the original, in oils, it would sell quickly and at a handsome price.

"There is much money in this city, Zachary, many wealthy merchants, traders, refiners, planters, all purchasing fineries for their beautiful homes. In fact, I will commission you myself to paint the crane I do so enjoy, and pay you two months of your lease."

Zack was convinced. He purchased, on credit at the mercado, the oil paints, brushes he needed, and yards of white canvas. He cut the canvas to size, stretched it over and nailed it to narrow slats of wood to make his canvas ready for a large easel and oil paints. He built the large wooden easel he needed, placed it near one of the huge windows in his studio so the light would be ultimate, and began work on the crane. Within a week, the black and white charcoal sketch of the crane in the Potomac River, with a skinny fish drooping out both sides of his bill, had been transformed into a two-foot by three-foot masterpiece in oil. With oils, Zack could nearly bring his sketched subjects to life. Zack went to work next on the mama bear frolicking with her playful cubs in the dismal swamp.

On days Rodie did not work at the mercado, he and Zack would set out for the day on an expedition. They took day trips through Bayou St. Jean, which ran between the great river and the huge lake called Pontchartrain. Zack came away from those short trips with drawings of alligators, crocodiles, wonderful turtles, and other creatures native to the region. He drew the city as well, with the picturesque streets of crushed coquina shells, bordered by plastered brick houses, walled up courtyards and gardens, and intriguing black wrought iron railed balconies. Zack knew some of these subjects, once put to oil, would sell.

Sundays were a special time in New Orleans for Zack and Rodie. After the citizens of town filed out of the large brick and timber St. Louis, King of France Church from Sunday's Roman Catholic mass, the town celebrated into the evening. There was feasting, games, conversation with other young people, and, especially enjoyed by Rodie, dancing with the girls.

Alejandro and Joaquin both had younger sisters. There were two Tamayo girls, Angelita at sixteen and the younger Margarita at fourteen. Joaquin's sister, Carmen Maria, was Angelita's best friend and had just turned seventeen. The three girls were always seen everywhere together. All three were charming with coal black hair, large brown eyes, and olive skin. Soon, Rodie was dancing with Angelita, while Zack took turns twirling Margarita and Carmen Maria around the improvised dance floor in the courtyard of the plaza.

The music was nothing like the sweet and restrained melodies of the minuet, played almost pensively on the harpsichord or pianoforte in Virginia. Here the sound of the guitar and brass instruments brought a faster tempo and the more spirited music of a more spirited people.

As Angelita and Rodie ended one dance, and Zack was sitting with Margarita and Carmen Maria on a terrace off the dance floor, the musicians began a song suited for the newly popular flamenco. Angelita put one hand on each side of her skirt, and started shaking the dress in tempo. Rodie had no idea what to do. Soon Alejandro saw Rodie's distress and ran toward the couple.

"You know not the flamenco?" Alejandro asked Rodie, as the older brother of the beautiful Angelita raised his hands and began hand-clapping in tempo.

"I am afraid they did not instruct me in the flamenco at William and Mary," answered the bewildered Rodie.

"May I?" Alejandro nodded to Rodie, as Rodie nodded and stepped away, joining Zack on the terrace. Alejandro and Angelita danced a marvelous flamenco as two other couples remained on the floor with them. When the song ended, Alejandro and Angelita took in the wild applause from the others, who like Rodie, had not yet mastered the artful footwork and clapping of the new dance.

As the sun began going down, the sky turned dark, the winds blew fiercely, and the rains began to come down. The dancing was forced to end, and all the celebrants began disappearing toward shelter. Zack and Rodie walked at a fast pace with Alejandro, Joaquin and the girls, to their homes on Calle Bourbon, between Calle Bienville and Calle Conti, at the west edge of the town.

By the time the young folks arrived, the rains were coming down harder than Zack and Rodie had ever seen. The winds were blowing stronger and even the stately tall royal palms, with their concrete-like trunks, were beginning to sway. Senor Avila ran out of his home as he saw the revelers approach. Senor Tamayo joined him.

"It must be a hurricane!" Avila shouted to the young people. "Come inside quickly!" he called to them. The girls ran for their homes.

"Yes children," Senor Tamayo motioned with his arm, "Quickly! Quickly!"

"You come as well," said Joaquin to Zack and Rodie. "If indeed it is a hurricane, you do not want to be caught out in it."

It was still a young evening, so Alejandro suggested the young men sit beneath the ceiling, formed by the upper level's balcony. The two families shared the courtyard patio, which was surrounded by the two massive homes. They sat in chairs on the side of the covered walkway, sheltered from the hurricane rains now pelting down.

"I've never been in a hurricane," Zack said somewhat excitedly. "How often do you have these storms?"

"This may just be a strong thunderstorm," Joaquin said in a calm voice. "We have hurricanes maybe every three or four years, sometimes several in one season though."

"They can be most devastating," warned Alejandro. "We fled our homes in San Juan after a hurricane destroyed much of the island of Puerto Rico and killed many. That is when we came here. We have not seen one so destructive since we have been here. Let me get us drinks. I shall be back in a moment."

"When these strong storms come," Joaquin said, "it's most enjoyable to just sit here, nice and dry, listening to the rains, and waiting for it to the end … a quite wonderful time for rum!" The guests chuckled, and looked forward to waiting out the storm with their new friends.

Alejandro soon arrived with a tray and four tall glasses, filled with a delightful rum punch, mixed with coconut milk and citrus juice. The four sat and drank, telling stories and laughing, until the sun broke through the storm and the rains ended. They ate breakfast on the verandah, and walked back to their rooms above yhe mercado, seeing the only real damage had been several up-rooted bushes, and a few palm trees standing tall, but missing many of their regal fronds.

Zack and Rodie had weathered their first hurricane, and quite frankly, it was quite a lot of fun. It was indeed enjoyable sitting under the courtyard verandah, drinking the delicious drinks and talking with their friends until the sun came up. They were anxious to weather their next hurricane.

The Elusive Victory

As 1776 was ending, Washington was searching for that victory, that one victory that had eluded him, as his army faced the far larger and much better trained and disciplined army of the British and their mercenary Hessians. While 1776 started out good for Washington, with the Howe brothers being forced out of Boston, with the retaking of the stolen arms plundered from the Williamsburg magazine, and with the successful movement of the entire army to New York, the war then seemed to turn bleak for the Americans. Except for the evacuation from Long Island to avoid disaster, and holding their ground at Harlem Heights, Washington had won no victories.

In late October, he was forced to retreat from White Plains, as Howe marched on the armory there. The American army retreated north and crossed the Hudson River at Peekskill.

In mid-November, Fort Washington fell to a fierce storming of the fort by the brutal Hessians. Americans lost fifty-nine killed, and a devastating twenty-eight hundred men captured. Three days later, Washington led the remaining army out of Fort Lee, and left it for the British.

For a month, Washington led the army west across New Jersey, crossing the Delaware River and headed south toward Philadelphia. Gen. Howe ordered Cornwallis to give chase to the Americans, and while doing so, to build a chain of small fortifications across New Jersey.

Washington's army made camp in mid-December within twenty-five miles of Philadelphia on the west banks of the Delaware River. Washington took William Keith's house as his headquarters, just a mile or so north of McKonkey's Ferry. Cornwallis had built forts at Morristown, New Brunswick and Trenton. He then sent his army into winter camp to wait for the better weather of summer to resume the war.

The fort at Trenton was garrisoned by Prussians, and sat just a few miles south and across the river from where Washington was headquartered. Washington had just four to six thousand men. Nearly two thousand of the men in camp were unfit for battle, due to injuries and infirmities.

With defeat followed by defeat in New York, and a long, cold, brutal march across New Jersey, morale was low. Many men had deserted during the retreat, and the army was running low on supplies and munitions. Compounding Washington's anxieties was the calendar. A large number of his men's commissions would expire on the first day of January, and, due to the low morale in the ranks, most of the men had no intention of staying with the army any longer.

Washington also had lost regular contact with two important generals, and the exact whereabouts of those troops remained a mystery. General Horatio Gates, still nursing bad feelings toward Washington, was somewhere in the Hudson Valley with fifteen hundred men, bogged down in the heavy early snows. General Charles Lee was somewhere in northwestern New Jersey, near Morristown. Lee, with his jealousy for Washington raging, had refused each order from Washington to rejoin the main army along the Delaware.

December 1776 was an enigma for the general. What to do about the morale of his men? How to get Gates and Lee and their men reunited with the main army? What could he do to bring about a surprise victory, something meaningful that could turn the tide of the war?

Thomas Paine, who had been the top-selling pamphleteer in the colonies in early 1776 with publication of his political treatise <u>Common Sense</u>, had just published a second pamphlet, which was quickly becoming just as popular, called <u>The American Crisis</u>. Washington had it read to his troops. It was a start toward lifting the morale, but Washington knew it was not enough.

"These are the times that try men's souls:
The Summer Soldier and the Sunshine Patriot will shrink
from the service of his country;
but he who stands by it now,
Deserves the Love and Thanks of man and woman."

On December 20th, General John Sullivan arrived in camp, leading the two thousand men under General Lee's command.

"What a welcomed sight you are, Sullivan!" Washington said, returning Sullivan's salute. "Where is General Lee?"

"A prisoner of the British, being held at Morristown," Sullivan told the story of how Lee had left the camp in the hills surrounding Morristown, to seek warmer and more comfortable quarters for himself. He went outside the sentry line protecting the camp, and was taken prisoner.

"All to find a warm and comfortable lodging for himself?" Washington queried Sullivan.

"Yes, general," Sullivan replied. "He deserted his men for a warm bed and hearth."

Later that same day, Horatio Gates finally arrived, but with only six hundred men.

"I lost nine hundred men whose commissioned have elapsed," stated Gates. "To a man, none would remain with the army. I can hardly fault them, given the pathetic strategies this army was forced to follow in New York," the jealous and the arrogant Gates chided his superior officer. "I am surprised I have not lost the rest to desertion!"

"I am surprised you did not lead them in desertion yourself," Washington harshly replied to the harsh criticism from his chief distracter, "but we are most thankful you did not."

Unexpectedly, one thousand fresh militiamen also arrived that day from Philadelphia. According to his estimations, Washington now sat alongside the Delaware River with more than eight thousand battle-fit troops, enough to carry out the surprise he had been secretly planning.

Two days before Christmas, Washington and Henry Knox, now a newly commissioned general, and the only officer Washington had let in on the plan, rode to the nearby Durham Iron Works. The iron works would be closing for the holidays. Washington secured use of the foundry's many high-walled, heavy, low drafted boats, used to bring iron to the foundry and slag away from it. They also made similar arrangements with several ferry operators to use a few of their large ferryboats.

On Christmas Eve morning, men from John Glover's Marblehead Regiment met with Washington to receive special instructions. These men were all New England fisherman and seamen, and knew how to maneuver boats. Washington ordered them to go and bring the boats to the secluded inlet at McKonkey's Ferry. All this was to be done as secretly as possible.

On Christmas Day, each man in the army was given three-days worth of rations, and fresh flints for their muskets. In late morning, the 3rd Virginia Regiment, under Washington's friend, General Mercer, was assigned to take all the horses and the eighteen pieces of artillery, and move out from camp. Washington led them himself to the ferry. When the regiment arrived, Washington ordered them to secure the horses and artillery onto the ferryboats, and camp there for further orders.

At one o'clock on Christmas Day, Washington finally had a meeting with his generals in the Keith House, after he hosted them with a Christmas dinner of roasted goose and turkey.

"Gentlemen," Washington said, "this army needs a victory for our men and for our country. We shall give them one."

No one spoke, but all knew Washington had some kind of plan. They were anxious to hear what Washington was finally about to divulge, the plan he had kept secret for days.

"We shall commence at dusk this evening on a three-pronged crossing of the Delaware River, and be in position at dawn for a surprise attack on the enemy's garrison at Trenton. We shall surprise the sleeping Hessians and win the battle we so need."

Without inviting comments or discussion, he laid out his plan.

The Virginians Wait

"I'm a freezin' ta death!" Garrett Hicks complained, as he paced near the fire beside where the Durham boats had been tied up. "An' I just betcha Washington's gonna be a orderin' us inta them boats ta freeze some more real soon!"

"Or fall off inta that icy-cold water out yonder!" added Malcolm Shepherd. "An' I cain't swim a lick! I'll be drown'ded fer certain!"

"You'll freeze afore ya've time ta drown'd," added Peter Patrick, laughing.

It started drizzling rain in the afternoon, and soon the rain turned to sleet. The army in camp on William Keith's farm formed up for their regular evening parade. Washington, sitting atop his white stallion, Nelson, told the men instead of a parade, they were leaving immediately on a secret mission. He ordered them to assemble in lines, eight abreast, and to march as quietly as possible. The men were each given sixty musket balls and enough powder. Even the fife and drummers were given muskets. They began their march to the ferry, and the sleet turned to snow.

Washington rode off with Knox, at a gallop, ahead of the men, for the inn at the ferry.

"Whatever this mission is," said Peter Francisco, sitting near the fire, "it's bound to be our first real taste of battle."

"Our first real taste o' battle?" Garrett p'shawed, as he continued stomping his feet and pacing to keep warm. "Then what'n the name o' Heaven did we do when we was a firin' at all them damned redcoats and Hessians off a Harlem Heights and at White Plains?"

"Oh, we fired a few shots at a few Redcoats," Peter replied, "but didn't stand and fight. We were ordered to retreat. This is bound to be a whole lot different."

"I think you are correct, Peter," said Lt. Monroe, the highest ranking of the Campbelltown-William and Mary boys. "I believe it will be a real fight."

"Do ya know where we're a headin'?" asked Pat.

"No, Pat, not for certain, at least. But if I were Washington, we'd be crossing the Delaware, and marching south to wait till daybreak, and surprise the Hell out of those drunken Hessians."

"Hessians?" Peter asked excitedly.

"Yes, Peter," answered Monroe. "I think we will be fighting the Hessians very soon."

"But we have ta give up our Chris'mas day, when we should be a celebratin' as everyone else is a celebratin'" protested Garrett. "It's the damnedest thing I ever heard tell of!"

"That's the point, Hicks," Monroe said. "Don't you think the Hessians, known for their beer-drinking, have been doing just what you said everyone's doing, celebrating all day long, and will keep it up well into the night. They will in no way expect a Christmas attack, and will not be fit to defend themselves early in the morning, following a day and night full of drunkeness."

"If that ain't Washington's plan," said Pat, "it sure should be!"

"If it turns out to be the secret mission," said Peter, "Lt. Jimmie here, should be promoted to the general staff just for his abilities at strategizin'!"

"All's I can say," Garrett complained some more, still freezing from the sleet that changed to a heavy snowfall as the sun went down, "I sure hope Gen'ral Washin'ton has put a whole bunch o' warm blankets in them boats, fer I'm surely a freezin' ta death!"

"Them're sure the biggest snowflakes I ever seen," said Malcolm, as the sky was a white blur.

"I'm sure ta catch a Chris'mas dose o' the croup!" Garrett moaned. "An' now we got us a God-fer-certain blizzard a comin'!"

The snow was getting heavier and heavier. It was difficult to see even five feet ahead. As well as it being Christmas evening, no one would expect a battle march in such a blizzard.

Crossing the Delaware

As the army marched its one and a half mile march, it was dramatically slowed. Two full hours after Washington expected them at the ferry, they had still not arrived. Washington waited out the delay, pacing like Garrett Hicks was pacing outside in an effort to keep warm.

"They most certainly shall be here soon," Knox tried to give Washington some relief to his anxiety.

"Why is it, Henry, every time we have an opportunity, something stands in our way?" Washington asked. "If it is not myself, allowing my generals to dissuade me from what I have already decided upon, it is my many officers failing to obey my very clear orders. Like Gates, telling me at our council after dinner, he shall not be joining us for he is apparently ill and shall remain in camp. And Lee, going beyond the perimeter and getting captured!"

"Gates simply ate too much of the Christmas goose," Knox chuckled. "And perhaps Cornwallis shall keep Lee locked away until the war's end."

"No," Washington said, shaking his head, not smiling at Knox' attempt to show levity, "we need him and shall get him returned soon in a prisoner exchange for that governor of the Bahamas we are holding at Williamsburg. Neither Gates nor Lee is my enemy this night, 'tis the weather. It has been dark ninety minutes, a full ninety minutes wasted away as the snows fly."

Outside the men of the 3rd Regiment still waited.

"I didn't sign up ta get frostbit an' froze!" Garrett continued his rantings, wishing for shoes without worn holes in the soles, and a warmer coat. Then he thought, 'at least I have shoes.' Too many of the men Garrett had seen in camp had none, and were forced to wrap their feet in pieces of old blankets and other cloth for protection from the elements.

"What ya gonna do when this here war's over, Pat?" Malcolm asked.

"I'm gonna marry Patricia Patterson and move to my tomahawk claim in the Ohio Country," Pat said dreaming.

"How you gonna marry someone name o' Patricia Patterson, an' saddle her with your name?" asked Garrett, poking fun. "She'd be Patricia Patterson Patrick … Pat Pat Pat! Yep, an' that's just what they'd all call here … Pat Pat Pat!" Pat slugged him.

"You'd know how I could marry her if you ever seen 'er," said Pat. "She's so easy ta look at. We wanted ta get married before I enlisted, but she promised ta wait for me. She can cook like the dickens."

"You oughtta see that tomahawk claim Pat made," added Peter.

"It's on the Scioto River," Pat said, "just before we got ta the Pickaway Plains. That's where I'm a takin' my Patricia, an' we'll build our homestead on that beautiful bottomland prairie."

"We all helped Pat make that claim," Peter said, chuckling. "He carved his initials in that old tree trunk…'P-e-e P-e-e', and we all took a pee pee right there in the creek running by the tree. We christened Pee Pee Creek for sure, right then and there!" Everyone laughed.

"Speaking of that, I think I need to christen the Delaware." Peter walked the short steps to the water's edge.

"You'll surely be a freezin' that thing right off, if'n ya pull it outta yer drawers in this weather!" Garrett laughed.

"Peter's gonna sure have one frost bit peter fer certain," Malcolm added, as all the men around laughed. Peter pee-ed into the icy Delaware River.

"Henry, they have arrived!" Washington said joyfully, as he turned quickly away from the window. He grabbed his heavy black wool overcoat, bright red scarf Martha had knitted for him, and his tri-corner hat. He headed out the door with the rotund General Knox fast on his heels.

Washington untied Nelson from the hitching post and led him toward the boats. The general handed the reins to the first soldier from the 3rd Regiment he met, one he remembered had been a visitor to Mt. Vernon with Judge Winston.

"Francisco, is it not?" Washington asked.

"Yes, general," Peter saluted his hero.

"Please take Nelson here and give him a good berth on board that ferryboat," Washington smiled and continued his walk.

Washington boarded the first of the Durham boats, stood in the center of the heavy boat, and faced his men on the shore.

"Gentlemen," Washington spoke, "we are ready to make a surprise visit to the other shore. You men shall take your berths, the 3rd Virginia Regiment, under General Mercer and General Lewis shall board first. General Knox is in command and will direct the boardings that will follow. When we arrive on the other shore, we shall need immediately to form a sentry line from the ferry to the River Road. We must do so in complete silence. No chatter amongst the ranks. None shall cross the sentry line without the passwords 'Victory or Death'! Is that clear?"

"Victory or Death!" shouted one soldier. "Victory or Death! ... Victory or Death! ... Victory or Death!" the other soldiers shouted in unison. Washington smiled. He was proud of the response his men were giving his orders. How could they fail?

The Battle of Trenton

The mission was already two hours late in leaving McKonkey's Ferry. The weather had grown worse through the evening. The river was clogged in many places with snow-covered chunks of floating ice to be maneuvered around and through. Washington knew the arrival on the Jersey shore would surely be delayed even more. He still hoped the crossing could be completed in time for the army to make the march to Trenton, undetected, before the sun rose.

The last boats arrived on the far shore at three in the morning, three full hours behind the timetable Washington had hoped for. With the snow still falling, there was no way now for a pre-dawn arrival on the edge of Trenton.

When the early morning sun was beginning to light the steel-gray winter sky, the snows stopped, but the army was still an hour from Trenton. About a mile north of Trenton, the army came across a cooper's shop where a handful of Hessians had made a small outpost. As the army approached, the unsuspecting commandant, dressed in his sleeping gown, stepped out to get a breath of fresh morning air. Seeing the army, the Prussian yelled to his sleeping men, *"Der Feind! Der Feind!"* ("The enemy! The enemy!")

The other Hessians ran out in their sleeping clothes and nightcaps, with the snow high on the ground. The Americans fired a volley at the Hessians, and the Hessians returned fire. Soon the commandant realized this was not simply a small raiding party. He ordered his men to retreat. Washington ordered the road to Trenton blocked to keep the men of the small garrison from warning the larger Hessian barracks at Trenton and ruining the surprise attack.

The army continued on its way, and within a half-mile, met up with Knox, Sullivan and their column. Washington spotted hills at the north edge of town, and decided he would position himself there to get a full view of the battle and dispatch orders. He ordered Gen. Knox to position the artillery at the heads of King and Queen Streets, between the Hessian barracks and their position at the north edge of town. The men would be stationed between private homes and shops along the streets, to fight back the enemy advance.

General Johann Rall, the Hessian commander who had led the storming of Fort Washington, was awakened from his sleep at the barracks by his adjutant. Immediately, Rall sprang into action. He ordered the full compliment of men at the barracks to dress and form up for an advance down King and Queen Streets.

Lt. Monroe and his men of the 3rd Virginia Regiment were formed between the houses on the west side of King Street, ready for the advance they knew would soon be coming. They would be among the first Americans to be able to fire upon the Hessians.

Rall ordered the placement of two three-pound cannons at the end of the King Street, close to the barracks. The Hessian cannons fired six rounds each up King Street at the American artillery, but all the men manning the big guns were killed when the American cannons fired back. Rall led the Hessians in a speedy retreat to a field just south of the barracks to regroup. The Americans from the head of King and Queen Streets began their own advance toward the barracks. It had to be taken.

"Monroe!" ordered General Mercer, "take some men and turn those cannons on them before they regroup!"

Lt. Monroe called out, "Francisco, Hicks, Patrick, Shepherd, you heard the general! Let's secure those guns!"

The five men ran from between the two houses where they were stationed and into the street, heading for the two important pieces of artillery. They turned them so they were now aimed at the Prussians.

General Rall ordered his troops to make a second advance up King Street and retake the captured Hessian cannons.

Heavy fire broke out and all of a sudden, Lt. Monroe let out a painful sounding cry and fell to the street.

"Jimmie!" shrieked Peter, who was squatted next to Monroe when he fell behind one of the captured cannons.

Peter stooped down. There seemed to be little life left in his eighteen-year-old friend. Blood was streaming out from his left shoulder where he had apparently taken a musket ball.

"Hicks!" Peter yelled. "It's Jimmie! He's dying! Help me!"

Garrett handed his musket to Malcolm and ran to Peter.

"He ain't gonna make it," Garrett spoke, holding back tears as he looked down at his good friend. "He, ain't gonna make it, Peter." He looked up at Peter.

"He might not," said Peter, "but we still gotta get him out of this street before the Hessians come at us with their bayonets."

"Bring him here!" came a cry from the east side of the street. "Bring him here!" an elderly man in his nightgown was standing at an open door, frantically motioning to Peter and Garrett. Peter reached down and grabbed Monroe around the shoulders, pressing one of his huge, strong hands over the open wound to try to stop the gushing blood. Garrett grabbed the lieutenant's feet. They ran, half hunched over with Hessian musket balls flying, and made it to the porch of the house and safely in through the open door.

"I saw him fall," the elderly man spoke as they carried Jimmie into the house. "Those damnable Hessians! I am a physician, Dr. Isaiah Riker. Follow me. I hope it is not as bad as it presently appears."

Dr. Riker led them through open French doors to a room that appeared to have been a dining room. Now it served as the doctor's examining room.

"Put him here," Riker pointed to a table, padded with a mattress. "Let me look at him." The doctor bent down and examined the young officer.

"Is he gonna live, doctor?" Peter asked. The doctor was silent as he continued his examination.

"You had the presence of mind, young man, to press down upon the wound," Riker looked up at Peter. "Your friend could easily have bled to death without what you did. Give me that gauze there," he said, pointing to a jar on a table. Garrett immediately handed the doctor the gauze.

Riker began dabbing gauze in the open wound to soak up the slowed bleeding.

"I need to prepare," Riker spoke, leading Peter and Garrett back into the parlor. "Remain here, if you are not needed in the srtreets. I must probe for the musket ball, cauterize the wound and dress it." He left the room and closed the heavy French doors behind him.

"Garrett," Peter spoke. "You remain here. I will try to report to General Mercer, and return as soon as I can." He left as Garrett stayed behind.

Doctor Riker worked behind the closed French doors as Garrett waited. A heavy-set lady soon appeared with a plate of breakfast.

"I dare say you have not had breakfast this morning, young man. I am Delilah Riker, the doctor's wife," the elderly lady said to Garrett, as she placed the tray on a table in the parlor. "You must eat, young man, if you are to defend us from the Prussian soldiers and win for us our independence."

"Thank you, ma'am," Garrett said, as he looked down hungrily at the plate with fried eggs and potatoes, sausage meat, flapjacks, butter and maple syrup. "Any word from Doc. Riker?"

"He is fast at work on your young friend," she answered, "but, no words as yet." She left the room and Garrett attacked the plate of breakfast. He hadn't eaten a breakfast like that in weeks.

Peter arrived a few minutes later.

"The battle seems to be won," announced Peter as he entered the parlor. "General Mercer said for us to remain here with Jimmie. He, being a doctor as he is, said as soon as possible, he will come to assist Dr. Riker.

The doctor's wife entered again with another plate of breakfast for Peter.

In a few minutes, the door opened and in came the others from the unit, accompanied by General Mercer. The doctor's wife showed Mercer through the closed French doors.

"You should have been there, boys," said Pat, "this day surely belongs to General Washington!"

"It's 'bout time we sent them damn Hessians a runnin'!" said Garrett. "I think I plugged me a Hessian er two, shootin' from behind that ole tree 'cross the street there, 'afore we took them cannons."

"But ya didn't see the half of it!" Malcolm said.

"Soon as you an' Peter carried Jimmie off," Pat said, "the Hessians had trouble with their muskets."

"Their guns just wouldn't go off," added Malcolm, as he started laughing. "Plumb funniest thing I ever seen. Them, dressed in their fine uniforms, a kneelin' an' takin' aim, pullin' the triggers, an' then 'click' nothin' comin' from out the barrels! Nothin'!" Malcolm laughed.

"They all took off a runnin' like a bunch of scare't rabbits," Pat added.

"Then, here comes ole Gen'ral Washin'ton hisself, a ridin' that beautiful white horse of his'n," said Malcolm.

"Nelson," Peter the horse lover said. "That's what General Washington calls him, Nelson."

"Well," Malcolm continued, "Washin'ton comes a ridin' down the street, ... on Nelson, ... yellin' out ta us as he approached, 'March on, m'brave fellers, after me!' We chased them damned Prussian fellers down the road, a firin' at 'em all the way, till we ran 'em into an apple orchard, where we soon had 'em all surrounded."

"As we was a chasin' them fellers" added Pat, "their gen'ral, that same damned Gen'ral Rall what we faced up at White Plains, took a few o' our musket balls himself, and died right then an' there under an apple tree."

"I think it mustta been m' musket ball that sent that Prussian gen'ral ta the Devil!" Malcolm bragged.

"So the battle's over?" Garrett asked, "an' it was victory ... not death."

"They surrendered as quick as fat ole Henry Knox offered it to 'em!" said Pat. "We captured 'bout a thousand of them Hessians, an' all their muskets, powder an' artillery ... an' even a whole bunch o' kegs of rum!"

"We only lost three men dead an' six, includin' Jimmie in there, wounded," said Malcolm. "The Hessians had more 'n' two dozen dead and near a hundred wounded."

About that time Dr. Riker and General Mercer came through the French doors.

"Your young lieutenant should be fine," said Riker, with a pensive smile at the boys crowded into his parlor. "That musket ball has severed an artery causing all the bleeding. I, with General Mercer, have clamped it back, and the bleeding seems to have been stopped. I shall keep close watch over him as he rests."

"Lt. Monroe is indeed in good and capable hands here, and needs a few days of rest," said Mercer. "Monroe will stay here and be well-cared-for, by Doctor and Mrs. Riker. I will come back for him in a day or so and return him to our camp when he is fit for travel."

"Can we talk to him?" asked Peter.

"He is sleeping now," said the general, "and will most likely sleep straight through until the morrow. We best leave him now and join our men."

Victory So Sweet

Washington was pleased with the performance of his army in pulling off the surprise victory over some of the most well-trained and disciplined European forces. He wanted to drive on while the morale was high among the troops. He planned to strike Princeton, then if possible, on to New Brunswick. But instead of marching the men without any rest, and considering the housing of the one thousand Prussian prisoners he needed to secure, he decided to re-cross the Delaware. The army was back at McKonkey's Ferry by nightfall.

Word spread quickly of Washington's victory in New Jersey. The victory at the Battle of Trenton did much to not simply build the morale of Washington's men, but also to build the confidence of the American people, who so wanted independence from the British crown.

During the last days of December, Congress voted a bonus of ten pounds to any soldiers who, at the expiration of his commission on January first, would re-enlist for an additional six weeks. Many of the soon-to-be-released soldiers re-enlisted immediately. Most would have re-enlisted without the bonus, after tasting victory at Trenton, but accepted the generous ten pounds happily.

The Hessian prisoners were marched to Philadelphia where they could be safely held. On the first day back in camp, Washington received intelligence reports that the British and Hessians at Princeton could be easily taken. The spies also told Washington that Cornwallis was preparing soon to leave New Brunswick with nine thousand British regulars, aiming for Princeton and Trenton. Washington drew up his plans.

On the morning of December 28th, General Mercer took Peter and Garrett in a wagon to the Trenton Ferry and crossed the river. They rode up King Street to Dr. Riker's home.

"It's sure mighty fine to see you," Peter said to Jimmie Monroe, who was lying asleep on the settee in the parlor.

"Peter!" Jimmie said surprised. "I am fine, and I heard all about our great victory."

"It surely was a fine day fer us independence-minded fellers," said Garrett. "Well, leastwise fer some o' us," he said looking at Monroe's bandaged shoulder.

"It was fine for me too, Hicks," said Jimmie. "I had some great friends who would not leave me for dead in King Street. And the doctor says I have a great souvenir ... a musket ball from a Hessian musket. I will show it to you when we get back to camp."

"Well, Jimmie ... er, I mean le'tenant Monroe," said Garrett, "are ya rested up 'nough ta comeback with us?

"I cannot wait!" Jimmie replied.

Washington began leading the army across the river, later that day. Mercer knew the plan and he took Peter, Garrett and Monroe to meet the army at Assunpink Creek, where Washington said they would make camp. The snows had stopped, but the air was bitterly cold, with heavy winds blowing. In many places, the ice on the Delaware was three or four inches solid, so, many of the men walked across the frozen river. It took the full army of ten thousand, with the injured and infirm, three full days to make the crossing. It was New Year's Eve before all the men and equipment had made it across.

Washington learned from his spies on New Year's Day, that Cornwallis had arrived with his nine thousand men at Princeton. The next day, Cornwallis was to leave twelve hundred men at Princeton, and would lead the rest of the army of regulars to confront Washington at Trenton. Washington sent out some snippers to meet Cornwallis' advance party, and delay them with ambushes and small skirmishes. Darkness was starting to set in as Cornwallis finally arrived on the outskirts of Trenton. The British general made three attempts to take the bridge over Assunpink Creek the Americans were holding, but failed each time. Cornwallis decided to pull back and delay the battle till the next day.

Washington planned a nighttime evacuation of his army, along the back roads to Princeton. Henry Knox had the men pad the wheels of the artillery, so the sound of cannons rolling would be stifled. The ground was well-frozen, so the wheels would not sink in mire and delay their travels north toward Princeton.

Washington left five hundred men behind with two pieces of artillery. Their orders were to keep the campfires burning all through the night, and work with picks and shovels, making noise so the British would hear them and think they were digging trenchworks for battle.

They were ordered to leave in time to join the main force at Princeton by dawn.

Washington and the bulk of the army rode out silently at two o'clock in the morning, while Cornwallis slept peacefully. Washington knew his army could not succeed at traditional European battlefield war. Surprise, however, could win American independence.

Within days of the victory at Trenton, the army aimed for Princeton. In the approach to Princeton, Redcoats chased General Hugh Mercer through an apple orchard. Thinking they had penned in General Washington, because the two men looked alike on their white stallions.

"Surrender you damned rebel!" shouted a British officer as he caught up with Mercer, and ran his bayonet into Mercer's gut, thinking he had killed the commander-in-chief of the Continental Army, not knowing he instead was, killing George Washington's close personal friend.

Mercer fell to the ground. Other Redcoat soldiers joined in the killing, beating Mercer's lifeless body with the butts of their muskets. They left him dead where he lay in the apple orchard.

Washington himself showed great courage and resolve that day. As one regiment began to retreat, Washington spurred them on, shouting, "Parade with us my brave fellows. There is but a handful of the enemy and we shall have them directly!"

The retreating men joined Washington without question, and soon other American re-enforcements arrived. Washington, still atop Nelson, rode through the troops, and with his hat in his hand, motioned the men forward, ordering them not to fire until he gave the order.

When they were within thirty feet of the enemy line, Washington rode Nelson in front of the American line, still advancing, and commanded, "Halt!" and then, almost immediately, "Fire!"

Both sides fired at each other simultaneously, causing a huge cloud of smoke to obscure everyone's vision. Many expected to see Washington dead, as he had been in the front of the American line, but when the smoke cleared, Washington sat in perfect posture, still atop Nelson. A great cheer rose up on the American side. There morale was lifted to new heights.

The Redcoats and Hessians retreated up the Post Road for Princeton. Washington ordered a continued pursuit of the retreating Redcoats, shouting, "'Tis a fine day for a fox chase my boys!"

After reaching Princeton, several of the retreating British took refuge in the main building of the College of New Jersey, Nassau Hall. A nineteen-year-old artillery captain, Alexander Hamilton of the New York Provisional Company of Artillery, stationed his company of sixty men and several artillery pieces in front of the stately hall. Hamilton ordered the artillery to fire upon the building. Some redcoats inside fired back, then Hamilton and a few of his men, stormed the front door, knocking it down. The soldiers hiding there waved white flags of surrender from the windows. They exited the building, laid down their arms, and were taken as prisons.

The Battle of Princeton was ended and Washington's army had won another victory.

Chapter Eleven

The Europeans

"Is she not a magnificent ship, Charles?" the young twenty-year-old Frenchman asked of his older mentor and one-time commander, Charles-Francois Comte de Broglie, as they stood at the wharf along the Garonne River at Bordeaux.

"She is indeed, Gilbert, she is indeed," replied de Broglie, dressed in his uniform as an officer of the French Army. "And you purchased the vessel yourself?"

"I did, when my yearly stipend came good," stated the younger man proudly. "I must sail to America, and join the noble fight there for the rights of man. I knew I must when I first learned of their struggle. Remember? ...When we dined with the Duke of Gloucester on his visit at Metz two years ago. Since then, you know I have thought of little else." The younger man was Gilbert du Motier, Marquis de LaFayette.

"Oh yes, the duke is an unusual one," stated de Broglie. "Upon meeting him and hearing him espouse the politics of independence, it is difficult to imagine him to be the younger brother of George III, King of England!"

"It is indeed," chuckled LaFayette, "but even Englishmen would welcome their rights. It is a growing tide here in France."

"So you are quick to disavow your own king and sail off to America?" questioned de Broglie.

"I do not renounce my country, my king, nor my title!" said LaFayette sternly. "I love France, and I love Louis XVI. You forget, I was 2nd Lieutenant in the king's Musketeers, before that fabled unit was dissolved. I now am only off to fulfill my appointment as a brigadier general in the American Continental Army...a commission given me by the American ambassador, Silas Deane."

"And disobey the orders given by your king to join your father-in-law's army at Marseille?" questioned de Broglie.

"When I received my American commission in December," spoke LaFayette, "I went to an audience with the king and informed him of my decision."

"And he went on to disapprove," noted de Broglie. "He saw no good coming from French nobility allying themselves on the battle-fields with Washington against King George."

"I am not a diplomat, Charles, I am a soldier," LaFayette defended his decision, "and one, like you my friend, who believes strongly in the inherent rights of man."

"I do indeed agree, Gilbert, but care for you, my friend, much more. Disobedience to the king carries the penalty of being held a prisoner at the Bastille," de Broglie warned. "The Americans will gain their independence without you. I do not wish prison for you."

"You and I have had many conversations in the discussion societies of Paris," LaFayette said, "and you my friend, if young as I am, would be joining me in America."

"Indeed I would, Gilbert," agreed de Broglie.

"You then approve?" asked LaFayette.

"And wish that I were thirty years younger," admitted de Broglie, "and I would be leading you there, not attempting to dissuade you." He hugged his young friend and they headed toward the café at the end of the wharf.

The two enjoyed glasses of wine. The region was noted for producing some of the best wines in the world, crushed from the grapes, which grew abundantly on the vines of the hillsides. They continued their conversation.

"When do you depart, Gilbert?" de Broglie asked.

"La Victoire has been being refitted for two weeks now," said La Fayette, "and I am told we can begin provisioning her in two days. I plan to sail within the week."

At that point, a young ship's carpenter rushed in and came up to the table where the two friends sat.

"Pardon, sir," the workman said to LaFayette, "but La Victoire has been seized by the British!"

"What?" LaFayette said, bolting out of his chair.

"And they intend to arrest you, sir," the workman added. LaFayette slumped back into his chair, as de Broglie pulled him back with a tug at his elbow.

"You must not confront them, Gilbert," warned the older friend. "You will surely be locked away in the Bastille, or even worse, taken off to the Tower of London."

The ship's carpenter left, having given the warning to LaFayette. As he left through the cafe's door, in walked an officer of the British Navy. The room grew still at his presence. While the sight of a British seaman was no rare occurrence in Bordeaux, the Frenchmen of the area despised the arrogance of the Englishmen. The officer paced around the room, eyeing every occupant, then stopped at LaFayette's table, and addressed the older uniformed man.

"I am Captain Percival Werther of His Royal Majesty's ship the Provident," the British officer introduced himself as de Broglie rose from his seat, extending his hand.

"I am Charles-Francoise, Comte de Broglie, general in the Army of my King Louis XVI. Welcome Captain Werther to Bordeaux. How may I be of help to you?"

"I shall get to the point of my mission," Werther said. "I have orders from London to commandeer the ship Victory, moored here, owned by one Gilbert du Motier. I have orders to arrest monsieur du Motier as a French propagator of the rebel army now fighting in America. We have uncovered documents detailing his intended mission, and his commission as a general in the American Army."

"I know this man," de Broglie admitted, slowly, "I know him as the Marquis de LaFayette."

"Yes, yes," spoke Werther, "he wears that nobleman's title. Your King has issued an arrest warrant for him as being insubordinate in disobeying orders from his highness. Do you know his whereabouts?"

"I do not, sir," responded de Broglie loudly, "in fact, I so hoped to dine with him this evening. I am myself, en route to Marseille, where his father-in-law, my good friend, the Marquis de Noailles, commands the king's army their. Will you not join us for dinner, in his absence?"

"And who is your friend, here?" asked Captain Werther.

"Oh forgive my discourtesy," said de Broglie. "May I present my *special friend* for the evening, Marcel de Moray." LaFayette blushed, as he heard his older friend introduce him as a gentleman's gentleman for evening pleasures. LaFayette then smiled, and in an effeminate manner, extended his hand.

"Oh yes," said LaFayette, playing the part he had been given, "do grace our dining table this evening...and, per chance, you might be enticed to join us later?"

Werther did not accept the extended hand, nor the invitation.

"I think not," the captain said. Directing his attentions to de Broglie, he warned, "If you do see du Motier...LaFayette, as you call him, have him come to me aboard the Provident, or you, as well, might face the gallows." He turned and began to exit.

"But of course, monsieur," spoke de Broglie. "I do obey the orders from my king."

When the captain had left the cafe, LaFayette smiled at de Broglie.

"You were marvelous," LaFayette said, "how you so quickly thought upon your feet."

"That is why I am so valuable to King Louis." Both men laughed.

De Broglie and LaFayette tried to decide how best LaFayette should react, in view of the loss of his refitted vessel, and the news of the warrant now issued for his arrest.

"Ride to Marseille," offered de Broglie, "report to your father-in-law, and the king will certainly rescind the warrant."

"I shall not patrol the wharfs at Marseille when independence calls me to America!" LaFayette nearly shouted. "I shall buy another ship. I have the funds enough."

"And a wife in Paris, and infant daughter you are deserting," added de Broglie.

"Deserting? Not! Adrienne is happy in her Paris residence," added LaFayette. "She is well-attended to. Ours is an arranged marriage, as you know. She has a pleasant enough disposition, and a life quite separate, and independent of mine. The love that comes to these marriages is not yet here. She knows of, and approves of my absence."

"You cannot remain in France one day longer, if you do not repent before the king," de Broglie warned. "You shall be arrested! And a bounty, a large one to be certain, will be upon your head to any scoundrel tempted by it.

"Buying another ship in France, refitting it and provisioning it, will cost you too many days. Go to Spain. You can be at the port in San Sebastian after three full days of travel. If you are so determined, I pray you leave this very night."

Winter Camp

The hills around Morristown made an ideal camp for the Continental Army to spend the winter months. General Washington communicated regularly with Congress, begging for even the most basic of provisions: food, shoes and blankets. He knew he needed to have his army better trained and disciplined, but had no idea how to do it, and no one he could rely upon to carry it out.

Washington did know he possessed the most viable weapon of the war ... men, however untrained and undisciplined as they were, fighting on their home soil for their own homespun way of life. They were fighting to make that life even better, with the vision of 'Life, Liberty and the Pursuit of Happiness.' The Americans faced an enemy from thousands of miles away, separated by a broad ocean, and a much more narrow vision and way of life.

Washington also needed to assemble his own coterie of advisors of like-minded men, and not rely simply upon the advice of his generals. That reliance upon his generals, even ones he took great stock in, had led Washington to his earliest disasters.

One man in particular had caught Washington's attention. Acting on his own judgment, seeing a way he could end the day with an American victory, this young artillery captain, acted. Wills Winkman summoned Captain Alexander Hamilton of the New York Provisional Company of Artillery to a meeting with General Washington at the farmhouse headquarters.

"Captain Hamilton," Washington addressed the young officer as he entered. "Please take a seat" Both men sat and Washington began the conversation.

"I commend you, Hamilton, for your quick actions on January third," Washington said. "How was it you acted so abruptly? Were you following orders?"

"Sir," spoke Hamilton, wondering if he was about to get a dressing-down for acting with no orders, "I saw the retreating Redcoats seek a refuge in Nassau Hall, and being but a few hundred yards away, saw we could end their refuge and make them prisoners."

"So, as I thought," Washington concurred, "you did indeed act without orders."

"I did, sir," admitted Hamilton. "Waiting for such specific orders would have allowed the Redcoats inside to fortify their position, retreat unnoticed out the rear of the building, or have been given time enough for re-enforcements to arrive. None of which would have been a desired consequence. I do take full responsibility for my actions."

"Full responsibility?" Washington questioned. "Do you not mean full honors? You put an end to the battling that glorious day, and your country is to praise you for the actions you took. When did you enlist, Hamilton?"

"Shortly following the battles at Lexington and Concord," Hamilton went on, proud to be telling his story to the most important military figure in North America. "I, along with other students at the college, joined the volunteer militia of New York, forming our own unit called 'Hearts of Oak.' I was given the rank of lieutenant. We took our duties most seriously and drilled daily in the churchyard of St. Paul's.

"When the British ship 'Asia' bombarded Manhattan," Hamilton was most happy to tell, "I led my unit in capturing the cannons at Arsenal Battery."

"Those cannons were most important to the army after we arrived from Cambridge," Washington related to his young friend. "And you were responsible for their capture?"

"My unit and I, yes sir," Hamilton's pride was clear. "Following that event, the 'Hearts of Oak' became a company of artillery. Afterwards, in '76, with the support of prominent New York patriots like John Jay, we became the artillery company we are today."

"So I have another young Henry Knox in my army!" Washington noted, with a smile. "Captain Hamilton, I have an invitation for you. I hope you shall accept it, unlike the refusals I hear you have given to similar invitations from other generals. I wish to invite you to become one of my advisers, an aide-de-camp, with the full rank of colonel in the Continental Army. When might I have your answer?"

Hamilton took no time to think the invitation through, and accepted immediately.

"Why then," Washington asked, as the two shook hands, "did you just as suddenly refuse the same invitations from General Greene and General Knox?"

"Because, General Greene and General Knox," Hamilton said, again without a moment's delay, "simply are not General George Washington."

Skirmishes in New Jersy

In the spring, General Howe in New York devised a two-pronged campaign for the British Army. He planned to drive a wedge cutting off the New England colonies from the southern colonies. Simultaneously, he would capture the city seen as the capital of the thirteen colonies, Philadelphia. In the tradition of European warfare, capturing the enemy's capital meant winning and ending the war. Howe's plan was to send Cornwallis, with the bulk of the army, to capture Philadelphia, while sending Lt. General John Burgoyne from Canada, to invade New York, taking and fortifying the Hudson River Valley all the way to New York City.

As warmer weather came, the armies of the British and Americans faced off in several minor skirmishes across New Jersey. Cornwallis decided not to attempt an overland march to Philadelphia, in the face of Washington's rested and ready army. He turned back toward New York. As soon as Washington received the intelligence of Cornwallis' move, he led his army in pursuit of Cornwallis, following the Redcoats until they crossed back over the Hudson River.

The start of the battle season of 1777 had gone well for the Americans, completely ridding New Jersey of the Redcoats. Washington now marched southeast to concentrate on defending Philadelphia from the British he knew would soon be on the way by sea.

In the north, General Burgoyne left Montreal with eight thousand men, and crossed the border into New York. He led the army south along the shores of Lake Champlain with the recapture of Fort Ticond-eroga being his first objective. By the second day of July, Burgoyne was in place on the highlands above the fort, looking down upon the three thousand men there under the command of General Arthur St. Clair.

The British began a siege of the fort that same day, and on July 6th, General St. Clair, waved the white flag of surrender. The British Union Jack was hoisted up the important fort's flagpole.

The loss of Fort Ticonderoga was a blow to American morale. Both General Phillip Schuyler, and General St. Clair, were blamed directly for the failure to hold the strategic fort. Schuyler was removed from his command, and demoted. Congress bypassed Washington, and replaced St. Clair with Horatio Gates to defend against Burgoyne's advance. Hearing the news of the fall of Fort Ticonderoga and Gates' appoint-ment, Washington sent seven-hundred and fifty men under Gener-als Benedict Arnold and Benjamin Lincoln, and another five hundred sharpshooters under Colonel Daniel Morgan, to march north and join Gates at Albany.

As Washington led the Army toward Philadelphia, a post rider met them, carrying a message from the president of Congress, John Hancock. Washington immediately halted the march of his eleven thousand men and rested to read the dispatch. He looked up from the message he had just read and spoke to Col. Hamilton, now his chief of staff.

"We must make camp immediately," Washington said. "Hancock has news of British ships spotted south of the capes of the Delaware, three days ago. What is their target? Is it truly Philadelphia? Or, is it possibly Charleston? We know they failed their previous attempt to take Charleston. Could that be their target again? We must not move further until those questions are answered.

"We are perhaps thirty miles north of Philadelphia," estimated Washington. "We need a week, perhaps two, to collect more intelli-gence, and plan for the defense of the city, if that be the case; or we shall be moving rapidly into the Carolinas."

Hamilton and six men rode up York Road, returning in less than an hour. They located the ideal spot for a few days encampment, about a mile further up the road. The camp was set up on both sides of York and Bristol roads, leading up Carr's Hill, with Little Neshaminy Creek running between the two roads. Hamilton arranged with the widow

Catherine Moland to use her spacious stone house for General Washington's temporary headquarters. Once settled, Washington sent the post rider back to Philadelphia with a letter informing Hancock of the army's encampment, and pleading for additional intelligence on the movements of the British.

"Bring my maps of the Chesapeake Bay," Washington ordered Wills Winkman. "It appears those ships will land as close to Philadelphia as they can. We must be ready for them."

Hair-Buyer Hamilton

Events on the frontier were moving closer and closer to actual war as well. Jacky and Tom Macneal had prospered with the buffalo, elk and other hides, horns and meats, when they returned from their hunting trip with Kenton, Clark and Boone at the Blue Licks. They stayed close to Annie's Port, hunting, fishing and building a half-dozen new flatboats, still planning to be ready for when the war would eventually wind down, and the settlers would head west.

One afternoon in late July, after a day curing deer meat and buckskin from two days of hunting, Tom and Jacky sat on their verandah looking out over the river.

"Ya know, Tom, I been thinkin'," said Jacky, as he took a swig from the jug of corn liquor they had bought at Nate Nevers' trading post.

"And what might you have been thinking about, Jacky?" Tom asked, taking the jug from his partner.

"One thing we ain't thought of is some good whiskey," said Jacky. "Those settlers might not've had a taste of it in weeks, by the time they get to Raven Rock."

"Well, you're right about that," said Tom, "We'll have to make arrangements with that farmer back at Pittsborough, what's his name … McKenzie?"

"This swill is alright, I guess," said Jacky, "but I sure wish it had the taste o' that whiskey we had last summer at the Blue Licks, that whiskey Preacher Borders brought from Boonesborough."

"That was a more refined tasting whiskey," agreed Tom. "Then this summer, we'll just have to make arrangements with a Kentucky distiller."

"Why can't we distill it on our own?" asked Jacky.

"Well...," Tom said hesitantly, "perhaps it is because we do not know the first thing about it, and haven't the equipment."

"We didn't know the first thing 'bout buildin' flatboats," Jacky argued, "but we sure learned how, an' a dare anyone ta find one better."

"I don't know, Jacky," Tom rebutted, "yes, I suppose we can build about anything, but knowing what measures of corn and grain and sugar and water and all, not to mention when to distill it and how long to let it set, that's a talent we simply do not have."

"We can build a still," Jacky said. "We've seen 'em enough, we can build one. As for the actual making o' the whiskey, I know I can get the recipe and learn, by experimentin' some. You've forgot I was a master at blendin' whiskey when I first met ya back on Lewis Street." That brought a laugh out of Tom.

"I guess we'll just have to start planning on a whiskey enterprise. Is that a canoe coming upriver?" Tom said, as he spotted a vessel in the water just coming into sight from the west. "Is it Kenton?"

"Is it Davy?" asked Jacky, jumping up from his seat and running to the western edge of the verandah. "It is! I think that's Davy!"

"If it is," said Tom, "there's someone with him."

"Is it Simon? Is it Dan'l Boone?" asked Jacky.

"I don't think so," said Tom. "It looks to be another young man, like Davy."

The canoe pulled up and moored at the dock. Tom and Jacky were at the dock to welcome their young friend they had not seen in months. Davy had a young man with him. Tom and Jacky led them to the verandah.

"Well, Davy," Jacky said, "did ole Dan'l marry ya off ta Jemima?"

Davy smiled and shook his head. "No, Jemima married one of her rescuers, Flanders Calloway, a very nice young man. But that is not why I came back to Annie's Port."

"This is your home, Davy," said Tom. "You need no reason to return home."

"But I do have a reason now," said Davy.

"The Shawnee are raiding and killing and scalping," said Davy, explaining what had happened since their hunting expedition to the Blue Licks.

"Every small settlement, standing alone with no stockade for protection, has been burned, with all the settlers killed and scalped, or taken as captives by the Shawnee," Davy said. "They are led by a fierce war chief, Kah-ta-wa-ma-qua, Blackfish. Blue Jacket and Chickseeka aid him.

"Blackfish led a siege against Boonesborough in April." Davy went on. "It was several days of battle. The fort ran low of food. Boone led a party outside the stockade, during a break in the siege, to herd some cattle into the fort to slaughter and eat. He took a musket ball. Only four of the twenty cattle were brought into the fort. The Shawnee slaughtered the rest, and destroyed the gardens before they finally gave up."

"Boone is dead?" Tom asked, horror-stricken at the thought.

"No," Davy answered. "Boone was carried into the fort. The musket ball did little damage. Boone was lucky to have been struck in the knee.

"On their way back to the Ohio Country," Davy continued, "the Shawnee raided settlers all along the way. Our friend Simon Kenton came to Boonesborough, after the Shawnee ended the siege. I joined his party to track them to the Ohio, leaving Boone to get well. We came across one burned out settlement after another, all the way to the river's edge.

"We found Jamie," Davy said, looking at his companion. "His family, and five others had homesteads on the Licking River. He was fishing when he heard the shots from the Shawnee attack. He hid in the thicket behind their cabin, and watched as his father and mother were killed and scalped. He watched as the torch was put to the cabin. He watched as his two young sisters were taken away as captives."

"Ya saw yer pa and ma kill't, Jamie?" asked Jacky.

"I was scare't and froze," said the fourteen-year-old boy. "I stayed in the thicket for two days, too scare't to run…too scare't ta even go ta the river fer a drink o' water."

"We found him there when we came across the burned out cabins," said Davy.

"So the Shawnee are bringing their terror to Kentucky again?" Tom asked.

"And the British at Fort Detroit are encouraging them," said Davy. "The governor, Henry Hamilton, is paying any Indian a heavy bounty for white prisoners, and an even larger bounty for just their scalps. He is now known on the frontier as 'Hair Buyer Hamilton' and is more feared than any general in the British army.

"Jamie came back to Boonesborough with us," said Davy. "He is now like my brother. Kenton wants me to ask you to build an army of men, and bring them to him and Colonel Clark, to help fight against Blackfish, Blue Jacket and Chickseeka."

Moland House

"Why have we no new intelligence?" General Washington ranted to Wills Winkman in the parlor of the Moland House. "The last we heard was on the seventh, now it is the twenty-first, and no further word...none whatsoever! I shall leave in the morning for Philadelphia and meet with President Hancock and Franklin, and what other members of Congress may be available."

"Dr. Franklin in now in Paris, with Arthur Lee and Silas Deane," Wills reminded the general."

"Silas Deane!" Washington fumed. "He gives the rank of general in the American Army to any European misfit who seeks him out! He sends to us the men the generals of Europe wish to banish! Men of the nobility with no talent for war, but with plenty of idle time on their hands!

"General Thomas Conway, that Irish fortune-hunting glory-seeker, simply because he fought in the French Army, was last sent to me by Deane. I have yet to see one reason he should be more than a captain. Diplomats and congressmen should never be allowed to make those decisions, and should not be the ones getting the intelligence we need!

"So Franklin is not in Philadelphia...is John Adams still with the Congress?"

"Yes," Wills answered.

"Arrange for Greene, Knox and Anthony Wayne, generals of my own chosing, to join me."

The minds of the general command of the American Army were stymied, their hands were tied, with no intelligence coming, as they camped waiting for two full weeks along York Road.

Lt. Winkman left headquarters to instruct generals Greene, Knox and Wayne of Washington's plans for them to accompany him in his carriage to Philadelphia the next day. As Wills was walking back up the steps of Moland House, he met Col. Hamilton coming out of with a newly promoted major, James Monroe. They stood on the porch and talked for a few minutes.

"Monroe here was just been appointed to General Lord Stirling's staff as aide-de-camp," Hamilton said. "We have just returned from General Washington with his blessings."

"That is good news," Wills said, extending his hand to Monroe. "Lord Stirling is a fine general, one of Washington's favorites."

"I am honored to have been so accepted," Monroe said with a humble smile.

At that time, two carriages with military escorts pulled up the lane in front of the house. Wills went down the steps to attend to the visitors as soon as the carriages stopped.

The door of the first carriage opened, and out stepped two ornately uniformed men, apparently of European nobility, accompanied by a man of more traditional American attire.

'Who has Silas Deane now sent to Washington?' Wills questioned in his mind.

The second carriage contained two other men in civilian attire and a lady. Wills immediately recognized one of the Americans in the second carriage as being his old Boston friend, John Hancock, now prsident of the Continental Congress.

"President Hancock," Wills said as he saluted, "what brings you and your party to us?"

Hancock looked Wills over, feeling they had met, but really could not put a name to the face.

"Should I not know you, young man?" Hancock asked. "I feel as though we have met."

"We have indeed, sir," answered Wills, "I am Lt. Wills Winkman, aide to General Washington. We had several discussions in the long room above Ead's Print Shop a few years back."

Hancock laughed and shook his hand in a most animated fashion. "We did indeed, young man," Hancock said, "we did indeed. And we threw many chests of tea into the waters of the harbor, did we not?"

"We did indeed, sir." Wills smiled.

"So you now serve as aide to our beloved general! Well, we have vital news for our general," Hancock said, "and have brought re-enforcements," he said, nodding, with a playful grin, toward the two uniformed Europeans.

"The general is most anxious for any news," Wills said, "and I am certain, for the re-enforcements as well," he laughed. "I shall take you right in to him."

"I have brought two members of the Congress the general will, I am certain, wish to discuss the news with as well," insisted Hancock. "Let me present Benjamin Harrison of Virginia and Benjamin Rush of Pennsylvania."

Wills immediately led the three congressmen up the steps, and introduced them to Hamilton and Monroe, who joined them in the meeting with Washington.

"You are that brave Virginian who was wounded at Trenton," said Harrison, anxious to shake Monroe's hand. "The Virginia Gazette was filled with news of how our 3rd Regiment helped win the day."

"We all did what we could that day, sir," answered Monroe humbly.

"It is so good to meet you, Monroe," Harrison added, "and now you are a major, and on the general staff. That is wonderful news for me to carry home."

Wills returned, after Washington gladly greeted Hancock and the congressmen. He went straight to the remaining visitors. Once introduced to them, he showed them into the parlor off the front foyer of the beautiful stone house. The two Europeans entertained the attractive lady, seeming to be in her mid-twenties, dressed in a stylish blue, yellow and white floral print dress, with auburn ringlets of hair framing her pleasant and very pretty face. Wills carried a wrapped bundle she had with her, and sat it on the table beside her chair in the parlor. Wills sent a private in with a tray of sassafras tea and sweet biscuits for the visitors, before joining the meeting in Washington's office.

"The British fleet has entered Chesapeake Bay," said Hancock, "and is certainly on its way to Baltimore, or even closer to Philadelphia, the mouth of the Susquehanna River. It appears they shall land in Maryland, and march overland to Philadelphia."

"We have awaited that word," Washington smiled, as if he had opened a Christmas present. "We now shall immediately make our plans. Lt. Winkman, pen a summary of the news to all my generals, and have them prepare now to break camp in two days. Set up a meeting of the general staff for in the morning."

As the meeting with the congressmen ended, Washington led the congressmen and his aides into the parlor. The Europeans immediately stood at attention as Washington entered the room. Hancock made the introductions.

"General," Hancock spoke, "we have two men I think you will find most valuable to our cause. May I present General Casimir Pulaski, a nobleman of Poland, and General Gilbert du Motier, the Marques de LaFayette of France, sent by our ambassador in Paris, Silas Deane."

"I am so honored," Washington said to the two, disguising his true sentiments toward more of Deane's generals being sent to him. "We shall meet presently."

Hancock turned then to the seated lady.

"General," Hancock added, "I should like to present the young widow Betsy Griscom Ross of Philadelphia. She has a presentation to make."

"Mrs. Ross," Washington reached for her gloved hand and kissed it, "I am delighted you have so graced my headquarters with your charm."

"The delight is indeed reserved for myself," she said, with a charming and blushing smile. She, remaining seated, handing the bundle she had brought with her to Washington.

"A gift?" Washington asked, puzzled.

"Yes, general," stated Hancock, "a gift for our new nation."

Washington seemed a bit perplexed, smiled and untied the ribbon, opening the bundle. He pulled from beneath the paper wrapping, a large, sewn flag, five feet in width, nine feet in length, with thirteen alternating horizontal red and white stripes, and a field of blue in the upper left corner, holding thirteen five-pointed white stars arranged in a circle.

"The Congress approved the design by resolution," Hancock said proudly, as it was his own design. "Mrs. Ross, a seamstress in the city, fashioned our flag from the design."

"It is indeed a beautiful flag for our new nation," agreed Washington, dropping one end in Betsy Ross' lap as she sat, holding the other end with the blue field of white stars in his hands.

"Lt. Winkman, take the flag," he handed it to Wills. "We shall have a dedication of it at the morning's parade." He turned to his guests. "You shall stay the night, all of you, dine with us this evening, and breakfast with us in the morn. Then we shall all see how our flag flies atop the standard?" They all agreed.

Wills took the flag, folded it and laid it on his desk. He then showed the congressmen and seamstress to rooms on the second floor, while Washington remained in the parlor to get the interviews with the Europeans over with.

"Ambassador Deane has certainly recruited several from Europe to fight in our cause," Washington began the interview.

"Congress certainly welcomed us," said LaFayette, reluctantly, "but gave the feeling they did not necessarily approve of Ambassador Deane appointing us officers, and even delayed sending us to you for well over six weeks. I am certainly honored now to finally meet with you, mon general," LaFayette bowed to Washington.

"I care nothing for your Congress," Pulaski spoke bluntly. "I came here, where freedom is being defended, to serve it, and to live or die for it! And they make me wait, because I am not an American!"

Washington chuckled. "I do understand your disdain for the politicians in our Congress," said Washington, with a smile and a disapproving shake of his head. "They control the purse strings, and the supplies so badly needed by the army. But, the Congress is, after all, a needed institution, to give us at the least, some semblance of a national government."

The three men took seats in armchairs as they got to know each other.

"I have a correspondence for you from Dr. Franklin in Paris," said LaFayette, pulling the missive from his inside coat pocket, handing it to Washington.

"I too have such a letter," echoed Pulaski, mirroring LaFayette's action. Washington took both, put a pair of spectacles on and read each.

"You are a renowned cavalryman, and it seems have had a great deal of success on the field of battle," Washington looked up over the spectacles and smiled at Pulaski. "And you, Marquis, come highly encouraged to join my staff as aide-de-camp." LaFayette nodded at the general.

"I come here, general," LaFayette said humbly, "to learn, not to teach."

"What better place from which to learn," said Washington, "than as an aide on my staff? You both are badly needed, and you both are welcomed with my open arms," said Washington.

Brandywine Creek

As the army assembled in ranks for the morning flag-raising, the new American Flag was raised to cheers from the men. Washington addressed the men, introducing the congressmen and Betsy Ross, then dedicating the new flag.

"To make this day even the more complete," Washington pulled a dispatch from his pocket, "I have further news from the north." He began to read.

"August 16th, 1777, New Hampshire and Massachusetts militiamen under General John Stark, aided by a company of Green Mountain Boys, under the command of Colonel Seth Warner, did intercept fourteen hundred British and Hessians soldiers and their Indian allies, raiding for supplies and livestock in the area of Bennington, on a mission from British General Burgoyne.

"Casualties were two hundred and seven enemy killed – thirty Americans killed; three hundred and twelve enemy wounded – forty Americans wounded; seven hundred and twenty-two enemy captured. Two hundred Indians laid down their arms, with a promise not to take up arms again against the Americans."

Washington looked up from the dispatch with a solemn smile, "To the brave men of the north, the Battle of Bennington shall be remembered as a great victory for America, and for American independence. We salute you!"

The men in the ranks cheered and flung their caps in the air in celebration.

With the new intelligence, Washington moved his army quickly, and set up camp at Chadd's Ford, in Pennsylvania southwest of Philadelphia.

He sent a company to Iron Hill, near the upper end of Chesapeake Bay, to spy on the British, expected any day. The British arrived two days later and began off-loading seventeen thousand five hundred men and artillery pieces. Off-loading was slow, because the river was narrow, and the shallow waters were muddy with a boggy bottom.

Washington wanted the advantage for the battle so, on September 9th, he stationed large guard units at all the fords of the Brandywine Creek, both north and south of Chadds Ford, hoping to force his selected position on Howe as the field of battle. Chadds Ford was the major crossing on the main road between Baltimore and Philadelphia.

September 11th opened with heavy fog that lasted until midday. Washington knew the British soldiers were now on land, and moving close, but the fog shrouded Howe's movements. The British rested at the town of Kennett Square, and Howe laid his plan for the day.

"I wish not this day to march into a trap," stated Howe to his generals while the troops rested.

"Washington and his farmers," Howe said, with a great deal of arrogance, "must surely think we to be green in supposing I should march up to where he sits, perched upon the high grounds at Chadds Ford. I shall end this war this very day."

On a table set up beneath a tree in the town commons, an aide laid out a map of the area between Chesapeake Bay and Philadelphia. The generals crowded around the map as Howe spoke.

"I shall send General von Knyphausen and his five thousand Hessians to advance directly toward Washington at Chadds Ford. Washington shall view this as the main army, thinking he has bested me in strategy.

"However, Cornwallis shall lead the balance of the army north, to here," he pointed to the map, "Trimble's Ford, and cross the west branch of the Brandywine, marching east to Jeffries Ford, crossing the creek's east branch. Here, Cornwallis shall turn back south to flank Washington with von Knyphausen at his front and Cornwallis at his rear."

At two o'clock in the afternoon, the fog finally lifted.

The Battle of Brandywine was not going well for the Americans. It seemed each time the Americans had a clear opportunity, they were out-numbered, and forced into retreat after retreat.

By six o'clock, the Hessians were on the west bank of Brandywine Creek, and began pounding the American centerline across Chadds Ford.

The 3rd Virginia Regiment, now part of the army of General Lord Stirling, was detached to stop the pursuing Hessians at a place called Sandy Hollow Gap, to allow the balance of the Continental Army to safely retreat north.

Peter Francisco, Garrett Hicks and Malcolm Shepherd were positioned behind a fallen tree trunk, firing their muskets almost continually at the Hessians across the creek. Peter Patrick and Major Monroe were doing the same just down from them.

"Damn, this sure has been one hellish day," complained Garrett.

"It surely has been," said Peter, while reloading his musket and getting off another shot.

"I hear this ain't even the main army o' Redcoats," said Malcolm. "Major Jimmie says 'twas only about a third of it. Cornwallis is a chasin' us from behind, he says."

"If this ain't the full army," said Garrett exasperated, "I sure hate to see it!"

"It's the Hessians, alright," said Peter, "and we've been facin' 'em all day."

"How long does Stirling 'spect us ta fend 'em off?" Garrett complained some more. "It's been near an hour I 'spect." He finished tamping down the powder, ready to fire another round.

"An' we just done the same thing less 'n a half-hour ago back on Meetin'house Hill," Malcolm added his complaints to Garrett's.

"And we were firin' on Meetinghouse Hill for a solid two hours straight," Peter said. "I guess we keep firin' till they tell us to quit."

"There sure ain't no restin' fer us this day," said Malcolm, getting off another shot.

"How many Hessians you bag today, Peter?" asked Garrett.

"Not near enough," Peter replied.

A Hessian musket ball struck the powder horn Peter had sitting on the ground beside where he was squatted behind the downed tree trunk. The force of the ball pushed the powder horn back a full ten feet behind him.

"Damn, that was a close one!" Peter said, surprised at how close the Prussian musket ball had whizzed by his head and landed.

"An inch er two closer an' that big ole Portugee head o' yer'n would've been gone for certain," said Garrett. "You're the luckiest man I know, Peter Francisco."

Peter chuckled and started to slither out to retrieve what valuable powder he still had left in the horn, after the last few hours of near constant fire.

"Watch out, Peter!" shouted Garrett. "You make too big a target!"

About that time Peter stopped moving. A musket ball drove itself deep into his left thigh.

"I'm hit!" Peter cried out. "I'm hit! Damn it hurts!"

Garrett and Malcolm, not worrying about the Hessian fire coming at them, both spontaneously stood in crouching positions, ran to Peter, and drug him to safety behind a huge oak tree. Garrett took his knife and sliced through the back of Peter's pants leg, exposing the wound.

"Damn! That sure ain't a pretty sight!" Garrett declared.

As Peter had done when he carried Jimmie Monroe to safety, Garrett put all his pressure on the wound to try and stop the bleeding. He ripped off his shirt and tore it into strips, making a square pad of cloth to soak the blood, and tied strips around the square of cloth covering the wound on the backside of Peter's massive thigh. Peter passed out.

A Farmhouse at Chester

The day had not been a good one for the Americans. Their frantic retreat did not end until midnight, when most of the army eventually had arrived at the town of Chester. Causalities were lopsided. The British lost ninety-three killed and over four hundred-eighty wounded. It was estimated the Americans suffered no fewer than eleven hundred killed and another one thousand wounded, with some four hundred more captured, most being wounded and left for dead where they lay during the pandemonium of the retreat.

However, the day could have been even worse for the Americans. General Howe, traveling with Cornwallis, was slow to act in his movements to out flank Washington. He did not arrive until the Americans were already in retreat. There was little or no British cavalry to cement the victory and truly vanquish Washington.

As the Virginia 3rd and others fended off the Hessians from across Brandywine Creek, to allow the bulk of the American Army to retreat, the sun was starting to go down. Within thirty minutes of sunset, Howe stopped his army's pursuit of the Americans for the night, allowing Washington's army to escape to Chester.

News spread rapidly to Philadelphia, and Congress evacuated the city, moving the capital west to Lancaster on September 26th, then a day later, further west to the town of York, across the Susquehanna River. Howe marched his army into Philadelphia, facing no organized resistance whatsoever, seeing the Congress had already fled.

All the news coming to Hancock and the fleeing Congress was not as devastating as the news of the close by Battle of Brandywine. As Washington was being forced into a disorderly retreat from Brandywine, the army of General Gates had given Burgoyne's advance a near-crushing blow at a place called Freeman's Farm near Saratoga, New York.

Within days, General Benjamin Lincoln led the counterattack on Fort Ticonderoga and hoisted the new American Flag up the fort's flagpole.

Peter woke up two days after being hit by the musket ball in his left thigh. He woke to strange surroundings. He found himself in a narrow bed, under a clean, white sheet and what appeared to be a homemade quilt. There was another bed to his left, where there was another wounded soldier sleeping. A window separated the two beds, with a mattress-high table beneath it that held a water pitcher and two glasses. There was a small fireplace on the wall beyond the second bed, and an interior door opposite the window. Peter raised himself up a bit, and felt the pains in his left leg as he tried to move. Then he suddenly remembered the musket ball, and how the pain had been so excruciating when it pierced the back of his thigh.

"I survived!" Peter thought out loud. Then he looked at the sleeping soldier in the other bed.

"I wonder what happened to him?" Peter continued his conversation with himself.

The body stirred a bit. His face turned toward where he had heard the voice. His eyes opened. He smiled. Peter smiled back, and thought how much like a fragile little china doll the strange soldier's face seemed. He could not be more than fifteen years old, Peter thought, just a boy. His eyes were large and deep blue, with thin, but dark brows. The eyebrows were a match in hue to the wavy, long, dark brown hair on the boy's head, that flowed down to his shoulders. His nose was a tad pointy, and his lips were narrow but full and dark pink. His complexion was very pale, very porcelain white. While Peter thought he was not a handsome boy, he would have certainly made a beautiful little girl.

"Bon jour, mon ami," came the first words out of the lad's mouth. Peter looked in puzzlement. The young boy was French.

"Pardon," said the boy, realizing his error. "I have forgotten for a moment, I am no longer at
my home in France."

"You are from France?" asked Peter.

"Yes," said the boy, "I am Gilbert du Motier, the Marquis de LaFayette."

"You cannot be more than a lad of fifteen," said Peter, amazed, "yet you have such a title?"

LaFayette laughed, "Oui, I became the marquis at the death of my father when I was but two years-old. I am also a brigadier general in the Continental Army, and aide-de-camp to General George Washington. I celebrated by twentieth birthday just five days before I took this Prussian bullet at Brandywine."

"I took one too," said Peter. "My regiment was holding off the Prussians across the river so our army could safely retreat. I took a musket ball in the back of my leg."

"I am sorry your regiment did not do a much better job," LaFayette said sarcastically, then smiled.

"Why do you say such a thing?" Peter asked with a frown.

"I was in that retreat you were assigned to cover, when I took my bullet," LaFayette said, giggling.

"We held those damned Hessians off for more than an hour, keeping them on their side of Brandywine Creek, so you could retreat to a safety!" Peter said with much distaste for the laughing French boy. "Why do you laugh?"

"It was said in jest," LaFayette laughed. "Please take it as such."

Peter thought for a moment, then smiled and joined in the laughter.

"You are quite a giant of a man, are you not?" LaFayette asked.

"I am taller and heftier than most my age. I turned twenty myself on the last day of June," Peter answered.

"How tall are you?"

"Just seven feet tall," answered Peter with a laugh.

"Seven feet? Mon Dieu!" LaFayette was amazed. "I have never seen such a tall man. Are you not too much a target for the enemy?" They both laughed some more.

"I guess I sure was back there at the gap," Peter admitted, and the two new friends laughed some more.

The boys enjoyed each others company as they both were being tended to by a Quaker family in their farmhouse, just a mile west of Chester. Andreas Huber had migrated to Philadelphia from the Swiss Palatinate, with his parents forty years earlier. He inherited the farm when his father died in 1760. He married Anna Eisenstadt one year later. Andreas and Anna were blessed with two quite attractive daughters, Anna Mary and Susannah. Andreas' mother, Katerina, also lived with them. The ladies of the house, including the teenaged daughters, tended to the two soldiers as they recuperated from their wounds. They brought them in their hearty Quaker meals three times each day, and followed every instruction given them by Dr. Mattias Schottmeister, who came by once every other day to check in on his patients.

"I will be extremely pleased when I get back to our camp," LaFayette said one morning as they ate their breakfast of oatmeal, eggs and flapjacks in their room. "I am afraid we shall yet be here as the army sets up winter camp."

"I miss the boys in my regiment," Peter said, "I boarded with several of them at school and at William and Mary. I don't want to miss any battles."

"I will miss all the attention we are getting from the Hubers," said LaFayette.

"I will surely miss these wonderful hot meals," Peter replied.

War Plans on the Frontier

Davy Danielson and his young friend, Jamie Salyers, stayed on at Annie's Port while Jacky and Tom changed their plans for the summer of 1777. Instead of a leisurely late summer hunting trip to the Blue Licks, they would now be forming a company from the settlers around Fort Pitt, who were waiting out the war like they were. The flatboats they had built for future settlers would become a flotilla down the Ohio River, to join Kenton by the end of September. The company of settlers would serve wherever needed by Clark and Boone, in an expedition against the Shawnee, Cherokee, Chickasaw and the evil Hair Buyer Hamilton.

Tom and Jacky met little resistance enlisting about fifty men in the area around Fort Pitt. They made arrangements for a pair of friends of theirs, John Hedrick and Robert Neff, who also had gone on hunting trips with them, to move in at Annie's Port and look after the place while they were gone. They didn't know how long that would be... maybe several months or a year...maybe even more.

On the 10th day of September, they pushed off in six flatboats from Annie's Port. This was the first time many of those in the company had been even as far down river as Annie's Port, let alone into the frontier of the Ohio Country and Kentucky. They were anxious to see the lands they had only heard about, and hoped someday to settle.

Late that first afternoon, the flotilla pulled ashore at Wheeling Creek, about fifty miles down river from Annie's Port. In 1769, Ebenezer Zane had laid out the settlement of Zanesburg there. Jacky, Tom and Davy had stopped at Zanesburg on their hunting expedition in 1776, and had made friends with the Zane brothers.

"So you're a headin' inta the Ken-tuck lands ta fight the injuns?" the thirty year-old Ebenezer Zane asked, as they sat beneath a big tree in the courtyard of the stockade at Zanesburg.

"Boonesborough has already been laid siege to earlier this spring," said Tom. "Kenton, Clark and Boone need us so we won't be hunting buffalo this year."

"No," said Ebenezer's brother Jonathan, "'pears like you fellers'll be a huntin' savages."

"Those damned British at Fort Detroit are stirrin' up the savages, an' payin' bounties fer white scalps," said Jacky.

"The governor there is Sir Henry Hamilton," added Tom, "and has rightly earned the name 'Hair Buyer Hamilton' for all his evil deeds."

"I knowed that damn war'd fin' its way ta the frontier sooner er later," said Ebenezer. "General Washing'ton sure surprised 'em the day after Christmas at Trenton, and stopped 'em good. I heard somethin' 'bout trouble in the Ken-tuck, but figgered it was nothin' but a few renegade Shawnee of Blackfish and Chickseeka bein' the menacin' sons-a-bitches they are. So ya say ole King George is behind it hisself?"

"It appears so, Eb," said Tom, "through the hair buyer he sent to Detroit."

"I reckon there be a dozen er so men right here might wanna join up with ya, Macneal," said Jonathan. "You give me a day an' I'll sure recruit 'em up. I'll lead 'em m'self."

Tom and Jacky decided they'd stay two nights there, if there was the chance of bringing another dozen or more men with them to help their Kentucky friends.

It was agreed the oldest of the Zane brothers would remain at Zanesburg, along with their eighteen year-old sister, Elizabeth, who was called Betty. Betty was taller than average women, just a few inches shy of six feet in height. Being a pioneer settler since the age of ten, she had a coarse and coppery, weatherworn, leathery complexion, which attested to hard work and a lot of time spent out of doors in the elements. She had long, slender fingers and calloused hands. Her hair was auburn and hung down around the shoulders of her homespun cloth dress that covered her from neck to ankles. Her feet were bare, and covered with the dust of the ground.

"These'uns a eatin' supper with us, Eb?" Betty asked her brother abruptly in her corn-husky voice.

"There's a plenty, ain't there?" replied Eb.

"I reckon there is," said Betty, unsmiling, as she headed to the cookhouse. "I'll go an' water down the stew what's left, an' fetch 'em some plates."

When the flotilla left the mouth of Wheeling Creek on the 13th day of September, there were two more flatboats carrying thirty more men bound down stream.

"We just now got ourselves a gall danged army!" Clark boasted, as he welcomed the Macneals and the Zanes, when the flotilla tied up at Corn Island.

"Do ya think we can put an end to ole Hair Buyer Hamilton with this army," asked Jacky.

"Macneal, if we cannot," answered Clark, slapping his arm around Jacky's shoulder and leading his guests away from the wharf, "then we are one pitiful lot! But we got ourselves more fish ta fry than what are at Detroit."

The men walked behind Clark and Kenton to the center of the long narrow island where about a dozen cabins were erected, and about sixty men tended the fires for supper.

Captain Benjamin Logan, Clark's second in command, sat with the leaders of the arriving re-enforcements at a long wooden table set just outside Clark's cabin.

"You could never know just how timely your arrival is," spoke Clark in gratitude. "I need ta send a compliment ta Boonesborough, as we know Blackfish and Chickseeka will soon return. We need ta continue our spyin' companies in the Ohio an' Illinois countries. An' I need a small company ta go down the Wilderness Road with me ta talk with Governor Henry at Williamsburg. I now have all the men I need ta do what needs ta be done, an' still guard our headquarters here on Corn Island."

"What's your business with Governor Henry?" asked Tom.

"Gov'nor Henry made me commander o' the Kentucky Militia," said Clark, "There's limits ta what I can do. I can do whatever I need ta do on this side of the Ohio River. I can send spies north o' the river, Hell, I can even chase them damned Shawnee bastards up inta the Ohio Country, if'n they been a raidin' in the Ken-tuck.

"From m' spies I sent to the Illinois Country in April," Clark continued, "they tell me the British forts're weak an' the towns're nothin' but French Canadians who hate the British.

"My business with Henry," continued the colonel, "is ta convince 'em ta let me go after them British forts in the Illinois Country, an' then go after the Hair Buyer at Fort Detroit.

"Our Ken-tuck settlements'll never be safe, so long as the British keep tellin' the Indians ta raid us, and pay them for our scalps," Clark went on. "If the British are run out o' the west, as they can easily be, General Howe's defeat will foller. But, I need the governor's approval."

Valley Forge

With General Howe now holding Philadelphia, the largest city in America, the season of war was closing badly for the Continental Army. The Americans made an attempt on the main British base at Germantown, a few miles northwest of the city, but failed as they had failed at Brandywine.

With Howe already comfortable and warm in Philadelphia, and Congress safely in the new temporary capital at York, Washington had not yet settled on an appropriate winter encampment site for his army. The army had been on constant move from town-to-town in eastern and southern Pennsylvania until finally, on December 19th Washington made a decision.

Washington led his twelve thousand men to a peaceful-looking valley about twenty miles northwest of Philadelphia. It was at the juncture where Valley Creek joined the Schuylkill River. The two hills of Mount Joy and Mount Misery, made the valley defensible. There was an iron forge along Valley Creek. The name of the encampment became Valley Forge.

As Peter and his new friend, LaFayette, walked down the staircase for breakfast, smelling the aromas of hot biscuits and sausages, the oldest of the teenaged Huber daughters, Anna Mary, met them in the foyer.

"There is a rider and a carriage from General Washington!" she announced, excitedly.

"We are finally to rejoin our army?" LaFayette asked in anticipation.

"It's about time!" added Peter. "We could have been sent for two weeks ago."

There was a rap at the door, Anna Mary ran and opened it. Standing on the threshold was a familiar face.

"Major Jimmie!" Peter broke out with the broadest smile, rushed to him, wrapped both of his huge arms around the young slim officer, and lifted him a full two feet off the ground. He kissed him on his right cheek, then on his left. "It is so good to see you!" He planted his superior officer back on the floor.

LaFayette stood and watched and chuckled at the sight.

"I did not realize you Americans greeted your comrades with kisses, as we French are so prone to do," LaFayette said, continuing his laughter.

"Peter," Monroe said smiling, once he had regained his composure, "I volunteered to bring you back to the regiment, since you were the one who saved me at Trenton." Monroe then turned to LaFayette and saluted the young general.

"General LaFayette, it is doubly an honor to collect you as well," Monroe said. "I pray you found your friend and chamber mate of the past three months as agreeable as I have over the past several years."

"Indeed," LaFayette said. "Private Peter Francisco has indeed helped make the long and monotonous weeks of our collective recuperation most enjoyable."

"When do we leave?" Peter asked impatiently.

"As soon as you are packed," replied Monroe. "It is about twenty miles due north of here, and if we leave within the hour we shall arrive before the sun sets."

"We were on our way to breakfast," Peter added.

"Will you not join us Major Monroe, for a hot Quaker breakfast?" LaFayette invited.

"Well," Monroe spoke, "since you do outrank me, I could not refuse." Anna Mary led them into the dining room.

Southern Pennsylvania winters were known to be typically moderate, with cold and damp days. Ice covered the streams, but few snows fell, and those soon melted away. The winter of 1777-78 was just that. Washington knew the first order of business was to cut trees, saw logs, and build cabins to shelter his men from the elements.

It took about three days for some cabins to be built, more than a week for others. It all depended upon how familiar with sawing logs and raising a cabin the men were. The dozen soldiers to occupy each cabin, built their own. The farmer-soldiers were well acquainted with cabin raising. The soldiers from the cities were not. Until their cabin was ready, the men slept in tents and lean-tos.

Sites for one thousand log huts were laid out along a grid of streets, paced off by Washington and his aides. LaFayette immediately took quarters at Washington's headquarters, as soon as he and Peter arrived. The house was Georgian in style, a relatively small, two-story, gray stone house. Isaac Potts had built it so he had a comfortable home when he spent weeks at a time on the property, where he operated a family grist mill on Valley Creek.

Peter was taken to a tent, which would be his home along with Monroe, Garrett and Malcolm, until they built their cabin. Peter Patrick and seven others from the Virginia 3rd would share the cabin. On Peter's first day in camp, the only part of the cabin finished was the hearth, and about one-third of the chimney.

"At the rate you boys are headed," Peter said when he first saw the laid-up stone hearth, "we'll be sleepin' in those damned tents till Easter!"

"We can't build a cabin till we have some logs," said Malcolm.

"Well, I see plenty of trees," said Peter pointing to a stand of tall pines at the foot of Mount Joy. "Fetch me an axe and I'll have all the logs we need by suppertime!"

"How we gonna get 'em from there to here?" asked Noel Chenoweth, from Caroline County, who became friends with the other boys.

"I'll cut 'em," Peter said. "Garrett and Pat'll trim 'em up, and everyone else will match up in pairs and tote 'em, one on each end, and stack 'em right here. I wanna be under roof by Christmas Eve!"

"That's jus'four days from now!" Garrett said. "I was thinkin' winter camp was ta be a time ta rest up for the summer war. You a plannin' on workin' us ta death, Peter?"

"I don't want to spend another Christmas with you belly-achin' like ya belly-ached last Christmas on the Delaware, Hicks!" Peter said. All the others laughed, remembering Garrett's complaints before they all boarded the Durham boats to cross the Delaware with Washington.

"Sounds like a plan that might just work," Major Monroe agreed, and the dozen men were off to the pine trees.

By sundown enough cut down and measured logs were stacked at the cabin site. The bark scraped from the logs would be the plank shingles to seal the roof from rain and sleet.

"Now, that we have the logs," Monroe asked, "how do we make a cabin out of it?"

"Well," Peter said, "we need about four fellers to dig a place over there for an outhouse."

"An outhouse?" Garrett questioned. "We need a cabin, Peter, not a damn place to shit!" The men laughed.

"We need the dirt ta make the mud ta mortar the logs," Chenoweth added. "Might as well dig it here an' have a place to piss an' shit when we do have the cabin built. We can build a frame an' nail up the canvas tents for that. I'll lead that project, Peter."

"Good," Peter answered. "Now while Garrett, Malcolm, Pat and me start placin' the base logs around perimeter, the rest of you can get buckets and go over to Valley Creek and fetch water for the mud."

By the end of the second day, logs were laid up forming a twelve-foot by eight-foot log hut about six feet high.

"Where you gonna sleep, Peter?" asked Malcolm. "This cabin's only six foot tall. You'll have ta be walking all stoopied over er you'll be a hittin' that big ole head of yer'n ever'time you try to stand up!" Everyone laughed at Peter's giant form.

"It'll be plenty tall when we add the eaves and rafters tomorrow," Peter said.

"I hope ya don't intend ta sleep up in the rafters," said Garrett. "If ya do, I sure as Hell don't wanna sleep 'neath ya an' wake up one mornin' flattened like a johnnycake after you done fell through in the night." The laughter continued.

The next day the rafters were in place and the roof shingled. The door was hung with a larger-than-normal six and a half foot plank door to accommodate, as best they could, Peter's seven foot height, without forcing the Virginia Giant, as he was now being called, to stoop too far to enter a normal six-foot doorway.

On Christmas Eve, the men built the bunk frames for both sides of the cabin, and floored and braced the loft on each side of the cabin with the center area open to the main room below. Eight men would sleep in the main bunks below the rafters, while four would sleep in the loft. Everyone voted Peter Francisco to have any bunk he wanted, as long as it was on the ground.

On Christmas Day, General Washington, accompanied by the Marquis de LaFayette, Lieutenant Hamilton, and General Anthony Wayne, walked from the Potts House into the encampment where most of the men were still sleeping in tents, and less than one hundred log huts had been erected. Only a few of the cabins seemed to be really ready for winter.

As they walked down the street where Peter and his friends had built their cabin, they stopped and walked to the door. Washington rapped on the door. Major Monroe opened the door from the inside.

"Major Monroe," Washington said, "I am certainly impressed with the cabin your men have raised."

"General Washington," Monroe saluted and seemed startled. "Will you not step inside?"

"These are men of the Virginia 3rd, gentlemen," Washington said, as the three generals entered the hut.

"You do my old friend, Hugh Mercer, a great honor," Washington spoke to Monroe. "You have a warm fire in the hearth, and no light shining through your roof. Others will envy you as the cold winds blow. You are to be commended."

"Begging your pardon, general," Monroe spoke up, "the man deserving the commendation is Private Peter Francisco. He organized the raising, the design, oversaw the work details, and single-handedly felled every pine tree that gave up its trunks for our logs and barks for shingles."

Washington spotted Peter by his height and near-three hundred pound bulk, and walked up to him, extending his hand.

"Peter and I are old friends," Washington said. "You have done fine work, Peter, and I am so pleased to see you have fully recovered from the musket ball you took for us at Brandywine. I believe in fact you convalesced with my aide-de-camp here, LaFayette."

Peter nodded and he and LaFayette shook hands.

"Private Peter Francisco is indeed mon ami," LaFayette said. "But I was unaware he was so talented in the building of cabins, and in building them so rapidly."

"I decided we needed to be under roof by Christmas," said Peter. "I remember how bitter the cold was last Christmas crossing the Delaware." They all chuckled and the visitors left.

The day after Christmas, the anniversary of Washington's victory at Trenton, LaFayette breakfasted with Washington.

"Mon general," LaFayette spoke. "Do you not think our friend, Peter Francisco, is already a hero in this war."

Washington chuckled. "I have known Peter a long time. He is the adopted son of dear family friend. He has visited at Mount Vernon, and was quite taken with my darling little daughter, Patsy. I think perhaps, if she had not died, he might be asking for her hand in marriage. But how is he already a hero of the war? He has quickly built a cabin, and has taken a bullet at Brandywine."

"One year ago at Trenton," LaFayette said. "As I have learned, when Major Monroe was ordered to take those Prussian cannons in King Street, and took an enemy musket ball, it was Peter who risked his own life to carry Monroe's lifeless body to safety, pressing his huge palm on the wound to slow the bleeding and keep Monroe alive."

Washington said pensively, "that was Peter?"

"It was," LaFayette said. "He also fired at the enemy at Brandywine constantly for over two hours, both at Meetinghouse Hill, then thirty minutes later, was again in the center line at Sandy Hollow Gap at Chadd's Ford, to allow the army's retreat. That's where he took a ball and woke up with me at the Huber farmhouse at Chester."

"He was also with me in New York," said Washington, "Harlem Heights and White Plains, and then with me crossing the Delaware."

"He is an outstanding soldier," LaFayette added, "but has some difficulties due to his size, especially, with his saber. He is called the Giant of Virginia, but with his standard issue saber in hand, he appears as a giant oaf with a butcher knife. He needs a sword to compliment his stature and his size.

"I know how you fight with your congress for adequate supplies," LaFayette continued, "so I propose we fit him with a sword, specially forged to be adequate for him. I shall pay all the expenses for such a gift myself."

Washington smiled. He liked the tribute LaFayette wished to pay Private Peter Francisco.

The Politics of War

"Here is another pathetic plea from Washington," said Thomas Mifflin, in his office at York, as he read a letter from the Commander-in-Chief. Mifflin was the thirty-three year old Quartermaster General of the army, and a member of the Congressional War Board.

"He requests twelve thousand blankets, new uniforms and shoes, enough palatable meat to feed the army through the winter, and so on and so on. He ends his request with a quite snide critique of us: '*Unless some great change suddenly takes place in your office, this army shall inevitably starve, freeze to death, dissolve, or be forced to disperse, simply to sustain life.*'"

"Why should the Congress send even one more blanket or one more slab of bacon to his filthy, undisciplined rabble of an army?" replied Benjamin Rush, a member of Congress who sat on the board. "He is the reason Congress had to flee from Philadelphia because his army could not keep the Redcoats out!"

"Mr. Adams made a huge mistake when he convinced us all to unanimously elect Washington Commander-in-Chief," Mifflin said. Mifflin, a Philadelphia merchant, had served in Congress, before becoming a general in the army. He was undistinguished on the battlefield, so Congress appointed him Quartermaster General, in charge of provisioning the army.

"Indeed," said Rush, "and I have written Adams on that very matter. General Washington is simply the puppet on the string of a few incompetent advisors. Washington brings us defeats, while Gates brings us victories.

"General Gates," Rush continued, "runs his army as a well regulated family, and gives us victories at Bennington, Ticonderoga and Saratoga. Compared to Washington and his uniformed mob of an army at Valley Forge, who has been outgeneraled and twice beaten. Gates is the pinnacle of military glory. We must replace Washington with Gates!"

Washington was constantly asking Congress for the necessities the army needed. There had only been occasional rations of meat and other foodstuffs coming into camp. Some even spoiled when it arrived. Blankets were scarce and those the men used were threadbare. A full one-quarter of the men in Washington's Army had no shoes at all, and many had not even one pair of socks. Most men wore badly tattered uniforms, and there seemed to be no new uniforms scheduled to replace the old ones.

It seemed that every request Washington made for vital supplies was seen in Congress as a low priority. Congress' attentions were turned to Paris, and the work being done by the diplomats Ben Franklin and Arthur Lee, making America's case for military and financial aid. Silas Deane had been recalled, and John Adams was then sailing to France as his replacement.

The troops at Valley Forge were making due on the barest of diets. With little or no food provisions, their daily diet became a concoction of boiled water and tasteless flour, called fire cake. If they were lucky, they might supplement their meal with a rabbit or other small game animal that got into their crosshairs. Occasionally, a deer might wander into camp and end up on a spit over the campfire.

Washington knew he was facing a real threat to his leadership of the army. Gates' victory at Saratoga made people remember only Washington's defeats at Brandywine, Germantown and the loss of Philadelphia. They had forgotten the removal of the British from Boston, the victories at Trenton and Princeton, and ridding New Jersey of the Redcoats altogether. His old friend and fellow Virginian, Richard Henry Lee, had even turned on him, joining the growing number of members of Congress supporting Gates.

Washington could hardly wait for Martha to arrive, as she was always the one person he could turn to when things frustrated him. But her plans were not to arrive until early March. He penned a letter to Mount Vernon, all but demanding she change her plans, and join him at Valley Forge as early as possible.

On the second day of the new year of 1778, General Benedict Arnold rode into Valley Forge to meet with Washington. He walked with the support of crutches, as he was still convalescing from a broken leg. At the Battle of Bemis Heights, the final victory at Saratoga, his horse was shot out from under him and his leg was broken in his fall. Wills Winkman showed him into Washington's office in the Potts House, where Washington was meeting with Lord Stirling, LaFayette and Hamilton.

"General," Arnold began the discussion he had asked for, "there is a dangerous cabal being formed against you."

"Go ahead," said Washington, "what do you know of it?"

"It centers around generals Horatio Gates and Thomas Conway," Arnold started his report. "Gates promotes himself to his friends in Congress as the one man who should be leading the army. Conway is simply an undistinguished general, an Irishman who once fought in the French Army, who seeks self-aggrandizement, and knows Gates shall give it to him."

"I care little about the politics of war," responded Washington. "I have dealt with Conway as best I could, opposing his pleadings to become a major general. When there are American-born men, who have earned such a promotion, I would never agree to the promotion of a foreign-born. We have been saddled with too many foreign generals, sent to us by Silas Deane as it is." He realized LaFayette was at the table and turned to him. "Please take no offense, marquis."

"None taken, sir," said LaFayette. "I agree with your premise."

"And your opposition to Conway is well known," Arnold continued. "After your refusal, Conway, being embarrassed, submitted his resignation, but Gates' friends in Congress had the letter sent to the war board, now controlled by Gates. The board refused the letter, gave Conway his promotion and moreso, appointed him Inspector General of the entire army!"

"My word means little to Congress and the war board," Washington said, "I cannot but get food, blankets and shoes for my army."

"And they continue their plotting for Gates," Arnold said.

"Gates has falsely reported to Congress about Burgoyne's surrender at Saratoga. He names himself, and himself alone for the victories. That credit belongs to his commanders in the field, Benjamin Lincoln, Henry Dearborn, Enoch Poor, Dan Morgan, and yes, myself.

"It was all Morgan and I could do to convince Gates to leave the fortress, and defend against Burgoyne's first advance, lest we be victims of a siege. But then Gates simply sat in his tent on the safe right flank at Freeman's Farm. He sent me along with Dearborn and Morgan to the left flank, knowing that was where the action would be. Gates gave us no orders ... no set strategy. In his own words, we were to do what we could.

"We did. Morgan's sharpshooters, from behind trees, carefully picked off all of the British officers and three-fourths of the artillerymen.

I led my men and Dearborn's light infantry to turn back the Redcoats. We stopped the advance, and heroically so, I might humbly add.

"In the weeks between the first advance at Freeman's Farm and the final Battle of Bemis Heights, Gates sent the Congress his false reporting, filled with omissions, taking the full credit, and naming no other names, even for commendation.

"His only strategy does seems to be defend or retreat," added Lord Stirling. "His mind is that of the European military thinker."

"Which is no way to think of war in North America," added Frenchman, LaFayette.

"I know General Gates well," said Washington, in an exasperated manner. "He and General Charles Lee have always begrudged my being named. They, the two of them, have been thorns in my side, always attempting to belittle my judgments and disagree, even disobey any strategy I might put forth."

"Saratoga was won not because of any assistance from Gates," said Arnold flatly, "but in spite of him. At Freeman's Farm, Gates retreated the right flank at the first sight of the Union Jack coming far off through the wheat field. I told him so, and likened him to someone's granny, running with her skirts flapping in the breeze, after seeing a rat in the hen house. The men started calling him 'Granny Gates', and the first time Gates heard it, he relieved me of my command."

Everyone broke out in laughter.

"We do not laugh at you being relieved of your command," Washington explained with a chuckle, "simply the vision of General Gates in a granny's dress, running is but too amusing."

"Based upon the report to Congress Gates sent," continued Arnold, "Gates has now been made head of the Board of War, his first step in replacing you. That is the cabal."

"I agree, Arnold," said Stirling. "I have had reports from Gates' army. I heard you, after being relieved of all command and ordered to remain in the fort at Bemis Heights, took to the field and led the two assaults of the British redoubts that clinched the victory. Granny Gates does indeed puff-up his undistinguished performance, and does take credit for other brave men's actions."

"General Stirling, as well, has intercepted a letter written by Conway to Gates," Washington noted, pulling the parchment letter from his coat pocket. "There is one line I would like to insert into our discussion." He put on his spectacles and read: *"Heaven must surely be determined to save your country, or the weakling General Washington and his band of bad counselors would have surely ruined it."*

"In France," LaFayette spoke, "what Conway and this Granny Gates are planning, we call a *coup d'etat*. But opinions now against you, *mon general*, would be changed, if a letter such as this, with the bold insubordinations and personal attacks against you it contains, would become public. The army and the people would come to your aid."

"Indeed! Their plot can be foiled with Conway's letter to Gates made public," said Arnold.

"Simply sending it to Congress will not change a thing," added Washington's aide-de-camp Alexander Hamilton. "It needs to be seen and read by the citizens."

"You would have me air the dirty laundry of the army, to all…to the citizens…to the enemy, that we fight amongst us?" Washington asked.

"It is laundry in need of a good airing," added Stirling.

"If it is not aired publically, and soon," Arnold said, "it will be the undoing of the army, and there shall be no victory for our independence."

The room remained silent for several long minutes as Washington paced the floor, pondering what had been said, trying to see the consequences of whatever action he might take.

"When the army assembles for the evening parade," Washington finally broke the silence, "I shall read the entire Conway letter to them all.

"Lt. Winkman," Washington continued, handing the original letter to his secretary, "make copies of the original, and see that they are delivered to each member of Congress, each general in the army, here and in the north. I wish to give this matter a public airing, but within our very own family. I wish not for it to come from my hand to the press. If others think that appropriate, so be it. That shall not come from me."

Wills knew Washington's frustration, seeing it first hand on a daily basis at the Potts House. He sent weekly letters to Priscilla in Cambridge. Her two sisters had married and moved out from the house on

Landsdowne Street. Wills and Priscilla's son, Rennie, would soon be three years old. They now had a daughter Wills had yet to see. Wills had received a letter at the Broadway headquarters in New York that informed him he had made her pregnant once more, in those fifteen short days and nights between the birth of their son, and when he left with the army.

Wills wrote home from Valley Forge the day of the meeting with Benedict Arnold. He wrote of the conditions at the camp, and asked questions about both his children. He knew that day was little Victoria's first birthday.

"I do wish you could be laying beside me this night," Wills wrote, "but I am happy you are safe, well-fed and warm in your bed at home in Cambridge. I would not have you suffering with the few wives, sweethearts and sisters of some of the men who follow the army. Their conditions are worse, by far, than I described they are for the brave men in camp. Perhaps this new year shall bring us victory, and an end to this war. My victory will be my return to you and to our bed!"

Clark's Journey

Before Clark headed out for Williamsburg in mid-October, he divided his army into three companies of fifty men each. He left his second-in-command, Captain Benjamin Logan, with a fourth company of twenty men on Corn Island. Logan would continue overseeing the spying operations across the river during Clark's absence. Clark was anxious for intelligence from up the Wabash, around the fort and settlement at Vincennes, and up the Miami River in the Ohio Country, toward the ultimate prize, Fort Detroit. The three other companies would protect the three settlements most prone to attack, Bryan's Station, Boonesborough and Harrodstown.

The three companies left Corn Island on October 12th, and arrived at Bryan's Station on the south bank of Elkhorn Creek. There, Clark gave Tom Macneal the rank of captain, and one of the companies, which would encamp at Bryan's Station. Forty cabins had been built by the expedition of North Carolinians led by the four Bryan brothers, Morgan, James, William and Joseph. Bryan's Station also was where the traveling church of Tolliver Craig was centered. The settlers gladly welcomed the additional men.

Clark asked Jacky Macneal to join his escort party to Williamsburg, but Jacky declined, wanting to stay back with Tom, and hopefully learn from the settlers the skills of distilling whiskey. Davy Danielson and Jamie Salyers jumped at the opportunity to be among Clark's escorts. Davy had still not found his family. Maybe on the journey he might find them.

For the remaining two companies, Clark placed Ebenezer Zane as a captain of one, and led them south for eighteen miles to Boonesborough, while Kenton led the other company southwest for to Harrodstown.

After two nights at Bryan's Station, Clark took his dozen-man escort down the Wilderness Road through the Cumberland Gap into southwestern Virginia. There the party headed north along the Great Valley Road, which ran up the west front of the Blue Ridge Mountains. At the small settlement of Lynchburg, Clark's party headed east. After a month of travel, Clark led his men down Duke of Gloucester Street in Williamsburg, and pitched their tents on the grounds of the Capitol.

Governor Patrick Henry was pleased to see Clark and learn of the events on the Kentucky frontier. Henry invited Clark to a meeting on December tenth with three of the governor's chief advisors, George Mason, George Wythe and Thomas Jefferson.

"I came here to speak with you, seeking permission to open a new war in the West," Clark said, stating the reason for his trek to Williamsburg, "and easily win all the western lands for independence. The total loss of the west to King George will bring him to the bargaining table, with or without France or Spain's aid."

Clark went on to discuss the results of his spying operations based on Corn Island. The governor was impressed with the large numbers of French Canadians residing in the Illinois Country, and how loosely defended the British frontier forts seemed to be. It was well known how bitterly the French hated the English. It was only natural to assume once Americans took the forts in Illinois, the local French-speaking settlers would greet the liberators, and join in the American cause.

Clark told of the atrocities suffered at the hands of the Shawnee, due to the influence of Governor Henry Hamilton, the "Hair Buyer," and the threat to the Kentucky settlements from Fort Detroit.

"I have done what my orders call for," said Clark. "I come across the Blue Ridge to ask for new orders. I need your approval for my army to march north across the Ohio River, into the Illinois Country, and take Kaskaskia, Cahokia, Vincennes and eventually, Fort Detroit."

Distilling Whiskey Along Elkhorn Creek

Before winter set in, Jacky and Tom built themselves a small cabin on the banks of Elkhorn Creek. Most days, new friends they had at Bryan's Station visited them. Two of their closest friends were the elderly Baptist preacher, Tolliver Craig, and his wife, Polly. The Craig cabin was only about fifty yards from Jacky and Tom's cabin, separated by the Craig garden of corn, beans, potatoes and other vegetables.

Another friend was Joshua Slone. Joshua was twenty-three and lived with his wife, Becky, and their infant son, Samuel, a few cabins further up Elkhorn Creek. Joshua had built a gristmill on the creek to grind the grains, grown at the settlement, into flour. He also had a still where he distilled whiskey from his take of each corn crop he ground for his neighbors into cornmeal. Jacky was anxious to learn the skill of distilling whiskey, and Joshua Slone was more than happy to trade an apprenticeship for free labor at the mill.

The first few months at the Kentucky settlements, there was no raiding by Blackfish, Chickseeka, and the Shawnee. The new year of 1778 was certain to bring more raids to the Kentucky frontier. Clark was not expected back from Williamsburg until spring, hopefully with word of expeditions across the Ohio, blessed by Governor Patrick Henry. In the meantime, the new militiamen would protect the Kentucky settlements.

"When we get back ta Annie's Port," Jacky said to Tom, as they slipped into their bed on Christmas Eve, "we'll order up the copper sheets and pipes we need from Nate Nevers."

"You do realize we may not see Annie's Port for at least a year," Tom reminded Jacky.

"That just gives me more time ta get even more skills at becomin' the foremost distiller o' spirits on the frontier," Jacky said with a broad smile, wrapping his bare arms around Tom. "Every settler a headin' west'll want a whole case o' 'Macneal's Old Raven Rock' ta lighten their load down the Ohio."

"You've already named our whiskey?" Tom asked, giggling, as he slid his hand down beneath the quilt.

"Yea," said Jacky. "What d'ya think 'bout it 'Macneal's Old Raven Rock'... 'blended whiskey' ... 'the finest on the frontier!'"

In early February, news came to Bryan's Station. Jonathan Patrick and Bryce Shepherd, two of Ebenezer Zane's men, came into Bryan's Station from Boonesborough.

"Dan'l Boone's been taken captive by the Shawnee!" Jonathan Patrick announced. "Him and about thirty others were taken captive."

Morgan Bryan was stunned. The Indians were raiding even as the snows were falling and even with the re-enforcements Colonel Clark had sent. Bryan's Station was the closest large settlement to the Shawnee villages in the Ohio Country. He wondered when his settlement on Elkhorn Creek would be raided?

"Do we know where Boone an' the others've been taken?" asked Morgan.

"All we know is all but two o' Boone's party at the salt licks was captured," said Jonathan. "Boone set out with thirty men the last week o' January, ta bring back salt an' game to Booneborough. Boone an' most o' the men left the salt party ta hunt game. Boone was captured an' taken back ta the camp at the salt licks. The two left stayin' in camp, hid, but seen it all."

"They say Boone promised ta give up Boonesborough if'n the Shawnee wouldn't lay siege ta the fort now," said Bryce Shepherd. "Boone said he'd surrender Boonesborough in the spring, an' gave no resistance ta turnin' his self an' all his men over ta the Shawnee."

"That sure don't soun' like Dan'l Boone," said Morgan. "He's no lover o' the Shawnee, that's a fact! He's justa buyin' time, mark m'words!"

"Well," Bryce continued, "the two men who were outta sight hidin' in the bushes, when the Shawnee were in the camp, sure said Boone told the Indians all whites would leave Kentucky in the spring."

"Well," said Morgan, "he must've said such a thing ta trick ole Blackfish. We gotta send out a search party an' find Boone."

"We're a waitin' ta hear from Benjamin Logan at Corn Island," said Jonathan. "We sent two messengers to him. He's Clark's second, and he may already have news o' Boone's whereabouts from his spies."

Jacky and Tom were invited to Sunday dinner at the Baptist preacher, Tolliver and Polly Craig's house, the first Sunday in March. Joshua and Becky Slone were baptized in Elkhorn Creek after the preacher finished his preachin'.

The young Slones had been saved at prayers with Preacher Craig on Wednesday night. They wanted to be baptized on Sunday, so they could claim Jesus Christ as their Lord and Saviour. Just after sun up Sunday morning, Jacky and Tom went to the creek with axes to break up the ice in Elkhorn Creek, and allow a path into the water for Preacher Craig and the new children of God to be baptized by submersion in the icy cold waters.

"I just don't understand why they couldn't go ahead an' be accepted as Christian, an' be baptized when there was no ice in the creek," Jacky said, as he swung the ax against the iced-over creek, "maybe sometime in June or July."

"According to Preacher Tolliver," Tom said, "you are to repent and be baptized, and when the spirit moves you to be baptized, you best be baptized."

"Well then" Jacky answered, "I guess if they both don't catch the pneumonia and die, that must prove it's the way o' salvation. I was sprinkled with holy water in the Catholic Church back in Boston. What about you, Tom."

"I never really paid much attention to religion, though I know there had to be some higher power helping me back after the massacre, other than just you and old John Adams. And I know another thing, I do like Preacher Craig's preaching."

"That was one fine service we had today," Jacky said to Preacher Craig, as they sat around the Craig's cabin. Polly tended to the table and all four waited for Joshua, Becky and baby Samuel to arrive in dry clothes.

"It is always a glorious day when another sinner becomes a saint," said Tolliver. "When are you boys gonna accept Jesus Christ and let him inta your hearts?"

"Well," said Jacky, "God has surely blessed Tom and me, and pulled us both out of a mess or two."

"One of these days, preacher ... one of these days," Tom smiled at the old man. "If you don't mind me asking, how many years has the Lord blessed you?"

"It'll be seventy-four years the eighth day of May comin'," said the old preacher, "but I didn't hear the lord knockin' at my heart's door till, twelve years ago. In 1766, Polly an' I both embraced the scriptural truth o' the necessity of man ta be born again in Christ Jesus fer the remission o' sin. That's not a practice accepted in Virginy these days."

"How so?" asked Tom.

"The Anglican Church is the only church recognized in Virginy," Preacher Craig lamented. "Just like them Puritans up in New England are intolerant of others' beliefs an' burned at the stake or stoned ta death nonbelievers as witches, just a few years back. Three of m' sons, Elijah, Lewis, an' Joseph, are all Baptis' preachers like me, an' held ta this day in jail at Fredericksburg, fer a preaching the gospel o' the Baptis' faith."

"An' Gov'nor Patrick Henry hisself," inserted Polly, wringing her hands in her apron after setting the last bowl of steaming vegetables on the table, "is defendin' 'em all three in the court, an' he shall surely win their freedom."

"It ain't neither Patrick Henry, Polly," Tolliver said, aggravated. "It's that Thomas Jefferson feller a defendin' 'em. Patrick Henry's the one what had 'em all three locked up."

The door opened and in walked the newest saints, Joshua and Becky Slone, and their baby boy.

"You're jus' in time," said Preacher Craig, rising from his chair. "Hang up yer coats an' join us at the table m'lovely Polly has set for us."

They all took seats at the oak table, Becky laying baby Samuel in a small cradle near the hearth.

"Brother Joshua," Preacher Craig asked, "would our newest saint lead us in askin' God ta bless our meal?"

Baron von Steuben

Through the early weeks of 1778, the situation remained miserably unchanged at Valley Forge for the Continental Army. Provisions of food, blankets, shoes and clothing, promised by the Board of War and Congress, arrived only sporadically. As the winter months grew colder in February and March, sicknesses and disease began claiming many of the soldiers. Typhoid, jaundice, dysentery, pneumonia and smallpox, along with simple exposure, killed over two and a half thousand of the twelve thousand troops encamped with Washington at Valley Forge.

After the letter from Thomas Conway to Gates was read in public and circulated, most of the support members of Congress had the so-called Conway Cabal had lost enthusiasm. Gates was still head of the Board of War. Conway tried the ploy that had worked for him when Washington first opposed his promotion. He submitted his letter of resignation to Congress. This time Congress accepted it, and Conway had no position at all in the army.

On March fifteenth, a sentry at the Potts House came inside and informed Wills Winkman a carriage, escorted by eight horsemen of a Pennsylvania militia regiment, was approaching Washington's headquarters. Winkman went out the door and watched as the ornate carriage pulled to a halt.

An officer of the Pennsylvania militia climbed down from his seat beside the driver. He opened the carriage door, and out stepped three younger officers, dressed in European-looking uniforms. When they had disembarked, out came a beautiful and sleek Italian greyhound on a leash. Holding the other end of the dog's leash was a short and rotund man, with a round face and powdered wig, wearing an elaborately ornate uniform. The Pennsylvanian turned and saluted Winkman.

"Captain Thomas Richter, 23rd Pennsylvania Regiment," the officer introduced himself. "I wish to present Freidrich Wilhelm Baron von Steuben of Prussia, with letters of introduction from ambassador Benjamin Franklin to His Excellency General George Washington, Commander-in-Chief of the Continental Army."

Wills returned Captain Richter's salute.

"General Washington will be most happy to meet the baron. He has been advised of his pending arrival," Wills said.

"May I also present Captain Benjamin Walker," Richter added, as the good-looking, blonde twenty-four year old took one pronounced step forward and saluted Wills. "Captain Walker is aide-de-camp to the baron, who speaks no English. Captain Walker is fluent in both languages, and serves as the baron's aide and translator."

"Welcome Captain Walker," Wills said, returning the salute, "You, as well, are most welcome at Valley Forge." Wills turned to Richter, "and the other guests, Captain?"

"These are the baron's staff, Louis de Pontierre, a second aide-de-camp, and Etienne Duponceau, the baron's sceretary. The dog on the baron's leash is Azor."

Wills stooped down and patted the greyhound on his head, "You are certainly a beautiful dog, Azor. You are most welcomed as well."

"The dog accompanies the baron everywhere," Richter whispered, "even to the latrine."

Wills smiled, and led the guests inside the headquarters.

Washington had been anxious for von Steuben's arrival, ever since receiving a letter from his old friend Ben Franklin in Paris. Washington had Wills send for his aides-de-camp, LaFayette, and Hamilton, as well as General Anthony Wayne, to join in the initial meeting with von Steuben and his young staff. Washington led his guests into the parlor to get acquainted while they awaited the others. Azor found a comfortable hooped rug in front of the blazing hearth to lay upon as the humans entertained themselves with glasses of sour mash poured by Wills.

"Tell the baron just how much we have looked forward to his arrival at Valley Forge," Washington directed Captain Walker. After translating Washington's greeting, German phrases came forth from the short, fat Prussian aristocrat, who appeared to be about the same age as Washington. Captain Walker translated the German's phrases back to Washington.

"The baron is most pleased to be here, general," said Walker, in an accent appearing to be proper king's English, "and is extremely honored to be able to assist the great General George Washington and his American army."

During the several minutes in the parlor, Washington learned, through the most able translator, the baron had served on the general staff of Europe's greatest military mind, King Frederick the Great of Prussia, and had been trained, with only twelve others, by the king himself at Frederick's famed Special Class for the Art of War at Berlin.

For fifteen years, until 1776, von Steuben had developed his skills on the general staff of the Prussian Army, helping build and streamline the army to its current greatness. Von Steuben possessed various abilities, not available in America at the time, which Washington could use to build a successful American army.

In 1776, due to von Steuben's own work, he had actually worked himself out of a position altogether. The baron's work had recognized there were too many officers for the streamlined new army. He found himself out of a position, so he headed to Paris, to get an introduction to the American diplomat Benjamin Franklin, then sailed from the Mediterranean port of Marseille to Boston. He traveled from Boston overland to join Washington's army.

LaFayette was extremely pleased to meet von Steuben, and the two conversed together in German and in French. Washington assigned Hamilton and Wayne to meet daily with von Steuben over the next two weeks to formalize a plan for the training of the Continental Army. Washington hoped the initial training would be ready to begin before the end of the month. He wanted to be able to leave his winter camp sometime late in May or early June, for a new season of warfare with a new, disciplined and well-trained fighting army, prepared and ready to defeat the Redcoats of King George.

Washington escorted the baron on a tour of the camp to show him the field where the men drilled, as best they could. Captain Walker went along to translate for the baron.

"Where are the latrines?" Walker interpreted the baron's first question.

"I am afraid," Washington admitted, "there really are none. A few of the men have built makeshift facilities on their own near their cabins."

"Where do your men shit and piss?" came von Steuben's crude question, "and what becomes of the filthy waste?"

Washington was speechless, having no legitimate response. The men of the Continental Army simply squatted in the woods, or urinated behind their cabins. The waste simply laid on the frozen ground.

"There is no wonder thousands of your men are ill and dying," the baron replied through Walker.

"This is not acceptable!" shot von Steuben. "In order to have men to train, we need healthy men, not men with dysentery! I see I must also train you, General Washington, in the building of an encampment, following guidelines for sanitation. That is a must."

"We attempted to lay out orderly street grids for the cabins," Washington tried to take at least some credit.

"Very well," spoke the baron, "it is a good start. But kitchen huts need to be on the one end of the streets sloping down toward the latrines at the far end, faraway from the food preparations. None of those, as you say 'makeshift' latrines shall be built, and those already erected must be taken down and filled in immediately. Our enemy is an army of bastard Redcoats, which we can defeat. We cannot defeat an enemy such as smallpox!"

"I shall see to it immediately," Washington agreed.

On the tour, the baron was pleased with the field Washington showed him where the training would take place. It was a large, flat, grazing land with trees butting against its eastern border. Von Steuben selected sites at the edge of the trees for two cabins to be built. One cabin, a large one, would be his field headquarters and private sleeping quarters. The second would be much smaller, and house his personal staff. Washington assigned Private Peter Francisco to select men to build the cabins, following directions from Walker. In the meantime, von Steuben and his three aides would use two rooms in the Potts House.

Seven days later, the two cabins on the edge of the pine forest were ready, and the Prussians moved out of the Potts House. That same day another carriage, escorted again by Captain Thomas Richter of the 23rd Pennsylvania Regiment arrived.

Out stepped Martha Washington and one black servant, Alexander. The general was happy to welcome his wife to stay with him during the final weeks at Valley Forge. He was also grateful her arrival coincided with the baron's moving out of the rooms at the Potts House.

"I have come to make life more agreeable for you," said Martha, as the general embraced her when she stepped down from the carriage, "and to make it much more agreeable for me as well."

Chapter Twelve

The Tide Turns

Baron von Steuben designed the plan for training the Continental Army. Alexander Hamilton and Anthony Wayne, appeasing Washington, sat at the table, basically nodding their heads in agreement to whatever the baron said, through Benjamin Walker, his translator.

The plan the baron devised was based on Frederick the Great's "Special Class for the Art of War", where von Steuben had been a student in Berlin, sixteen years before, and an instructor afterwards. There would be extensive training in marching, field maneuvers, and battle strategies, along with the effective use of bayonets.

The plan called for the baron to select a company of one hundred twenty of the most capable officers, to be the first trained in four smaller thirty-man units. "Men learn better when trained in smaller units," von Steuben professed through Benjamin Walker. The model company was to train two hours each day, every day except Sunday. The model company's training would last four weeks. Each of the officers in the company would then train up to one hundred twenty regular soldiers, the same way they had been trained, until the full army was ready for the battles of summer.

"We can have a completely trained army by the fourth day of June ... at the latest," the baron said.

Washington was well pleased with the training plan, and immediately agreed with it. He was extremely pleased, as he sat down to dinner with Martha the evening before the training of the model company would begin.

"That is all very well and good, I suppose, George," said Martha, in reaction to his exuberance with the thought of real training for his army about to begin, "but do you truly trust this man you cannot even converse with, without the interpretations from another?"

"Oh, the baron is indeed a difficult man, Martha," replied Washington, "but he is the one man in all the world who can see just where we are now failing, and change that for us. He is a master of modern warfare, trained himself by the greatest master, Frederick the Great."

"He is such an odd sort," added Martha, shaking her head and taking a fork full of noodles from her plate. "He has such an odd manner about him."

"Well, my dearest," Washington said, "he is German." They both giggled and concentrated on their roast beef.

The next day, the first forty men the baron was to personally train, were assembled on the field promptly at eight o'clock. Von Steuben came out of his cabin, dressed in full Prussian military uniform and regalia, the huge and sleek greyhound, Azor, on a leash he held in his gloved hand. The American soldiers formed on the field in front of him were dressed in their tattered uniforms. Washington had received word Congress was sending twelve thousand new uniforms by the first of May.

Walker stood beside von Steuben to call out the marching orders, and to interpret any instructions.

At one point, early during the morning drills, von Steuben called out an order, *"Recht gesicht!"* and Walker interpreted, "Right face!"

The lines marching on the field followed the order, with about one third of the men turning the wrong way, and bumping into their comrades. Von Steuben, who had a short temper, fumed.

"Here! Come swear for me!" he said in English words with heavy Germanic accents, one of the few English phrases he had taught himself. He immediately started swearing at the offending soldiers in German,

"*Du bist nichts als ein heards von disesed Schweinegrippe!*" as Walker translated, word for word: "You are nothing but a heard of diseased swine!

"*Schweine! Alle von euch! Schweine!... Wer weil nicht eure Arsche aus deine Titten!*" "Pigs! All of you! Pigs!... Who know not your asses from your tits!"

"*Wenn Sie wissen nicht Ihrem Recht aus Ihrem Links...*"

"If you know not your right from your left..."

"*...wie zum Tuefel soll ich dich lehren ... zu toten das verdammtes Rotrocke?*"

"...how the Hell am I to teach you... to kill the fucking Redcoats?"

"*Recht gesicht! Recht gesicht! Recht verdammt gesicht!*"

"...Right face! Right face! Right fucking face!"

The baron got his point across.

Running the Gauntlet

Twelve of the white captives from the Blue Licks were taken to the Shawnee main town of Chalagawtha, in the Ohio Country, along the Scioto River. There they would either be adopted into Shawnee families, or be burned at the stake or boiled in a pot. The other eighteen captives were given to the renegade white man, Simon Girty. Girty took the captives to Hair Buyer Hamilton at Fort Detroit, and would bring the bounty paid for the captives to Chalagawtha in a few weeks.

When Boone and the other eleven arrived at Chalagawtha, they were taken into a lodge and stripped naked. Outside, the Shawnee braves formed a gauntlet, a pathway with braves on both sides of the path, each holding willow branches in their hands. The captives were ordered to run naked down the pathway, passing in front of each of the more than a hundred braves with their threatening sticks. The captives were told that if they made the run without falling to the ground from being struck by the sticks, they would live and be adopted. If the stick-wielding braves forced any of the captives to their knees, the fallen captives would be burned alive at the stake.

"I've sure heard tell o' this," said Boone to his fellow captives. "Whatever ya do, keep yer footin' an' don't ya dare fall down, even on one knee. They'd really like ta see ya burn, an' I don't much like the idea o' bein' the only white man left here."

"Dan'l," said one of the men, Perry Higby, in a shaky voice, "ya gotta run first so's we can see how ta do it."

"Doubt I'll have any say in the matter," Boone said, "just do ever'thin' ya can ta stay on yer feet."

Two braves came in and took one of the naked captives at a time, leaving the rest inside, not able to watch their comrades run the gauntlet. Boone was the last to be taken out to run and attempt to evade as many stinging willow branches being swung at him as possible.

When the ordeal was over, Boone and nine others had successfully run the gauntlet, and were immediately adopted into Shawnee families. Two had fallen during their run. Perry Higby and Hugh Gray were bound and taken to a small lodge, guarded until their penalty would be extracted.

Boone was led to the chief, Blackfish, who had decided he would adopt the frontiersman into his own family.

"I will call you Shelk-to-wee, Big Turtle," Blackfish spoke to Boone in the English tongue he learned from Simon Girty and other English frontiersmen. "You are now my son." The chief placed his hands, one on each of Boone's shoulders and smiled. "You will shed the ways of the white man and live as a Shawnee."

"Might yer new son speak?" Boone boldly asked Blackfish.

"Speak my son," replied the chief.

"I'm sure honored ta have such a great warrior as you select me as his own son," Boone spoke. "I'll wear the buckskins an' robes o' the Shawnee, an' wear the name Shelk-to-wee. I ask but one thing," Boone bravely spoke.

"Speak my son," answered Blackfish.

"The captives ta be burnt at the stake and sacrificed ta Manitou, are good men with good hearts," Boone spoke. "But they are ta be burnt ta death 'cause they could not run the gauntlet. Is a good man's life o' so little value in the eyes o' my new family...o' my new god, Manitou? I ask my new father ta spare them, an' let them join our new family."

"But, my son, that is the way of the Shawnee," spoke Blackfish proudly.

"Then burn me at the stake too," Boone spoke, "as I will never serve a father, a tribe, or a god who views the life o' any man to be o' such little value."

Blackfish did not speak for several moments, thinking of Boone's words. Finally he spoke, after forming his defense of Shawnee custom in his mind.

"The white man invades our country," Blackfish spoke firmly. "He kills our game. He burns our towns. He kills our braves, our women, our children. If Blackfish frees the captives, Blackfish turns his back on his own people...on the ways we know. I will never do as you ask!"

"Some whites do as ya say," Boone answered, "as some Shawnee follow Cornstalk west, but you stay behind. Evil men should be burnt at the stake, but good men should not. Does Manitou expect ya ta kill all who simply can't run the gauntlet? Or does Manitou want ya ta kill the evil man who burns yer towns an' kills yer people? I have never led men ta do so. Those two men have never done so...why should they be put ta death?"

"I will hear no more of this," Blackfish said angrily, waving his hand in front of Boone's face and beginning to turn away.

"My father has heard my promise," Boone spoke. "I'll lead the white settlers back across the eastern mountains, an' give all the lands of Kentucky ta the Shawnee. No more need be put ta death. No more Shawnee...no more white, need ta die. If the two are tied ta the stake and burnt," Boone concluded his plea, "the killing will not end, and the white man will stay on the frontier forcing the Shawnee ta go west of the Wabash."

Blackfish turned back to Boone. "There is wisdom in what you say, Shelk-to-wee," spoke Blackfish. "I will burn no man at the stake this day." He turned and left Boone.

In the following weeks, Boone dressed as a Shawnee, as did all eleven of the captives. They took part in the chores and in hunting for game on the Pickaway Plains. They became friends with many of the Shawnee, and lived as the Shawnee lived.

Chickseeka, his younger sister, Tecumapese, and two younger brothers, Tecumseh and Tenskwatawa, lived in the lodge alongside the lodge of Blackfish. Their parents had both died just after Tenskwatawa's birth two years before.

Boone especially took a liking to the ten year-old boy, Tecumseh. He had a son Tecumseh's age, named Ezra, and started substituting Tecumseh for his son. He taught the young Shawnee boy many skills of the forest, and took Tecumseh off many days to hunt and fish.

Perry Higby and Hugh Gray, the two saved from burning at the stake, had been adopted into Chickseeka's family. Both were becoming attracted to the beautiful Tecumapese.

Tecumapese was a beautiful girl with coal black hair that streamed down to the middle of her back. She had a beautiful oval face, with large dark eyes and luscious lips. She had a sweet spirit that caused her to smile often, and go about her chores singing or humming pleasant melodies. She had been married at age fourteen, and was a widow at age fifteen, with no child. Her husband had been killed during a raiding party into Kentucky. She too soon began to see both Perry and Hugh as possible new husbands.

Boone knew he had to escape and began making plans. He felt certain the Shawnee would wait until late spring, or sometime during the summer months, before getting anxious for Boone to keep his promise.

The Settlement at Sapling Grove

Colonel Clark and his escort party left Williamsburg in mid-March, just after word reached Williamsburg of the capture of Daniel Boone. Governor Henry authorized Clark to "do what you need to do to rid the Ohio, Illinois and Michigan countries of the British and the Shawnee."

As they crossed the Blue Ridge and marched down the Great Valley Road, the dogwood and redbud trees were in full bloom. The early wildflowers were adding their whites and yellows, golds, pinks, and blues to Mother Nature's pallet, as she painted the reborn hillsides and meadows. The robins, starlings and blue jays were singing their songs of springtime.

The Clark party made camp at the small settlement of Sapling Grove, where they left the Great Valley Road, heading west for the Wilderness Road into Kentucky. They were a full day from the southern edge of Boone's Cumberland Gap. About three more days after that, they would be at Boonesborough.

Sapling Grove was the last real settlement before Boonesborough, with about fifty or more cabins with small settler gardens. Davy learned, when they were in Richmond, that Clinton Deerfield, who had married Davy's mama, fled his farm, being hunted down by the constable for killing a man. Davy had, at every settlement on the trek to and from Williamsburg, asked if any of the settlers had heard of a settler by the name of Clinton Deerfield. No one seemed to know anything until their stop in Richmond on their return trip.

"I don't know him," said the trading post owner at Sapling Grove, "but I heard tell o' that name."

"Clinton Deerfield?" Davy asked again with enthusiasm.

"No, not Clinton Deerfield," the settler said. "I heard the name Deerfield though. A woman … believe her name's Deborah. I know she has three young'uns." Davy smiled broadly and looked at his friend Jamie Salyers. He turned to the settler. "Is she here?" Davy asked. "She's my mama."

The settler directed him to the cabin near the creek where the woman lived. Davy and Jamie found it, and saw the woman stooped over in her garden. Davy walked up to her.

"Mama? Is that you?" Davy spoke softly to the stooped over woman. The woman craned her head and looked up at the eighteen year-old young man who had just spoken.

"Davy?" she was barely able to utter. "Is that you boy? Davy, is that you?"

"Yes, Mamma," he said falling to his knees and hugging her. "I have finally found you!"

"Colonel Clark!" Jacky shouted, as he saw the frontiersman approach the settlement on Easter Sunday afternoon. Tom, hearing Jacky's shouts, came running out the door of their cabin.

"Macneal, it's surely good ta see you fellers," Clark said as he approached. "Any sign of Injuns?"

"Not a one," said Jacky. "Where's Davy and Jamie?"

"With Davy's mama back at Sapling Grove," Clark said as Jacky looked at Tom and smiled.

"That is such good news," said Tom with a huge grin.

"Yep," Clark said, "Davy's mama was sure glad ta see him. Her no'account husband kilt a man in Richmond, and headed to'ards Boonesborough. She's now twice a wider, her man bein' eat up by an ole mama bear. When he was kilt, she was with child an' had a boy. That was two years ago. Yep, ole Davy's now the man o' the house with two brothers and a sister. Strappin' good lookin' young'ns fer certain."

"How was your time with Governor Henry?" Tom asked.

"Yeah, we be headin' for the Hair Buyer at Detroit?" asked Jacky.

"After we find Boone," said Clark. "we'll march on the Shawnee towns on our way ta Fort Detroit. Gov'nor Henry approved our plans, an' we're ta run the Redcoats out o' all the frontier lands. Has Zane arrived yet from Harrodstown?"

"Haven't seen him," answered Jacky, "but we weren't expectin' him."

"I sent word from Boonesborough fer him ta meet up with us here today," said Clark. "I wanna move out tomorrow at first light fer Corn Island."

Tom and Jacky started packing up for the march to Corn Island early the next morning. They made arrangements with the Craigs and the Slones to store what they could not carry on the expedition. They would return for their belongings before heading back to Annie's Port in the fall.

Boone's Escape

One day in late April, Boone overheard Blackfish and Chickseeka talking in the Shawnee tongue. With his years on the frontier, Boone had picked up enough of the language to know what they were saying. Blackfish was calling a council of warriors to assemble that evening in the cave at the cliff that overlooked Chalagawtha from the high hills across the Scioto. Blackfish also told Chickseeka, the warriors would wait until early August to raid Boonesborough. Boone knew it was time to escape, and return to Kentucky to warn of the coming attack.

Later that day, he met with each of the captives, one or two at a time, and told them to prepare. Eight of the captives were told to leave soon after supper on walks, with no more than two leaving together. They were told to go west along Paint Creek to the Scioto trail. They were then to go south on the trail for three miles, without speaking or making any noise at all. They were to meet at the old Indian burial mound, and wait till all eight had arrived. Perry Higby would then lead the eight to the west banks of the Scioto, a half-mile away. There they would wait for Boone.

Hugh Gray and the two others would watch to see when the warriors left camp, and then head toward the river. They were to go to the walnut grove, within sight of where the canoes were tied. When Boone gave the sign, each man would untie one of the canoes and follow Boone. If everything went as Boone planned, they would have at least a four-hour jump on their Shawnee pursuers.

As darkness fell, the braves headed down the trail and crossed the river in dugout canoes. Boone watched from the western shore of the Scioto, as the warriors climbed the mountain and disappeared into the cave. Most council meetings went on for several hours. Hopefully this night's would be no different, and their escape would not be discovered until morning.

Boone took a dugout canoe and quietly drifted several yards off the shore of the broad Scioto. Three other canoes followed. When at a safe distance from the town, he began paddling downstream, keeping an eye on the opposite hillside where the council was meeting.

The canoes paddled quietly down the moonlit river, with stars shining brightly in the dark sky. They stopped for Higby and the others, who were there waiting on the bank where Boone told them to wait. Now the journey became more difficult. It would have been easier for one man, like Boone, to easily escape, but he could not have left the others behind. They would have been scalped, burned at the stake, or sold off to the hair buyer at Fort Detroit, out of revenge for Boone's escape. Now, not one captive, but twelve were missing at Chalagawtha. It now was not just one quiet canoe with one man paddling down the Scioto; but four canoes with three men in each. They had to make good time.

As the sun began to rise, Boone's party of captives was at the mouth of the Ohio. He paddled to shore at the broad, flat beach under the high rock that resembled a bird's beak. He had heard Tom and Jacky Macneal refer to it as Raven's Rock. Boone ordered the men to hide the canoes beneath the branches of the low-hanging weeping willows, and found an inviting grassy area about twenty feet back in the forest for the men to get a couple-hours' nap.

A day later, Boone led the men up the buffalo trace that led back to Simon Kenton's cabin. Before they left the riverside, they pitched large boulders into the canoes to sink them. Kenton was no where to be found, so Boone went inside the cabin and fixed the first meal the men had eaten since their escape. He went to the smoke house and took a side of venison from a curing hook, pulled some wild onions and wild carrots, and the men feasted.

Two days later the captives arrived home at Boonesborough.

"A day later, Boone, an'd you'd a sure missed us. I was ready ta lead an expedition against the Shawnee towns up the Miami, and take it all the way ta Hamilton's fort at Detroit," explained Clark, when Boone came to Corn Island five days later. "We were a leavin' at first light."

"I need 'least a half company ta help us defend Boonesborough," said Boone. "We know they're comin', an' by the sound of it, it will be one Hell of a fight."

"I'll send Kenton's company with you to Boonesborough," said Clark. "I want Kenton with me, though."

"What about Bryan's Station and Harrodsburg?" asked Clark.

"Blackfish an' Chickseeka want Boonesborough," said Boone. "If Boonesborough falls, they feel all the other whites will skee-daddle back through the Cumberland Gap.

"If I'm not marching up the Miami in search o' your burly ass," Clark said, "I can go back ta my 'rig'nal plan. Within three weeks I'm settin' off down the Ohio an' takin' them British forts in the Illinois Country. From what our spies tell us, it'll be an easy feat. We'll then go east ta Vincennes an' take that fort, an' hopefully return here in time to join you in defense o' Boonesborough."

"If it works as well as ya think," Boone added, "this war can be won right here on the frontier."

A Sword for Peter

On April 30th, Washington submitted the name of General Friedrich Wilhelm Baron von Steuben to Congress to succeed the departed

General Thomas Conway as Inspector General of the Continental Army. If there had been months of disappointed officers plotting against Washington in the so-called Conway Cabal, that had been laid to rest. Washington also saw much needed supplies now coming regularly to his troops, along with new uniforms, as demanded by von Steuben.

Word of the French alliance with the United States, and recognition as a free and independent nation, came to Valley Forge on May 6th. Washington was anxious to lead his newly trained army into battle within the next few weeks.

Martha was also pleased to see the hurt and anguish on her husband's face replaced by a new boyish and jovial spirit of confidence and anticipation. She knew, as she boarded her carriage for Mount Vernon, that the war season of 1778 would fare much better for her beloved George and his Continental soldiers.

With the French now aligned with the Americans, and pledging financial and military aid to the American cause, the British Prime Minister, Lord North, saw the need to change strategy in the war. With the bulk of the British forces sitting in Philadelphia, Lord North felt, the French Fleet, then in the Caribbean, could easily sail into New York Harbor and isolate his army, one hundred miles away, rendering it useless. General Howe had resigned in late March, and was replaced by Sir Henry Clinton. Lord North ordered his new commander-in-chief to prepare to evacuate Philadelphia, and return, in all haste, to New York, to defend that city from the French Fleet.

Washington's spies in Philadelphia had learned of the plan, and Washington wanted to have his entire army ready to march, chasing Clinton in his exodus. He knew Clinton's travels to New York across New Jersey, would not be rapid. Washington knew Clinton had about fourteen thousand Redcoat and Hessian soldiers, as well as perhaps another thousand Loyalists, and all the baggage of the army. The exodus march would stretch at least ten miles from forward advance to rear guard. His agents in Philadelphia were assigned the task of obtaining details of when the army of the Redcoats would be evacuating Philadelphia. When Clinton would begin his march, Washington would be ready to begin his the following day.

Shortly after General Benedict Arnold left Valley Forge when he had visited Washington there in February, his doctors in New York advised amputation, but Arnold protested, and opted instead for a painful operation to attempt to mend the severed bones and reset them. It had been a long period of healing, but heal it did. He arrived in his carriage at the Potts House as the army was planning to break camp.

"What a welcome surprise, General Arnold!" Washington said, rising from his seat to shake hands with Arnold as Wills showed him in.

"There was indeed a time when even I wondered if ever again I would be returning to my country's service," Arnold said, as he shook hands with the commander-in-chief.

Pleased as Washington was to see General Arnold once more, he now wondered how best to use the man, the hero of Saratoga, who had such limited use of his legs. He no longer was a horseman. He only traveled painfully by carriage. He walked with the support of crutches or, on good days, with two sturdy walking sticks. He could not effectively command a regiment in the field. The army was soon to march into heated battle in just a matter of days. What was Washington to do with Benedict Arnold?

"Arnold could command a non-combatant force," spoke John Laurens.

Laurens was the twenty-four year-old son of Henry Laurens, a member of Congress from South Carolina. He had been sent to London and Switzerland for his education, and due to pressure from his father and, out of pity for the poor girl, married Martha Manning, the daughter of Laurens' London agent. Within a few weeks of his marriage, he sailed back to Charleston in 1776 with his father, leaving his new wife, newly pregnant, in London.

John accompanied his father to Philadelphia for the session of Congress, but, over his father's protests, left Philadelphia to join Washington before the battle of Brandywine. After the way Laurens performed at Brandywine, and later at Germantown, he was made a lieutenant colonel. At Hamilton's suggestion, Washington appointed Laurens to his staff as a third aide-de-camp, along with Hamilton and LaFayette.

"When Clinton and the Redcoats evacuate Philadelphia in a few days, and Congress returns," added Laurens, "we shall need a military commander of the city we can depend upon for the city's defenses."

"I agree," said Hamilton. "General Arnold has served us well in battle, and has a most affable personality that will be well-received by the citizens there."

"He would see it as the important position it is," added LaFayette. "He would not think for a moment he was being drummed out of the army."

"I agree as well," said Washington. "I will speak to General Arnold about this at supper."

On May 28th, Washington mounted his white stallion, Nelson. His high command of Generals LaFayette, Greene, Stirling, Wayne, Charles Lee, and Baron von Steuben, and their aides-de-camp, mounted up with him. They rode to the training field together for the morning muster of the troops.

The various regimental and brigade commanders, in their new uniforms, marshaled their men into ranks, and paraded them before Washington and the general staff. With all eleven thousand men standing at attention before the mounted generals, Washington spoke.

"I see before me this morning," Washington said, "men of an army capable of fighting and winning a war for the independence of the American nation. For the first time since its conception, the Continental Army stands ready to enter its fourth season of war, trained ably and prepared well, and in striking new uniforms, ready to face the most powerful land army ever assembled in the history of man.

"We will face the enemy," Washington went on, "and they shall be ours."

A cheer rose up to the heavens, as the men of Washington's army accepted the words of encouragement and congratulations.

Washington went on to congratulate Baron von Steuben through his aide and translator, Benjamin Walker. Then Washington spoke once more in a voice of sheer authority.

"Private Peter Francisco, 3rd Virginia Regiment, front and center."

As the seven-foot tall private, stunned at being singled out, began making his way to the front, Washington reined Nelson several steps forward. The Marquis de LaFayette, hearing this as his cue, dismounted his steed, and walked to a spot alongside Washington. Peter stood in front of the generals and saluted. Washington and LaFayette returned the salute.

"Private Francisco," Washington spoke, "I am well aware of the valor you exhibited at the Battle of Brandywine, when you took a

Hessian musket ball at Chadd's Ford, and would have been left for dead had it not been for the actions of your fellow comrades. Your rescuers remembered how you had performed the similar rescue of your captain in King Street at Trenton.

"You were saved to fight again. And this army is proud to have you standing amongst us this day, prepared to continue with us in our noble fight. Others of this army have shown similar valor and suffered similar injury. Others are to be so-honored this day as well. I have selected to honor you myself." Washington dismounted from Nelson and walked to LaFayette. The marquis handed him a medal with a purple and white ribbon.

Washington pinned the newly commissioned medal to Peter's new uniform coat, after reading the inscription on the back of the medal.

"Let it be known by all...He who wears the Military Order of the Purple Heart has give of his blood in the defense of his homeland and shall forever be revered by his fellow countrymen."

Washington stepped back and saluted Peter who humbly returned the salute.

Two men stepped forward to LaFayette, carrying a huge sword, near six feet in length, in a leather sheath and shoulder strap. Washington again began to speak.

"General, Marquis de LaFayette, who befriended you as the two of you convalesced together from your wounds at Brandywine, suggested the standard issue saber of the army appears as a table knife in your giant hands, alongside your extreme height and girth. He suggested, and I assented, that there be a special saber forged for you to more effectively wield upon the battlefield. Please accept this special sword as a mere token of your country's gratitude for your service thus far. Wield it well."

The Beautiful Peggy Shippen

Peggy Shippen was a beautiful eighteen year-old, known to and admired by all society in the city of Philadelphia. She lived with her widowed father, Judge Edward Shippen, in his elegant home on Chestnut Street, just a few doors down the street from the home of Benjamin Franklin.

On the first day of June, the late spring sun was a bright and warm harbinger of the coming summer. Peggy dressed in her favorite pink and white flowery dress, with white lace around the neck and sleeves. She put on a large, broad-rimmed hat with cherry-colored silk ribbons tied under her chin, grabbed her pink parasol and headed down the stairs and out the front door. She did hope the dress the widow Betsy Ross was making for her was ready. She hoped no alterations were needed once she tried it on. She really wanted to wear it that evening to the dinner party at the home of Philadelphia merchant, Joseph Stansbury.

She slowed her pace as she passed in front of Franklin's house. With Franklin abroad negotiating for the rebellious Americans with the Europeans in Paris, Sir Henry Clinton, the commander-in-chief of the British Army, and his handsome young aide, Major John Andre, now occupied his home. She slowed her pace a bit, hoping perhaps Major Andre was at one of the windows, and would see her as she passed by. She was very much enamored of the twenty-seven year-old she had met the past winter during the social season in the city.

It had been such a wondrous time, she thought, as she continued her walk. Not since she was fourteen, back in 1774, was the city so gay and carefree. All that independence talk had stifled any real gaiety in the city. People seemed so intent on politics, and cared little about the important things, like cotillions, balls and dinner parties in proper society. Of course, Peggy thought, if the Continental Army was to bring independence, all semblance of civilized society would board vessels for London, and Philadelphia would become a denizen for common people, uncouth common people, with no sense of style, breeding or decorum. She, like her father and all of her friends, was loyal to King George III, and of course, to his Queen, Charlotte of Mecklenburg. The royal house of Hanover was the epitome of proper society. How could anyone wish to cut ties with the society that British royalty brought with it?

She once again picked up her pace as she was now beyond Franklin's house, and Market Street loomed. Perhaps she would have more success on her return from the widow Ross' dress shop. If not successful, the major would most definitely be a guest at the Stansbury house that evening.

Major John Andre had been the most sought after guest in any Philadelphia home during the past nine months. He was a fine singer, and enjoyed serenading the dinner guests, when the guests retired to the parlor. He was a talented writer of poetry, and always repeated his verses when asked. But his most acclaimed charm was his capable talent of drawing and cutting silhouettes. Peggy, herself, was honored when he begged her to sit for her silhouette. She presented it to her father as a present last Christmas.

All of her friends of her age were already married, many with children. Major Andre would certainly be a wonderful husband for her, and she was determined to pursue that goal.

She arrived at Betsy Ross' dress shop, and the glorious dress was ready. It was made from the luxurious lavender satin fabric Peggy had chosen weeks before. She tried the gown on and it was a perfect fit. Mrs. Ross made arrangements for the boy who lived next door to the dress shop, to deliver it to the Shippen house by mid-afternoon.

Peggy went from the dress shop and headed back home, again slowing as she passed the Franklin house, and again, having no luck in seeing the handsome young major. She went back to her home and rested until it would be time to bathe and dress for the evening's gaiety.

Sir Henry Clinton enjoyed being General Howe's successor, and thoroughly enjoyed the cosmopolitan atmosphere of America's largest city. He had declined to move into the mansion Howe and his brother the admiral had shared in the countryside. Clinton much preferred the friendly society of the city to being isolated on a farm with the chickens and hogs. With the Franklin House sitting empty when the army marched in the last of September, he ordered it seized and set his headquarters there.

Clinton spent most days in Philadelphia at his mahogany desk in his second story office overlooking Chestnut Street. Major Andre, his most trusted aide and friend, sat at a desk alongside the windows. For the past weeks, they had been preparing to carry out Clinton's new orders from Lord North. They would be evacuating Philadelphia entirely, and relocating the army to New York, to defend against the expected French Fleet.

"John, I wish for you to remain here in Philadelphia," Clinton spoke to Andre, "until perhaps the first of July, to see to some to my commercial interests here, and then take a carriage to New York to join me there at that time."

"I would be delighted to see to your affairs here," answered Major Andre. "I can perhaps give you reports on General Washington's plans."

"Yes, Washington will no doubt take the city as his headquarters," said Clinton. "Perhaps the loyalist townsfolk here will lynch him for us." The two men laughed.

"You know, John," Clinton rose and walked to the window, "that despicable Benjamin Franklin used this very room as his library, and used these very windows to give him his infamous air baths." Clinton raised the window.

"An air bath?" Andre questioned. "What, pray tell, is an air bath?"

"Doctor Franklin swore by the curative powers of fresh air blowing in upon one's naked body, seated in an armchair, as the wind rushed in upon it," Clinton answered. Both men laughed again.

"John, I actually joined Dr. Franklin in one of his air baths in his house in London, oh perhaps fifteen years ago," admitted Clinton. Clinton, a man of near fifty years, a man of the nobility, was in good physical shape, standing at average height, and rarely seen without a freshly powdered white wig. His white wig contrasted beautifully with the bright scarlet red of his uniform. Andre could not imagine Clinton in his thirties, naked in an armchair, sitting alongside the short and flabby Ben Franklin, naked in the armchair beside him, both being bathed in the strong-blowing fresh air of a London night.

"Oh yes, John, we did, with his illegitimate son, William. Now, unlike the old man, William Franklin is a strong Loyalist, and was our governor of New Jersey," Clinton opened the window.

John rose and stood beside Clinton, as they looked out the open window. "There is no breeze today," Clinton noted.

"We must," said Andre, with a mischievous smile.

"We must what?" inquired Clinton, smiling at his young friend. Andre placed his arm around the older gentleman's waist. "We must get naked and sit in Franklin's armchairs, and take an air bath together".

"Perhaps," Clinton said. "Perhaps, after we return from the supper party this night, we shall."

479

"Judge, it is so good to welcome you again to my home," said Stansbury, as he turned to Peggy and took her white gloved-hand. "And it is always a pleasure, my dear, to welcome the beautiful Peggy Shippen to my table." He kissed the top of her gloved-hand.

"That is such an exquisite gown," Deborah Stansbury said, "such a beautiful shade of lavender! Let me show you to your seats. We are just awaiting Sir Henry's arrival. Lord Cornwallis has already arrived." She led them away to seats at the dining table. Soon Major Andre arrived, appropriately a few moments before Clinton. Andre was shown to the vacant seat alongside Peggy.

Once Sir Henry had arrived and all the guests were seated, Stansbury rose to greet his guests before the servants brought forth the lavish supper fare.

"We have just learned this very day, that our dear friend and his valiant army shall be departing from our city in just a matter of days. We shall all miss dearly, Sir Henry Clinton, Lord Cornwallis, Major Andre, and the officers who have graced our soirees and entertainments for the past months," Stansbury lifted his glass of claret. "Let us drink to their safe passage across New Jersey to New York, and a successful end to this horrid conflict."

Peggy enjoyed her evening very much, being seated alongside the charming major, the most handsome man in the room. Their table conversations were about all things other than the evacuation of the city, the politics of the war, and the vile General Washington and his rag-tag army of farmers and street ruffians. They discussed civilized matters such as the theatre, music, literature, the glorious weather, and how society in Philadelphia was far superior of that to be found one hundred miles away at New York.

After dinner, the sated diners filed out onto the terrace, where musicians had been serenading them through open French doors as they supped, and was now ready to play for them as they took to the dance floor set up in the garden. Andre and Peggy found a table set up at the edge of the dance floor. Another couple was seated there.

William Franklin, the last royal governor of New Jersey, and prisoner of the rebels for two and a half years, now a leader of the loyalists in New York, was visiting Philadelphia. He sat with one of Peggy's friends, Caroline Oliver.

"Governor Franklin," Andre spoke, as he and Peggy took their seats, "it is such a pleasure meeting you this evening."

"I am similarly fortunate to meet you, Major Andre," replied Franklin. "The loyalists of New York are most pleased to hear news of the army's pending return to our city. And I understand you are the one officer who has Sir Henry's ear."

"We are indeed, soon to be leaving here," Andre said, "I, however, shall remain in this lovely city for several weeks, attending to Sir Henry's commercial dealings here." Andre turned to Peggy, smiled at her and squeezed her hand. She smiled back, not yet having heard this grand news.

"Philadelphia is a lovely city," spoke Franklin. "Tis is the city of by birth."

"Yes, governor, I have found the home of your youth to be most accommodating as our headquarters," replied Andre.

"I was pleased to hear Sir Henry was residing in the old place," spoke Franklin. "Do you suppose you might arrange an audience for me with Sir Henry, on matters I feel could turn this drawn-out war toward a rapid and victorious end."

"I would suggest the two of us meet first," said Andre, "as he is so consumed presently in our preparations to move fourteen thousand men, baggage, and arms across the breath of New Jersey in a matter of days. When shall you be returning to New York?"

"I hope to be returning within one week," Franklin noted.

"Let us meet in the morrow, at your convenience," Andre suggested. "I shall arrange for General Clinton to meet with you when he has set his headquarters at New York."

"Splendid," agreed Franklin. "I shall meet with you at my old home in mid-afternoon. It will be good to see the old house once more…and not have to endure my traitorous father."

"This will not be your first encounter with Sir Henry, I assume," added Andre.

"Oh yes, it shall be," noted Franklin, "and I am most grateful for your assistance in arranging for such."

"I was told this very day, by Sir Henry himself," stated Andre, "that he met you after King George first named you his royal governor, one evening at your father's London residence, when the three of you enjoyed one of your father's infamous air baths."

Franklin grew red in the face, but then remembered that event from fifteen years before. Andre took Peggy's hand and they danced the minuet.

Andre escorted the lovely Peggy back to her home. As they walked, with her arm draped through his, they spoke of his remaining in Philadelphia for a time after the army would be leaving. Judge Shippen walked with them.

"Andre," spoke the Judge, as the three walked up Chestnut Street, "you have not shared in the joys of marriage yet, have you?"

"Father!" Peggy blushed and expressed her embarrassment at her father's brashness.

"Oh, Peggy," the judge said backhandedly, "if you shall not broach the matter for yourself, I certainly shall. You see, major," the judge continued to Andre, "the two of you appear to be a beautiful couple, you both seem to relish in the company of the other. Have you considered taking a wife?"

"Well sir," spoke Andre, searching for the right words, "I have never before shared in those joys you refer to. I do, as you say, relish being in the company of your beautiful and intellectual Peggy." He smiled a charming smile at her. "I feel however," he turned back to Judge Shippen, "during the current station of my life, being on battlefields and in danger of my well-being on a near-daily basis, it would only be in the greatest of selfishness should I take the hand of any woman, until my service to king and country is concluded."

"Well spoken, Andre, well spoken indeed," said the judge, deliberating the defense the major had spontaneously given for not having married, nor wishing to marry now at the age of twenty-seven. "Should you ever so decide," the judge added, "I could only but give my good countenance to a plea for her hand." They arrived at the stoop of the Shippen house. The judge opened the door and walked in, leaving the two on the stoop.

"John, I do so apologize for Father's impertinence," Peggy spoke, as soon as the judge was safely out of earshot.

"So your father sees me as a future son-in-law?" Andre said jokingly. He pulled her toward him and the couple kissed.

"While he did so embarrass me," Peggy admitted, "I shall make it no secret. I have thought at length of the possibility that some day you and I might wed. But I have kept those feelings to myself, and certainly never broached the subject with Father." Andre chuckled, and again kissed the lovely young Peggy.

"Some day, perhaps, we shall see," Andre said. "For now, I shall hold these conversations near to my heart, and be proud someone so lovely as you should like to walk to the altar with me." He kissed her once more, then headed down Chestnut Street.

"So the young Lady Shippen desires to become the wedded Lady Andre?" Clinton joked with the major as the two men sat naked in armchairs in Ben Franklin's old second-floor library in front of the open window. There was no breeze.

"It seems so," said Andre, chuckling "though it comes as no surprise to me. I have enjoyed these months with the fairest marriageable daughter of Philadelphia society attempting to set her snares for me. Have you not noticed, Henry, how each day she walks just a bit slower as she passes by our windows, hoping I shall notice her and come to her?"

"I have, John, indeed I have," answered Clinton, giggling. "Now are you certain I can trust leaving you in Philadelphia, and not have you come to me at New York attached to a wife?" Both men laughed. "I simply do not know how I should survive without the pleasure of your nightly company."

"You do have not one thing to worry about, Henry," Andre smiled.

"I saw you speaking with Governor Franklin this evening," Clinton said inquiringly.

"Yes," admitted Andre, "and I reminded him of the time you and he and his father bathed in the air in London."

"You did no such thing!" Clinton was appalled.

"I most certainly did," Andre chuckled, "and achieved seeing the former governor blush the brightest red."

The two laughed at Governor Franklin's expense, and continued to enjoy their nakedness, even if there was no breeze.

The Battle of Monmouth

It was well after dark on June 17th. Wills was still at his desk at the Potts House, writing a letter to Priscilla in Cambridge. General

Washington had retired to his bedchamber and the house was quiet. Wills told the wife he loved so much and missed even more, how the British would soon be leaving Philadelphia, and the Continental Army would give the Redcoats a chase through New Jersey. He knew Washington's plans to headquarter the army around New York.

"I am so anxious to see how little Rennie has grown, and to at last lay my eyes upon baby Victoria," Wills wrote. "God willing, I will be blessed with a leave to visit my dear family soon."

Then there came a loud wrap at the door of the Potts House. Wills put his writing aside and went to the door.

"News from Philadelphia," the rider at the door said. Wills recognized him as Col. Benjamin Tallmadge, Washington's chief of intelligence, given the post after Nathan Hale's capture and hanging.

"Come in, Col. Tallmadge," Wills said and showed him in.

"Have a seat," Wills said, "I will inform the general. I am certain he will want to see you."

"It is news of great importance on the movements of the Redcoats," Tallmadge said.

"I will hear it," said Washington from the top of the stairs. He had heard the knock and had been expecting the news. He walked down the stairs and sat in a chair beside Tallmadge. Wills took his seat at his desk.

"Clinton is moving the entire army from Philadelphia at first light," Tallmadge spoke. "The move will be in one single march, with all fourteen thousand British and Hessian soldiers. None shall be left behind to hold the city."

"None whatsoever?" Washington asked with a smile as he started down the steps.

"Not even one Hessian," confirmed Tallmadge. "The city will be totally devoid of Redcoats."

"How will they move?" Washington asked.

"They shall be borne across the Delaware River to Camden, then march northeast toward Perth Amboy, then north to Manhattan," Tallmadge answered.

"Is there an estimate as to when the city will be cleared?" Washington pushed for more information.

"From what I hear, General Clinton plans to have Cornwallis see the last boat leave the west shore of the Delaware before four o'clock in the afternoon, so the exodus can set up camp before darkness sets in," Tallmadge informed Washington.

The advance party, led by the Marquis de LaFayette with the 3rd Virginia Regiment under Major Monroe, arrived at the old statehouse, now called Independence Hall, by five o'clock in the afternoon, and pitched tents on the lawn. General Benedict Arnold's carriage pulled in front of the house of Joseph Stansbury, shortly thereafter. Arnold had had dealings with the famed merchant previously, and knew he would be accommodated there as the new military commander.

"Arnold! It is most wonderful to see you here!" beamed Stansbury, as he opened the door and saw his old friend. "Come in! Come in!"

"Joseph I am indeed happy to see you as well," Arnold spoke. "You are honestly the only man I know here in this city." Stansbury escorted the general into the parlor.

"You will join us for supper, will you not?" Stansbury asked.

"I was hoping I might seek accommodations here until I find suitable ones for myself," Arnold spoke. Stansbury beamed again.

"I would be most delighted to take you in as my houseguest, and for as long as you need," Stansbury beamed. "And what brings you to my city?"

"With Sir Henry Clinton fleeing for New York," Arnold spoke, "Washington has made me the military commander of the city, with a small force of five hundred men to secure the city and keep the peace."

"Wonderful news!" answered Stansbury, keeping his loyalist sympathies under wraps. The butler showed another man into the room. Stansbury was surprised with Major Andre's arrival, dressed in civilian clothing, but thought quickly.

"And this young man," Stansbury said, before the young major introduced himself, "is another friend, a merchant from New York. General Benedict Arnold, let me present my friend John Anderson."

LaFayette invited Major Monroe, and privates Francisco, Hicks, Shepherd, Patrick and Chenoweth, to join him for a proper dinner at the Tun Tavern. The men had not enjoyed a proper dinner in many months. The tavern sat on Water Street at Tun Alley near the wharf. Ben Franklin had recommended it to LaFayette as a good accommodation, and the marquis had stayed there during his weeks in the city, before finally being sent to General Washington at the Moland House in Bucks County.

"I hope we are not the ones selected to stay here with General Arnold," said Peter. "I am anxious to again be on the battlefield."

"I will see to it, Peter," LaFayette said, as they awaited the serving wench with their suppers. "I will make certain you will soon be wielding that giant sword of yours!"

"Yea," said Garrett, "I'd sure hate ta see the fat ole baron's hard work a trainin' us not be put ta good use, runnin' a few o' his Hessian countrymen through with our dang bayonets...now that we leastwise know how ta use 'em."

"I'm sure glad someone taught us how ta use 'em," said Malcolm, "though I wouldn't mind a bit sittin' right here an' squirin' some o' them beautiful looking Pennsylvany gals. A little Pennsyvany lass would do me no harm a'tall!"

"You wouldn't know what on earth ta do with it if it came up an' bit ya on the ass!" Garrett said laughing.

"Ain't nothin' to it," said Noel.

"Now how in Hell would you know, Chenoweth?" asked Garrett.

"I told ya I been courtin' Molly Darnell back home," Noel said. "We tried it once er twice."

"Ya *tried* it once er twice, did ya?" asked Garrett. "Doesn't sound a'tall ta me like ya *did it* er ya wouldn't've said ya just *tried it*." The tabled roared with laughter.

"Give our friend the benefit," said Pat. "He prob'ly did *try it*... just couldn't get his little feller down there ta stan' up an' salute!" The laughter continued until the supper of fish and potatoes was served.

By midday the next day, General Washington, astride Nelson, rode down Chestnut Street in Philadelphia. The townsfolk came out of their houses and cheered the Continental soldiers as they passed by. Washington dismounted at the statehouse, and held a meeting of his general staff inside, where the Congress would soon be returning. Washington had sent a team of riders west to York to inform Congress the city was free of all British, and they could now safely return.

He then gave orders to his second-ranking general, the despicable Charles Lee. Lee was to lead four thousand men as an advance guard on the heals of the Redcoat army, and engage the enemy in a rear assault.

"I do not countenance such a move," Lee objected, as he always did object to any strategy Washington laid out. "I do not think it prudent to engage the British in a full assault at this point. It is much more wise to simply harass the British with a few sporadic, small, annoying skirmishes."

"I do not intend to play parlor games of cat-and-mouse with Clinton and Cornwallis!" Washington said. "I intend to have them hear our thunder and see our lightening! But, ...very well, Lee, ... I shall then send General LaFayette. I also think it best LaFayette lead five thousand men."

"Very well, general," Lee conceded, "I shall lead the advance. If there be such an action, I insist I be the one to lead it. I am afterall your second."

For a week, the Continental Army moved northeast across New Jersey, with Charles Lee leading the advance guard of five thousand, and Washington leading the remaining six thousand an hour behind Lee's advance. Washington's strategy was for Lee to keep the enemy engaged with Washington joining Lee for the kill.

On June 28th, the advance guard under General Lee, met the British rear flank as the Redcoats were leaving Monmouth Courthouse. Lee commanded the attack and General Charles Lord Cornwallis turned the British forces and answered the attack with heavy fighting for more than two hours in one hundred-degree heat. Lee decided not to send riders to alert Washington to race to join him. Instead, Lee did not stand and fight, but ordered a full retreat.

Washington, riding at the head of the main American forces, ran directly into Lee's quickly retreating men. He immediately rallied the men to turn from their retreat and form up once more under his lead. With the first men in retreat following Washington, they encountered Lee in retreat.

"What in Heaven's name do you think you are doing, General Lee?" Washington shouted at his second-in-command. "I have given you orders as clearly as I possibly could, for you to hold your line until my re-enforcements arrived! I have privates in the field more competent at following orders! Your's is not to question...not to question me! Your's is to obey my orders, regardless of how you may feel about those orders! Is that clear?"

"It is, your Excellency!" screamed Lee bitterly.

"Then you now are relieved of your command forthwith! Report, at once, to the rear, as I have a battle to lead!" Washington shouted as he rode off to the front.

Washington repositioned the troops on the small heights of a ravine, running along the west side of the Monmouth-Freehold Meetinghouse Road. He placed Lord Stirling and his men to the left, and General Greene to the right. Both sides met heavy fire during the next several hours, well into the afternoon. The British Light Infantry came from the right flank and met with heavy fire from Stirling's men. The British were pushed back. Private Peter Francisco took his second musket ball of the war, but continued the fight. It had not been the serious wound he had taken at Brandywine.

As the British push began, Washington led his troops to a better location atop nearby Comb's Hill. He ordered General Knox to set artillery pieces on each flank, and at the center of the American line.

One of the camp followers, who had wintered at Valley Forge, the wife of an artilleryman, carried pails of water to the troops along the artillery line. She had done so at Brandywine and at Germantown. Her name was Mary Ludwig Hays, the wife of John Hays.

Mary Hays, better known among the ranks as "Molly Pitcher," was a common sight along the American lines, bringing water to the thirsty soldiers posted at their cannons. At Comb's Hill, as the fierce gunfire raged and the American cannons fired constantly at the British, Molly gave drinks from her pitcher to her husband and the men firing his cannon. A bullet struck John in the head, just after he had taken the refreshing drink from Molly. He slumped to the ground, dropping the huge cannon tamper he held. Molly shrieked, seeing her husband lying on the ground dying. Amid tears of anguish over John, and hatred for the Redcoats, she picked up the tamper and took his place at the cannon as the battle continued.

The battle raged on and the Americans held the high ground through attempts by both Cornwallis and Clinton to mount aggressive attacks. The sun was going down and, as was the custom, the battle ended for the day, with both armies holding the field.

Washington met with his general staff to discuss the day's battle, and to plan the strategy for the next day.

"I feel we have made good use of the artillery this day, and feel we should remain on our present line with the addition of more artillery from Knox," spoke Washington. "Our position is superior to the Redcoats, and we can win here, even if it means several days of battle. I do believe we can win our independence here at Monmouth."

"We certainly fought well," said Anthony Wayne. "We must take note that this is the first day of battle where we have held the field, even if the bloody British have held their field as well."

"I agree," said General Greene, "our men did fight extremely well, with the exception of one abysmal general being insubordinate to his orders. We could easily have won an all-out victory, if that damned arrogant son-of-a-bitch Lee had obeyed his orders."

"What are we to do with General Lee?" Washington posed the question he knew was on the minds of his generals.

"Hang the son-of-a-bitch!" shouted Greene. "That's what the scurvy bastard deserves!"

"I do not think that appropriate," answered Washington.

"His resignation from the Army must be demanded," added Lord Stirling. "We need not be saddled with such the sunshine patriot Thomas Paine has so nobly warned against."

"Do what his insubordination requires," spoke Wayne solemnly. "He must be taken into custody to stand before a general court martial."

"I agree, *mon general*," said LaFayette, "a court martial is indeed more appropriate than the noose around his neck. Let a court martial decide his fate."

"Then a court martial it shall be," agreed Washington. "Major Winkman, order the sentries to arrest him at once."

Unbeknownst to Washington and his spies, Clinton ordered his army to leave the field of battle at midnight, and continue its exodus on to New York.

Kaskaskia, Cahokia and Vincennes

On June 24th Col. George Rogers Clark took to the flatboats and went down the Ohio, heading west with one hundred and seventy-five men.

On June 28th, as George Washington was turning back the retreat Lee had ordered at Monmouth, Clark's flotilla camped at the mouth of the Tennessee River, a little over one hundred miles from his first target at Kaskaskia.

Jacky and Tom slept on the flatboat they had poled down the Ohio River for five days, with the men assigned to the company Tom led. The summer night was warm and the sky was black, filled with tiny sparkling stars. They made their bed atop the covered storehouse of the flatboat, and laid down, using their crossed arms as pillows beneath their heads. They enjoyed the sounds of the gentle river, as ripples of water lapped onto the pebble-laiden shore. They had enjoyed a supper of river mussels, steamed in water with a touch of some of the whiskey Jacky had brought from Bryan's Station.

"When we finish this expedition with Clark," Tom said, "I for one will be damned anxious to return to Annie's Port."

"I can't wait ta set up m' own still right on the creek bank when we get back home," Jacky added, handing a flask of some of his whiskey to Tom. "I'll produce some o' the smoothest, best tastin' whiskey ta ever cross the lips o' man."

Tom smiled. "I hope Johnny and Robert are taking care of Annie's Port for us."

"There good fellers," Jacky said. "I'm sure they're a doin' fine."

They laughed and soon fell asleep.

At nine o'clock the next morning, the army was taken by the flotilla to the site of the ruins of the old French outpost at Fort Massac. There they started the one hundred-twenty mile overland trek to the northwest. Two men were stationed on each of the flatboats, would turn back and meet the returning army on the Wabash River.

Taking few trails, the three companies trudged for five days through swamps and soggy bottoms, thickets and dense forests, and all sorts of rough, but relatively flat terrain. On July 4th they arrived at the edge of the Kaskaskia River, with the settlement and fort in sight At midnight, as the settlement slept, the expedition crossed the waist-high deep water of the river, carrying their muskets, rifles and powder bags high above their heads, to keep the powder dry. On the other shore, they walked into the settlement and, without firing one shot, took the settlement.

A small party, led by Tom and Jacky Macneal, walked through the unguarded and open gate of British Fort Gage. They woke a guard, sleeping in a chair near the gate.

"Lead me to your commandant," said Captain Tom Macneal, as he tussled the Frenchman awake. The Frenchman did not understand Tom's English, so Tom drew from his schoolboy days in England where he learned the French language, and repeated his orders in French. *"Emmenez-moi a votre commandant!"* The guard smiled at Tom, and led him inside the commander's private quarters.

Tom, Jacky and two others from the company, opened the door to the commandant's bedchamber. The commander, a French soldier named Rocheblave, hired by the British to command the fort, was in bed with his young French wife. Tom lit a lantern and the room became bright. The commander stirred and opened his eyes, staring at four musket barrels taking aim at the bed. Tom, still speaking French, ordered Rocheblave and his wife to get dressed. They marched the prisoners out of their quarters to the fort's courtyard, where the men of Tom's company had rounded up the fort's thirty men, all French soldiers.

The company marched their prisoners into the settlement. By this time, the three hundred or so French settlers had been awaken and, because the French had an inbred hatred of the British, cheered and applauded the Americans. Even Rocheblave and his wife cheered.

Clark went to the Catholic Church in the settlement to speak with Father Pierre Gibault. He used Tom as an interpreter. The priest confirmed that the settlers at Kaskaskia would be more comfortable with the Americans in control of the area than with the hated British.

Gibault was concerned for his parishioners, and them being permitted by the Americans to practice their Roman Catholic faith.

"We are fighting a war for our independence," stated Clark, through Tom's French interpretation. "One of the freedoms we cherish so dear, is the freedom to worship God as we damn see fit, without the intrusion of a government-backed church. Be assured Father, the Catholic settlers of the Illinois Country will be free to worship as the Catholics they are."

"*Je suis heureux*...I am pleased," said the Catholic priest, "as I am certain God is happy."

Clark went on announce his plans to have the French settlers swear to an oath of allegiance to the American cause. Anyone, so swearing, would be left alone, all others would be forced to leave for the western shore of the Mississippi River, now governed by the Spanish in New Orleans, or be taken prison. Father Gibault was certain everyone in the settlement would pledge to the oath, and truthfully do so.

After resting two days and feasting on meals prepared by the grateful French settlers, now pledged to the American cause, the Illinois Regiment headed north to the other French settlements along the Mississippi. Being welcomed at each settlement, and adding more and more French settlers pledging their allegiance to the Americans, Clark took the settlements at Prairie du Rocher and Saint Phillippe before arriving on July 15th at the oldest white settlement in the Illinois Country, Cahokia, founded in 1699.

There was a growing settlement on the heights of the west bank of the Mississippi River, planted in 1763 by a French trader from New Orleans, Pierre Laclede, and his thirteen-year-old stepson, Auguste Chouteau. Laclede's settlement, Saint Louis, sat across the river from Cahokia, south of the mouth of the wide Missouri River, a river gateway to the vast western plains and mountains. By the time Clark's regiment was at Cahokia, the St. Louis settlement had a population nearing five hundred. The trading post Laclede established was buying furs and pelts from the French and Spanish mountainmen, who spent most of the year in the Rocky Mountains to the west. They brought their furs and hides to St. Louis to sell to Laclede. Laclede would then send hides and furs down river for sale in New Orleans, or across the Atlantic to Spain and France.

After one day of rest at Cahokia, the expedition headed east for Vincennes on the Wabash. When Clark left Kaskaskia for the three settlements on the Mississippi, Father Gibault left immediately for Vincennes. Clark sent him in advance to begin negotiations with the French settlers, in secrecy from the few British stationed at the fort. By the time Clark arrived, the Catholic priest had gotten the townsfolk all to sign the oath of allegiance.

The men of the local French militia were also anxious to join the American cause, storming Fort Sackville held by the small British force Henry Hamilton had sent to secure it. The British Union Jack was lowered and an American flag was raised.

Clark appointed the local commander of the French militia to man the fort. Clark was pleased with the campaign, and the taking of all the British forts south of the Great Lakes. Fort Detroit and the Hair Buyer would be his next target, but that would be put off till the following spring. The men were back on Corn Island at the falls of the Ohio by the first week in August, ready to help fend off the threat to the settlements from the Shawnee.

The Hudson Valley

By early July, Sir Henry Clinton was well established at new headquarters on Broadway in New York. Washington led his army around Manhattan Island, on the west side of the Hudson River to Brunswick, Newark, then Paramus, before tracing the Hudson River north above the city to the towns of Haverstraw and King's Ferry. Washington established his headquarters at the home of Elijah Miller in White Plains on July 20th.

A portion of the French Fleet, under the command of Admiral Comte d'Estaing, had arrived, but was prevented from landing at New York. The fleet also carried soldiers, needed as re-enforcements for the Continental Army. D'Estaing ordered the fleet north to Narragansett Bay and Rhode Island, where the Americans, under General John Sullivan, were attempting to drive the British and Hessians from the northern half of the island, north of Newport. The Americans held the port, and wanted the British pushed off the island entirely. Washington sent LaFayette and Greene to assist Sullivan, and to welcome d'Estaing and the French soldiers.

Washington received unexpectedly good news from the West, that Colonel George Rogers Clark and his frontier militia had taken control of the western frontier lands all the way to the Mississippi River. The only British presence remaining in the West was now at Fort Detroit, and the more remote Fort Michilimackinac, many miles north at the far northern tip of the Michigan peninsula, where three of the Great Lakes met at the Mackinac Straits. It was wonderful news for the American cause.

During the weeks of stalemate, with the British strongly in control of New York, and Washington's army encamped closeby at White Plains, Washington used this time to fortify the Hudson Valley north of Manhattan. He took tours of the region, and laid out sites for American positions. Since the American victory at Saratoga, the Americans had held the northern Hudson Valley from the Canadian border to Albany, and on south to the settlements at Kingston, Kinderhook, Newburgh and Poughkeepsie. The British remained solidly in control only of Manhattan Island and the important harbor.

South of King's Ferry, the narrowest crossing of the Hudson, was a rocky site on the palisades overlooking the river called Stony Point. Washington saw it as a strategic site, near the town of Haverstraw on the west shore. North of there, Washington found another strategic site known as West Point. These sites were well-worth fortifying with American troops. With other troops staged in the towns of Tappan, Tarrytown, Dobbs Ferry and Nyack, Washington spent the remaining months of summer fortifying the Hudson Valley to keep the British pinned-in on Manhattan Island.

Washington's army broke camp at White Plains in early October, and camped at Fishkill for a week, then six weeks at nearby Fredericksburg. As the end of November was approaching, Washington called Wills Winkman into his office.

"Wills," Washington asked, "how old are your son and daughter now?"

"Young Reynolds, Rennie we call him, turns three years in March, on the twentieth," said Wills, "and baby Victoria will be two years old on the second day of January."

"Do you not think it not time for you to see your son again, and meet the daughter you have never yet seen?" Washington asked as Wills smiled broadly.

"By my recollection," Washington continued, "you have been by my side, near every day, since June 1775...nearly three and one half years. Unfortunately, I have taken you further and further away from Cambridge, and your lovely wife. Now we are, what, six...seven days ride from Cambridge? December is coming in two days and the war rests until the summer.

"You have not asked, but I have seen it upon your face, and have heard it in your voice," Washington continued. "As of first light, I order you to take an extended furlough."

"A furlough?" Wills beamed. "I have so wanted to ask, but never felt the time to be the right time."

"'Tis the right time," Washington added, placing a fatherly arm about his shoulders. "The army will be encamped these winter months at our positions here along the Hudson. I shall join Lady Washington in Philadelphia before the Christmas celebrations, and remain there until the springtime. Report back to the commandant in charge at West Point on or about the first day of May. He will send you to me if I am not there. If I do need you in advance of May, I shall surely send for you. Have a wonderful Christmas in Cambridge with your family."

Philadelphia

In Philadelphia, the Congress had moved back into Independence Hall. Henry Laurens was elected as the new president, and General Benedict Arnold was enjoying the social scene of Philadelphia as the city's military commander. Arnold commanded few men and had little official business to conduct. From his first night as a guest of Joseph Stansbury, Arnold had enjoyed Stansbury's social circle, without being aware the lot of them were loyalists. Arnold never pegged Stansbury as the important loyalist leader he was. His new best friend became the young merchant from New York, John Anderson.

Anderson always had one reason or another not to be seen in public with the city's American military commander. He could not chance a greeting from any one of the many loyalists who might see them together in public. Major Andre wanted to learn what he could through his friendship as John Anderson, with the American commander, without that important man learning his true identity. Andre wanted to be able to relay what espionage he could to Sir Henry, when he would join the commander-in-chief in New York later in the summer.

Everyday that first week, Arnold and Anderson were together at Stansbury's home. Arnold had not yet found an appropriate permanent accommodation, so he remained in one of the guest rooms at Stansbury's home. His friend occupied another guest room down the hallway.

After supper one evening, Anderson and Arnold joined Stansbury for brandy in the second floor library. After a snifter of brandy, the host retired early for the evening, as he was sailing to Williamsburg on business the next morning. He invited his two guests to help themselves to more brandy and excused himself.

"I am so fond of this beautiful city," said Anderson. "I visit here often, and simply dread it when I must leave."

"New York is a wonderful city as well, do you not think?" Arnold asked. "I am a native of Connecticut ... New Haven, and am as enamored with New York, as you seem to be enamored with Philadelphia."

"Yes, it is lovely, Ben," John said as he sipped, "I imagine the familiarity I have with New York appears to make it seem all too commonplace and inferior for me. Did you inquire into the Franklin House on Chestnut Street?"

"Yes, and thank you for the suggestion, John," Arnold answered. "It is a beautiful place and convenient to the capitol. I do not think Dr. Franklin would be the least bit distressed knowing I have taken over his lovely residence. I shall move in there on Monday."

"I am certain the old man would not object," John added, "in fact, he will no doubt credit you with kicking out that damnable Sir Henry Clinton and his aide, and as I hear it, his apparent lover, that vile Major Andre."

"What?" Arnold asked, laughing at Anderson's bit of gossip.

"That is what the talk has been," said John. "The commander-in-chief had what proper society calls a 'love unspeakable' with his young and handsome major."

"Disgusting," Arnold chimed, shaking his head in disbelief, "simply disgusting."

"It is indeed," agreed John, as he took another sip from his snifter. "Ben Franklin is such the treasure of this city," said John, hoping for some insight into Franklin's plans. "Do you hear when he shall return from Paris to join us once more here in Philadelphia? We do so miss him."

"I would assume Dr. Franklin shall remain at Paris for the duration of the war," spoke Arnold. "He has, after all, secured alliances from France, the Netherlands, and Spain. There are yet other nations on the continent who despise the British, and may be willing to join in an alliance themselves. If Frederick the Great comes aboard, now that Louis XVI has, who knows, those damnable Hessians may be left with no option other than to join their own countrymen against the Redcoats. Franklin is fighting the American Revolution along the River Seine." The two new friends toasted Franklin.

Andre left three weeks later for New York and Sir Henry's headquarters on Broadway. That same evening, two dinner guests arrived at the Stansbury home. Mrs. Stansbury had invited Judge Edward Shippen, the corpulent jurist, and his attractive daughter, Peggy. Stansbury had just returned that day from his trip to Williamsburg.

With Major Andre having left Philadelphia, and pledged to seek no wife until the war was ended, Peggy was now seeking a new suitor. At nineteen, she viewed herself as not able to wait until the war's end. She would soon be turning twenty, and needed to be married before she aged much further, and be left to face the future life of a spinster. This handsome American, General Benedict Arnold, might be just the man. He was nearly twice her age, but had maintained a youthful appearance, despite his handicap. He was a patriot and the Shippens and Stansburys were loyalists. That could change, if an invitation to the altar called for it.

As she had once set her sights on Major Andre, she now set her sights on the American general. He had finally taken the Franklin home on Chestnut Street, just as Andre had lived there with Clinton. So her daily routine of passing by on the sidewalk, slowly, did not change. It did not change, except for the fact that most days General Arnold saw her, and did indeed come out to speak with her, or drop whatever it was he was doing, and escort her in his carriage on her daily rounds of shopping. It was not long before Peggy Shippen was seen regularly on General Benedict Arnold's arm.

In early December, Arnold received word from General Washington that he planned to winter in the city. He would arrive before Christmas, staying with Henry Laurens, probably until May. Arnold was not happy at the prospects.

"I have been the face of the American Army here in the capital since June," stormed Arnold to Judge Shippen, Peggy and Stansbury, at the supper table in the Shippen home one evening. "Now, I shall be over-shadowed by our glory-seeking commander-in-chief. That bastard!"

"Glory has escaped Washington, no matter how much he has sought it," said Shippen. "He could not even keep Howe and Clinton out of our capital. The war rightly should have been ended then and there, with Clinton taking the city."

"The Congress had to flee like old maids," added Peggy, "flee to some town in the hinterlands on the Susquehanna. It was such a disgrace." Due to Stansbury's instructions, none of his loyalist friends dared hint their true leanings to Arnold...not just yet, at least.

"There was talk of having Washington replaced," said the judge. "Why that did not occur, I shall never understand. At least Horatio Gates is a proper gentleman."

"I admit," said Arnold, "I am the reason he was not replaced."

"You, Benedict? How so?" asked Peggy.

"As the real hero of Saratoga, I stood up for Washington against his detractors, Gates especially. Gates is no field commander, but took all credit for what the others and I did. We called him Granny Gates," explained Arnold. "That is all I need say."

"May I talk frankly, Ben?" Stansbury asked. "We have grown to become such excellent friends from your first night here."

"Your words are always welcome, Stansbury, you know that," Arnold spoke.

"I take my chances when I speak," Stansbury started. "I for one, am no lover of the so-called cause. I do not feel any one's life will be bettered in any way, if we separate from the king and his realm.

"This war is a great distraction for us all, and quite an inconvenience," Stansbury continued. "Even many, who once legitimately supported the cause of independence, have since become sickened of this war, and want to return to the sanity of being British subjects."

"I had my suspicions," admitted Arnold, "my new friends in Philadelphia are, to a man, Tories and loyalists to the king." Arnold smiled slyly.

"Ben," continued Stansbury, "you are an intelligent man, and a highly successful military commander. Surely you can see the writing upon the wall. If we remain loyal subjects of King George, we are citizens of the most powerful and the richest realm in all the world. We are to share in those riches. These colonies in America are just the start of the empire to come for Britain, with colonies in India, Asia, Africa, colonies on every continent. We have the glory of the realm in our grasp, and all the fortunes that come with that glory.

"On the otherhand," Stansbury went on, "should that independence be won, all that will be lost to us. We shall become merely a small and insignificant backwater nation of thirteen loosely bound together states, open to attack and war on all fronts, and doomed to poverty and stagnation.

"I have never before broached such thoughts in public that I have broached with you this evening," Stansbury confidently continued, "but I feel now is the time. You are wasting your talents on a cause that is lost. Your talents could lead you to the heights in service to the king. ...and to riches untold. Surely you do see that."

"Surely you do, Benedict," added Peggy, "surely you do."

On the Mississippi

"I want to see those mountains," Zack said to Rodie, the evening before they were to arrive back in New Orleans from their four month long journey up the Mississippi. The flatboat lazily drifted with the currents down the muddy river, lit only by the late autumn moon. "I want to see this whole land, all the way to the Pacific Ocean!"

They had been invited along on a trading trip with Alejandro and Joaquin. They had taken a full load of goods from the Mercado in New Orleans to Laclede's Trading Post, and were coming back to New Orleans with the flatboat laden with piles of hides and pelts from the mountain men who hunted and trapped in the Rocky Mountains.

They had met and befriended Auguste Chouteau, the adopted son of Pierre Laclede, who had built the trading post. Auguste was now the sole owner of the booming business, as Laclede had died earlier that year midway down the Mississippi on a trip to New Orleans.

Zack and Rodie spent a full month and a half at the large settlement called Saint Louis, that was growing up around the trading post. The settlers were predominately French families who remained in their new world cut out of the wilderness, after the French lost their American holdings to the British following the French and Indian War.

Zack and Rodie arrived at St. Louis soon after Col. George Rogers Clark's army saw victories in taking the British forts at Kaskaskia, Cahokia and Vincennes. While Rodie had kept up on news of the war through newspapers arriving from Havana, San Juan, Savannah and Charleston, he and Zack were surprised to learn the war had spread as far west as the banks of the Mississippi River.

"I don't know, Zack," Rodie said, somewhat reluctantly about Zack's thoughts of heading even further into the frontier. "I thought this trip would be enough for you. I've been thinking about getting married and settling down with Angelita."

"Getting married," Zack admitted, "is not in my plans at all. As long as there's a huge new world of nature to explore and sketch and tell others about, that's where I wanna be."

"You haven't seen enough of this land?" Rodie questioned his friend. "Don't you want to marry someone like Carmen, and settle down in your own hacienda, and have about four or five little Winstons to raise."

"Settle down?" Zack answered. "That sounds like something you have no choice over, something that happens when you're ready to die," replied Zack. "A water-logged tree branch settles down to the bottom of the river, after there's no life left in it. I am still young and healthy enough to explore those unknown worlds, and that's what I intend do while I still can. I plan to go back to Laclede's Landing, as soon as I can, and join up with Auguste and a party of mountain men, and head off to the Rocky Mountains. I want to spend a year, maybe two there, sketching the animals that lived in these pelts and furs we are taking to New Orleans."

"I don't know, Zack," I hoped we would both settle down, and then head back to Virginia some day. I know you miss your folks."

"I love them," Zack said, "and do miss them. But they recognize the fact that they are not my real parents, just my uncle and my aunt.

They know I have this spirit of adventure, and talent for art. They know if I lost that, I would have very little to live for, like that water-logged branch.

"I hoped you would want to go west with me. Imagine it...flat grassy plains as far as the eye can see...herds of those mammoth bison... mountains with snowcaps all year round! Can you imagine the vistas seen from their summits? And the Pacific Ocean!"

"I know how the unknown draws you, Zack," Rodie said, "that's why I wanted so to be with you on this journey. I thought this long journey would satisfy that wanderlust you have inside.

"I have no family I ever plan to see again. But I am in love with Angelita. She is such a beautiful girl. I can dream only of marrying her at the altar in the church on the plaza, honeymooning with her in Havana or San Juan, settling in our own hacienda on Calle Bourbon, and raising ten or twelve beautiful little children. That is my dream, Zack, and I plan to make it real."

Zack smiled. Rodie did not know if his friend was smiling, pleased with Rodie's plans to marry the woman he loved, or if he was day dreaming of all that yet waited for him to discover, west of the river they were currently floating down.

Chapter Thirteen

The Making of a Traitor

Wills arrived in Cambridge on the tenth day of December. It was an unseasonably warm day for December in New England, as it felt more like Indian summer, with bright sun and blue skies that had not yet turned to gunmetal gray. Many of the trees along Brattle Street still had some of their leaves. He passed the house where Washington had his first headquarters as commander-in-chief, and where he was first taken on as Washington's secretary.

Wills smiled, as he thought back to that time when Henry Knox introduced him to Washington, and suggested Wills serve as his secretary. He thought then it would be a short-term appointment, until a better and more skilled army officer would replace him. But he and the general had gotten along well, and Washington had never indicated any desire to replace him. He was proud he had been at Washington's side through what would soon be four years, and felt certain he would be alongside him to the very end. The stories he was anxious to tell Priscilla flooded his brain. These were stories he would tell, in later years, to his children and grandchildren.

Wills smiled even more broadly when his walk down Brattle Street led him to the small and narrow cross street called Landsdowne. Three houses down from Brattle was 21 Landsdowne Street, the house he had leased, and where he and Priscilla had stood in the parlor on June 30th 1775, to become Mr. and Mrs. Wills Winkman. He rushed up the three-step stoop and banged the doorknocker. The door opened and there stood Priscilla!

Not expecting to see her husband for the Christmas holidays, she dropped the pitcher of milk she was taking to the children for their mid-day meal. The pitcher shattered and white creamy milk spewed all over the stoop porch and Wills' boots.

"Why did you not write to me and let me know you would be coming home!" Priscilla said as she threw her arms around her husband.

"It was all so sudden," Wills told her how General Washington had given him his furlough at the last moment.

"My but do you not look so handsome in your uniform, Lieutenant Winkman," she said, looking him up and down. "Come in and meet your daughter, and see how your Rennie has grown," Priscilla said, taking his hand and tugging at him.

"Should we not tend to this spilt milk first," Wills said, without moving.

"The birds can do that," Priscilla said, insisting he follow her. "I shall broom up the glass shards later."

She led him to the room at the top of the stairs. There he saw a charming boy sitting near the hearth, playing with some toy soldiers. In a high chair by the window, with a bowl of oatmeal in front of her, sat what appeared to be a fragile little baby china doll. She had the same blonde curls framing her milky white face, and bright blue eyes as her beautiful mother. She was indeed her mother's daughter, and as beautiful a child as his Priscilla must have been.

"Rennie," Priscilla said, getting her son's attention. "Do you know who this man might be?"

The young toe-head blonde boy turned his head, stood up at attention and said, "Yes, General George Washington!" the boy saluted the man in the army uniform. Wills smiled and returned the salute.

"No, silly," said Priscilla, "it's your Papa."

The boy beamed, "Papa?" He ran toward Wills, who squatted down with open arms to welcome his son's coming hug. Wills picked him up. The hug lasted long moments.

"Papa, you're here," Rennie said. "Is the war over?"

"Not yet, son," Wills said with a chuckle, "not yet. Can you tell me who this little angel is, sitting so sweetly in her highchair?"

"She's no angel, Papa," said Rennie. "She just my little sister, Victoria."

"Well, she certainly looks like a little angel to me," said Wills. Priscilla picked Victoria up from her highchair and turned to her daughter.

"Victoria, this is your father," Priscilla said to the child. She handed Victoria to Wills who had set Rennie back down. Wills took his daughter for the first time in his arms. Her big, bright blue eyes looked straight into his face. She gave a tentative, closed-lipped smile.

"Hello, Victoria," Wills said, kissing her on her small white forehead. "I have waited far too long to see my beautiful daughter. The girl let out a huge whimper and turned her head and little arms toward her mama for a rescue.

After the family had supper, Wills and Priscilla immediately headed to bed. They had not been together in months, and both missed lying naked in bed with each other. They got very little real sleep that evening, making up for all the evenings they had been forced to sleep alone, divided by many, many miles.

"Perhaps, in September," Wills whispered gently in Priscilla's ear, "there will be another little Winkman coming into this world." He kissed her and hugged her as the first light of day was coming in through the window.

Major Jimmie

On that same day, Major James Monroe and the 3rd Virginia Regiment who had led General Washington south toward Philadelphia, was told they would break camp the next day, where they had stayed the past two nights at Paramus, New Jersey. Peter Francisco, and the comrades from his school years, were looking forward to being in the capital for the Christmas holiday.

"It's sure gonna be better than Valley Forge!" Garret Hicks said, at the thought of wintering in Philadelphia. "We gonna get ta spen' the whole winter in Philadelphy, Major Jimmie?" asked Garrett, as some of the men fished in the river beside their camp.

"I hear," said Major Monroe, "we will set up a winter headquarters at Middlebrook. Only one or two companies will actually be stationed in the city."

"Surely Washin'ton'll want his favorite comp'ny with 'im," Malcolm supposed. "After all we crossed the Delaware in his own boat, an' he's always assignin' us some o' the fiercest fightin'!"

"We've surely been there for him every step o' the way," said Noel Chenoweth.

"An' we've fer sure taken enough musket balls for 'im," said Peter Patrick, "specially ole Peter over yonder."

"Oh he could've batted that dang musket ball what hit 'im at Monmouth, with that dang ole giant sword Washin'ton gave him," added Garrett, "an' saved himself from another bullet hole."

"Naw," said Malcolm, "He's too dang slow reactin' an' just too dang a big ole target for them Redcoats." Everyone laughed, as their friend Peter sat fishing, with a smile but no response.

He finally spoke.

"I was too busy swinging my sword and loppin' off the arm of a Hessian, when that tiny little musket ball barely hit me. I fought on my feet the rest o' that day, with the ball in my back, makin' better use o' my sword against the enemy than any o' you slackers did with your guns and bayonets. You tell 'em Major Jimmie."

Monroe smiled.

"I will not be staying with you fellows," added Monroe rather solemnly. He laughter died down. "I will be traveling south... back to Fredericksburg."

"You got some kinda promotion an' field command we don't know 'bout, Jimmie?" asked Malcolm.

"It appears there is to be no colonelcy, nor any field command for me," Monroe answered. "I will be mustered out of the army in ten days, a few days ahead of when my commission ends. I will not be re-enlisting."

"We need ya Jimmie," said Garrett. "Me an' Peter picked yer ass up off o' King Street back at Trenton an' saved yer gangly ass so as ya'd be our leader throughout this damn war."

"I will always be grateful," said Monroe, "but if I wish to command a unit in the field, it appears I will have to recruit and train one, just as General Mercer did for us."

"Why?" asked Peter. "You have been a fine leader, Jimmie. You made us into one of the best-trained companies in the entire regiment…in the whole army. Even Baron von Steuben was impressed with how easily we picked up his training, and didn't once cuss at us, all because of how well you'd already trained us. You should have been on Washington's staff as one of his aides, right along with LaFayette, Hamilton and Laurens."

"I feel Lt. Hamilton is the reason my career in the army is about to end," stated Monroe. "I met with him just after he and LaFayette were brought onto Washington's personal staff. I could tell in that first meeting with Hamilton that his own ambitions were getting in my way. That's when I was placed with Lord Stirling instead.

"I will ride south and be at my sister's home in Port Royal by Christmas Day," Monroe continued. "After the first of the year, I will start recruiting a Virginia regiment of my own command, and ride back to join Washington."

"You want some comp'ny, Jimmie?" asked Garrett. "I'm at the end of my commission too. In fact, we all are. I was gonna sign-up again, but if 'n you ain't gonna be m' major, I'd just as soon leave, an' come back with you in yer new regiment."

"Why not? Our commissions all end on the thirtieth," said Malcolm, "Pat's an' Noel's too. We could all be back at home for Christmas, an' then re-enlist in yer regiment. Peter, too."

"That's what we all should do," said Peter. "We joined this outfit together. We can leave it together, and then come back together."

"Well, if you all wish, I would certainly appreciate your support and understanding," Monroe said, not expecting that show of support from his old school chums. "I will speak to the general and see if he will give you each early releases," Monroe offered, "if you really want it, that is."

Garrett and Malcolm led the men, formerly of the 3rd Virginia, to the Hicks Homestead at Manassas on their second day out of Philadelphia, after spending the night in Baltimore. The following morning, Monroe led the rest on to Fredericksburg, where they took rooms at the Rising Sun Tavern, owned by General Washington's younger brother, Charles. The tavern keeper would not accept any payment from the men in uniform for his hearty food, drink and warm beds for the night. The next morning, their young classmate, Bushrod Washington, home from

William and Mary, heard they were at the tavern, and came by with his father, Jack, and his mother, Hannah.

On Christmas Eve morning the four split up. Monroe and Chenoweth headed east a half-day's ride to Port Royal in Caroline County. Chenoweth's family lived on a large farm about one mile away from the plantation of Nathan Buckner, Major Monroe's older sister's husband. Peter and Pat headed south to Winston Woods.

The sun was slowly going down as the two Peters, turned up the tree-lined lane leading back to the Winston Woods manor house.

"It will sure be good to be home for a spell," said Peter. "I haven't really seen this place since we stopped off on our march with Lord Dunmore back in '74!"

"It'll sure be good to see Pa," said Pat. "He sure hated to see me march off to Williamsburg to train with General Mercer, but was sure proud I did. And I can hardly wait to see my Patricia."

"We should have stopped by Cedar Forks on our way," Peter said.

"No," said Pat, "I'll surprise her tomorrow an' call on her at the Patterson home. I bought her a locket when we was in Baltimore. I sure hope she likes it."

"I hope ole Zack is back from the Carolinas," said Peter, "and if he is, I'm gonna drag his ass off with Jimmie's new regiment, and let him get a taste of Redcoats and Hessians!"

The men rode up to the manor house unnoticed, and tied their mounts to the hitching rail beside the steps. The two soldiers walked up the steps and banged the doorknocker. Soon, the old Negro, Malcolm, dressed in his valet's attire, opened the door. Malcolm saw the two soldiers in uniform and smiled a bright pearly white smile.

"Mistah Petah, Mistah Patrick," Malcolm spoke, "it sure is a fine day o' jubilee!" He led them into the parlor.

"You'uns just sit a spell right here in the parlor." Malcolm said in a whisper with a smile, "I'll send in the judge and Miss 'Della straight away." He smiled a sly grin, "I'll not let on it's you'uns, and they'll be sure surprised."

In just a moment or so, the judge and Adella came to the parlor to greet whatever guests it might be who dropped by so unexpectedly on Christmas Eve. As soon as they saw the two soldiers, they both froze in their steps. Their faces quickly were decorated with beaming smiles, and the both rushed in with outstretched arms.

"Peter! ... and Peter!" Adella near screamed. If she hadn't, she probably would have fainted dead away.

"Look at the two of you," the judge said, excitedly, "I do not know whether to salute or hug you both!" He hugged them.

"It is so marvelous to have you with us on Christmas Eve," Adella said.

"Jimmie, you have served enough in this war," Major Monroe's sister, Elizabeth Buckner, scolded him after presents were exchange Christmas morning. "You were so badly wounded at Trenton, all but left to die in the street," she continued, showing her disapproval in his ambitions to recruit his own regiment and return to the battlefields, "and you do have the scars of battle to prove that fact.

"You, at your young age, are the head of this family, like it or not," his two-year older sister went on with her scolding. "Our parents are both long dead. You now have the responsibility to tend to our younger brothers, Andrew and Joseph. It falls upon your shoulders, not mine."

"I did not come here to get a tongue lashing from you, sister," Jimmie defended himself. "I came back to Virginia to recruit soldiers willing to fight for our independence. You are married to a fine husband and a man of wealth. Is it not logical you tend to our young brothers' needs till I have the inheitance? You know I will pay you every shilling for what their raising has cost you and Lucien."

"You cannot be dissuaded? You still plan to run back to the army?" Elizabeth said, wringing her hands in her apron, continuing her disapproval.

"I cannot be disuaded!" Jimmie stood up to his older sister. "Why have Andrew and Joseph not yet been enrolled at Campbelltown?"

"I could not touch your inheritance, brother," Elizabeth replied snidely. "It is not my responsibility, but yours."

"I cannot touch the inheritance myself, until I come of age on April 28th," Monroe snapped back. "On the 29th I shall ride to the academy and make their arrangements for enrollment in the fall. Andrew should have been enrolled two years ago! Now he can enroll with his brother and they shall study together. The Campbells will prepare them well for William and Mary. I shall appoint an agent to see to their needs in my absence."

"Lucien will gladly oversee their stipend from the inheritance," Elizabeth said sternly.

"I think it best an attorney oversee the needs of Andrew and Joseph," Monroe said, not wanting his brother-in-law to have access to the inheritance.

"You seemed unable to put forth the funds to enroll the boys two years ago, knowing full-well I would repay you! Why should I expect you to tend to their education!" He left the manor house, slammed the door, and mounted his horse.

The Way of the Frenchmen

A few days before Christmas, General Washington's carriage pulled up in front of the house on Chestnut Street where Henry Laurens, now the president of Congress, was living. Martha had arrived from Mount Vernon the day before, and would stay with the general through the coming Christmas holiday and well into the spring.

President Laurens was happy to greet his friend, General Washington, and was also most happy to see his twenty-four year-old son, John, who was then a lieutenant colonel. He was proud his son was now serving on the commander-in-chief's staff as an aide-de-camp.

The next day, Laurens sat in on an informal meeting Washington was having with his aides, before LaFayette and Hamilton would return to the army's camp at Middlebrook. As the men gathered in the library, Laurens casually asked how his son John had performed on the field of battle.

"Well," said Washington, "he was heroic in all his battles...Brandywine, Germantown and Monmouth."

LaFayette chuckled. "He certainly has been heroic."

"How so, LaFayette," asked Laurens for more details.

"I saw him first hand at Monmouth," LaFayette said. "He had a horse shot out from beneath him. By the actions I saw him display on the battlefield, it was certainly not his fault he was not killed or seriously wounded. He did everything he could possibly do to achieve either one or the other." The entire room laughed at Lt. Col. Laurens' expense.

22

2222

2

"Henry," Washington spoke, as the levity was dying down, "what war business is on your mind that you wished to speak to LaFayette and me about?"

"Well, general," Laurens began, "dispatches from Paris tell me talks with the king are stalling. The French have recognized our independence, and given us aid, but talks for Rochambeau to lead additional French land forces are going no where."

"Do they not understand, the mere presence of the Comte de Rochambeau on American soil, leading his own army alongside the American army, will shorten the war, and we can all return to our normal affairs," Washington asked.

"My government," LaFayette added, "can certainly spare Rochambeau. He is not needed in Europe, as the whole world awaits the outcome of the American Revolution, cheering our victories. Mon Dieu! Does King Louis not realize what a benefit to the prestige of France it would be to defeat Great Britain in North America?"

"That is what is on my mind," added the president of the Congress. He looked directly at the marquis. "I propose we send you, LaFayette, back to France immediately, so you can join Franklin and Adams when negotiations with the king begin again in the new year."

"I will certainly do so," LaFayette said, "so long as when the negotiations are rightly concluded, I can return to my post here."

"What about that warrant the king has issued for your insubordination at coming here in the first place," Washington asked with a smile.

LaFayette smiled. "He will give me a day and night at the Bastille, then all past differences will be set aside. That is the way of we Frenchmen."

The Capture of Henry Hamilton

While the army in the east sat in camp for the winter, events on the frontier were looking as if the winter weather might, out of necessity, have to be ignored. Colonel George Rogers Clark, along with Simon Kenton and Benjamin Logan, had left Corn Island for a winter headquarters at Kaskaskia on the Mississippi.

On a sunny, yet cold wintry day in late January, an Italian-French soldier turned fur trapper and trader, Francis Vigo, arrived at Kaskaskia.

"May I speak with Colonel Clark," the fur trader requested as he arrived. "I have just left Vincennes an' have terrible news the colonel needs immediately."

He was quickly taken to Clark in his quarters.

"That devil, Governor Hamilton, the hair buyer they call him," began Vigo, "marched inta Vincennes, easy as ya please, with ninety men an' that many savages, an' took the fort the local militia had been holdin' after you claimed it for Virginia durin' the summer."

"Hamilton led this attack himself?" Clark asked, bolting up from his chair.

"Yes," Vigo affirmed, shaking his head, "He sits there this very day, pretty as ya please."

"What are his plans?" Kenton broke into the conversation.

"It appears," Vigo said, through his tartar-encrusted teeth, "Vincennes will be his headquarters now, not Fort Detroit, an' Cahokia an' Kaskaskia will be his summer plans...taking them back for King George."

"How many men are presently at Vincennes?" Clark inquired.

"I counted sixty-three men an' maybe a dozen or so Injuns," Vigo said. "Hamilton sent the rest back to Fort Detroit, with orders to bring two more companies to Vincennes in the spring."

Clark stood and began to head to his desk in the corner by the window.

"When do ya think the re-enforcements will arrive?" Kenton asked the trapper.

"Well, knowin' the Michigan lands as I do, the snows lay deep till sometimes as late as mid-May. An' from the talks I had with Hamilton an' his officers, I feel they don't expect 'em till the end o' April at the earliest, an' prob'ly won't march on Kaskaskia till June or July."

"Vigo, I appreciate yer news," said Clark. "Remain here as long as ya wish."

"Oh no colonel," Vigo said, as he rose from his chair. "I'm bound fer Laclede's Landin' an' the Rocky Mountains. I knew you'd be here, so I could give ya the news from Vincennes. The settlers there wish ya well, and will welcome yer return ta retake the fort an' their settlement at Vincennes." They shook hands and Vigo left as swiftly as he had arrived.

"How many men are now here?" Clark asked of Logan.

"Two hundred and seven," answered Logan.

"We march with all but a handful to watch this place in one week, Kenton an' me," Clark announced his intentions. "You keep charge here, Logan. Kenton, I should've taken yer advice last fall, an' made my headquarters at Vincennes then, not a hundred an' fifty miles away to the west."

"At least, we know the way there," said Kenton with a sly smile. "We marched across the Illinois Country last summer an' it's not that bad of a trek."

"We'll just have ta see how bad it is in the wintertime," Clark retorted.

Clark and Kenton led the army out of Kaskaskia in early February. They reached the Little Wabash River after one week of marching through half-frozen forests, and the swampy valleys of muck, sometimes knee-high. They found the Little Wabash flooded, making it an uncrossable, swiftly running river, a flooded land that appeared to be a good five miles wide. They stopped and built rafts to carry their men on. They then marched for four days to the Embarrass River, and it too was flooded, too high again to ford. They were now just nine miles from Vincennes. They made their camp.

In the headquarters tent, as the winter sun was quickly sinking on the horizon, and the cold winds blew, Clark and Kenton unrolled a map.

"We are now here," Clark pointed, "an' we need ta be here," he pointed again. "How do we get there?"

"Well, with the Embarrass flooded here," Kenton said, pointing, "we can just imagine how flooded the Wabash will be," said Kenton. Kenton looked at the map, trying to imagine the flooded lands between them and the fort.

"In stead o' buildin' rafts here, what if we march the army along the west bank o' the Embarrass to here," he pointed to where the smaller river emptied into the larger Wabash. "We build the boats there, where we'll be what ... maybe within three miles from the fort? We ferry our men across. Quietly during the night ... we enter the settlement an' lay siege ta Hamilton in his fort as he sleeps."

Clark smiled.

The next day the army moved south along the banks of the Embarrass, and arrived at the Wabash in the mid-afternoon. They set their camp and began immediately chopping down trees to build their makeshift flotilla. In three days they had their frontier navy built.

"We must take that fort an' Hamilton as a prisoner now," stated Clark. "He's not expectin' us, an' has no idea we're just three miles from his gates. Hell, in this weather he'll be thinkin' no one in their right mind would plan what we're 'bout to do."

The next day, the army made its crossing of the flooded Wabash. Clark sent a dozen men from the French militia at Kaskaskia, into town, dressed in common clothing, to blend in with the townsfolk, and warn them of the army's approach. Clark wanted the townsfolk to be quiet as the army marched in after dark, so as not to arouse Hamilton and the British men at the fort.

With the conditions of flooding in the area south of Vincennes, the army moved out at dusk, carrying their muskets high above their heads, as they waded water, in many places, up to their waists. They marched into the settlement, still undetected by Hamiliton and his men. The plan had worked.

Immediately, Clark and Kenton quietly placed their army within siege position of the fort. The siege began at midnight and continued until dawn. As dawn broke the next day, Clark sent a messenger to Governor Hamilton inside the fort. It was a demand for Hamilton's surrender. The Hair Buyer refused, so Clark continued the siege of the fort.

In two hours, Clark sent a second message to Hamilton.

"That backwoods commandant expects me to surrender, with no conditions what so ever!" Hamilton read the message, crumpled it up, and pitched it into the fireplace. He sat at a desk and took a quill pen, dipping it in ink. He wrote a missive to his opponent outside his gates.

"I propose a three-day cease fire, so as to allow us to meet, as the gentlemen we are, and determine an adequate outcome for this unpleasant situation."

He folded the message and handed it to the messenger. "Give this to your commandant," Hamilton said. "Those are my terms, and the terms of His Royal Majesty King George III!"

After Clark received and read Hamilton's response, two Frenchmen, having been held for weeks in the fort's stockade, were escorted out of the fort by four of Hamilton's Indian allies. The Frenchmen were released to the town, but the townsfolk grabbed the four Indians and the tomahawks they carried. They used the tomahawks on the Indians, and left them for dead in plain view of the British inside the fort.

Holding the siege lines as darkness began to set in, Clark sent one final message to Hamilton. Clark would suspend the siege until mid-morning. At that time, Clark expected Hamilton to leave the fort, and come to the Catholic Church in the town for a meeting with the town's mayor, the priest, and Clark, or he would storm the fort.

At ten o'clock in the morning, the gates of the fort opened, and Hamilton, dressed in his finest red coat uniform and freshly powdered white wig, appeared, and marched quietly to the church, followed by threatening hoots and hollers of the townsfolk. The remaining soldiers in the fort came out and laid down their arms in surrender. Kenton accepted their surrender, and ordered no harm be done to the Redcoat prisoners. A small force of Americans rushed inside the fort and immediately pulled down the Union Jack, replacing it, once more, with the stars and stripes of the new American flag. The sign at the fort's gate came down, and a new one was nailed up in its place: *"Fort Patrick Henry"* the new sign proclaimed.

Governor Henry Hamilton was manacled and taken under heavy guard to flatboats waiting on the Wabash landing. The town had made all the boats available for their liberators.

Most of the boats would carry the bulk of the French-speaking army back to their families at Kaskaskia along the Mississippi River. One company, made up of a dozen volunteers from Kentucky, and three-dozen French militiamen, were posted at Fort Patrick Henry, under Clark's command. It was planned that the march on Fort Detroit would leave from Vincennes sometime during the summer.

Kenton, with the remaining Kentuckians, left that day from Vincennes for Corn Island and the new settlement, now starting to grow on the Kentucky banks opposite the island. The settlers were calling the settlement Louisville, in honor of the French king, now an official American ally.

With the Hair-Buyer in chains, his days as a threat to the American settlers were now effectively ended. He was bound for Williamsburg, where Governor Patrick Henry had him imprisoned in the old powder magazine.

News of the victory was cheered in the East. Washington was thrilled with the news. In Paris, the news from the American frontier gave Franklin and Adams a new reason to negotiate with King Louis XVI.

Gilbert and Adrienne

In February, LaFayette returned to Paris, and was welcomed as a hero for his service as aide-de-camp to the famous American General George Washington. However, the king could not welcome LaFayette as a hero as his people had. The king remembered all too well just how the young and impertinent nobleman had left for America, flagrantly disobeying the orders of the king. Louis knew he could not allow such a precedent to be set. LaFayette was immediately seized, and taken to the infamous Bastille in Paris, which housed the most vile of prisoners. For two weeks, the marquis slept on scattered hay and straw, in a cold, dark, damp cell, and shared his rations of stale bread and tepid water with rats and all form of diseased vermin, all simply to prove the king's absolute rule.

Soon he was freed, and immediately went to the home of his wife and daughter on the Rue de la Madeleine, on a rise of land overlooking the River Seine, and the skyline of the city. LaFayette was proud to have been asked by the president of the American Congress and General Washington to travel back to France as a diplomat. He was anxious to meet with Franklin and Adams at Passy where Franklin resided. But first, he was anxious to see his wife, the beautiful Adrienne, and his daughter.

LaFayette's mother had arranged for his marriage, to insure the du Motier's family name, fortune, and survival after the death of her husband. In 1774, Gilbert, at age seventeen, married the beautiful Marie Adrienne Francoise de Noailles, the fourteen-year-old daughter of one of the wealthiest men in France, Jean-Paul Francoise, 5th duc de Noailles.

Young Gilbert much enjoyed his life in an arranged marriage, as was commonplace among the European nobility. It allowed for freedoms from being tied down to one woman, especially in the realm of the physical pleasures of marriage. Who could fault any young man, saddled with a wife not of his own choosing, and a marriage not secured by love?

LaFayette had actually found his young wife quite pleasing in appearance, and in spirit as well. He could easily have fallen in love with Adrienne on his own, but was thankful his mother had intervened, and selected a bride for him.

Soon after they were married, Gilbert and Adrienne were expecting a child. Marie had been born in the late autumn of 1775.

"My how my little Marie has grown," LaFayette said.

"Oh, Papa," the young girl spoke, "I am no longer your Little Marie. I am just Marie and all grown up."

He kissed her on her forehead. "No no, mon cheri, you shall always be my Little Marie."

She kissed him, jumped down from his lap, and ran out of the parlor to her playroom, smiling.

"And how beautiful she is!" the marquis turned to his beautiful, young wife.

"She is beautiful," agreed Adrienne, "but so strong-willed!"

"That is good," Gilbert added. "She is beautiful, as her two parents are beautiful, and as any child we might bring into this world would be so destined for beauty. But strong-willed, no! Marie is simply determined and self-confident. I would have it no other way! She needs a brother or a sister, Adrienne," Gilbert said, "so perhaps she becomes less, as you say, strong-will."

"Oh, Gilbert!" Adrienne seemed to immediately dismiss any such suggestion.

"I shall make certain," LaFayette said flatly, "before my work is finished here and I sail back for the war in America, I shall provide a baby brother or baby sister for my little Marie. Yes I shall," LaFayette said with a huge smile.

"We shall see, Gilbert," Adrienne said, rising to leave the room. "Perhaps."

"You know you cannot resist my romantics," LaFayette said to Adrienne before she left the room. "I am, as you said our wedding night, so irresistible! No?"

She turned, blushed, and smiled at the husband she had grown to miss lying beside her in her bed.

"The king is hosting a ball at Versailles to welcomne you home, marquis," the aged Ben Franklin said, as he and John Adams met with him at what was considered the American Embassy, Franklin's home at Passy, a small village on the edge of Paris. "This will be our first invitation to the palace since October. I pray your return will give us entrée to return to our mediations."

"You must now be in good standing with the king," Adams added. "The king must be satisfied with your short prison term. If you had been insubordinate to George III, I dare say you'd be rotting away in the Tower of London."

"King Louie is a noble and fair man," laughed LaFayette. "I have now reclaimed my favorable position at his court, as if not a thing had come between us. It did, however, take two full weeks in the Bastille instead of the simple over night stay I felt would be called for," he laughed some more. "But whatever the delay, we shall soon welcome the Comte de Rochambeau and his army of six thousand Frenchmen to the American shores."

"We must leave the ball tomorrow with a set date for restarting our deliberations with the king," Adams added.

"Why should we wait?" LaFayette questioned Adams. "Let us deliberate with Louie at the ball over pate de foie gras and petits gateaux. We can set a date for the signing of the treaty as we enjoy champagne with the king, and pleasure ourselves in watching his beautiful Queen Marie Antoinette dancing the minuet."

"King Louie does so enjoy the subtle negotiations," Franklin said, having much preferred mixing business with pleqasure as his style of diplomacy.

Remembering Boston

"I'll be home for supper," Wills shouted from the front door of the house on Landsdowne Street. He walked off, securing around his neck, the red scraf Priscilla had knitted him for Christmas, to ward off the day's winter winds. It was March 5th and the city was celebrating the ninth anniversary of the Boston Massacre.

Wills didn't plan on going to Fanuiel Hall for the orations, although the popular pamphleteer, Thomas Paine, was to speak. Wills wanted to spend the day seeing how things had changed, since the days he led the Plug Uglies in protest to Parliament and King George. Back then, he had no idea he would some day become the secretary to George Washington, and see the battlefields of a war for independence.

He wanted to go to the harbor, and visit old man Eads at the print shop. He wanted to stop in the tavern at the wharf, and his old rented rooms at Susan Estridge's house, where Rennie had been conceived the night the minutemen rode to awaken countryside.

Things had changed little at the harbor. The most apparent change was the absence of British British ships, flying the despised British Union Jack. All the ships and fishing boats now flew the new American flag with the thirteen red and white stripes and the blue field with thirteen white stars. There were a couple of French merchantman ships flying the Fleur de Lis of France, and a Dutch ship flying a Dutch flag. He saw two ships of the Continental Navy flying the American flag along with the coiled rattlesnake with the words, "Don't Tread On Me!"

"Wills Winkman!" Josh Beadle, wearing the apron of a printer, cried out as he saw Wills coming into the print shop. "It is so good seeing you."

"And you Beadle, as well," said Wills. "Is Mr. Eads here today?"

"I am sorry, no," Beadle said, in an almost whisper. "Benjamin Eads was killed at Bennington. They brought his body back for a proper burial at the Granary."

"So many of our old friends populate that place now," Wills said.

"Indeed they do, indeed they do," Beadle agreed. "All of the victims of the massacre, the Seider boy, Christopher, they're all planted there."

"I must add a stop there on my way back to Cambridge," Wills said. "Who, then now owns the print shop?" Wills asked.

"I manage it for the widow Eads," Beadle said. "I am buying it m'self. I have left the sign alone. Some day, when I own it free and clear, I'll hang a new sign proclaiming 'Joshua Beadle Printer,' but I may not change it at all, just keeping Eads on the shingle in our old mentor's honor."

"He was a great man, and a great teacher," Wills said.

"He wanted to see you run it, Wills, but you headed out with Washington," Beadle said. "I'm sure glad you were gone, or I'd never have had the chance. You are still with General Washington, are you not?"

"Yes, and this is my first visit with my wife and children in Cambridge, since we marched to New York in '76. Might I go up to the long room and look around for old ghosts there while I'm here?"

"I'm afraid I have rented it out to a merchant for storage," Beadle said. "I haven't a key."

"Well then, I think I will head off to the tavern, and get a hot toddy to warm up m' insides."

"I would join you," Beadle said, "and there is really no business today with the celebrations going on, but I rarely have quiet time enough to catch up on pending orders. If I would have known you were stopping in, I'd have damn-certain put an apron upon you and set you to work. I'll never be the printer you were, Wills."

"I would have enjoyed it," Wills smiled, "but don't put yourself down. I remember you as a quite good man at the presses." Beadle smiled, and Wills headed to the door.

"You'll probably run into some of your old friends at the tavern," Josh yelled. "Apollos Revere, Alex Seider and others are seen there most days. I even saw ole Johnny Kilkenny there a day or so ago."

"Johnny Kilkenny?" Wills stopped in his tracks and turned back. "Is he not still with the navy?"

"Oh, yes indeed, and the captain of a fine frigate," Beadle said, as Wills smiled. "His ship, 'The Enfield' is moored just there," Beadle pointed out the window to the beautiful Navy ship he had seen flying the coiled snake flag.

"I was on the Enfield with Kilkenny when he brought those captured cannons to Rhode Island," Wills said. "I hope I run into him at the tavern."

Wills smiled and walked out the door. He headed to the tavern, took a seat by a window, and ordered a hot rum toddy.

"You bastard of a no good for nothin' Englishman's whore!" a voice came from behind him. Wills knew it was Johnny. He jumped to his feet and turned facing his tormentor.

"Johnny Kilkenny!" Wills yelled. "You measley no good for nothin' imbecile of an Irish teague!" The two old friends hugged and Johnny pulled up a seat.

Johnny had had quite a career in the navy, even after sailing with Admiral Hopkins in the Bahamas, and capturing Lord Dunmore's stolen arms from Williamsburg. He, at the wheel of the Enfield, and Jeremiah Prevost in the Cambridge, had raided British merchant ships up and down the east coast, making quite a name for themselves, as the rest of the fledgling fleet was bottled up in Narragansett Bay. He and Prevost then captained their ships alongside John Paul Jones, raiding the Irish coast during the past year. Now, for the most part, he shuttled diplomats to and from Europe.

"I just returned from Marseille takin' the Marquis de LaFayette home ta France," Johnny said. "Ole King Louis XVI's been a stallin' at sendin' more French troops to fight those damned Hessians. Washington sent him over ta help out old Ben Franklin and our own Johnny Adams."

"LaFayette is a great man," spoke Wills. "I remember the day he arrived at headquarters, and I introduced him to Washington. He's been with Washington ever since. I didn't know the general was planning on sending him to Europe though."

"Oh, he's there alright, but he'll be back by the end o' the year," Johnny said.

"How long are you in Boston?" Wills asked.

"This is me home port," Johnny said. "I'll be back in Marseille in the summer sometime, prob'ly ta fetch John Adams and his son back home. An' who knows, maybe LaFayette too by then. I took the Adamses over last year, Mr. Adams an' his ten-year-old boy Johnny, who's a servin' as the father's secretary. When you goin' back ta the army?"

"Washington told me to report in May to West Point on the Hudson."

"You have a boy o' yer own, don't you?" Johnny asked.

"Yes, Rennie, we call him. He turns three on the twentieth," Wills said proudly, "and a daughter too, Victoria, who just turned two. Priscilla is once more with child," Wills smiled proudly.

"Damn!" Johnny said, "Are the two o' you not just the prolific ones in the bed!" Wills laughed.

"Join us for supper tonight, Kilkenny," Wills invited. "Priscilla would love to see you once more, and you could meet Rennie and Victoria for yourself. You know the way. Lord knows you took many a meal at that dinner table."

"Let me take ya on a tour o' me ship, then I'll just come along with ya," Johnny suggested to his friend. "She's been total refitted now, from when you were aboard 'er at Charlestown. You wouldn't recognize the ole Enfield now."

They finished their toddies and walked aboard the beautiful ship, "Enfield," then stopped by for tea and cakes with Sarah Estridge at the house, where Wills had rented the upstairs rooms.

On their walk back to Cambridge, Wills and Johnny walked through the Granary Burial Grounds, stopping at several headstones proclaiming names of old friends ... Samuel Maverick, Christopher Seider, Crispus Attucks, Annie Macneal, Benjamin Eads and Miles Reynolds, Wills' father-in-law, who was struck down in the Battle of Bunker Hill. He was anxious to get back to Cambridge.

"Leastwise," Johnny said, "our names ain't etched in any o' them stones ...yet."

Changes at Winston Woods

Peter put down the leather bound copy of <u>Captain Jack</u>, by Daniel Defoe, the judge and Adella had given him on Christmas Day. Peter had always said his favorite novel had been Defoe's <u>Robinson Crusoe.</u> This new book was about an orphaned youngster, who grew up in poverty on the streets of London, with the ambition of becoming a gentleman. Peter enjoyed the new book, as he knew he would when he first opened it on Christmas Day.

Peter had spent almost three months, waiting at Winston Woods for news from Jimmie Monroe of his recruitment plans. He was disappointed Zack had not returned, and in Zack's absence, Peter was missing the companionship of the men of the 3rd Virginia.

The judge and Adella had not seen Zachary since both Peter and Pat last saw him, in Williamsburg, when he and Rodie Murray headed off with the Magruder party for the Carolinas.

"We hear from Zachary about every month or so," said Adella at the breakfast table. "The mails are so slow getting to us from the Spanish territory."

"The Spanish territory?" Peter asked.

Adella continued, "They went on to New Orleans, Peter, and have been there for over two years."

"Zachary's last letter was from a small French settlement called Saint Louis, along the Mississippi River, somewhere north of the Ohio River," added the judge. "They were there taking a supply of goods to a trading post. Mountainmen from the Rocky Mountains bring their pelts and furs there, and the boys took a load of furs back to New Orleans."

"Knowing Zack," Peter added his impressions, "he'll be heading west to those mountains before long."

"I so wish he does not," pined Adella. "He has a thriving income painting portraits of the noble families in New Orleans. I so hope he settles down and tends to that...or decides to come back to Virginia."

"Yes, we both miss him tremendously," said the judge. "But the lad does have that wandering nature about him."

"He does indeed," agreed Peter. "I am just happy to hear he is happy."

Many things had changed on the plantation since he had left nearly eight years before.

The Winston girls were pretty little things. The oldest, Angelica Christmas turned nine on Christmas Day. She was the judge's little Christmas angel. Angel, as she was called, was a sweet spirited youngster, petite in appearance, with blonde curls like her mother. She seemed older than her young age indicated, and seemed not to cause any trouble at all.

Angel's sister, Christina Noelle, called Noelle, as a reminder of the season of her birth, had celebrated her sixth birthday five days before

Christmas. Noelle was also beautiful, but with dark red hair, like the judge, and piercing large blue eyes. Unlike Angel, Noelle seemed to have a mean streak in her. She was undoubtedly spoiled, and seemed to feel forced to compete against her older sister for affection. She was clearly jealous of Angel, and if she didn't get her way, she took her vengance out on her older sister.

Adella was pregnant a third time. She was due in April, and hoped the baby would come on Easter Sunday. She had also picked out a name, Della Easter. Adella was so proud of her "little ladies" as she referred to Angel and Noelle, but the judge really hoped their third child might be a son.

The judge also told Peter that Christina Donnelley had married the legislator Calvert McGowan.

"Are they living at the tavern?" Peter asked.

"No, they are living on a plantation McGowan bought in Buckingham County, west of Richmond," the judge answered Peter's question. "But the tavern is still there, being operated by your old playmate, Joshua."

"Joshua Donnelley?" Peter asked.

"Yes," the judge said, "he's near twenty years-old now, and doing a right fine job with the tavern. Auntie Savannah is still there, making those famous rum buns. But she doesn't light the hearth fires before daylight any more. Joshua does most of the work. She is nearly seventy years old now, Peter. She keeps herself in the kitchen, cooking her flapjacks for breakfast and seeing to the mid-day meals. She retires to her room upstairs in the afternoon."

"It would be so good to see them again," said Peter, "before she joins old Nico in the graveyard."

"Well, perhaps you can accompany me the next time I go to City Point," the judge offered. Peter smiled.

"Perhaps we could all go," Adella said, "and go on to Williamsburg and stay at the Governor's Palace with Patrick. He's the governor now, don't you know?"

The household slave girl, Cassia, now twenty-five, and a beautiful ebony-skinned young mother, had been married to the slave Alexander, who was the most-able carpenter and cabinetmaker on the plantation. She still helped her aging parents with the serving duties in the manor house, and was the favored seamstress. The judge had set up a room in the house for her and Alexander, and their two-year-old son, Ezekiel.

Peter's friend, Pearlie, was now a plantation carpenter. His brother-in-law had trained him. Pearlie moved into the attic room over the carpentry shop, as soon as Alexander moved into the manor house with Cassia. When Peter visited him in his attic room, Pearlie told him he was going to start preaching the gospel to the slaves, with the judge's permission, and Rev. Gadsden's encouragement.

"I want to give them the understanding of God's mercy to all men…all his creations, not just to the white masters," Pearlie said.

"That's wonderful! Do we now call you Preacher Pearlie?" Peter asked

"Some do already call me that," Pearlie smiled.

"And I hear you are quite good with the skills of cabinetry," Peter asked further, as Pearlie smiled and nodded.

"I enjoy working with wood," Pearlie said. "You know Jesus was raised by a carpenter named Joseph, and he, Jesus himself, learned as a boy to be a carpenter as well. I pray I can be able soon to tell those stories to my people, and give them the same knowledge I have, that Jesus died for all men's sins."

Peter spent time in the plantation cemetery. There he'd stop beneath the long-limbed weeping willow, for a few moments to talk to his papa and mama. He knew their bodies were not there, but also knew the place was where he could commune with them, and with God.

"Papa," Peter said one morning, "I have tried my best to be the man you and Mama would want me to be." He shared some stories with them, but knew in his heart he really didn't have to. He knew their spirits had been with him as he crossed the Delaware with Washington, and lay in the Huber farmhouse with LaFayette, mending after being hit by a Hessian musket ball at Brandywine. He just needed to tell them himself.

As Peter sat in the study that day with the closed copy of <u>Captain Jack</u>, he heard footsteps and a voice.

"I'm marrying Patricia!" Pat blurted out.

"What!?! When?" Peter questioned Pat, jumping up and hugging his friend.

"On Palm Sunday," Pat explained, "Rev. Gadsden will marry us at the end of the services. Will you stand up for me, Peter?"

"Of course, I will," said Peter. "Of course I will."

The Courtship of Benedict Arnold

"This simple-minded town is all a-buzz with celebrations, for some band of frontiersmen taking some insignificant British outpost called Vincennes," fumed the military commander of Philadelphia. "They assume, stupidly, that their independence is now all but assured." Benedict Arnold now sounded more like a loyalist than a member of George Washington's command.

"And that insipid Washington, wants you to give up your residence in this fine home," added his new fiancé, the lovely Peggy Shippen, as they sat in the parlor of the Franklin House.

"Oh yes. He says Clinton stayed here only as an enemy occupier," Arnold went on, "and feels people may view me as such. Where would he have me live? ... in a tent on the edge of town? I think not! I shall stay put right here in my home!"

"At least that impossible man and his plump and dowdy wife will soon leave our city," said Peggy, "Lady Washington actually invited us to honeymoon at Mount Vernon, of all places. Can you imagine, spending our first days of marital bliss dining on a pig roasted in the ground, and watching the slaves pick cotton, or pick whatever slaves pick in Virginia?" They both laughed.

"Well, the wedding does approach, dear," Arnold acknowledged, with a smile. "April the eighth is just a few weeks away."

Peggy pulled him closer to her on the sofa.

"Ben," Peggy said, in a soft, flirtatious voice, "I think I should begin sending packed trunks over, so I shall be ready to move in upon our wedding night." He kissed her on her cheek.

"Feel free to do so, my love," he said, and kissed her again, this time much more amorously on the lips.

"That way," Peggy said between kisses, "should the time arise and our passions build, I can stay the night in your bed to help you satisfy those passions."

Arnold pulled back, red in the face.

"I should think not," he said, staring at his intended. "We must control those passions best left unfulfilled until the vows be spoken, Peggy. We must." He again kissed her gently on the cheek.

"Yes, Ben," Peggy said, showing a slight disappointment, "you are, as always, correct… we must."

A sentry came into the parlor and announced a visitor. The Philadelphia merchant Joseph Stansbury entered and took a chair.

"Forgive me general," Stansbury said, "but I have some important papers I feel you must sign, regarding some of those lucrative commercial affairs you have ask me to see into for you."

"Wonderful," Peggy said, as she rose from the couch. "Joseph, pay heed that all dealings you do for General Arnold must be most lucrative, for in just a few weeks, the profits of those ventures shall be for him to pamper his lovely new bride. Now I have rounds I simply must attend to, so I shall take my leave, and you gentlemen might tend to those affairs with which I wish not to trouble my mind." She smiled and departed.

"What do you hear from Washington?" Stansbury asked, after Peggy had left the room.

"The great victory on the frontier won at Vincennes, proves the war is all but won, according to the wise general," Arnold replied, as both men laughed. "He turns his attentions now toward the Hudson Valley, to defend against Clinton's army, that has now, three months ago, taken Savannah, a full one thousand miles to the south! Such a military mind Washington does possess!" The two friends laughed at the expense of the American general.

"Well," Stansbury said, through tears of laughter, "it is nothing akin to victory, but, unfortunately, it does appear to be a legitimate set back for the British. The Governor stationed at Fort Detroit on the Great Lakes, was captured in that raid at Vincennes, and is, it has been learned by Clinton, a prisoner in Williamsburg to sit out the war."

"Hamilton was a fool," commented Arnold.

"But he was our fool, Ben, he was our fool. He did a splendid work in inciting the tribes to burn and scalp those American settlers in Kentucky," Stansbury said. "If that George Rogers Clark fellow marches now on to Fort Detroit, it can be taken more easily than even Vincennes was taken. That would leave the British with but a twenty-man garrison in the far north of the Michigan Peninsula. We can only hope Clark sits and waits, and does not attack Detroit."

"But Washington, concentrating on the Hudson Valley, with the bulk of the British forces now at Savannah, and soon no doubt at Charleston as well," Arnold criticized the American strategy, "tells us just how wrong Washington is."

"I feel you are wrong, Ben," Stansbury went on. "Clinton's reason for opening the southern strategy at Savannah is because he plans to march on the Hudson Valley, and finally divide the New England colonies from the rest, and end this war.

"The real reason for my visit today is not at all about your commercial interests, which by the by are reaping extreme good profits," Stansbury said, "but to arrange a meeting, perhaps this evening if it please you, with the merchant from New York you met your very first week here in Philadelphia."

"John Anderson?" Arnold smiled excitedly, in anticipation of seeing the handsome young man again.

"You do remember him," Stansbury responded. "Good!"

"Certainly I remember Anderson," Arnold added, "he is a most charming young fellow. I was about to ask why he has not yet returned to us here."

"Well, Benedict," Stansbury said, preparing to pass on a secret, "he arrived last evening. I needed to see you first because, he is not who you think him to be. He is actually General Sir Henry Clinton's most important aide, and his name, I know you have heard it much, is Major John Andre."

"Major Andre!" Arnold shot up from his chair. "Yes, I have heard quite often that name...the Major Andre who courted my Peggy, the same Major Andre who is Sir Henry's lover?" he sat back down.

"Yes, the same. Forgive me, Ben, but we could not let you in on his true identity until we knew where you really stood on the issues of this war," Stansbury explained. "Now it is vital for you and Andre to meet and to make plans for us to end this war."

"Does he know Peggy and I are to be married?" Arnold asked.

"Indeed he dose," assured Stansbury, "and is well pleased Peggy has finally found a husband. He most courteously turned down her proposal to him before leaving Philadelphia."

"Well then, at least there seems to be no cause for a duel between us," Arnold said. "I should find no pleasure in having to put an end to such a handsome young mnan's life."

"Absolutely none whatsoever," Stansbury chuckled. "Now Ben, might I extend an invitation to the major to join you here for dinner tonight?"

"I would be delighted to have Major Andre as my dinner companion this night," Arnold agreed.

Andre arrived at the Franklin House and dined alone with Arnold.

"Ben, I am so sorry for my role in the charade of not being truthful to you from the start," Andre said, as they sat at the dining table.

"No apology is needed," Arnold said. "If I had known your true identity, as the American commander of the city, I would have been forced to arrest you." They both laughed. "Now, as it turns out," Arnold went on, "we are the best of friends, and it appears there is much we now agree upon."

Chapter Fourteen

Riding Off to Camp

Washington knew he had to keep Sir Henry Clinton bottled up on the island of Manhattan. He knew, from the intelligence he was getting, that Clinton saw an end to the war and defeat for the patriots, if he could take back the Hudson River Valley. That way the five colonies east of the Hudson would be effectively isolated from the eight in the South. As he remained in Philadelphia in April, he was anxious to leave for the North in the coming weeks.

He had gotten favorable reports from the companies which had wintered along the Hudson, that a series of fortifications along the river could easily be built to make Sir Henry's plans hard to undertake.

Ships of the British fleet still patrolled up the river about halfway to Albany, with few American fortifications there to stop them. General Mad Anthony Wayne, one of Washington's favorites, was in charge during Washington's absence. Wayne was putting together an extensive plan to fortify the Hudson Valley as soon as the weather broke and Washington would return.

A Visit to Monticello

"Any word from Major Monroe, Peter," the judge said, as they sat on the back verandah, looking out over the Pamunkey, one Sunday afternoon..

"None!" Peter said, showing his angst and impatience. "The army will be breaking its winter camp at Middlebrook, probably by the first of June. I'd surely like to be there with them. While I feel much loyalty to help Jimmie, I do not think I can afford to wait much longer."

"You have fought in the army for over two years, Peter," said Adella, resting her hands on her now huge belly. She had hoped the baby would have been born a week before on Easter Sunday, but it was late in arriving.

"Have you not already done your duty? Why not shake the war off your boots and get on with your own life? With Pat now married, I'd think you might want to follow. Turn your attentions to a young lady. Settle down and raise a family right here."

"This land gave me a home when I was an orphaned boy dropped on the wharf at City Point," Peter said. "I love my new country, and feel I must do more than those privileged with birth here. I must be there with the army, until the Redcoats surrender and sail away from our shores."

"Then, with that in mind," the judge said, rising from his seat, "let's you and I go for a little afternoon stroll."

Peter immediately shot up from his seat.

"Now, Angel, you look after Mama," the judge said as Angel smiled.

"I will. Papa, let me," chimed in Noelle. "I'm a much better nursemaid than Angel!" The judge tousled her red curly head and smiled. "This is important enough a chore for you both to see to." He smiled at Adella, and walked off around the side of the house with Peter.

They soon came to the stables and paddock. The judge stopped and looked out into the pasture as his eight beautiful riding horses were grazing.

"Have you developed a personal friendship with any of the steeds in the army, Peter?" the judge asked.

"No, that is the one disappointment," Peter admitted. "For the most part, my feet have been my horse on our marches. Except for being given the old nags we were given at Philadelphia to come home at Christmas, horses ready for the pasture, I have seldom sat in a saddle. I hoped you might agree to me borrowing Lucifer, or maybe Hannibal."

"Why don't you go into the stable?" the judge suggested, "I think there is a horse not with the others in the field."

Peter had a perplexed look on his face, but obeyed the judge and went into the building.

"Coronado!" came the shriek from the stable. A horse's loud whinney followed. Peter ran to the horse and hugged his face.

"How did you come by Coronado?" Peter asked.

"Dr. Campbell had read of General Washington and LaFayette presenting you with that giant sword, and wished to present you with Coronado," the judge laughingly answered. "I picked him up last week. That was the business I had in Fredericksburg. I hid him in the stable yesterday when I returned home late, and hoped you'd stay away."

"I think," Peter said, "if you do not mind, I shall saddle Coronado, and take him on a ride."

"He's all yours, and I'm certain he'll be happy to take you off to New Jersey. It is a lovely day meant for a ride, Peter. You'll find your old saddle and tack in the box. Have a great ride." The judge turned and disappeared."

On Monday, in the late afternoon, a rider rode up to the manor house. Peter was just coming back from a ride on Coronado as the visiting rider dismounted.

"Peter Francisco! Is that you?" the dismounted rider shouted at him.

"You are one of the Madison boys, are you not?" Peter asked as he dismounted Coronado.

"Yes, Ambrose Madison," he replied, shaking Peter's hand and smiling. "I remember you joining us for a fox hunt at Montpelier a few years back."

Peter led the Ambrose into the house. They walked through to the verandah on the river.

"I am returning to Montpelier from Williamsburg," Ambrose said, "and Jimmy asked me to stop here with a message for you."

"Regarding Jimmie Monroe's regiment?" Peter asked anxiously.

"Somewhat," Ambrose said. "Jimmy said Monroe is meeting him at Montpelier tomorrow, and Jimmy is taking him to meet with Jefferson at Monticello. Jimmy wants very much for you to join them."

Ambrose spent the night at Winston Woods, and the two saddled up and rode for Madison Mills after breakfast the next morning. They arrived at the Montpelier estate in late afternoon, and were greeted by Jimmy Madison, and Jimmie Monroe.

The next morning, they all mounted their horses, even the small-statured Jimmy Madison, seemingly in much better health than he had been saddled with in his youth.

The journey was one new to Peter. It went south, then west into the town of Charlottesville. The road from town wound up the eastern face of the Blue Ridge Mountains. It passed by a tavern, just at the base of the winding packed dirt lane. At the top, they passed a small cemetery with a few Jefferson family members interred there. Then the lane turned flat and ran south across the summit of the mountain for about a mile, passing the beautiful columned west front of the graceful Paladian mansion, called Monticello.

When the three riders were shown into the mansion by the liveried valet, Jefferson was seated in the library with a young militiaman.

"Come in my fwiends," Jefferson said with his pronounced lisp. His red head of hair was unruly atop the handsome and noble head. He was dressed in a flowing maroon silk house robe and slippers.

"I apologize fo' my casual appeawance, gentlemen," Jefferson explained, "but these past thwee days, I have been confined to the bed with the most inconvenient indigestion twoubles. Have seats, please."

The three new arrivals found seats as Jefferson introduced his other guest.

"This young man is a captain in the local militia, Nathaniel Massie," Jefferson said. "I took the libe'ty of inviting him, due to the topic we awe to discuss."

The conversation dealt with Monroe's attempts to recruit a new regiment for the Continental Army, and Jefferson's coming elevation to the governor's chair in June. Monroe had received little encouragement from his efforts so far. Governor Henry would not give him an official commission to build a regiment, knowing he was leaving the office, and felt it better to leave such an appointment to Jefferson, his intended successor.

"With the Bwitish now concentwating on the southe'n colonies," Jefferson said, "I feel it to be pwudent we concentwate any such militawy effo'ts on the militia hewe, instead of the a'my as a whole."

534

"Washington will undoubtedly send an army south, under General Greene or Mad Anthony Wayne," Monroe began to plead his case. "My intentions would be to join that army, being ready to join them as they march through Virginia to the Carolinas."

"The Fwench, it is lea'ned," added Jefferson, "awe sending six thousand men. I should think that should be a sufficient fowce for Washington.

"My concewn must be fo' the safety of the citizens of Vi'ginia," said Jefferson. "We sit between the two coming together ... New Yo'k's Hudson Valley and the piedmont of the Cawolinas. If the Bwitish open two fwonts to the southe'n campaign, Vi'ginia is destined fo' an invasion of Wedcoats. Vi'ginia shall be the final battlegwound. That I feaw."

Jefferson would commence his term as governor on the first day of June, in six weeks. He was not going to make any definite decision, one way or the other, until then.

Peter was disappointed with the tone Jefferson set for the meeting. Certainly, if the war came to Virginia, Washington would send the army. But until then, men were badly needed along the Hudson. Peter had faith in Washington, inviting Peter and the others to join the Virginia Militia with Captain Massie.

Jefferson ended the meeting, and instructed his valet to show his guests to rooms in the mansion for the night. After the meeting, there were a couple hours before dinner, so Jimmy Madison, Peter and the young Captain Massie took seats on the mansion's east front portico, where the view was panoramic, taking in the Virginia landscape for a hundred miles or more, as far as the eye could see.

"There, over there," Madison said, pointing, "is Montpelier."

"And there," he pointed to a spot about midway between Charlottesville and Montpelier, "is Shadwell. Shadwell is where Jefferson' father had his estate, where Jefferson was born. The manor house burnt to the ground years ago."

With Madison and Jefferson having been members of the House of Delegates, they had not only become close political allies, but also the very best of friends. Madison spent many days and nights at Monticello, the most beautiful mountaintop estate in Virginia.

"He wanted to build a mansion on this mountaintop ever since he was a boy," Madison told his friends. "He and a young friend used to hike here. His friend died and is buried in the cemetery we passed. Jefferson is a student of classical architecture, and designed Monticello himself. He started building ten years ago. He has a brilliant mind, and will lead this nation some day."

Monroe soon came out of the mansion to join his friends.

"So, what business did Mr. Jefferson have with you, Jimmie?" Peter boldly asked, hoping Jimmie had convinced the author of the "Declaration of Independence" to change his mind and authorize a new Virginia regiment for the Continental Army.

"He wants me to read law with him, and become a lawyer," Jimmie said.

"What?" Peter said, stunned.

"Wonderful," Madison chimed in. "You could not learn the law from any one more capable. He was trained by George Wythe, the best legal mind in any one of the states."

Jefferson and his frail-looking, but lovely wife Martha, hosted them at an elegant dinner that evening. A feature of the dining room Jefferson had invented fascinated Peter. It was a panel in the wall that when opened, displayed a flat serving board. Servants in the ground level kitchen would place hot trays of food, then raise it one floor up to the dining room, tugging on ropes on pulleys. Servants in the dining room could then serve the hot meals to the guests. When the dirty dishes needed to be removed from the dining room, servers in the room would stack the used plates and glasses on the serving board, and kitchen servants would lower them. Jefferson was proud of what he called his "dumb waiter", as he was proud of all the inventions his immaculate mind had come up with, and he had found places for them in his beautiful mansion.

After dinner they all went into the music room for wine. Jefferson was a connoisseur and collector of rare wines. Aside from the wines, the highlight was Martha sitting at the harp, and Jefferson at his cello, playing light aires to their dinner guests.

The Jeffersons had two young daughters, Martha, called Patsy, age six and Mary, called Polly, just an infant. They had had two others, born between Martha and Mary, but those two, a daughter Jane and an unnamed son, were under two of the small headstones in the estate's cemetery.

There was another young girl in the mansion, a delightful five-year-old household slave girl. Sally, as she was called, was a beautiful light-skinned child, who could easily pass as a white child. Sally had helped serve the dinner that evening. She was what was called a "quadroon", because she was three-quarters white throughout her ancestry. Because her female ancestors were all black African slaves, the white blood in her veins legally meant nothing. According to Virginia statutes, she too must be considered a black slave.

Young Sally was the daughter of the main house slave, the forty-eight year-old Elizabeth Hemings, who, like Sally, could easily pass as white. Martha Jefferson's father, John Wayles of Charles City County, near Williamsburg, had bought Elizabeth years ago. When he died in 1773, his will left the Hemings slaves to Martha, who had recently married Jefferson. Elizabeth was "with child" at the time, probably the child of her master, John Wayles. Sally was born shortly after the Hemings slaves arrived at Monticello. She soon became the favored household slave of the Jeffersons, mainly because they felt, as most people felt, the infant Sally Hemings was indeed Martha Jefferson's half-sister.

On the ride back to Montpelier, and then on to Winston Woods, Peter thought back to the wonderful time he had just experienced with the Jeffersons at Monticello. He was very disappointed in Jimmie Monroe not being able to win his case for a new Virginia regiment for Washington's army. How could Jimmie turn down an invitation from the man who was soon to be governor, and study law privately under the tutelage of Thomas Jefferson himself? He smiled, knowing Jimmie Monroe was embarking on an important career, but he himself, atop Coronado, would, in a few days, ride north to rejoin Washington.

Peter spent just a few more days at Winston Woods before he was ready to ride north. The newly wedded Peter Patrick rode back to the army with him. They stopped in the early afternoon of their second day at the Hicks homestead near Manassas. They wanted to see if Garrett and Malcolm were as anxious to get back to the army as they were.

"Oh m' god!" shouted Garrett sitting in the yard under a big willow tree, eating his midday meal at a small table with two others, "I jest saw me an ugly ole giant! Quick boys, run fer yer lives!"

He laughed, got up and ran over to Peter, sitting atop Coronado, and Pat atop his dapple gray stallion, Frank.

"That looks all the world like ole Coronado," Garrett said, as he approached and grabbed the horse's face in his hands. "It is! Is ole Peter still a thinkin' he can talk ta ya boy?" The horse nodded his head up and down.

"You doin' alright, Pat?" Garrett asked, shaking Pat's hand.

"He up and got married three weeks ago," Peter announced.

"Ta, ...what was her name, ...Patty Pat?" Garrett asked.

"Yes, Patricia Patterson," Pat said proudly. "She is now Mrs. Patricia Patterson Patrick, but we all call her Tricia.

"Pat Pat Pat's what I'd be a callin' 'er," Garrett chuckled. "Well," he said in a loud whisper, putting an arm around Pat's shoulders and slowly starting to walk with him, "what's it like a 'doin' it' with Pat Pat Pat?"

"He's already got her with child!" Peter shouted. Garrett stopped dead in his tracks.

"Ya don't mean ta tell me ya figgered out jest how ta plant your tiny little feller up inside that sweet young thing, an' your seed actually up an' took root?" Garrett roared with a smile ear-to-ear.

"Please promise me one thing," Garrett was bent over in laughter. "Promise me that that young'in o' yer'n won't be named anything that starts with the letter 'P'!" Everyone laughed.

Peter and Pat told Garrett how Jimmie Monroe's plans had not worked out. They told him they didn't want to miss out on any action in the war, and were heading to Middlebrook before Washington broke winter camp and moved out.

"Im sure ready," said Garrett, "Malcolm too. We're both as homesick as Hell fer more o' that god awful food, marchin' miles on end every day, and duckin' them dang Hessian musket balls. Hell yes, we'll go."

"We'd like ta head off in the morning," Pat said. "Can ya be ready ta mount up so we can leave at first light."

"Let's head on over ta the Shepherd place an' light a fire up un'er neath ole Malcolm's tail," Garrett said. "We can be ready...but can we wait till Mammy sets out her biscuits an' gravy in the mornin'? You 'member them biscuits and gravy don't ya mister giant man? It'll only delay us 'bout an hour...but well-worth not havin' ta listen ta that giant gut o' yer'n a growlin' all the way to Maryland!"

The Storming of Stony Point

Sir Henry Clinton sent eight thousand men north from Manhattan, up the Hudson Valley in late May, in an attempt to draw Washington out from the scattered American outposts in the mountains there. Washington, however was still in New Jersey, but receiving the news from West Point, headed north immediately, arriving in the Hudson Valley on the seventh day of June.

Washington took a position atop Buckberg Mountain, where, through his telescope, he could watch the Redcoat soldiers and their American Loyalist allies, build their fort. They did not build a fort in the traditional sense, using wood or massive stone works, but simply dug a system of earthworks. Washington watched as they downed trees and sharpened one end of the logs to make wooden structures called 'abatis' to make any assault from invading ground troops more difficult.

Washington spent the best part of a week, sitting atop Nelson on the mountaintop, out of sight of the Lt. Col. Henry Johnson and his Redcoats at Stony Point. He spied what men Johnson had in his command, and estimated the numbers to be under one thousand. It appeared to be about two-and-a-half regiments of infantry, as well as fifteen field artillery pieces, seven cannons, four mortars and four howitzers. There was also a Royal Navy gunboat and a British sloop, 'the Vulture,' patrolling the river.

One of the most strategic features of the outpost at Stony Point was its physical location. It set on a promontory, jutting out into the Hudson, surrounded on three sides, the north, east and south, by a steep, rocky riverbank. The land to the south was marshy. The outpost appeared to be accessible only from the west. Stony Point sat directly across the river from Verplanck's Point. With the British outpost at

Stony Point, the most usable crossing of the river, King's Ferry, was now unavailable as a safe crossing for the American Army.

Washington needed a victory to start the war season of 1779. Using the intelligence he saw through his telescope, and what intelligence he received from traders passing through the area, he began to set a plan of attack. Wills Winkman, back in camp after his extended furlough at Cambridge, sent for Major General Anthony Wayne to help plan the attack.

"Col. Johnson expects any attack to come from the west," Washington spoke, pointing to the map. Wills had drawn the map from his many hours alongside Washington, as the general spied on the British from the mountaintop. "The southern and northern flanks of the fort have little artillery to defend with."

"Then we orchestrate a three-pronged attack," Wayne suggested. "Our men, under the cover of darkness, can quietly scale those rocks, cross the breastworks, and storm the fort from both of the least defended sides."

"My thoughts are similar," said Washington. "There is a narrow beach running here," he pointed to the map. "It runs along the south, and is very accessible at low tide. The main assault would come from the south, along the beach and up the rocks."

"By making it appear the main assault is coming from the west, as they suspect," offered Wayne, "I can lead four-to-five hundred of the best light infantry from the south, and take it quickly. The force coming from the north would be our support."

"I demand total surprise," said Washington, as he seemed to agree with the one general on his staff he had the most respect for in the way of strategic competence. "I order the men to attack only with bayonets. I want not the sound of rifles and muskets firing to alert the enemy."

"Very well, general," said Wayne, "but I suggest the attack straight on the center from the west be a galling burst of fire with weapons blaring. Therefore, diverting all attention from the north and south, from where the storming of the fort will be coming"

Washington smiled. He agreed and knew the plans would give General Sir Henry Clinton a taste of surprise and devastation.

On July 11th, General Wayne formed the special Corps of Light Infantry from the best and bravest infantrymen among the soldiers in

Washington's army. Wayne had been impressed with several Virginians, and named Peter, Pat, Garrett and Malcolm to the special force that he himself would lead in the main assault from the south, across the narrow beach, and up the steep, rocky bank to the breastworks.

On the morning of the 15th, the army marched out to the east, following a circuitous route through the mountains west of Stony Point, so as not to be detected by Lt. Col. Johnson and the men of his garrison. Just before sunset, they had arrived at the Springsteel Farm, undetected, one and a half miles west of the British fort. For two hours the men sat and relaxed, as best they could, before they would receive their actual orders.

"It mus' be somethin' big we're a settin' out for t'night," Garrett said, as the Virginians sat and drank their ration of rum General Wayne had ordered for each man. "They don't pass out this good o' rum if'n it ain't somethin' mighty they want out o' us."

"An' we're gonna be right smack-dab in the thick of it," said Malcolm, "elsewise, ole Mad Anthony wouldn't've handpicked us fer the job."

"General Wayne picked us 'cause we're the best," said Pat.

"Nope," said Garrett, "he picked us cause we're fool 'nough ta hang 'roun' this damned ole giant over here," he said, looking right at Peter, who was rubbing a rag up and down his six-foot long, specially-made broadsword from Washington and LaFayette. Peter smiled, but didn't add to the conversation.

"Ole George Washin'ton jus' wants ta make gall-darned sure his money wasn't wasted on that ole sword fer Peter," added Malcolm. "If'n Peter don't run through a pack o' Redcoats with that there sword, I hear Peter's joinin' the prison train down ta Easton." They all laughed.

At ten o'clock, the men were formed into their attack columns, and given their actual orders.

"We're sure a fightin' right 'longside Mad Anthony," Malcolm said.

"An' not able ta use nothin' 'ceptin' our bayonets," added Garrett.

"An' he's ordered us to keep quiet," said Peter. "You think you can manage that Hicks? ...Shepherd?"

"I'm just a wonderin' how in Hell you're gonna climb up them rocks with that three hund'erd pounds o' lard ya carry in that seven-foot body o' yer'n," Garrett said, getting one last jab in at Peter while he could still talk.

"Lordy, lordy," said Malcolm. "I surely don't wanna be a'hind 'im, an' have ta somehow maneuver 'roun' his moldry carcass, if'n he falls off'n them rocks."

"Hell, Malcolm, if'n he does falls ya, won't have a thing to fret over," added Garrett. "His fall'll take us all down with him." Peter smiled at their ribbings as all his friends joined in on the laughter.

The men were all handed pieces of white paper and a stick pin to pin the paper to their hats. With the darkness of the night, Wayne wanted some way for his men to identify themselves from the enemy. And it was a dark night. There was heavy cloud cover, totally obscuring any moonlight. At half-past eleven, the army moved out in their assigned columns to their jumping-off spots, to be ready to begin the assault exactly at midnight.

The column Peter and his Virginia friends were assigned to was delayed about half-an-hour by the marshes not being a low tide as expected. They had to walk in river water of two-to-four feet in depth. Their trudging through the water necessarily made some noise, and sentries on the east side of the fort opened fire.

General Wayne was the first one hit by the sentries' fire. A bullet grazed his head with enough impact to knock him to the ground. Wayne was right in front of Peter, who saw his general fall, and felt the whiz of the British bullet zinging by his own head. He ran to Wayne.

The men inside the fort suddenly saw and heard what they assumed was the main invading force coming from the west. The Americans, as planned, fired loud and constant barrage at the fort from the west. The Redcoats assembled on the west wall to return that fire.

"Go on Francisco," Wayne ordered him. "I shall be fine, and will join you men inside the fort. Pull down that damn flag of their's Francisco...capture the flag!"

Peter rushed ahead furiously with his orders, leaving Wayne on the ground where he had fallen.

"Come on boys," Peter shouted as he led the men over the first of the breastworks. "I'm gonna get me a Redcoat or two." Peter drew his gargantuan sword and ran through two grenadiers, leaving them dead on the ground. He rushed on with Garrett, Malcolm and Pat alongside. They were the first ones inside the fort, along with a half-dozen Pennsylvanians who came in from the north.

Peter ran to the flagpole and pulled down the Union Jack. As he turned, with the British flag under his arm, a third British grenadier slashed him deeply across this stomach. In pain, Peter stayed on his feet, drew his sword and killed his attacker.

"Dammit man!" came a cry from one of the Pennsylvanians, "that was some fine sword play." Peter smiled and slumped to his knees, then down fully onto the ground.

"You gonna be alright?" the Pennsylvanian bent down to Peter. Peter just nodded.

"Well, I'll stay with ya," he said. "This here battle's about through with anyways, and we done won the day."

Garrett, Malcolm, Pat and the handful of Pennsylvanians, all with bayonets drawn, marched in a long row toward the Redcoats defending the diversionary assault from the west. Seeing the Americans with their bayonets, the Redcoats dropped their guns, raised their hands, and gave up the fight.

"The Fort's our own!" yelled Garrett. That was the watchword the soldiers outside the fort were waiting to hear.

"The fort's our own!" Garrett yelled again, as the other men yelled too. The Storming of Stony Point was ended after only twenty-five minutes.

Soon, General Wayne was back on his feet and came into the fort himself. He saw Peter lying on the ground.

"Are you going to make it, Francisco," Wayne stooped over and asked the fallen giant, with the torn down Union Jack clutched under his arm.

"I'll be fine, sir," Peter said.

"We need to get this man to Fishkill for attention to that nasty wound!" Wayne yelled out. "We cannot have gangrene set in upon this brave young man."

"I will see to it sir," said the Pennsylvanian who hadn't left Peter once he fell. Garrett rushed over to Peter. "How ya doin' big man?" Garrett asked Peter, as Malcolm and Pat rushed up too.

"Guess I'm headin' to Fishkill to recuperate," Peter said. "Maybe I'll share another bedchamber with Lafayette."

"Nope, don't think so," said Malcolm, "I hear he ain't back from France yet."

Before dawn, having surveyed the battle scene and the new American fort, Wayne wrote a brief summary of the battle for Washington.

"The fort and its garrison, along with the British commandant, Johnson, are ours. Our men behaved like men determined to be free."

Sailing Home

The heat of July in Paris was unbearable. John Adams, his work complete as an American ambassador, having secured the important alliance with France, working with Ben Franklin and the Marquis de LaFayette, now was anxious to set sail for Boston. King Louis XVI had agreed to send General Rochambeau and his army to aid in the fight for American Independence. He felt free to sail for home.

Adams could hardly wait to visit his lovely Abigail and their children at Braintree. He had been away for well over a year, and that was too long, in his estimation, to be away from his three young children he had left behind. The letters he had received from Abigail were very much welcomed, read and re-read. They were love letters in one sense, but among the words she wrote reaffirming her love for him, were missives about the humorous activities of the nine-year-old Charles and the seven-year-old Thomas...oh, and of course, of their fourteen-year-old daughter, Nabby. The letters were also accounts of what was going on in the Congress and on the battlefields of war. The letters were a wonderful respite from the diplomatic deliberations in Paris, but were read with a strange happy sadness and melancholy. With every letter, he was strongly left with the feeling of being in exile.

The Marquis de LaFayette was also missing America and the war, fighting as an aide-de-camp beside General Washington, who was quickly becoming the most admired military man in the world. He also enjoyed seeing Adrienne again with child. Adrienne agreed with LaFayette's choice of a name for the child, if it was a son. He would be called Georges Washington du Motier de LaFayette. Now little Marie would have a little brother for a playmate.

He had also enjoyed renewing his role as a French nobleman, entertaining at the palatial home of his wife on the Rue de la Madeliene, or being entertained in the salons of the French nobility, and especially, as a favored guest of the young King Louis XVI and his beautiful young Queen Marie Antoinette, at the Palace of Versailles.

The king had fully forgiven LaFayette's earlier disobedience. The king in fact now gave LaFayette his blessings in sailing once again for America. When he heard of Adams' plans to sail, he arranged to sail with him.

Adams was very pleased with the education his oldest son, twelve-year-old John Quincy had been getting in France, but did not want to sail without him. He knew he would most likely be returning to Europe as a diplomat in a year or so. Young John would simply have to be signed out of the Academie Passy, where he had been a good student, and where his bunkmate for the past year had been Ben Franklin's eleven-year-old grandson, Benjamin Franklin Bache.

Adams would have allowed young John to stay in the school instead of returning to Boston, but did not really trust Franklin to see to Johnny's care. Franklin was too much of a character for Adams' liking. He had a reputation with the ladies, while his devoted common-law wife, Deborah, stayed at home in Philadelphia. Franklin enjoyed parties seemingly every night, where the level of drunkenness created, measured the party's success. Franklin was a freethinker, and known for his infamous and appalling 'air baths', not limited, in Franklin's case, to all male co-bathers. No, Ben Franklin was simply too vile and too sinful for the Puritanical John Adams, to see as a fit guardian of his son.

The day came for their departure, and a carriage took them to the port of Calais where the USS Enfield was moored and ready for a three-week crossing of the Atlantic to Boston. Captain Johnny Kilkenny welcomed his distinguished passengers and they set sail.

"I do hope we arrive in time for me to join cousin Sam and James Bowdoin in writing the new constitution for Massachusetts," said Adams at dinner in the captain's quarters their first evening at sea. "I do hope the Congress does not send me back until that work is done."

"I, as well, hope we shall anchor in time for me to join Washington at West Point," spoke the marquis, "before Sir Henry moves against the Hudson Valley."

"Barrin' any thing unforeseen," assured the young Captain Kilkenny, "we should dock in Boston Harbor the tenth day o' August. As ta the plans o' Sam Adams," he turned to John Adams, then turned to

LaFayette, "or ta the plans o' that rascal Sir Henry Clinton, I've no control." The guests chuckled and took forkfuls of prime rib.

"You sailed to Nassautown and captured Dunmore's stolen munitions, did you not, Captain Kilkenny?" the inquisitive young Johnny asked.

"Yes, Johnny, I did indeed," answered Kilkenny.

"Please tells us about it," the twelve-year-old implored the young captain.

"John, do not pester the captain," his father admonished his son.

"'Tis no bother," Kilkenny came to the boy's defense, "but I s'pose the ambassador an' the marquis might not be int'rested in hearin' o' me adventures at sea with the navy fer the first time in me life.

"Perhaps though," Kilkenny, in a whispery voice said, "I'm certain we might fin' the time, just the two o' us mind ya, during these coming weeks o' the crossin', an' I'll tell ya all about it." Adams and the marquis smiled at Kilkenny's marvelous personality with the young and inquisitive lad. The lad smiled as well.

"Mister Adams," Kilkenny turned to the ambassador, "when might I be transportin' ya back ta France?"

"Hopefully not at all," Adams spoke his true feelings, "but I fear within the year."

"Mr. Adams feels his talents would be best used shaping the new nation," LaFayette spoke up, "not treating with the crotchety old monarchs of Europe, pleading for alliances and loans."

"I shall, of course, go where my government feels I might serve best," conceded Adams. "If I do return, it shall be with my entire family this time. I shall never again live on one side of this damned ocean while they live upon the other. If I am sent back, as I do expect to be, I want my son here to continue his education in Europe, perhaps at Leyden. I hear it to be a fine institution."

The Enfield docked at Boston Harbor, as Captain Kilkenny planned, on the tenth day of August. The homecoming was much anticipated at the Adams farm in Braintree. John did join his cousin Sam and others for the Massachusetts State Constitutional Convention on September the first. He arrived and received the news of his appointment by Congress to the post of Minister Plenipotentiary. He was to sail for France again in November, with instructions to begin negotiations in London with the government of King George III for the eventual peace.

LaFayette spent the better part of a week in Boston before riding to General Washington, headquartered at West Point.

"Gilbert!" Washington shouted a greeting as he had seen LaFayette arriving, and ran out of the Moore House at West Point. The two generals hugged and kissed each other's cheeks. "It has been too long, my friend," Washington exclaimed, as he led the marquis into his headquarters.

"We will launch an attack on Savannah in less than thirty days," Washington said to LaFayette. "If General Lincoln can take back Savannah, and capture or expel the British there, this war can be won by the new year."

"And Sir Henry simply waits in New York?" asked LaFayette.

"General Wayne's victory at Stony Point was a great surprise and disappointment to Clinton," Washington said. "None but small skirmishes have been made since, and our army has stood its ground. The south is the where Sir Henry's attentions must now be directed."

"Charleston?" LaFayette continued his inquiry.

"Most assuredly," said Washington, "but there, Lincoln and Moultrie have answered and pushed back every advance of the British from Savannah. They cannot win directly on land. If Charleston is to fall, it will be from the sea."

Portrait of a Wealthy Family

One of the oldest, most prominent and wealthy families in New Orleans were seated in Zack Winston's studio, above the Mercado Tamayo y Avila. The family elder, Francois Maison-Pierre, was a man of near ninety years, with a weather-worn and deeply withered face, and eyes set back deep in his head, hidden behind narrow slits. Thin white tufts of hair, necessarily unruly, tried futilely to adorn his oblong head. His skin seemed to be just a thin, almost translucent, wrinkled veneer covering his bones just beneath the surface. He sat in the center of the small sofa, dressed in his finest, with his wrinkly hands resting atop an ivory-knobbed walking stick, which seemed to prop up the ancient man's gaunt and skeletal frame. Zack knew the old man had not the strength to sit erect without the support of the cane.

Monsieur Maison-Pierre was part of the original expedition of the Frenchman Bienville, who set up the original settlement of Nouvelle-Orleans in 1718. He did not go back to France with Bienville, but as a twenty-nine-old unmarried man with no family left living in France, stayed and opened a lucrative trading post, and oversaw trappers and fur traders. For four years in the 1720s, after a devastating hurricane hit when New Orleans served as the capital of all of French Louisiana, Maison-Pierre served as the royal governor, appointed by King Louis XV. It was Maison-Pierre who oversaw the original street grid for the city Bienville had drawn, but had not implemented before he sailed back to France. Maison-Pierre actually named the streets on that grid, most notably Rue Bienville and the Rue de Bourbon, after the French Royal House of Bourbon.

By 1763, when all of French Louisiana was ceded to the Spaniards, Maison-Pierre, then in his mid-seventies, had amassed a fortune trading furs, and owning the huge six-thousand acre plantation, of course named "Maison-Pierre" just to the west of the city. He owned more than a thousand slaves to grow his rice, indigo, cotton and sugar cane, and work his sugar mill and rum distillery.

He had also amassed a huge Catholic family, of four sons, six daughters, thirty grandchildren and seventeen great grandchildren. Zack had been commissioned to paint the family portrait of the dying local icon of the Mississippi delta. Fortunately, Zack was not to paint all fifty-eight Maison-Pierres living then, just a good representation of them.

The grand sire himself, was seated in the center of the sofa, flanked by his two surviving daughters, seated beside him. His lone surviving son, and his eldest grandson, stood behind the sofa, while his youngest great granddaughter, a beautiful two-year-old, was seated on the carpet at the old man's feet, holding a small china doll.

Zack was also happy that this day he had simply to add the finishing touches, get the family's approval, and receive the handsome, near-obscene amount of money the family had offered to pay. He had only dealt with the oldest daughter, Heloise Maison-Pierre d'Estaing, who was the grand duchess of the family, and the sixty-year-old widow of a cousin of the famous French Admiral. Zack had worked for weeks on the portrait, requiring the subjects to dress the same for a total of ten one to two-hour sessions on and around the sofa in his studio. He knew them all very well, and convinced himself, except for the money they were willing to pay, he liked none of them very much at all.

"I am now finished," Zack said with pride as he invited them each to stand and come to his side of the large canvas resting on the easel.

Heloise, of coarse was the first to dart around to view Zack's work. She stood back about ten feet and gazed at the oil paint that replicated every mole, wart and wrinkle on the family Maison-Pierre. She stood silently, with an arm across her stomach bulge, propping the other bent arm with its hand resting beneath the flab of her fat jowls. Silently she gazed at Zack's latest piece of art. Silently the others came too, and struck similar poses as Heloise, all but the old man who was too afraid to try standing up, after a solid forty-five minutes of sitting without twitching a muscle. The young great granddaughter remained at the old man's feet, now able to actually play with her china doll.

"Well?" Zack fished for a verbal response. He noticed a tear in Heloise's eye. Was it a tear of grief, sadness, sheer pain, horror or, perhaps ... joy?

"Splendid!" Heloise finally let the word escape. "I cry because I did not realize just what a beautiful family I have!"

"It is indeed a marvelous likeness," said the lone surviving son, Auguste. The other sister, Camille Maison-Pierre Rochelle, was non-committal, as she had been at each sitting. She simply smiled her approval.

"Well worth every hour of our toil," said the only handsome part of the family, save the two-year-old. Etienne Marcel Maison-Pierre du Vallier, was the eldest grandson at twenty-six, son of the old man's dead oldest daughter. "Pay the man, Auntie and I shall call for the carriage."

Heloise opened the drawstrings of her purse, and pulled out a rolled and banded wad of bills. She handed it to Zack.

"Monsieur Winston," she smiled, "it is all there...two thousand livres...a small fortune we pay, but for such a splendid remembrance of our dying papa."

"I am not yet dead, and placed in the family crypt with my three dead wives!" the old man coughed out his response to his daughter's words of doom.

Soon the studio was empty and Zack flipped through the wad of French livres, still very spendable, if not preferred, by the Spanish bank in New Orleans. They were all there, all two thousand of those beautiful little pieces of paper, with not very good likenesses of French kings and queens, generals and admirals. He saw the one of Heloise's brother-in-law. The Maison-Pierre plantation carpenter would not come until the following day, to measure the portrait for a fitting frame. Zack would head immediately to the Banco de Nuevo Orleans. When he returned, he'd have plenty of time to dress for Rodie's wedding.

The wedding would be a huge affair that Friday afternoon at the Saint Louis, King of France Catholic Church. After the ceremony, the newlyweds would board the ship La Gloria de Cadiz, and sail for Havana for their honeymoon. They would likely return within a month.

Rodie and Angelita had been forced to attend several sessions with the monsignor at the church. Rodie had agreed to revoke his membership in the Presbyterian Church of Scotland, and take the vows of a Roman Catholic. His uncle, John Murray, Lord Dunmore, would certainly disown him for good now, if he had not done so already. Only Catholics could be married in the church sanctuary itself. If Rodie did not become a Catholic, his wedding to the beautiful senorita could not be consecrated, and out of necessity, would be a simple private affair in the monsignor's library, with no guests, just two witnesses.

Nothing was too good for Senor Tamayo's daughter, and no expense would be spared. Everyone in New Orleans would flood into the church to witness the recitation of the vows of marriage, and take Holy Communion with the newly wedded couple, Senor y Senora Stephen Roderic Murray.

"I hope the Maison-Pierres will not be there," Zack said to himself, as he walked toward the waterfront. "I have seen quite enough of that one ugly family for a lifetime."

He got back to the rooms above the mercado. Rodie had returned and was dressed and ready to go. There were about forty minutes remaining before the guests would be arriving, and an hour and a quarter before the ceremony was set to start. Zack dressed in his finest suit of clothes.

"Let me buy you one last cold rum punch at the taverna," Zack invited his old friend, "while you are yet a single man, untethered by the bonds of matrimony."

"Thanks," Rodie said, "I just might need one to calm my nerves."

Chapter Fifteen

The War Moves South

Lt. Col. Lewis Campbell was feeling comfortable as the conqueror of Savannah, the port settlement of the Georgia colony. He had landed on nearby Tybee Island with three thousand men on December 23rd, and was greeted by balmy temperatures in the high fifties and mid-sixties, sunny skies and calm breezes...and it was just two days before Christmas! The Battle of Savannah, six days later, had been brief, with the American commander offering only an obligatory exchange of fire before ordering a devastating retreat. Most of the American force was taken as prisoners. Of the seven hundred defenders of Savannah, five hundred and fifty were either killed or captured, along with all the American guns and artillery.

"I am the first British officer to force that damned American Congress to remove one of those stars and one of those stripes from their damned flag!" Campbell crowed proudly to his staff. "With the fall of Savannah, we have taken the entire colony of Georgia!"

Campbell thoroughly enjoyed the pleasant climate at Savannah, like none he had ever enjoyed previously. Every morning, he started the day strolling through the conquered city's streets, made of crushed coquina shells, and lined with beautiful palm trees. Flowers bloomed the year round, with fragrant aromas of hibiscus, magnolia and jacaranda. He had heard of other British soldiers being fortunate enough to be stationed in such warm and exotic locations as Jamaica, Barbados, and the Bahamas, but he had never been so fortunate. He had now been in Savannah for nearly a full month. He would be most happy to see Savannah as a permanent base for his remaining military career.

"Sir," a sentry saluted Campbell as he returned from his morning stroll to the beautiful house he had secured for his headquarters. Campbell acknowledged the salute.

"There are guests," the sentry said, "two generals from St. Augustine in East Florida. They are seated on the east verandah."

Campbell seemed a bit puzzled, smiled hestitantly, then headed to greet his guests. He had no knowledge of any such high-ranking officers coming to see him. Were they sent from General Clinton in New York? Being stationed in St. Augustine, less than one hundred miles south along the Atlantic coast, they had no doubt heard of the capture of Savannah, and perhaps simply wanted to see for themselves, and congratulate him on the easy victory?

The headquarters house had a large roofed-over verandah that ran around three sides of the house. Campbell preferred having his staff meetings on the east verandah, to take in the beautiful climate, and look out over the Savannah River, and the seemingly forbidden jungles on the far shores of the South Carolina colony.

Before going out onto the verandah that morning, he paused a moment and spotted the two uniformed men, seated in chairs made of local bamboo, and covered with upholstered cushions, placed with other chairs around a rectangular table of the same manufacture. One man appeared to be in his mid-to-late fifties, with a gaunt-looking face and naturally white, thinning hair. The other seemed younger, by ten years at least, and had a much more athletic look about him, and rich-looking dark brown hair. Both appeared older than his thirty-nine years, and both assuredly outranked him. He opened the glass-paned French doors and walked onto the verandah. The men stood and saluted. He returned the salute.

"Brigadier General Augustine Prevost, sir," the older of the two introduced himself, "and my brother, General James Mark Prevost." He pulled folded papers from his breast pocket and began to hand them to Campbell. "If you are Lt. Col. Lewis Campbell, I have my orders from General Sir Henry Clinton to relieve you of this command."

Fort Moultrie

One week later, in the small fort on Sullivan's Island in Charleston Harbor, about eighty miles up the coast from Savannah, Lt. Col. John Laurens was a guest of General William Moultrie, awaiting the arrival of General Benjamin Lincoln and several other officers of the American forces in the south. Lincoln had been appointed the commander of the Southern Department of the Continental Army, and the retaking of Savannah and all of Georgia was foremost on everyone's mind.

Moultrie, who had led a successful raid on a large encampment of runaway slaves on Sullivan's Island in 1775, built the small fort there. In 1776, from his command post at the fort, he successfully repulsed the early attempt by Sir Henry Clinton to take Charleston. Congress promoted him Brigadier General, and the South Carolina Legislature named the fort in his honor, Fort Moultrie.

Congress had dispatched Lt. Col. Laurens, former aide-de-camp to General Washington, and the son of the president of Congress, to Charleston with the commission to build a regiment of three thousand black slaves to fight for the American cause.

In early 1778, Laurens and his father promoted enlisting slaves, freeing them from their bondage, and paying them like any other soldier. There was a great need for soldiers, and what better source than freed slaves for recruitment? That was not a popular stand in the South, even if coming from two South Carolina slaveholders like the Laurenses.

Laurens, now was also a member of the South Carolina Legislature. He had proposed his idea of freeing and arming the slaves in a legislative session. He found very few allies among the fellow delegates, and absolutely no ally in Governor John Rutledge, who would also be coming to the fort that day to meet with General Lincoln.

"We should never have lost Savannah," Moultrie fumed to Laurens and Lt. Col. Francis Marion, "and that damned general of ours should have been run out of the army, or hanged for his decisions that cost us three-fourths of our brave men there!"

"If he had retreated," added Marion, who was Moultrie's second-in-command, "we would have had an army saved to fight another day."

"Five hundred and fifty brave and able-bodied men!...patriots all! ... killed or taken prisoner by a low-ranking Redcoat!" Moultrie ignited his disdain. "That son-of-a-bitch lost, for no other reason than his own total incompetence, an entire army! I can abide an out-and-out defeat, well fought, well selected, but I cannot abide our own stupidity!"

The three men walked the wooden planked gun deck floor of the fort's upper level, overlooking the Atlantic Ocean, Charleston Harbor and the beautiful city in the background. They discussed the southern campaign of the war Clinton had just opened from his headquarters in New York. They expected their new commanding officer, General Lincoln, to arrive within the hour.

Laurens had heard the name Francis Marion, but had never met him. Marion was a man about the same age as Washington and Moultrie, a good twenty years Laurens' senior. Marion was from a well-known plantation family of several generations. The Marions were descended from French Huguenots, and had made their fortune and good name growing rice and indigo in the area around Georgetown, sixty miles north along the coast from Charleston.

In 1759, Marion, even though unmarried and without a family of his own, moved from Georgetown and built his own plantation, Pond Bluff, on the edge of the swamps along the Santee River. He made a name for himself as lieutenant and Indian fighter under then Captain Moultrie, during the French and Indian War, battling the Cherokee tribe on the Carolina frontier.

Later, in 1775, he became a member of the South Carolina Provisional Congress, and was commissioned a militia captain under General Moultrie to defend Charleston. After the British were repulsed from Charleston in 1776, due to the efforts of Moultire and Marion, Congress commissioned Marion with the rank of Lt. Col.

Soon they spotted the boat carrying Lincoln and Governor Rutledge, so they went to greet them, then led them to the council room.

"We have received some important dispatches from Savannah," said Gen. Lincoln, as he opened the council. "The British have replaced Campbell with Brig. Gen Augustine Prevost of the Florida Rangers. Prevost and his brother, also a general, have arrived, and have launched a two-pronged campaign."

The men hovered around the table where a huge map was laid out. Lincoln pointed to sites on the map as he shared the intelligence.

"Campbell will lead one thousand, of the four thousand British and Loyalist troops now at Savannah, along the Savannah River, north and west toward the Augusta settlement. They hope to double their force by recruiting from the many loyalists along the way. They will have few artillery pieces with them.

"In the meantime, a Major Valentine Gardiner of the Rangers," Lincoln continued, "will sail up the coast toward the settlement of Beaufort and Port Royal Island at the Broad River, twenty-four miles north of Savannah. Gardiner will lead men and artillery units.

"I feel the drive toward Beaufort to be simply diversionary, with the real aim being Augusta," Lincoln concluded.

"I wish for you, General Moultrie, to move immediately in defense of Beaufort. You, with Col. Marion and three hundred men, should easily be able to repulse Gardiner. I shall move toward Savannah itself, opening a third front, while the large part of the Redcoats are out of the city.

"I will need a strong group of militia to meet Campbell at Augusta. What units have you available?" asked Lincoln.

"Major Andrew Williamson of the South Carolina Militia has fourteen hundred," Moultrie offered. "He can march, but I feel his strengthen might not be sufficient."

"General Ashe has a sizeable force just over the border in North Carolina," Marion suggested. "We could get word to him to meet up with Williamson on the Carolina side of the river, across from Augusta, and double Williamson's force."

"Splendid suggestion," Lincoln said. "I want nothing short of a rout. It is imperative we drive the British out of Georgia, and not allow Clinton to have further thoughts on a southern foothold, nor a prize so valuable as Charleston."

"Begging the commander's pardon," spoke Laurens, "but you have just broached an issue that weighs most heavily upon the minds of our Congress in Philadelphia…the vital need for more troops than are at this time available."

"If you speak of arming slaves," Governor Rutledge spoke defiantly, "as you have in the legislature, we may as well just surrender now and forestall further bloodshed. The patriot planters, and those planters currently neutral in the southern colonies, owning slaves and standing true to the heritage of our Carolina society, will go over to the British side, when the first black man is given a musket!"

"We fight, do we not, for American independence?" questioned Laurens, just as defiantly. "That is for the independence of the states from Britain, as well as for the independence of every American. How can we advocate for independence, and turn blind eyes upon the fact we hold thousands of black individuals in bondage, not to share in the greatness of freedom?"

"Talk of the sort," Rutledge fumed, "will change minds presently for independence. If the independence we fight for frees the slaves needed to work our plantations, the idea of independence will quickly flee from South Carolina, and from every state south of New England!"

"Gentlemen," Lincoln interrupted the debate, "this is a subject best left to be debated in the Congress, not in the councils of war. Our role is to make certain the British leave our shores. We shall debate the issue of the slaves at another time more appropriate, and in another place."

Men of the Waxhaw

Francis Marion made a trip to the Waxhaw region on the South Carolina-North Carolina border in the days following the victory at Port Royal Island, defending Beaufort.

Moultrie and Marion had made quick work of the Redcoats at Port Royal, and joined Lincoln at Purrysburg, waiting to march into Savannah. News reached Lincoln of success in driving Campbell back from Augusta, but also of a devastating loss for the Americans at Brier Creek. It was now impossible to stop Campbell's retreat back to Savannah. Lincoln felt it better to fall back to Fort Moultrie, and prepare for an advance on Charleston from land.

With there being a great need for men, Marion wanted to pay a visit to a friend in the Waxhaw, who was seen as a leader of Scotch-Irish settlement there. They had been soldiers together with Moultrie fighting the Cherokee on the Carolina frontier. At one time or another, they each had saved the other's life, amid the brutality of the savages.

Gabriel Mathias was Marion's age and they had become great friends. Marion tried to make a trip to the Waxhaw about every year or so. Gabriel had married a Cherokee woman, before the war with the Cherokee had broken out. She took the English and Biblical name, Naomi, never speaking her Cherokee name again. They had three sons. Their oldest, Micah, was now twenty, living in a cabin of his own nearby. Micah had married Theresa Henderson, and they were expecting a child in the late fall. Angus, seventeen, and Grant, sixteen, were still living at home with Gabe and Naomi.

"Francis Marion!" Gabe shouted, as he saw his old friend approaching the cabin, "what brings you all the way out here?"

"Can't an old friend just come by for a visit?" Marion answered, as the two old friends hugged one another. "You got somethin' or another on yer mind," Gabe laughed.

"Naomi have some good vittles fixed up to feed a hungry traveler?" Marion asked.

"I'm sure she does," said Gabe, "I'm sure she does. In fact she's prob'bly skinned that fat ole mama possum Grant up an' shot this mornin', an' got him on the spit b'now."

"Sounds good to me," Marion said as the men went inside the rustic cabin. Naomi was tending to the pot on the hook that had vegetables stewing to go with the possum, skewered on the spit above the flames.

"I'm here," Marion said, "to recruit as many men as the Waxhaw can spare, to kick those damned British out o' Savannah, and make certain they don't try again to take Charleston."

"Well, Marion," Gabe said, lighting a pipe of local grown tobacco, and handing it to his friend, "this here is sure one settlement those Redcoats had best leave be. Patriots, ever' one of 'em, 'ceptin' ole Joe Finerty." He spit on the floor and wiped the corners of his mouth. "Loyalist to the last devilish bone in his rotten soul!"

"I did not know souls had bones, Gabriel," Naomi corrected her husband of twenty-five years, as she left the hearth and walked to join the men.

"You know what I mean, N'omi," Gabriel pulled her onto his lap, as if the two were still newlyweds. He continued his talk with his friend. "You need ta talk ta Thad Henderson. He's the one what knows ever'one for miles around. He's at his trading post, ya know."

"Wanna come along?" Marion asked.

"No, you go on Marion," Gabe said, "just don't tarry too long or the possum'll sure be burnt to a crispy. But stay gone a little whiles, case N'omi and me might wanna ... oh, you know! Just go!"

Marion walked down the dusty streets of the settlement, which probably now had two hundred or more cabins. As more and more Scotch-Irish came on boats to Philadelphia, Ansley Magruder kept leading more and more to the Waxhaw. The settlement stretched across the border between the two Carolinas, and no one really seemed to know when they were in North Carolina or South Carolina. They just never paid any mind to borders at all. Marion was soon walking inside Thad Henderson's trading post.

"I heared you an' Moultrie sure sent them Redcoats a runnn' at Port Royal," the old man laughed.

"Yes we did, Thad," answered Marion with a smile, "but then they sent our militias a packin' down at Brier Creek."

"That they did," Henderson said, much saddened at that thought. "So you're a needin' more soldiers, are ya? Well, I can have ya a company if'n you give me a week."

"A week I have," Marion said, "but I need to get back to Sullivan's Island in a day or two."

"I got just the man ta lead 'em too," Henderson said, "my grandson-in-law, Micah Mathias...fine young man. I'll have Micah take the boys an' meet ya back at Fort Moultrie in a week...week-and-a-half at the most."

"Send 'em to my plantation at Pond Bluff on the Santee," Marion said. "I wanna give 'em some trainin' before they march off ta fight the Redcoats."

They shook hands and Marion walked back to the promised roast possum and vegetable stew at the Mathias cabin. He paid a visit to Gabe and Naomi's neighbor in the cabin next to their's, the widow Betty Jackson.

Marion had always stopped in to see her on his trips to the Waxhaw. Several folks in the settlement expected Betty to marry Marion, from all the attentions he paid to her, but nothing but a true friendship ever seemed to develop. In two days he left the Waxhaw.

As promised, a week later Thad Henderson sent off a company of fifty-nine men and boys from the settlement and throughout the region. Micah Mathias, was the captain. He kissed his wife good-bye, as the company assembled in the big common area in front of the trading post at sunrise. The whole settlement turned out to see their brave husbands, sons, nephews, uncles, and cousins, head off to do their part in fighting the Redcoats. Many of the Scots who settled there were related and intermarried. It was one of the closest-knit settlements on the American frontier.

Betty Jackson was there with her boys. Hugh, her eldest, at sixteen, was in the company, marching with his two best friends, Angus and Grant Mathias. Betty knew her eldest was anxious to join the army, and knew too, that if the war didn't end in the summer of 1779, there would be little she could do to prevent the two younger Jackson boys from going off to war as well. Her second son, Robert was fifteen, and it was all she could do to convince him not to go off that day with Hugh. Her youngest, Andy, had just turned twelve two days earlier, so she used Andy as an excuse to convince Robert to stay put at home for at least another year or two.

Andy Jackson was a strong boy, a leader type, and really seemed older and more mature than Robert in many ways, at times even more well equipped than Hugh. But war was no place for a twelve-year-old boy, no matter just how well equipped he might be. Betty stood firm and held tight to both boys' hands as the others marched off. Two days later, they were camped at Pond Bluff.

"Mama told me not ta take nothin' off o' them rascally Redcoats," said Hugh Jackson, as he and the Mathias brothers sat around the fire after a supper of rabbit.

"That wasn't your mama, Hugh, that was your baby brother Andy!" said Grant, as Angus started laughing. "I heard it plain as day! I was standin' right there! "

"Robert an' Andy should've come 'long with us," said Hugh, "but mama wouldn't stand for it a'tall."

"Robert surely could've," said Angus, "afterall, he's near as old as Grant."

"Not near the man I am though," said Grant. "Ole Robert's a might puny boy in my way o' thinkin'."

"I guess Mama didn't want ta send off the last o' her family ta die together an' leave her total alone in life," said Hugh.

"Why Hugh?" asked Grant, "you plannin' on lettin' some rotten ole Redcoat pluck ya off?"

"I ain't near as worried 'bout me as I am worried 'bout you, Grant Mathias," answered Hugh. "I'd just hate ta have ta dodge bullets ta carry your measley shot-up carcass of'n the battlefield, an' dig a hole in the groun' ta bury ya in."

"Ya needn't worry 'bout that," said Grant, as Angus and Hugh laughed. "You'll prob'ly faint an' die straight away at the first sight o' one o' them Hessian bayonets! "If'n ya do, please do it a'fore the fightin' commences, so's I don't have ta worry 'bout getting' my ass shot up as I'm a carryin' your ass away!"

The company trained for two weeks, then marched into Fort Moultrie for inspection by Gen. Moultrie.

On May 10th the Americans, under Gen. Isaac Huger, met the leading edge of Prevost's Redcoats, seven miles from Charleston, at a ferry over the Ashley River. The men of the Waxhaw Patriot Company had been assigned to Huger's army, and saw their first action at the brief skirmish with the Redcoats there that day.

The significance of the day's battle was that Prevost decided to retreat back to Savannah, knowing Lincoln, with the main army, might arrive at any time. Before he left, Prevost moved to Stono Ferry, another ferry with the mainlang connecting John's Island. There he stored his supplies for a later advance on Charleston. He left nine hundred men there to guard his military stores. The British built a bridgehead to defend against an attack, dug readouts with abatis works, and fortified the area around where the supplies were stored.

When Gen. Lincoln's army arrived, Lincoln ordered an attack on the outpost at Stono Ferry. After a nighttime march south from Fort Moultrie, the battle began at dawn on June 20th. The Waxhaw men were among those to first open fire on the Redcoats. The Scots Highlanders, dressed in their regimental kilts, defended the British outpost. They stood and fought till they had only eleven men left standing. The Hessians were doing no better. The heat of the day was growing, and the humidity was becoming unbearable.

"Damn! This is one god-awful heat to be a figthin' in!" said Angus Mathias. "I'm a sweatin' heavy as a hot water rain."

"The way things 'pear," said his brother Grant, "those damned soldiers in those sissy-lookin' skirts'll be a flappin' them skirts an' a runnin' away real soon." He got off another shot at the Highlanders.

"It'll ...be over...real soon," Hugh Jackson panted his affirmation as to what Grant had said. Hugh fired another musket shot, then slumped to ground.

Hugh was dead. No musketball from a Highlander's musket had got him. The heat of the day gave him a severe heat stroke, and there was no way of saving the widow Jackson's oldest boy.

Clinton and Tarleton

General Sir Henry Clinton was indeed perplexed as he sat in his headquarters on Broadway on Manhattan Island. He had been surprised by General Mad Anthony Wayne's success at Stony Point, dashing a crucial blow to Clinton's hope of taking control of the entire Hudson Valley. His most recent success had been the taking of Savannah, but that success had not shown any real advancement toward the goal of marching on to Charleston, and ending the American drive for independence once and for all.

Major John Andre was placed in charge of all espionage activities for the commander-in-chief. Andre had developed an important clandestine relationship with the American General Benedict Arnold in Philadelphia, and was cultivating Arnold as a useful spy in service of Britain.

"We need to turn the American rout of our forces at Stony Point into a great victory for us, and stop this licking of our wounds," Andre said, speaking bluntly to Sir Henry, one day in the headquarters.

"Do you have even the most remote of ideas as to how this might come about," Sir Henry asked skeptically.

"Indeed," answered Andre emphatically.

"Washington will be breaking his camp and headquarters at West Point in late November," Andre went on, divulging the intelligence his espionage agents had given him. "Washington will again winter near

Philadelphia, most probably in the hills scattered around Morristown, to ease Lady Washington's travel plans to spend the winter with him.

"Washington will travel with the largest portion of his army, leaving West Point, and other strategic outposts in New York, without sufficient defenses," Andre went on. "I have spoken with our friend General Arnold, and he is politicking, as we speak, for appointment as commandant of the northern forces at West Point."

"What are the chances of Arnold being assigned to the post?" Sir Henry asked, showing great favor in Andre's idea.

"Well," Andre began to answer, "we, of course, have no guarantees, but Arnold is authentically held in good esteem, and indeed qualified well for such an assignment. He has served well as a military strategist, and most of all, is not in the least suspected for betrayal."

"We can certainly hope," Sir Henry stated, "but war strategy is best not left to happenstance."

"We must plan a siege of Charleston from the sea as well as land. If the pieces are all in place in the Hudson Valley, with Arnold the new commandant at West Point, and Washington at Morristown, we can take West Point, and finally split the colonies in two."

An orderly rapped on the door.

"Enter," commanded Sir Henry. A uniformed orderly entered and saluted.

"A major of the dragoons, Lt. Col. Banastre Tarleton, First Baronet," the orderly announced as a splendidly uniformed officer appeared and saluted.

"Come in, Tarleton," ordered Sir Henry.

The young, handsome dragoon, dressed in an emerald green uniform coat with golden brocade, tight-fitting white riding breeches, and shiny black knee-high riding boots entered. He carried a riding crop in one hand, while the other hand and arm supported a dazzling high hat with black ostrich plumes.

"Have a seat," Sir Henry said, directing him to the seat beside Major Andre. "What can I do for you Tarleton?

"I am here, Sir Henry," the brash young officer said, "to ask you quite bluntly why we have not yet sailed south to end this damend war!"

"I share your impatience," Sir Henry spoke with reddened cheeks, from the dressing down the leader of the dragoons had just given him.

"We shall wait but a little longer. I was about to summon you here myself, so you might help plan our strategy, and I am so happy you saw it upon yourself to arrange your own audience."

"My dragoons are trained and ready to scorch the earth of the Carolinas, once given the chance," Tarleton spoke agrresively. "We are impatient with how this war seems to have no real strategy at all. Give the damned Americans their independence ... or get us to the Carolinas so we can do what we came across the waves to do!"

Honorably Discharged

Peter Francisco recuperated at the army field hospital at Fishkill, from the deep saber gash across his stomach he received during the storming of Stony Point. Peter's injuries were more severe than first thought. While healing well, the physicians at the field hospital doubted Peter's ability to return to the battlefield, at least for another six months.

As September turned into October, Washington received dispatches from Charleston that General Benjamin Lincoln, with the help of one of the first French units to arrive, had begun a siege on the British at Savannah. Washington was not an advocate of the siege, as he much preferred a frontal surprise attack, especially from the high ground. A siege, in his estimation, was too hard to predict the outcome. It would last until one side was tired and ready to give up.

The British General Prevost and his brother seemed not to be interested in giving up.

"With all the new French re-enforcements," Washington fumed at his aides, LaFayette and Hamilton, "why did they simply not attack with full force on the enemy's weakest point, as I instructed?"

"The Europeans love a siege," Hamilton said, as LaFayette nodded in agreement. "I feel certain they convinced Lincoln of their strategy."

"What good did we achieve by getting them to agree to send more troops!" Washington spoke his disgust aloud. "We are not Europeans, and we will not win our war fighting the Europeans on their terms. The French are to be here as allies, and nothing more...certainly not to run our war for us. I believe my orders have been clear. Yet again, they are disobeyed."

Dispatches arrived in mid-October that General Lincoln had lost the siege and retreated back to Charleston.

"Clinton thought wisely when he took Savannah...the farthest possible port city from where we now sit upon the Hudson. That devil wants me to go south, so he can march into our valley here, and split the colonies in two. I shall not be budged!"

"We will lead half the army to winter camp in New Jersey on November 27th," Washington said to Wills. "Half shall remain here to guard the valley. Dispatch the orders to all the commands here. The men, not battle ready due to their wounds or illnesses, are to be discharged honorably."

When they arrived at Morristown on December 1st, Peter Francisco was honorably discharged from the Continental Army. Two weeks before the army marched out of West Point, Peter Patrick fell from his horse as he was jumping a log. He broke his leg, and was deemed by the physicians as not being battle-ready. Like Peter, Pat received an honorable discharge.

With his leg in a cast, Pat rode his own horse alongside Peter atop Coronado. Pat could ride in his condition, he just couldn't walk without suffering excruciating pain, and he certainly could not mount or dismount. Peter easily lifted Pat up into his saddle, down from it, and propped him up when he did need to walk.

Garrett Hicks and Malcolm Shepherd again obtained winter furloughs from the army, as long as they signed a pledge to return to Morristown no later than the first day of May. They rode with Peter and Pat. They all boarded at the Hicks homestead in Manassas on the third night and were treated to a fried chicken supper.

"They sure don't feed us like this back at camp," said Garrett, taking a bite out of a drumstick.

"They surely don't!" echoed Malcolm.

"I bet you can hardly wait ta see that ole bride o' yern, Pat," Garrett said, taking another bite.

"You're sure right about that," Pat admitted. "Why I wasn't married six weeks a'fore ole Peter here drug me off ta war again. It's been six months since I seen her."

"An' six months since you planted your bayonet up inside her," Garrett started laughing until he was surprised by a gravely voice.

"Garrett Riley Hicks! You nasty boy!" shrieked his mama, Jane, as she came into the dining room from the kitchen with a fresh platter of biscuits and a pitcher of buttermilk. "I never raised you ta talk that a way! Now shame on you, boy!"

"You up an' done it now, Garrett! Ya surely did!" Malcolm eagerly joined his Aunt Jane in the reprimand of his cousin and best friend.

"Now you can jes' hesh up too, Malcolm Lonnie Shepherd!" Jane chided her nephew. "I 'magine you're jus' as ign'rt as Garrett is 'bout sech as that!" Peter and Pat laughed.

"Do you think that'll be my life in twenty years?" Pat asked Peter, as they rode away from Manassas the next morning.

"What do you mean?" Peter asked.

"Farming my own farm with stair-step children, born every two years," Pat painted the picture.

"Yes," Peter said matter-of-factly, "ten children in twenty years, all starting with this one who's coming with the new year."

"Really?" Pat asked, with fate staring him in the face. He didn't know whether to be ecstatic or scared to death.

"Of course," Peter assured his friend as they rode, "and you'll be happy as any man in our new country, sitting on your front porch alongside Pee Pee Creek up in the Ohio Country, rocking in a chair, and looking out over your Pee Pee Prairie fields toward the Scioto River."

"I cannot wait to start," Pat smiled, as he accepted Peter's vision of his future.

Peter insisted on riding with Pat across the shallow ford to Cedar Forks, if for no other reason than to make certain Pat didn't hurt his bad leg trying to dismount.

"You are home!" Tricia was shocked. She ran out of the house to greet them. She was heavy in weight, protruding from mid torso, having carried a baby eight full months. She ran to Pat, as best she could, as Peter helped Pat down from his horse.

"What on earth happened to you?" Tricia shrieked. "Oh my God, were you shot?"

"My horse threw me over a log," Pat said, grimacing as Peter held him up on the ground. "I just broke a leg." Tricia threw her arms around her husband and kissed him.

"Are you home from the war for good?" she asked pleadingly.

565

"We'll see," said Pat. "I should heal well-enough by summer and, well, if they need me, I guess I'll go."

"We'll see, I suppose," Tricia heard not what she had wanted to hear, but at least he would be home when she was ready to give birth to their first child. Pat put his palm on her protruding stomach and smiled.

"And how is our son...or daughter?" Pat asked.

"Doing wonderfully," she said, "at least according to Doctor Lowe."

"And you? How are you doing?" Pat asked, taking his palm from her stomach to her cheek.

"Quite well, sir, now that you are home."

She insisted Peter come in for a piece of coconut cake and tea, and rest a bit before finishing the last hour of his trip to Winston Woods.

Locust Grove

Peter always enjoyed Winston Woods at Christmastime. This year Peter would not be riding off again to war. He realized just how close he had come to dying at Stony Point. He had had enough of battlefields.

Zack was still in New Orleans. "He is still determined to travel to the Rocky Mountains," said the judge, showing what Peter picked up as more disappointment than anger. "He will travel with some of those so-called mountain men that live like hermits, nine months at a time, trapping and cavorting with the savage tribes, and who knows what!"

"Now, dear, Zachary said he will sail for Virginia this year," Adella spoke up. "Rodie Murray is now married, and a papa in his own right. He wants to bring them to Virginia, and Zachary will accompany them."

"Yes, dear, then he plans to leave from here to St. Louis and the mountains," the judge added.

"Well, then," Adella said, not wishing to think about that, "we shall simply have to convince our boy to stay."

"I wish you to join me, Peter, on a trip, as soon as we can arrange it," the judge said, changing the subject. "I have come into a fine farm, about eight hundred acres, in Buckingham County. It was my pay for settling an estate. I want to see it, and, if you like it, sign the deed over to you and Zachary."

"Land?" Peter said, surprised at the thought. "When can we go?"

"Well, we could leave Monday, I suppose. The weather should still be fair. If the farm is the fine land I have been told it is by Christina and Calvert McGowan, I think you might just be able to tempt Zachary to forget about the Rocky Mountains."

"I am most anxious to see it," added Peter.

"Oh Peter, you will surely like the old Manners place, Locust Grove, they call it," Christina said, as the judge and Peter joined her for dinner. "I wish Cal were here to go with us tomorrow. But we can take my buggy, and I will be happy to show you around."

"We don't want to be a bother," the judge said. "I think I can find it. Peter and I can ride over on our own."

"I insist...and it tis no bother a'tall," Christina said. "I look forward to a ride in the country, with my old friend, Peter." She smiled. "I can just not get over your size, young man. You are no longer the small, helpless little boy we found coiled up with the ropes on the wharf." They all laughed.

They left early, just after breakfast. Christina took the reins of the buggy and drove them about a half-hour when they came to a gravel lane.

"Well," Christina announced, "we're here. This is the lane that leads back to the farmhouse. We can go up there first, then I'll take you to see the fields and outbuildings." She drove the horse and buggy on.

I believe they call this Payne Creek," she said, as the buggy began across a slate ford of a shallow creek. "It runs behind the garden that sits beside the house. You'll see."

The house was a relatively small wooden, one story house with a second dormer story. It had a central hall running front to back. A parlor sat on one side of the front door, a dining room on the other. A wooden staircase headed up. Beyond the parlors on one side of the hallway was a kitchen. On the other side was a small room for a farm office or library. Upstairs were two equal-sized rooms, one on either side of the second floor hallway, each with slanted dormer ceilings. There were two chimneys, one on each end of the house. Each room of the house had a small fireplace hearth. There was a full cellar beneath the house.

Near the house was a summer kitchen to keep the cooking heat out of the main house in the warmer months. There was a smoke house in the barnyard, a chicken coop, a barn and stables. A long kitchen garden ran parallel to the creek.

"Well what do you think of Locust Grove so far, Peter?" the judge asked.

"The fields are flat, and it looks like good soil," Peter said. "I don't know much about farming," Peter admitted, "but maybe I could talk Pat and Tricia into movin' here with me. He could be our foreman. We could build a house on the other side of this garden. In the meantime, there's room aplenty in the house for us to share."

"That sounds like a grand idea," said judge. "I'll give you a few slaves and plenty of supplies to get a good crop of tobacco. That does indeed look like good tobacco ground."

"Is that an orchard across there?" Peter pointed across the wide field.

"Yes," said Christina. "I believe there are apple and peach trees there. Perhaps even some cherry trees."

"You have plenty of field land here for other crops than simply tobacco," the judge said. "Enough for corn, barley, oats."

"I bet there's some fine hunting in those woods," Peter said. "And I bet there's plenty o' fish in that creek."

"Well, Peter, it's yours and Zachary's, if you want it," the judge said. "Of course, it's further away from Winston Woods than I would have liked."

"It's wonderful," Peter said, "with those beautiful Blue Ridge Mountains so close. And it's an easy day's ride into Richmond or Charlottesville. And knowin' one of my closest neighbors in gonna be Christina and Calvert just makes it all that much better."

The Life of a Farmer

Peter Francisco was now a Virginia landholder. He was excited about his prospects and immediately began making plans for the land he was going to share with Zack, if and when Zack ever came back to

Virginia. In the meantime, Peter planned to save one-third of the farm profits for Zack, give one-third to his new farm foreman, Pat, and take one third for himself.

He missed the army and the camaraderie with all his friends. He was proud of the huge sword General Washington and LaFayette had given him. He could see it hanging above the fireplace mantel in the dining room at Locust Grove.

There was no real news coming from the war that winter, although most newspapers were expecting some sort of action coming from the British soon, with Charleston as the most-likely objective. Peter tried to put the war behind him.

The first week of March, Peter set out from Winston Woods with Pat and Tricia, and little Gadsden Campbell Patrick, who had been born on January 12th. Pat was anxious to start the spring planting. The judge had given Peter two wagons, with two two-horse teams to pull them, an old plow, bags of seeds and other planting equipment. The judge also made good on the promise and gave Peter eight slaves.

"You gotta be the luckiest man I know," said Pat, as they rode out. "You get kidnapped in the Azores an' dropped on the wharf at City Point, only ta be adopted by one o' the wealthiest an' nicest families in Virginia. Then, we come back from the army an' you get a farm... eight hundred acres, just handed right to ya! I swear you are the luckiest man on earth!"

"Not to mention bein' hit by a Hessian ball at Brandywine, and another at Monmouth, and my guts nearly riped outta me at Stony Point," Peter said, laughing. "Yes, I'd say I'm lucky alright!"

"Well 'least ya lived ta tell about It!" Pat laughed.

"I hope you like Locust Grove as much as I do when you see it," Peter said. "I'm thinking this is for sure the place for you and Tricia to settle, till the Ohio Country is safe for white families, that is.

"This year, we'll all live in the house that's already built there," Peter said, "then we'll go ahead and raise a house for you and Tricia, a house of your own."

"You don't know how much I want my own place," Pat said, "at least a way to make my own livin' to support Tricia and little Gadsden, until I get my own land. I like Tricia's papa and all, but living under his roof and helpin' my Pa out at the judge's plantation, well, that's just not my idea of a proper start in life for a married man startin' a family. I don't know how to thank you."

The Fall of Charleston

Clinton landed at Savannah with eighty-five hundred men. General Augustine Prevost and his brother General Mark Prevost were happy to see the re-enforcements. Sir Henry and Major Andre took over the house the Prevost Brothers had used, and began, immediately directing the land invasion of Charleston.

"Tarleton," Sir Henry spoke, "you will command your dragoons and march north for Charleston." He pointed to the map as Tarleton and Andre looked on.

"The main force will march for James Island, and hold that island to forbid any Americans from an exodus route," Clinton continued. "That will also end important supply lines into the city and Fort Moultrie.

"You shall head swiftly and directly northeast, and approach the city from the west," Clinton spoke to Tarleton. "I want siege lines built, penning the American Army and the fair citizens of Charleston inside the city, which sits upon this peninsula. They shall not enter nor leave the city.

"Of course," Clinton added, "any American troops you encounter, baggage or supply wagons, magazines and arsenals, are to be anhilalated."

On the North Carolina-South Carolina border, the widow Betty Jackson saw how her boys, were getting the fever to get into the fray. She had already buried her eldest boy, Hugh, who had died of heat stroke at the Battle of Stono Ferry at the age of sixteen.

"Mama, mama," Andy came running to his mother, as she hoed the garden at her cabin. "Mama, there's a feller down at ole Thad's general store, an' he's a sayin' them damn ole British've landed again at Savannah, an' they's a fixin' ta march on Charleston!" Betty rested on the handle of her hoe.

"Don't you be a gettin' no notions 'bout joinin' up," she said, as she slowly walked down the row and onto the porch of her cabin. She sat on the floor of the porch beside where a pail of fresh spring water sat with a dipper. She sat on the porch floor like it was a chair with her bare feet on the ground. "It's sure a hot day for March," she said, fanning herself with a newspaper laying on the porch floor. She took a dipper of water and drank.

"I wonder if it was this hot a day when Hugh passed out an' died o' the heat stroke. I surely do wish we'd a been able ta fetch his body an bury it over yonder by his pa."

"Mama," Andy said in a more plaintive tone, as he sat crossed-legged on the ground in front of her. "This may be it. It may be the end o' the war a comin', an' Robert an' my only one chance ta be o' any service a'tall to our country."

She handed him a fresh filled dipper of water. "Here, drink son," she said. "I reckon I don't be a wantin' another o' my sons ta pass out an' die o' the heat." Andy drank from the dipper, then threw it to the ground. "I don't be a wantin' one a dyin' in the war either." She rose again and started back toward the garden.

"Mama!" Andy yelled after her. "I'm a gonna ride as a messenger fer the militia. Me an' Robert both. We won't be a wearin' no uniforms. We won't be a lookin' like no soldiers. Hell, we're too young appearin' to be shot at as enemies ta the Redcoats."

Betty stopped in her tracks, stood like a statue, not turning around to face her youngest boy. There was silence, and one tear trickling down her dust-caked right cheek. Andy thought she must have been like Lot's wife in the Bible, when God turned her into a pillar of salt.

"We'll do our ridin' from right here, just ridin' messages ta the other militia units," Andy explained. "Hell. Mama, we'll be home an' in our own beds ever' night. We won't be no where near all the fightin'… but we are a fixin' ta do it, an' there just ain't no stoppin'' us!"

The British armada of ninety ships appeared in Charleston Harbor in mid-March. General Charles Lord Cornwallis sent cavalry and infantry units to march around the north, west and south sides of the city to report back on the siege lines Tarleton's men had been ordered to erect.

On April 1st the siege began, with cannons firing from the British ships, answered weakly by General Lincoln's limited artillery. There was no way out for the Americans, and they knew it. At least thirty-eight hundred of the American troops were trapped inside the confines of the city. The others were reconnoitering at different locations outside the siege lines.

Lincoln surrendered the city to Cornwallis on May 12th. It was estimated a total of five thousand Americans were taken captive, as well as all the American artillery in the city, and at Fort Moultrie. Among the prisoners were Generals Benjamin Lincoln and William Moultrie, along with John Laurens of the South Carolina Legislature, and three signers of the "Declaration of Independence": Arthur Middleton, Thomas Heywood, Jr. and the governor's brother, Edward Rutledge.

Major Francis Marion had not been captured. He had stayed at Pond Bluff nursing his ankle he had broken in a nasty fall earlier in the spring. He was kept aware of the devastation in Charleston. He sent riders out to the frontier, the Waxhaw and other areas, to form one of the units he saw as being the only hope left for the Americans. He began assembling his men on an island in the swamp west of Pond Bluff. He would wear no uniform, just that of a frontiersman. He would lead his men in a sniping war against the British Regulars, to harass their every move. Soon he become feared by the British, who started called him "the Swamp Fox."

Ban the Butcher

Governor Rutledge had been spirited out of town to a nearby plantation, to remain for days, as the siege was going badly. Colonel Abraham Buford, leading about four hundred Virginians on their way to help defend Charleston, stopped at the plantation where Governor Rutledge happened to be staying.

"Charleston has surrendered to Cornwallis," stated the governor, as he sat and reported to the Virginian.

"Then there is no cause for me to lead my men to Charleston just to have them captured or killed," Buford replied. "We shall turn back north to Charlotte, and we ride within the hour."

"I agree," said Rutledge. "I am in need of an escort to Charlotte, myself. Might I enlist your services, Buford?"

"You may indeed, sir, if you can be ready to ride within the hour," Buford spoke bluntly, "and not delay us on our march."

"I have packed lightly, sir," Rutledge rose to gather up his baggage.

A rider came to the British headquarters in Charleston with word that Governor Rutledge, a person very much wanted in shackles by Clinton, was fleeing and had been seen with a small band of Virginia troops on the way to Charlotte. Clinton, not wanting the governor to escape and remain in the region, ordered his favored dragoon, Tarleton, to pursue the fleeing patriot. Tarleton left immediately with about two-hundred-fifty mounted men, and a three-pounder cannon.

On the second day of their journey toward the North Carolina border, news came to Buford and Rutledge that Tarleton and his men were quickly advancing on their rear. Buford ordered fifty men of the cavalry to take Rutledge on a secondary route toward Charlotte, so Tarleton would continue in pursuit of the main army, and allow the governor to arrive safely in North Carolina.

The following day, May 29th, two riders rode to meet Col. Buford at a crossroad just a few miles from the main Waxhaw settlement.

"Who goes there?" Buford shouted at the riders.

"News from the militia at Waxhaw," shouted back the young voice of Andy Jackson.

"Are you the leader of this army?" Andy's brother Robert asked.

"Col. Abraham Buford," the colonel replied.

"The gov'nor rode through Waxhaw three hours ago," said Andy, "told Captain Mathias of your sit'iation with the dragoons on your asses. He's a sendin' his brothers, Angus and Grant with 'bout forty more men to help ya out."

"They should be right behind us," added Robert. "See," he turned around and pointed, "here they come now!

"Very well, boys," Buford said. "Now you boys high-tail-it back to Waxhaw, before the bullets start a flyin'!"

Andy and Robert turned their horses around and started heading back to Waxhaw, facing Captain Mathias and his brothers as they approached.

"Where ya goin' Andy," cried out Grant Mathias, as Andy and Robert approached.

"Col. Buford ordered us back to Waxhaw," said Robert.

"Dang it all!" said Grant, "I thought the Jackson boys surely wouldn't wanna miss out on a chance to see us kill a Redcoat or two!"

"Let's stay, Robert," Andy began to beg. "We can hide over yonder in the tall weeds there in those pines, and get a real view of the battle."

"But Mama said we had to stay 'way from the fightin' or else," Robert said then smiled, "but if'n we was ridin' back an' the ole Redcoats jus'came up on us a'fore we could get away, I think she'd un'erstan'." The boys ran for the rise above the crossroads, and hid in the weeds on their bellies under the pine trees.

About then, Tarleton caught up with Buford's army at the crossroads. Buford kept his men marching north toward Waxhaw. Tarleton, a real spectacle to the Jackson boys, dressed in his bright green uniform and hat with plumes, halted to wait for his entire army to catch up.

"That surely is one beauteous lookin' dragoon a mounted up on that white stallion," said Andy. "I ha'int never seen such a purdy green coat, an' look there at that fine hat he's a wearin' with all them feathers on top. Looks like a peacock ta me." The boys snickered from a safe distance.

Tarleton sent Captain David Kinlock with a white flag toward Buford. Buford paused as Kinlock approached. He read the arrogant demand for an unconditional and immediate surrender. He wrote a response for Tarleton.

"I reject your proposals and shall defend myself to the last extremities!" was Buford's reply.

"I wonder what that was all about?" asked Robert Jackson, laying flat on his belly alongside his younger brother, Andy. Andy shook his head and shrugged his shoulders.

Buford turned back toward Waxhaw and started marching again.

"Why ain't we standin' and fightin'?" asked Grant as they started to march again.

"I surely don't know," replied Angus. Then a bugle sounded 'Charge' and bullets started flying from the rear. Some of Buford's men sought out the tall grass for cover. Angus and Grant Mathias ended up laying on their bellies beside the Jackson boys. Buford gave no command to fire until the charging, saber-ready cavalry were within ten yards of his musket-holding men. The volley the Americans finally fired had little effect on the dragoons, and having no time to reload, most of the militiamen threw down their guns. Col. Buford raised the white flag of surrender.

A musket fired and the ball hit Tarleton's stallion, felling the horse. Tarleton was pitched to the ground, but not wounded. The dragoons saw this as a planned assault on their commander. Captain Kinlock began an indiscriminant massacre. The dragoons followed Kinlock's lead, and began thoughtlessly swinging their sabers and stabbing even the helplessly wounded Americans, as they lay on the ground. The dragoons wanted nothing less than total annihilation of the Americans.

Dragoons charged their horses through the tall grasses on the rise, where dozens of the men from Waxhaw were hiding. They swung their sabers at the ground, cutting many of those in hiding. Grant Mathias screamed as his ear got in the way of one dragoon's sharp blade. Andy screamed as he felt the pain from a charging horse's hoof landing on his right calf.

Tarleton lost five men killed and twelve others wounded that day, compared to one hundred thirteen Americans killed.

Andy Jackson and Grant Mathias were taken, along with some of the wounded men not already dead, or too far gone to help, to the Moravian Church house. There they were tended to by the local Moravian settlers. Betty Jackson came running to help.

"Why in Heaven's name, son?" Betty shouted at Andy, as the doctor was tending to his leg leg. "Why did ya not do as I said? Why didn't you an' Robert get back home a'fore all the fightin' started up?"

"I don't know, Mama," Andy said sniveling, "but I surely do wish I had."

"What you cryin' 'bout?" Robert asked. "Poor ole Grant had one o' his ears chopped clean off'n his head!"

"Don't ya go cryin' fer me," Grant said, from his bed where his head had been salved and bandaged, "cry for Angus. He caught a musket ball smack dab in his chest, then another dragoon ran him clean through with his blade! We'll be a buryin' him in a day or two."

To Now Face Cornwallis

On June 10th, General Washington broke winter camp from the hills surrounding Morristown, New Jersey. It had been the worse winter the Continental Army had to endure. The news coming into Washington's headquarters was not good. While little intelligence had come in the autumn, reports from the spies now flooded in, and the news did not bode well for the Americans cause.

"Charleston has fallen to the British," Washington read the message Wills Winkman had just handed him. He threw it across the desk. Washington instructed Wills to assemble a council of his general staff for that afternoon.

A second messenger rode into camp. Wills took the message into Washington immediately. Washington opened it and read it silently. He took his spectacles off and shook his head at Wills.

"Our Congress has again imposed its will," Washington said reverently. "With General Lincoln a prisoner, they have voted to assign the command of the Southern Department to Horatio Gates. The vote on the appointment was unanimous, for the exception of the newest member of the Virginia delegation," he smiled, "the youngest delegate, I might add, and a good family friend, James Madison."

Generals Greene, Wayne, Stirling and LaFayette, along with Baron von Steuben with his interpreter, Captain Benjamin Walker, and Major Alexander Hamilton, Washington's aide-de-camp, met with Washington at the appointed time.

"Charleston is lost, sirs," Washington opened the council, "and with it, five thousand of our finest men. Generals Lincoln and Moultrie, as well as Col. Laurens, are all now prisoners of war."

The room fell silent for a long period of time as the general staff mulled over in their minds the devastating news they had just received...news they might well have expected, but devastating just the same.

"You can lead us south," General Greene seemed to express the thoughts of his colleagues in the room, "and if the British chose the Carolinas as the battlefield, so be it, we shall fight them there!" More nodded and verbal agreements came from around the council table.

"But there is more gentlemen," Washington spoke solemnly. "The Congress has now appointed General Gates to replace General Lincoln, and lead the Department of the South. I am to return to West Point and defend the Hudson Valley." Again, silence filled the room.

"How can a Congress of politicians implement the strategies of the war?" spoke Wayne, not believing what he had heard. "Gates is no strategist! He now sits without a command on his farm in western Virginia, where he belongs. Let him stay put!"

"Are there details from Charleston?" asked LaFayette.

Washington relayed to his command all the news he had learned. General Lincoln had surrendered the city on May 12th.

Following the surrender of Charleston, the man now known as "Bloody Ban the Butcher" led horrific slaughters, like the one at the Waxhaw, at Monck's Corners, and other settlements. Tarleton's dragoons followed the scorched earth policy Tarleton had spoken to Clinton about, ravaging the South Carolina countryside, plundering and pillaging like medieval barbarians, burning fields, trampling gardens, slaughtering livestock and burning the carcasses.

On the first day of June, General Sir Henry Clinton and Major John Andre sailed back to New York, leaving General Charles Lord Cornwallis in command of the Southern war.

Chapter Sixteen

Under the Union Jack

B enedict Arnold was anxious to talk to Major Andre. While Clinton and Andre had sailed to South Carolina, Arnold had left Philadelphia on a tour back home to Connecticut, by way of the Hudson Valley, with an important stop at West Point. While there, he had taken an extensive tour of the American outpost, and drew plans of the fortifications from memory, to turn over to the British...for a price. Arnold also learned of a plan Washington and the French had laid-out, as a surprise of their own, and knew Sir Henry would want to know. This bit of intelligence, Arnold felt, would prove his value to Clinton, and he would turn that over at no additional cost to the British.

He arrived in New York City the same day the HMS Carolina docked and Sir Henry and Andre disembarked at Murray's Wharf. Arnold took a room at Fraunces Tavern, and sent word to Andre to meet him that evening.

"It has been too many months since we have seen one another," Major Andre said, smiling as he approached Arnold at a table by a window. "I have so longed to get back from the hot and humid Hell they call the Carolinas." Andre wiped his forehead with a handkerchief.

"And you have chosen the hottest and most humid day to return to this Hell they call Manhattan," Arnold said as both men laughed.

"So," Andre prodded, "what news have you?"

"I have some news I feel Sir Henry needs to know immediately," Arnold started the conversation. "General Washington and the French General Rochambeau have a plan to move up the Connecticut River Valley, and invade Quebec."

"Quebec?" Andre questioned in a surprised and puzzled manner. "When?"

"I know not when, but it is to make good on a promise to King Louie to secure Canada again for the French," Arnold said, "in exchange for the loans, the fleet, and the soldiers he has already sent."

Andre pondered the news his friend had just given him. There had never been any such thoughts in Clinton's headquarters at all about the possibility of the French expecting the Canadian lands they had lost two decades before. Nor had there been any notion the Americans, if successful, would not desire Canada for their own, or would be comfortable with the French at their northern border.

"Do you realize just how valuable this information will be to Sir Henry? ... and to the king?" Andre said, showing how startling the news was. "Can you imagine Sir Henry's fate as he takes Charleston, but loses Canada?"

"Please do discuss this with Sir Henry at your earliest," Arnold said.

Andre smiled at Arnold. "Information such as this must be given to Sir Henry immediately," Andre agreed.

"Now to the information Sir Henry is most anxious to have," Arnold went on. "I have drawn the complete layout of the fort at West Point. The drawings are accurate, and from my own firsthand inspection. They note every possible egress into the fort, most useful to an army wishing to capture the fort by surprise.

"Also," Arnold went on, "I am assured assignment to command West Point in but a few weeks time."

"That is wonderful news, Ben!" Andre said excitedly, seeing his and Clinton's plans coming to reality.

"General Schuyler," Arnold went on, "has assured me the post. All that is left is Washington's assent. That, I am told, will come within days.

"Washington is now headquartered at Passiac in the Dey Mansion there. I met with him as I started my journey to New Haven."

"That is indeed good news, Ben, good news indeed," smiled Andre. "Now, much as I would like to stay, I feel duty bound to take the news to Sir Henry right away."

"There is one further item I wish to bring up," Arnold said. "It is the matter of an American general's just compensation for such vital information…the drawings of West Point and the actual surrender of it."

"I am certain you will be well compensated, Ben, for all your service," Andre concurred.

"That is not really sufficient," Arnold went on. "The drawings alone are invaluable to Clinton, but I, as commander at West Point making certain the fort remains an easy target, unsuspected of a storming, agreeing to surrender the fort without a fight, is beyond value. I shall agree to give over the drawings and my pledge to surrender West Point, upon agreement of a payment of twenty-thousand pounds sterling, deposited in my London bank. Half now, and half when the Union Jack flies above the Hudson."

Off to Fight Again

"Stockard!" Peter called out to the man riding up the lane. He had spotted him while sitting with Pat on his porch. Peter shot up out of his chair and ran to meet his old friend. "What brings you to Locust Grove, and why are you wearing your old uniform?"

"I'm heading back to the war," Peter's old mentor from William and Mary said, as he dismounted and tied his horse to the hitching post. The friends hugged and Peter led him to a seat on the porch.

"I was wondering if my old friend, the Virginia Giant, might be itching to come along?" Stockard said as he sat.

"Not me," said Peter, shaking his head. "I am now truly enjoying my life as a Virginia planter. What caused you to re-enlist? Are you not still a delegate?"

"Oh no," Stockard said, "I was voted out last election."

"So you wanna get back into the army, Samuels?" Pat asked.

"It is not so much that I wish to, Pat, it is more that there is a need," Stockard explained. "We can still win this war and gain our independence as a nation of our own. Congress is sending Horatio Gates to the

South to fight Cornwallis and Tarleton. He is marching south from his farm at Shepherdstown with three thousand men, and heading to Charlotte. Many, like me, will be joining him as they march through.

"We simply can not suffer here in Virginia what our cousins in South Carolina are now suffering," Stockard went on. "If we can win back South Carolina and Georgia, Washington will march from the north, and trap Cornwallis as he tries to flee. We can win and end this war once and for all!"

"I am happy for you, Stockard," said Peter. "I wish you well. Let Pat and me show you around our farm."

"I'd enjoy seeing it," Stockard said, and the three mounted and rode.

They passed the fields where corn was growing high, tobacco was a deep green, and soon ready to be cut and hung up to cure. Oats and clover were standing, taking in the warm July sun. They stopped at the orchard and dismounted. They walked over and sat in the shade of a peach tree.

"This reminds me so much of the orchard where General Mercer was slain at Princeton," Stockard said, as he looked around the stand of fruit trees. "I will never forget that day."

"We lost a good man there," Pat said.

The three men reminisced about some of the battles they had fought. The 3rd Virginia Regiment had seen action from the closing months of 1776, all the way through the fall of Charleston, where several companies had been sent south with General Lincoln, when he first took over command in the South. There had been great victories like Trenton, Princeton and Stony Point. There had also been defeats at White Plains, Brandywine, and Germantown. There were partial victories as well, like at Monmouth. The only battle wounds among them had all been suffered by Peter.

"Peter's just too big a target," said Pat, as they all laughed.

"But my musket and sword brought much more Redcoat blood to the ground than the Redcoats ever took from me," Peter said proudly.

"I thought certain you would want to join me, Peter," Stockard made a last attempt to recruit his giant of a friend.

"I just can't," Peter said, shaking his head. "You saw the fields, you see the trees here heavy with fruit. There is just too much work needed here, and harvest time will be soon upon us. We're cutting the clover just next week"

"If we lose the war now," said Stockard, "we lose our nation as well, and Locust Grove will be governed by Parliament, ... if Tarleton does not march right through it and torch it, as he's been doing in Carolina."

"Peter," Pat spoke up, "we have enough slaves here, and I can oversee 'em," Pat said. "I can put up the clover an' tobacco, sell off the fruit, an' get the best price fer the grains.

"I know your heart's been a pinin' to get back into the fray. Hell, I see it ever' night when you an' me an' 'Tricia are sittin' at the supper table, an' you're a eyein' that giant ole sword a yer'n, hangin' over the mantle. Don't be a usin' the excuse of the farm keepin' ya from marchin' off with Stockard, if'n ya want to. An' don't feel I can't han'le your affairs while you're gone, an' be a cussin' ya fer doin' it."

Stockard Samuels slept on a cot in the small office in the house for three nights, until a messenger rode up the lane saying Gates was camping for the night at Sprouse's Corners, and any volunteers should be ready to march at first light.

Peter pulled his uniform and tri-corner hat out of the trunk. He pulled the six-foot long sword down from above the mantle, and cleaned the rifle the judge had given him last Christmas. He mounted Coronado as Stockard mounted his steed, and the two friends rode off to join the army again.

There is Espionage Afoot

Benedict Arnold took his newly commissioned post at the American fort at West Point on the third day of August. He was now in place to deliver to the British, perhaps the most important American fortress, and more importantly, an end to a five-year-long and very costly war for the king's treasury. He sat at the outpost at West Point with a relatively small contingency of General Washington's army posted there. The army was scattered between the other outposts in the area. Arnold simply sat at West Point, waiting for word from Clinton's, and, of course, a favorable response from Sir Henry, agreeing to the payment of twenty-thousand pounds sterling for his services.

Washington kept busy in those weeks riding between the various posts in the Hudson Valley, still seeing it as vital to keep Sir Henry Clinton bottled up on Manhattan Island. Washington did not set up any real headquarters for himself that summer and into the fall. He and Wills Winkman, with a small escort party, simply rode between New Jersey, just opposite Manhattan at Fort Lee, and the Hudson Valley, lodging a day or two at various farmhouses as they saw fit.

Washington had received intelligence that Clinton had indeed learned of the plan to attack Quebec from the Connecticut River Valley.

"There is espionage afoot!" screamed Washington at Wills Winkman in front of officers at every outpost they visited. "We shall lose this war, mark my word," Washington would rant and rave, "because our plans become known to the British, as soon as those plans are set! We seem to learn what moves Clinton shall make only as he makes them!"

When Washington would leave the outpost after excoriating every man in sight, hunting for the breach in his security, Washington would chuckle with Wills.

"If they only knew I planted that scheme of the French wanting Quebec, and marching up the Connecticut River to get it, as a simple ruse," Washington would say to Wills, as Wills smiled, knowing the general's real secret. "And Clinton has fallen for it! He is sore afraid to leave Manhattan for the Hudson Valley just yet, and has near-barricaded the entire coast of New England in anticipation of Rochambeau, who is not coming there at all. Clinton does play so into my hands... thanks much to the spy in our midst, whoever he is. I shall smoke the scoundrel out of his hole, and treat him as the traitor he is!"

Joshua Hett Smith, brother of a Hudson Valley farmer at West Haverstraw near Stony Point, and an avid loyalist, unbeknownst to the patriots of course, was a regular visitor to General Arnold at West Point. Arnold had approached Smith on his inspection tour of West Point a few months earlier, as Andre had told Arnold to seek him out. From the day of Arnold's arrival at the post, he and Smith planned ways to weaken the defenses of the fort, without causing blatant alarm. As new deliveries of supplies arrived at West Point, Arnold began shipping those new supplies, with some similar supplies already in the arsenal and store houses at West Point, to other, smaller and less strategic outposts in the area. Not one delivery made to West Point stayed there more than overnight.

Arnold kept the deliveries coming, as he was constantly complaining to the Congress for more supplies. With Smith nearly a constant companion of the general, the men at West Point started assuming Arnold was selling the much needed supplies on the black market with Smith's assistance. It was only rumor, and none of the officers seemed to really believe it. Arnold had been known as a lavish entertainer when he was in Philadelphia, and a slave to costly and fashionable clothing and furnishings. But he was already a wealthy man and a loyal patriot in their minds.

"When can you arrange for Andre to meet with me?" Arnold asked Smith after Arnold had been at West Point for about two weeks. "It is imperative that we act quickly, before Washington sets a permanent headquarters, possibly here. If Clinton is to move on West Point, it must be done before late fall. There are details I must work out now."

"I will be in Manhattan in three days," said Smith, as he was getting ready to mount his horse and ride out. "I will see Major Andre and set it up before the middle of September."

The Swamp Fox

Francis Marion had recruited over seventy men, mostly from the frontier settlements of South Carolina. He had them meet with him on his island in the dense swamplands along the Santee River. The swamp began along the west side of his Pond Bluff plantation. The men were promised no pay and wore no uniforms. They supplied their own horses as well as their own guns, powder, balls, and any other supplies they might need. They would cook their own meals from the game they shot or the loyalist livestock they might capture and butcher, along with any eggs they might pilfer from hen houses.

The men went through several weeks of rigorous training in backwoods warfare, sniping from behind trees, ambushing small units of men, infantry and cavalry, from hiding places along their march, and in general, any operation that might work well in an unconventional manner, foreign to the British and the hired Hessians.

Within a week of Sir Henry's sailing from Charleston, Marion's men began putting their training to work. As Tarleton established stations of men at nearly every town in the interior of South Carolina, the "Swamp Fox," as Marion had become widely known, would lead his men on harassing attacks of the men Tarleton had stationed in those towns. The raids were speedy, like sudden lightning strikes and totally unexpected.

There was no way to figure out where the Swamp Fox would strike next. Following a raid in one town one day, the next raid, the next day might be sixty miles to the north. The third raid on the following day, might be eighty miles to the east, or it might be just five miles to the west. There was no sure way to think like the Swamp Fox was thinking.

While the Swamp Fox's raids seemed minimal, with the British suffering only dozens of casualties at a time, Marion lost no men, and the word of the Swamp Fox's success built the confidence of the patriots. On August 9th, much inspired by the success of the Swamp Fox, American General Thomas Sumter led eight-hundred men against fourteen-hundred Redcoats at the station Tarleton had set up south of Heath Springs, near the settlement called Hanging Rock. Among the British soldiers there was the much-renowned Prince of Wales Regiment under the command of Major John Carden.

A regiment from the Waxhaw eagerly joined Sumter, hoping to pay back the British for the Waxhaw Massacre led by Tarleton. Major William Davie became leader of one of Sumter's three main thrusts of the three-hour long battle. Robert and Andy Jackson, as well as Grant Mathias were among Major Davie's men.

"We gonna get us some Redcoats in the morning,' sure 'nough!" said Grant, as he sat with the Jackson boys and ate a supper of roast rabbit. "Yes siree, I wanna walk off'n that battlefield with one o' them kilt skirts them Highlander boys are a wearin'! Yes, siree."

"You gonna wear that kilt skirt you a fixin' ta take as a souvenir?" asked Andy.

"I sure will," said Grant. "I'll wear it all the way right on back to the Waxhaw, jes like our Scots ancestors a'fore us wore 'em!"

"How you plannin' on getting' that ole kilt in the firs' place, Grant?" asked Robert. "You jes gonna walk right up ta one of 'em an' ask him fer it?" Andy laughed.

"I'll rip it right off'n his dead bones a layin' on the groun'! Them bastards took off my ear, didn't they?"

Major Davie's men from the Waxhaw were assigned the first attack on the enemy as the sun was coming up the next morning. Davie's men opened fire on a group of British soldiers, called Bryan's Corps. The men from the Waxhaw made quick work of their assignment, and routed the corps after only a few minutes.

As Bryan's men were fleeing, a British Captain McCulloch began firing volleys at Davie's Waxhaw men, but was immediately answered by American riflemen firing from the woods.

The famed Prince of Wales Regiment came under heavy fire and suffered many losses. Major Carden was wounded, and began to lose his will to continue the fight. Instead of surrendering, Carden relinquished his command to a junior officer. The British formed up in an open field with a three-pounder cannon left behind by the Americans. The junior officer led a brave charge against the Americans, forcing Sumter's men to retreat.

Sumter's army was running low on ammunition and therefore, Sumter ordered the retreat. With a few more rounds of ammunition, it would have been a total victory for the Americans. The British lost nearly two hundred killed, compared to the American losses of only twelve.

The Battle of Camden

General Horatio Gates arrived near Charlotte on the North Carolina-South Carolina border on July 25th. When he set up his camp at a place called Deep River, Gates had a fresh army of thirty-seven hundred men, ready for battle. Gates was determined to give them a battle quickly that would turn the tides of the war, and prove himself, once and for all time, as the hero he knew in his heart he was. He had, after all, been the commanding general at Saratoga, to date, the most successful battlefield victory for the Americans.

Francis Marion received news of Gates' commission and his arrival at Deep Water with mixed feelings. While Marion had no real confidence in Gates as the commanding general, he was pleased to see a major general of the Continental Army replacing the now imprisoned

Lincoln. He rode to Gates' encampment to offer his services, and the services of his men who had proven themselves well during the past few weeks.

"Why would you assume I need the services of such an undisciplined backwoods fighting unit of marauders," Gates said abruptly as Marion made the offer.

"We have made our mark," Marion said in a protesting manner. "When the army and the militia were unwilling to fight, we fought and lost not one engagement, nor lost not one man."

"You took matters into your own hands," said Gates dismissively. "You are now talking to a man trained in the army, and trained to fight the warfare the British fight. I am not George Washington, whose strategies are more open to your unconventional manner of thinking. They call you the Swamp Fox. Many do not even know your Christian name, nor your military rank. Why is that, sir?"

"I fight, yes, as the Swamp Fox, if that is what others may call me," Marion answered. "I do not fight to obtain glory or rank for myself, as you may. I fight only for the glory of my future nation."

"I shall not refuse your offer of service, Colonel Marion," Gates said, still not seeing Marion and his backwoodsmen as anything short of a nuisance. "I shall be marching with the full army on the British at Camden, where their most men are encamped, and their precious supplies are stored.

"When I rout them from Camden, they will attempt to pull back to Savannah," Gates said clairvoyantly.

"If you should still make your offer, knowing what I think of your tactics," Gates said, "I will send you to the Pee Dee Valley, to block any possible escape Cornwallis and Tarleton might seek."

"You see no need for seventy hardened fighters with you at Camden?" Marion could not believe the only offer Gates was willing to give him. It was no more than a way to get Marion faraway and out of Gates' sight.

"I have thirty-seven hundred disciplined and battle-ready men, trained in the art of war," Gates said. "That should be most sufficient."

"There goes the man they call the Swamp Fox," Stockard said to Peter, as Peter stirred a pot of vegetables over the campfire.

"I've sure heard of him," Peter said, looking up and watching the man walk toward where a band of men dressed in buckskins and coonskin caps were huddled. "I'd sure like to march with him."

"He's certainly been keeping the British on the run," Stockard added. "They say that Tarleton, Bloody Ban as they call him, is going quite mad trying to hunt him down."

"I hear Marion and his men run the countryside during the day," Peter said, "killing as many Redcoats as they can, and then go all the way back to their camp in some swamp somewhere every night, just to get up at the crack of dawn and do it all over again."

"Before Gates got here," Stockard said, "they were the only Americans left to harass the British. Cornwallis has offered a reward for his head."

"What about this Gates?" Peter asked Stockard. "I hear he ain't much of a general. What do you think, Stockard?"

"Well, some say he was the hero of Saratoga," Stockard said, "but many would dispute that claim. They say the real heroes were the field commanders, especially Benedict Arnold and Dan Morgan."

"I heard that too," said Peter. "I heard he stayed safe inside his fort and didn't see the battle at all. He just sent out the field commanders and let them do as they saw fit."

"That is what they say," Stockard confirmed.

"Well why did Washington send him to be in charge down here?" Peter asked.

"Washington didn't," said Stockard. "Congress voted unanimously to commission Gates here. It was unanimous, except for one vote. Our friend Jimmy Madison voted against it."

On August 15th, Gates and his nearly four thousand men made camp at Rugeley's Mills, about six miles north of Camden, within a mile of the British garrison of eleven hundred, commanded by Lord Rawdon. Gates' original thirty-seven hundred had been increased by militias from North Carolina and Virginia. Peter and Stockard had been assigned to Colonel William Mayo.

General Cornwallis received word of Gates' move toward Camden the day Gates moved out from Deep River. Cornwallis left Charleston the next morning with one thousand re-enforcements for Rawdon to hold Camden at all cost. Cornwallis and Tarleton arrived at Camden on the same day Gates arrived at Rugeley Mills.

On August 16th, Gates was first to form his army on the battlefield, and waited for Cornwallis to do the same, as was the European style of battlefield war Gates had been trained. Both armies were in position by dawn, and shortly after the sun rose, both armies simultaneously advanced toward the other. The British began firing volleys into the right flank of Gates' army, inflicting many casualties on the Americans. Cornwallis, seeing the devastation already done to Gates' right flank, ordered fixed bayonets, and the buglers sounded "Charge!"

The American militiamen, who had made up the right flank and already saw many of their comrades fall to the ground wounded or dead, had no bayonets to fix, so they turned and ran in retreat. The left flank saw the right flank fleeing into the piney woods, so they too began to retreat. Disaster was in the wind for Gates immediately, so he too mounted the fastest steed he could find, and sped away north, leaving the battlefield altogether. Gates did not stop to look back until he was safely sixty miles away, back in North Carolina at Charlotte.

As others were fleeing, the German-born French ally of the Americans, General Johann de Kalb, attempted to rally his Maryland and Delaware troops. In his attempts, he was struck eleven times by musket fire. He died the following day.

The Battle of Camden was over within an hour, but misery to the Americans continued into the night and beyond. "Bloody Ban" and his two-hundred fifty green-coated dragoons began chasing down the retreating patriots as they tried to run to safety.

Peter and Stockard found themselves in retreat. Col. Mayo wanted not to see his men slaughtered under Tarleton's Quarter, as was the case at the horrific Waxhaw Massacre. Mayo saw the faulty strategic logic Gates had put his men in, and wanted to save his men to fight another day. Mayo agreed with Washington…to win a war in North America, it took new thinking, quick assaults, surprise actions and stamina; not parading one army against the other, as if in some sort of feudal tournament. During the retreat, Peter and Stockard were soon separated.

With Tarleton's fierce dragoons in hot pursuit, Peter ran into the piney woods following his comrades. In a matter of minutes, he spotted Col. Mayo. Rushing to get to Mayo, Peter saw a British cavalryman taking aim at his colonel. Peter, thinking quickly, took his rifle and fired, killing the Redcoat instantly. The Redcoat's horse ran off. Peter and Mayo ran off together in the direction of the retreating men.

Col. Mayo and Peter ran together for nearly half an hour, when one of Tarleton' green-coat dragoons spotted them and charged at them with full force. Shouting as he charged them, "Surrender or die!" Mayo turned and ran off into the woods. Peter stopped and stood his ground, awaiting the dragoon's approach.

"Shall you be my prisoner or shall you become a corpse?" the dragoon shouted from his horse.

"I shall be neither," answered Peter boldy, "I shall live as an independent American!"

The dragoon rode circles around Peter, swinging his saber, as Peter ducked at each lunge. Peter swiftly pulled his giant sword from its scabbard and struck the dragoon with all his strength on his shoulder, lopping off the green-coat's arm. The dragoon fell, and Peter jumped on the captured horse.

Peter rode through the woods, and when the woods opened, he saw British troops marching in front of him, pursuing the Americans. He paused at the edge of the woods, at the rear of the British troops. He had to make a plan. "How can I get through all these Redcoats?" he asked himself. He came up with an idea. He threw his uniform jacket to the ground, so he felt he could then easily pass as a loyalist. He spurred his commandeered horse forward. He wished he had Coronado, but had kept him safely back at the camp at Deep River.

"Huzzah, boys!" Peter shouted in a booming voice. "Let's go after those damn rebels!" The Redcoats cheered him as he rode through their ranks and into the woods ahead of them.

Several minutes later, several hundred yards into the woods ahead of the approaching troops, he again spotted Col. Mayo on foot, now the prisoner of a British officer. Peter rode up furiously to where the officer held Mayo, and with not a word spoken, Peter swung his sword and lopped off the officer's head with one swing of his sword. Peter jumped from his captured horse, freed Mayo of the ropes binding him, and gave Mayo the horse. Peter ran alongside his colonel and they soon caught up with more retreating patriots.

As they came up to the rear of the Americans in retreat, Peter spotted a dead horse, fallen near the path. The horse had been pulling a small field artillery piece attached to its carriage. Peter ran over to it. He crouched down and cut the harness from the horse, loosened the artillery piece from its carriage, lifted it to his shoulder, and carried the eleven-hundred pound piece of artillery to an army unit a hundred yards in front of him.

"Here boys," Peter said, crouching back to the ground and sliding the heavy piece off his shoulders. "We might need this next time we run into Bloody Ban." It took four men to lift the piece onto the back of a buckboard wagon. Peter laughed as he watched them.

Being exhausted, Peter felt he deserved a rest, and slid underneath one of the many pine trees in the woods. The army unit was already continuing its retreat when Peter shut his eyes. He shut his eyes for maybe ten minutes. He was awakened when one of Tarleton's dragoon surprised him and yelled, "Surrender or die!"

Peter opened his eyes, rifle in hand, smiled at the dragoon and started to hand the gun to him.

"Take it, sir," Peter said, "It is spent of all its ammunition."

The dragoon smiled and reached for the barrel of the gun. Peter pulled the trigger and blew a hole in the Greencoat's chest.

Peter jumped to his feet and onto the dead dragoon's stallion and galloped away. He rode back to Deep River where he again met up with Stockard.

The Battle of Camden was the most devastating defeat for the American cause thus far. Most considered it more costly to the Americans than Burgoyne's defeat at Saratoga had been to the British. The British suffered sixty-eight killed, two hundred and forty-eight wounded, with eleven missing. American casualties numbered over nine hundred killed or wounded and another one thousand taken as prisoners. The Americans also lost all of their pieces of artillery, (except for two, one being the one Peter had carried on his shoulders). All the baggage of the army was taken, and all their supply wagons were lost. Many prisoners were taken back to Camden and held there in a fenced-in open corral. The others were marched to Charleston for imprisonment there.

At Charlotte, Horatio Gates knew his military career was ended in disgrace. He left hastily for his farm at Shepherdstownm, making the one hundred-seventy mile retreat in three days.

Unravelling the Plot

Peggy Arnold arrived at West Point after Arnold had been there about six weeks. The meeting between Arnold and Andre was set for September 20th.

"This is such a lovely place," Peggy said to her husband, as he took her on a stroll around the encampment at West Point the morning after she arrived. "On these heights, overlooking that most beautiful river, one feels to be standing on top of the world, looking down upon all creation. The leaves are turning to their glorious hues of autumn. It is such a beautiful time to be here."

"But there is no city," Arnold said, "no society, save that of the army life."

"But Ben, I have lived all my life in the city. I have never before lived in such a beautiful setting," Peggy went on. "I have only imagined of such a place. It must be exactly like the panoramas seen in Switzerland, or Austria...perhaps Bavaria."

"Enjoy it, my dear," Arnold said, "for in a matter of weeks, it will either be ours, living here as the King's commandant of his newly reclaimed realm in North America, or we shall flee to London as traitors to the American cause."

"These are such exciting times, Ben," Peggy squeezed his hand between her two gloved hands as they stood on a cliff overlooking the Hudson River below them.

Major John Andre left Manhattan the morning of the 20th, aboard the HMS Vulture, sailing north up the Hudson. In the early afternoon, the Vulture dropped anchor. Andre was lowered into a rowboat, and rowed to the western shore, south of Stony Point.

From the shore, Andre walked through the woods to the Smith farmhouse, where he was to meet Arnold and set the plot against West Point.

"I'm gonna leave you two to your work as I finish up of some chores," Joshua said as he started to leave the house. "My Sarah baked a rhubarb pie, and there's a baked ham on the table and a pot of coffee on the hearth." He left the two alone.

"I, for one, am ravished with hunger," said Andre.

"Well, I hear there's a ham and pie awaiting us," said Arnold with a smile. "You suppose there's something other than coffee we might tipple?" Arnold asked.

"Josh keeps a bottle of whiskey in the pantry," Andre said with a smile. They sat at the table and ate as they started planning.

They plan for a British force to sail up the Hudson, and begin a siege on the West Point garrison. Arnold, as commandant, would, shortly after the siege began, order the American flag down the flagpole, and the white flag of surrender raised. Arnold would seemingly be taken prisoner by the British. Sir Henry would move his base of operations to West Point, having effectively cut off the New England colonies all together.

Clinton would eventually expose the plot, and name Arnold commandant and governor of New York. Then ten thousand pounds sterling would be deposited into Arnold's London bank account. The first ten thousand pounds had already been deposited.

Washington's surrender would be forced by Christmas, and the war would be ended by New Year's Day.

They talked of the plans, looked at maps and drawings of the fort for hours, and consulted the calendar.

"How soon can we act?" Arnold asked.

"One week," Andre offered his most optimistic guess, "perhaps two at most."

"I wish we could move before Washington himself comes here," Arnold said.

"What are Washington's plans?" Andre asked.

"He is now at Hartford, then will spend two days at Litchfield before coming here," said Arnold. "I am to host him for breakfast the morning of the 24th."

"Do you feel he will use West Point as his permanent headquarters?" Andre asked for further details.

"I believe not," said Arnold. "He favors Tappan, closer to Manhattan, and where he has a large garrison. A Dutchman, invited Washington to stay at his farmhouse when he was inspecting the redoubts in August. It's a small Dutch house, but the general rather enjoyed the Dutch hospitality. I believe he will headquarter at Tappan."

"Let us plan to move on West Point three days after the breakfast you are to serve him," Andre suggested.

"I think that is a safe timeframe," agreed Arnold. "Washington should be in the mountains heading to Tappan by then, so he shall not spoil our plans."

"Then it's settled," Andre said.

At that time, Smith came rushing in from his chores.

"The Vulture has sailed without you, major."

"What?" Andre said, bolting up from the chair. "I lost all track of time. What am I to do now? How am I to get back to Sir Henry? Why did they sail? They had orders to wait till sundown!"

"The Rebels fired on the Vulture from the east shore at Verplank's Point," Smith said. "The Vulture turned and sailed back towards Manhattan. That's what I was told."

"How can I get our plans to Clinton?" Andre asked, frantically."

"For the time being," Arnold said, "we stay here, if Joshua and Sarah do not mind."

"Not a'tall," offered Smith. "There's a downstairs bedroom there," he pointed to a door on the end of the parlor. "Sarah and I sleep upstairs."

The next morning at the breakfast table, Arnold laid out his new plan.

"Joshua," Arnold began, "I think it best he get out of that damned British uniform, and dress like a common American farmer."

"I'll go fetch him some clothes," Smith said, as he got up and ran up the stairs.

As Andre dressed, Arnold asked Sarah for writing paper, a quill pen, and bottle of ink. He drafted a passport for safe passage for Andre. The major would become John Anderson, a Hudson Valley farmer, traveling to tend to a sick mother at Hoboken. Smith had a horse ready for Andre to use on his thirty-mile ride to Manhattan.

Arnold gave Andre his drawings of West Point, holding up his end of the bargain with Sir Henry. Andre folded the papers, with their plans for taking the fort, and put them in the bottom of his right boot. He put the passport in his jacket pocket.

Andre crossed the Hudson on a ferry to Tarrytown on the eastern shore and stopped in at a tavern for food.

After eating, he headed south on the post road. Within an hour he came across three armed men in common clothes.

"Gentlemen," Andre said, as he approached the men he thought to be some of the loyalist watchmen he had heard tell of, "I do hope you belong to our party!"

"And what party might that be?" one of the men, John Paulding, asked.

"The lower party," Andre announced, as the loyalists in New York were referred to as being members of the lower party.

"We are, indeed," said a second man, Isaac Van Wert, deceivingly, hoping to catch a prisoner.

"Thank the stars!" Andre said. "I am Major John Anderson, an officer in the King's Army, and I must not be delayed. I am expected at New York."

"Anderson is it?" asked the third man, David Williams.

"Yes," affirmed Andre.

"Major Anderson," added Van Wert, "We are Americans and you are our prisoner."

Andre was fast thinking on his feet in such a situation.

"Good!" Andre said, reaching into his jacket pocket. I, too am an American, but feared you to be one of those many loyalists I have encountered on my journeys from Peekskill." He handed the fake passport to Van Wert. "That should prove my true identity to you."

Van Wert read the paper. "So this is a passport signed by General Benedict Arnold, himself." He looked at Andre, smiled and handed the passport to Paulding.

"Well, that should do it," said Paulding, as he handed the document to Williams, who started to read it.

"But before we take this paper as fact," said Williams, "it would do no harm to search Mr. Anderson." He turned toward the captive and smiled. "If ya have nothin' to hide, what's the harm?"

"No harm, at all," Andre said, raising his arms ready to be frisked. "But please be quick. I have a dying mother in Hoboken. I'm hoping to get there before she passes."

Paulding ran his hands up and down Andre's sides, legs, chest and back. Van Wert took Andre's farmer's hat and turned it inside out, feeling the lining. Van Wert nodded at Paulding.

"Well, things 'pear you are free to go," Paulding said. Andre smiled, thinking his ruse had worked.

"We haven't searched his boots," said Williams, stooping down to lift the left boot off his foot. There was nothing to be found, and Andre began to protest.

"I shall report this insolence to General Arnold at West Point!" Andre said.

"What harm is there if nothing's found in the other boot?" Van Wert said.

"Well...nothing...I suppose," said Andre, "but it is a gross inconvenience, and holding me from my journey." He pulled a gold encased watch from his pocket Paulding had found when he searched Andre. "This watch cost me dear," Andre said, "here..." he handed it to Paulding, "take it and let me be upon my way."

Paulding handed the watch back to Andre, and nodded at Williams.

Williams immediately grabbed the toe of the boot with one hand and the heel of it with the other. He wriggled it off Andre's foot. The folded papers landed on the ground.

Paulding, Van Wert and Williams marched their prisoner to the garrison at Sands Point. There they were told to report to the main headquarters at Tappan. Andre was housed in a locked cellar on the De Wint farm, with a sentry posted.

The next day, Lt. Col. John Jameson, the post commandant, sent a dispatch to Dobbs Ferry, across the river, for Major Benjamin Tallmadge, the head of Army Intelligence. Tallmadge arrived in the afternoon and conducted an interview with the prisoner.

Tallmadge walked to the De Wint cellar and the sentry let him in.

"Mr. Anderson," Tallmadge greeted the young prisoner, "I am Major Benjamin Tallmadge, Chief of Intelligence of the Continental Army. I have a few questions for you."

"Certainly," the prisoner agreed, being quite the gentleman. "In truth, I am Major John Andre, aide to Sir Henry Clinton, commander-in-chief of the British Army of North America. Anything I might do to help clear up this unfortunate situation."

"Who is your American accomplice, Major Andre?" Tallmadge asked, not expecting an answer.

"I am a British officer," Andre said, "I certainly have no American accomplice, as you suggest."

"Who told you about the plan to invade Quebec?" Tallmadge wanted to delve into a subject with which he had no direct link to Andre.

"I know of no such plan to invade Quebec," Andre said, laughing and feigning ignorance. "By the Americans?" he laughed some more, "that would be quite stupid, when your army is now engaged in a full-scale revolution facing Lord Cornwallis in the Carolinas."

"When is the siege on West Point to begin?" Tallmadge continued, using something in the papers found in Andre's boot.

"I have just couriered information," replied Andre. "I know not what that information contains."

"To whom, and from whom were you taking the information?" Tallmadge persisted.

"To General Sir Henry Clinton," Andre said, hoping that would be enough, "from a ferry boat operator at Tarrytown, an intermediary from some one else I am quite certain."

"You came upon the Vulture," Tallmadge said, laying out a scenario he thought might be the truth, but had no real evidence. "You landed south of Stony Point, north of Haverstraw, and were rowed to the west bank. You spent last evening ashore in meetings nearby. When you came back to the Vulture to return to New York, it had left without you, the result of a firing upon it from Verplank's Point. Now, with whom were you meeting?"

"I assure you that is not what occurred," Andre was devastated at the major's description of events.

"It was General BenedictArnold, was it not?" Tallmadge shouted at his prisoner. "Arnold was asway from West Point all night and did return till late yesterday. It was General Arnold."

"I stated I met with a ferryman only," re-iterated Andre firmly.

"That ferryman at Tarrytown is a cousin of one of your captors, Isaac Van Wert, and neither are involved in any clandestine dealings with the British," Tallmadge objected, not knowing at all the Tarrytown ferryman.

"Then it was a ferry further upriver, perhaps," said Andre unconvincingly.

"Benedict Arnold filled out and signed your passport of safe passage, did he not?" Tallmadge said with the document in hand.

"It is his name," Andre admitted, "but I'm certain it to be a forgery."

Tallmadge pulled another paper from his pocket containing Arnold's signature, and set the two documents side-by-side examining the two signatures.

"No," Tallmadge said matter-of-factly. "The man who signed both are the same man."

"It was Arnold, and you have proven it so," announced Tallmadge. "Why else would you not place the blame upon him squarely when you had the chance? If General Arnold is not your important associate and means nothing to your plot, you would have quickly pinned the blame upon him."

Andre sat without speaking another word. He knew he had spoken himself into a corner.

After several silent minutes he spoke. "What is to become of me?" Andre asked of Tallmadge.

Tallmadge told the story of his college chum, Nathan Hale, how he had been hanged.

"Do you think Hale's crimes and mine are similar?" Andre asked Tallmadge.

"Yes, strikingly so," Tallmadge answered, "precisely similar, and similar shall be your fate." Tallmadge turned and walked to the cellar door, calling for the sentry.

"From what Andre did not say," Tallmadge told Jameson, "and the way he did not say it, I am cartain the defector among our officers is General Benedict Arnold."

"And what if you are incorrect in your surmising?" Jameson asked.

"I will take all of the scorn," said Tallmadge. "I think you should make copies of each of the eight pages found in Andre's boot. Keep them safe till Washington is here within the week. Send the originals in a packet for Arnold at West Point, and send the messenger tonight with instructions to give the packet to Arnold as soon as he arrives. Let us unravel this plot that could cause us our independence."

The horseman left Tappan at midnight the evening of September 24th, and rode the post road to West Point, arriving at six the next morning. He stopped at the Moore House, a gray stone house that housed General Arnold and his lovely wife Peggy. The rider dismounted and rapped on the door. Arnold, already dressed for his busy day that would start with a breakfast for General Washington in just two hours, opened a second story window and leaned out.

"A message from Jameson at Tappan," cried out the courier.

"I shall be down momentarily," Arnold answered.

Major Wills Winkman was lying in his bed in a small bedroom on the second story of a second gray stone house opposite the Moore House. The courier's cries awakened Wills, as he had always slept with an ear open for such cries in the night hours from couriers. He went to the window, opened it and leaned out. He was glad someone else would be taking the packet this time, as General Washington was no doubt still soundly sleeping in the bedchamber next door to his.

Wills saw General Arnold open the door and bring the courier inside. The door closed behind them.

Arnold took the packet and dismissed the courier.

"If this requires an answer, I shall send for you at the stable bunks," Arnold instructed the courier.

He sat and read the messages he had penned for Andre, as well as the drawings of West Point he had made. He read the final attached sheet:

"One Major John Andre, a spy, captured at Tarrytown, now held at Tappan. Enclosed pages apprehended from Andre's person at time of arrest. Andre promises to divulge name and rank of defector from within our ranks for mercy shown him in this matter."

Lt. Col. John Jameson and Major Benjamin Tallmadge, Army Intelligence had signed the letter.

Arnold's face immediately loss all hints of color. He was devastated, and now very desperate. He grabbed a blank sheet of paper and penned a note to Peggy.

"Dearest Peggy, ***dispose of this immediately***
JA captured. I must flee. Entertain GW this morning. Make excuses for me---ill son in

Philadelphia---left immediately. Join me soon. All my love... BA"

He quietly went back to the bedroom and left the note for Peggy on her dressing table. He wanted to waste no time.

Wills Winkman had not gone back to bed. He was to have breakfast with General Arnold and Washington in less than two hours, so he dressed and sat at the desk by the open window. He started a letter to Priscilla and the children in Cambridge. He looked out the window and saw General Arnold, limping toward the stables on his bad leg and crutches. Within a few minutes a horse carrying the general galloped by the gray stone houses and headed down the post road.

Wills and Washington walked across to the Arnold house and rapped at the door. Peggy Shippen Arnold opened the door and made her apologies.

"I am so very sorry, general," the lovely Peggy announced as Washington entered the house, "but just after General Arnold greeted you and showed you to our guesthouse, a rider came in with news of his eldest boy, Alexander, being tragically ill with the fever. He left immediately for Philadelphia. He asked that I beg your pardon. He shall attempt to return within two weeks."

"Pardon is granted," Washington said graciously, though disappointed, "as I know what it is to lose a child. Lady Washington and I lost our dear, sweet Patsy. I shall see General Arnold when he returns."

As Peggy Arnold led Washington and Wills into the dining room, Wills knew the apology Peggy had given was not the truth. He had just seen Arnold less than an hour before. They passed by the general's desk as they walked to the dining room. Wills saw what looked very much like the packet he had watched the courier carry. Unnoticed, he picked it up and folded it, slipping it inside his jacket.

Lafayette, Anthony Wayne, Arthur St. Clair, Lord Stirling, and Baron von Steuben arrived for breakfast shortly after Washington's arrival. Nothing was mentioned of Arnold's absence, other than Peggy's explanation. As soon as breakfast was finished, Washington thanked Lady Arnold and left the house for the parlor of the guesthouse, so as not to impose upon the general's wife.

"Sir," Wills said to Washington, having pulled him aside from the others, "I think you should read this dispatch I witnessed General Arnold receive by courier just an two hours before we breakfasted." He handed the packet to Washington. He read it and passed it to General Wayne.

"I think, gentlemen," Washington said most earnestly as they sat for a council, "I think we have just caught our rat."

On October 2nd, John Andre was hanged in the orchard of the De Wint farm at Tappan.

The Overmountain Men

A week after the retreat from Camden, Col. Francis Marion came into the camp at Deep River. "Is there a Private Peter Francisco here?" he kept asking as he walked between the men at the camp. "I am looking for Private Peter Francisco."

"I'm Private Peter Francisco, sir." Peter stood from where he was sitting on a log under a big elm tree, polishing his sword. He saluted the fabled Swamp Fox.

"Are you the one who captured that British cannon at Camden, and carried it off on your shoulders?" Marion asked.

"It was me," Peter answered.

Marion smiled, then chuckled. "That word has spread all around camp, even to the Redcoats at Camden. We heard it when we were coming in from the Pee Dee. Where you from?"

"Buckingham County Virginia," Peter answered, as the two men sat down on the log.

"Where the Hell did you ever get that giant sword?" Marion asked, pointing to the sword laying on the ground in front of them.

"General Washington and LaFayette had it special made for me before we left Valley Forge," Peter smiled.

"Well then, how many Redcoats and Greencoats did you send to meet their maker back at Camden?"

"I lost count." The two soldiers laughed.

"Well, private, it appears we might get a new commanding general down here to take the place of old Granny Gates," Marion turned the conversation. "It will probably be some weeks before that happens, and we still have a war to win, to keep Cornwallis and Tarleton busy. How would you like to join me and my men in the swamp?"

Not only Marion and his men were harassing the British, but bands of patriot militias were forming in what was called the over mountain region of western North Carolina. Like at the Waxhaw, many Scotch-Irish had gone across the Great Smoky Mountains of the Appalachians, settling there as far away from the British colonies in the East as they could. Now, they were seeing the war was getting closer to them. Even some militias from the Kentucky region of Virginia were marching. Col. Isaac Shelby led the Kentucky militia, and joined with Col. John Sevier and his Western North Carolina men.

Cornwallis ordered a British officer, Major Patrick Ferguson, to take his loyalist troops, and enlist other loyalists on the frontier, to suppress any efforts of the Swamp Fox and the overmountain men of Shelby and Sevier.

In early September, Peter Francisco and a band of men led by the Swamp Fox, were in the settlement of Gilbert Town for supplies. Ferguson led his army of thirteen-hundred into the settlement. Ferguson stood on the steps of the mercantile and ordered all the settlers to assemble for what he had to say. When they had congregated, Ferguson spoke.

"That damnable Swamp Fox has laid the torch to Greeley Mills, killing all inhabitants and eighteen of the king's men."

"Did not!" yelled one man in the crowd. "I was there an' no torch was lit an' not one settler harmed, jes them damned Redcoats!"

"Sieze that man!" Ferguson ordered, as four soldiers brushed past Peter and rushed the man who had spoken.

"This man will be strung up for all to see," Ferguson announced. "I have an ultumatum to lay down for you all. Lay down your arms, or I shall lay waste to your country by fire and by sword."

Shelby and Sevier were, at the time meeting with Col. Marioin in the attic of the mercantile, unaware Ferguson and his men were coming. The three heard what Ferguson had said.

"I say," said Sevier, "we can unite our forces an' put an end ta that wind bag!"

"He's heading west," Marion said. "I heard Cornwallis ordered him to enlist more loyalists here on the frontier. He's ta track me down as well as you two fellers."

"That don't seem ta be no way ta enlist support," said Shelby, "threatenin' 'em with the torch and sword. I agree, Sevier. With yer men and mine, we can put an end ta that bastard."

"Do it," Marion encouraged them. "We're headin' back toward Camden. There ain't a handful of loyalists left on the frontier."

Shelby and Sevier made camp at South Mountain. They heard that Ferguson and his men were camped on top of the mountain. They took nine hundred men on horseback to the steep base of the mountain, which was an area of steep hills and forests. There they divided into nine units. They devised a plan of attack, with most of the units, led by John Crockett, charging up the steep face of the mountain, screaming as they charged. Shelby and Sevier would circle around, and come up from behind Ferguson on the mountaintop. Their plan was to surround and destroy the loyalists by shooting from behind rocks and trees.

At three o'clock in the afternoon, the first charge up the mountain began. Ferguson ordered a charge with fixed bayonets, down the steep front of the hill, as the rebel force charged up. The patriots, having no bayonets, when faced with the charge, retreated back down the mountain. Ferguson's men, over-shooting due to the terrain, retreated back up the mountain. Ferguson ordered a second bayonet charge, and as his men charged back down the mountain. A second time, the patriots again charged up. Ferguson rode his horse back and forth across the edge of the mountaintop, ordering his men on, blowing a silver whistle as he shouted out his orders.

This same action repeated a third time, with the loyalists suffering heavy losses during the one-hour battle. By the time the loyalists retreated back to the mountaintop, preparing another charge down hill, Shelby and Sevier's units had made their way around to the rear of Ferguson's men on the mountaintop.

Shelby and Sevier pushed the loyalists across the mountaintop to the far side, where they began to wave the white flag of surrender. Ferguson, irate at the sight of white flags coming from his men, took his sword and began knocking the flags out of his own men's hands. He ordered a frontal charge on Shelby and Sevier, and was immediately struck by seven different bullets. He fell from his horse and layed dead on the ground.

John Crockett shouted "Give 'em Tarleton's Quarter!" Many agreed, especially those from the Waxhaw region where Tarleton's men had slaughtered the patriots waving the white flag. Sevier spoke up loudly, joined by Shelby, and put an end to a possible atrocity. The loyalists suffered two hundred and ninety killed, one hundred and sixty-three wounded, with another six hundred and sixty-eight captured. American losses were twenty-nine killed and fifty-eight wounded.

Tarleton's Legion

On October 5th, after the devastating loss at Camden in August, and the humiliating retreat of Horatio Gates, Congress argued the war strategies. The twenty-nine year-old James Madison, the one vote against Gates' original promotion, stood and addressed his colleagues in Philadelphia.

"Gentlemen, I did not cast a vote in favor of General Gates to direct our war in the South," Madison said. "I cast that vote not because my politics opposed General Gates, but because I am not a military mind, and because this is not a military body.

"My vote was to express my confidence in the work Congress did in 1775, appointing General George Washington as our one commander-in-chief, to lead our army, and wisely to direct our war for independence. Congress' role is to fund and support the army and the struggle, not to plan the specific strategies of this war, nor to assign what each general shall do. When we make military decisions, best left to our commander-in-chief and his generals, we increase the inevitability for disaster on the fields of battle, as recently seen at Camden. When we make military decisions based solely upon our personal political beliefs, we ensure that disaster.

"I rise to offer a resolution that we unanimously call for a new military commander to be placed in the southern department of the war, and reassert the authority of General George Washington, our commander-in-chief, to fill that position, when he sees fit, and with whom he feels best fit to serve there."

The Congress accepted Madison's resolution without decent. Ten days later, General Washington named General Nathaniel Greene as the new Commander of the Department of the South.

General Greene arrived on December 2nd at Charlotte, and found his army weak and low on supplies. Greene knew his army could not successfully stand against the superior numbers of the British. He divided his forces in two, and devised a totally new strategy.

He appointed Brigadier General Daniel Morgan, who was the leader of the Light Infantry Corps of nine hundred, to raid any loyalist settlements and small British encampments, as well as forage for supplies. Morgan was ordered not to provoke an all-out attack on the enemy. Greene would lead the main army from Charlotte, thus forcing Cornwallis to split his forces as well.

Lt. Col. William Washington, a commander of Virginia dragoons, and second cousin to George Washington, was assigned to Morgan's command. Col. Thomas Watson's cavalry unit that now included Private Peter Francisco atop Coronado, was attached to Washington's dragoons. The Swamp Fox, once Greene arrived, disbanded his private army of marauders to join Greene's army.

Morgan left Charlotte on December 21st, and by Christmas day was at the Pacolet River.

Cornwallis soon learned of General Greene's new strategy for the Americans, and ordered 'Bloody Ban' Tarleton to capture Morgan, as he had ordered him to capture the elusive Swamp Fox, with no success.

Tarleton learned Morgan was then at the Pacolet. Morgan learned Tarleton was in pursuit of him, so he retreated north, so as not to be trapped between Tarleton and Cornwallis's armies.

On January 16th, Morgan arrived at the flooded banks of the Broad River, and knowing Tarleton was but a few hours behind him, stopped before dusk at a place called Cowpens.

Cowpens was a popular cattle-grazing meadowland used by settlers in the area. Morgan saw it as an ideal battle site, and decided to plan for a battle with Tarleton the following morning. He knew he was disobeying direct orders, but also felt firmly, this place could bring a turning point for the Americans. He set a plan, unlike any used on any battlefield in the war. He relied on the natural lay of the land, and on the accuracy of the Virginia sharpshooters that he had put to good use at Saratoga.

Morgan lined up his men between the two rivers to prevent Tarleton's men from an escape route. The first line was made up of the

Virginia sharpshooters. The next, unseen by the charging enemy, were the militiamen, and finally, on a hilltop, again unseen, were the regular army troops, and Washington's cavalry.

Tarleton's vanguard arrived just before sunrise, tired from the long ride through the night without rest, and famished, having nothing to eat in two days. The Americans performed as Morgan had planned and instructed them throughout the night.

The first two lines of sharpshooters sent a volley at the advancing British, inflicting heavy casualties on the green-coated dragoons. The first line then turned their backs on the British, and squatted to reload their muskets. When the charging dragoons were at their backs, the patriots abruptly turned, aimed at the enemies' faces, and fired at point blank range. The marksmen rose and retreated around the next two lines of the American defenses behind them, still unseen by Tarleton's men.

The remaining dragoons, feeling that had been the extent of the American force, charged within seconds, only to be met by the second fresh line of the Americans. That exchange went much like the first, with the second line ending their skirmish quickly, and again retreating to the rear.

Again, Tarleton's men were convinced they had seen all the American fire they were in for, but then they saw the third and largest line of the Americans, charging down at them from atop the gently sloping hillside.

The Battle of Cowpens on January 17th 1781, lasted less than an hour, with the British seeing one hundred and ten of their best men killed, and more than two hundred wounded. Eight hundred and thirty British were taken as prisoners, and their two field artillery pieces were captured, as well as all of Tarleton's supplies. Twenty-five Americans died on the battlefield, and one hundred and twenty-four were wounded. Tarleton escaped capture with about ninety men. Cornwallis had, that day, lost one of the most feared units of the British army in the South, Tarleton's Legion.

Guilford Courthouse

Peter Francisco was invigorated by the victory. He was thrilled to charge down the hill atop Coronado, sword in hand, to do as much damage to the Greencoats of Tarleton's Legion as he possibly could do. He had vindicated the devastation of the Battle of Camden.

Greene was happy with the news from Cowpens, even if General Morgan had disobeyed the order not to provoke an attack. Greene had marched east and south, and won a few skirmishes, but failed with the Swamp Fox, now in uniform as Brigadier General Francis Marion, to take Georgetown on the Atlantic coast, north of Charleston.

In the weeks after Cowpens, Cornwallis was determined to squash the American Army led by Nathaniel Greene, whatever the cost. To lighten the load of his army on the march, he burned his own supplies. Cornwallis knew Greene was marching to cross the Dan River into Virginia for re-enforcements he had asked Patrick Henry and Governor Thomas Jefferson to send. Cornwallis chased him without success in what was called the race to the Dan, but Greene crossed the river just hours before Cornwallis arrived.

Cornwallis turned back immediately toward Charlotte, and camped at Deep River on March 14th. There he learned Greene's re-enforced army was close by at Guilford Courthouse. The new re-enforcements for the Continental Army had now given Greene superior numbers to Cornwallis. Cornwallis sat with nineteen hundred men, while the best estimates showed Greene now was in command of between four and five thousand. Cornwallis chose to attack at Guilford Courthouse, regardless of knowing he was out numbered.

Cornwallis led the British Army into Guilford County, arriving at the Quaker New Garden Meetinghouse at midday. Between the Quaker meetinghouse and the Courthouse, Tarleton's remaining dragoons, met and exchanged fire with General Light Horse Harry Lee's dragoons before Tarleton could be re-enforced by a British foot regiment. Lee's dragoons made a brief retreat, with Greene's main army following.

Knowing Cornwallis and Tarleton were in pursuit, Greene set his men on a rise. The first line, manned by the North Carolina Militia flanked by the best Virginia sharpshooters, and two six-pound cannons on each side, ran along a fenced-in wooded area. Virginia Militia manned the second line of defense, and the third line was Greene's main army, with General William Washington's battle-tested dragoons at the rear. Two more six-pounders were set at the center of the line atop the rise.

At half-passed one, Cornwallis' Army advanced on the Continental Army's and met with a heavy cannon barrage. They continued the march and advanced to within one hundred and fifty yards of the fence. Heavy long-gun fire came from the Americans. The long guns had a greater range than the British muskets, but the British continued their advance until they were within a mere fifty paces of the patriots.

The North Carolina Militia rested their long guns on the picket fence and fired a single volley, then fled into the woods. The woods were too dense for a pursuit, so Cornwallis ordered his men on. They met the second line of defense and heavy fire, so the Redcoats flanked the line, and were then forced to face the final line of defense.

The British had already suffered heavy casualties, but marched on through the wooded area, coming out onto the open yard of the courthouse. There, the British faced the American Infantry until the infantry fell back and the British took two of the cannons. The British followed in hot pursuit of the American Infantry retreating through woods. There stood General William Washington's dragoons. Peter Francisco was astride Coronado with his giant sword drawn.

During the next few minutes of the fight, Peter killed nine Redcoats with his sword. A Redcoat infantry man, with bayonet fixed, had seen Peter killing another of his comrades, and was determined to put an end to this giant of a man, who seemed to be an army of one. The Redcoat charged toward Peter and thrust his bayonet into Peter's leg, pinning his leg to Coronado's side. Peter took one swing with his sword and the Redcoat's head came flying off his shoulders. The headless Redcoat became Peter's eleventh kill of the day.

Peter freed the bayonet from his leg, and, although wounded badly, did not leave the field, but fought on as long as he could. Coronado's flesh wound from the bayonet did not seem to bother the horse, so in the final assault of the day, Peter rode Coronado, swinging his sword, killing two more enemy soldiers.

The initial thrust of the Redcoat's bayonet had entered just above Peter's knee, ran up his thigh the entire length of the bayonet, and exited at his hip socket. Peter finally slumped from the horse to the ground where he was left for dead.

What Now?

The Battle of Guilford Courthouse was a tactical victory for the British, even though a full one-quarter of the King's Army was lost. The battle took all of ninety minutes to fight. Cornwallis, at his camp that evening, after going over the statistics of the battle and replaying it in his mind, said to Tarleton, "another such victory shall certainly ruin the British Army."

Following the Battle of Guilford Courthouse, Cornwallis headed his army east to the coast at Wilmington. There the army could re-supply and he would spend days surveying the situation in the South, and devise a new strategy to end the war long war.

Cornwallis saw the British in control of the Carolinas and Georgia, but knew that control was not secure with Greene and the marauding sorts like Pickens, Sumter and the Swamp Fox. He felt he had to move north to Virginia. If he could present a substantial British presence in Virginia, the largest of the colonies in rebellion, it would place the British in control of the entire South, and war would come to an end.

Cornwallis corresponded with Clinton in New York. Sir Henry was not happy with Cornwallis' tactical victory at Guilford Courthouse, and criticized his planning severely. But Clinton agreed with Cornwallis that Virginia was now, out of necessity, the key to a British victory, and agreed with the general plans for Cornwallis to leave Wilmington.

In December 1780, Clinton had sent the defector, Benedict Arnold, now a brigadier general in the British Army, to command British forces in Virginia. In a surprise attack in February, Arnold took the new state capital at Richmond, and followed that with a rampage of raiding and burning the Virginia countryside. General Washington at his head-quarters at New Windsor in New York, dispatched General Lafayette to Virginia to hunt down Arnold.

"My orders to you," Washington said to the marquis, "is to find that bastard, capture him, and hang him at the first tree you come upon!"

LaFayette was cunning in his new assignment from Washington. He harassed Arnold's army of sixteen hundred, as much as Arnold had harassed the Virginia countryside. Arnold retreated south to Portsmouth to await re-enforcements, or evacuation back to New York. In March, Clinton advised Arnold to wait at Portsmouth for the re-enforcements he was sending. In late April, Cornwallis and Tarleton headed north across North Carolina, arriving at Petersburg on May 20th. Arnold's re-enforcement from Clinton had finally arrived, and the total British Army at Petersburg was now fifty-five hundred men.

"Clean My Boots, Boy!"

In April, along the Carolina border, many of the militias from the southern states were mobilizing against the British stations around the settlements in the area. Grant Mathias, adjusting well to having an ear lopped off by an enemy saber, joined his friends Robert Jackson and the fourteen-year-old Andy Jackson, as couriers between the militia commanders. Their work for the American cause kept them close to their homes in the Waxhaw, and generally able to sleep at home in the own beds most nights. They would report at the nearby militia encampment at Lancaster, receive their orders, deliver their packets to other encampments in the area, then return home.

"I betcha we won't make it home fer supper t'night," Andy said, as the three young couriers were about to split up for the day, after getting their packets they were to deliver.

"We oughta meet at Thomas Crawford's place fer the night," Robert suggested. "Cousin Tom's always ready to put us up. We can meet there when we're finished, have some o' Molly's shepherd's pie fer supper, an' start back inta Lancaster tomorra mornin'." The three friends agreed.

Thomas Crawford, the twenty-five year-old nephew of Betty Jackson, was putting his mules in the barn at his river bottom farm as his young cousin, Andy, came riding up from the post road.

"Hey, Tom," Andy yelled out waving, "care if me an' Robert an' Grant spen' the night?"

"Come on, Andy," Tom waved back, "you can sure help me put Lucy an' Linus away fer the night." Andy rode his horse toward him, and helped put the mules in the barn.

Soon Robert and Grant arrived, and it wasn't long until the beautiful Molly had set the supper table, with her delicious shepherd's pie and platters of hot biscuits. When supper was finished and Molly started clearing the table, there was a sudden rap at the door. The cabin door flew open, and three British Grenadiers stood in the threshold.

"Are you the proprietor of this farm?" the ranking grenadier looked at Tom and asked.   "I am," said Tom. "I'm Thomas Crawford, an' this here's m' wife, Molly, an' m' cousins, stayin' the night."

The grenadiers entered.

"I am Major Byron Simms of the Chippenham Guard," stated the officer, as the three soldiers walked to the table. "We are bound for Camden, but the smells from your hearth have tempted us so."

"Why sure, come on in fellers, an' sit yerselves down," said Tom. "Molly has a plenty o' her shepherd's pie left."

"Why should we be forced ta share our supper with the likes o' you?" The fourteen-year-old Andy blurted.

"Andy!" Tom admonished his young cousin, "mind your tongue, Andy! It's the Christian thing ta do."

"What have we here?" Major Simms answered, "a patriot?"

"A patriot an' a proud one!" chimed in the impertinent teenager.

Simms and the others laughed, and took their seats at Molly's table. They dined on the common meal Molly served, but when Simms was nearly finished eating he stared once more at Andy and the two other boys.

"So you are a patriot, lad?" Simms looked directly at Andy, "and your brothers here? Are they patriots as well?"

"I speak for m'self," Andy answered, again in an obstinate fashion.

"They are just young cousins o' mine," spoke up Tom. "Their mama's away in Charleston, where she's tendin' to yer own wounded on ships in the harbor. They don't know what they are. They's jus' youngins."

"Very well," Simms spokes as he stood and walked to stand in front of Andy, seated in a cane-back chair.

"Clean my boots, boy, and I shall consider it pay enough for your talk of treason," Simms barked.

"I'll do no sech a thing!" Andy bolted up from the chair, shouting at the Redcoat. Simms drew his saber and slashed his left hand and face. Andy slumped to the dirt floor of the cabin.

Within minutes, Simms ordered his two men to take the three boys as captives. They left the Crawford cabin with the boys tied up, and marching alongside the grenadiers on their horses. They set off on the thirty-mile trek to the prisoner of war compound at Camden.

An Orphaned Boy

Betty Jackson had left the Waxhaw just weeks before her two sons and Grant Mathias were taken prisoners at her nephew Thomas Crawford's cabin. Tom rode hard the next two days, after the boys were taken, to find his aunt in Charleston. Betty had come to Charleston to help an elderly aunt and uncle, and volunteer as a nurse on British ships in the harbor, where both British and America wounded were being treated. A smallpox epidemic had also broken out.

When Thomas arrived with the news that her sons had been taken to the prisoner camp at Camden, she set out with him the next day to plea for the boys' release.

"You've made a terrible mistake," Betty said to the commandant of the prisoner camp. "They ain't no soldiers, my sons an' my nephew. They're jest fool-hearty boys what don't know a British soldier from an overmountain man. I've been, these past weeks, volunteerin' as a nurse ta the brave wounded men o' both sides, on the British ships in Charleston Harbor. I beg ya, let me take m'boys home, an' they'll be o' no further trouble ta you, nor ta King George!"

Her pleadings worked on the commandant. Soon she and Tom were on their way back to the Waxhaw. All three of the boys were violently ill with smallpox, so Tom walked alongside his horse with Andy and Grant, in their worn out state of health, riding. Betty rode her horse with her eldest boy, Robert, the most ill of the three, sitting in front of her.

When they had completed the thirty-mile trek to the Jackson cabin, well after dark, the boys were taken to their beds. Betty nursed the boys with sassafras tea, honey and other herbs, but Robert died after two days, and joined his father in the small cemetery.

In a week, Betty and Andy said a final goodbye to the Waxhaw, and moved to Charleston, and the home of Betty's elderly uncle and aunt. When Andy recuperated fully from his bout with the smallpox, he apprenticed with a Charleston saddlemaker. Betty continued to volunteer aboard the hospital ships, but in the fall, contracted cholera and died. Andy Jackson was then an orphan at age fourteen.

"Capture That Damned Rebel Jefferson!"

In early June, the traitor Benedict Arnold led a second raid on Richmond, and this time the legislature and Governor Thomas Jefferson were forced to flee for their safety. Jefferson and the legislature exiled themselves in Charlottesville, on the eastern front of the Blue Ridge Mountains, near Governor Jefferson's palatial estate, Monticello. When Arnold reported to Cornwallis that Jefferson and the legislators had fled, Cornwallis ordered Tarleton to lead his newly re-enforced dragoons, and hunt down and capture Jefferson, and capture as many of the legislators as they might.

"Capture that damned rebel, Jefferson!" Cornwallis ordered Tarleton. "Kill him, if need be. He is credited with authoring their damnable dreams of independence. Let us bring an end to it now!"

News spread quickly among the patriot Virginians, that "Bloody Ban" Tarleton was in hot pursuit of Governor Jefferson and the legislature. Along with Jefferson, Tarleton also hoped to capture or kill other famous Virginians in the legislature, especially Patrick Henry, Benjamin Harrison, and Richard Henry Lee.

Jack Jouett was a twenty-seven year-old Virginia planter, living in Louisa County. He had returned from the war as a captain of the 16th Virginia Regiment, having seen action at Brandywine and other battles during the early years of the war. Jack had heard all the news of Tarleton's pursuit, and assumed Tarleton's men would probably pass through on their ride to Charlottesville. He had taken supper at the Cuckoo Tavern in Louisa Courthouse, and decided, if he could learn the location of the bloody dragoons, he, dressed as a common farmer with a fast steed, might be able to ride ahead to his friend Thomas Jefferson at Monticello, and warn him and the legislators of Tarleton's approach. After supper, Jack spread a blanket under a tree in the side lawn of the tavern, and tied his horse.

At ten o'clock, Jack was aroused from his light sleep by the sound of hundreds of horses' hooves. It was Tarleton's Greencoat dragoons, about one hundred and seventy of them. Jack mounted his horse, and took a back road out of town, as Tarleton ordered his men to a much-needed rest.

In case Tarleton had sent a small advance party out ahead on the main road toward Charlottesville, Jack stayed on the back roads he knew well. Jack's ride was unobstructed, and about an hour before dawn, hitched his horse at the Swan Tavern in Charlottesville, where he knew most of the legislators were staying. He pushed open the tavern door, and announced in an alarming voice, "the British are coming! You must all flee!" Within half an hour, all but seven of the legislators had been warned, and the targets of Tarleton's march were now crossing the mountains to Staunton on the western side.

Jack did not waste time at the tavern. As soon as he had seen that Henry, Harrison, and Lee were alerted and making new plans, he left to ride the two miles from town up the winding mountain road to Jefferson's mountaintop estate. As the lane to Monticello ran along the rear gardens of the mansion, Jack spotted Jefferson, always the early-riser, in the garden tending some of his plantings.

"Governor Jefferson," Jack cried out, "the British dragoons are on the way!"

"Jouett? Jack Jouett, is that you?" the governor, still in his night-gown and silk robe asked.

"Yes, governor," Jack said, as he dismounted and ran toward his friend. They shook hands and Jefferson led him to a table on the rear portico of the mansion, where a bottle of fine Madeira Port stood amongst some cut-crystal glasses.

"Tell me the news, and enjoy a glass of Madeiwa with me," Jefferson said. "Tell me all you know about this Ban Tawleton," Jefferson lisped. A butler appeared and Jefferson instructed him to arouse his wife and daughters, and have breakfast set on the table within a half hour. Jouett told Jefferson of his sighting Tarleton at Louisa Courthouse.

"With this info'mation," Jefferson said, "Tawleton could a'wive in Cha'lottesville by seven o'clock. It is now half-past five." Jefferson sipped calmly and rang the butler's bell.

"I think delays will put theiw a'wival sometime just befo'e half-past seven," Jefferson surmised, and sipped again, as the butler came onto the portico.

"Wayles," Jefferson said to the butler, "take the telescope to the patio ove'looking the city." He turned to Jack and rose.

"Come, Jack," said the governor, "let us take our Madeiwa to the patio, and watch fo' the a'wival of the dwagoons."

As they walked, Jefferson said the carriage and wagon were already packed for the family to leave at a moment's notice, and all would be ready to depart well before seven. He had made plans to travel south to his retreat at a second plantation, the biggest part of a day's ride south. His wife Martha would take the carriage with their two daughters, Patsy and Polly. Elizabeth Hemings, his main household slave and her four children, along with the other house servants, would follow in the loaded wagon.

Breakfast was soon set in the dining room and eaten. The family boarded the carriage and the slaves followed in the wagon, driving down the mountain lane before Tarleton's men were seen through the telescope.

Jefferson gathered up the state papers he wanted to keep from the enemy, and ordered his steed saddle and tied at the patio.

Jack and Jefferson, now dressed in riding clothes, took turns looking through the spyglass until, at a quarter till eight, Jack spotted the first dragoons arriving at the Swan Tavern. They had already seen Patrick Henry and the others leave for safety in Staunton an hour before.

"Well," Jefferson said, rising to take a look for himself, "I assume it is time fo' my depa'tu'e."

"I'd be pleased to escort you," offered Jack.

"I would be most happy to have you," agreed Jefferson.

They left riding through the woods, as they saw the first of the dragoons remount, and head up the two-mile long mountain road toward Monticello.

Francisco's Fight

June 30th 1781, was Peter Francisco's twenty-fourth birthday. Having been left for dead on the ground at Guilford Courthouse, with what seemed to be a fatal saber slash laying open his thigh. He was found by a Quaker farm boy after the battle. Seeing Peter was breathing, but unconscious, the boy ran back to the farm for his brothers and father. They saw Coronado standing near the fallen Peter, and assumed the loyal horse was the fallen man's horse. They hoisted Peter's lifeless seven-foot torso across Coronado's back, and led him to the farmhouse in the New Garden Quaker settlement.

Jasper Robinson, at fourteen, was the oldest of four sons born to the Quaker couple Andrew and Matilda Payne Robinson. Andrew and Matilda were then living at her father's plantation, Sweet Gum, in Goochland County, Virginia, where the boys were born. Matilda's brother, John Payne, and his wife, Mary Coles Payne, lived with their daughters, Dolley and Lucy, on the New Garden farm they owned. When John and Matilda's father died, the estate went to his eldest son, which was the custom. John gave his prosperous farm at New Garden to Andrew and Matilda, and packed his family to make the trek back north to Sweet Gum. Andrew and Matilda moved with their young boys to New Garden to live on their new farm there.

Peter was taken to a bedroom in the Robinson farmhouse, and Matilda immediately started dressing his wounds, as Jasper rode to his uncle's farm to bring the settlement's doctor, Absalom Robinson, Andrew's younger brother.

Peter's recuperation took just over six months, because the severe gash should have killed him. But now, the last day of June, Peter was almost fully recovered, and planned to travel home to Locust Grove within the week.

"I will miss this place," Peter said, as he sat on the verandah with Andrew Robinson that afternoon."

"Thee must visit John and Mary, and their daughters at Sweet Gum," insisted Matilda, as she came out the door of the farmhouse with a pitcher of lemonade. "A strapping man like thee needs a wife. How old his young Dolley, now Andrew?"

"Too young for thee to be marryin' her off," Andrew smiled and held a glass for Matilda to fill.

"She is not too young, Andrew," Matilda smiled back. "I was just fouirteen when I wedded thee. Life has worked well for us and the Lord has blessed us mightily." She sat beside them in a rocking chair.

"He has," agreed Andrew, "but I was just sixteen at the time. A man can marry a woman nearer his age, and have a better way of it.

A younger woman brings with her too many younger ideas. That Matilda is hard on both."

The door open again and Jasper came out holding a freshly baked and iced coconut cake, followed by his brothers.

"Happy birthday, Peter Francisco!" the boys said in unison as Jasper handed the large cake on it's large plater to Peter.

"Thank you," Peter said, looking down at the big white frosted cake in his lap. "It looks so good! Now what are you folks going to eat?" They all laughed at Peter's joke.

"Now the very next time thee goes into Charlottesville, stop and visit Sweet Gum," Matilda said as Peter sat on Coronado, ready to ride north for Locus Grove. "The plantation is just two miles east of the main post road, about three miles north of Goochland Crossing. Thee shall find them all most hospitable."

"I will," agreed Peter. "I know the area, and have passed by there many times."

But what was on Peter's mind as he headed northeast toward Virginia and his Locust Grove Farm, was that he had missed all the springtime planting. He had sent a letter to Pat and Tricia Patrick, informing them of his survival at Guilford Courthouse, and his planned early summer return to the farm. Now it was the sixth day of July, later than he hoped to return. He had gotten a response from his letter to Pat which had raised his spirits. He had been reported among the causalities of the battle, and proclaimed dead. Pat replied that, "all in the area receive this wonderful news with great joy." He also said he had sent word to the judge at Winston Woods.

On the third day of his journey home, as the sun was going down, he approached Ward's Tavern in Nottoway County. He decided to end his day's journey there, get a good supper of the fried chicken the inn was known for, and a comfortable night's sleep, before starting his final day of travel back to Locust Grove. He rode Coronado to an oak tree in the yard, tied him, and dismounted. Peter started walking toward the door of the tavern. He could already smell and imagined tasting that fried chicken.

Eleven Greencoat dragoons on horseback appeared, coming around the tavern. Peter knew immediately who these men were, and wanted no more trouble from them. He had seen his share of "Bloody Ban" Tarleton's green-coated dragoons. Peter continued toward the door.

"Halt!" cried out one of the dragoons. Peter stopped dead in his tracks without turning toward them.

The leader of the eleven began questioning Peter, and did not accept Peter's story that he was a Virginia farmer, divorced of the war, just wanting it to end. He claimed to have no sympathies for either side, being a peace-loving Quaker, like the Robinsons were.

"There can be few Virginians who stand near seven feet in height!" barked the captain. "I have seen you wielding that giant sword on the battlefield, and have seen the heads of my comrades fly. You are under arrest!"

The eleven dismounted and surrounded Peter. The captain ordered the paymaster to guard the prisoner, as the others went into the tavern for drinks.

"Oh, you shall be quite the prize," said the paymaster arrogantly. "What valuables have you I might keep as a souvenir of this great day?"

"I am but a modest Quaker farmer," Peter repeated. "My valuables are stored up in Heaven."

"None?" the paymaster continued his query, as he began patting Peter down. Peter hoped he would not discover his dead father's pocket watch. The paymaster stood abruptly upright. He pointed to the golden buckles on Peter's shoes, "P" and "F," the same golden buckles he had proudly worn everyday since before he had been kidnapped from Terceira. While at the time of his arrival on the wharf at City Point, they seemed gargantuan on a small boy's shoes. They now were seemed quite small, compared to the giant-sized shoes he wore that day.

"I shall have those golden shoe buckles!" the paymaster proclaimed, pointing to the ground. "Give them here!"

"Those I shall never give you!" Peter replied bravely. Peter knew, if seeing the opportunity, with his hands not yet bound, and with the other ten drinking in the tavern, he could fool the paymaster and make his escape.

"I say, I shall have those buckles!" the paymaster said, just as bravely.

"Then you shall have to take them yourself!" Peter said determinedly.

"Very well then, I shall," the paymaster replied. He stupidly put the sword he had been holding on Peter under his left arm, bent down and placed his right hand on Peter's left shoe. Peter grabbed the sword's handle and pulled straight up with all his strength, severing the paymaster's arm from its shoulder. The paymaster fell to the ground fainting. Peter picked up the paymaster's pistol, lying on the ground, jumped up and ran toward Coronado.

The door to the tavern flew open and another dragoon came out and yelled for the others as he saw the paymaster lying dead on the ground. The other dragoons came running out. Peter shot the first dragoon dead between the eyes, with the paymaster's pistol he had taken. He tucked the pistol into his trousers and ran to Coronado to retrieve his giant sword. He charged the nine, swinging his sword, and in one stroke, sliced the head off one and an arm off another. Seeing the slaughtered dragoons, the others ran to their horses and mounted to ride away.

The leader of the retreating dragoons drew his pistl on Peter. It misfired and Peter charged him. Peter wielding his giant sword slashed his shoulder and pulled the dragoon to the ground. He ran him through with his sword.

Peter had killed five of the eleven members of Bloody Ban's eleven dragoons who had arrested him on the lawn of Ward's Tavern at Nottoway. Five dead bodies were scattered across the lawn. Six of the defeated dragoons raced down the road and out of sight with two of the riderless horses. Three horses were left behind. Peter tethered them, holding the tethers in his huge hand, and rode away with Coronado and his equine prize from the fight.

"I can make it to Rice Crossroads before the sun goes down," Peter said to himself. "I think I'll stay the night at the inn there. I hope the fried chicken at Rice Crossroads is as good as it is here at Ben Ward's Tavern." Peter rode off up the post road.

Chapter Seventeen

Return to Mount Vernon

Martha Washington was excited. Any moment she expected her husband to ride up the lane to the mansion house she had shared with him for twenty-four years. For the past six years, he had been away, leading the Continental Army. Their only times together in those six years had been when, each winter, she traveled to him at his winter encampments. But now, he was leading the combined American-French Army to Yorktown, where the British General Lord Charles Cornwallis was stationed, and now sat, bottled up by the French Navy from the Caribbean, which had just arrived. General Washington and the French Comte de Rochambeau planned to spend four full days and nights at Mount Vernon on their way to Yorktown.

Martha's only son, the twenty-six year-old John Parke Custis, whom she and the general called Jacky, was staying with her along with his wife, Nellie, and their four young children. It was surely a wonderful time at Mount Vernon, with Jacky, Nellie, and the grandchildren there, filling the house with the excited energy of family. The Washingtons had not been blessed with children of their own.

Martha rushed about the house making certain everything was just so for when the general arrived. She shouted instructions to the servants, and every ten minutes or so, ran to the front entry to watch for the general riding Nelson up the lane. Occasionally, she even climbed to the cupola that held the weather vane above the roof, for a more panoramic view than she could get standing in the doorway.

"Here Hassie, put this vase of fresh-cut lilies in the guest room for General Rochambeau," Martha ordered the teenaged Negro. "Vespacia needs a full set of bed linens in the guest room for General LaFayette. Rowena run to the washhouse and get them for her. I know they will be arriving shortly. Hurry, hurry. I do wish everything to be ready when they arrive."

"Here they comes!" shouted the butler Josiah. "Surely as I'm a standin' here, theys a comin'. I can hear them fifes a blowin' and them drums a drummin.'"

Martha heard the fifes and drums as well, in the near distance. She tore the apron from her dress and handed it to Vespacia. She primped her white hair, sticking out from under a calico bonnet, then rushed to the front door stoop to see for herself.

There they were indeed, riding up the lane from the post road to Alexandria. She saw a uniformed French general, which she assumed to be the Comte de Rochambeau, and beside him her very own husband, with the September afternoon sun glistening off his freshly white-powdered wig. He looked so handsome! On each side of them were two riding flag-bearers, one with the stars and stripes of the new American Flag, the other holding the blue and white of the "Fleur de Lis" of King Louis XVI of France. She could not make out the young General LaFayette.

Martha beamed as the fifes and drums came into sight, and the generals entered the circular lane, heading to the entry stoop where Martha stood. When the riders stopped, General Washington saluted his Martha. He smiled, dismounted, and ran to her, as she ran to him, and they hugged and kissed.

The troops made camp for four days, spread out all across the acreage of Mount Vernon. The French General Rochambeau was shown to a guest room in the mansion, as were Washington's second, General Benjamin Lincoln, who had been forced to surrender Charleston, but released in a prisoner exchange. Washington's aides-de-camp, Major Alexander Hamilton, and Major Wills Winkman, who had remained Washington's private secretary since 1775 in Cambridge were also boarded in the mansion.

"Where is the marquis?" Martha asked, somewhat disappointedly. "I was so hoping he would be with you."

"La Fayette has been superbly shadowing Cornwallis and Tarleton, in hopes of capturing that damnable traitor, Benedict Arnold," Washington answered his wife. "He will join us at Fredericksburg after we leave Mount Vernon. Might we have refreshments on the verandah?"

"I shall see to it," Martha said, leaving for the kitchen, as the general led his staff to chairs on the splendid columned palazzo overlooking the broad Potomac River and the green fields of Maryland.

Heading to Yorktown

Peter Francisco was happy to be home on his farm in Buckingham County. He took great pride in hanging the sword Washington and La Fayette had presented him, which had severed heads and arms from many an enemy torso. There it would stay put, never to see a battlefield again.

Pat had certainly done a fine job planting and cultivating his crops and fields, and with harvest quickly coming, Peter knew another good year on the farm would add to his and Zack's growing bank account. Pat and Tricia were now comfortable in their own house across the large vegetable garden. Their two children were delightful. Gadsden would turn two in January, and baby Emmaline, who had been born in July, was the apple of her father's eye.

It was now the 9th of September, a beautiful late-summer day, and Peter and Pat sat on the porch sipping lemonade Tricia had made.

"What do you think these fellers want?" Pat asked as he pointed to a couple dozen soldiers approaching on the lane.

"I have no earthly notion," answered Peter, with a note of foreboding in his voice. He stood up from his chair and stared at the riders approaching. "My God! That's LaFayette!" said Peter, "and that 'pears to be Jimmie Monroe with him!" He stepped off his porch and walked slowly to greet them. Pat followed.

Peter, with a huge smile across his face, saluted LaFayette, as the marquis reined his steed to a halt just in front of his old friend. LaFayette and Monroe returned Peter and Pat's salutes and dismounted.

"What brings you to Locust Grove?" Peter asked.

"Word that the news of your tragic death at Guilford Courthouse was inaccurate," LaFayette said, as he hugged Peter, "and that you killed another five of Tarleton's men on your long ride home."

"We were in the area," spoke Monroe, "and wanted to see for ourselves." Monroe and Peter hugged.

"Join us for some cool lemonade on the porch," Peter invited.

"I'll go see if Tricia's taken that peach cobbler from the hearth yet," Pat said, as he went inside the house.

"This war is about to end," LaFayette said, as he filled Peter in on the recent events that found Cornwallis and Tarleton penned-in at Yorktown. "The entire American and French Army, near twenty thousand in all, are now in Virginia, to arrive at Mount Vernon this very day. The French Fleet has sailed into Chesapeake Bay, and have cut off any escape route by sea for the British. The war will end in a matter of weeks."

"We are to join up with Washington at Fredericksburg in four days," added Monroe. "Then we march to Williamsburg for the finish."

"My men, about eight hundred, are camped at Sprouse's Corner," LaFayette said. "Maj. Monroe and I decided to invite you to join us for the final victory. You so deserve to be part of the glory."

"I'll have to think about it," Peter said, knowing he had vowed to never again walk upon a battlefield. "But the last I heard. Major Jimmie here was readin' law with Jefferson and had swore off war."

"Governor Jefferson appointed me his military aide," Monroe said. "He felt I, like you, Peter, had earned the right to witness the final glory at Yorktown."

"We will leave tomorrow and march to Hewlett," Monroe added.

"Hewlett?" Peter seemed puzzled. "That's where Winston Woods is."

"I know. We'll camp there three days," LaFayette added, "then march into Fredericksburg on the thirteenth to join Washington and Rochambeau. General Washington would certainly be honored to have you along with us."

"It would surely be nice to visit with the judge and Adella," Peter said, looking plaintively toward Pat.

"Tricia an' the babies an' me could take the wagon an' visit our families there as well," Pat added, "an' still come back in plenty time

624

to put up the harvest. Jezrah can see after things while we're gone. I know ya wanna go, Peter. Your brave on the battlefield, but too coward to admit you wanna go." Everyone laughed.

"Then it is decided," said LaFayette. "Meet us at our camp in the morning and we shall ride."

"You and Monroe will stay here for the night," Peter insisted. "Tricia will have the supper table set at seven. Pat will pack the wagon for his family, and we will not delay you one moment."

"All Peter needs ta do is pull that damned giant sword from off'n that nail above the hearth once more," Pat laughed.

Reunions

Jacky Custis joined his stepfather on a morning walk along the Potomac, after breakfast on the day after Washington's return to Mount Vernon. It was the first time the two, who had never really been close before, took a walk together after breakfast.

"Jacky," Washington began the rather awkward situation, "I have been so proud of you for the service you have given these past four years in the legislature."

"I have enjoyed it, general," Jacky admitted. "It has felt good to be a member of the state legislature, knowing, in some way at least, I am following the path my station in life requires of me."

"And you have fulfilled your role in an exemplary fashion, I am told," Washington added.

"I only regret one thing," Jacky admitted. "I was once invited by you to join the army and do my part for independence. I regret now, I did not, and was not there with you in the battles."

That admission startled the general, who always viewed his stepson as too prissy and effeminate to ever want the physical and common life of a soldier in the army.

"I am most serious," Jacky said.

"Well, son," Washington said, "it may not be too late. Oh it is too late for you to join the army, but I could always use a civilian aide-de-camp. I have left Col. Laurens' post vacant."

"You would yet take me on as an aide?" Jacky seemed excited.

"For this final campaign of the war," Washington answered, "I certainly would, and would be honored to have you with me."

Jacky beamed ear-to-ear.

"You will tent with Major Hamilton," Washington said, "and sit with my aides when I meet with them and the general staff. It should be an easy victory, and you will be there, by my side, when General Lord Charles Cornwallis surrenders his sword to me, and we end this damned war. With the French fleet surrounding them by sea, and our near twenty thousand men surrounding them by land, the victory shall be ours."

The two hugged. It was one of the few times the two had ever done so since Jacky had been just a lad. It felt good to them both.

When La Fayette's army made camp at the town of Hewlett, Peter led the marquis, Monroe, four escorts, and the wagon carrying Peter Patrick and his family up the lane to Winston Woods. The house servant Malcolm appeared at the door and shouted.

"Lord have mercy!" Malcolm cried out. "It's Mista Peter! Mista Peter Francisco!"

Soon the portico was crowded with the judge, Adella, and three daughters, as well as the household servants. Peter jumped off Coronado and ran to the portico, giving hugs and kisses all around.

"Do I not get a welcome hug as well?" came the voice of a young man from inside the foyer. Peter looked up.

"Zachary Winston!" Peter was startled. "That cannot be you!" He rushed to his long-lost brother and friend. They hugged him. Peter lifted Zack high off the ground. "When did you come home?"

"Zachary surprised us two weeks ago," said the judge. "He sailed from New Orleans to Cuba, then Saint Augustine, Savannah and Charleston, before going on to Williamsburg."

"You must see his marvelous art," Adella added.

"But after we gather on the verandah to catch up with one another," added the judge, "and become acquainted with our guests," he said referring to the marquis and Monroe.

"I am so sorry," Peter said, remembering his important guests. "Judge, Adella, Zack, you remember Jimmie Monroe. He's now a military aide to Governor Jefferson. And this is my good friend Gilbert du

Motier, the Marquis de LaFayette and Brigadier General of the Continental Army."

The party moved to the portico overlooking the Pamunkey, where they took seats and Mammy Jane brought out cider and cookies.

"Rodie's back in Virginia as well," said Zack, as he and Peter walked along the Pamunkey after excusing themselves from the others.

"He is?" Peter asked excitedly.

"Yes," Zack explained. "We traveled together from New Orleans with his wife, Angelita and their baby Roderic. He purchased Christina Donnelley's tavern at City Point. You heard Christina married Patrick Henry's friend, Calvert McGowan."

"Yes," Peter said, "she's a neighbor to our farm, Locust Grove, in Buckingham County. I want to show you Locust Grove after the war ends at Yorktown," offered Peter. "City Point is an easy journey from our farm."

"Our farm?" Zack questioned.

"Yes," Peter answered. "You haven't heard?" Zack indicated he had no idea of what Peter was saying. "Yes, we are both of the landed gentry now. I have saved your earnings and intend to share everything with you."

"I don't know," Zack pondered. "I do not see me settling down on a farm, and being content plowing fields and overseeing slaves."

"Pat manages the slaves and the fields," Peter explained. "It would make a peaceful place for you to really concentrate on your drawings."

"What about that Pee Pee Creek tomahawk claim Pat made along the Scioto River in the Ohio Country?" Zack asked. "I thought he'd have surely been off to settle it by now."

"Oh," Peter answered, "the Ohio lands are still not safe to settle for whites. He married Tricia Patterson, the daughter of the merchant at Cedar Forks, and now lives with Tricia and their two children in a house we built for them at Locust Grove."

"I just don't know if I am ready to settle down on a farm, but I will promise you this...I will visit, and then decide on that," Zack said. "It would be good to be near you, and with Rodie and Angelica not being far away."

"You should ride with us to Yorktown, and sketch the final battle of the war," Peter suggested. "Then we can visit Rodie at City Point, then go to Buckingham County and Locust Grove."

"I would like that," agreed Zack. "It will be like it was when we marched with Lord Dunmore."

It was good to be back at Winston Woods!

On September fourteenth, Washington, Rochambeau, Lincoln and LaFayette, led the allied troops into the old colonial capital of Virginia, Williamsburg. The town was not deserted, but many of the townspeople and merchants had moved to the new capital at Richmond. The palatial Governor's Palace and the old Colonial Capital sat empty and idle.

The army would camp there, throughout the city and its environs, as the high command surveyed the situation at nearby Yorktown. Washington and his vgeneral staff opened the old palace to use as headquarters.

Martha Washington, along with Jacky's wife, Nellie, and the children, had followed along as far as New Kent. Martha had made arrangements to stay with her widowed younger sister, Fanny Dandridge Bassett. They would wait out the end of the war there, as their husbands rode off, at the lead of the army.

Peter had been able to convince Pat to join for the final battle. Tricia stayed at Cedar Forks with her father, and Peter and Pat arranged for their trusted slave foreman, Jezrah, to manage the early harvest at Locust Grove. They camped with their old unit, the 3rd Virginia Regiment, on the back lawn of the old Governor's Palace.

"Damn it all!" came a loud shout, as they began pitching the tent they would share. "I jes seen me a gall darned ghost!"

Peter turned and beamed at his old friend Garrett Hicks, of course standing beside Malcolm Shepherd. Peter and Pat ran toward them and they all hugged.

"We heard tell ya was kilt on the battlefield at Guilford," said Garrett, "then we heard y single-handed lopped the heads off'n five o' Tarleton's nasty dragoons at Ward's Tavern."

"Guess ya cain't keep a good man down," added Malcolm.

"I swore never to set foot on another battlefield, after near dyin' at Guilford Courthouse," Peter said, "but LaFayette and Major Jimmie rode up to my farm in Buckingham, and gave me a personal invitation to see this war end."

"We're a gonna end it all right here, by damn, an' create that there free an' independent United States of America!" said Garrett proudly. "Me an' Malcolm wouldn't've missed this here party for all the tea that was a throwed inta Boston Harbor!"

As the four old friends sat around a fire ring, LaFayette, Washington and Baron von Steuben approached from Washington's headquarters in the palace. Washington spotted the newest hero of the war, the Virginia Giant, and headed directly to where the four men sat.

"Private Peter Francisco, I believe," Washington said, as Peter immediately stood and saluted.

"It is so good to know that you have weathered this war from its very start," Washington said, "and with, as I have been told, some very sever wounds." The general extended his hand to shake that of his the private.

"I am honored to be with you, General Washington, to the end." Peter responded.

"I do not know if you realize it, private, but you have been a one-man army in this war," Washington said. "If not for you, we could easily have lost at least two of those battles that eventually have led us here." Washington saluted him, embraced him, and walked into the palace.

Camp Fever

September 28th was the day many of the units of the combined allied army of French and Americans began to move to within sight of the British. It was also a day General Washington received disturbing personal information.

Two days before, Washington invited Jacky to dine with him, LaFayette, Rochambeau, de Grasse and General Wayne at the Raleigh Tavern. After dinner as the men sat and drank brandy and smoked pipes, Washington noticed a pallid look on his stepson's face.

"Jacky," Washington asked in a fatherly tone, "are you well?"

"I have had a near-constant headache these passed two days," Jacky replied. "This is the first meal I have eaten, if I can keep it down."

"Camp fever is making its rounds at camp," General Wayne spoke up with a warning. "Pay heed to it and special heed to your personal hygiene. It is painful, and has caused death to many a fine soldier."

"I shall, general," Jacky said with a pleasing smile, "but I think I shall beg your leave and return to my tent now."

Washington followed him out, placing his arm around Jacky's shoulders.

"General Wayne is right," Washington spoke calmly, as they walked out into the evening's fresh air. "Camp fever is nothing to ignore. Get rest. Drink fluids. If you can keep the dinner down that you have partaken of this evening, tis a good sign."

"I feel much better simply breathing the fresh air this evening," Jacky said with a smile. "I think it is just all the excitement of camp and the coming battle."

"I am certain of it," Washington assured the boy. "Just remember, Jacky, I fear camp fever has taken more lives than British muskets have. With God's grace, a good night of sleep will find you well again in the morrow." He hugged his stepson and watched him walk down Duke of Gloucester Street before he himself turned and went back inside to his generals.

Two days later, as the army's last units broke camp at Williamsburg, Washington received word from Alexander Hamilton, Jacky's tent mate, that Jacky was in a near unconscious state and had gotten no better. He indeed had an extreme case of the camp fever.

Washington sent Wills Winkman to the Bassett House in New Kent, to advise Lady Washington and Jacky's wife, that soon he would be arriving with Jacky to recuperate there. He went immediately to the tent Jacky shared with Hamilton. He had a bed prepared in the back of a wagon for Jacky to be as comfortable as possible on the two-hour journey to New Kent. A dozen cavalrymen escorted them to the Bassett House.

Leaving command of the troop movements to General Wayne, Washington stayed at New Kent until the sun rose the next morning. When he returned to his army, Jacky had had a good, restful sleep, and seemed to be comfortable with his mother, aunt and wife tending to his every need with cups of broth and warm quilts. He was also pleased with the new encampment of his army, in easy sight of the penned-in British redcoats.

The Giant's Shoe Buckles Tavern

Rodie Murray, the new proprietor of the tavern on the wharf at City Point, bought from Christina Donnelley McGowan, was happy with the delivery that had just come to the wharf. Two teamsters had just brought it from Romney Hoffman's carpentry shop in Richmond. The teamsters propped up the sign, ready for hanging, but needing Rodie's approval. Rodie looked at it from every angle. He stepped back a few paces, and looked some more, then up a pace or two.

"Angie! Come here," Rodie shouted out to his wife who was tending the kitchen. "Come here, I need you!"

"What is it?" the beautiful young Spanish lady came out, wring her hands in her apron.

"The sign, Angie?" Rodie asked. "Is the sign beautiful or is it not?"

The sign depicted a giant wearing green knee breeches, white stockings, and black leather shoes. The giant was sprawled the length of the sign, resting on an elbow, with a grin on his face. Each shoe had a gold buckle "P" on one, "F" on the other, with the lettering forming a half circle above and one below: "The Giant's Shoe Buckles Tavern" in bright red. In small letters in the bottom right corner stated: "Roderic Murray & son, proprietors."

"It is beautiful," agreed Angelita, "now can I return to making my rice pudding?"

Rodie ran to her, hugged her, kissed her, and put his arm around her waist as they watched the teamsters hoist the large shingle sign up to where Christina's smaller sign had been.

"I cannot wait until all the fighting is over, and Zack and Peter come for a visit," Rodie said. "You will truly love Peter Francisco. He is a wonderful friend, and such a gentle spirit, for a giant. He will be so embarrassed to see I have named the tavern in his honor...but he is a legend now...and this is where it all started." Rodie was like a small boy on Christmas morning, filled with so much anticipation. Angelita smiled, looking up at the man she loved and sailed to Virginia to be with. She was so in love.

"It all started right here," Rodie went on, as he pointed toward the James River, "right there on that coil of rope…well not that exact coil of rope, but exactly there!"

"Yes, yes, I know the story, many times I have heard the story," Angelita said, wringing her hands in the apron and pulling away. "But if I do not get back to the hearth, there will be no rice pudding fit to eat. And if you cause it to scorch, I shall never forgive you." She kissed him and smiled. He smiled as the sign was secured into place.

The Siege of Yorktown

For nearly three weeks, George Washington was overseeing the most important military campaign of his near twenty-year career. He led the French-American siege against the British, isolated in Yorktown. As Providence would have it, he also, out of necessity, had to deal with his young stepson's seemingly slow recuperation from a severe case of camp fever. Washington would nearly split his days between the events of the siege at Yorktown, and the suffering Jacky was going through in New Kent, thirty miles away.

On September 28th, as the army moved from Williamsburg, Jacky was moved to the Bassett house at New Kent. The next day, there was some fire from the British, as the redcoats became nervous with the closeness of the Americans and French. Cornwallis, receiving news Sir Henry Clinton was sending an additional five thousand men from New York, feared they would not arrive in time, or be repelled by the formidable French fleet. He decided to regroup his army and abandon all but three of the redoubts closest to the town. Immediately, Washington ordered his army to secure the abandoned redoubts before he headed off to New Kent to check on Jacky.

When Washington returned to the army on the first day of October, he ordered the placement of the allied artillery pieces in the newly taken and abandoned British redoubts. He had learned from a courier, while at New Kent, the French had failed in a primary assault on one of the remaining British redoubts. That did not dampen his resolve.

On October 4th, he learned from Col. Tallmadge that the feared Banastre Tarleton of the dragoons, had been on a foraging expedition on the opposite side of the York River, where he came back empty-handed, and had lost seventy-five of his best men in the effort. Washington then returned back to New Kent.

The day Washington again returned to his headquarters outside Yorktown, October 6th, was a day threatened by storms. As the sun was setting, Washington ordered a massive digging operation, using nature's cover of stormy weather and a moonless night. Washington ordered a two thousand yard long parallel line be dug to the York River. This would be the first such trench built by the allies, and Washington himself took an axe and shovel, and joined his men as the Redcoats slept. Within three days, the field artillery pieces were in place along the recently dug parallel line. British fire upon the allies lessened when Cornwallis saw the impressive artillery all too close for his comfort. Among the pieces were three twenty-four pound cannons, three eighteen pounders, two eight-inch Howitzers and six mortars.

At three o'clock in the afternoon on October 9th, the French guns on the left side of the parallel, opened fire on the HMS Guadalupe, which was at anchor near the far side of the river. At five o'clock the Americans began the bombardment of Yorktown. Washington, always visible atop his beautiful white horse Nelson, dismounted, as the order was about to be given for the Americans to open fire. Washington walked over to one of the artillery pieces, took the torch, and lit the cannon. The first shot, fired by Washington, struck a table where British officers were eating.

The American shelling was devastating to the British defenses. It was clear that it was simply a matter of time. Washington ordered the Americans and French to fire throughout the night, so as to hamper any repair work Cornwallis might order. A large number of Redcoat deserters showed up at the allied line to surrender. On October 11th, Washington ordered a second parallel line be built before he again headed out of camp to see to Jacky in his bed at New Kent.

"How is he?" Washington asked Martha as they sat beside the fireplace in the parlor of the Bassett house. "How is he really faring?"

Martha sniffled. "No better. No better at all. Oh he has his day, when it seems he might win the battle, but then, within moments, he slips back into his dread. I fear he will not rise from his bed."

She sobbed openly. "Imagine. Colonel Custis blessed me with four children. Two died as infants and are buried in the ground at White House, just down the road. Precious little Patsy we enjoyed till she died in your arms. Now I am to lose my Jacky."

"Now now, Martha," Washington moved to the settee where she was seated and put his arm around her, kissing her temple. "I have seen many a fine soldier suffer months with the fever, and then return to their former good health. Jacky will do so, if it be the will of Providence."

"Providence be damned!" Martha cried. "Providence gives us the blessings a child brings into your life, then takes the very blessings away. Jacky is too frail of health to win this battle. He is all but dead to us now. Providence be damned!"

On October 14th, Washington was back at Yorktown, fearing, as Martha feared, the end of time was coming quickly, and unjustifiably so, for Jacky. He wished he had never invited Jacky to come to camp in the first place. He blamed himself and his own personal selfishness to be closer to his stepson. Had he not encouraged Jacky, Jacky would never have come down with camp fever in the first place.

He saw the finished allied lines completed, and now within one hundred and fifty yards of both British-held redoubts called Redoubt Nine and Redoubt Ten. The night, promising to again be without moonlight, was ideal for Washington to order an evening assault under cover of a pitch-black sky.

Redoubt Nine was manned by seventy Redcoats and stood at river's edge. Redoubt Ten was a half-mile inland and manned by one hundred and twenty. Both were well fortified, with rows of abatis works behind broad and muddy ditches.

Washington met with his staff. His plan was for the French to create a diversionary firing upon the British fusiliers, then, in half-an-hour, turn and assault Redoubt Nine with four hundred men. In the meantime, Colonel Hamilton would assault the abatis works of Redoubt Ten with four hundred men and axes. The plan was agreed to and executed.

When the French turned from firing on the fusiliers and began the assault on Redoubt Nine, they were initially stopped at the abatis works by Hessian gunfire. They withdrew, regrouped and charged again. This time, the Hessians threw down their arms and waved the white flag of surrender.

Hamilton was under heavy British fire as his men chopped through the abatis works of Redoubt Ten, but were unflinching in executing their orders. Throwing down their axes and taking up their muskets and bayonets, they climbed the parapets into the redoubt to Hamilton's urging them on crying, "Rush on boys! The fort's ours!"

As the two remaining redoubts were being taken, the balance of the American and French forces not engaged in the plan, presented the look of being ready at a moments notice to launch a final assault on the town itself. This created great fear in Cornwallis, as his officers and men watched the redoubts fall, and the American and French flags raised over them. When the redoubts were in allied hands, Washington ordered a shelling of the town.

That evening, in a last attempt to bring something favorable out of the debacle, Cornwallis ordered Col. Robert Abercromby to commence storming the Americans as they slept in the wee hours of October 15th.

As he started the too little, too late effort, Abercromby cried out to his men, "Push on my brave lads and we shall skin these bastards!" A French force answered the call and pushed Abercromby and his men back into the town.

On the morning of October 16th, Washington ordered the bombardment of Yorktown to resume. Cornwallis, desperate to evacuate his army across to Gloucester Point on the far side of the York River, and march his army safely to Clinton in New York, set a plan to move the men across in every boat available in the town. The first wave of boats loaded with Redcoats made it to the other side just as a squall rose up, ending any further hopes of evacuation. With the fire from the allies seeming to grow heavier by the minute, Conwallis met with his staff. It was agreed the situation was beyond hopeless.

As the sun rose on the morning of the 17th, seventeen British soldiers and drummers appeared with a white flag. Washington ordered the bombing to stop. The soldiers were met, blindfolded, and led behind the American lines.

635

On October 18th two British officers and four American and French officers, led by Col. Hamilton, met in a private house to enter into negotiations. They worked throughout the day, and into the night. On the morning of October 19th, the Articles of Capitulation were signed.

The World Turned Upside Down

At two o'clock in the afternoon, American and French forces marched across the British lines and formed a corridor, with the French making up the left side and Americans on the right. Washington and his staff formed a line at the end of the two columns, to receive the British officers in surrender. The vanquished British and Hessians rode or marched down the corridor, as their fifes, drums, and bagpipes played the popular tune of the day,*"The World Turned Upside Down."*

But even if this day belonged to George Washington and his American and French armies, Cornwallis saw to it, some of the glory was absent, notably the British General himself. Claiming illness, Cornwallis refused to ride to where his adversary was waiting in person to receive his sword of surrender, as was the custom. Cornwallis saw Washington not as a military man, but simply as a common man, not adequate to meet with someone of his own military stature and prowess. Certainly, he saw Washington as no man adequate enough to be presented with his sword of surrender.

Cornwallis sent his sword with his second, Brigadier General Charles O'Hara, with instructions to present the sword to Rochambeau, who, in Cornwallis' estimation, was at least on a par with himself.

When O'Hara offered the sword to Rochambeau, the French general refused and shook his head, indicating Washington was the one to take the prize. O'Hara then offered the blade to Washington.

Washington, not enjoying this insult on his field of victory, shook his head at O'Hara as well, and motioned toward his second, General Benjamin Lincoln. Lincoln took Cornwallis' sword, admired it, looked at Washington, who nodded to Lincoln. Upon the nod, General Lincoln returned the sword to O'Hara instead of keeping it as a spoil of war. O'Hara saluted, turned and rode his horse back to Cornwallis in Yorktown.

All told, there were eight thousand soldiers taken as prisoners, two hundred and fourteen artillery pieces, thousands of muskets and bayonets, twenty-four transport ships, many supply wagons and horses captured. The war in effect was now ended and American independence had been won. The world, indeed, had been turned upside down.

Finis

Epilogue

Swords into Plowshares

Surrender of Lord Cornwallis
by the artist John Trumbull [PD-US]

Whether the British General Lord Charles Cornwallis showed up on the field of battle at Yorktown to surrender his sword to American General George Washington or not, America had won its

War for Independence, and, as the British Army fifes, drums, and bag-pipes played their song … the world had in fact, turned upside down.

Thirteen colonies, from the Maine District of Massachusetts, stretching down the entire Atlantic seaboard to the Georgia Colony, had won their independence, after six long and uncertain years of war, against the largest and greatest army the world had seen since the times of the Roman Empire. A Continental Congress had met in Philadel-phia to declare independence, and "with a firm reliance on the pro-tection of Divine Providence," pledged their lives, their fortunes, and their sacred honor to the cause. Many died in the struggle for independ-ence at places with names like Harlem Heights, Bennington, Chadds Ford, Stono Ferry and Kings Mountain. There were dramatic victo-ries and devastating defeats. But the Congress, and the spirit of the American people pressed on with belief in what they were fighting to achieve.

After Yorktown, no American living under their newly won inde-pendence knew what the new nation they were left with would develop into. They did know there would be no more taxation without repre-sentation, nor a parliament, sitting faraway across the Atlantic, passing old world legislation on the residents of the new world. Many wanted George Washington to become their king, because governments by monarchs were all they knew.

The Continental Congress carried on as the central government of the new nation, sanctioned by the Articles of Confederation enacted in 1781. It was no real federal government at all, with no real authority. Each state governed itself, and laws in one state were different from laws in other states. Some states even started not dealing at all with their neighboring states. Soon it was apparent there was a need for "a more perfect union" of the states.

By the end of the decade of the 1780s, the United States Constitu-tion was ratified, and the government of the United States of America began with the inauguration of George Washington as the first Presi-dent of the United States on April 30th 1789.

"Dr. Franklin, what sort of governmnent have you given us?" a lady asked Ben Franklin, as he was returning home, after the adjournment of the Constitutional Convention. He thought for a moment before he replied.

"A republic, madam, ... if you can keep it." The answer Franklin gave in 1787 resonates today, as many feel we have done a poor job of *"keeping it,"* especially during the 20th century, and now into the 21st.

George Washington, as the first President, had no guidelines to follow. He knew everything he did would set precedent for future presidents to follow. He was opposed to alliances with foreign powers, which might entangle the new nation in foreign wars. He was also opposed to the growth of political parties, but knew there was little he could do to stop their growth. He created a cabinet of advisors, and appointed men of opposing thought. Thomas Jefferson was made the first Secretary of State, while Jefferson's main political foe, Alexander Hamilton, served as Secretary of the Treasury. Henry Knox, one of his favorite and most trusted advisors during the Revolution, was made Secretary of War. Edmond Randolph of Virginia became the first Attorney General. The patriot leader, John Adams of Massachusetts, had been elected the first Vice President.

James Madison, and member of the first Congress, drafted the first ten amendments to the Constitution, to fulfill the promise that individual rights and responsibilities would be the hallmark of the new American government. Those amendments were ratified by the states in 1791, and have become known as the *"Bill of Rights"*.

The Bill of Rights guaranteed there would be no state established religion, and that individuals had the right to worship as they saw fit, with religion not being interfered with by the government. It was Freedom *of* Religion, not Freedom *from* Religon, as some today seem to believe. The Bill of Rights also gave the individual the right to speak freely, the freedom of the press, the right to peaceably assemble, the right to own and bear arms, and the right to a trial by a jury of one's peers. The Bill of Rights also guaranteed the individual protection against undue search and seizure, excessive bail, and cruel and unusual punishment. What was not laid out as a constitutional function of the federal government was to be the implied right and responsibility of the states. All other rights and responsibilities were left to the local governments, and to the individual himself.

John Adams became the second President, Jefferson, the third, Madison, the fourth and James Monroe the fifth. John Quincy Adams, the son of John Adams, became the sixth president, winning the volatile

"Disputed Election of 1824", defeating Andy Jackson of Tennessee, formerly a boy of the Waxhaw Region of the Carolinas. Jackson defeated Adams in 1828, and became the seventh president.

The next volume to follow **Cornerstone** will carry the saga of our new nation through the Jackson presidency. It is my plan to publish it in the fall of 2012.

As far as the characters in the follow-up novel, Peter Francisco will remain a major character, along with others including Jacky and Tom Macneal, Wills Winkman, Johnny Kiklkenny, Zack Winston, Rodie Murray, Garrett Hicks, Malcolm Shepherd and Peter Patrick. New historic figures will be introduced as well, notably the vivacious Dolley Madison, along with the explorers Lewis and Clark, Henry Clay, John C. Calhoun, Aaron Burr and others.

I hope **Cornerstone** has been as enjoyable for my readers to read, as it has been enjoyable for me to write.

Jim Murray

About the Author

James Allen Murray

James Allen Murray is an exciting new author who began his love of American History in the 4th grade, and his love of creative writing in high school. At age sixty, he was finally able to devote the time needed to combine both into his first historical fiction novel, <u>Cornerstone</u>.

He likes to say he was born *"smack dab in the middle of the 20th Century"* on Friday, June 30th 1950. He was born in Southern Ohio at the Murray family farmhouse on Denver Road in Pee Pee Township, alongside Crooked Creek, near Waverly in Pike County.

Growing up he was active in the high school marching band as drum squad leader, member of the scholarship team (competing in American History, World History and French), served as editor of the school newspaper, and was member of Future Teachers of America, the <u>Waverly Novel</u> yearbook staff, and the Waverly Tigers Varsity Golf Team. He won statewide honors in the American Legion's Ohio History, Government, and Citizenship Test, and was chosen to represent Pike County in the All-Ohio Youth Choir at the Ohio State Fair. In 1968, he won first prize in the Bristol Village Men's Club's *"What Democracy Means to Me"* Essay Contest.

Adding to his love of American History was another love of American politics. In 1960, as a ten year-old fifth grader at Waverly East Elementary, he was taken out of school for a day to attend a whistlestop train rally for Vice President Richard M. Nixon. He was caught up in all the excitement of a political rally. In the winter of 1962, he stood on the corner of 4th Street and 5th Avenue in Columbus to watch President John F. Kennedy's motorcade pass by. In 1966, he made his first-ever political contribution. He used money he made during the summer mowing lawns in Waverly's Bristol Village retirement community, and sent $55 to Ronald Reagan's first campaign for Governor of California.

He graduated Waverly High School with the Class of 1968, and attended Miami University in Oxford, Ohio, 1968-72. He was a member of the Kappa Sigma National Fraternity, where he served as Grand Scribe for the Theta-Upsilon Chapter, and was chairman of the Miami University Young Republican Club. As a college freshman, he was invited to the 1969 Presidential Inauguration for serving as state chairman of Ohio Students for Nixon. During the summer of 1971, he served on the staff of Ohio Congressman William H. Harsha, Jr. as a summer intern, writing Harsha's press releases, district newsletters, and re-writing Harsha's campaign biography.

A short career in politics, began for Jim during his senior year at Miami, when he ran for a seat in the Ohio Legislature. He lost to a seven-term incumbent Democrat, Vern Riffe. Riffe later became the most powerful Speaker of the Ohio House of Representatives.

In 1976, Jim was elected as the youngest-ever member of the Ohio Republican State Central and Executive Committee. In 1978, he was elected state chairman of the Ohio Young Republicans. In 1980, Congressman Harsha announced his retirement, so Jim sought the Republican nomination for Congress in Ohio's 6th District. He came in third in an eight-way race.

As a "Reagan Republican" he was a maverick in the eyes of the local and state GOP organizations during the era of Governor James A. Rhodes. He served on the Ohio Reagan campaign committee from 1975 to 1980. He attended the 1976 GOP Convention in Kansas City, working on the Reagan staff as a delegate-hunter in the cliffhanger race against President Jerry Ford. He attended the 1980 convention in Detroit as chairman of the State Chairmen's Caucus of the Young Republican National Federation. He managed the Pike County Reagan Headquarters that year, and escorted his first motorcoach tour in January 1981, taking a busload of local Republicans to the Reagan Inauguration.

In the work-a-day world Jim worked for, then managed the Murray family's ready-mix concrete and building supplies business in Waverly from 1967 to 1984. He opened a Christian book, music and gift shop in Waverly in the historic Emmitt House Hotel of the canal era. After that, he describes his career as *"spotted,"* working variously as a cruise and motorcoach tour guide, hotel night auditor and desk clerk, apartment resident manager, local newspaper reporter, columnist and special editor, and in call centers in Ohio, Virginia, Georgia, Florida and California. He says, *"the most unusual job I ever had was as a pet butler, scooping dog poop from other peoples' backyards."*

During his career as a journalist in southern Ohio, he edited an award winning *"Historical Edition"* of the *Pike County News Watchman*, wrote a popular political opinion column, *"Strictly My Opinion"*, and edited a company-wide monthly travel tabloid to spur tourism in Southern Ohio called *"The Southern Ohio Traveler."*

He married in 1978, and had a daughter, Susan Eliza, born April 21st 1980. He became a born again Christian July 6th 1980, and a member of the Waverly Church of Christ, where he served as a trustee and teen advisor. He divorced in 1985-86, and met his life partner, Gary Hicks, in 1994, in Columbus.

In 2010, the business he had worked for since returning to Ohio in 2006, shut down without notice. Shortly thereafter, he had some medical issues, which confined him to a wheelchair, having lost his right leg. His born again Christian faith reminded him ... *"God gave me sixty years use of two legs, and I made good use of them. Now I simply have to adjust."* He found himself now with enough time to devote himself to writing and publishing his first work, **Cornerstone**. *"When God closes a door, He opens a window!"*

Currently, he lives in Columbus, Ohio, with his life partner of eighteen years.

Keep up with the progress of his next novel, and join Jim's American History blog at *www.cornerstone-book.com*.